COMMUNITIES, CONTEXTS AND CULTURES
LEICESTER STUDIES IN ENGLISH LOCAL HISTORY

GENERAL EDITOR
CHARLES PHYTHIAN-ADAMS

CONTINUITY AND COLONIZATION

THE EVOLUTION OF KENTISH SETTLEMENT

ALAN EVERITT

LEICESTER
UNIVERSITY PRESS
1986

First published in 1986 by Leicester University Press
First published in 1986 in the United States of America
by Humanities Press Inc., Atlantic Highlands, NJ07716
and also distributed by them in North America

Copyright © Alan Everitt 1986

All rights reserved. No part of this publication may be
reproduced, stored in a retrieval system, or transmitted, in
any form or by any means, electronic, mechanical, photo-copying,
recording or otherwise, without the prior permission of the
Leicester University Press

Designed by Douglas Martin
Phototypeset in Linotron 202 Baskerville
by Wyvern Typesetting Limited, Bristol
Printed and bound in Great Britain at
the Bath Press, Avon

The publication of this book
has been assisted by a grant from the
Isobel Thornley Bequest

British Library Cataloguing in Publication Data
Everitt, Alan
Continuity and colonization: the evolution of Kentish settlement.
1. Human settlements – England – Kent – History
2. Kent – History
I. Title
942.2'301   GF552.K4
ISBN 0–7185–1255–3

IN MEMORIAM
R.A.E. & G.B.E.

'And I may say that though I have now arrived at what I believe to be the true solution of the case, I have no material proof of it. I know it is so, because it must be so, because in no other way can every single fact fit into its ordered and recognized place. And that, to my mind, is the most satisfying solution there can be.' Hercule Poirot in Agatha Christie, *Murder in Mesopotamia* (1962 edn), 163.

CONTENTS

List of maps   x
List of tables   xi
Note on orthography   xii
General editor's foreword   xiii
Preface   xvii

1   PROBLEMS AND APPROACHES   1

     1. Continuity or colonization?   1
     2. Regional approaches   3
     3. Landscape and society   6
     4. Analysis and synthesis   13

PART ONE
THE COMMUNITY OF KENT

2   LANDSCAPE AND ECONOMY   17

     1. Antiquity   17
     2. Reappraisals   20
     3. Woodland   25
     4. Pasture and transhumance   32
     5. The settlement pattern   39

3   REGIONS AND *PAYS*   43

     1. Regional patterns   43
     2. Foothills and Downland   45
     3. Holmesdale and Chartland   49
     4. The Weald   52
     5. The Marshland   57
     6. Regional interdependence   65

PART TWO
THE FOUNDATIONS OF SETTLEMENT

4   THE JUTISH BASIS   69

Contents

    1. The structure of settlement 69
    2. The pattern of river-estates 76
    3. The pattern of springhead-estates 87
    4. Conclusion 90

5 BEYOND THE JUTES: PRELIMINARY CONSIDERATIONS 93

    1. The problem 93
    2. Archaeological complexes 95
    3. Pre-Jutish place-names 103
    4. Early problem-names 107
    5. Names in 'stone' 113
    6. Seminal settlements 116

PART THREE
THE EXPANSION OF SETTLEMENT

6 THE FIELD AND THE FOREST 119

    1. The expansion of settlement, c.600–1050 119
    2. Forest and field 121
    3. The testimony of the woods 127
    4. The chronology of Downland colonization 135

7 THE DOWNLAND ECONOMY 141

    1. Pastoral place-names 141
    2. Boundary pastures 144
    3. Dependence and transhumance 155
    4. Pastoral usage 163
    5. The freedom of the Wold 172

PART FOUR
THE ECCLESIASTICAL TESTIMONY

8 ECCLESIASTICAL DEVELOPMENT 181

    1. The church and the landscape 181
    2. Minsters and primary mother-churches 187
    3. Secondary and 'bookland' churches 196
    4. Chapel and chantry 205
    5. Contrasting communities 222

9 CHURCH-DEDICATIONS 225

1. The evidence and its problems   225
      2. Dedications and *pays*   234
      3. Early dedications   239
   4. Early cults and cult centres   243
   5. The church in the wilderness   250
      6. Towards a chronology   255

PART FIVE
TOPOGRAPHICAL RECONSTRUCTION

10   TOPOGRAPHICAL METHOD: ANALYSIS   259
   1. The evidence and its problems   259
   2. Settlement direction and place-names   264
      3. Lanes and droveways   267
      4. Territorial relationship   270
      5. The parochial unit   274
      6. Parish boundaries   278
   7. The church and its situation   293
      8. Holy wells and springs   296
         9. Conclusion   300

11   THE LANDS OF MILTON REGIS: SYNTHESIS   302
      1. *Regio* and minsterland   311
         2. The heartland   315
   3. Outlying lands to the east   320
   4. Outlying lands to the west   320
         5. The Minnis   325
         6. Conclusion   331

---

12   LANDSCAPE AND SETTLEMENT IN ENGLAND   333
      1. Parallels and contrasts   333
         2. Settlement and *pays*   338
      3. Landscapes of continuity   341
      4. Landscapes of colonization   343
   5. The communities of England   348

      List of abbreviations   350
         Notes   352
         Index   395

LIST OF MAPS

1	Droveways and tracks crossing the Downland	36
2	Kentish *pays*	45
3	Early Jutish estate-centres and principal related settlements	76
4	Early Jutish estates in East Kent	80–1
5	Early Jutish estates in Holmesdale	84–5
6	Faversham: early place-names and archaeological sites	110–11
7	Downland woods: Meopham and Luddesdown area	134–5
8	Upland pastures of settlements on the Darent and Cray	148–9
9	Downland boundaries between Rochester and Hollingbourne	152–4
10	Downland farms and pastures: Alkham and Swingfield area	166–7
11	Minsters and mother-churches	188
12	Ecclesiastical development in Mid-Kent	200–3
13	Evolution of the minsterlands: Shoreham, Wrotham, and Aylesford	208–18
14	Interlocking boundaries near Elham	282–3
15	The Hoo Peninsula: pastoral development	285–91
16	The lands of Milton Regis	303–10

LIST OF TABLES

1	Estate-centres: place-name elements	91
2	Settlement-names in pre-Conquest charters	120
3	The *dens* or detached summer pastures	125
4	Downland place-name elements	130
5	Pastoral elements on the Downs: I	142
6	Pastoral elements on the Downs: II	143
7	Downland place-names: elements in pre-Conquest charters	162
8	Landownership in Kent, c.1086	173
9	Landownership in Kent, TRE	176
10	Church typology and parish size	223
11	Dedications in Kent and in England generally	228–9
12	Dedications and *pays*	235
13	Dedications in the Original Lands and the Wilderness parishes	236–7
14	Dedications in Kent and in Leicestershire	246–7
15	Dedications: a tentative chronology	254–5

Note on orthography Except in the citation of name-forms, the spelling, punctuation, and capitalization of quotations have been modernized unless there seemed special significance in retaining the original.

County boundaries Throughout the book county boundaries are taken as they existed before the Local Government Act of 1974, except in the cases of Kent, Surrey, and Middlesex, where boundaries antedating the formation of the London County Council are utilized.

GENERAL EDITOR'S FOREWORD

The need for a series of full-length monographs devoted to the furtherance of English Local History as an academic discipline requires little explanation. With the subject increasingly being studied at sophisticated levels in practically every university in the country, usually on a regional basis, and at Leicester nation-wide; with the accompanying genesis of scholarly journals devoted respectively to *Northern History*, *Midland History*, and *Southern History* in which short localized studies may find regular outlets; and with the continuation of the Leicester Departmental series of *Occasional Papers* (published since 1952 by the Leicester University Press) as a medium for work of middle length, irrespective of region; the absence of some established vehicle by which influential full-scale studies may reach a wider audience is glaring indeed. To point the moral, one has only to look at the cumulative publishing achievements of the discipline perhaps most closely related to English Local History, that of Social Anthropology, which also concerns itself with the study of small-scale societies. In the historical field, by contrast, there are still too few extended analyses of, for example, the various types of past local societies and their ever-differing evolutions, yet to allow either of sufficiently detailed comparisons between them, or of the means to test the broader interpretative or evidential frameworks within which such investigations tend to be set. More than this, it may be claimed that only in the full-length study is it possible effectively to demonstrate the continuing wider relevance of the subject, and so establish that vital link between the particular and the general which is so necessary for the academic advance of the discipline.

This new series of occasional monographs, therefore, is designed to respond to these needs. In it will be published only studies that are of broader significance than the geographical confines of their subject matters might be taken to imply. Each, in its different way, will contribute to the conceptual or methodological development of the discipline as well as to the illumination of some instructive corner of the English past. For this will not be a series of local or regional histories *per se*; rather will it represent a sequence of discrete approaches to *how* we may more closely identify and understand, at any period of the pre-industrialized past, not only the locally differentiated experiences of

English peoples on the ground, but also the ways in which these experiences may have related to the ever-changing nature of the greater society to which all those peoples severally belonged. While the character of the series will thus reflect the general concerns of the 'Leicester School' of *English* Local History, and the more specific approaches to the subject which it favours, it should be emphasized, nevertheless, that challenging contributions from any source will be welcomed.

The approaches to be stressed are four-fold and interrelated. First and foremost, we are concerned with the historical analysis of particular societies and their activities. It matters not whether these represent groupings of people inhabiting rural or urban settlements, or definable districts, regions or even quarters of the nation, nor whether such societies may be described in precise sociological terms as 'communities'. What does matter is that they should be studied both as entities in themselves (and thus not merely as illustrative of a single specialism like, for example, the history of crime), and as entities related to, and indicative of, the wider world of their times. Above all, such societies should be understood in their geographic contexts. The second approach, therefore, is topographical: the analysis not only of the landscapes of the past and those other physical surroundings which pre-industrialized societies created, but also of the interplay between man and his environment – a study which involves the exploitation of both visual and documentary evidence. Equally fundamental, thirdly, is a temporal and human form of context: the extent to which over the years, and within broadly definable territorial limits, regional families persisted, proliferated or perished. Patterns of physical mobility throughout the generations in a region and their temporal and spatial relationships to 'communities' of relatively short-term residence may be reconstructed in a number of ways. In this series, it would be appropriate to complement, from other points of view, and perhaps for narrower periods, the pioneering work that continues to be published in this respect for a growing number of counties over many centuries by the *English Surnames Survey*. Finally, and far from least, there is the study of regional popular cultures. It is at this level of *mentalité* in particular, perhaps, that eventually we may reach a more precise understanding of how the several 'peoples' of this country both differentiated themselves from each other and yet also combined to characterize the English as the richly variegated society they remain to this day.

But if all historians should be concerned ultimately to connect the

Foreword

past with the present, one major lesson that academic local historians have learned over the last 30 years has been to do with the extraordinarily powerful influences or restraints on so many subsequent local developments that were generated as long ago at least as the periods of Anglo-Saxon and early medieval settlement. Parish, manor and shire – those dry topics so much beloved by an older generation of institutional historians – not only become real again when their various origins and early forms are traced to specific geographic and social contexts; such gradually accumulated patterns may also now be seen to have helped to shape all manner of local social tendencies over an entire millennium.

It is especially appropriate then that this series should open with a highly original illustration of how such a provincial matrix for the future may have evolved in one of the two best-documented areas of early settlement in the land, the ancient kingdom of Kent. The author of this major study, our leading practising local historian, is too well known to require further introduction. With his unrivalled knowledge of the county's history and with his inimitable prose, it is not too much to say that Alan Everitt here recreates a lost landscape, a whole world of the past, in a fashion which those who follow after, in their pursuit of this the most shadowy period of our history, will wish to emulate and test in other areas. Never before, I believe, has a whole region received such detailed treatment in this respect; and never before has quite such systematic and exhaustive use been made of what, at first sight only, may appear to be unpromising forms of evidence, like minor place-names or church, chapel and well-dedications. In the hands of a master, however, the insights that may be so derived are such that no student of Anglo-Saxon settlement in other regions of the country will henceforth be able to ignore them. Above all, there is in this study a marvellous and sensitive blend of the general and the particular. Kent may not be England, but in what follows, we come close to the earthy realities that lay behind the making of English society as a whole.

Charles Phythian-Adams
Head of the Department of English Local History
University of Leicester

PREFACE

This is a book about the evolution of Kentish settlement from the end of the Romano-British period and the coming of the 'English' down to the thirteenth or fourteenth century. It is not about the Romano-British period itself, or about the ultimate origins of Kentish settlement in the Iron Age or Bronze Age, since those are matters for the archaeologist. I have endeavoured to indicate places and neighbourhoods where continuity of occupation with the Roman era seems likely; but I have not discussed pre-English settlement as such except where there seems reason to suspect that occupation was indeed continuous. However important the older strata of colonization may be to the archaeologist, however absorbing to the student of landscape, they are relevant to the historian of English society only where settlements actually survived, or where an older population or system of organization was incorporated in the new. If the origins of English society are my theme, however, I must also stress that this book is not a study of the social and political institutions of Kent, such as J. E. A. Jolliffe undertook in his brilliant monograph, *Pre-Feudal England: the Jutes* (1933). Like Jolliffe, I believe that the roots of these institutions may be traced in the early Jutish *regiones* which moulded the structure of Kentish settlement; but the relationship between *regio* and institution was more diverse, more complex, more evolutionary than Jolliffe recognized, and it demands an understanding of English medieval society as a whole which I do not possess.

Historiographically Kent is both fortunate and unfortunate. This is not the place for detailed discussion, but a few points must be made. There is no county record society and many basic sources long since published for other shires are consequently still in manuscript or available only in antiquated editions. The more important printed records, such as D. C. Douglas's edition of *The Domesday Monachorum of Christ Church, Canterbury* (1944), have generally been published by outside bodies, in that case the Royal Historical Society. There is little or nothing in print on the agriculture and rural society of Kent to compare with the work of W. G. Hoskins on Leicestershire and Devon, Joan Thirsk on Lincolnshire, Margaret Spufford on Cambridgeshire, or some of the more recent volumes of the Victoria County History. Many elementary themes in the history of the county are still virtually

Preface

unexplored, such as the cloth industry of the Weald and the recession of settlement in the later medieval period. In other areas topics like these have given rise to an extensive literature which in some respects has revolutionized our understanding of medieval society. Two notable exceptions to these shortcomings are Dr A. R. H. Baker's authoritative investigation of Kentish field-systems and Professor F. R. H. Du Boulay's classic study of *The Lordship of Canterbury* (1966). There are other works of this calibre, and there is much of detailed value in the numerous local histories produced over the last two centuries. At the professional level, however, the historiography of the county has far indeed to go before it approaches that of its rivals, and its limitations will be apparent in my own.

There are two matters, nevertheless, regarding which the student of early Kentish society must be accounted fortunate. Readers will find that I have devoted much attention to reconstructing the primitive jurisdictions of the county, since these often shed light on the course of settlement, and in this task Edward Hasted's great *History and Topographical Survey* of the eighteenth century has been my principal standby. In Kent itself there is a long and not entirely honourable tradition of belittling Hasted; after two centuries his outlook inevitably seems dated, and in his many hundreds of pages it is all too easy to find errors of detail. What needs to be remembered, however, is that he wrote at a crucial period in Kentish history when much of the ancient jurisdictional structure of the county still remained intact, or else was readily recoverable by a man of his inclinations and connexions. His systematic account of matters like these thus furnishes us with an unrivalled historical record in its own right, and one to which there is little parallel in most other counties. For the student of settlement his *History* is a more valuable source than a work like John Nichols's *History and Antiquities of the County of Leicester*, though that is one of the finest of the classic county histories of England, and is generally more accurate as a work of scholarship.

Secondly, I have also devoted much attention to the topographical and onomastic evidence in which Kent is so rich. There are more place-names recorded for the county in pre-Conquest charters than for any other part of England, and these were subjected to detailed scrutiny by J. K. Wallenberg in his pioneering study, *Kentish Place-Names: a Topographical and Etymological Study of the Place-Name Material in Kentish Charters dated before the Conquest* (1931).[1] My debt to this work, and to Wallenberg's second volume, *The Place-Names of Kent* (1934), is pro-

xviii

Preface

found; without them this book could never have been written. Since great advances have been made in this field over the past 50 years, however, some assessment of Wallenberg's work in the light of recent opinion seems necessary.

It cannot be claimed that Wallenberg provides a definitive study of Kentish nomenclature as a whole; for that we await publication of the English Place-Name Society's survey, now in progress. His two volumes cover only about a third of the 12,000 or so settlement-names of the county, though that includes all the 'major' names, of parishes, hundreds, lathes, and towns. There are three types of name that are seriously under-represented in his work, since they rarely occur in the kind of medieval sources he utilized: those of rivers and streams, those of regions and districts, and – by far the most numerous – those of woods and other topographical features. It is no disparagement of his achievement to say that these urgently demand intensive investigation. In the interpretation of the onomastic evidence Wallenberg devoted particularly close attention to local topography, making extensive use of the six-inch Ordnance maps; as a student of landscape he was far more knowledgeable and scrupulous than his English contemporaries, D. C. Douglas and J. E. A. Jolliffe. Though he sometimes advanced wire-drawn or occasionally absurd interpretations, he was a cautious scholar, and the bulk of his work has stood the test of time remarkably well when the scale of the undertaking is borne in mind. His identification of minor place-names was at times necessarily tentative, and for many of the notoriously difficult 'problem-names' of Kent he could only advance inconclusive explanations. In cases like these I have not generally thought it appropriate to recapitulate his arguments or those of other scholars in detail, except in a few special instances like Faversham. To have done so would have inordinately expanded an already lengthy book, and on the linguistic aspects of the subject my judgment would have been worth little. I hope, however, that readers will accept that I am not unaware of the problems involved, and that I have endeavoured to examine each dubious case afresh in the light of recent research and the topographical context of the place in question. On etymological matters I have received invaluable assistance from Dr Margaret Gelling, who with characteristic generosity has devoted many patient hours to investigating some scores of place-names for me, correcting many of my mistakes, and endeavouring to check my wilder flights of fancy.

For these and other reasons this book is to some extent necessarily a provisional study; but that is a malady incident to all interpretative history.[2] There are many matters which I should have liked to go into more deeply, particularly in connexion with post-Conquest society; but if I had done so I should never have completed the book. In concentrating attention on the general development of Kentish colonization there are also many intriguing oddities and exceptions which I have not been able to discuss in these pages, but which in some cases might open up new vistas in settlement-study if subjected to intensive scrutiny. In endeavouring to visualize the kind of primitive society which lies beyond the formal evidence of documents, place-names, and jurisdictions, and in trying to reconstruct a complete picture of settlement from countless isolated fragments of the past, a certain element of speculation is at times unavoidable. I hope I have kept it within bounds; but where topography in particular is concerned we are only at the beginning of scientific understanding; there must be many pointers I have failed to recognize; and on some matters I have changed my mind in drawing the evidence together. I hope, therefore, that no one will suppose I have said the last word on Kentish settlement history, or that I am offering my conclusions as a 'model' for other counties or as a 'paradigm' of English settlement in general. I made a similar *caveat* in an earlier book on Kentish society in the seventeenth century, though apparently to little purpose, and I can only hope that students of settlement will be more observant of it than some historians of the Stuart era. If this island, as Chesterton said, is 'like a little book, full of a thousand tales', there may well be a certain similarity of form from one area to another, but there must also, by definition, be a contrast of substance.

The maps to this volume have posed a special problem. My originals were drawn on single sheets based on the $2\frac{1}{2}''$ Ordnance Survey. For topographical detective work that is essential, but to have reproduced them on this scale would have necessitated large-scale fold-outs, which were impracticable on grounds of expense. By dividing the maps into sections, as in an atlas, and by an ingenious system of signs it has been possible to incorporate virtually all the detail on my originals, though many minor place-names have had to be indicated by numbered dots together with a key. In the index these minor names are listed under the page on which the *number* appears, not under the page on which they appear in the key, though it is necessary to refer to the key to ascertain the relevant number. I owe a great debt to Mrs Susan Martin of Leicester University Press for working out the sign-system, to Mr and

Preface

Mrs Ian Lovett for their labour in redrawing the maps, and to Mrs Elizabeth Fowler for compiling the index. It is no reflection on their work to say that cartographically the final result is inevitably more difficult to follow than it would have been on a single sheet. If it taxes the reader's patience, I must plead that I have had in mind those who may wish to follow my argument in the text in some detail and imitate my methods in turning to other areas. The evolution of settlement in this country can only be unravelled by microscopic attention to detail in this way, and I make no apology for burdening the maps with so much.

Many people have contributed to this book and it is a pleasure to acknowledge their assistance. I owe a particular debt to Dr Margaret Gelling, Professor G. W. S. Barrow, and Mr Charles Phythian-Adams for reading the final text in its entirety, for raising many expert points of detail, for suggesting lines of thought I had not considered, and above all for encouraging a temerarious alien in the field of settlement studies. More help than I can recount has been given to me by my colleagues at Leicester, particularly Mr Phythian-Adams, but also Richard McKinley, Harold Fox, and Margery Tranter, and my former colleagues Peter Eden and David Hey. Many of the points made in this book have arisen from the frequent discussions we have had together and from the references they have so generously given me. Mrs Tranter has also devoted much time and thought to compiling the list of Kentish chapels and chantries discussed in Chapter 8 and to proof-reading my typescript. A debt of another but equally important kind is due to Mrs Muriel Phillips and Mrs Dorothy Brydges for their expert typing and retyping of an often intractable manuscript. In Kent itself I have received hospitality of the most generous description when working in the field, particularly from Professor and Mrs T. C. Barker at Faversham, the late Mrs Mary Wagstaffe of Tunbridge Wells, Mr and Mrs W. Key, lately of The Priory, Pembury, and Mr and Mrs G. Fletcher, lately of The Kennel Holt, Cranbrook. I must also thank those many students of mine who over the years have listened to successive versions of this book in the form of lectures: I owe more than they know to their patient attention, their shrewd questions, and their sense of humour. Finally, it has been a pleasure once more to leave my publishing problems in the expert hands of the Leicester University Press, with the calming assurance that they will all be solved by Peter Boulton and Susan Martin.

Alan Everitt

1

PROBLEMS AND APPROACHES

1. CONTINUITY OR COLONIZATION?

In recent years the view has gradually been gaining ground that the English landscape was more or less fully cleared and settled at a much earlier period than we used to suppose. The evidence of aerial photography in particular and the discoveries of 'rescue' archaeology are now often adduced as proof of an intensively colonized countryside as early as the Romano-British era.[1] There can be little doubt that a number of areas once regarded as uncolonized forest during Old English times had in fact been cultivated for centuries, sometimes on a substantial scale, though not necessarily without a break. Some of our leading historians have added eloquent voices to those of the archaeologists, and Professor Peter Sawyer has argued that the English settlement pattern 'is, in general, much older than most scholars have been prepared to recognize'. Not without reason he questions the reliance of some earlier historians upon Domesday evidence in dating the origins of a settlement. He also questions the view of Professor Loyn that 'the story of Anglo-Saxon settlement, when looked at in depth, yields more of the saga of man against forest than of Saxon against Celt. It was a colonizing movement in the true sense of the word.' For Professor Sawyer the Anglo-Saxon period was not one of gradual colonization, it seems, as settlement spread out into the wild from more ancient centres: on the contrary, 'the rural resources of England were almost as fully exploited in the seventh century as they were in the eleventh . . .'[2]

The present book does not set out to resolve these problems in the country as a whole. It is limited to an examination of a single county, and one which in some ways was untypical. Its scope is confined to a reconstruction of the English settlement of Kent, and of the extent to which it may have been continuous with that of the Romano-British period, or may represent 'a colonizing movement in the true sense of the word'. Ever since H. P. R. Finberg wrote *Roman and Saxon Withington* (1955) the evidence for continuity has been steadily accumulating, and in Kent there are important areas where the facts bear out Professor Sawyer's view that the settlement pattern is much older than we used to suppose. In a region where woodland was unusually extensive, however, there are also areas where the evidence supports Professor

1   *Problems and approaches*

Loyn's interpretation, and in the county generally we cannot say that rural resources were as fully exploited in the seventh century as they were in the eleventh. In other words there were in Kent distinct 'landscapes of continuity' on the one hand, and 'landscapes of colonization' on the other. That does not mean that these latter areas remained wholly unoccupied during the Roman period, but that if they were occupied – and at present there is singularly little evidence of it – we must posit a widespread recession of settlement at the end of the Roman era, followed by massive regeneration of woodland, and subsequent recolonization by the English.[3]

How far in these respects the Kentish experience may have been characteristic of other parts of England is a complex problem which cannot be considered until the evidence itself has been discussed. It was not unique; but more systematic investigation of other areas is necessary, such as Mr W. J. Ford has undertaken for Warwickshire and Dr Della Hooke for the West Midlands, before detailed or positive parallels can be drawn.[4] There is one general observation, however, which may be made here, and which leads the present writer to feel that the extent of early English settlement is possibly in danger of being oversimplified.

I came to the study of the pre-Conquest period with the landscape and the agrarian economy of the sixteenth and early seventeenth centuries in mind.[5] That landscape was one where in some counties substantial woods and forests still remained; where the waste was not yet everywhere reclaimed and settled; where squatters were still able to put up cottages at the edge of commons; where new hamlets and 'rows' were appearing on parish boundaries and extra-parochial tracts; and where extensive intercommonable stretches still survived in highland and heathland areas, and in old forest counties like Kent and Sussex. Naturally, these features were not everywhere equally apparent; in much of East Anglia and the Midlands they were rarely in evidence; yet taking the country as a whole, they were a striking feature of the period. In other words, what we see in the countryside of the sixteenth century is an uncompleted landscape: a landscape which in places was undergoing a final phase of colonization, and in whose features we can still trace, at many points, the vestiges of a more primitive environment. By that phrase I do not mean a virgin environment, unaffected by human activity, but one that had not yet everywhere been intensively colonized or wholly reclaimed. Obviously the widespread retreat of settlement during the later medieval period accounts for some of the surviving

1   *Problems and approaches*

waste-lands of the sixteenth century: yet when the topographical development of particular localities is reconstructed in detail, and their agrarian evolution traced back beyond the fourteenth century, it generally becomes apparent that late-medieval decay cannot explain all those vestigial features of a more primitive world.[6] What we see in the sixteenth century, in short, is a landscape that has only gradually yielded to the axe and the plough, only reluctantly succumbed, acre by acre, to the piecemeal and persistent labours of generations of English peasants. Essentially it is a landscape of evolution. Seen in the light of that age-long process, in places extending over more than a thousand years, and involving a more exhausting process of clearance than is sometimes envisaged, the belief in a countryside more or less fully exploited by the seventh century is not everywhere easy to accept; and certainly the Kentish evidence does not support it.[7]

Topographically speaking, the evolution of English settlement was thus more varied, and in many areas more gradual, than may at first sight appear. In endeavouring to trace its progress in Kent, a number of basic convictions have consequently forced themselves on my mind, and moulded the general strategy of this book. Briefly summarized, these convictions are of three kinds: first, the extreme regional diversity to be found in the chronology of settlement, even within a single county; second, the profound influence of topography and environment upon the course of settlement, and the importance of the landscape itself as an historical document; and third, the danger of drawing conclusions where settlement is concerned from isolated or selected examples, and the necessity, as in so many branches of history, of a systematic approach to the evidence. It is to these three topics that the remainder of this chapter is devoted.

2. REGIONAL APPROACHES

Before describing the kind of regional framework adopted in this book, it may be useful to discuss some of the difficulties involved in regional definition generally. Where settlement is concerned, the problem of defining a region is not necessarily a straightforward matter, and if regional boundaries are misconceived to begin with, the interpretation of settlement itself is in danger of distortion.

Broadly speaking, there are perhaps four different ways in which the English landscape has most frequently been divided in approaching the problem of settlement. First, it has often been envisaged in terms of

1 *Problems and approaches*

counties and kingdoms, such as Devon and Kent, or Wessex, East Anglia, and Northumberland. There are obvious advantages in this approach, since political and administrative divisions are readily grasped, and they have clearly influenced colonization, though in Kent that influence has probably been exaggerated. Second, settlement may be thought of in terms of large and loosely-defined areas, such as the Midlands, the North, and the West Country. Such categories as these also have their uses, provided we remember the diversity of settlement to be found within even a relatively homogeneous region like the Midlands. To these larger regional categories a number of others may be added, such as the Pennine Counties for the six northern shires, and the Forest Counties for Kent, Sussex, Surrey, and Hampshire. These phrases indicate the dominant environmental factor in the settlement history of the regions concerned, though they obviously gloss over a number of fundamental contrasts between each shire and within each region. Some of the resemblances between the four forest counties were pointed out nearly fifty years ago by J. E. A. Jolliffe in *Pre-Feudal England: the Jutes* (1933), though he attributed them to racial rather than environmental influences.

Third, historians have sometimes borrowed the concepts of the geographers and thought in terms of the larger division of Highland Zone and Lowland Zone. There can be no doubt that this is a real division for settlement history as well as geography; but for topographical purposes it is too large to be of much local use, and tells us nothing about the contrasts to be found within a single county, or between two counties within the same zone, such as Kent and Northamptonshire. Behind it there is often a further idea, perhaps only half-realized, that in some sense the Anglo-Saxon invasion of this country resembled a tidal wave, gradually spreading across the face of Britain from the south and east to the north and west, little by little engulfing everything in its wake, and eventually driving any Britons who happened to survive into the fastnesses of the Highland Zone. Each area the English invaded in turn was thus more or less fully colonized before they moved on to the next, so that English settlements in counties like Kent and Sussex are necessarily older than those in Lancashire and Devon. Nowadays, no doubt, few informed people would subscribe to the 'tidal wave' theory of settlement when expressed in such simplistic terms; yet the spirit of it still lingers, and on a superficial view there seems much to commend it. The earliest English settlements in Kent and Sussex no doubt are older than those in Devon or Lancashire. Since Wales and Cornwall are

1 Problems and approaches

obviously Celtic in a sense that Kent and Sussex are not, it is easy to assume that as one moves towards the north and west one will find a deepening Celtic imprint: and in some respects one will. Yet when the settlement history of any particular county is reconstructed as a whole, from every available line of evidence, the reassuring simplicity of the idea tends to dissolve away. The topographical reality is not only likely to be more complex, but different in kind. There are parts of Kent where the landscape bears a markedly Celtic imprint, whereas much of the Pennine countryside of the northern counties is a landscape of English and Scandinavian ancestry. There are also more Celtic place-names in Kent than there are in a supposedly 'Celtic' county like Devon, though of course they form only a small percentage of the total. This does not mean that the 'Highland Zone' and the 'Lowland Zone' are figments of the imagination, but that in both zones we are likely to find 'landscapes of continuity' alongside 'landscapes of colonization'.

The fourth division that is sometimes now adopted is that of our contemporary regional vocabulary. The disadvantage of this approach is that most of our current terms are of recent origin. Expressions like Tyneside and Merseyside, the West Midlands and the North-East, have no very lengthy lineage; such phrases as the Home Counties did not come into general use before the railway era; the present usage of a genuine historic name like Wessex is no more than an antiquarian revival; while the current re-animation of Mercia seems to be chiefly attributable to a contemporary police force. In other words, behind many of our regional terms, ideas and preconceptions lie implicit that were not necessarily of any significance to the people of earlier centuries. A phrase like 'the Home Counties' implies a kind of regional unity between the shires surrounding London which until recent centuries is fallacious. There was no connexion between the origins of settlement in Hertfordshire and in Sussex, for example, or between settlement in Essex and in Kent. In the latter county colonization owed nothing to the influence of London, and most of the earliest places in the shire lay well away from it, to the east of the Medway. In studying the evolution of settlement, in short, our modern regional terms not only give rise to spurious generalizations but impose the wrong *kind* of regional pattern upon the landscape of colonization.

To avoid the danger of reading these terms back into the past, a more fundamental reappraisal of regional definition is needed. In this matter the landscape of the sixteenth century again provides a useful point of departure, for what we see in that period is a landscape that was

1   *Problems and approaches*

sharply divided into contrasting countrysides or *pays*. There was nothing new about these divisions at that time, moreover; they had long been fundamental to the structure of provincial life. The evolution of the English economy was intimately related to them, and it is inconceivable that they had no effect on the origins of settlement. The fact that most of our historic regional names, apart from those of counties, are the names of *countrysides* is significant in this connexion: the Chilterns, the Mendips, and the Weald, for example; or Dartmoor, Bowland, Charnwood, and Arden. It was their character as distinctive *pays* that impressed itself on the primitive peoples who named them.

Owing to the unusually varied physical structure of this island, these different types of country often occur within quite short distances of one another. They give rise to marked regional variations within most English counties; they regularly stretch across the borders of one county into the next; and their characteristics are often echoed on similar landforms elsewhere. There are obvious resemblances between the settlement of the Weald of Kent and the Weald of Sussex, for example, and the Weald as a whole is more like the Forest of Arden in Warwickshire than the marshlands or the coastal plains of Sussex and Kent. There are also closer resemblances between the scarp-foot settlements of the Kentish Downs on one hand, and the Oxfordshire and Buckinghamshire Chilterns on the other, than there are between those of the Kentish scarp and Romney Marsh. This does not mean that the areas in question are historically identical, or that the course of settlement can be explained by crude determinism, but that it was moulded by complex human responses to a varied yet indigenous environment. The fact that in Kent nearly a thousand years elapsed between the oldest English settlements of the coastal plain and the latest English settlements of the Weald and the Chart bears testimony to the effect of these differences of *pays* upon the progress of colonization. It is the perception of these contrasting *pays*, therefore, and the light which systematic investigation of their evolution sheds on the chronology of settlement, that forms the framework of this book. They furnish the basic outline to which other lines of evidence, such as place-names, archaeology, topography, and ecclesiastical development, need to be related.

3. LANDSCAPE AND SOCIETY

In the evolution of settlement both human institutions and environmental circumstances play a part, and there can be no simple

1   *Problems and approaches*

answer as to their relative importance. In Kent itself settlement has hitherto been explained largely in terms of social institutions, while relatively little attention has been paid to the landscape evidence in which the county is so rich. The outstanding example of the institutional approach is J. E. A. Jolliffe's reconstruction of early Kentish society in *Pre-Feudal England*. When I began my work, I was much influenced by this luminous study; but as my research proceeded I became increasingly sceptical of some of Jolliffe's conclusions. Since he was primarily concerned with society rather than settlement as such, I have not felt it appropriate to offer a critique of his work within the limits of this book; but it raises two general points which need to be considered here before turning to the evidence of the landscape itself.

First, like Jolliffe, I have adopted the traditional expressions 'Jutes' and 'Jutish' to describe the original English settlers of Kent; but I have done so with reluctance, and in the absence of an adequate alternative. Wherever the early Teutonic peoples of Kent came from, if indeed they came from any single area, it seems clear that they did not come from Jutland and that they probably did not call themselves Jutes. Just as they retained the Celtic name of their kingdom of Kent or *Cantium*, so the terms they used to describe themselves were the *Cantware* or Kentings. Yet while this circumstance is itself significant, and forms an instructive contrast with the habits of their neighbours in Sussex and Essex, it would savour of preciosity to revive these expressions in a contemporary book. Of the other alternatives, 'English' is insufficiently precise, and 'Saxon' or 'Anglian' are misleading. While following Jolliffe's practice on this point, however, I do not subscribe to his further belief in what he called 'the Jutish South-East'.[8] Important parallels there certainly are between the settlement of Kent and that of Sussex and Surrey; but it is unlikely that these were due to a racial or tribal connexion. The original colonization of the three counties proceeded from different points on their outer margins – from the Thames valley in Surrey, the coastal plain in Sussex, and the north-east coastlands of Kent – while Jolliffe's attempt to limit the Saxon connotation of Sussex to the area around Chichester has never seemed convincing. It is more probable that the resemblances in question arose largely from environmental and topographical circumstance than from a common 'Jutish' ancestry.

Second, something needs to be said about the difficult problem of the lathes. Just how important were these local institutions in moulding the course of Kentish settlement? Were they indeed of any importance?

1   *Problems and approaches*

Can we accept Jolliffe's view of their profound antiquity, and their crucial role in the early evolution of the kingdom of Kent? It was Helen Cam's view that we could, and that 'with their antiquity, their origin as *regiones* dependent on royal vills' was likewise established.[9] More recently, in a wide-ranging survey in *The Kingdom of the Scots* (1973), Professor G. W. S. Barrow has re-examined the problem of early English and Scottish territorial units generally, and his findings plainly reinforce the argument.[10] There seems no reason, in short, to question the early existence of the lathe in some form or other, while its association with recognized *villae regales* like Eastry, Wye, and Milton Regis, as Jolliffe himself indicated,[11] evidently points to an ultimate connexion with the early *regiones* of Kent. Nevertheless, it is doubtful if the connexion was simple or straightforward. In the settlement period it is imperative, I believe, to envisage the lathes as evolving rather than mature institutions. They cannot be thought of as the elaborate organizations that Jolliffe described at Wye and other places, and to read the conditions of the eleventh century back into the fifth or sixth is surely anachronistic.[12] Extensive and populous territorial units or 'provinces', established as a result of massive folk-migrations, and based on a complex administrative structure imported from the continent and imposed from above, seem to me altogether out of place in considering the ultimate roots of early 'Jutish' settlement in Kent. If it is easy to make the early Anglo-Saxon village too large, as others have remarked, it is equally easy to make the early Kentish lathe and the *regio* from which it developed too sophisticated and extensive. In other words, Jolliffe's view of the early lathe as a highly developed folk-institution of continental origin is very difficult to reconcile with the settlement evidence. As we move backward in time, what we find in Kent is not an increasingly systematic territorial structure, but on the contrary a more diverse and irregular one, and one whose roots were clearly in some sense indigenous.

What exactly do I mean? There are two matters here that demand consideration. First, in the earliest phases of settlement, I see administrative districts as ultimately developing from those territorial or agrarian units which in this book I have ventured to describe by the term 'estates'. I use this term in a neutral sense, and quite what is meant by it must be left to unfold itself in subsequent chapters. It is not intended to imply any specific form of social organization, still less any theory of property. In the period when such 'estates' originated, we are moving in a profoundly shadowy world where very little can be known

1 *Problems and approaches*

about such matters, and it is important not to venture beyond the evidence. In Chapter 11 the colonization of one such territory – that of Milton Regis – is described in detail; but so far as the social framework behind it is concerned, there are several possible permutations, and there is no reason to suppose that other estates necessarily developed along identical lines: there was a family likeness between them, but they did not all conform to a single mode. At the elemental level, however, we must visualize the estate as in origin an agrarian territory, generally compact in form though occasionally discrete, sometimes extending to as much as 40,000 acres though in places to less than 15,000, and always centred on a focal settlement, a *caput*, which was often, though not invariably, a *villa regalis*. From these centres both the colonization and the organization of the estate developed, and eventually a quasi-administrative unit also emerged.

If this interpretation is correct, we are still faced with a second problem, that of relating the 'estate' to the 'lathe'. In response to this I can offer only a tentative solution. If the *regio* fathered the lathe, it seems plain that there must have been some kind of relationship between lathe and estate, for the coincidence between the *capita* of the estates and the *capita* of the *regiones* is altogether too pronounced to be fortuitous. Yet once again it is important not to visualize too schematic a development, since it would not be true to suggest that every estate-centre became the *caput* of a *regio*. There can be no doubt that this occurred at many places, such as Milton, Maidstone, Faversham, Eastry, and Wye, which are known to have been *villae regales* or other kinds of early administrative centre.[13] But while the number of recognizable *regiones* was substantially greater than the six or seven lathes recorded in Domesday Book or the possible nine or ten existing before the Conquest,[14] it can hardly have been as great as the 40 or more early Jutish estates. What we must envisage, in short, is an evolutionary situation in which some of the largest estates, such as Milton, probably survived but little altered in extent in the *regiones*, whereas others must have been amalgamated or grouped together to form precursors of the lathes. There are, in fact, a few places mentioned in later chapters where there seems reason to suspect fusion of this kind; it is arguably, indeed, the only feasible explanation; but it must be stressed that the evidence is sketchy, and it is important not to make it seem more positive than it is. Nevertheless, the conclusion that the primitive *regiones* were more numerous and at once smaller and simpler institutions than the mature lathes remains inescapable.

1 Problems and approaches

The belief that lathes and *regiones* ultimately developed from primitive agrarian estates in this way is not one that may find universal acceptance. I hesitate to advance it in the face of some established views, and strictly speaking it is not essential to the main arguments of this book. Early administrative districts in England have more usually perhaps been thought of as imposed from above. Stenton, it is true, regarded the *regiones* as originating in what he called 'tribal settlements' – a term about which I am not very happy – and 'not in any deliberate division of the land for administrative purposes'. But Chadwick seemed to be more or less positive in visualizing a coherent system imposed by the king, and his view has been echoed by subsequent scholars like Helen Cam.[15] Since the *regiones* were certainly based on *villae regales*, moreover, there is obviously much to commend it. But is it not possible that we are being too simple? There is a clear sense in which administrative units must derive their authority from above; but surely they also develop in response to existing circumstances? As I understand English institutional history, both in the Anglo-Saxon period and subsequently, they often arise from an attempt to rationalize a confused and unsystematic situation, frequently incorporating older territorial units and developing what already lies to hand.

When we look into the detail of local circumstances in Kent, it seems to me that this is by far the most likely explanation of institutional development. In reconstructing the *regiones* one cannot but be impressed, to begin with, by the influence of topography in shaping their evolution, and even in the case of an important royal estate like that of Milton Regis, on a major Roman road, by the extent to which in the early English period they often remained separated from one another – though not of course wholly isolated – by tracts of uncolonized woodland. Then, further, it seems clear that there was a good deal of diversity between individual *regiones*, both in scale and in structure, particularly as between those in East Kent and those in West Kent: and this diversity argues in favour of a piecemeal and localized origin rather than a uniform or alien system imposed from above. Finally, there can be little doubt that the *regiones* sometimes incorporated relics of older territorial units, and that they were almost everywhere based on Romano-British settlements like Maidstone, Milton, Reculver, Faversham, and Otford, where the case for continuity is cogent. If archaeological opinion is any guide, this should not surprise us, since it now seems that the belief in massive 'folk-migrations' may be mistaken, and that the early 'Jutish' settlers often arrived in small bands accompanied

1   *Problems and approaches*

by their families. In that case they are more likely to have fitted themselves wherever possible into an existing framework, or to have adapted an old one, than to have imposed a wholly novel system of their own.

There can thus be no real doubt that the *regio*, and its offspring the lathe, exerted a significant influence in the development of settlement in Kent: that much is plain. But there can likewise be little doubt that the *regio* and the lathe were themselves evolving institutions necessarily moulded, as settlement expanded, by the intractable circumstances of locality and environment. If in recreating the landscape of settlement we confine ourselves to the documentary evidence and fail to explore that of the landscape alongside it, we are likely to forget this basic reality, and to attribute too great a role in the evolution of settlement to political circumstance and royal administration. The highly ingenious attempts of some of our older historians to do so, and to erect a systematic theory solely on the basis of a few records like the Tribal Hidage, seem to me to have been little more than playing with moonbeams. What I have set out to do in this book is rather to envisage the real world beyond the documents, the world of peasants and colonists, and to reconstruct the evolving landscape of woods and farmsteads of which the king, though so much more than the figurehead, was so much less than the creator. For this purpose there is not only an unusual abundance of pre-Conquest place-name evidence in Kent, and an institutional structure which until Hasted's day still incorporated the outlines of its pre-Conquest past, but an extraordinary wealth of documentation in the landscape itself. These three types of evidence are in no sense rivals or substitutes, of course, and it is only by continually turning from one to the other, and exploring each in the light of the others, and in the light of written records, that the evolution of settlement, in all its complexity, can be unravelled. Yet because there is a sense in which the landscape itself is our most important historical document, and because it is also an enigmatic record which scholars like D. C. Douglas and J. E. A. Jolliffe were strangely perfunctory in examining, it seems necessary at this point to indicate its crucial place in the interpretation of settlement.[16]

Probably in all parts of England the landscape has more to tell the student of settlement than most of us yet realize. In counties of old enclosure like Devon or Kent, however, it is a more revealing document than in areas of parliamentary enclosure like the Midlands. In Kent itself there is infinitely more primitive evidence incorporated in the

1 Problems and approaches

surviving maze of woods, lanes, fields, farms, and boundaries, and in the *corpus* of some 12,000 settlement-names, than there is in a Midland county like Leicestershire.[17] When I began my work on the colonization of Kent, it was this wealth of topographical detail that most impressed me. Yet as I puzzled over the 60 sheets of the $2\frac{1}{2}''$ O.S. map, I was perpetually haunted by the question, How am I to decipher its message? What do these myriads of obscure *minutiae* mean? What do the shapes of the woods mean, or the network of lanes and holloways, or the situations of the farmsteads, or the courses of the parish boundaries? Why are there so many isolated churches, and why are they so eccentrically placed within their parishes? Why are the parishes themselves so irregular in form, and why are there so many farmsteads situated on their borders? Why are there so many thousands of scattered shaws and copses, sometimes as many as 60 or 70 to a parish, yet in parts of Kent no woodland whatsoever? Above all, what do these thousands of place-names mean? What do the names of parishes, chapelries, churches, hamlets, 'boroughs' (*borghi*), farmsteads, hills, valleys, streams, springs, ponds, woods, heaths, marshes, minnises, forstals, greens, and commons actually tell me about the evolution of Kentish settlement and the origins of Kentish society? They certainly mean something: but what is it?

Some of the solutions to these enigmas, and to others like them, will come to light in the course of this book; but there are four general points that ought to be briefly mentioned here. First, there can be no real understanding of the evolution of settlement without reference of every other type of evidence to that of the $2\frac{1}{2}''$ O.S. map, or without minute familiarity with the local topography of the landscape. Second, in interpreting that landscape, it is the *relationship* of one settlement to another, of one line of evidence to another, and one element in the landscape to another, that forms the first underlying principle, so that distribution maps marking only settlements, or only place-names, or churches, or archaeological sites, or the like, are pointless unless those features are also related to one another or to other types of topographical detail. Third, it is important to recognize that in Kent we have a different *kind* of landscape from that of the Midlands, not only on account of its old enclosure, but on account of the dispersed character of local settlement, and the absence of any true agricultural villages, or common-field settlements, in the Midland sense of the term. For this reason direct comparison with Midland experience, and direct extrapolation from the Kentish evidence, may be misleading, and such

1   *Problems and approaches*

features as isolated churches bear quite a different signification in the two regions.

Finally, how far can we be certain of the authenticity of the landscape evidence of Kent? How reliable is it as an indicator of the evolution of settlement? It is part of the purpose of this book to explore this problem; but there is one general comment that should be made here. In describing the landscape as our most important historical document, it is not so much the scattered archaeological remains or the individual details, taken in isolation, that one has in mind. It is rather the fact that in the surviving network of woods and farmsteads, of churches, lanes, and boundaries, we have the outlines or vestiges of a complete tapestry of settlement. Behind its daunting complexity, there is nothing formless or haphazard, but a consistent structure and a coherent pattern of development – a more subtle, varied, intricate, localized, and indeed kaleidoscopic pattern than we might have expected; a pattern that can only be interpreted, moreover, in the light of its constituent countrysides or *pays*, and yet one in whose infinite detail a whole millennium of settlement history is inscribed, parish by parish, as the experience of a lifetime is inscribed in the lineaments of the human face. As we shall see in subsequent chapters, it is this sense of structure and coherence behind the landscape evidence that forms one of the arguments in favour of its authenticity.

4. ANALYSIS AND SYNTHESIS

Over the last generation there has been much fruitful generalization in the field of settlement history by the intensive scrutiny of individual places. One thinks, for example, of Withington in Gloucestershire, of Wharram Percy in the East Riding, or of Lullingstone in Kent, each in its way a name to conjure with and awaken the historical imagination. Such studies are essential if the subject is to advance; but the time has perhaps come when a period of consolidation is needed, and a more systematic if less exciting approach. How typical, in other words, are places like Lullingstone, Wharram Percy, and Withington, and what exactly do they typify? In approaching the past there seems to be a natural tendency to notice the eccentric and overlook the typical, and for that reason it is imperative to keep the general framework of development in mind, and to see where such places fit into it. There are two ways in which this may be done. The first is to take a single topic and explore it over a more or less lengthy period in the country as a

1 Problems and approaches

whole. Maurice Beresford's book, *The Lost Villages of England*, is a notable example of this approach, and for many people it opened up a new dimension in settlement studies when it appeared in 1954. The second method is to select a particular region, a county or a kingdom perhaps, and as far as possible examine every aspect of its development on a systematic basis: this is the approach adopted in the present book.

Such an approach demands the combination of two methods of analysis if it is to yield valid conclusions. It entails the comparative study of particular types of settlement or settlement feature, and where possible all the available examples of each type, or at least a substantial sample of them. For instance, there is much to be learned about the evolution of Kentish settlement from a comparative study of church-dedications, a subject which is investigated in Chapter 11, although individual dedications, considered in isolation, can often be misleading. Similarly, there is much to be learned from a comparative study of topographical features, such as church sites and parish boundaries, and these are investigated in Chapter 10. There are many other matters where this kind of comparative method is followed in the present book, for example, in the examination of boundary settlements (pp. 144 ff.), in the pattern of Downland woods (pp. 127 ff.), and in the identification of minster churches (pp. 187 ff.). Such an approach has long been familiar to place-name scholars and in their hands it has yielded important conclusions.[18]

The second requisite is, as already remarked, the need to follow up each available line of evidence, and to examine each in the light of the others. There may be some matters where only one line is available; but in general it is wise to be wary of grandiose theories based on a single type of source. There are many settlement problems where the solution is not a matter of absolute proof but of devising the best possible hypothesis to fit all the known facts, and where any single argument, taken in isolation, can be misleading. One thinks, for example, of the primitive origins that used to be claimed for place-names in *ingas*, and of the theories that were based on them, through failure to test them against the distribution of pre-Christian burial sites. In reconstructing the evolution of settlement in Kent, I have therefore sought to keep each line of evidence in view – documentary, onomastic, ecclesiastical, manorial, agrarian, jurisdictional, archaeological, geological, and topographical – and wherever possible to relate them to one another, or if they conflict to strike a balance of probabilities between them.

It is this systematic approach to the problem of settlement, and the

1 *Problems and approaches*

consequent necessity of evaluating each line of evidence individually, that underlies the organization of this book and its division into five parts. In places it entails repetition, and perhaps a tedious catalogue of facts; but if a regional survey is to be of use to scholars generally, the analytical method is imperative to establish the basic principles of investigation. I have therefore attempted in the first part of the book to identify the dominant characteristics of the community of Kent, not only in the settlement period but over a wide time-span, in the belief that there is a certain inherent bias or genius in each local or regional society that tends to mould its historical evolution.

In the second part of the book, the broad framework of the original 'Jutish' settlement of Kent is reconstructed in Chapter 4; this is followed in Chapter 5 by a consideration of the evidence for continuity between Roman and Jute in the 'Original Lands' or 'Old Arable Lands'[19] of the Kentish kingdom. In Part Three, the discussion turns from these 'landscapes of continuity' to the 'landscapes of colonization', and more particularly to the colonization of the great Downland forest or *wald*, some 300,000 acres in extent, between the seventh century and the eleventh. The evidence for this development is particularly instructive in Kent, and has led me to believe that the solution to many problems in English settlement history may well lie in devoting more attention to these zones of 'intermediate' or 'subsequent' colonization. For that reason, although this is not a book about the Kentish economy as such, a chapter has been added at this point in which the evolution of the early Downland economy is investigated.

In the fourth part of the book, the method of approach changes. Chapter 8 returns to the sixth century and traces the ecclesiastical development of the county from its origins in the Augustinian period down to its abrupt cessation in the fourteenth century. Owing to the early establishment of Christianity in Kent, the structure of church foundation was perhaps more closely linked with the progress of settlement than in some other parts of England, so that the ecclesiastical evidence as a whole is peculiarly revealing. It is noteworthy, for example, that the original Kentish minsters were almost without exception sited either within the old estate-centres themselves or else in adjacent settlements. The gradual development of daughter-churches and chapels in the outlying parts of their 'minsterlands' or dependent territories thus sheds a flood of light on the colonizing process and the local clearance of the *wald*. These circumstances were further reflected in the evolving pattern of church-dedications in Kent, and Chapter 9

1 Problems and approaches

attempts to reconstruct a tentative chronology of this subject, and to indicate its regional peculiarities in a county widely noted in the medieval period for its religious cults, its pilgrimages, and its devotion to the saints.

In the fifth section of the book the approach changes once again, and the topographical evidence is investigated. By systematic analysis of such matters as settlement direction, the course of lanes and droveways, parochial nomenclature, parish size, ecclesiastical relationship, manorial structure, church siting, parish boundaries, and so forth, Chapter 10 sets out to identify the basic elements of the subject, and to show how they illuminate the progress of settlement generally. If the ultimate purpose of analysis is synthesis, however, it is also necessary to draw the threads together, and to see how they bear upon one another, by reconstructing an individual territory in the round. For this purpose, there are several places in Kent that might have been selected, such as Maidstone, Reculver, and Faversham; but the complexity of the evidence, and the manifest need to follow it out in all its bearings, have restricted my choice to a single study, based on Milton Regis. It is the evolution of Milton and its dependent *regio* and minsterland that forms my final theme, therefore, and Chapter 11 in a sense sums up the argument of the book. It cannot be claimed that Milton was an altogether typical estate; with its fertile soils and relatively dense population, its development was very different from that of Wrotham, for example, with its outlying heaths and late-settled chartlands in West Kent; or from that of Eastry, with its discrete jurisdictional structure, in the extreme east of the county. Nevertheless, while it is part of my argument that every *regio* and estate was in some sense distinctive, there was necessarily a certain resemblance between them, and the methods that have been employed to reconstruct Milton have likewise served to reconstruct other territories, though these are not discussed in detail.

How far these methods may be relevant to other regions is a problem that has constantly been in my mind in writing this book, and one which is tentatively explored in my concluding chapter. We should never forget that England is a country of infinite diversity, however, and on the origins of English settlement generally, in that fascinating twilight world beyond Domesday Book, I cannot claim to have cast more than 'a little glooming light, most like a shade'.

PART ONE
THE COMMUNITY OF KENT

2

LANDSCAPE AND ECONOMY

1. ANTIQUITY

The character of the Kentish countryside, as we see it today, has been formed over a period of nearly 2,000 years. Many of its features, such as the rock-shelters of Oldbury Hill, the Coldrum Stones near Trottiscliffe, and the hill-forts at Squerryes and Holwood have a much longer ancestry. Generally speaking these primitive features are visually less prominent than in areas like Dorset and Wiltshire, where they form a more vivid element in the bare downland scenery than in the wooded hill-country of Kent. Perhaps the most striking relics of the pre-Roman world are the megaliths of the Medway valley – the only group of the kind in south-eastern England – and the prehistoric track erroneously called the Pilgrims' Way, which in Kent survives almost complete. To these we may add the dramatic earthworks of Dover castle, if we accept their identification as an Iron Age encampment. But apart from isolated features of this kind, the landscape of Kent that we now see has evolved, by and large, during the 19 Christian centuries.

The extent to which an older network of settlement, perhaps much older, underlies the general landscape pattern of the county is a question of the deepest interest, and one to which we shall return in later chapters. The name of Kent itself, together with those of its regions like Thanet, its rivers like Medway, Darent, Cray, and Dour, and a substantial number of its oldest settlements all derive from primitive Celtic roots, or perhaps in a few cases from a pre-Celtic origin, and so dimly hint at a more ancient stratum beneath that of the Romano-Jutish period. But on our present knowledge we cannot be so certain of the precise influence of that pattern on the modern landscape as we can of that of the Roman era. There are important parts of Kent, particularly along its northern side between the Downs and the seacoast, which still bear the imprint of the Roman world more obviously

PART ONE *The Community of Kent*

than most other parts of England save perhaps the Border counties. Scenically, most people would probably regard this part of Kent as its least attractive area. As a rule the great Roman roads of England, like that which traverses the area between London and Canterbury, make for a singularly unromantic countryside. And yet for the student of history they possess a certain kind of fascination: the beauty of a land long since begun.

The antiquity of the Kentish landscape, its very gradual evolution over an exceptionally lengthy period of time, is an important point to grasp for two reasons. In the first place many of those features commonly regarded as essentially characteristic of the county, such as orchards and hop gardens, are merely the latest of many inscriptions on the scenic palimpsest, so that this book will be chiefly occupied in deciphering the older layers beneath. But also, despite these changes, the rural landscape of Kent has in general been less subject to dramatic changes over the last two centuries than that of many counties, particularly those of the great heartland of England, the 20 or so Midland shires between the Thames valley and the Yorkshire Ouse. Although there are everywhere elements of great antiquity in the landscape of England, such as village sites and churchyards, much of the rural scenery of these Midland shires has been transformed over the last two or three centuries in a way that did not occur in Kent.

In the parish of Kimcote in south Leicestershire, for instance, the roads, farmhouses, and field-boundaries are almost entirely a creation of the last 200 years, as a result of parliamentary enclosure in George III's reign, though of course they have also been affected by older historical factors. None of the outlying farmhouses dates from before that period; most of them are either Victorian or modern; and few, if any, occupy a site of much antiquity. The only old buildings are to be found in the two villages of Kimcote and Walton themselves, and apart from the parish church and Walton Hall it is doubtful if any of these antedate 1550. In Kent the nearest approach we have to this kind of transformation is perhaps to be found in the orchard country of the Weald around Paddock Wood, which was largely a creation of the railway era. Yet even here there is nothing to compare with the totally modern landscape created by fruit-farming around Histon in Cambridgeshire within the last three or four generations. For although the development of the rural landscape of Kent has been continuous, extending over many centuries, it has taken place to a greater degree than in most counties within the old framework of roads, fields, and

2 Landscape and economy

farmsteads, without fundamentally destroying it. There are probably at least 8,000 settlement sites that have been continuously occupied for seven or eight centuries, as a consequence, and many hundreds for more than a thousand years. There is no real parallel to this situation in the Midland counties. Although in some parts of the Midlands farms still occupy their original sites, these are mainly areas of old woodland like the Forest of Arden, where permanent settlement as we know it often did not take place until the tenth or eleventh century. In such areas farms have remained on their original site for much the same reason as in the Weald of Kent, that many of them were enclosed farms from the outset, so that they were not affected by parliamentary enclosure in the eighteenth and nineteenth centuries.

A striking illustration of the characteristic contrast between the Kentish and the Midland scene may be found by placing a sheet of the $2\frac{1}{2}''$ O.S. map of the Downland area of Kent beside a sheet for the Lincolnshire Wolds. These are two regions where on grounds of solid geology, land-forms, and in some respects early history, one might have expected a somewhat similar countryside to develop. Both are chalk uplands, intersected by dry valleys; both are relatively accessible to the coast; both are areas of 'wold' settled principally in the centuries preceding the Conquest; and neither is among the more fertile parts of the Lowland Zone. Yet the Ordnance sheets reveal wholly different kinds of landscape. The immediate impression in Lincolnshire is of an exceptionally bare countryside, with few farms, few villages, little woodland, straight roads, and surprisingly little detail of any kind. The impression in Kent is the opposite. Here we have a countryside crowded with detail: dozens of scattered farms, scores of narrow twisting lanes, countless little shaws and copses, and several large stretches of woodland: in short a broken, parcelled, varied countryside, thick with tiny settlements and ancient place-names. These contrasts have little or nothing to do with such matters as density of population; both areas are among the more thinly-settled parts of the Lowland Zone. To some extent they are occasioned by differences of drift geology; but in the main they are due to the fact that in Lincolnshire we have a countryside that was virtually reconstructed in the eighteenth century, when the evidence of earlier centuries was largely obliterated by parliamentary enclosure: whereas in Kent there was very little enclosure of this kind, so that the evidence of earlier centuries is still inscribed upon the modern landscape.

On the sheet covering Lyminge and Elham, for instance, more than

PART ONE *The Community of Kent*

170 settlements are marked by name, and another 50 names relate to woods and other topographical features. Nearly half these names are discussed by Wallenberg in his two volumes on the county and certainly relate to medieval or pre-Conquest colonization, while most of the remaining half, to judge by their name-forms – in *lēah, hām, hamm, dūn*, and so on – are also probably of medieval or pre-Conquest origin. The name of Lyminge itself has a Celtic root, and its parish church is one of the earliest in Kent, an old minster founded on the site of a Roman temple and within a mile of an early Jutish burial ground. A little to the west, the Roman Stone Street runs from Canterbury to Lympne, another place with a Celtic name and probably the mother-settlement of Lyminge itself; and for most of its length this road is followed by medieval parish boundaries. North of Lyminge, names like Waltham commemorate the great Downland forest or *wald* that once covered all this upland country of East Kent. Scattered about among the hills are the numerous *steads* or forest lodges of some of the early settlers – Exted, Elmsted, Maxted, and Palmstead, for instance – which probably originated as summer shielings in the Old English period. A little to the east is Shuttlesfield, or 'boundary field', a farm first recorded in a charter of 838, and still occupying its original site on the parish boundary 1,100 years later.[1] Many additional farms in the area came into existence in the two or three centuries following the Conquest; and late in the medieval period Stelling Minnis or *gemǣnnes*, 'land held in common', originated as a squatters' settlement on the heathy commonland between Stelling and Lyminge. Later still, Bunker's Hill must have been squeezed in on the boundary between Elham and Denton during the American War of Independence. About the same period the old manor house of Acrise ('oak brushwood') enclosed itself with its rustic little park; whilst Ebenezer Chapel originated as late as 1862, when it was founded in the woods of Stelling Minnis by the Primitive Methodists. Almost every century since the time of the Romans, in short, has contributed to the formation of the landscape in this characteristic corner of Kent.

2. REAPPRAISALS

It is in the light of this antiquity that we must re-examine some of those characteristics which are commonly thought to be all-pervasive in Kentish history, but which on the long view are more recent in origin and more limited in effect than is generally realized. The first and

2 Landscape and economy

perhaps the most difficult to eradicate is the view that Kentish history has been chiefly shaped by the proximity of London. Now no one would deny that over the past century the metropolitan impact has been very great; but taking a longer view what are the facts that need to be remembered? First, that London was a Mercian not a Kentish town, and that it had virtually no influence on the early settlement history of the county. Second, that all its historic transpontine suburbs were in Surrey and that its continuously built-up area did not extend as far as Deptford, the first parish in Kent, until after 1800.[2] Third, that although it has always been England's largest city, until Queen Elizabeth's reign it was no larger than modern Maidstone and only half the size of modern Norwich. In the development of Kentish society, moreover, the pull of the capital has been counterbalanced by the size of the county and its peninsular position, which in many ways created an unusually inbred and introverted community.[3] Nowadays Kent has lost nearly 70,000 acres to Greater London, including (through historical accident) a sizable stretch of genuine countryside around Cudham and Downe; but originally it comprised about 1,040,000 acres and was substantially exceeded by only six other counties: Yorkshire, Lincolnshire, Devon, Norfolk, Northumberland, and Lancashire.[4] Since its extremity lies 75 miles or so from London, moreover, much of Kent until relatively recently lay beyond the orbit of the metropolis. If one draws a circle of 40 miles around the capital, the area so described comprises the whole of Middlesex, Surrey, and Hertfordshire, more than half of Essex and Buckinghamshire, and about half of Bedfordshire, whereas more than half of Kent lies beyond it. Forty miles is no great distance in modern terms; but in terms of settlement history it is substantial, and as late as George II's reign it represented a day's journey by stage-coach along the Dover road.

One further factor limiting the influence of London has been the topography of the Kentish road system and the geographical configuration of the landscape underlying it. Until the seventeenth century the county was traversed by only one primary route, the Roman road to Canterbury and Dover. After the Conquest this became one of the principal roads in the country, linking England with the continent; but it traversed only the northernmost edge of the shire, leaving its hinterland still untouched and remote. Originally this fact was more apparent than it is today, since beyond Canterbury this road continued to Richborough, the chief point of entry in early Roman times at the mouth of the Stour, whilst the extension to Dover was a subsidiary

PART ONE *The Community of Kent*

branch passing through heavily forested countryside.[5] In these respects there is a marked contrast between Kent and the counties to the north of the Thames. The great Roman road through Essex traverses the middle of the shire on its way to Colchester, unimpeded by geographical considerations. To the north-west, the Chilterns have never offered the same barrier to communication as the North Downs in Kent, since their valleys tend to converge on the capital, and the escarpment itself is breached by numerous wind-gaps, so that trunk routes have developed through Hertfordshire and Buckinghamshire with relative ease. In Kent, by contrast, the valleys of the Downland tend to run north and south and so lie athwart the lines of communication fanning out from the metropolis. Apart from Watling Street, the original road system of the county was thus not oriented upon the capital, and this was a point of great importance in its settlement history. Behind it lie not only problems of geography, but the fact that in origin Kent was an independent kingdom whose wealth and power were predominantly centred upon Canterbury and the countryside of East Kent. Although the presence of the Dover road opened the county to continental influences from a very early date, the fact that it skirted along the northern edge of the shire for most of its length thus limited the penetration of those influences. That is one reason why until recent generations Kent has always been a region not only of advanced civilization but of primitive survivals: a region of contrasts and paradoxes where poverty and plenty have always existed side by side.

It was for reasons such as these that until the nineteenth century the wealth of Kent, and the inspiration behind its evolution, lay in the east and centre of the shire rather than in the west. Many little signs indicate this historical predominance of the east. The overwhelming majority of the most ancient settlements, apart from those of the Darent valley, are to be found in east and central Kent. All its 15 ancient incorporated boroughs except Gravesend, and most of its historic market towns, lay east of the Medway. The capital of the ancient Kentish kingdom – Canterbury, or the '*burh* of the men of Kent' – is situated nearly 60 miles from the western edge of the shire. And until the time of the Hearth Tax, fiscal records generally indicate the relative poverty of the western third of the county outside the half dozen or so parishes in the immediate neighbourhood of London, such as Greenwich, Woolwich, and Deptford.[6]

The second misconception that needs to be disposed of is the legendary wealth of Kent as compared with other parts of England.[7]

2 Landscape and economy

Until the sixteenth or seventeenth century that reputation is largely mythical. In the medieval period, it is true, there were some very wealthy stretches of countryside, particularly in the rich arable lands of the north-eastern corner. But there were also extensive poor districts, and as a whole the county was not among the richest in England, in the thirteenth century ranking only twelfth in terms of taxable capacity per square mile.[8] At the end of the medieval period, there are grounds for thinking that its wealth expanded rapidly; but it is not until the Hearth Tax of the 1660s that we can be positive that it was among the five or six richest counties of England.[9] The truth is that there have always been sharp contrasts between its rich and its poor districts.[10] As a rule, it was only the wealthy countryside of the coastal plain, alongside Watling Street, that travellers saw in passing through the county, while the fortunes of the Downland, the Chartland, and the Weald escaped their attention. If the main routes had traversed these latter districts instead of the coastal plain, they would have told a very different story. Ever since Caesar's time contemporary comment has thus tended to overemphasize the prosperity of Kent. It was the plain that Caesar saw, and it can only have been this area that he had in mind when he described Kent as the most civilized part of Britain. Against his comments must be set the impressions of Bede, eight centuries later, when he described the Weald as still a region 'thick and inaccessible, the abode of deer, swine, and wolves'. These contrasts of wealth and poverty lie at the heart of all Kentish history, and in the settlement period they moulded both the basic pattern of colonization and the structure of Kentish society.

For similar reasons the popular image of Kent as the fabled Garden of England is also a misleading one. Historically speaking, fertility of soil and the consequent development of hop-growing and fruit-farming during the last four centuries are not its most prominent characteristics. 'One must not think of the whole county as a fertile garden,' wrote G. H. Garrad in 1954. 'There is a larger proportion of good and medium-quality land in Kent than in the other Home Counties, but there is also a great deal of poor land . . . there are also large stretches of poor, dry chalk downland and wide belts of wet, stubborn clay.'[11] Though in Romney Marsh and in the fruit- and hop-growing areas some of the most fertile lands in England are to be found, these tracts are of limited extent and the county as a whole is not generally fertile like such Midland counties as Leicestershire and Northamptonshire. Orchards and hop gardens have never covered more than a tenth of its

PART ONE *The Community of Kent*

area and the remaining nine-tenths comprise much comparatively unrewarding land whose intractability has been one of the most important factors in shaping the evolution of settlement.[12] It is a sure sign of that intractability that oxen remained the draught beasts of the Weald until Queen Victoria's reign, while the cumbrous turn-wrest plough survived in universal use in the early nineteenth century.[13]

Finally, though it may seem surprising, Kent has probably never been amongst the most densely settled English counties. It has not, of course, been one of the most thinly populated; as a rule it seems to have occupied a position about a quarter or a third of the way down the national scale. At the time of the first census in 1801 it ranked tenth, alongside Somerset and Nottinghamshire, with one inhabitant to every 3.8 acres. It was surpassed at that time by London (with one inhabitant to 0.08 acres), Lancashire (1:1.8), Middlesex (1:2.1), Staffordshire (1:3.0), Warwickshire (1:3.0), the West Riding (1:3.0), Worcestershire (1:3.1), Gloucestershire (1:3.1), and Cheshire (1:3.4).[14] Before 1801, comparative figures are more questionable; but in the latter half of the eighteenth century the Kentish population seems to have expanded at an unprecedented rate of 88 per cent, so that in 1750 its ranking was probably below that of 1801. It may also have been below that level a century or so earlier, since the population apparently remained almost static between 1600 and 1750.[15] What the county ranking may have been in the early settlement era it is impossible to say; but at the time of the Conquest there are grounds for believing that most of the East Anglian and East Midland counties were more densely populated than Kent. The average size of their early medieval parishes was substantially smaller, and their surviving woodland and waste seem to have been much less extensive.[16] More important than comparison with other counties at this time, however, is the local variation within Kent itself. By 1086 all the indications are that the coastal plain and Holmesdale were already thickly settled, whilst the Downland and Chartland were relatively sparsely inhabited, and the Weald and much of the Marshland had only recently begun to yield to permanent colonization.

In a sense perhaps the most important fact to realize about the Kentish population in earlier periods is its remarkable sparsity by the standards of the twentieth century. In 1801, for example, despite the massive expansion of the previous 50 years, Kent was more thinly peopled than any modern English county save Westmorland and Herefordshire, and more thinly than Welsh counties like Anglesey and

24

2 *Landscape and economy*

Caernarvon. With a little over 300,000 inhabitants it had only one-third the population of modern Devon or Northumberland, only one-eighth that of modern Warwickshire. That does not mean that we should envisage vast open spaces like Dartmoor or the Northumbrian fells: it was a different kind of landscape and the population was very differently distributed throughout it. But it does mean that if we are to visualize the situation in 1801, we must think away at least five people out of six in the modern county. If this was the situation in 1801, in 1086 the sparsity of settlement would have seemed far more striking. With an estimated population of perhaps 40,000 or 50,000,[17] Kent was then more thinly inhabited than any English or Welsh county of today, and almost as thinly as the remotest Scottish Highlands in Ross-shire. This is a sobering reflection, and one which needs to be borne in mind in approaching the settlement history of the county; otherwise we may easily make false assumptions in attempting to explain it.

3. WOODLAND

If in the light of antiquity neither wealth nor fertility, neither orchards nor hop gardens, neither density of population nor metropolitan impact are the dominant characteristics of the community of Kent, what are its most enduring features? The first to note is the extent of woodland. As is well known, the word 'weald' is derived from the Germanic *wald* and specifically means 'forest'. Less well known is the fact that the Downland also is a well-wooded area, and the county as a whole is still one of the most heavily forested in England. Its woods are exceeded only by those of Sussex and Hampshire and extend to nearly 100,000 acres, or more than all its orchards and hop gardens.[18] Very little of this woodland is strictly speaking 'natural'; but the great bulk of it is 'ancient woodland' rather than modern plantation. Its characteristic lacelike network on the modern map represents the remains of a more or less continuous tract of forest which has gradually been eaten away by piecemeal clearance and assarting. The topography of the surviving woodlands of Kent, and the extraordinary number of woodland place-names, thus provide a major body of evidence for reconstructing the evolution of local settlement. In a typical stretch of Downland country between the Stour valley and the English Channel, 1,135 woods are marked on the $2\frac{1}{2}''$ Ordnance sheets, and in the county as a whole there are probably at least 10,000 woods altogether.

One of the outstanding characteristics of these woods has always

PART ONE *The Community of Kent*

been the variety of their tree-cover. Oak, beech, birch, elm, and hornbeam; alder, elder, willow, yew, wild cherry, and hazel; ash, holly, whitebeam, crab apple, pear, plum, and field maple: most of these and other species are represented in early Kentish place-names, and all are still common in the area. Along the foot of the Downland escarpment in particular, and wherever the holloways cut down into the chalk, trees and shrubs may be found growing in wild profusion that are rarely met with outside a few southern counties: spindle, dogwood, and guelder-rose, for example, wayfaring tree and wild service tree, often half-smothered in summer-time by the gigantic tangles of the wild clematis. Yet in the midst of this profusion there are two species that have perhaps always been predominant in Kent: the oak and the chestnut. On the heavy clays the oak is still ubiquitous, and on the lighter soils of the ragstone and sandstone it is in many places very common. It was principally the oak forests of the Weald that gave rise to an early transhumant economy in Kent, since their mast provided pannage for livestock, so that indirectly they have shaped both the evolution of settlement and the pattern of roads and tracks. It was also the oakwoods that furnished the principal material for the county's unrivalled legacy of timber-framed buildings, and in later centuries gave rise to a major shipbuilding industry. The unusual prevalence of the sweet chestnut is in part attributal to post-medieval plantation for hop-poles; yet in much of the county there can be little doubt that this species also has long been widespread. In an attempt to prove that it was indigenous, Edward Hasted adduced the manifest antiquity of the chestnut woods of Borden and Milton Regis, where he found trees often used as early boundary-marks and ancient rents paid to the Crown in chestnuts in 1575.[19] Since he wrote, the names of Chestnut Street and Northwood Chasteners in this area have been traced in early thirteenth-century records and are now known to contain the rare Old French word *chastaignière*, 'place where chestnut trees grow'.[20] If the species is not indigenous, there can thus be very little doubt that it has formed a major element in the Kentish landscape for a thousand years, and perhaps for very much longer.

Historically speaking, the importance of woodland is further attested by the large number of local words, some 25 in all, used to denote different types of wood. Some of these words, like *hurst*, *frith*, and *shaw*, were originally of general significance; others have always borne a more limited or specific meaning. Several are still in current use, though their historic definition is not always easy to establish, and in some cases has

2 Landscape and economy

varied over the centuries. *Hurst* is the characteristic word for a wood in the later-settled parts of the county, especially in the Weald, where it occurs in more than 200 place-names and is much more common than on the earlier-settled Downs. In Kent, in contrast with some areas, it is not necessarily associated with hill-top sites, and it is just as common in the Low Weald as the High Weald. *Frith* and *shaw*, by contrast, are especially common on the Downland, though they are not infrequent in other parts of the county. In later centuries *shaw* and its local doublet *shave* came to refer particularly to the irregular strips of woodland left along the steep flanks of Downland combes or around the edges of medieval assarts as settlement advanced; in many places they are still a faithful indicator of medieval assarting. Of words with a more limited connotation, *copse* and *spring* refer to woodland which has been 'coppiced' and allowed to spring up again on the old stocks; *toll* signifies a grove or clump of trees, usually on a hill-top; *hanger* a wood hanging on a hillside; and *carvett* a length of woodland beside a field. *Snode* is often used in Kent of a stretch of woodland once belonging to the king;[21] while *roughs*, *ruffits*, 'shrubs', 'scrubs' and 'bushes' are common local expressions for poor scrub. Several other words only gradually acquired their distinctive historic meaning, and originally referred to other topographical features. *Trench*, for instance, originally indicated a track through a wood, but gradually came to be used for the long strip of woodland left on either side of the track. Both *hurst* and *grove* often came to signify a woodland pasture as well as the wood itself. *Hoath* is the dialect form of 'heath', but in West Kent it often came to refer to small heathy woods, as at Chiddingstone Hoath and Hill Hoath, rather than to the open heathland itself. *Warren* must originally have referred to a rabbit warren; but on the steeper slopes of the Downs trees and scrub quickly recolonize the area if the warren dies out, so that eventually the word came to signify a particular kind of dense hanging woodland, as at Boarley Warren and Boxley Warren.[22]

The survival of so much woodland after more than a thousand years of unremitting reclamation is directly attributable to the intractability of much of the local terrain, so that its historic distribution is generally associated with the poorer lands of the county. Woodland often imparts an air of luxuriance to a landscape, but that look is deceptive: acre for acre its yield is generally much lower than that on arable land or pasture, so that it tends to survive only in areas that will support nothing more profitable. On the richest lands of Kent there has for many centuries been very little woodland. There is practically none in

PART ONE *The Community of Kent*

Romney Marsh, the North Kent marshes, the Isle of Sheppey, or the whole north-eastern segment of the county between Canterbury and the North Foreland. There is relatively little on the fertile Foothills north of the Downs, or in the Hoo peninsula between the Medway estuary and the Thames. Apart from the difficulty of growing forest trees in marshy areas, the land is generally too valuable in these parts to waste on timber or coppice. Much of the remaining woodland of Kent thus still lies where it has always lain: on the sandy or stony soils of the Chartland; on the heavier clays and hungry sandstones of the Weald; along the steeper sides of the Downland valleys; and on the crest of the Downs where they are mantled with that terrible clay-with-flints which has been the despair of so many generations of Kentish farmers. It is the abundance of woodland that most clearly distinguishes the chalk country of Kent from the bare whale-backed hills that are usually associated with downland. It forms a less dramatic countryside than that of the Sussex downs or Salisbury Plain; but for those familiar with its sombre woods and winding combes it has its own haunting beauty.

How far in earlier centuries the areas now woodless were bare of trees is a question of the utmost importance in Kentish settlement history, and one that will figure prominently in later chapters. Even as late as the eighteenth century, there was substantially more woodland in some parishes than there is today: 540 acres in Rainham, for example, 634 in Ash-by-Wrotham, and 1,100 in Longbeech Wood alone in the parish of Challock.[23] Between Maidstone and Sittingbourne, the historic chestnut woods of Milton Regis still stretched for five miles up into the Downland valleys of Stockbury and Borden, where relatively little woodland now remains.[24] In the topographical accounts of Edward Hasted, woodland thus figures prominently, and his comments, though tinctured by eighteenth-century prejudice, often give a vivid impression of the densely forested environment which shaped the lives of so many generations of Kentish people and gave rise to many local occupations. In the parish of Rainham, for example, he tells us that 'the ground rises southward to a dreary barren country among the woods, which is exceeding hilly, the soil at places chalky and much covered with flints, over which it extends till it joins Bredhurst, its southern boundary.' In Bredhurst itself, meaning 'board wood' or perhaps 'broad wood', the whole parish was then 'surrounded by an extensive range of woods ... the north-east part of this parish being almost covered with them.'[25] In both these places there is still a fair amount of woodland remaining; but in some parts of Kent the coppice woods have now given way to orchards,[26] and on the heavy clays of the Weald the development of clay-pipe drainage in the nineteenth century facilitated the last major clearance of woodland.

At the time of the Norman Conquest, the forested area of Kent was substantially more extensive, and certainly far more so than the evidence of Domesday Book would lead us to suppose.[27] On the Sussex border nearly all the parishes formed about this time bear woodland place-names – Ashurst, Speldhurst, Lamberhurst, Goudhurst, Hawkhurst, Sandhurst, and so on – and in all probability more than half the county was then still under wood. Before the coming of the Jutes, there are grounds for thinking that not only was the whole of the Weald, the Downland, and the Chartland once forested, but also much of Romney Marsh, the Isle of Thanet, and the Foothills north of the Downs. Certainly in the south-western part of Romney Marsh there were extensive woods around Lydd,[28] and great trees 'as black as ebony' – perhaps bog-oak – were often dug up in this area in the early nineteenth century.[29] Beyond the Swale, both the Isle of Elmley, 'elm wood' or 'elm clearing', and the Isle of Harty, 'stag island', must once have been wooded, though for many centuries now they have been entirely given over to sheep pasture. In Thanet, as Hasted pointed out, there was at one time much more woodland than in his day; for although almost all of it had long since been 'grubbed up and converted into tillage ... several of the little vills in [the island] still preserve the memory of these woods, viz. Westwood, Northwood, Southwood, Colyswood, ... Villawood, ... Frisket Wood near Hoo, a wood called Bobdale in St Nicholas, and Manston Wood, a copse of about five acres, which is the only woodland of all these now left.'[30] The Thanet countryside is so bare of trees today that it is difficult to imagine it as anything but an arable district; yet in the very centre of the island the name of Woodchurch Farm still reminds us of the vanished parish of Wood.

Perhaps the most interesting evidence of a former forest landscape is to be found on the Foothills between Blean Forest and the hundred of Hoo. The whole of this fertile area was settled very early, much of it in the Roman period; yet the countryside between Canterbury and Hoo was probably at one time almost entirely wooded, so that the 8,000 surviving acres of the Blean itself in fact represent the last vestiges of a forest once extending for some 40 miles between the Thames estuary and the Stour Levels. That this area was indeed once woodland is suggested by the occurrence of the British word *cēto* or *caito*, signifying 'wood' or 'forest', in five of its place-names: Chatham, Chattenden in

PART ONE *The Community of Kent*

Frindsbury, Chetney in Iwade, the lost *Chathurst* attached to Swalecliffe, and the lost *Chetham* in Ospringe.[31] The name of Blean itself has not been satisfactorily explained, but it may be that the whole wooded area between the Medway and the Wantsum was at one time called the Blean.[32] Its former character is further attested by the survival of many minor place-names, such as Norwood, Grovehurst, Woodstock, and Wildmarsh or 'weald marsh' near *Chetham*.

Until well into the Jutish period, in fact, Kent needs to be thought of as overwhelmingly a region of forest. For many centuries the evolution of local settlement and the development of the local economy were very largely moulded by this brooding presence of the *wald*. At its maximum extent, in the Romano-British period, the great forest of Kent and Sussex stretched for nearly 100 miles east and west, between Petersfield and Deal, and 40 miles north and south, between Watling Street and the South Downs. Its sheer size, the density of its woodland, the poverty of its resources, and the difficulty of communication across it, imparted to the region an isolation which more than counterbalanced the fragile early civilization along its outer rim.[33] In many ways what the fells and moorlands were to the North, the *wald* or forest was to these southern counties. That is one of the principal reasons why the colonization of Kent, which began so early, took so much longer to complete than that of Midland counties like Leicestershire and Cambridgeshire, whose woods seem to have been almost entirely reclaimed by the time of Domesday Book.

Although the inhospitable character of the *wald* thus inhibited clearance and delayed colonization for so long, it was nevertheless not wholly unexploited, and its gradual development as a region of forest pasture left a permanent mark on the landscape and economy of the county. Quite when the woodlands of Kent first began to be utilized for this purpose it is impossible to say; but there can be no doubt that the custom of transhumance behind it goes back to the early days of the Jutish kingdom, and perhaps to the Romano-British period or indeed beyond. Pasture of some kind, after all, is the most obvious elementary use to which uncleared woodland can be devoted, and for this purpose there are broadly speaking two ways in which it may be exploited. The first is the fattening of livestock on the mast or pannage of certain types of tree, chiefly oak, but also chestnut, hornbeam, and beech, during the late summer and autumn; this is a well-known aspect of early Kentish history, and one which we shall return to in the following section. Less well known, and at present less well documented, is the custom of

2   *Landscape and economy*

feeding livestock off the foliage or *browse* of the trees. In some countries peasants still keep their sheep in the woods, pulling branches from the trees to feed them, and in England this was a widespread custom in the medieval period.[34] In Kent, woodland names like Shepherds Hill (*scēap* + *herst*, 'sheep wood'), Cowden ('cow pasture'), Cowlees ('common cow pasture'), Milsted ('milking place'), Woodstock ('wood vaccary'), and Shiphurst in Marden indicate that both cattle and sheep were at one time pastured in the forest and fed off the browse.[35] In some parts of the county this custom of woodland pasture was more important than the right of pannage, and on the Downs it was a major factor behind clearance and colonization: that is why the Domesday evidence, which in Kent is limited to the record of pannage rights, is often misleading.

It is the use of woodland for pastoral purposes in this way that eventually necessitates the development of some kind of management; for otherwise sheep and cattle will eventually clear an area of its trees more or less completely by eating seedlings and saplings. Probably from a very early period, as a consequence, and certainly since the early medieval era, much of the woodland of Kent has been 'managed' woodland rather than natural forest, carefully tended and regulated, like any other crop, for certain specific purposes. This is still evident today in the fact that as much as 75 per cent of it is in coppice, mostly coppice with standards, a higher proportion than in any other county.[36] What the historian of settlement would like to know is how far back this preponderance of coppice or spring-wood may be traced. In recent centuries it has been largely determined by the demand for hop-poles;[37] but there can be no doubt that the practice of coppicing, by tradition every 13 years or so, goes back far beyond the development of hop-farming and very probably far beyond the Conquest. Coupled with the fact that the Kentish woods are generally sited on the poorer land for which little alternative use could readily be found, these circumstances have tended to preserve their place-names and their individual identity over many centuries, and in a considerable number of cases they are recorded in pre-Conquest charters. Like the Suffolk and Cambridgeshire coppices studied by Dr Rackham,[38] the many thousands of spring-woods in Kent are thus of great significance as historical evidence. Their names, their forms, their distribution, and their topography will frequently be referred to in this book in tracing the evolution of settlement.

PART ONE *The Community of Kent*

4. PASTURE AND TRANSHUMANCE

The rights and customs of a pastoral society have thus had a profound effect on the evolution of Kentish settlement. They had their origins in the heavily wooded environment of the county, and their consequences have continued to affect the character of Kentish agriculture until very recently. It is perhaps not generally realized that Kent has for long been the least arable and most pastoral of the corn-growing counties of England – those east of a line from, say, Scarborough to Bournemouth – and it is possible that this has always been the case. That is not to say that there have not always been important arable areas too, particularly on the Foothills and in the Isle of Thanet. During the late eighteenth century there was a substantial extension of arable farming, moreover, and it is possible that for a time cornland exceeded pasture. But whereas in 1900 about half the area of all the eastern counties of England from the East Riding to Essex was under crops, in Kent the comparable figure was less than one quarter.[39] That was at the depth of the agricultural depression; but in the mid-nineteenth century too the proportion of cornland in Kent, at 34 per cent, was well below that of the leading arable counties, such as Essex, with 51 per cent, Suffolk with 52 per cent, and Cambridgeshire with 57 per cent. The area under permanent pasture, meadow, and grass, by contrast, was greater than elsewhere in the Lowland Zone. At not far short of 300,000 acres, it exceeded the figures for Sussex and Norfolk by some 70,000 acres and those for Suffolk and Hampshire by about 150,000.[40] In reality the area devoted to pasture was probably nearer 325,000 acres owing to the widespread practice of keeping sheep in the orchards.

That this predominance of pasture in Kent is of great antiquity is evident from the place-names of the county. Many different kinds of animals, both wild and domestic, are recorded in its nomenclature: sheep, swine, oxen, cows, goats, and geese among the latter; deer, boars, bears, wolves, badgers, otters, fitches, and wild cats among the former. For wild animals a wooded countryside provides an area of refuge, so that several species survived relatively late in Kent: the wild boar until the sixteenth century, for example, the red deer until the end of the seventeenth, and the pine-marten into the late nineteenth.[41] For domestic stock, a wooded country often comes to be used as pastureland, as we have seen, and this accounts for the frequent reference to farm animals in early Kentish place-names. Oxen, for instance, are recorded in 20 or more names, such as Oxenden, Oxenhoath, and

2 Landscape and economy

Oxney; so too are swine, in names like Swanley, Swinford, and at least six Swantons, or 'swineherd's farms'. But the most widespread evidence of early stock-farming is to be found in those many names that indicate some kind of pasture. In Kentish usage such elements as 'tye' (*tēag*), 'lees' (*lǣs*), 'bere' (*bēr* or *bǣr*), 'minnis' (*gemǣnnes*), 'stead' (*stede*), and 'den' (*denn*) all connote pastoral use. The two last are particularly frequent and are more common than in any other county.

In more recent centuries the emphasis in Kentish pastoral farming has always been on sheep. In earlier times, before the Conquest, it was on both sheep and swine. When reasonably reliable statistics of livestock first become available, in the Agricultural Returns of 1866, there were more than 730,000 sheep in Kent, and that figure was exceeded in only two other counties, Lincolnshire and Devon, both of which are considerably larger than Kent.[42] Subsequently numbers increased substantially, and during the depression of arable farming in the late nineteenth century they hovered around the million mark. In the most famous grazing area, Romney Marsh, more than three-quarters of the land was under grass at the time of the Tithe Surveys about 1840, and in this district there are still more sheep to the acre than in any other part of England.[43] Historically almost as important were the marshlands of North Kent, particularly alongside the Swale. In the little island of Harty (2,600 acres) 4,000 sheep were fed on the marsh in the late eighteenth century and all the inhabitants of the parish whose occupation is recorded were shepherds. In the neighbouring Isle of Elmley (1,860 acres) there were more than 6,000 sheep and the annual wool crop was sometimes sold for as much as £1,000, or perhaps £50,000 in modern terms. In the Isle of Sheppey four-fifths of the land, or more than 18,000 acres, was under grass, and the marshes provided very valuable fattening grounds.[44]

The marshlands were not the only part of Kent where the economy was traditionally based on sheep-farming. Until recently much of the Downland and parts of the Weald were also sheep country. During the winter months the carrying capacity of the marshes was greatly reduced, so that in autumn the bulk of the flocks had to be sent to upland farms until the spring. Many up-country farmers, moreover, used to buy in wether-lambs in August, feed them on the Down, fold them at night, and sell them lean at two-and-a-half years to the fattening graziers of the marsh. These are the underlying reasons why the great arc of Downland countryside, particularly between the Medway valley and Dover, was for so many centuries essentially a

PART ONE *The Community of Kent*

region of sheepwalks and woods: an unusual combination. In the 1820s parts of this area were described as having been sheepwalk 'time out of mind', and there can be little doubt that the same might have been said of the Downs generally, save perhaps to the west of the Darent valley. Nowadays, much of the pasture has been ploughed up; but traditionally tenants were often restrained in their leases from breaking up the old Downland pasture. Poor though it was in comparison with that of the marsh, it played a crucial part in the stock-farming of the county as a whole, and the perennial interdependence of marsh and upland has long been a fundamental feature of Kentish husbandry. Every autumn and spring witnessed a great migration of flocks and herds between the two regions, and all the narrow little lanes leading up from the Levels were alive with the plaintive bleating of the droves.[45]

Until the definitive history of Kentish husbandry has been written, it is very difficult to say with certainty how far back this widespread preoccupation with sheep-farming may be traced. It is clear, however, that it extends back far beyond the first reliable statistics in the nineteenth century. About 1700 Kent was second only to Lincolnshire in total wool production, and in the early fourteenth century it was surpassed only by Norfolk.[46] In c.1322 sheep were twice as numerous on the Kentish manors of Christ Church as on those elsewhere in England, and if the Christ Church figures were typical of other manors in Kent at that time there may have been about 400,000 sheep in the county as a whole.[47] The fact that Sheppey, or 'sheep island', is recorded in one of the earliest Kentish charters, dating from the late seventh or early eighth century, shows how ancient is the preoccupation with sheep in that district,[48] and in all probability the economy of the Marshland has always been based predominantly on fattening or wool production.

The evidence for the importance of swine in the economy of Kent before the Conquest is well known. It consists in the fact that the whole of the Kentish Weald, together with Blean Forest and other stretches of woodland in the east and north-west of the county, formed the swine pastures of the Jutish kingdom. This fact is still apparent in the extraordinary prevalence of Wealden place-names terminating in *den*, normally signifying a swine pasture, of which more than 500 are said to have been recorded and some 250 are still marked on the $2\frac{1}{2}''$ O.S. map. Swine pastures in the forest were a feature of Anglo-Saxon England generally, wherever oakwoods or beechwoods predominated; they were in no sense a peculiarity of Kent. But the Weald was a larger stretch of

2   Landscape and economy

forest than most similar areas; in Kent alone it extends for upwards of 40 miles from east to west; and there is no other part of England with the same concentration of names ending in *den*, or where the swine pastures of a primitive people have left so marked an effect on the modern landscape. In this connexion it is worth pointing out that, although at many points the early history of Sussex closely mirrors that of Kent, and despite the fact that the Sussex Weald was apparently utilized as a pastoral region in much the same way as that of Kent, place-names in *den* become relatively infrequent as soon as one has crossed the county boundary. That fact in itself is an indication that, although the two kingdoms developed equally early and in many ways along similar lines, they also developed independently of one another: from different origins, under different auspices, and with partially distinct linguistic traditions.

Many of these detached pastures of the Weald were identified more than a century ago by Robert Furley in his three-volume *History of the Weald of Kent* (1871–4). As a local solicitor and steward of paramount manors like Aldington, Furley's knowledge of local records was unrivalled, and though his work has obviously dated, it remains very valuable. Other studies, such as Professor F.R.H. Du Boulay's 'Denns, droving, and danger' in *Archaeologia Cantiana*, LXXVI (1962), have dealt with more limited or specific aspects of the *dens*. More recently the area has been subjected to intensive scrutiny by Mr K. P. Witney in *The Jutish Forest: a Study of the Weald of Kent from 450 to 1380 A.D.* (1976). Mr Witney's book is a remarkable piece of topographical detective work, and at many points he has been able to correct or amplify Robert Furley's evidence. The Weald is thus the one area of the county whose early evolution has been intensively examined, and for that reason its settlement history will not be described in the same detail in this book as that of other areas. There is one fundamental matter, however – the custom of transhumance – regarding which its development has affected the settlement and topography of the county as a whole, and to this matter we must devote some attention.

One of the most obvious ways in which the swine pastures of the Weald have left their mark on the topography of Kent is to be found in its road system. With a few obvious exceptions, such as the Roman Watling Street and the Pilgrims' Way, most of the ancient roads and tracks of the county still display a marked tendency to run across the grain of the county, from north-east to south-west, often descending the steep escarpments of the Downs and the Stone Hills by narrow,

PART ONE *The Community of Kent*

twisting holloways (see map 1). It is still difficult to travel directly for any distance east and west along the Downs; by car it is often quicker to descend to the A2 or A20, and then return to the hills nearer to one's destination. These difficulties, which have preserved the remoteness of much of the Downland, arise from the fact that early Kentish society, particularly in the centuries leading up to the Norman Conquest, was based essentially on the practice of transhumance. Certainly many, and probably most, of those sunken lanes running across the grain of the county to the south-west are the droveways of a people whose swineherds, during the summer months, migrated with their herds from the settlements north of the Downs to their detached pasturelands in the Weald and Romney Marsh. In a number of cases, as at Kettleshill near Under River, these lanes are still locally referred to as 'the Drove' or 'the Drift', although the expression has not often found its way on to the Ordnance Survey map and its topographical significance is perhaps rarely recognized by those who use it. That they originated as droveways rather than cart-tracks is evident from their

MAP 1. *Droveways and tracks crossing the Downland*

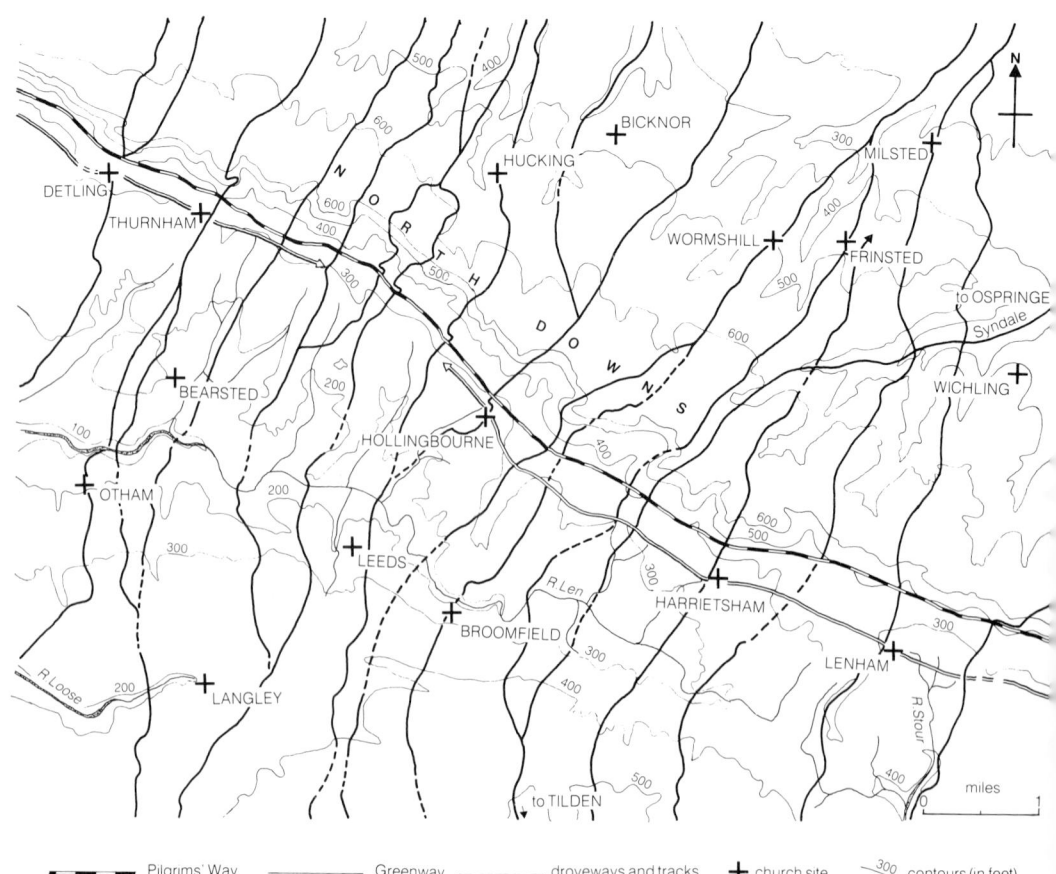

gradients in negotiating the Downland escarpment, which are generally too steep for horse-drawn vehicles. They are not too steep to have been utilized by packhorses, and some of them were so used in later centuries; but they are too numerous to have generally originated in this way, occurring as they do every half-mile or so along the escarpment.

There are still many places in Kent where these droveways can be traced on the map and in the field with reasonable certainty, though not necessarily in every detail of their course. The pasture of the men of Ospringe near Faversham, for example, is known to have been situated at Tilden, 15 miles away to the south-west in the Wealden parish of Headcorn. Although Tilden, like most *dens* of its kind, subsequently became an independent farm and so remains to this day, the old droveway linking it to Ospringe may still be traced by means of lanes, tracks, and parish boundaries from the point near Ospringe where it leaves Watling Street by way of Syndale direct to Tilden itself. There is only one stretch of a few hundred yards where it has disappeared, at the marshy spot where it crosses the water meadows of the infant River Len by the aptly-named Water Lane. Further west, the detached pasture of the men of Meopham was situated 12 miles to the south in the Tonbridge area, no doubt in the vicinity of Meopham Bank in that parish. In this case there are two possible droveways that may have been used, one by way of Culverstone Green and Wrotham, the other by Stansted and Ightham, the two uniting at Bewley Bar above Fairlawne and proceeding together to Meopham Bank by High Cross, Tinley Lodge, and Coldharbour.

Further west again the summer pastureland of Lewisham, Woolwich, and Greenwich lay nearly 30 miles away, near the borders of Surrey and Sussex, and gave its name to the hundred of Somerden, or 'summer pasture'. This name still survives in the farm settlements of Somerden and Somerden Green in the parish of Chiddingstone, from which droveways lead northwards over the Stone Hills and the Downland escarpment near Sundridge. The name of Sundridge itself is worth noting in this context, for it means 'sundered or separated pasture', though in this case we cannot be certain which place it was attached to, and it is not in the Weald itself but on the wooded dip-slope of the Stone Hills. It may be that, like Somerden, it was attached to the Lewisham district, as an enclosed pasture or halting-place half way to the distant Wealden pastures. In that case it would have some parallel with Thanington in the Stour valley, which probably means the *tūn* of the

PART ONE *The Community of Kent*

men of Thanet and lies 15 miles or so along the road between Thanet and its Wealden swine pasture at Tenterden – the *den* of the men of Thanet. In both cases, at Tenterden and Somerden, the pasture is situated unusually far from the parent community, at Tenterden more than 40 miles away. Lewisham, Woolwich, and Greenwich, it will be observed, have no connexion with London at this early period but look southwards for their livelihood to the forest country around Sundridge and Somerden.

In Kent, then, more obviously than in most parts of England, we have a road system and a countryside that in these respects have been largely shaped by the needs of a pastoral society based upon the practice of transhumance. Although with the permanent settlement of most of the Weald between about 1000 and 1300 this practice was on the wane, the vestiges of it survived until at least the seventeenth century. The Weald itself had by then ceased to be used as an area of detached pasture – though it remained a pastoral region – and sheep had taken the place of swine in the economy of the county as a whole. But Romney Marsh was still an area to which the upland shepherds used to migrate with their sheep-flocks in springtime; and there they spent the summer months in their 'old removable houses' or 'summer lodges', just as the Swiss cowherds today still migrate to their mountain shielings with the melting of the snows. In a sense, as we have seen, these customs continued to influence farming practice even in the nineteenth century, with the annual movement of sheep between marsh and upland. It is for these reasons, amongst others, that so much of the primitive road system of the county still survives within the maze of narrow lanes and trackways of the present day.

The pastoral economy of Kent left its imprint not only on the roads and place-names of the county, moreover, but also on the historic framework of its social organization. Behind the vestiges of an archaic countryside, behind the network of droves and pastures, we can also discern an archaic form of society in Kent, fossilized or encapsulated, so to speak, in the later parochial and manorial structure of the county. The ultimate reasons for this survival are too obscure and complex to be followed out in this book; but among the more important was the well-known fact that at the Conquest the county retained its own distinctive legal system.[49] Owing to the fact that the system was codified as the Law and Custom of Kent in the medieval period, moreover, the outlines of early territorial organization were still at many points substantially intact when Edward Hasted took up his pen in the last quarter of the eighteenth century.⁵⁰ Since it was local custom of this kind that particularly interested his somewhat dry and legalistic mind, his *History and Topographical Survey of the County of Kent* is thus one of the most important records we have for unlocking the secrets of early Kentish settlement history. Notwithstanding its errors of detail, his documentation of the structure of parochial organization, and of the framework of paramount and subordinate manors, with their intricate and at times conflicting jurisdictions, their scattered members and detached outliers, provides an unrivalled body of evidence for reconstructing the course of settlement, and for tracing the influence of transhumance upon its evolution.

If transhumance played so large a part in shaping the rural settlement and economic structure of Kent, when did it originate? There is little concrete evidence that it originated earlier than the Jutish period; but there are several tantalizing indications that the droveways traversing the Downland and Chartland may sometimes be much older than that. That many of them are of very considerable antiquity is evident from the depth of the holloways they have cut in the chalk and ragstone, in some places as much as 15 or 20 feet below the surface of the land. But perhaps the most interesting piece of topographical evidence is the fact that these droves frequently cut across the prehistoric route of the Pilgrims' Way without changing course. Where tracks of this kind meet an older road, they generally tend either to terminate at that point or to continue ahead by a zig-zag or 'dog-leg' alignment. The fact that these droveways often do not change course but run directly across the Pilgrims' Way does not definitely prove that they antedate it; it may be due to other circumstances; but it is one of many little details in the Kentish landscape that probably point, in the last resort, to those Celtic peoples who gave *Cantion* its name.⁵¹ In that connexion the fact that transhumance is a well-attested feature of early Celtic society in other parts of Britain may well be significant.

5. THE SETTLEMENT PATTERN

The last general characteristic of the landscape to note is the marked dispersal of the settlement pattern. Though Kentish settlement has often been described as 'mixed', comprising both villages and isolated farms, it is an open question whether there are any true 'villages' in the county in the Midland sense of the word: that is to say, nucleated places, historically based solely on farming, and organized on a

PART ONE *The Community of Kent*

communal basis, such as W. G. Hoskins described at Wigston Magna in *The Midland Peasant* (1957). Many of the places commonly called villages today, such as Lenham, Wrotham, Biddenden, Chilham, and Goudhurst, were in origin little market towns rather than agricultural communities as such. Of the remainder, some are relatively modern developments, like Ham Street in Orlestone; some are late expansions of medieval green-hamlets, like Throwley Forstal; some are probably late-medieval industrial communities, like Staplehurst; some are post-medieval encroachments on intercommonable land, as at Stelling Minnis and Brabourne Lees; some are eighteenth- or nineteenth-century settlements for farmworkers or quarrymen, as at Borough Green; and a number have developed gradually over the centuries through infilling between older scattered houses. Of the last, Boughton Street between Faversham and Canterbury is a typical example; for although it originated in the medieval period and still contains several early timber-framed buildings, it was not until the eighteenth century that it became continuously built-up; the original centre of settlement was more than a mile away, at Boughton church.[52] The further back we go in time, in short, the fewer genuine villages do we find in Kent and the more evident does it become that they originated either as small hamlets or as single farms.

Is it not possible, however, that old market centres like Lenham and Wrotham were genuine villages before they developed as trading-places in the late Saxon or early medieval period? Although at present there is little evidence of the fact, this is a possibility that should not be ruled out, since they were often ancient *capita* of great Anglo-Saxon estates, so that they always exercised some kind of administrative function and some kind of attraction as meeting-places. Nevertheless, in two respects they were distinct from the classical Midland village. In the first place, they were probably never the only centres of settlement in their parishes. There are very few rural parishes in Kent, if any, where as far as we can see settlement has ever been centred in a single community. Everywhere there are outlying farms, frequently a dozen or more to a parish, sometimes as many as 60 or 70, mostly on sites that have been occupied for six or seven centuries, and many for more than a thousand years.[53] Nowhere are ancient farmhouses generally sited in the villages themselves as they are in the Midlands. In other words, places like Lenham and Wrotham were never communities of farmers pure and simple: as far as can be seen they have always exhibited signs of some alternative activity to agriculture, whether of trade, of crafts, or

2 Landscape and economy

of industry. In the second place, there is no clear evidence in Kent of that great hallmark of the Midland village, the communally-organized open field. True, there were once many places with 'common fields' of a kind. Hasted often mentions them in the Foothill country east of Canterbury, and Dr Alan Baker has made an intensive study of them in such places as Wrotham, Gillingham, and Deal. But as Dr Baker has shown, no proof has yet come to light that these fields were communally organized like those of the Midlands.[54] The scattered holdings in the unenclosed arable land of parishes like Wrotham were owned individually and farmed in severalty. The villages themselves were not centres of co-operative farming as they were in central England, and in some places where there were so-called 'common fields' there was no village at all.

In the Midlands generally there is no real parallel to the general dispersal of settlement characteristic of Kent. Although there are areas where farms are scattered, and indeed they are more extensive than is commonly supposed, they are usually associated with old woodland country whose colonization often did not take place until the end of the Anglo-Saxon period or after the Norman Conquest. In these respects there are close resemblances between areas like the Forest of Arden in Warwickshire and the Weald of Andred in Kent and Sussex: in both cases clearance of woodland and colonization of the waste took place relatively late and was probably the work of individuals rather than organized communities. From the dispersal of settlement in such areas as these we can clearly deduce nothing directly about the original phases of Anglo-Saxon colonization five or six centuries earlier. But in Kent the point to note is that scattered settlement has always been characteristic of every part of the county: of the early-settled Foothills and Holmesdale as well as of the later-settled Downland, Chartland, Marsh, and Weald.

What are the reasons behind this scattered pattern of settlement in the early-colonized parts of the county? It certainly did not arise from the development of an advanced economy, supposedly farming for the market, such as encouraged the dispersal of farms from old Midland villages at the time of parliamentary enclosure. There can be no doubt at all that Kent was a county of isolated farms and hamlets many centuries before there was any question of commercial agriculture, for most of its outlying farmsteads are recorded in early medieval records or pre-Conquest charters. In the earlier-settled parts dispersal may well arise, as some scholars have argued,[55] from an underlying Celtic

PART ONE *The Community of Kent*

stratum in the landscape, and in this respect there are marked parallels between Kent and areas like Devon, Cornwall, and Wales. Yet it is also clear that in districts like the Downs and the Weald settlement was profoundly affected by the prevalence of woodland and the pastoral character of early Kentish society: for pastoral farming does not necessitate communal organization like tillage, and it is often preferable for stock-farms to stand isolated rather than grouped in villages.[56] In this respect the relative importance of pastoral husbandry and Celtic tradition are obviously difficult to define with any certainty; but it is probably safe to say that both factors lay behind the origins of dispersal in Kent. It may be, indeed, that pastoralism itself was a concomitant of Celtic tradition.[57]

Whatever the ultimate causes of this dispersal of settlement, the fact itself needs to be firmly grasped if we are to avoid advancing false parallels with other parts of England, such as Leicestershire, where true agrarian villages have long been the norm. It implies, amongst other things, that the isolated parish churches which are so marked a feature of Kent, particularly on the Downland, cannot in themselves be taken to indicate deserted village sites, as they normally would be in the Midlands and sometimes have been in Kent.[58] Although there are more than 300 lost churches and chapels in the county, at least 70 of which were at one time parochial, only a tiny handful of these definitely indicate deserted villages. Hitherto their neighbourhood has been searched in vain for vestiges of those earthworks that betray so many vanished communities in the Midlands and the North. It is possible, of course, that excavation may yet bring evidence of nucleation to light; but the fact that villages are rarely found at any point in the Downland parts of the county today, where isolated churches are most numerous, does not suggest that this is in general likely. The conviction remains that in this respect we have an essentially different kind of countryside in Kent from that of the classic Midland plain.[59]

3

REGIONS AND *PAYS*

1. REGIONAL PATTERNS

The evolution of settlement has been moulded not only by the environment and economy of Kent as a whole, but by the regional structure of the county and its contrasting countrysides or *pays*. Historically it has long been divided into two parts, East Kent and West Kent, respectively based on Canterbury and Rochester or Maidstone; but although this division is probably of great antiquity, its significance is primarily administrative rather than topographical.[1] In most respects more fundamental to the settlement of the county are its divisions north and south. It is these that have given rise to the sharply contrasted countrysides on which so many writers have remarked. The modern motorist following the main roads to Thanet, Dover, or Folkestone scarcely notices this diversity because he is following the grain of the country. But take one of the old droveways across Kent from north to south and you will traverse half a dozen distinct types of landscape within the space of 30 or 40 miles: cornland, downland, chartland, clayland, woodland, and marshland. It was this kind of variety that G. H. Garrad was thinking of in his *Agricultural Survey of Kent* (1954) when he wrote: 'Kent, in fact, is a county of contrasts. . . . Owing basically to the geological conditions, the nature of the soil probably varies more frequently and more abruptly than in any other county of similar size.' At the beginning of the nineteenth century William Marshall made much the same point: 'Kent, more than any other county, I think, of equal extent, naturally separates into well-defined districts.'[2] Marshall's comment is the more telling in that he was not a local man and spoke from wide acquaintance with other parts of England. His point may be illustrated by a comparison of Kent with Essex, five-sixths of which is based on a single formation, the London Clay.

Underlying these types of countryside is the exceptionally varied geological structure of the county. Although the effect of geology upon topography is never one of simple determinism, in Kent it is impossible to get away from its influence on almost every aspect of settlement history. Landforms and terrain, periods of colonization, forms of settlement, patterns of farming, types of local community, the evolution of roads and tracks, the distribution of population: all these and other

PART ONE *The Community of Kent*

matters have been more or less closely affected by the geological structure of the county. The old adage that sums up so much of its history, that the Marshland is wealthy but not healthy, the Upland both healthy and wealthy, and the Downland healthy but not wealthy, is ultimately a reflection of this fact. From north to south it is based on a series of nine successive formations, each overlying the next and giving rise to a distinct belt of countryside: the London Clay, the Thanet Beds, the Chalk, the Upper Greensand, the Gault Clay, the Lower Greensand, the Wealden Clay, the Wealden Sandstone, and the alluvial deposits of Romney Marsh. Within these formations there are important subdivisions, and the drift geology of the county gives rise to a bewildering variety of local soil-types, often within a single parish, and often decisive in their influence on local settlement. The basic historical divisions or *pays* to which these formations give rise are the Foothills, the Downland, Holmesdale, the Chartland, the Weald, and the Marshland (see map 2). Most of these terms have long been familiar and call for little comment; but two need a brief word of explanation. The phrase 'the Foothills' is not an historic term, and it is used here with some reluctance in the absence of any unambiguous alternative. Holmesdale is the name of the wide upland vale lying between the Downs and the Chart, and strictly speaking it is confined to the area west of the Medway. In discussing the settlement history of the county, however, it will be convenient to extend it to the valley as a whole.

The fundamental differences between these six regional divisions lie at the root of Kentish history and need to be kept in mind throughout this book. The first point to note is that they varied greatly in fertility and economic potential, a fact which has shaped both their individual development and the settlement history of the county as a whole. In early centuries it entailed a certain interdependence between them, and subsequently it facilitated their increasing independence of one another. It also entailed wide variation in the period of settlement as between different parts of the county. The two earliest-settled zones, from which virtually all subsequent colonization ultimately developed, were the Foothills and Holmesdale, and these may be described as the Original Lands of Kent, or to borrow Professor Du Boulay's useful expression, the Old Arable Lands. The other four regions were in origin dependent on the Foothills or Holmesdale, although eventually each developed a life of its own and its own idiosyncrasies of settlement and society. Only in the Marshlands did the local economy never become truly independent, and in a sense this area has always remained a

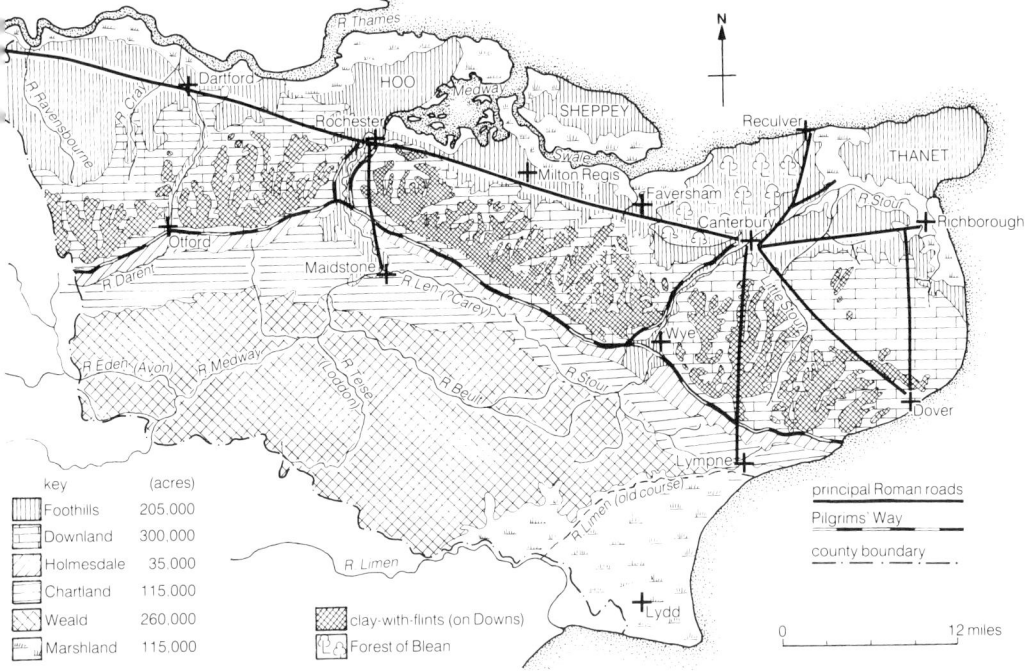

MAP 2. Kentish *pays* (based on the Ordnance Survey map with the permission of The Controller of Her Majesty's Stationery Office; Crown Copyright reserved)

tributary region to the rest of the shire. Its lands are among the richest in Kent; but for reasons which will be discussed below they have always been exploited by landowners and farmers living elsewhere, so that their wealth has been largely employed in enriching other parts of the county.

In many respects these regional divisions have continued to shape the agrarian structure of Kent down to the present day. The historic character of each *pays* is in most parts still imprinted on the contemporary countryside. For an understanding of this character in earlier centuries, before it was transformed by the coming of the railways, we must turn once again to the topographical descriptions of Edward Hasted at the end of the eighteenth century. He was the first writer to explore the county on a systematic basis, parish by parish, and the picture he presents of its sharply contrasted *pays* is of the greatest use for an understanding of its traditional society before it was subjected to the pressures of the nineteenth century.[3]

2. FOOTHILLS AND DOWNLAND

The first belt of countryside to consider is the low-lying but gently undulating coastal plain along the northern borders of the county

PART ONE *The Community of Kent*

between the Downs and the Marshes. In area this important region extends to about 200,000 acres, though it is rarely more than three or four miles in width. Formerly it was sometimes known as the 'Upland', a name which it acquired not in relation to its height above sea-level, which is often no more than 40 or 50 feet and rarely more than 200, but because it lay dry and breezy above the damp unhealthy marshes. In later centuries the term 'upland' was widened to cover the hill-country of the county generally, and it is for this reason that the area is referred to in this book as the Foothills. The accessibility of the region to the sea, and the generally fertile and easily worked soils of the Oldhaven Beds, Thanet Sands, and Brickearths, were circumstances of the first importance in the early settlement history of the county. They facilitated the development of the area as the Original Lands, and by and large it has probably always formed its richest and most thickly settled *pays*, as well as its chief corn-growing district, and the nursery of its orchards and hop gardens. Nowadays, much of the Foothill country is heavily populated and far from picturesque; but that fact in itself indicates something of its wealth, and of its history as the busy workaday part of the shire. It was not only its fertility and its proximity to the coast that contributed to this prosperity, but the fact that it was traversed by the one major Roman road of Kent, and penetrated by its three navigable rivers, the Medway, the Darent, and the Stour. There are more ancient boroughs and market towns on the Foothills, as a consequence, than in all the rest of the county, so that the wealth due to natural fertility has been augmented by the wealth arising from trade: in Canterbury, Sandwich, and Deal, for example, in Faversham, Sittingbourne, and Milton Regis, in Rochester, Chatham, Gravesend, and Dartford.

Together with the Downland to the south, the Foothills will therefore figure prominently in later chapters of this book, and their riches are frequently referred to by Edward Hasted. Between Sittingbourne and Blean Forest, for example, he tells us that the land was so valuable that hedges were dispensed with and 'most of the farms are thrown into two or three, or perhaps only one field, several of which contain sixty, seventy, one hundred acres, or more, and this makes the country more open and champion than the other parts of this county usually are.' It was the fertility of the soil in this neighbourhood that gave rise to the local custom of 'roundtilt land', or continuous tilth, according to which the fields were never allowed to lie fallow but were regularly cropped, year after year, with the same rotation of barley, beans, and wheat.[4] Although the 'open and champion' appearance to which Hasted refers

3 *Regions and* pays

was characteristic of much of the Foothills, and in many places was probably of great antiquity at the time he wrote, there were substantial stretches of this countryside, especially between Rochester and Faversham, where the Downland woods still came down as far as Watling Street in the Romano-British period. There were places, indeed, where they were not wholly cleared until the nineteenth century.

To the south, the Foothills gradually merge into the next region, the chalk Downland, the largest *pays* in the county, and historically closely connected with the Foothills. The Hog's Back or Backbone of Kent, as it has often been called, stretches for 70 miles east and west in a continuous range of hills from the Surrey border to the South Foreland, severed only by the river valleys of the Darent, the Medway, and the Stour, and the narrow windgap of the Elham valley, itself at one time watered by the Nailbourne or Little Stour. In breadth the Downland varies from five or six miles to ten or eleven, generally broadening out towards the east, and its total area amounts to rather more than 300,000 acres. Mile after mile its steep escarpment faces south, with immense views over the Stone Hills and the Weald. At its highest point it rises to 824 feet at Westerham Hill; it rarely falls much below 600, and it terminates in the tumbled cliffs of Folkestone Warren, 540 feet above East Wear Bay, the highest point on the coast between the North Riding and Dorset.

The chalk country of Kent is quite unlike that of most other parts of England: the sweeping Wolds of Yorkshire, for instance, the whale-backed hills of Sussex and Berkshire, or the wide expanses of Salisbury Plain. For the most part it is a quiet land of woods and combes, of sudden winding valleys, lonely farms, and solitary churches, everywhere laced with an intricate network of narrow lanes, steep hills, and shady holloways, peaceful, silent, and in many parts remote. It has remained remote because the trunk routes of the county pass on either side of it, as we have seen, and because it is still devoid of urban settlement. The only Downland town in the 70 miles between Surrey and the Channel is Dover, at its seaward extremity, although the suburbs of the Medway towns now reach up into the wooded valleys around Walderslade (*wald* + *slæd*). The few little market centres that there used to be, such as Elham and Chilham, have long since lost their urban status, and in modern terms are no larger than villages.

Owing to its extent and its broken character, the Downland of Kent forms a very distinctive countryside, with its own peculiar economy and historical evolution. As one rises up from the bare undulating

PART ONE *The Community of Kent*

Foothills around Adisham and comes suddenly upon the valley of the Little Stour, one seems to look across to another land, almost another country, thickly wooded, deeply scored, stretching away as far as the eye can see towards Wootton, Waltham, and Walderchain: the 'wood-farm', the 'forest *hām*', and the 'chine of the forest-dwellers'. To the early settlers this was a much less fertile and attractive area than the Foothills, bitterly cold in winter when the cruel north-easters blow up its narrow valleys, blocking the lanes with snow, and often severing farms and hamlets from the outer world. For that reason its clearance and colonization came later than that of the Foothills, except where the three major river valleys cut down through the chalk and form fertile shelves of land above the course of the stream.

The relative poverty and infertility of the area in the Hanoverian period are frequently depicted in the pages of Hasted, and his comments give a vivid impression of the kind of countryside the early settlers had to contend with. Take what he says of Lower Hardres, or 'the lower forest', for example, four miles south of Canterbury: 'this parish extends up to a dreary wild country of high hills and deep dales, the land in which is very poor, mostly chalky, and covered with sharp flint stones, having frequent woodlands interspersed over it, and carrying a face of rustic poverty throughout it.' Or take Stalisfield, six or seven miles south-west of Faversham: 'an unfrequented and obscure place, situated in a wild and dreary country', its soil 'a red cludgy earth, of very stiff tillage, very barren, wet, and flinty', its inhabitants as poor as the country, and even its coppice wood 'from its sort, and its out of the way distance from markets . . . not of any great worth'.[5] Or take Paddlesworth, on the Downs above Elham: 'a lonely and unfrequented parish, situated very high, among the hills . . . the inhabitants of which are poor indeed. The soil is much like that of the last described parish of Acrise, only still more barren, with a great deal of heath or common throughout it, a wretched and miserable country.'[6] These comments of Hasted's are worth pondering. They are refracted through eighteenth-century eyes, but the basic facts cannot seriously be disputed, and they were paralleled in a number of other poor chalkland districts, such as south-east Cambridgeshire. Modern methods of cultivation have ameliorated some of the problems of Downland farming, and improvements in transport have overcome the absence of markets. But at many points the margin of early colonization is still plain to see, and beyond it the unreclaimed woodland and the waste. Where greedy modern farmers have ignored it and tried to wring more from the land than

3   *Regions and* pays

nature will give, one may still see cornfields in summertime whose verges are nothing but barren chalk. Medieval people knew what they were doing when they left land like this uncultivated, and reconciled themselves to its use as a tract of poor wood-pasture.

It is one of the curiosities of Kentish historiography that so little attention has yet been paid to the historical evolution of the Downland. If discussed at all, it is often loosely bracketed with the Foothills; yet its landscape, its colonization, and its economy were in every respect dissimilar. Though it was a relatively poor countryside in terms of agricultural potential, moreover, it played a crucial part in the development of the Kentish economy as a whole, and its evolution sheds a good deal of light on that of other regions of early-colonized *wald*. For these reasons, the settlement of the Downs will be discussed at some length in the sixth and seventh chapters of this book.

3. HOLMESDALE AND CHARTLAND

South of this region again, at the foot of the Downland escarpment, Holmesdale forms a narrow yet fertile and well-watered tract of countryside which, like the Foothills, played a prominent part in the original phases of Kentish settlement.[7] Much of the vale lies on the intractable Gault Clay; but in Kent the Gault has been ameliorated by downwash from the chalk and by admixture with the Upper and Lower Greensand. All along these warm southerly slopes, as a consequence, where the springs gush out at the base of the Downs, a line of very ancient places is to be found, from Chevening, Otford, and Wrotham in the west to Hollingbourne, Lenham, and Charing in mid-Kent, and beyond the Stour at places like Wye, Stowting, and Folkestone. Some of these settlements, such as Otford and Wye, are sited on the Pilgrims' Way; but the great majority are on the Greenway, which runs parallel to it, and which is also thought to be of prehistoric origin. Like the early settlements on the Foothills, many of these places probably go back beyond the English invasions and in some cases beyond the Roman period. Many of their churches, as at Otford and Kemsing, are sited by sacred springs that may have been objects of heathen veneration before the advent of Christianity. Although the area is no more than a narrow corridor of countryside, rarely more than a couple of miles wide, it has thus exerted a profound influence on Kentish history, traversing as it does the centre of the county between the poor chalk on one hand and the poor Chart on the other. Its total extent is less than 40,000 acres;

PART ONE *The Community of Kent*

but it has given rise to a characteristic belt of open country still notable for its great arable lands and ever-changing skies, and largely devoid of those little copses and enclosures characteristic of the county generally; for the land is too valuable to be squandered on woods.

Beyond Holmesdale, and forming a sudden contrast with it, rises the Chartland, on the Lower Greensand formation: in origin a poor hill-country like the Downs, fretted with narrow valleys, and in many parts still heavily wooded. Its steep escarpment rises to a height of 810 feet at Toy's Hill near Westerham, gradually dropping to 600 or 700 beyond Sevenoaks, and rarely exceeding 500 between the Medway valley and the Stour. Beyond the Stour it eventually merges into the Weald, though reappearing in the sea-cliffs between Folkestone and Hythe. Altogether, the Chartland of Kent covers about 115,000 acres. Although less extensive than the Downs, and nowhere more than five or six miles in breadth, its broken character and narrow wooded combes, particularly in West Kent, make it seem larger than it is and emphasize its individuality. Much of its character arises from the fact that it forms one of the few genuine stone-belts of south-eastern England. The hard grey Kentish rag, a limestone embedded in the Greensand, has been quarried in many places on the Chart since before the Roman period, giving rise to the other names for the region, the Stone Hills or Quarry Hills. The early fortunes of Maidstone owed much to the export of ragstone to other parts of Kent and to London, where it was extensively used for building and paving from Roman times until the seventeenth century. Apart from the great quarries of the Maidstone district, a few of which are still worked for roadstone, the Stone Hills are peppered with hundreds of local stone-pits, or *petts* to use the vernacular word, most of them now unrecognized and buried in trees. These little disused petts may often be found in the vicinity of old farmsteads and manor houses in the area, many of which, like Stonepitts in Seal and Outridge in Brasted, are first recorded in the thirteenth century and were built literally out of the ground they stood on. Locally, the stone was still widely used for building purposes in the nineteenth century, and it has given rise to a series of characteristic stone villages, such as Ulcombe and Egerton.

The stony and infertile character of much of the Quarry Hills is also what gives the area its name of the Chartland. *Chart* is a word which is cognate with the Norwegian *kartr*, meaning 'rough, rocky, sterile ground', and it is an element found in many place-names on the Stone Hills, from Brasted Chart and Seal Chart in the west to Chart Sutton

3 *Regions and* pays

beyond the Medway and Great and Little Chart near Ashford. In a few favoured spots, the Greensand gives rise to a fertile countryside, and around Maidstone it forms one of the richest and earliest-settled parts of the county. Elsewhere, however, its infertility is indicated by minor place-names like Starveall, Starvecrow, Phen Farm ('fen'), Hothfield Bogs ('heathfield'), Roughway ('rough *(ge)hæg* or enclosure'), Rats Castle, and Whitley Scrubs. It is further indicated by the fact that most of the remaining stretches of commonland in Kent are to be found on the Chart: at Crockham Hill, Hosey Common, Goathurst Common, Brasted Chart, Sevenoaks Common, Fawke Common, Seal Chart, Hothfield Common, and elsewhere. In the pages of Hasted we can see just how poor much of this wood-heath country was in his time, before its natural beauty came to be appreciated. Of the parish of Westerham, for example, he writes: 'From the town southward, to the summit of the sand hill, is about two miles, over a very hilly infertile soil, interspersed with commons, waste rough grounds, and woods . . .' Further east, on the Chartland of Seal parish, there was also 'much waste ground . . . a dreary barren sand, consisting in this and the adjoining parishes eastward, of several hundred acres, being in general covered with heath and furze, with some scrubby wood interspersed among the hills. . . .'[8]

Except where the Medway valley cuts through it, there was thus little or no primary settlement on the Chart. Although several of the Iron Age hill-forts of Kent are to be found there, as at Squerryes and Oldbury, it is unlikely that these had any direct connexion with subsequent colonization, save perhaps at Boughton Monchelsea, near Maidstone. Originally, most of the area was utilized as the common pasture of primary settlements in Holmesdale, much as the Downland formed the outlying pasture of the Foothills. In the more fertile central reaches, between the Medway and the Stour, a few of these forest shielings began to develop into permanent settlements as early as the seventh or eighth century, particularly in the neighbourhood of Great Chart and Sutton Valence. By the tenth or eleventh century much of this central area seems to have been relatively well settled, and most of its churches are recorded in the contemporary *Domesday Monachorum of Christ Church*. Nevertheless, the fact that these churches were originally dependent on the mother-churches of Holmesdale plainly indicates their subordinate origins. To the west of the Medway, colonization seems to have begun a good deal later than this, and the only parish church to be established on the high Chart was at Sevenoaks, some 500 feet above sea-level. Then in the post-Conquest period a great wave of

PART ONE *The Community of Kent*

new settlement spread right across the area, and scores of outlying farms and manor houses were established in the woods at places like Squerryes (first recorded in 1216), Everlands (1239), Outridge (1270), Knole (1281), Black Charles (1292), and Blackhall (1313). Later again, in the Tudor period, some of the characteristic little green-villages and heathland hamlets of the region came into existence, such as Godden Green and Whitley Row; finally, at the time when Hasted was writing, there was yet another wave of settlement, when cottagers' communities like Hothfield Common and Brabourne Lees developed.[9]

In many ways the Chartland of Kent was a typical forest countryside, originally settled by small freeholders, often hacking out their own farms from the woods, and sometimes, as at Squerryes and Black Charles, giving them their own names. Yet it was also in some sense differentiated from that other great region of forest, the Weald, though immediately adjoining it. Until the nineteenth century most Chartland parishes consisted of an upland 'borough' (or tithing) on the Chart itself, and a Wealden borough below the escarpment, as at Sevenoaks Weald, and there was plainly a vital distinction between them in the eyes of contemporaries. Despite the development of a good deal of parkland in the early modern period, much of the Chart seems always to have remained something of a backwoods country, like Blean Forest in East Kent, whose strange ways and lawless customs often survived until a remarkably recent period. When one learns that the early nineteenth-century cleric, Beilby Porteus, found his fellow-parishioners at Ide Hill in Sundridge so ignorant of Christianity as never to have heard of the name of Christ, one has a sudden glimpse of the inner life of one of these outlying Chartland hamlets, though within 30 miles of St Paul's. That is a salutary fact to bear in mind in connexion with the settlement history of the region nine centuries earlier.[10]

4. THE WEALD

Beyond the Chartland, again to the south, lies the Weald, which is itself divided into the heavy-soiled Low Weald on the clays, and the generally light-soiled High Weald on the sandstones. This is the second largest region of the county, some 45 miles in length from Edenbridge to Lympne, and varying in width from eight or nine miles on the Surrey border to 15 or 16 between Egerton and Sandhurst. Viewed from the Chartland escarpment, the great expanse of wooded countryside

3 *Regions and* pays

stretches away as far as the eye can see to the Sussex border. When the county boundary was eventually fixed, some 260,000 acres of the Weald of Andred were included in Kent, and the remaining 500,000 unequally divided between Sussex, Surrey, and Hampshire: a total area of some 760,000 acres, or almost double that of the Lake District.

Nowadays, most of this area has long been cleared and colonized. Yet many hundreds of shaws and copses and some considerable stretches of woodland still remain to give the illusion of a forest countryside, and on a distant view suggest its original character. Rich woodland generally denotes poor country, however, and until the mid-nineteenth century the Weald was for the most part still a pastoral region, retaining much of its inhospitable character in the eyes of contemporaries. Although more variously endowed than the Stone Hills, and in places blessed with rich tracts of grazing land, its arable had never been of more than local value, and its terrible clays were still ploughed by oxen, a sure sign of their intractability. Since 1840 two developments have partially transformed substantial stretches of the Weald, particularly in the central parts of the Vale of Kent. The first was the invention of satisfactory clay-pipe drainage, which facilitated the cultivation of the more fertile areas of wet clayland. The second was the building of the main line railway through the county in 1840–2, which in its course to Dover traversed the heart of the Weald between Edenbridge and Ashford, and for the first time opened it up to easy communication with the London market. The area around Paddock Wood, the new railhead village which sprang up where the lines branched off to Maidstone and Cranbrook, was thus gradually converted into one of the fruit- and hop-growing districts of the county. Yet even the changes of the nineteenth century did not create a wholly new landscape; by and large the new orchards and hop gardens were fitted into the ancient pattern of farms and fields, and everywhere linked to the old network of twisting forest lanes. As so often in Kentish history, the original fabric remained, though shot through with vivid threads of change. There are still many places, as a consequence, where the evidence of woods and shaws indicates medieval assarting, and where the pattern of contemporary farmsteads still bears the imprint of the Jutish summer pastures.

Until the nineteenth century the great problem everywhere in the Weald was the state of the roads. During the autumn and winter months most farms and hamlets were isolated for weeks on end in a wet season. In the 10,000-acre parish of Cranbrook, for example, the bye-

PART ONE *The Community of Kent*

roads were 'so very deep and miry, as to be but barely passable till they are hardened by the drouth of summer'. In Benenden the roads were so deep in winter that Sir John Norris of Hemsted 'was forced to have his coach drawn to church in the common waggon track, by six oxen, one before the other, as the only means of conveyance to it.' In High Halden, the roads were 'hardly passable after any rain, being so miry that the traveller's horse frequently plunges through them up to the girths of the saddle; and the waggons sinking so deep in the ruts, as to slide along on the nave of the wheels and axle of them.'[11] Such conditions necessarily bred an isolated and inward-looking countryside, and this was a Wealden characteristic on which many contemporaries commented from the time of William Caxton down to the early nineteenth century.[12] Even at the present time, indeed, something of the traditional inscrutability of the area may still be sensed if one leaves the roads and takes to the woods and footpaths: in Bedgebury Forest, for instance, or in the wooded dingles of the Isle of Oxney, or the steep gills and shady valleys of the Sussex border.

With so adverse an environment, it is not surprising that the Wealden hinterland of Kent was relatively late in yielding to colonization. The clearance of the forest was a formidable task, particularly on the heavy clays and ill-drained gleys of the Low Weald. Although periodically exploited for pastoral purposes from a very early period, it was probably not until the tenth century that the woods began to give way to permanent settlement, and not until the fifteenth or sixteenth that the work of reclamation was complete. In this lengthy process five successive though overlapping phases of development may be distinguished. In the first phase, the Weald formed the common pasture of the Jutish kingdom of Kent as a whole, and it may have been so utilized before the advent of the Jutes. Then, by the seventh or eighth century the old primary communities of the Foothills and Holmesdale began to acquire independent *dens* or pastures of their own in the area, and each summer the swine were driven down to be fed on the mast, while the swineherds spent the pannage-season in their forest lodges or shielings.[13] In the third phase, these summer lodges gradually developed into permanent farmsteads, occupied all the year round, so that many places in the Weald today are first recorded as summer pastures or shielings in early Kentish charters. Though we can rarely be positive that they had become permanent farms until after the Conquest, there can be no doubt that the process of independence was beginning before the end of the Anglo-Saxon period, and in a few cases they are recorded

3 *Regions and* pays

as established settlements in Domesday Book. In the fourth stage of development many new farms were carved out of the forest, particularly during the two centuries or so following the Conquest, and some of these still bear the names of their early owners, as at Jenkeys in Shadoxhurst, first recorded in 1313, and Silver Locks in Staplehurst, in 1327. The final phase of settlement seems to have come at the very end of the medieval period, and may well have been on a more substantial scale than is generally recognized. There are numerous Wealden farms whose origins can be traced back to the fifteenth or sixteenth century, but not beyond; and while some of these may have been in existence for generations, there can be little doubt that places like Blindgrooms in Shadoxhurst (first recorded in 1500) and Highlands in Woodchurch (1473) are relatively late foundations. The development of the local cloth industry, moreover, and the widespread rebuilding of Wealden churches and farmhouses bear witness to a substantial growth of population at this time.

The gradual evolution of the medieval Weald as a separate region, with a life of its own apart from that of the Foothills and Holmesdale, forms one of the cardinal themes in the later settlement history of Kent. Since the area has recently been subjected to intensive scrutiny by Mr Witney in *The Jutish Forest*, it will not be explored in detail in the present volume; but there is one aspect of its history that ought to be mentioned. Like that of other late-settled forests, the society that eventually developed in the Weald was one with a good deal of individual freedom from manorial control, and with a notably independent yeoman class. Visually, the most impressive evidence of that freedom today is the extraordinary wealth of substantial yeomen's houses, built or rebuilt for the most part in the fifteenth and sixteenth centuries. Since the Weald was essentially a tributary or dependent region in origin, and since the paramount manors of the Original Lands still retained some control over it even in the eighteenth century, the question arises as to how this freedom developed. While no detailed answer to this question can be given in the limits of this chapter, the underlying causes need to be borne in mind in any consideration of Kentish settlement history, and in this context there are four points to take into account.

In the first place, with the decline of transhumance after the Conquest and the development of a permanent, settled society in the Weald, it became increasingly difficult for distant upland landlords to exploit their Wealden resources. In the adverse economic circumstances of the later medieval period, they were driven to commute their

PART ONE *The Community of Kent*

rights in the area, as a rule for a fixed money rent, which in the long run necessarily favoured the tenant and weakened the landlord's power. Secondly, the fact that the Weald always remained a pastoral region in a sense encouraged individual freedom; for pasture-farming, as remarked earlier, does not necessitate communal organization like arable husbandry, and it is often preferable for stock-farms to stand isolated from one another. Thirdly, the fact that the original settlements still retained manorial control over their detached Wealden territories, and refused to grant them full independence, in the long run weakened their control and paradoxically tended to foster a certain freedom. For where the centre of jurisdiction is remote, independent action is likely to be encouraged, and the distance of the parent-manor inevitably militated against its manorial authority. Even those omnipotent landlords, the medieval archbishops, were thus gradually driven to grant greater liberties to their forest tenants than to those on their Upland estates, particularly in the later Middle Ages.[14] Finally, the sheer size of the Wealden parishes, and the fact that their farms were often remote from the parish church and isolated for lengthy periods of the year, inevitably made them difficult to govern. The scale of these parishes was a characteristic which the Weald shared with many late-settled regions of forest and moorland, and it was basically due, no doubt, to the sparsity of the local population at the time when parishes were formed. Later in the Middle Ages, when the Wealden population was expanding, the age of parish-formation had passed, and no new churches were established until the nineteenth century.[15] Even a moderate-sized parish like Smarden, with 62 separate farms and hamlets scattered over its 5,400 acres, cannot at any time have been easy to govern: and some places, such as Goudhurst, Cranbrook, and Tonbridge, were two or three times the size of Smarden.

In these respects the Weald forms an instructive contrast with that other great woodland region of Kent, the Downland. Both areas originated as outlying pastoral territories of the Original Lands and up to a point there were marked resemblances between them. But only up to a point; the parishes on the Downs originated at an earlier period and were generally much smaller than those in the Weald, so that they developed an ecclesiastical and manorial structure of their own which was largely separate from that of the Foothills, and very different from that of the Weald. Broadly speaking, the Weald as a consequence became the classic home of the yeomen of Kent, and the Downland of its manorial gentry. Although the importance of this distinction must

3   *Regions and* pays

not be overstressed, since neither social structure nor agrarian economy were uniform or unchanging, its basic features were still apparent in the nineteenth century, and its visual consequences are still evident in the countryside of today.

5. THE MARSHLAND

In contrast with the other regions of the county, the Marshes do not form a single continuous territory but are split up into three areas, each with certain characteristics of its own and more particularly related to its own hinterland. Altogether the three areas comprise 115 parishes, in part or in whole, and cover some 115,000 acres. Of these, nearly 47,000 acres are in the Romney district, the largest continuous stretch of marshland in the county, with another 4,000 in the Rother Levels, which form an irregular extension of it into the Weald. A further 47,000 acres extend along the northern shores of the county, partly bordering the Thames, but principally alongside the Swale and the Medway estuary with its maze of saltings, oazes, and uninhabited islets. Finally, beyond the Forest of Blean the wide alluvial Levels of the Stour account for a further 17,500 acres between Thanet and the mainland.

Though all the marshland areas of Kent have fulfilled the same essential function in its economy, fertilizing the rest of the county with their riches, there are two essential distinctions to note at the outset between the Levels of North Kent and the Stour on one hand and of Romney Marsh on the other. In the first place, in the two former districts there are no parishes entirely composed of marsh: all the 54 places in North Kent and the 20 in the Stour Levels comprise both Marsh and Upland. Although in many cases an essentially marshland economy developed and the Upland may be no more than a couple of hundred acres 40 or 50 feet above sea-level, it was the Upland that formed the original area of settlement whilst the Levels formed the outlying pasture. One indication of this fact is that there is only one parish in North Kent, Lower Halstow, where the church itself is situated in the Marsh. With its little hithe on Stangate Creek, Halstow lies hard by the shore, behind massive embankments, and at high spring tides below sea-level. Presumably it marked the landing-place of some particularly saintly figure in the early Christian history of Kent – perhaps from Sheppey Minster – for its name means 'holy place', and its church still contains Roman bricks and Saxon workmanship in both nave and chancel. But in every other parish the church is sited on the

PART ONE *The Community of Kent*

Upland and indicates plainly enough the original centre of settlement. In the Stour Levels, moreover, there are still many places where the relationship of Marsh and Upland is evident in local droveways linking the Level itself with its Upland farmstead. Goldstone and Paramore Street in Ash-by-Wingham, for instance, are early medieval farm-settlements on the Upland and each has its own droveway – Goldstone Drove and Paramore Street Drove – leading down to its stretch of the Level. Much the same relationship must have given rise to other tracks in the area, such as Snake Drove and Gilling Drove in Chislet. These Marshland droveways were not long-distance 'drifts' like the droves elsewhere in Kent, linking the Original Lands with their detached pastures in the Weald: they were local tracks between one part of the same farm or estate and another.

In Romney Marsh, by contrast, although the parishes along the northern edge of the area, such as Appledore, comprise both Level and Upland, most parishes have no Upland at all: they are purely Marshland communities, and they have always been so. The reason for this difference is not simply that Romney is larger in area, but that it was a region of detached pasture, like the Weald, for the most part exploited by distant communities practising transhumance: whereas the Levels of North Kent and the Stour were regions of attached pasture exploited mainly by neighbouring parishes. Thus Burmarsh in the Romney area was the 'borough marsh' of the people of Canterbury, 17 or 18 miles to the north, and Dengemarsh of Denge, a vanished community 25 miles away, near Denge Wood in the Stour valley. In very early times, it is true, certain Foothill communities exercised rights of transhumance in the North Kent Levels and a number of Wealden parishes exploited the marshland areas adjacent to them in the Romney district. Nevertheless, in the historic period North Kent and the Stour Levels have formed the pastureland, by and large, of adjacent settlements, whereas Romney Marsh has always been a region of detached pasture.

The second difference to note between the North Kent Levels and Romney Marsh is the fact that the former seem to have attracted exploitation at an earlier date than the latter, and several of their place-names are recorded in charters dating from before 800. In Romney Marsh, by contrast, only Lydd, recorded in 774, and perhaps Romney itself, recorded by 1052, can with some assurance be assigned so early an origin. Both were somewhat exceptional in that they were ports, and Lydd was established on what was probably a natural island when the area as a whole was still under water. Few other places in Romney

3   *Regions and* pays

Marsh are recorded as distinct settlements before Domesday Book or the roughly contemporaneous *Domesday Monachorum of Christ Church* – though they may have existed as marshland pastures – and several not until the late twelfth or thirteenth century: Snargate in 1197, Fairfield in 1203, and Hope All Saints in 1240. Like that other great region of detached pasture, the Weald, much of Romney Marsh was thus reclaimed and settled relatively late.[16]

These differences between the Romney area and the Levels of North Kent and the Stour have in some important respects continued to influence their history down to the present day. In other ways, however, owing to their basically similar environment, they have always borne an obvious general likeness, and for the purposes of this chapter it is on their common features that attention will be concentrated.[17] What are those common features, then, that historically speaking have set the Marshlands apart from the rest of the county, and in a sense necessitated their dependence on other areas as essentially tributary regions? There are several points to take account of, and these will be discussed here at some length because the settlement history of the Marsh needs to be seen as a whole and hence is not explored in detail in the following chapters.

The first general characteristic to note is the fertility of much of the Marshland. Of course it is not everywhere equally productive and there are infertile districts. The 12,000-acre parish of Lydd, for instance, contains hundreds of acres of agriculturally worthless shingle as well as some of the richest land in the shire. In North Kent there are parishes like Upchurch with a good deal of poor gravelly land, much of it until recent generations covered with broom and bracken.[18] Nevertheless, when every allowance is made, the Levels have always provided much of the most productive land in the county. The phrase 'very rich and fertile' runs like a refrain through Hasted's descriptions of the Marshland parishes: of Midley, Burmarsh, and Lydd in the Romney area, for example; of Murston, Teynham, Bapchild, and Tonge in North Kent.[19] In most parts, moreover, the absence of woods and hedges provides further evidence of the exceptional value of the land. Once the Levels had been drained, woods could certainly have been planted with profit; but what trees there are seem to date mostly from the nineteenth century, when they were planted as windbreaks around the farms. Until that time there were many parishes with scarcely a tree or hedgerow throughout them: Fairfield and Orgarswick, for instance, Ivychurch, Dymchurch, and Hope All Saints.[20] Almost everywhere the

PART ONE *The Community of Kent*

fields were separated only by fences or drainage ditches, as indeed they still are at the present day. Of the typical marshland scenery of Burmarsh Hasted tells us that there are 'very few hedges either on the sides of the roads or to part the property of different persons, deep and wide ditches or dikes, with post and rail fencing, being everywhere made use of, so that there is an uninterrupted view over the whole marsh; a very few houses with stacks of hay and corn thinly scattered about, and a low tree or pollard of willow or ash growing at long distances here and there, with the cattle grazing over the whole, fill up the prospect as far as the eye can see.' The only area with any woodland to speak of was the strange tract of the Holmstone in Lydd, where a miniature holly forest stretched for two miles, wild and stunted, among the shingle ridges of Dungeness.[21]

The second point to note is that Marshland fertility was everywhere a precarious fertility, dependent on unremitting attention to embankments, dikes, and 'sewers', or drainage channels. Much of the vast network of walls and ditches of today is of medieval origin, and some of it is probably more than a thousand years old. In Romney Marsh it still depends on maintenance of the great sea-wall of Dymchurch, three miles in length, 20 feet in height, and wide enough at the top to carry the high road from Hythe to New Romney. In Hasted's time Dymchurch Wall alone, with its elaborate pileworks, its 'jetties, knocks, and groynes', required an expenditure of £4,000 a year, or probably more than £150,000 in modern terms. Only very valuable land could have supported such an expenditure, and even so there were still swampy areas. South of the Rhee Wall defective drainage involved frequent inundation of exceptionally good land in Walland Marsh; along the derelict course of the old River Limen hundreds of acres were 'under water for the greatest part of the year;' and much of Fairfield, that green enchanted spot today, was then 'a most forlorn and dreary place, and ... seemingly the sink of the whole marsh', its church accessible only by boat or on horseback during most of the year.[22] Similarly in North Kent, a good deal of the Marsh has always had a precarious history, and much of it has from time to time been wholly lost to the sea, never to be regained. Nearly 500 acres of the notorious Slayhills in Upchurch, for instance, were lost when the tides broke through the neglected medieval embankments and destroyed the alluvial pastures.[23] The wealth of the Marshlands, then, has always been both hardly won and expensive to maintain.

The third characteristic to note is that the Marsh has always been

3   *Regions and* pays

utilized chiefly as pastureland, and for the most part as sheep pasture. Even in the Napoleonic Wars, when the acreage under corn greatly expanded and probably reached its maximum extent, there seems to have been very little ploughland in the area generally, though there was clearly an increase of it in places. Only 30 acres were then under the plough in Brookland, for instance, and only 50 in Brenzett.[24] Everywhere it was the marvellous pastures that impressed contemporaries, and the 'great quantities of sheep continually feeding on them'.[25] According to G. A. Cooke, writing about 1820, there were then more sheep to the acre in Romney Marsh than in any other part of England, as indeed there still are at the present day.[26] These celebrated sheep-flocks of the Marshlands, however, were only to be seen there in the summer months. In winter the carrying capacity of the area was so drastically reduced that the great bulk of the sheep had to be put out to farms on the Upland. It was this circumstance that gave rise to the pattern of seasonal transhumance which dominated the whole economy of the area from the earliest times until the seventeenth century, and in a modified form until the nineteenth or twentieth. As Dr Roger Kain has shown, in the early Victorian period most of the land in Romney Marsh was still linked with Upland farms, and every autumn and spring still witnessed the age-old drift of sheep between one region and the other. The work of R. A. L. Smith on the estates of Christ Church indicates that much the same customs were probably in operation in the medieval period; and the fact that Burmarsh is recorded as an outlying pasture of St Augustine's, Canterbury, in the ninth century suggests that they go back to the early phases of Marshland exploitation.[27]

The fourth characteristic to note is that, despite its agricultural potential, the Marsh has probably always been the most thinly settled part of the county. Visually this is apparent in the relative paucity of secular buildings dating from before the nineteenth century, except in New Romney and Lydd. It is also evident from the Compton Census of 1676, which suggests that there were then 6 acres of land to every inhabitant on the Foothills, 7 or 8 acres in the Weald and on the Chartlands, 11 on the Downland, 18 in the North Kent Levels, and as many as 44 acres in Romney Marsh.[28] In the eighteenth century much the same pattern is recorded by Hasted, who tells us that there were only four or five dwellings in Burmarsh, only two in Hope All Saints, only one in Orgarswick, and none at all in Blackmanstone. In the Stour Levels, the only village of any description was Sarre, and that consisted of merely 'a few straggling houses', while the rest of the area was virtually uninhabited, as indeed it still remains.[29] For the medieval period, taxation records suggest that in general the Marsh was scantily populated at that time also, although one of the unresolved problems of Kentish history is the remarkable scale of many Marshland churches. Some of these churches are urban buildings, as at New Romney and Lydd, and others, as at Brookland and Ivychurch, may have been financed by their rich absentee landlords, the monastic houses of Canterbury. But whatever the explanation, there can be little doubt that there was no real parallel in Kent to the populous fenland villages of medieval Lincolnshire and Cambridgeshire, with their big arable fields and numerous substantial peasant families. The Kentish Levels belonged essentially to a different type of *pays*: their economy was based on sheep and their society was mainly composed of sheep-farmers, fishermen, and lookers or shepherds: in other words they were marshlands pure and simple.

The ultimate reason for this scanty population was the notorious unhealthiness of the area, and this is the fifth characteristic to take note of in connexion with its settlement history. Until the nineteenth century 'marsh ague', apparently a form of malaria, was endemic throughout the Levels, and mortality rates seem everywhere to have been very high. No doubt it was the malaria mosquito that was generally responsible for this ill-health rather than the fogs and vapours blamed by contemporaries; but whatever the cause, the consequences were plain to see. Throughout the Romney Marshes, says Hasted, 'both the air and water make dreadful havoc on the health of the inhabitants of this sickly and contagious country, a character sufficiently corroborated by their pallid countenances and short lives.' In the Stour Levels, too, the inhabitants were 'much subject to intermittent fevers and agues', and the village of Sarre was inhabited only by those 'whose occupations among these sickly marshes oblige them to reside in it'.[30] In North Kent similar conditions had given rise to the local proverb:

> He that will not live long,
> Let him dwell at Murston, Teynham, or Tonge.

The parish of Iwade, for example, was 'hardly ever free from fogs and noisome vapours, and in summer in dry weather, the stench of the mud in the ponds and ditches, and the badness of the water, contribute so much to its unwholesomeness, that almost every one is terrified from attempting to live in it, and it is consequently but very thinly

3 *Regions and* pays

inhabited.' As for Murston, its inhabitants were so continually subject to agues that their 'complexions from those distempers become of a dingy yellow colour, and if they survive [they] are generally afflicted with them till summer, and often for several years, so that it is not unusual to see a poor man, his wife, and whole family of five or six children, hovering over their fire in their hovel, shaking with an ague all at the same time; and Dr Plot remarks that seldom any, though born here, continuing in it, have lived to the age of twenty-one years.' These accounts may sound exaggerated, but in the main they must be accepted. Hasted not only visited each parish himself but inherited property in the vicinity, whilst Robert Plot was a native of Sutton Baron, only four or five miles away. In Romney Marsh one of the reasons advanced for incorporation in Edward IV's reign had been the decline of population due to 'the unwholesomeness of the soil and situation'.[31]

The sixth characteristic of the Marshland to note was a natural consequence of these conditions, and that was the development of an absentee society. Despite its fertility, nobody would live there unless they had to, and ultimately this is why it remained a tributary region. By the eighteenth century there were virtually no gentry resident anywhere in Romney Marsh or the North Kent Levels, and in earlier periods they can never have been numerous. These 115,000 acres of wealthy countryside have always been owned and governed by absentee landlords and yeomen, and that is why there are few manor houses to speak of in the Marshes today. In the sixteenth and seventeenth centuries, it was often the old armigerous families of the county, like the Twysdens, who owned these pastures, and such families usually lived many miles away, in the case of the Twysdens at Roydon Hall on the northern edge of the Weald. In the medieval period they were widely colonized and exploited by those most powerful of all Kentish landowners, the monastic houses of Canterbury. In a sense, indeed, absenteeism had originated with the practice of transhumance itself, and was a natural consequence of the basic difficulty of keeping stock on the marsh during winter. The draining away of wealth from Marshland to Upland that resulted has thus been one of the most persistent and fundamental themes in Kentish history for the best part of a thousand years.[32] There are still many evidences of it in the countryside of today, and not only in the Levels themselves but elsewhere in the county. Both the poverty of secular architecture in the Marsh and the extraordinary wealth of it in areas less well endowed by nature, such as the Weald and the Chart, are partly due to it. Until recently it formed an essential feature of the economy of these latter districts and was a more important factor in their prosperity than the outflow of riches from London.

In the Levels themselves, the inevitable consequence of absenteeism was an impoverished and alienated society: and this is the final characteristic to note. In the rest of the county the marshfolk were regarded with something of the same suspicion and disdain as the tin-miners in Devon and Cornwall; their lowly status was commented on by many contemporaries. 'The inhabitants of these villages,' says Hasted of the Romney area, 'are but of very mean condition, being mostly such as are hired to look after the grounds and cattle, the owners and occupiers of which live in general in the neighbouring towns or Upland country.' At Dymchurch, the inhabitants 'are of the lower sort, and like others dwelling in the rest of the Marsh, are mostly such as are employed in the occupations and management of the level, or a kind of seafaring men, who follow an illicit trade, as well by land as water.'[33] Only at Brookland, and in the two little boroughs of New Romney and Lydd, was there a sprinkling of more substantial families: and even at Lydd the generality of the inhabitants 'are such as follow a contraband trade between this kingdom and France, and fishermen who are employed . . . in a herring fishery . . . and for the purpose of carrying it forward, they have cabins, and a common dining room, erected on the shore . . . where they remain the whole time of the fishing season.'[34] These comments receive clear confirmation from the absence of substantial family monuments in local parish churches, an absence which is the more remarkable when compared with their abundance elsewhere in the county.

It was not only the poverty of Marshland society that struck contemporaries, but its strange alienation from the ordinary ways of mankind. It was this aspect of it that attracted Dickens in setting parts of *Great Expectations* in the hundred of Hoo: the last place God made, as the local proverb has it, and never finished. Even the unimpressible Hasted was affected by the brooding desolation of Lower Halstow, 'so enveloped among creeks, marshes, and salts . . . that it seems a boundary, beyond which the traveller dreads to hazard his future safety.' One of the few books to depict life in the Marsh from the inside relates to this area, and the author, in describing his boyhood in the mid-nineteenth century, gives many vivid details of the customs of the marshfolk: the confused web of their religious beliefs, their many magical practices, their faith in corpse-lights, their superstitious dread of owls, their veneration for the sacred ring-dotterel, their morbid puritanism during the cholera epidemic, their oddly localized forms of Nonconformity, their fatalism and fierce dislike of outsiders.[35] These matters lie beyond the scope of the present volume; yet they afford an insight into the *mentalité* of the marshfolk that must have been no less characteristic of earlier centuries. Behind it we should envisage a profoundly localized way of life, an isolated and outcast society, and the perpetual warfare of its people with a daunting environment by land and sea.

6. REGIONAL INTERDEPENDENCE

The foregoing account does not exhaust the regional diversity of the county. There are important subdivisions within some of its regions which generalization unavoidably obscures. The two islands of Sheppey and Thanet had their own characteristic history, and differed in several major respects both from the rest of the Foothills and from one another. The Forest of Blean, that last remnant of the *cēto* that once stretched from Canterbury to Chatham, formed a distinctive district which in some ways resembled the poorer Chartland, and was certainly very different from the rich Foothills on either side of it. There were fundamental differences between the Low Weald and the High Weald, moreover, which in certain contexts may rather be regarded as two separate regions. Enough has been said, however, to indicate the general framework within which the settlement history and topographical development of the county need to be examined. What are the main conclusions to bear in mind?

At the risk of oversimplifying a complex pattern, they may be said to be fivefold. First, of the six dominant divisions of the county, two, the Foothills and Holmesdale, together with the three major river valleys connecting them, in general formed areas of very early settlement and may be regarded as the Original Lands of the Kentish people. In both regions, as we shall see in the following chapters, the case for continuity between Roman and Jute is at many points a strong one, particularly on the Foothills. Of the other four *pays*, two, the Weald and the Marshland, were on the whole areas of late settlement, much of it post-Conquest in origin; one, the Downland, was an area settled mainly in the middle-to-late Old English period; and one, the Chartland, partly in the Old English period, like the Downs, and partly after the

PART ONE *The Community of Kent*

Conquest, like the Weald. That so much of Kent, in comparison with other counties of the Lowland Zone, such as Suffolk or Leicestershire, was settled relatively late is a vital point to bear in mind. Nellie Neilson long ago pointed out the remarkable combination in Kent 'of advanced civilization, on one hand, which prevailed along Roman roads, . . . and on the other, of the very primitive conditions natural to fen and deep wood.'[36] That combination has always characterized the county and is perhaps the most important single clue to its settlement history. It was closely paralleled in the neighbouring county of Sussex, and to a large extent for somewhat similar environmental reasons.

Secondly, two of these regions, Holmesdale and the Foothills, formed predominantly arable areas and together comprised about 240,000 acres, or rather less than one-quarter of the county. The four remaining regions were predominantly pastoral in character and covered 800,000 acres, or more than three-quarters of the county. Of the four, the Downland, Chartland, and Weald were essentially areas of wood-pasture, and comprised two-thirds of the county; the fourth, the Marshland, was an area of grassland pasture which in historic times has always been almost bare of woodland. These pastoral areas must not, of course, be thought of as entirely given over to livestock, or the Original Lands as entirely devoted to corn. Neither must the figures be taken to suggest that three-quarters of the *wealth* of the county was derived from livestock; for by and large it was the poorer areas, apart from the Marsh, that were utilized as pasture. Over the centuries, moreover, the relative extent of cornland, woodland, and pasture has necessarily varied with the gradual clearance of the forest, with the changing needs of manorial lords and monastic houses, and with the eventual development of a commercial market for agricultural products. Nevertheless, the fact that so much of Kent has until recently been predominantly occupied with stock-farming needs to be firmly grasped in approaching its settlement history.

Thirdly, the four pastoral districts of the county all originated as dependent areas of the Foothills and Holmesdale, and in general were at first exploited seasonally rather than permanently colonized. Most of the Downland, though not all, formed the pasture of places on the Foothills, and much of the Chartland of neighbouring settlements in Holmesdale. The Weald and Romney Marsh, by contrast, were essentially regions of detached pasture, for long exploited by the settlements of the Original Lands, though in time, with the permanent colonization of the central Chartland, by certain places in that region

3 *Regions and* pays

too. The early relationship of the Stour Levels and the North Kent Marshes to the Foothills is more difficult to reconstruct. In places there were certainly at one time stretches of detached pastureland in these areas too; but in more recent centuries they seem on the whole to have been exploited rather by neighbouring settlements.

Fourthly, all these dependent regions eventually came to be permanently colonized and, except for the Marsh, developed an indigenous and independent society. The Marsh never really obtained this kind of independence, and for agrarian as well as manorial reasons it has always remained a tributary countryside, everywhere closely linked with farms and estates in the Upland. In the Weald, too, the outlines of dependence long survived in the manorial and ecclesiastical structure of the area; but there, for most practical purposes, the economy not only became independent of its Upland origins, but developed marked idiosyncrasies of its own, with its numerous yeomen and graziers, its clothiers and its ironmasters. Naturally, no area acquired a totally separate individuality, and in some sense they always remained dependent on one another. One of the dominant themes in the evolution of the Kentish countryside, indeed, is their changing relationship over the centuries, and the subtle shifts of emphasis in their influence on one another. The gradual clearance of the forest and the varying rates of population growth in each region were two of the main underlying factors in this changing relationship.

Finally, it is instructive to look beyond the settlement period and note the contrasting types of society to which these different countrysides gave rise in subsequent centuries. The point may be illustrated by a brief account of their contrasting demographic development. Each region, it is clear, has always sustained a very different level of population, and from an early period this occasioned a good deal of migration between one region and another. In a sense, indeed, the tradition of mobility goes back to the custom of transhumance itself; but the pattern that eventually developed did not exactly repeat that of transhumance, and in recent centuries it was also affected by other, more elusive, factors. By and large the Marshland and Downland seem always to have been the most thinly-populated parts of the county, and for many generations they have evidently been regions of emigration to other parts of Kent. In the former area emigration was encouraged, as we have seen, by endemic ill-health, and in the latter by the apparently well-attested longevity of the inhabitants, coupled with the intrinsic poverty of the countryside, and the absence of alternative occupations to agriculture. The Foothills and Holmesdale, by contrast, seem always to have been the most populous parts of the county, and in recent centuries at least to have attracted substantial immigration from other *pays*. In the late medieval period it seems probable that much of the Weald, and parts of the Chartland, gradually came to rival the Foothills in these respects, and certainly by the mid-seventeenth century they were among the more populous parts of the county, save in the extreme west. On the Foothills and in Holmesdale, it was the numerous towns that attracted immigration, and the fact that the husbandry of these areas required a large labour force, both on the arable lands and, at a later date, in the orchards and hop gardens. In the Weald and on the Chartland, by contrast, immigration must generally have been encouraged by different factors, such as the relative freedom from manorial control, the availability of unappropriated waste, and the development of by-employments and local industries.

Although little systematic work has yet been devoted to the demographic development of Kent, there can thus be no doubt that it was everywhere characterized by regional contrasts, and in this connexion two points need emphasizing.[37] First, the motive force behind the pattern of migration was an indigenous one, occasioned by differences of potential between its varying countrysides, and not by the relative proximity of London. Second, mobility was at once accompanied and in a sense encouraged by that continuous movement of riches between Marshland and Upland which was for so many centuries the great irrigating force in Kentish society. In examining the settlement history of the county, this varied demographic development is an important factor to bear in mind, for it indicates a very different kind of rural society in each type of countryside and in each *pays*.

PART TWO
THE FOUNDATIONS OF SETTLEMENT

4

THE JUTISH BASIS

1. THE STRUCTURE OF SETTLEMENT

Traditionally, the study of English settlement in this country has usually been divided into a 'primary' or original phase and a 'secondary' or post-Conquest one. For the purposes of this book it is more appropriate to adopt a threefold division. The first or 'primary' phase will here be restricted to the original Jutish settlements that either go back to the invasion period or else were established shortly after it; in point of fact, as we shall see in the following chapter, many of these primary communities originated in the Romano-British era. For the second phase of colonization the expression 'subsequent settlement' will be adopted, and broadly speaking this is intended to cover the succeeding period to within a generation or two of the Norman Conquest. For the final phase, extending from the eleventh century to the thirteenth or fourteenth, the traditional expression 'secondary settlement' will be retained. By no means all places can be made to fit into this broad categorization with complete certainty. Since the process of colonization was essentially evolutionary, no system of classification can be altogether satisfactory. Nevertheless, owing to the many thousands of minor place-names in Kent and the unusual abundance of topographical evidence and pre-Conquest charters, it is possible to identify the basic zones of colonization and to plot the progress of settlement from one to another with greater precision than in counties like Leicestershire or Cambridgeshire, where most rural parishes contain few places of any antiquity outside the church-village. With these resources, amongst others, it is also possible to discern a distinctive pattern in the kind of local community to which each period gave rise, and something of those forms of human organization which shaped their early development.

With relatively few exceptions the original Jutish settlements of

PART TWO *The Foundations of Settlement*

Kent, as already remarked, were to be found on the Foothills and in Holmesdale. Where the three major river valleys cut through the Downs, there was a further line of early places, reaching as far as Otford on the Darent, probably Teston or Yalding on the Medway, and Wye or perhaps Ashford on the Stour. Beyond these three points, and to the south of Holmesdale generally, the original primary settlement of the county came to an abrupt halt on the edge of the Chartland and the Weald. From the Foothills subsequent colonization then tended to press southwards, up into the wooded valleys of the Downs; from Holmesdale it also pressed southwards into the wooded recesses of the Chart; from both areas the herdsmen migrated each summer in a southerly or south-westerly direction to the drovedens of the Weald; and eventually, from about the tenth century onwards, these summer pastures themselves gave rise to independent settlements of a permanent kind. The general direction or movement of settlement that resulted, from the north and north-east across the grain of the county towards the south and south-west, forms one of the most striking features of Kentish colonization. Naturally, there are exceptions to the general rule, such as Dover, Lympne, and Folkstone on the southern side of the county, from which settlement pressed inland in a northerly direction. Nevertheless, when every exception has been admitted, the overwhelming trend was from north to south; except in the neighbourhood of Dover and Folkestone the lines of penetration rarely ran inland from the Channel coast. Until the marshes were drained and the forest cleared, much of the countryside west of Folkestone and Lympne was too intractable for the first English settlers to exploit, save in a few isolated spots such as Lydd. It was simpler to enter the county from the northern or eastern side and settle where others had settled before them, on the Foothills and in Holmesdale, which provided that nucleus of arable land essential even to a pastoral people. That is why there are five places in Kent called Sutton, or 'south farm', but only two called Norton, and none called Easton or Weston.[1]

This general outline or *schema* of Kentish settlement is clearly a simplified one, and one important rider must be added to it. In thinking of the Foothills and Holmesdale as zones of very early settlement, or of the Downland and Chartland as areas of subsequent colonization, it must not be imagined that every hamlet and farm in those areas dates from the period in question. Owing to the prevalence of late-cleared woodland in most parts of the county, there are outlying farms and hamlets even in the most ancient territories that were not founded until

4 The Jutish basis

late in the Old English period or after the Conquest. In each of the six settlement zones there are thus wide variations in the date of individual settlements and, as in other woodland regions, new farms and hamlets were still appearing on marginal land in the sixteenth century, and in a few places as late as the eighteenth. Nevertheless, the broad outline here described indicates fairly enough the *characteristic* period of colonization in each zone: the period, by and large, when settlement tended to originate. Places founded subsequently were generally minor ones, sometimes established by cottagers or squatters, and these clearly fall into a different category from the original settlements of the areas in question.

The whole of this complex process of colonization was necessarily a very gradual one, commencing before the fifth century and ceasing only with the drastic decline of population in the fourteenth: as long a period as separates us from the age of William the Conqueror. By the fourteenth century, however, the basic colonization of the county was virtually complete. There were still numerous stretches of common, woodland, and waste, and there were three subsequent periods which saw widespread changes in local settlement: the end of the Middle Ages, the end of the sixteenth century, and the end of the eighteenth. But the general framework of colonization had been completed by the time of the Black Death. There was then no region of the county that remained wholly uncolonized, and there were no further parishes created until the nineteenth century.[2] All subsequent changes in the settlement pattern were fitted into the established structure without fundamentally altering its outlines, though often modifying the distribution of population.

When the network of primary Jutish settlement in the Original Lands is plotted on the map, the most striking feature to emerge is its association at most points either with riverine sites or with major springheads. Some of the basic geographical factors behind this association are not far to seek. In a heavily wooded countryside like that of Kent, rivers provide in the first place a natural line of penetration and a guideline back to base in event of attack. In some cases navigability also influenced the choice of site; for along the north coast there are many lagoons and tidal creeks bordered by early communities like Faversham and Milton Regis, and the rivers themselves were then navigable further inland than today. The Stour, for instance, was probably navigable as far upstream as Wye; the Darent apparently to Riverhead or 'rother hithe', that is 'cattle wharf'; and even the insignificant Dour

PART TWO *The Foundations of Settlement*

for some way inland from Dover.³ On the Medway, the name of Hadlow Stair or 'hithe', first recorded in 1327, suggests that the river was then navigable almost to Tonbridge, although the present navigation above Maidstone dates only from the eighteenth century.⁴ The principal factor, however, at both springhead and riverine sites, must generally have been the need for fresh water, without which no invader or settler could have survived for more than a few days. In later chapters we shall see that there were also more ineluctable circumstances behind the association of early settlements with rivers and springheads; but there can be no doubt that the problem of water supply has been an important one in Kent in anchoring the original colonization of the county to the banks of rivers and the springline on either side of the chalk.⁵

These early waterside settlements of Kent must not be thought of as wholly isolated places, or as simplex communities like the nucleated villages of the medieval Midlands. They must rather be envisaged as centres of a dependent territory or estate which often extended to 20,000 acres and occasionally to double that size, and was frequently of royal origin. Part of the estate always seems to have consisted of a fertile stretch of well-watered land around the parent settlement, which in the case of a minor river like the Cray might comprise most of the valley. The rest of the estate generally formed an outlying region of wooded Downland or Chart, which was normally developed as a pastoral area. On the Foothills, and in a few places in Holmesdale, the estate often comprised a more or less substantial stretch of marshland as well, though it is doubtful how much of this had actually been reclaimed when the original settlement itself was founded. In course of time, often quite early in its history, the parent community began to establish subsidiary farms and hamlets in these outlying lands, retaining a certain suzerainty over them, however, and hence gradually evolving as the administrative *caput* of a substantial economic unit. It was partly for that reason that in later centuries many of these early settlements in the Original Lands also became local market towns, as at Maidstone, Milton Regis, Faversham, and Dartford. In a sense they must always have acted as meeting-places to which the people of the territory brought their food-rents and the surplus produce of their farms, so that the development of an early market was a natural consequence.

Before describing the network of these Jutish estates in detail, it will be well to place them in their wider setting; for they were not a peculiarity of Kent. Some 30 years ago, in an essay on 'The Making of

4 *The Jutish basis*

the Agrarian Landscape of Devon', W. G. Hoskins suggested that some of the earliest settlements in that county were associated with the names of rivers.[6] More recently, Margaret Gelling and Terry Slater have made the same point regarding early places in other parts of the kingdom.[7] Professor Hoskins cited the examples of Tawton with Tawstock on the Taw and Plympton with Plymstock on the Plym. The *stocks* and the *tūns* on these rivers have long been separate places, in some cases situated several miles apart; but originally each pair of names probably formed a single unit or estate, and each estate appears to have been called simply after the name of its river – Taw or Plym – without the addition of an English suffix. It was only at a later date that the element *tūn* was added to the river-name, and the *stock* came to form the outlying cattle farm or dairy farm of the estate. Tawstock, for instance, was the *stock* or dairy-farm belonging to Tawton, and the whole estate of *Taw* (or Tawton) originally extended to some 21,000 acres. Professor Hoskins then went on to suggest that there may have been other very early estates of this kind in Devon, named after the rivers flowing through them and called Tavy, Culm, Coly, Creedy, Clyst, Claw, Teign, and Ashburn. More recently, in a personal communication, he has added Exeter to the list, the *Isca* of the *Dumnonii*, and this is perhaps the most striking Devonshire example of all.

Now these early river-estates, or settlements of the river peoples, were not a peculiarity of Devon any more than of Kent. They were to be found in many parts of the country. There were several in the neighbouring county of Dorset, for example, such as Wimborne, whose original territory of about 21,000 acres extended for some eight miles along the parent stream, the Wim Bourne, from Wimborne Minster to Wimborne St Giles, and included all the six later parishes lying between them, which were subsequently carved out of the original territory: Knowlton, Hinton, Moor Crichel, Chalbury, Gussage, and Witchampton.[8] There are clearly other examples in Dorset, besides Wimborne, such as the Cernes and the Tarrants, though the present writer has not worked on them. There are also many instances in other areas, in counties as far afield as Wiltshire, Hampshire, Oxfordshire, Bedfordshire, Lincolnshire, Yorkshire, Somerset, and Essex: places like Calne, Meon, Thame, Luton, Louth, Leeds, Frome, and the Essex Colnes, for example, probably all come within this category.[9]

Two further points of a general kind may be made in regard of these estates of the river peoples before turning to examples in Kent. First, in many cases they are significantly associated with river-names of Celtic

PART TWO *The Foundations of Settlement*

origin, and where they are not they generally incorporate some very early English element in their place-name. Most of the examples here cited derive from Celtic rivers, except Ashburton and Wimborne, both of which incorporate the word *burna*, which can often be taken to indicate an early origin although it does not necessarily do so. Second, like their counterparts in Kent, a remarkable number of river-estates gave birth at some subsequent period in their history to market towns, such as Wimborne Minster, Crediton, and Cullompton. There is also reason to think that in many cases these towns date from an exceptionally early period. Although, generally speaking, they did not acquire formal market grants or borough charters from the crown until the twelfth or thirteenth century, it is clear that the grant of a charter often only confirmed in law trading rights which had been exercised by customary or 'prescriptive' right from before the Conquest. Certainly Calne, Louth, Wimborne, and Luton are cases in point; for at Luton the market is recorded in Domesday Book, while Wimborne, Louth, and Calne all appear as boroughs in the same record. They are examples of what I have ventured to call elsewhere 'primary towns', that is to say market towns of pre-Conquest origin.[10] It is remarkable, in fact, how many primary towns originated as *capita* of riverine estates in this way.

In many counties these estates probably constitute the earliest type of agrarian organization of which we can form any distinct impression. Together with the basically similar springhead territories, they provided the essential nucleus from which much of the subsequent colonization of this country ultimately sprang. In Kent they are to be found on all the main watercourses of the county save the Wealden rivers and the Thames, which in Kent is not a fresh-water stream, and by many of the more copious springs at the base of the Downs. Between them, these places seem to have accounted for virtually all the original Jutish settlement of the shire, and in many cases they originated long before the Jutish invasions. A few exceptions there naturally are, such as Lydd at the tip of Romney Marsh, which has no obvious association with springs or rivers at the present day. But such exceptions are rare, and some of those that appear to be so, such as Lyminge and Keston, turn out on closer inspection to have been situated by streams or springheads now no longer flowing due to the lowering of the water-table.

In the two following sections an attempt will therefore be made to identify the general network of early Jutish territories. Much of the

4   *The Jutish basis*

evidence from which they have been reconstructed will be discussed in greater detail in subsequent chapters; but a brief résumé of the main lines of argument may be useful at this point. Quite a number of estates survived in outline in the unusual manorial structure of the medieval county, with its elaborate complexes of paramount, subordinate, and reputed manors.[11] Others were partially preserved in the primitive jurisdictions of early minster churches, whose forms often lingered on in Kent in the ecclesiastical structure of later centuries. In several cases, of which Wrotham and Milton Regis are the most obvious examples, they were incorporated in the hundredal structure of the county, though in Kent this was unusual. In yet other cases they may be reconstructed from the topographical evidence of parish boundaries, church-siting, farm-siting, woodland features, place-names, and the course of droveways. Most frequently it is from a combination of these and other varied lines of argument that the outlines of the early territories may be pieced together. In some cases the evidence is fragmentary and at times conflicting, and it must be admitted that it is not always possible to recreate the territory as a whole. Nevertheless, we can generally identify its original *caput* or centre, and this is the fundamental point to grasp (see map 3). For with few exceptions these old estate-centres continued to exert a peculiarly magnetic influence on each subsequent phase in the history of Kentish colonization. For this reason they may appropriately be described as the 'seminal settlements' of the pre-Conquest peoples, a point we shall return to later.

2. THE PATTERN OF RIVER-ESTATES

Quite a number of the old estate-centres of Kent still bear unaltered the names of their parental streams and are not difficult to recognize. One striking example is that based on the Cray valley, which included St Mary Cray, St Paul's Cray, Foot's Cray, North Cray, Crayford, and *Cray Ewelme* or Orpington.[12] Together with Bexley, Farnborough, Downe, Knockholt, and a sizable stretch of the surrounding Downland, these once formed a single continuous territory simply called *Cray*, deriving its name from the Celtic word for the river running through it (see map 8). That word is probably identical in meaning with the Afon Crai in Breconshire and signifies 'fresh' or 'clear': a description which nowadays, alas, is singularly inappropriate, but which naturally appealed to a primitive people. Another instance is Dover, deriving its name from the little River Dour, a place of Roman

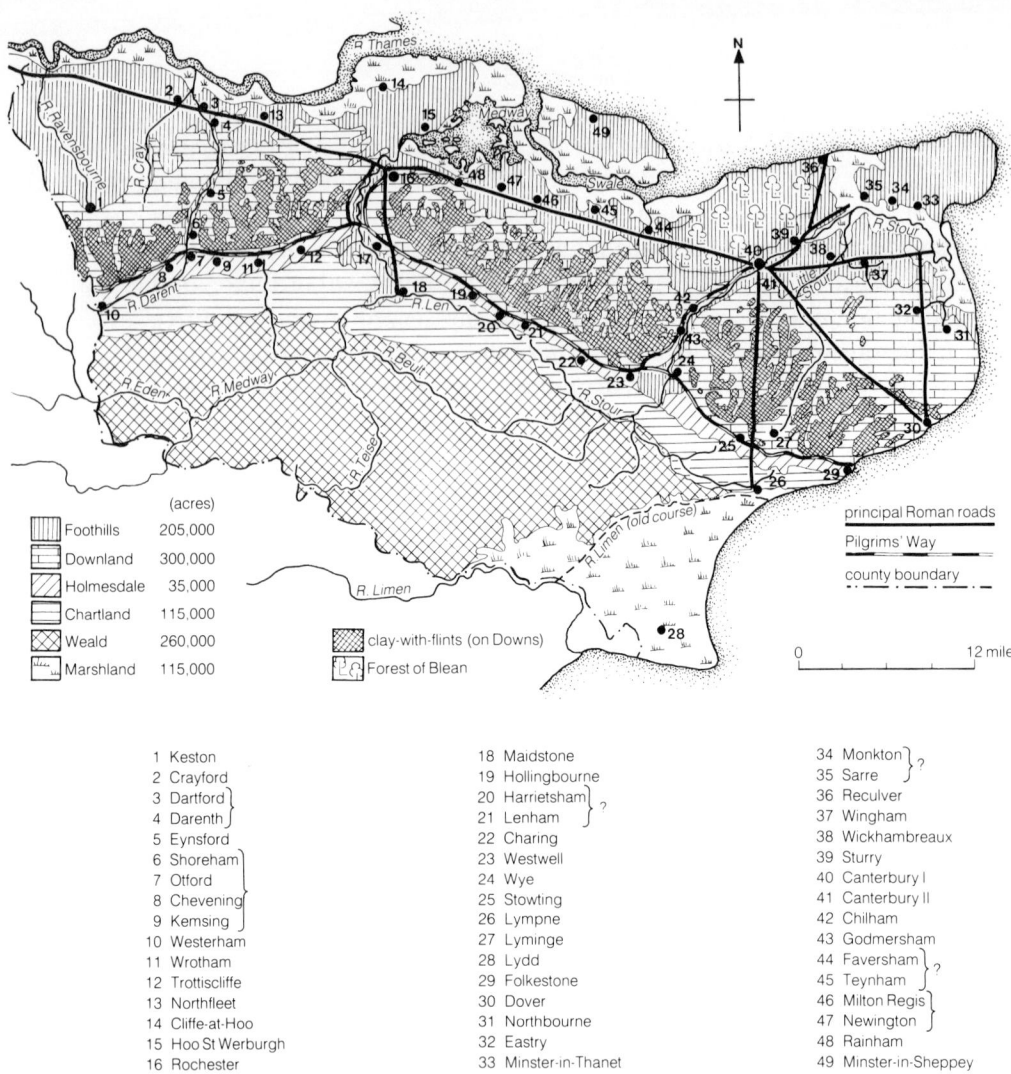

		(acres)
	Foothills	205,000
	Downland	300,000
	Holmesdale	35,000
	Chartland	115,000
	Weald	260,000
	Marshland	115,000

1	Keston	18	Maidstone	34	Monkton
2	Crayford	19	Hollingbourne	35	Sarre
3	Dartford	20	Harrietsham	36	Reculver
4	Darenth	21	Lenham	37	Wingham
5	Eynsford	22	Charing	38	Wickhambreaux
6	Shoreham	23	Westwell	39	Sturry
7	Otford	24	Wye	40	Canterbury I
8	Chevening	25	Stowting	41	Canterbury II
9	Kemsing	26	Lympne	42	Chilham
10	Westerham	27	Lyminge	43	Godmersham
11	Wrotham	28	Lydd	44	Faversham
12	Trottiscliffe	29	Folkestone	45	Teynham
13	Northfleet	30	Dover	46	Milton Regis
14	Cliffe-at-Hoo	31	Northbourne	47	Newington
15	Hoo St Werburgh	32	Eastry	48	Rainham
16	Rochester	33	Minster-in-Thanet	49	Minster-in-Sheppey
17	Aylesford				

MAP 3. *Early Jutish estate-centres and principal related settlements mentioned in the text* (based on the Ordnance Survey map with the permission of The Controller of Her Majesty's Stationery Office; Crown Copyright reserved)

or pre-Roman origin, which in Jutish times gave birth to several subsidiary settlements in the Downland combes converging on the seashore beneath Shakespeare's Cliff. As in the case of Cray, Dover has retained its Celtic river-name in a simplex form unchanged throughout its history, without acquiring the suffix *tūn* which was usually added to the river settlements of Devon. Its name is in fact identical with the Welsh word *dwfr*, of which it was the plural form and simply meant 'the waters'. A third example, similar in origin to Dover and Cray, was

4   *The Jutish basis*

based upon Lympne and stretched inland for several miles to include Lyminge and perhaps also Lymbridge Green.[13] Lympne is the old name of the River Rother or Limen, and is another Celtic word, identical with Lac Léman in Switzerland, signifying 'elm [river]'.[14] Originally the Limen flowed into the sea at Lympne, where it gave rise to *Portus Lemanis*, Lympne's Roman predecessor. Lyminge was not on the river itself but in the outlying part of the estate, about five or six miles inland, its name meaning 'the *gē* [or territory] of the Limen people,' and its site marking another early settlement of Romano-British origin. In the Darent valley, in West Kent, we find yet another of these estates based on a river-name, and centred on Darenth. Like its tributary the Cray, and like the Limen and the Dour, Darent too is a Celtic word, identical with Derwent in Cumberland and Dart in Devon – the form that also appears in Dartford – and signifying 'oak [river]'.

The fact that Darenth, Dover, Lympne, and Cray thus retained the simplex form of their names and never acquired the suffix *tūn*, as in Devon, probably points to a very early origin for these river estates in Kent, perhaps to a period before the word *tūn* had become current in local speech.[15] Such an early origin cannot be doubted in the case of Dover, the Romano-British *Dubris*, or at Lympne, the Romano-British *Lemanis*, and it is what we should expect to find in the heavily-Romanized Darent valley. The presence of pagan Saxon burial grounds in the vicinity of Darenth itself reinforces this view, while the Celtic name of the settlement, its neighbouring Roman villa, and the Roman brickwork in its church probably point to a greater antiquity than that of the Jutish period: perhaps much greater, if we may judge from the Neolithic remains in the vicinity.

The territory of the Darenth people is a particularly interesting one since its original extent can be reconstructed with a fair degree of certainty, so that it is worth describing in more detail. It was a great estate, kept entirely in the king's hands until the tenth century, stretching ten miles and more from the Roman ford across the Darent at Dartford far up into the wooded valleys of the Downs, at its highest point touching 730 feet near the prehistoric Downland ridgeway. Its original area seems to have extended to about 21,000 acres, or much the same as at Tawton and Wimborne, and it was eventually divided into as many as ten separate parishes: North Darenth, South Darenth, Dartford, Stone, Wilmington, Sutton-at-Hone, St Margaret-at-Helles, Horton Kirby, Maplescombe, and Kingsdown (see map 8).[16] The fact that it was a royal estate is what gave Kingsdown its name – the king's

PART TWO *The Foundations of Settlement*

dūn or stretch of downland. In Kentish usage that does not normally denote bare hill-country like the Berkshire Downs or the South Downs in East Sussex, but a densely wooded upland, deeply scored by narrow combes. Kingsdown, in short, formed part of the outlying forest or wood-pasture of the estate, just as the neighbouring parish of Stansted formed part of the wood-pasture of an estate based on Wrotham.[17] In much the same way Downe and its adjacent hill-country around Walden (*wald* + *denn*) formed the outlying wood-pasture of the Cray people,[18] and Kingsdown near Faversham the royal pasture of a territory based on Milton Regis.

At Dartford itself this estate of the Darenth people gave birth to what was probably one of the earlier post-Roman towns of Kent. For although it is not specifically recorded by that name until 1086, its ancient *port-street*, that is to say 'market street', is recorded in an Anglo-Saxon charter of the year 995, by which date the town may also have had its own mint.[19] Domesday Book makes no mention of this market, but then there are many other towns where it does not do so; and it does record two hithes or havens, and three chapels besides the parish church, so that the settlement was probably a sizeable trading centre of some kind. Dartford, in fact, bears most of the marks of a primary market town: it may have been the economic centre of the estate; it was certainly the ecclesiastical centre; it was sited at an important river crossing; it was also on a major Roman road; it was at or near the point where the lost Roman route following the Darent valley branched off this major road to the south; and it was situated in a neighbourhood thickly strewn with Roman and Romano-British relics.

The whole of the Darent valley has long been recognized as one of the earliest cradles of English settlement in Kent. Practically every church-site in the 12 miles between Dartford and Otford is neighboured by its Roman villa, and with the excavation of the villa at Lullingstone it has become increasingly evident that here the gap between Romano-British and Jutish, if gap there was, was of the narrowest description. It is therefore no surprise to find other early river-estates developing in this valley, besides that of Darenth, based on such centres as Eynsford, Otford, and Westerham, though these cannot all be reconstructed with the same certainty. The Eynsford estate probably comprised both Farningham and Lullingstone as well as Eynsford itself, together with parts of Chelsfield and perhaps other parishes; it may have been associated in some way with the Iron Age hill-fort at Hulberry as well as with the Lullingstone villa and other Roman remains (see map 8).

4   The Jutish basis

The Otford estate originated at the point where the Downland ridgeway and the Pilgrims' Way unite to cross the Darent valley, extending southwards over Sevenoaks and a large tract of forest lands beyond it, which were known as Otford Weald until quite recently. At one time it also included Shoreham, in which the mother-church of the estate came to be sited, and to which Otford itself was later subordinated as a dependent chapelry, together with Halstead and Woodlands (see map 13). Like Eynsford, Otford, may have been associated with an Iron Age hill-fort, on Otford Mount, as well as with extensive Roman remains, and it was probably sited on the lost Roman road following the valley from Dartford; its association with Kemsing is a point we shall return to later in this chapter.

The Westerham estate, as its name implies, was the most westerly to develop in the Darent valley, and was situated near the source of the river. At one time it extended for nine miles along the Surrey border, from the Downland ridgeway on the north, across the Stone Hills, and down into the Weald beyond Edenbridge. Like Otford and Eynsford, it may have been associated with an Iron Age hill-fort, in Squerryes Park, and perhaps also with the Roman temple at the headspring of the river, though that is just within Surrey.[20] Like Dover and Darenth, Westerham was an important royal estate,[21] and possibly for that reason gave rise to one of the early market centres of the county, as at Dartford, though in this case there is no proof that the market antedated the Conquest. The original area of the Westerham territory seems to have been unusually extensive, and in addition to Edenbridge may have included the neighbouring territories of Brasted and Hever, and parts of Chevening, Chiddingstone, and Cowden. The boundary enclosing the former parishes has remained a strikingly regular and continuous one,[22] with the internal boundaries abutting upon it without passing through it, and these circumstances, amongst others, hint at the original unity of the area and its subsequent subdivision.[23] If this reconstruction is correct, the Westerham estate must have extended to about 30,000 acres; but this somewhat exceptional scale is paralleled in a number of other places where the territory included a substantial stretch of poor Chart and uncolonized Wealden forest.

Some 50 miles to the east of Westerham, in the beautiful valley of the Little Stour, another of these ancient river-estates developed, that of the Bourne people (see map 4). Like the Darenth territory, it can be reconstructed with some confidence. As well as the four parishes that still bear the name of the Bourne – Littlebourne, Bekesbourne, Patrix-

PART TWO *The Foundations of Settlement*

MAP 4. *Early Jutish estates in East Kent*

Note The southern boundary of the Bourne estate, based on Wickhambreaux, is indefinite; only parts of Denton and Wootton lay within it. Adisham and its daughter Staple lay outside both the Bourne and the Wingham territories. Settlement from Eastry and Northbourne followed similar directions to that from Wingham and Wickhambreaux; but the estate boundaries are difficult to determine in these cases. The parish boundaries indicated are the contemporary ones; broadly speaking these follow the historic boundaries, but in this area there were many small detached parts of parishes which have now been eliminated.

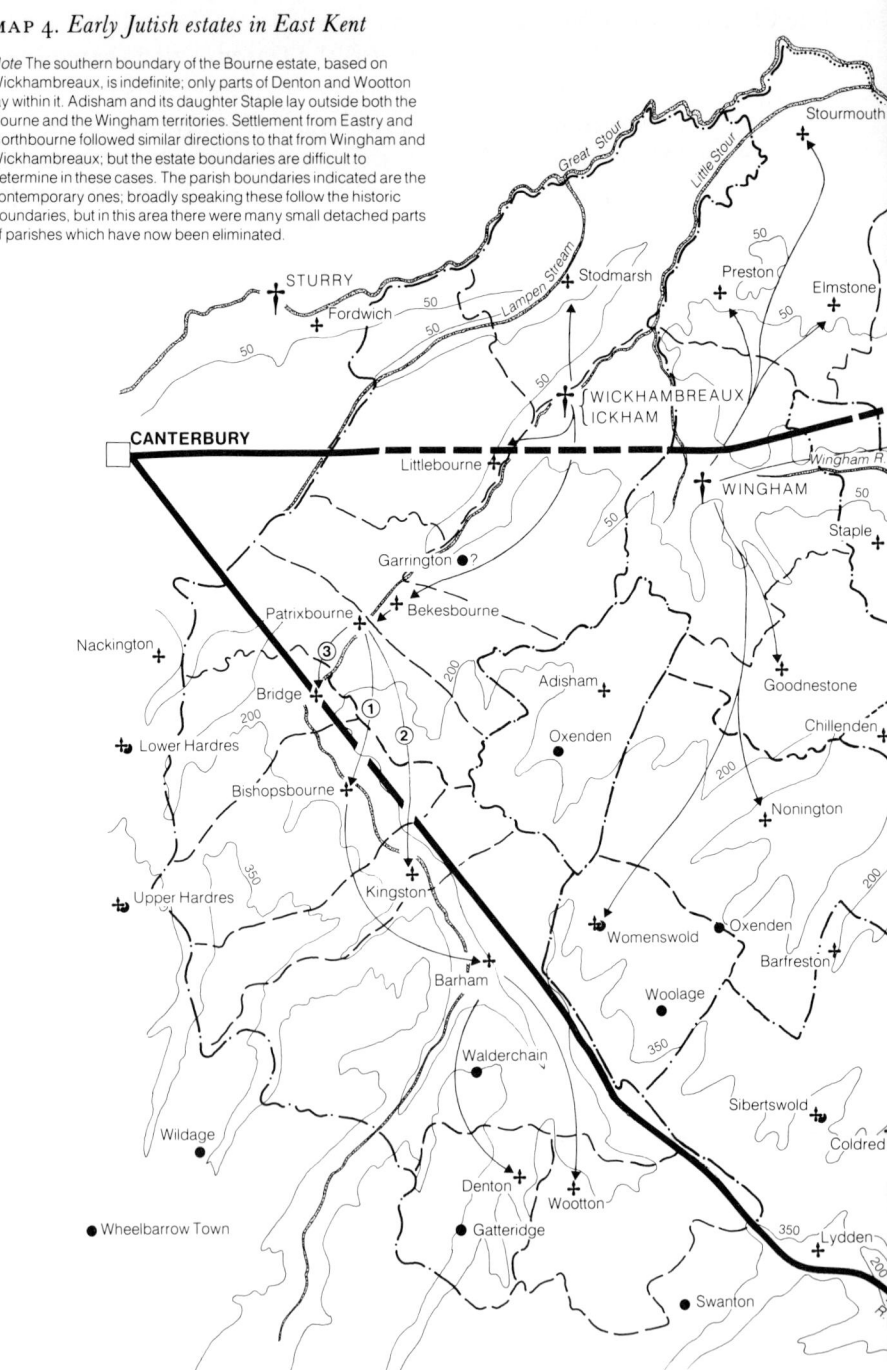

4 The Jutish basis

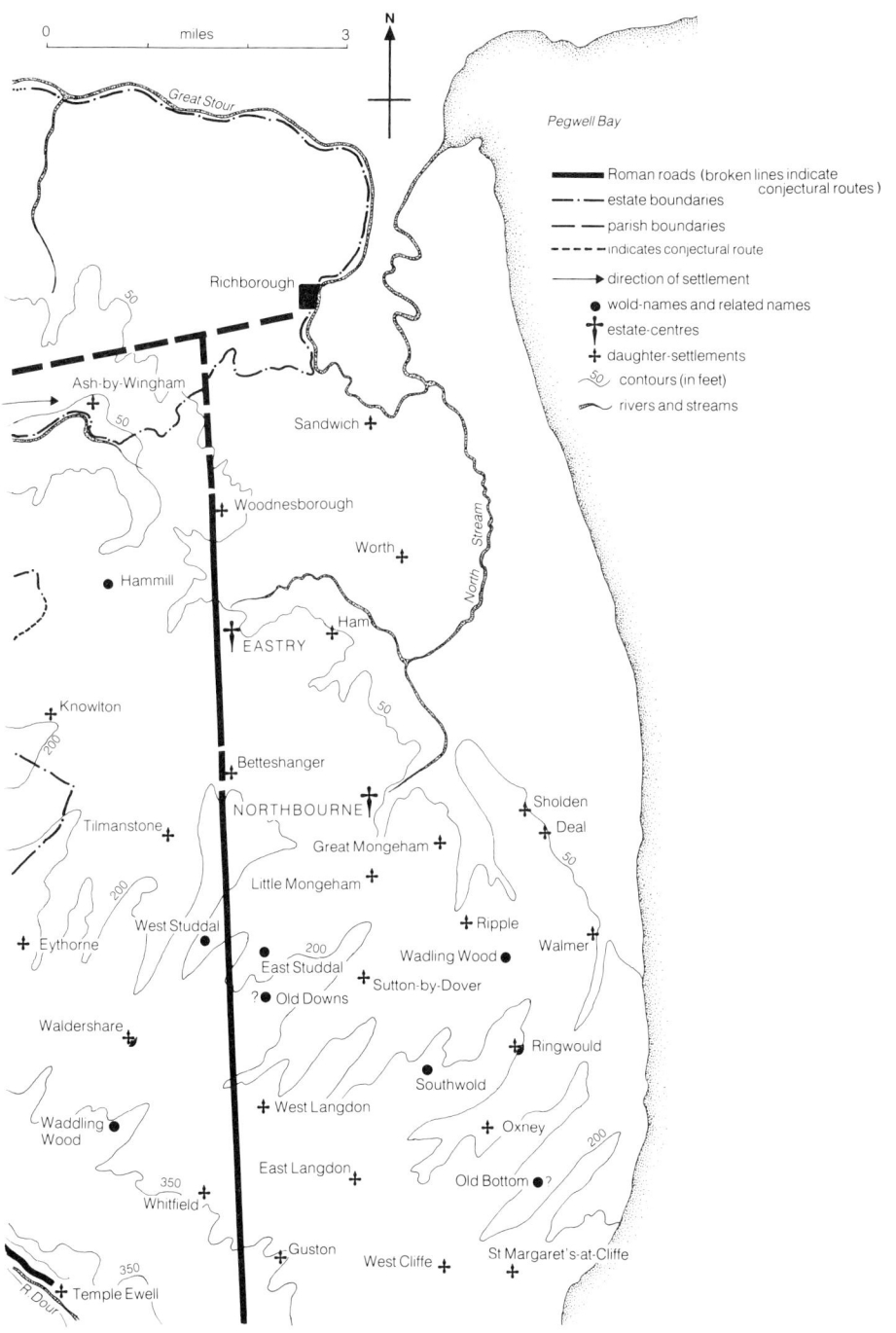

bourne, and Bishopsbourne – it comprised five or six other parishes – Wickhambreaux, Ickham, Bridge, Kingston, Barham, and probably Stodmarsh – together with parts of Denton and Wootton.[24] All in all, it probably extended to about 21,000 acres, or very much the same area as those of the Darenth and Wimborne peoples. In this case the name of the estate did not derive from a Celtic root but, like Wimborne and Ashburton, from the Old English word 'bourne', which was an early alternative name of the Little Stour. As so often in the river peoples' territories, settlement on the Bourne began near the mouth of the river, and then gradually moved upstream, in this case in a south-westerly direction into the wooded recesses of the Downs, though not in an exactly regular progression. The earliest settlement recorded in a written document is Littlebourne, which is found by that name in a charter relating to the year 696.[25] But the name Littlebourne must imply an even earlier place once regarded as the 'Great Bourne', and although no place of this name now exists, it can safely be identified with the neighbouring parishes of Wickhambreaux and Ickham, which lie immediately below Littlebourne. These two places stand adjacent to one another on either side of the stream, near its original mouth, and historically they have always been intimately connected. Like Darenth and Dartford, they are situated on or close to a major Roman road;[26] they have significantly early types of place-name;[27] they are associated with important Roman and Romano-British sites; and taken together they cover about 5,000 acres, or nearly three times the extent of their daughter community, which was thus aptly named Littlebourne.[28] In this case the centre of the estate was probably based on Wickhambreaux.

The next settlement of the Bourne people to be formed after Littlebourne must have been Bekesbourne, which immediately adjoins it upstream. Bekesbourne was subsequently divided into two parts and its daughter-settlement, which eventually came to be called Patrixbourne, gave birth at different dates to three distinct places. Bishopsbourne was the earliest and most important, and this in turn gave rise to Barham, which itself seems to have been the mother-community of most of Wootton and part of Denton. Probably well before Denton and Wootton were created, Patrixbourne had formed its second subsidiary settlement, which came to be called Kingston, and which, though a name in *tūn*, was a royal pasture-farm like Kingsdown in West Kent rather than a 'king's town' or *villa regalis*.[29] Its third foundation, Bridge, was almost certainly the last to be established in

4   *The Jutish basis*

the territory and was probably of quite recent origin when first recorded in Domesday Book in 1086. Though it lies in the centre of the estate, sandwiched between Patrixbourne and Bishopsbourne, Bridge bears the marks of a relatively late street-migration. As its name implies, it is situated at the point where the Little Stour is crossed by the Roman road from Canterbury to Dover, on which it forms the only settlement in a stretch of ten or eleven miles. It is eccentrically sited on the very edge of its own parish, moreover, and directly abutting on that of its parent community, a sure sign in Kent of its dependent origin.[30] Although there appears to be no record of a market-grant to Bridge after the Conquest, and indeed it was too near Canterbury to develop into a genuine town like Dartford, the possibility that it originated as a small pre-Conquest trading centre for the Bourne people should not be ruled out. Certainly its topography suggests that possibility.

The territory of the Bourne people is closely paralleled in East Kent by a number of other estates in the same stretch of country between the Stour valley and the Channel coast. Next to Bourne, adjoining its eastern boundary over much of its length and originating from the Wingham River, was that of the Wingham people. This also extended for some 20,000 acres, from the Stour Levels on the north to Womenswold high up on the Downs to the south. The name 'Wingham River' is a relatively modern one and the meaning of Wingham, like that of many early places in Kent, is much disputed; but one possibility advanced by both Karlström and Wallenberg suggests that its first element may incorporate an old name for the stream.[31] Like the Darenth estate, that of the Wingham people may have given rise to another of the pre-Conquest markets of Kent; for although, as at Westerham, there is no documentary proof that Wingham was a trading centre until after 1086, its topography and early history, like that of Dartford, display the characteristic features of a prescriptive or pre-Conquest market; its High Street forms part of a prehistoric ridgeway, and it adjoins the old Roman trunk route from Canterbury to Richborough. Beyond Wingham, again moving east, lies Eastry, a *villa regalis* whose name means the *gē* or territory of the 'eastern people', situated at the source of its own small stream, and giving rise at Eastry to yet another small market. Finally, between Eastry and the coast there was a second 'Bourne' territory, originating from Northbourne, and like the others stretching up into the Downs. Towards the southern, upland end of all these territories of East Kent we find a series of place-names in *wald*, such as Walderchain, Womenswold, Siberts-

PART TWO *The Foundations of Settlement*

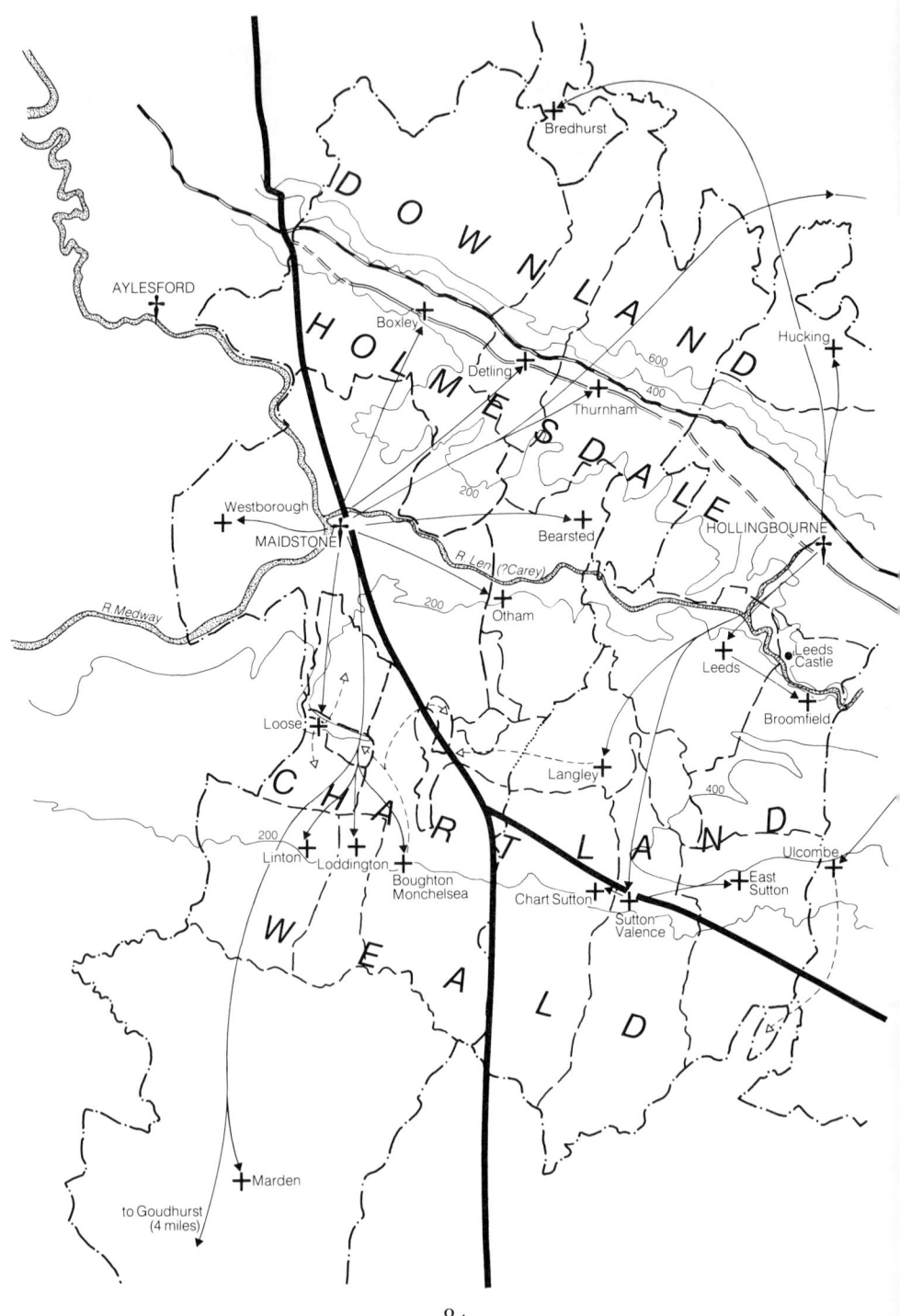

4 *The Jutish basis*

MAP 5. *Early Jutish estates in Holmesdale* (based on the Ordnance Survey map with the permission of The Controller of Her Majesty's Stationery Office; Crown Copyright reserved)

PART TWO *The Foundations of Settlement*

wold, and Waldershare, indicating the outlying forest pastures of the area.[32] These point to much the same pattern of subsequent colonization as in the estates further west, and we shall return to them in this connexion in Chapters 6 and 7.

The valley of the Great Stour was also the home of a number of river territories, based on early centres like Sturry, Chilham, Godmersham, Wye, and Canterbury. Sturry is recorded as *Sturigao*, 'the Stour district', in one of the oldest Kentish charters, relating to the late-seventh century, and is therefore of particular interest. It may possibly have been the first estate in the valley to develop, bearing as it does the name of the river and lying near its former mouth. In its early phases at least it was evidently an important one, comprising Westbere and Chislet as well as Sturry itself and much of the densely wooded stretch of Blean Forest between Canterbury, Swalecliffe, Whitstable, and Herne.[33] It was sited, moreover, at the junction of two Roman roads and in the heavily-Romanized area to the east of Canterbury, so that here, as at Dover, Darenth, and Lympne, we must suspect a pre-Jutish origin behind the pre-Jutish name. Neither Wye nor Chilham bears the name of the river, but both were none the less centres of major territories, and settlements of great antiquity. With its castle, church and market-place situated on a hill-top, on a branch of the Pilgrims' Way, Chilham occupies a dominating defensive bluff above the river, perhaps the site of an unrecognized hill-fort, and certainly occupied during the Roman period.[34] Wye also stands on the Pilgrims' Way, on its main branch, and like Otford at a point where the Downland ridgeway joins it to cross the river valley. Like the Darenth territory, it formed an estate of the Kentish royal house, and Wye itself became an important *villa regalis*, the *caput* of a Kentish lathe, an early market centre, and a focal point of heathen worship, as its name $w\bar{\imath}g$, 'idol' or 'idol house', implies.[35]

On the Medway there were several early estates, based on places like Aylesford and Maidstone, though in this area the general pattern of development is more problematical and the settlement of the Medway valley raises a number of difficult questions. There can be no doubt, however, that a major estate was centred on Maidstone, certainly comprising Boxley and Detling to the north, together with Thurnham, Bearsted, and Otham to the east, and Loose, Linton, and Boughton Monchelsea with its hill-fort on the Chartland to the south. That would have given the Maidstone territory an area of some 22,000 acres; but originally it seems to have continued southwards into the Weald, as at

4 *The Jutish basis*

Westerham, at its maximum extent reaching as far as Goudhurst on the Sussex border, 16 or 17 miles away, and probably covering more than 40,000 acres (see map 5). In that case it would have been the largest identifiable estate in the county; but this should not surprise us. For although it was many centuries before Maidstone eclipsed Canterbury as the county capital, in a sense it has always formed one of the two focal points of the shire owing to its proximity to Penenden Heath, the Old English and perhaps prehistoric meeting-place of the community of Kent, on the border of Maidstone and Boxley. The origins of Maidstone as a Romano-British settlement, as an early religious centre, and as a pre-Conquest town are important topics that we shall return to in later chapters. Here it is sufficient to note that it was certainly a major focus of Roman influence; it is situated on a Roman road significantly known as Week (*vicus*) Street and Stone Street; its neighbourhood is thickly strewn with Roman remains; and its place-name probably indicates a megalith once known as 'the maidens' stone' or possibly 'the people's stone' (*mægd*).[36] At this point, as at Dover, Darenth, Lympne, and other places discussed earlier, the origins of the territory probably go back beyond the Jutish era, and in this connexion the unusual scale is perhaps significant.

3. THE PATTERN OF SPRINGHEAD-ESTATES

In their general structure, the springhead-estates of Kent do not seem to have differed in any essential respect from those based on rivers, and may be discussed more briefly. They were often less extensive, and those in Holmesdale usually lacked marshland; but otherwise they were closely similar, and a number of territories might be classified under either heading.[37] In every case they were associated, as has been remarked, with the springline at the foot of the chalk: near the Pilgrims' Way and the Greenway to the south, and on Watling Street or its prehistoric predecessor to the north. They are not found at any point on the springline of the Greensand, by contrast, which was not traversed by any comparable prehistoric route and did not provide an early line of penetration into the county. North of the Downs early territories developed at places like Faversham, Teynham, Milton Regis, Newington, and Northfleet, in all of which the outlying pastureland stretched up into the Downland valleys to the south in much the same way as in the river territories.[38] Of these, the estate based on Milton is a particularly interesting and well-documented one, and will be

PART TWO *The Foundations of Settlement*

reconstructed in detail in Chapter 11. South of the Downs a great arc of early estates developed along the springline of Holmesdale, centred on such places as Kemsing, Wrotham, Trottiscliffe, Hollingbourne, Lenham, Charing, Westwell, Folkestone, and probably Stowting. Except at Hollingbourne, Wrotham, and Lenham, these rarely stretched far over the chalk escarpment to the north, and west of the Darent their northern boundary followed the Downland ridgeway. As a rule their outlying pastures stretched instead over the Chartland to the south, and in some cases seem to have merged into the common pastures of the Weald without any very distinct boundary, a point we shall return to in later chapters.

The territory based on Hollingbourne, about six miles east of Maidstone, may be taken as a typical example of these springhead-estates of Kent (see map 5). The lands of Hollingbourne extended to nearly 18,000 acres in all, and comprised the whole area subsequently divided into the parishes of Hucking, Leeds, Langley, Broomfield, Sutton Valence, East Sutton, Chart Sutton, and Hollingbourne itself, together with the detached chapelry of Bredhurst near Rochester. The original unity of the estate, and the way it was subdivided internally in successive stages, are still apparent in the local boundaries of the neighbourhood, in very much the same way as at Westerham.[39] Typically enough, Hollingbourne itself occupies the more fertile land near the Greenway, sheltered and lush by its undying spring, 'the bourne of the people in the hollow'.[40] Hucking, by contrast, stands high above it, a tiny parish of 1,200 acres, starved and bleak on the flinty summit of the Downs. All the remaining settlements were carved out of the Chartland to the south, in the inferior wood-pasture of the original territory, as their place-names indicate. Sutton Valence and East Sutton, for example, formed Hollingbourne's 'south farms', on the ragstone outskirts of the estate; Langley derived its name from some *lang lēah* or 'long clearing' in the forest country beyond Leeds, and may have been intercommoned with Maidstone; Broomfield developed very late, probably after 978, and was situated on a patch of heathland where the wild broom must once have flourished;[41] while Chart Sutton, or more properly Chart-next-Sutton, developed on the very edge of the Stone Hills, looking far away across the Weald towards Sussex. Very much the same pattern of development is repeated elsewhere in Holmesdale: at Kemsing in West Kent, for instance, with its daughter-community at Seal or 'hall', and its wood-pasture on Seal Chart, which is first recorded as Kemsing Chart; at Charing in mid-Kent, with its old

4   *The Jutish basis*

forest-clearings at Egerton, Pevington, Pluckley, and Little Chart; and again at Lenham, with its outlying Chartland pastures in Boughton Malherbe. In each case the original settlement is situated by the springs towards the northern edge of the estate, while colonization extended principally to the south, up into the wooded hills and heathy valleys of the Chart.[42]

The relatively modest scale of many of these springhead-estates of Kent raises a point of some interest which, in concluding this section, ought to be briefly touched on. Not all of them were small: Faversham, for example, may have covered more than 20,000 acres, and Milton and Wrotham, as well as Hollingbourne, nearly 18,000. Newington, however, did not extend to more than 15,000 acres, Charing to barely 12,000, and Kemsing and Teynham to little more than 8,000. Since territories of this kind originated from essentially localized circumstances, and were clearly moulded by their immediate topography and environment, it would be surprising if they all approximated to the same size. In several cases, however, it seems likely that the disparity between them arose through subdivision of an older and more extensive territory. There can be no real doubt that Newington, for example, developed as a subdivision of Milton, whose original area must therefore have exceeded 30,000 acres. There is also reason to think that Teynham once formed part of the Faversham estate, and Kemsing part of Otford, while Lenham very probably included the small neighbouring territory of Harrietsham, which is a *hamm*-name, not a *hām* like Lenham itself. The ultimate circumstances behind subdivision of this kind are of course unknown to us, but amongst them we must probably envisage an increasing population; in the Milton Regis area, and in the central stretch of Holmesdale where Lenham is situated, there is some reason for postulating an early increase. Even the smaller springhead-estates, however, originated at a very remote period; for place-names like Kemsing and Charing are recorded in very early charters, and incorporate the primitive name-forming suffix *ing*, which is also found in such unquestionably early places as Wantage, and which in these cases produced a name probably referring to the springhead itself.[43]

4. CONCLUSION

It would be misleading to imply that there was any simplistic uniformity about the organization of early Kentish settlement. At present there are many facts that cannot readily be fitted into the basic framework

PART TWO *The Foundations of Settlement*

outlined in this chapter. There are some places, like Lydd, that may never have been integrated into estates of the kind described here. There are several ancient settlements, like Cuxton near Rochester and Adisham near Canterbury, whose regional context is problematical. There are some parts of the county, such as the stretch of Holmesdale beyond Wye and much of the Medway valley, where the outlines of early territorial organization remain obscure and elusive. The development of an estate based on Lyminge is particularly intriguing, since Lyminge is five miles from its eponymous river and must once have formed part of the outlying territory of Lympne. The primitive crisscross of conflicting jurisdictions in the neighbourhood of Eastry and Northbourne is equally difficult to interpret, and in this area may well derive from pre-Jutish arrangements. Yet such problems as these are themselves significant, since they show that the early Jutish estates of Kent did not stem from identical origins and only gradually approximated to a common form.[44] They arose from essentially localized circumstances; they developed in response to a very varied environment; and they were moulded perhaps more than we realize by the legacy of a Romano-British past. Certainly they should not be thought of as administrative units systematically imposed from above on a largely virgin countryside.

Nevertheless, the burden of the evidence indicates that the kind of territory described here, with a riverine or springhead community at its heart, and a substantial tract of outlying *wald* or wood-pasture, was the characteristic unit of early English settlement in Kent. Altogether some 40 or 50 territories of this kind may be distinguished, and in conclusion it may be useful to survey their nomenclature. The subject is a complex one and the following tabulation is deliberately limited, in general, to the names of the estate-centres themselves. Since these form the earliest clearly identifiable group of Teutonic settlements in Kent, their place-names are plainly of more than ordinary significance;[45] altogether about 80 elements appear to be represented.

The figures in table 1 speak for themselves. The most obvious point to note is the surprisingly small number of habitative elements represented and the very large number specifically referring to rivers, streams, wells, pools, and springheads. In the neighbourhood of estate-centres like Maidstone, Milton, Faversham, Wingham, and Wickhambreaux there are also many minor names in 'well', 'spring', 'bourne', 'ford', and the like which are not included in the table. The significance of this onomastic pattern in the context of Romano-Jutish continuity,

90

Table 1. Estate-centres: place-name elements[a]

1.	Pre-English river-names		7/10	
2.	Other water elements		24/28+	31/38+
	burna, 'a spring, a stream, a bourne'	4/6+		
	flēot, 'a fleet, a rivulet'	2		
	ing[b]	3/4		
	celde, 'a spring'	1		
	cille, 'a spring'	1		43/52+
	wella, 'a well, a spring, a stream'	3/4+		
	ēwell, ēwelm, 'a river-spring'	3		
	wēl, 'a deep pool, a place in a river'	1		
	spring	1+		
	ford	5+		
3.	Other topographical elements		12/14+	
	clif, 'a cliff, a bank'	2		
	hōh, 'a spur of land'	1		
	ēg, 'an island'	1/2		
	stān, 'a stone'	4+		
	hlid, 'a slope'	?1		
	gē, 'a district'[c]	4		
4.	Habitative elements		15/19	
	hām	10/13		
	wīchām	3		18/23+
	tūn	2/3		
		3/4+		
5.	Religious elements			
	monasterium, 'a minster, a mother-church'	2+		
	wīg, 'an idol, idol house'	1		
	beorg, 'a hill, a tumulus'	?1		
6.	Pre-English place-names (excluding those from rivers)		4/8+	
	Total		65/83+	

[a] Only major place-names (i.e. of estate-centres) are in general included. Maximum and minimum numbers (as 3/4) are given in cases of doubt. A plus sign indicates the existence of associated place-names of a minor kind incorporating the element in question.

[b] Not in itself a topographical element, but a suffix which in Kent seems to have produced place-names referring to springs.

[c] This element should perhaps be classified as 'administrative' rather than 'topographical'.

PART TWO *The Foundations of Settlement*

and in connexion with the early well-cults and springhead-minsters of Kent, is a point we shall return to in subsequent chapters. How far it was a regional characteristic is a question that demands more detailed investigation before it can be adequately answered; there are grounds for believing that it was particularly striking in Kent; but it was not an entirely local peculiarity. The prevalence of early names in 'ford' is now widely acknowledged, while primitive territorial names derived from those of rivers are to be found in most parts of the country.[46] The fact that so many Celtic river-names have survived, even in counties where there is relatively little other trace of British occupation, must often be connected with the development of early estates on their margins. Rightly interpreted, it is probably one of the major arguments in favour of continuity, and in Kent the evidence seems particularly convincing.

When St Augustine landed in Thanet in 597, it seems probable that Kentish settlement was still predominantly confined to the Original Lands, and largely organized on the basis of these river and springhead territories. Most of them must still have been in the hands of the king, and it was these circumstances that led to the establishment of minster churches in the old estate centres, and the granting out of many of them to the early Kentish church. Both the structure of ecclesiastical development, as a consequence, and the structure of colonization were moulded by the subsequent evolution of these estates: and eventually it was from these circumstances that the territorial organization of the *regiones* and the lathes emerged, and the legal and administrative framework of the medieval county.[47] That is why the administrative evidence and the ecclesiastical evidence are so illuminating in Kent in seeking to reconstruct the progress of settlement.

5

BEYOND THE JUTES:
PRELIMINARY CONSIDERATIONS

1. THE PROBLEM

The question of continuity between Roman and Jute poses two historiographical difficulties to which there is no ideal solution. By its nature, to begin with, the evidence is partial and amorphous; such indications as we have are more in the nature of clues or pointers than absolute proofs. Of the several lines of argument available, none taken by itself is likely to be altogether convincing; it is only when individual settlements are studied in the round and the whole syndrome of evidence is brought together – archaeology, place-names, topography, early religious development, and so forth – that the case for continuity becomes manifest; only when each particular line of argument is placed alongside others, and found to point in the same direction, that its significance comes to light. Yet it is also imperative to examine each line of evidence on its own, on a comparative basis from place to place, if we are to arrive at valid conclusions. For example, it is only when the numerous Kentish place-names in *stān* are examined systematically, as a group or species, that their bearing upon pre-Jutish settlement begins to become apparent; individual examples, taken in isolation, prove nothing whatever.

In the present chapter the argument is therefore limited to a preliminary survey of two types of evidence which are obviously basic to any consideration of continuity – archaeology and place-names – while other aspects of the subject must await consideration in subsequent chapters. If this approach seems unduly artificial or frustrating, it can only be said that neither the topographical nor the religious aspects of continuity can usefully be discussed until a systematic survey has been made of such matters as early ecclesiastical development, the pattern of church-dedications, the topography of parish boundaries, the structure of manorial evolution, the association of holy wells with mother-churches, the evidence of prehistoric tracks and pilgrim ways, and other topics which remain to be explored in the later parts of this book. For this reason I must beg the reader to be patient before passing final judgement on the general hypothesis advanced in this chapter.

PART TWO *The Foundations of Settlement*

The second difficulty that faces us is the fact that continuity of occupation is an historical problem which cannot be solved by the historian alone. Essentially it also demands the special skills of the place-name scholar, while the final proof depends on expert excavation and must be left to the archaeologist. In recent years the three disciplines have expanded so greatly, and become so specialized and recondite in their respective techniques, that it is not possible to be expert in all three. In this connexion it is difficult to improve on the words of Margaret Gelling in *Signposts to the Past* (1978);

> It is a commonplace of Dark Age studies that philologists, historians and archaeologists do not always appreciate each other's points of view. Historians may feel that philologists are not particularly well equipped to evaluate the historical significance of their material, and archaeologists may feel that philologists lack the practical sense needed for the realistic interpretation of names bestowed by peasant farmers. Philologists, for their part, are acutely aware that historians and archaeologists are embarrassingly disaster-prone when discussing place-names. An earlier book on the interaction of the three disciplines in Dark Age studies [F. T. Wainwright, *Archaeology and Place-Names and History* (1962)] was mainly concerned with the logical foundations of the three subjects and the possibility of a single scholar mastering all the fields sufficiently to achieve a satisfactory balance between co-ordination and specialization. . . . Assuming that Dr Wainwright's co-ordinating scholar is an ideal unlikely of attainment, the disciplines of history, archaeology and philology must remain to some extent distinct. There will continue to be demarcation problems, and accusations are sometimes made that the philologists operate a sort of closed shop. There is some truth in this, but long experience has convinced me that a closed shop is something of a necessity on the etymological side of place-name study.[1]

In discussing the onomastic and archaeological evidence, therefore, the historian's task must necessarily be limited to investigating the *correlation* or *association* between archaeological sites, early place-names, and historic settlements; and this is all that will be attempted in this chapter.

With these limitations in mind, how far is it possible in Kent to press back the broad pattern of primary settlement in the Original Lands, as

5 Beyond the Jutes: preliminary considerations

described in the last chapter, beyond the coming of the Jutes? It is not seriously possible to trace the precise boundaries of pre-Jutish estates, although some of those described probably antedated the Jutes in their main outlines. Neither is it possible to trace continuity of settlement in any substantial form beyond the closing centuries of the Iron Age, the last generations before the Roman invasions. Naturally, there are archaeological sites of much greater antiquity than that; but much of this very primitive settlement may have been shifting and impermanent, the work of huntsmen rather than farmers, so that it has left little proof of continuous connexion with subsequent occupation. With the Celtic-speaking peoples of the late pre-Christian centuries we reach firmer ground. It was they or their ancestors who gave Kent its name, *Cantion* or 'border [country]', and so in a sense first recognized its individuality.[2] It was also they who gave the county its principal river-names and its earliest settlement-names, so that they may justly be regarded as the first people to shape the countryside of today. Their work of colonization was carried further by their Romano-British successors, and in Kent, as has been remarked already, the Roman contribution is particularly important. Though it is rarely possible to determine the boundaries of Roman farms or estates, it is thus certainly possible to identify the general areas, and in many cases the specific sites, colonized by Celtic, Belgic, or Romano-British peoples. By and large place-names and archaeology confirm one another and point to the same districts and the same places as the earliest centres of colonization. These places frequently correspond remarkably closely with the original Jutish estate centres, moreover, so that the case for continuity of occupation between Roman and Jute is at many points a cogent one. Though there may well have been a drastic decline of population during the twilight period following the Roman withdrawal,[3] and extensive advance of secondary woodland, it seems likely that a substantial native population must have survived, and that many of the 'seminal settlements' of Kent described earlier, if ever wholly deserted, were quickly reoccupied.

2. ARCHAEOLOGICAL COMPLEXES

In approaching the archaeological evidence the historian of Kent is faced with one insuperable problem at the outset: the absence of an up-to-date distribution map. In many areas of England 'rescue' archaeology and aerial photography have in recent years revolutionized the

PART TWO *The Foundations of Settlement*

accepted pattern of distribution, and this may yet prove to be the case in Kent.[4] In practice, however, the extent to which the major complexes of archaeological evidence tend to be centred in the Original Lands, and in the immediate vicinity of the early Jutish estate centres, is too manifest to be wholly fortuitous. Sometimes it may simply be due to the fact that these are the areas archaeologists happen to have looked at; yet the dense cluster of sites around places like Maidstone has come to light through chance discovery[5] rather than systematic investigation, and on any count presents a fundamentally different picture from that for a later Kentish settlement like Tunbridge Wells. On the whole, therefore, though these reservations must be emphasized, and the following account makes no claim to finality or to authoritative scrutiny, the general pattern of major archaeological complexes in Kent is plainly significant in the context of continuity.

A survey of the more obvious printed sources for the county yields a total of nearly 500 major sites of the kind under discussion in approximately 200 parishes. These relate to a very varied range of settlements, villas, forts, farms, cemeteries, coin-hoards, potteries, temples, and so forth, dating from the Iron Age, Belgic, and Romano-British periods.[6] Not far short of 400 of the total relate to the latter era, and while this figure is no doubt affected by the greater popularity of Roman archaeology, it also illustrates the formative character of the Roman occupation. Although at first glance these 500 sites seem to be widely distributed, moreover, closer inspection, coupled with the precise local mapping on the $2\frac{1}{2}''$ O.S. sheets which is essential to any understanding of continuity,[7] reveals a sharply contrasted regional pattern. More than 70 per cent of the total are to be found on the Foothills, in the three major river valleys, and in Holmesdale, in those same Original Lands where early Jutish settlement is also found.[8] The remarkable concentration of sites in these areas obtains in all archaeological periods, moreover, and is no peculiarity of any particular wave of settlement, though it tends to increase in later centuries.[9] The whole of the rest of the county, by contrast, amounting to three-quarters of its total area, accounts for less than 30 per cent of the 500 sites: the Downland for 12 per cent, the Marshland 7 per cent, the Chartland 6 per cent, and the Weald only 3 per cent: and that despite the fact that both Weald and Downland are more extensive than the Original Lands. In reality the concentration of prehistoric evidence in these latter areas is more striking than the crude figures suggest; for the vast majority of the more important complexes are to be found there, including almost all the

5 Beyond the Jutes: preliminary considerations

numerous Roman villas, whereas those in other areas are in many cases comparatively minor. Most of the sites in the North Kent Marshlands, moreover, do not relate to settlements as such but to pottery kilns along the coast and near the Swale, many of which were probably attached to neighbouring places on the Foothills. It is also noticeable that the Downland sites tend to lie towards the northern edge of the area, near the Foothills, and those on the Chartland near Holmesdale, from which in some cases the settlements in question had probably originated.[10]

Obviously these figures do not represent genuine statistics; the sites under review vary greatly in archaeological significance, moreover, and the present writer is not competent to assess their relative importance. Nevertheless, it is plain that when the Jutes first settled in Kent they were not colonizing a virgin countryside, and that by and large they settled in the same zones or areas as the Romans, the Belgae, and the Celtic peoples before them. Even if substantial evidence of pre-Jutish occupation should come to light in other parts of the county, moreover, it is doubtful if the pattern of continuity itself would be affected; for in this respect the archaeological evidence is only one strand in a complex skein, and each other line of argument also points to the Downland, the Chartland, and the Weald as essentially regions of 'discontinuity', or colonization. In that case we should have to postulate a major recession of settlement in these areas at the end of the Roman period and subsequent recolonization by the English; there are certainly some places where this is likely to have happened, and even in the Original Lands we must probably envisage a relatively rudimentary way of life and the desertion of a major urban centre like Canterbury in the period following the Roman withdrawal.[11] Nevertheless, despite these reservations, the current evidence of archaeology obviously points to the Foothills and Holmesdale as the likely regions of continuity in Kent. This view receives striking confirmation from the fact that Roman brickwork is frequently found in the parish churches of these areas, and very rarely in those of other parts of the county, save occasionally on the Downs. In the limits of this book it is impracticable to discuss the context of every major archaeological site in the Original Lands in detail – altogether there are nearly 350 of them – but at the risk of burdening the reader with a tedious catalogue the broad outlines ought to be indicated.

In the stretch of countryside between London and the Cray, the first major complexes that need to be mentioned occur at Keston and Crayford, some 12 or 13 miles from St Paul's (see map 3).[12] The relative

PART TWO *The Foundations of Settlement*

sparsity of early evidence between London and the Cray valley is noteworthy and has been commented on by others before now.[13] It may partly be due to suburban development; but much of this development is recent, and elsewhere in Kent suburban building has often brought prehistoric evidence to light. Actually, it is one of several indications that colonization rarely proceeded from the London end of the county or from the Thames, and probably in no case from London itself. Few though such sites may be, however, both Keston and Crayford are places of unusual interest. Crayford is situated at the point where Watling Street crosses the river, and seems to have formed the original centre of the Jutish river-estate based on the valley, and the site of its accompanying minster. The fact that it developed near the Roman station known as *Noviomagus*, while the mother-church of St Paulinus of Rochester[14] stands adjacent to the Iron Age settlement site subsequently occupied by the Belgae, is thus particularly significant. Keston is situated at the source of the Ravensbourne on the northern edge of the Downs, and its role as a springhead estate-centre is more difficult to reconstruct. It was certainly a very early settlement, however, whose place-name incorporates the element *stān* which in Kent is so often associated with Roman buildings and prehistoric megaliths. In Keston itself, Baston Court occupies the site of a Roman building;[15] about a mile to the north a further Roman building is associated with the parish church of Hayes; and a major Roman site has been excavated at Warbank, near the Iron Age hill-forts in Holwood Park and on Keston Common.

Two miles to the east of Crayford is Dartford, the first of that long line of early primary settlements in the Darent valley which, as we have seen, also included Darenth, Eynsford, Shoreham, Otford, and Westerham. In this area a further chain of early archaeological complexes occurs, strung out on either side of the river. Dartford itself, at the lowest bridging-point, is a place of great antiquity, having yielded a succession of Palaeolithic, Neolithic, Bronze Age, and Iron Age evidence, as well as a Roman settlement north of Watling Street in the neighbourhood of a Jutish cemetery. Archaeologically, it is closely associated with its neighbour Stone, which was later incorporated along with it in the Darenth estate, and which has also yielded important evidence of Roman and Belgic settlement. Sandwiched between Dartford and Stone, Darenth is associated with a major Roman villa, whose flourishing farm was later converted into a fulling establishment,[16] and whose remains were subsequently re-used in the

5 Beyond the Jutes: preliminary considerations

Saxon parish church. At Eynsford, below the Iron Age hill-fort at Hulberry, Roman brick is also re-utilized, in this case in the castle, perhaps taken from an undiscovered villa beneath the village itself, or else from the neighbouring villas at Farningham and Lullingstone. At Otford and Kemsing, which lie below the hill-fort on Otford Mount, no fewer than six Roman occupation-sites are strung out on either side of the Pilgrims' Way: by the river, by Otford church, at Twitton, and near the significant place-names of Wickham, Copstone (*stān*), and Springhead.[17] Several of these sites have also yielded Iron Age pottery, whilst a seventh lies north of the hill-fort, on the boundary of Otford and Shoreham, where there was yet another Roman villa close to the village of Shoreham.

Between the Darent valley and the Medway there is only one major archaeological complex that needs to be noted here, at *Vagniacae* on the boundary of Northfleet and Southfleet. Other sites occur at reputedly early places like Meopham and Cobham, where there was perhaps an Iron Age hill-fort and where Roman brick is again used in the church; but these places did not become estate-centres, and archaeological evidence of the crucial Roman period is at present far to seek. *Vagniacae*, by contrast, was a Roman posting-station alongside Watling Street, and an important religious centre based on the springs at the source of the Ebbsfleet, which gave *Vagniacae* its English name of Springhead.[18] Although Springhead itself did not develop into an English settlement of any consequence, it was probably the parent of the Jutish Ebbsfleet estate, which was subsequently divided into Northfleet and Southfleet along the line of the springs, and of which Northfleet must have been the original centre. Like Dartford and Crayford, Northfleet itself is also a place of great antiquity, moreover, having yielded evidence of the Palaeolithic, Mesolithic, Neolithic, Bronze Age, and Roman periods, in addition to that at Springhead itself.

In the Medway valley we reach another major series of archaeological complexes, headed by the Belgic and Roman town of Rochester or *Durobrivae* at the chief river-crossing. Four miles below Rochester two Roman burial grounds and an occupation site have come to light at Hoo St Werburgh, the estate-centre of the Hoo Peninsula. On the further side of the peninsula, Cliffe-at-Hoo formed an estate-centre based on a Roman occupation-site, in this case well known for its military connotation and its evidence of centuriation. Upstream, a long line of early settlements associated with Roman remains stretches for 15 miles or so between Cuxton and Teston, though in this area the

PART TWO *The Foundations of Settlement*

Jutish *capita* cannot always be definitely identified. At Cuxton (*stān*) the church adjoins the site of a Roman building, and the grounds of the rectory have long been noted as a source of Palaeolithic implements.[19] At Snodland the church also stands close to a Roman building, at Stone Grave, and half a mile from a cemetery at Holborough which has yielded both Roman and early Jutish remains. At East Barming the church is once again associated with a Roman building, and also with a walled cemetery and two cremation sites. At Teston (*stān*) there is a Roman villa, and at East Farleigh there are three Roman sites within a mile or so of the parish church. At Aylesford prehistoric evidence is especially abundant, and includes the notable Roman villa at Eccles (*eclēsia*), a Belgic cemetery yielding Iron Age finds next to the church, and the great series of megaliths on the outskirts of the parish at Kits Coty, the Countless Stones, the White Horse Stone, and elsewhere.

The most important centre of early settlement in the Medway valley, apart from Rochester itself, was undoubtedly Maidstone. Nearly 40 major archaeological sites may be plotted on the $2\frac{1}{2}''$ O.S. sheet covering the town, more than on any other save that covering Milton Regis and Ospringe. Almost all of these are within two or three miles of the town centre, and many of them are close to its Roman spine-road, Week Street and Stone Street. For the Roman period these finds include: six cemeteries, six cremation sites, at least two villas, a bath-house, four or more other Roman buildings, three 'settlement' sites, two 'occupation' sites, two major coin-hoards, several minor finds, and a pastoral enclosure on the edge of the town at Mangravet. For earlier periods they include Iron Age 'B' pottery, Belgic cremations, and an Iron Age hill-fort near Boughton Monchelsea. The surviving evidence of pre-Jutish settlement at Maidstone is thus very substantial; yet it is probably only a tithe of what still lies buried beneath the built-up area, where there has been very little systematic excavation. With its extensive quarries and its easy water transport, the neighbourhood formed the chief source of building stone in the south-east under the Romans, and the town itself was clearly a community of some consequence at that time. At this crucial river-crossing the case for continuity between Roman and Jute is thus particularly cogent and would repay more detailed investigation.

In the Stour valley and the Foothills beyond Canterbury we find a further series of major archaeological complexes headed by Canterbury itself, a Roman, Belgic, and Iron Age community known to the Romans as *Durovernum Cantiacorum*.[20] Upstream from Canterbury, evidence of

5 Beyond the Jutes: preliminary considerations

Roman occupation has come to light beneath the Norman castle at Chilham, an estate-centre also associated with the important Iron Age, Belgic, and Roman site at Julliberries Grave across the river. At Wye, further upstream, Iron Age pottery has been found and a pagan Jutish burial ground, though as yet there is curiously little evidence of the intervening Roman period. Below Canterbury, Roman remains are to be found in the neighbourhood of almost every major Jutish settlement, and at many minor places too. At Richborough and Reculver there were important Roman forts; at Ickham, Wingham, and St John's-in-Thanet, Roman villas; at Sturry, a Roman settlement with a quay by the river; at Chislet and Wickhambreaux, Roman pottery sites; at Eastry, a Roman ritual site; at Worth, a temple and a burial ground; at Sarre and Minster-in-Thanet, cremation sites; at Northbourne, a cemetery and an occupation site; and so on. In several of these places there is also evidence of pre-Roman occupation – of the Iron Age at Richborough, Reculver, Sturry, Northbourne, and Worth, for example – and at many there are early Jutish burial grounds. Not all these places beyond Canterbury developed into estate-centres; but Wingham, Sturry, Eastry, Reculver, Minster, Northbourne, and Wickhambreaux come within that category; while Chislet, Richborough, and Sarre, if not *capita* themselves, were certainly ancient Jutish settlements in their own right.

Between the Stour valley and the Medway lies the last major series of archaeological complexes to note, in the Foothill country bordering Watling Street and the Swale. Once again most of these are associated with early Jutish estate-centres. They stretch in a continuous line from Rochester and Chatham on the west, through Gillingham, Rainham, Newington, Milton, and Teynham, as far as Ospringe and Faversham, where there was probably another Roman station, *Durolevum*.[21] All of these places lie immediately to the north of Watling Street except Rainham and Ospringe, which adjoin it to the south.[22] The relative sparsity of pre-Jutish evidence to the south of the road is one of several signs that the continuation of Blean Forest still came down to Watling Street at many points in this part of Kent in the Roman era. Apart from Faversham, which is discussed later in this chapter, the most interesting settlement in this area is Milton Regis, one of the seats of the Kentish kings. In the neighbourhood of Milton there are at least 25 major sites, mostly dating from the Roman period. These include no fewer than 16 cemeteries, a Roman settlement of some kind alongside Watling Street, perhaps a posting station, together with Roman

PART TWO *The Foundations of Settlement*

buildings at Milton itself, and other evidence of occupation at Great Grovehurst and elsewhere.[23] About a mile north of the Street, Milton parish church adjoins the site of a Roman house and stands within an enclosure which may also be of Roman origin;[24] between church, Street, and creek there are two Roman burial grounds and an early Jutish one. At this point, as at Maidstone, the case for continuity between Roman and Jute is thus especially strong, and quite possibly the origins of settlement reach back in a continuous line beyond the Roman period. For at Murston, on the other side of the Creek, there is evidence of Belgic and Iron Age occupation, and at Grovehurst, north of Milton church, an important Neolithic settlement.[25]

The remaining archaeological complexes of Kent occur in smaller and more scattered groups, and though often of great interest must be dealt with more briefly. Dover, Folkestone, Lympne, and Lyminge formed important Roman centres on the southern side of the county. Lydd is an isolated site near the Sussex border, and Minster-in-Sheppey, with its Roman and perhaps pre-Roman connotations, on the north coast. Apart from these, the only places calling for special comment are the spring-line settlements of Holmesdale. In this stretch of country, Kemsing, Wrotham, Trottiscliffe, Thurnham, Detling, and Stowting all seem to be more or less closely associated with Roman remains, and perhaps a few other places such as Westwell and Kennington. In general, however, it is noteworthy that in this area the link between Roman and Jute is at present less pronounced than on the Foothills. At a few early Jutish estate-centres, such as Hollingbourne, little or nothing in the way of Romano-British evidence has yet come to light, and what there is is sometimes, as at Charing, at some distance from the crucial centre of occupation around the church. It may be that in this area some of the original Jutish settlements were indeed sited on virgin territory, and had no connexion with earlier waves of colonization. But the use of Roman brick in local parish churches like Lenham, where no other finds have yet been recorded, suggests that there may be archaeological evidence still awaiting discovery. Some of the old market villages of Holmesdale are sizeable nucleated places by Kentish standards, so that there may be evidence of previous occupation beneath the built-up area.

Of the 40 or so definitely identifiable Jutish estate-centres, at least four out of five are thus directly associated with major Romano-British remains. This association does not in itself prove continuity of occupation at these places; but it suggests that they are the places where

5 *Beyond the Jutes: preliminary considerations*

archaeologists are most likely to find it. Moreover, almost every major Roman site in the county, including Dover, Rochester, Richborough, Reculver, Lympne, Northfleet, Milton Regis, and Faversham, has produced early Saxon or Jutish burials.[26] At places like Eastry, Woodnesborough, Sturry, Rainham, Maidstone, Rochester, and Dartford it is further noteworthy that the main street of the Roman settlement still forms the principal street of the community today, so that in Kent the early Germanic colonists did not necessarily shun places occupied by their predecessors as they appear to have done in some other areas. If it is true that the English settlement of the South-East was a process of gradual infiltration rather than catastrophic invasion, a piecemeal settlement 'by comparatively small bands of immigrants, men, women, and children together', these facts should not surprise us.[27] In such circumstances it was only natural that the new Teutonic settlers should attach themselves to extant communities, and in places the onomastic evidence seems to reinforce this view.

3. PRE-JUTISH PLACE-NAMES

In the context of continuity between Roman and Jute, there are three major groups of place-names that need to be considered: those deriving from a Celtic root or indicating a pre-English population; the early-recorded 'problem-names' of Kent, for which no generally accepted explanation has yet been advanced; and certain specialized groups of place-name generally associated with primitive settlement in Kent, of which those in *stān*, 'stone', are the most numerous. Like the archaeological evidence, these early names are largely confined to the Original Lands, and in most cases relate to old estate-centres or settlements immediately adjacent to them.[28]

As in most English counties, names of undoubted British lineage in Kent are not numerous in relation to the nomenclature of the county as a whole. They are more plentiful than in many Midland or eastern counties, however, and probably more so than is generally acknowledged. Altogether there are about 35 names whose pre-English origin may be regarded as established; a further dozen or so that possibly indicate Celtic-speaking communities; and another dozen or 20 for which a Celtic root has been suggested by reputable scholars, such as Ekwall, Wallenberg, or Zachrisson, though it has not found universal acceptance and in most cases must probably be accepted with caution. This total of 60 or so names at the most represents only a small fraction

PART TWO *The Foundations of Settlement*

of the 10,000 or so ancient settlements of Kent; but the point to note is that these names are not scattered at random through the county as a whole but are largely confined to areas of early Jutish occupation. Only one-third of the place-names in the county are discussed by Wallenberg, moreover, so that there may be some further names of British provenance still awaiting discovery. In interpreting onomastic evidence it is also important not to assume, as early authorities on the subject like Mawer too readily assumed,[29] that settlements with English names are necessarily of English origin. Canterbury bears an English name, 'the *burh* of the men of Kent', and if it had not been an important place attracting archaeological attention, and figuring in Old English records under its British name *Durovernum* as well as under its English name, it might have passed as an English foundation. There may well be other places in Kent that gradually acquired a new name in this way, but which are not recorded so early and cannot be so readily recognized. There are several, such as Richborough and Lyminge, where a Celtic and an English element are combined.

The linguistic evidence for the Celtic foundations in Kent is thus obviously incomplete, but it is of crucial importance for an assessment of continuity. It comprises two groups of names: those of regions and rivers on one hand, and those of settlements on the other. Of the regional names the most important is that of the county itself. The fact that Kent alone among the regions of the South-East retained its British name, *Cantion* or *Cantium*, and never acquired an English substitute for it, is worth pondering. It is one of those facts in its history – the Medway megaliths are another – that in some ways connect it more intimately with distant Celtic or pre-Celtic lands than with regions close at hand. The people that we call Jutes on the strength of a reference in Bede did not christen their territory anew, as their Germanic neighbours did in Sussex, Essex, and Middlesex, and described themselves as Kentings or *Cantware*. In Thanet they also retained a Romano-British regional name, *Tanatos*, an obscure word, perhaps meaning 'bright island', and apparently cognate with the River Tanat in the Welsh borders. For the Weald they retained the name of Andred, and it is possible that the Forest of Blean, between Canterbury and the north coast, also derives from a pre-English root.[30] Some of their rivers, as in other counties, later acquired alternative English names, such as Wantsum and Swale; but many river-names in Kent stem from a Celtic (or perhaps in a few cases a pre-Celtic) root, and if Wallenberg had covered them more systematically, we should

5 Beyond the Jutes: preliminary considerations

probably know of further examples.[31] The fact that such rivers and streams as the Medway, Darent, Cray, Dour, Limen (Rother), *Carey* (Len), *Colne* (Westbrook in Herne), *Sarre* (Wantsum), and perhaps *Daven* (Fishbourne in Faversham) originally retained their pre-English names is probably in some way connected with the development of early river-estates along their margins.[32]

The evidence for settlement-names of pre-Jutish significance is more complex. Four types of place need to be considered. First, there are 12 or 13 major primary settlements of obviously British lineage, such as Dover, Reculver, and Lympne. Second, there are nine or ten lesser places like *Pennycrych* and *Billerica*, which, though unimportant in themselves, are closely linked with Jutish estate-centres. Third, there are several names in *wealh*, 'foreigner, Briton, etc.', which probably indicate a Celtic-speaking community brought into servitude by the Jutes, and which are once again connected with old estate-centres, as at Walton by Folkestone and Walton by Eastry. Finally, a more difficult problem, there are more than 50 Kentish names in 'combe'. This has usually been regarded as an early English loan-word from the British, and predominantly a West Country one in consequence, so that its frequency in Kent is of some interest. In most cases, however, it relates to minor settlements like Ranscombe, Winchcombe, and Combwell, in the wooded valleys of the Downs, the Weald, or the Chart, where it bears no pre-English significance.[33] There are seven or eight places, however, where names in 'combe' are significantly associated not only with early estate-centres, like Faversham, Maidstone, Otford, and Lympne, but also with early archaeological sites or with some other significant place-name element. Like the names in *wealh*, therefore, these particular names may just possibly go back to a Celtic-speaking population, though the derivation of 'combe' from a British word is now questioned by Dr Gelling.[34]

Clearly this total of 40 or 45 settlement-names of British ambience does not in itself prove continuity of occupation, and in some cases, such as Lympne and Reculver, the evidence is obviously more convincing than in obscure spots like Combe in Otford. What it indicates, however, is the presence of an important Celtic strand, at many points, in the local fabric of Kentish settlement. Viewed in conjunction with the archaeological evidence, the concentration of these names in the Original Lands of the county and in the immediate neighbourhood of Jutish estate-centres is thus surely significant. Apart from the special case of Dover, there are none on the Downs,[35] none in the Chartlands or

PART TWO *The Foundations of Settlement*

Marshlands, and only two – both doubtful cases – in the Weald: the lost *Brickenden* in Biddenden and *Wallinghurst* in the neighbouring parish of Frittenden.[36] Otherwise all 40 or so places are to be found on the Foothills or in Holmesdale, though they are not evenly distributed over these regions.

In Holmesdale itself there seem to be few names of pre-Jutish significance, probably not more than seven or eight in all, and not all of those conclusive. Although in turning to the 'problem-names' of the area we shall find some cause to question this conclusion, it is clear that names of proven British provenance are rare. Among them are the following, with their relevant elements in brackets: Chevening on the Pilgrims' Way (*cefn*, 'a ridge');[37] Eccles in Aylesford (*eclēsia*, *eglēs*, 'a church' or a 'Christian community');[38] Walton in Folkestone; perhaps Combe in Brabourne, Combe Bank in Sundridge, and Combe in Otford; and the two Carings on the River *Carey* or Len (?*car*, *caru*, '?pleasant stream'), in Leeds and Maidstone, where there is a further early name in 'combe'. Of the major place-names in this list, Aylesford, Otford, Maidstone, Brabourne, Folkestone and possibly Chevening were early Jutish estate-centres, and several of these are also associated with major archaeological sites. At Combe Bank in Sundridge, for example, there is a Roman cemetery, and while Sundridge itself did not belong to the first phase of Jutish settlement, Combe Bank is near the prehistoric Greenway and not far from Chevening.

On the Foothills there is a marked difference between the eastern and western parts of the county. In West Kent there are only four names of pre-English origin: Darenth (*Derventio*, 'oak river'), Cray (*Crei*, 'fresh, clean'), and Northumberland Heath in Erith (*humber/amber*, 'river').[39] East of these there is nothing until we reach *Briogoningwara* in Cuxton (*brigā*, 'hill'), and Rochester or *Durobrivae*, 'the bridges of the stronghold'.[40] Then by the Medway estuary (British ?*medu* + *gwy*, 'meadow water') and the Swale we find five settlement-names derived from the British *cēto* or *caito* which once covered this region: Chatham, Chattenden in Hoo St Werburgh, Chetney in Iwade/Milton, the lost *Chetham* in Osprange, and *Chathurst*, whose exact site is not known but was apparently near Swalecliffe.[41] As in Holmesdale there are possibly other names of British origin in this stretch of the Foothills, as we shall find in turning to the local problem-names; but in the present context the significant point to note is the association of most of these British names, once again, with Jutish estate-centres or other very early settlements and with major archaeological sites: Darenth, Cray, Cux-

5 Beyond the Jutes: preliminary considerations

ton, Rochester, Chatham, Hoo St Werburgh, Milton Regis, and Ospringe are all places of this kind.

Most of the remaining Celtic settlement-names of Kent lie on the Foothills to the east of Canterbury and the Blean. These include: *Durovernum* or Canterbury itself (*duro*, 'fort', + *verno-*, 'alders, swamp'), Reculver (*Regulbium*), Richborough (*Rutupiae*), Sarre (probably a British river-name for the Wantsum), *Pennycrych* in Bishopsbourne (perhaps containing the British word *crouco*, 'a barrow, a mound'),[42] Walton in Eastry, Walmer near Deal (*wealh* + *mere*, 'Briton + pool'), and perhaps Coombe in Woodnesborough.[43] Separated from these by the Downs, but also in East Kent, are Dover (*Dubris*, 'the waters'), Lyminge (*Limen* + *gē*, 'elm [river] district'), Lympne (*Limen*) with its lost *Billerica* (a doublet of Billericay in Essex), and Walton in Folkestone, which has already been mentioned.[44] Of the major place-names in this list Dover, Lympne, Lyminge, Folkestone, Canterbury, Reculver, and Eastry were all, as we have seen, centres of Roman settlement and *capita* of early Jutish estates. Both Sarre and Woodnesborough were also early sites, of which Sarre may have formed the original *caput* of the territory later based on Monkton, which comprised the western half of Thanet. Richborough does not seem to have become the *caput* of any estate, but it is one of the major Roman sites in Kent where excavation has definitely proved continuous occupation into the Jutish period and it became the site of an early Augustinian church.[45] In this area too, then, there is at many points a close relationship between Celtic place-names, major archaeological sites, and early Jutish settlements.

4. EARLY PROBLEM-NAMES

It is this topographical association between early Jutish places and names of pre-Jutish significance that lends interest in Kent to the numerous problem-names of the county; for many of the places to which Wallenberg and others have devoted lengthy and often inconclusive discussion are recorded in very early documents, and are known on other grounds to be of great antiquity. Some of this discussion is probably due to Wallenberg's penchant for seeking a topographical origin for names perhaps more readily explained on other grounds. Yet when all is said, we are still left in Kent with a substantial body of very difficult names, as is widely recognized. What lends interest to these places is the fact that at many points they fill out the basic network of

PART TWO *The Foundations of Settlement*

pre-English settlement-names indicated by the Celtic evidence. That does not mean that the names in question are necessarily of Celtic origin; in most cases it may rather suggest a very primitive Germanic lineage, perhaps going back to the Teutonic peoples brought into Kent in the Romano-British period. It is perhaps worth remembering, however, that unless places like Richborough had been settlements of some importance, well-evidenced in early records and easily recognized archaeologically, the Celtic origin of their names might not have been suspected, since their second elements are undoubtedly Germanic. It must also be remembered that several generations elapsed between the decline of Imperial rule and the first written record of Kentish place-names. There may be a number of places that are not so readily recognized as Richborough because they were less important and are not recorded so early. Within the limits of this book it is not possible to follow out the conflicting philological arguments for these problem-names in detail, and the present writer's opinion would in any case be worth very little. Nevertheless, it is important to indicate their distribution and to examine them afresh in the light of their local topography and archaeology. At the conclusion of the discussion, one particular locality, that of Faversham, will be described in more detail in order to illustrate the suggestive complex of evidence with which such names are often associated.

The first point to note is that the early Jutish settlements of Holmesdale, where Celtic evidence is relatively sparse, often seem to bear problem-names of this kind. Otford, Kemsing, Wrotham, Trottiscliffe, Aylesford, Detling, Hollingbourne, Lenham, Charing, and Stowting have all given rise to lengthy debate, and the formal evidence for them seems to be exceptionally difficult and contradictory.[46] In view of their markedly primitive topographical context this circumstance is interesting. All of them are certainly places of great antiquity, whether they go back to the original Jutish colonization or beyond. All of them are traversed by the Pilgrims' Way, which in most cases passes close to the principal settlement. All are sited on the prehistoric Greenway, which at Kemsing, Wrotham, Trottiscliffe, Detling, Hollingbourne, Lenham, and Charing passed directly through the churchyard, a matter we shall return to in Chapter 9. Several, such as Otford, Wrotham, Aylesford, and Detling, are associated with Roman remains of some consequence. Almost all became sites of early Christian minsters or mother-churches; and several were associated with sacred springs that may have been objects of pagan veneration before the

5 Beyond the Jutes: preliminary considerations

advent of Christianity (see further in Chapter 10). They are all, in short, the kind of places where we might expect to find pre-English settlement, and in a few cases the possibility of a pre-English element in their names has in fact been suggested. Wallenberg tended to reject these suggestions, sometimes on the ground that in Kent the onomastic evidence is overwhelmingly English in character; but strictly speaking the point at issue is not the character of Kentish place-names as a whole but the likelihood of a pre-Jutish strand in the fabric of local settlement *at these particular places*. In the light of their local topography and archaeology it may be that their names would bear re-examination with this in mind.

The place-names of Holmesdale form perhaps the most obvious group of problem-names in the county; but there are many others elsewhere, such as Chilham in the Stour valley, Wingham and Chislet east of Canterbury, and Rainham, Teynham, Ospringe, Davington, and Faversham in the Foothill country between Rochester and the Blean. Like the Holmesdale settlements, all of these were estate-centres or other very early communities, associated with major Roman remains, and sited on prehistoric routes. Rainham, for example, is situated on Watling Street, and Ospringe adjoins the Street to the south; Faversham lies between Watling Street and the pre-Roman trackway running parallel to it to the north; Davington is sited directly on this trackway, and Teynham a short distance beyond it; Chilham is on a branch of the Pilgrims' Way connecting Canterbury with Eastwell; and Wingham is situated on a prehistoric ridgeway where it joins the Roman road from Canterbury to Richborough. Most of these settlements also became sites of early mother-churches or minsters, and several of them were associated with prominent holy wells and springs.

The names of the Faversham neighbourhood will serve to illustrate in more detail the substratum of primitive settlement with which places of this kind are often associated (see map 6). Faversham itself bears a name of unusual interest, first recorded in 811. Its initial element is generally explained as an old English loan-word *fæfer* from the Latin *faber*, 'a smith', so that Faversham apparently signifies 'the smith's ham'.[47] Perhaps because places in *hām* are more usually combined with names of people than of occupations, A. H. Smith suggested that 'Faver' probably represented a personal name derived from this

MAP 6. *Faversham: early place-names and archaeological sites* (based on the Ordnance Survey map with the permission of The Controller of Her Majesty's Stationery Office; Crown Copyright reserved)

PART TWO *The Foundations of Settlement*

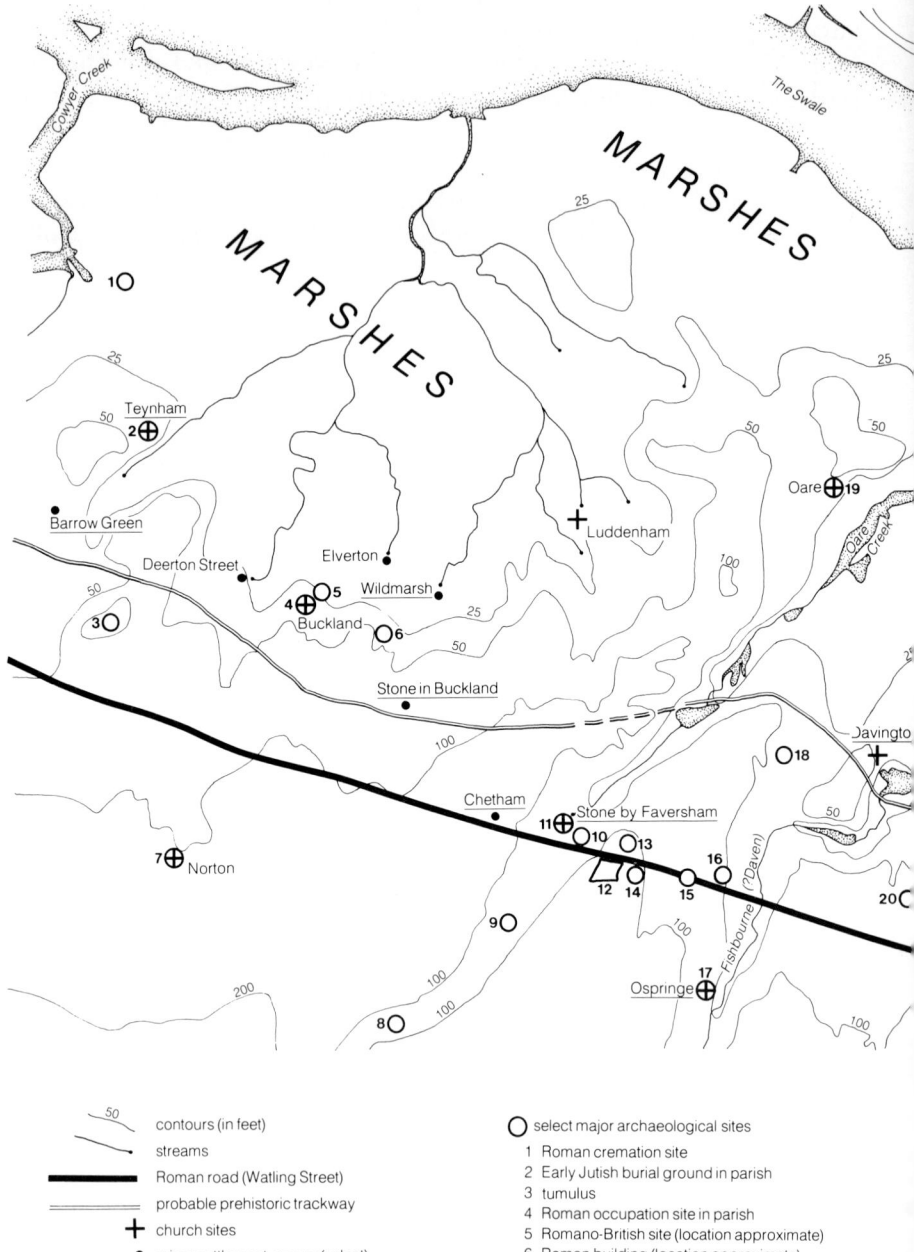

contours (in feet)
streams
Roman road (Watling Street)
probable prehistoric trackway
church sites
minor settlement-names (select)
underlining indicates
significant early place-names

○ select major archaeological sites
1 Roman cremation site
2 Early Jutish burial ground in parish
3 tumulus
4 Roman occupation site in parish
5 Romano-British site (location approximate)
6 Roman building (location approximate)
7 Early Jutish burial ground in parish (?)
8 Romano-British burial ground
9 Romano-British burial ground
10 Roman hut
11 church ruins incorporate part of Romano-British mauso

5 Beyond the Jutes: preliminary considerations

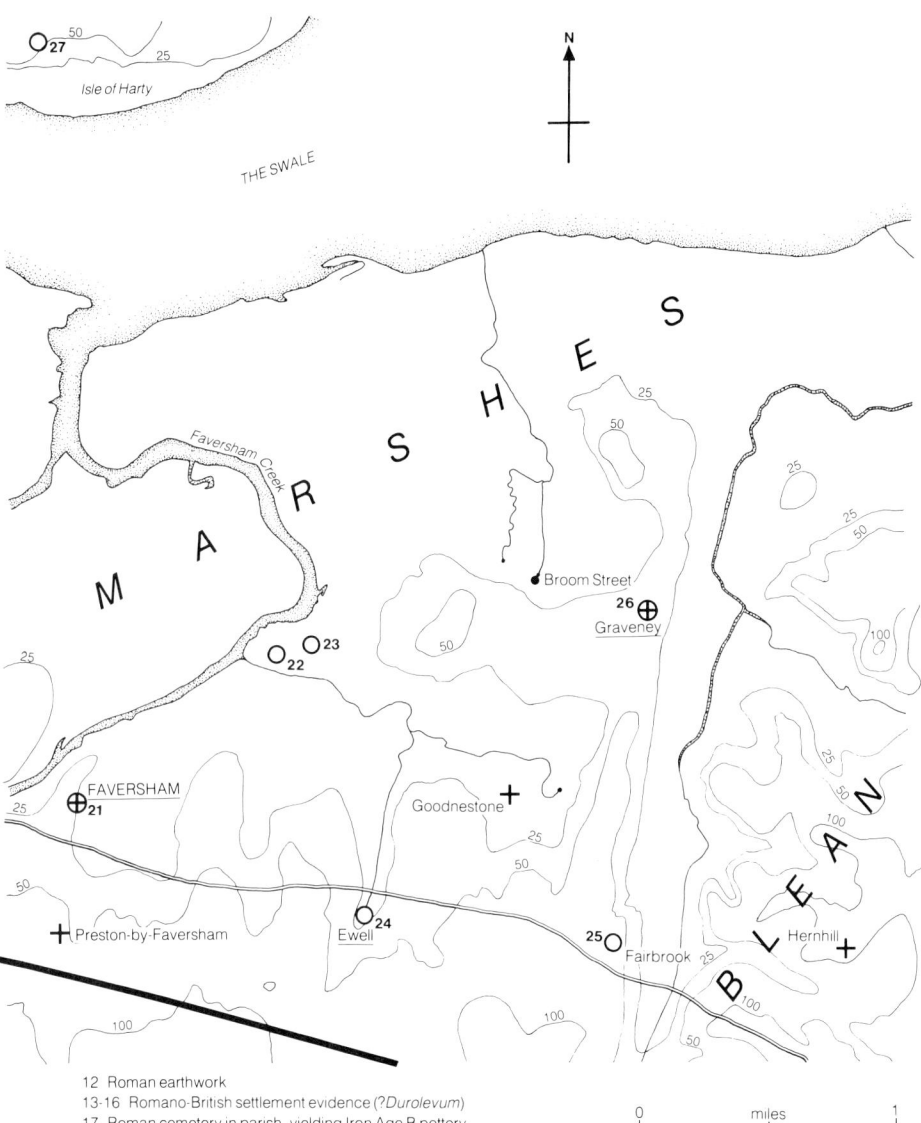

12 Roman earthwork
13-16 Romano-British settlement evidence (?*Durolevum*)
17 Roman cemetery in parish, yielding Iron Age B pottery
18 Roman settlement site
19 Roman cremations in parish
20 pagan Jutish burial grounds in vicinity (location approximate)
21 minster church on site of Roman building; Belgic and native Romano-British settlement in parish (?*Durolevum*: see 13-16 above); evidence of Roman ironworking in vicinity; Romano-Germanic pottery site in vicinity (?third or fourth century); Romano-British building at Blacklands
22 Romano-British site (location approximate)
23 Early Jutish site (location approximate)
24 Romano-British site
25 Roman pottery found
26 Roman cremation site in parish; pagan Jutish site at lost *Ealhfleot*, from *ealh*, 'a heathen temple'
27 Romano-British site

PART TWO *The Foundations of Settlement*

supposed *fæfer*.[48] There can be little doubt that the first element in Faversham in fact derives from the Latin *faber*, for it appears as *Febres hām* as early as 815 and 858; but the only evidence that such an English word as *fæfer* existed is the name of Faversham itself. On the ground of its well-attested Roman remains, Wallenberg suggested instead that Faversham might rather be an anglicized version of a Roman settlement once called *oppidum fabri* or *villa fabri*.[49] Since he wrote, archaeological evidence has come to light that seems to support this suggestion. It is now known to have been a centre of ironworking in the Roman period, perhaps employing numerous smiths, and probably drawing on the adjacent Blean Forest for its ironstone and its fuel.[50] Though the evidence of ironworking at present relates only to the first century, Faversham remained a substantial native settlement throughout the Roman period. The cluster of archaeological sites in the vicinity is suggestive in this connexion, and there can be little doubt that occupation continued without a break into the time of the Jutes.[51] If the settlement of the South-East was in fact undertaken by small immigrant bands accompanied by their families,[52] what could be more natural than that these immigrants should adopt the Latin place-name in use amongst their Romano-British neighbours, merely adding their own English suffix to it, as they are known to have done at Richborough and Lyminge?

The Romano-British origins of Faversham itself lend interest to a number of other place-names in the vicinity. Like its neighbour Milton Regis, Faversham early became an important 'king's town' and the centre of a major royal estate,[53] which included, *inter alia*, Davington, Ospringe, *Chetham*, and a substantial stretch of Blean Forest. The Celtic element in *Chetham* has already been referred to. For Davington, on the northern edge of the town, a number of conflicting explanations have been advanced and Wallenberg devotes one of his longest articles to it. The Romano-British context of the neighbourhood seems to reinforce his suggestion, somewhat reluctantly advanced, that it might incorporate a British name for the Fishbourne, the stream that flows into Faversham Creek. The *Daven* or *Deven* would thus be identical with the Cheshire River Dane, from *daven* or *dafn*, 'a drop', which gave rise to Davenham and Davenport, so that Davington would in fact mean 'the *tūn* by the *Daven*'.[54] For Ospringe, too, at the headspring of the Daven or Fishbourne, a number of conflicting explanations have been suggested, none of them altogether satisfactory. The second element is said to be the English word 'spring' with the final 'g' softened as so often in Kent;

5 Beyond the Jutes: preliminary considerations

but for the first element at least five different explanations have been advanced: *ox-*, *or-*, *of-*, *ōs-* ('god'), and *Ōsa* (a personal name).[55] Of these perhaps *ōs* is the most likely; but in the light of its association with Faversham, Davington, and *Chetham*, and in view of the major Romano-British settlement at Syndale on the edge of the parish, is it possible that Ospringe too contains an unrecognized pre-English element?

Faversham is a place, like Maidstone and Milton Regis, that one returns to again and again in the early settlement history of Kent. With its evidence of Belgic and Roman colonization, its Romano-Saxon pottery site, its early Jutish cemetery, and its church, like so many Kentish minsters, on the site of a Roman building, it is one of the most instructive seminal communities in the county.[56] Like Maidstone and Milton, it would warrant a brief monograph on the lines of H. P. R. Finberg's *Roman and Saxon Withington* (1955). But the case for continuity between Roman and Jute that seems so manifest at places like Faversham is also echoed, if less distinctly, at many of these primitive Kentish settlements whose names at present appear so perplexing.

5. NAMES IN 'STONE'

Of the various specialized groups of place-name associated with primitive settlement in Kent, those in *stān* or 'stone' are the most numerous, and in some respects the most interesting. Other groups, such as those in *campus*, as at Swanscombe, and *wīc* + *hām*, as at Wickhambreaux, have been discussed elsewhere by Dr Margaret Gelling and are already familiar.[57] Of these the most significant are probably Wickhambreaux, the centre of the Bourne estate; Wickham in Cuxton, on the Medway opposite Rochester; and Wickham in Otford, which has come to light since Dr Gelling wrote.

The stone-names of Kent are at least 50 in number; but about half of the total have no relevance to continuity, and must be left out of account. These include places where the word refers to stony ground, as at Stansted; to a natural stone outcrop, as at Chiddingstone; to a stone quarry, as at Stonepitts in Seal; or to a stone building of post-Conquest origin, as at Stonehouse in Frindsbury. Apart from these, there are about 25 places where some important stone object seems to be referred to. In about a dozen cases the word occurs in its simplex form, as at Stone-by-Faversham and Stone-in-Oxney;[58] otherwise it is usually combined either with an obviously significant early element, as at

PART TWO *The Foundations of Settlement*

Maidstone and Folkestone; with a Celtic element, as at Bredenstone in Dover; or with a 'problem' element, as at Cuxton, Teston, Keston, and Copstone.[59] The great majority of these 25 places are closely associated with early Jutish estate-centres, and most of them lie notably remote from the major stone-belts of the county. In the context of continuity they raise three points of interest.

In the first place, they are almost invariably associated with major archaeological remains of the Romano-British period. It has long been recognized that names like Stone Street bear a Roman connotation;[60] it has sometimes been suggested that other names in 'stone' also do so; and in Kent this view receives striking confirmation from the places under discussion, several of which have already been mentioned. Stone Grave in Snodland, for instance, marks the site of a Roman house. Bredenstone near Dover derives its name from the fragment of a Roman lighthouse or pharos, the Breden Stone, on the Western Heights. At Stone-in-Oxney, by the old course of the River Limen, a Roman altar is preserved in the parish church.[61] At Cuxton, or '?Cucola's stone', the church adjoins a Roman building, and at Stone-by-Faversham the ruins of the parish church incorporate part of a Romano-British mausoleum.[62] Near the Surrey border Baston occupies the site of a Roman building, and Keston (?*Cysse* + *stān*), as we have seen, is associated with Roman, Iron Age, Neolithic, and Palaeolithic remains. On the Medway, Maidstone is also associated with a lengthy sequence of Roman, Belgic, Iron Age, and Bronze Age relics.[63] Elsewhere, Folkestone ('the people's stone'), Maxton near Dover ('consort's stone'), Teston (?'stone with a cleft or hole'), Copstone in Otford (?'peaked stone'), Lullingstone ('Lulling's stone'), Stone-by-Dartford, Stone in Bapchild, Stone in Saltwood, and Stone in Thanet are similarly associated with major Romano-British remains.[64] Of these places Maidstone, Folkestone, and Keston were centres of early Jutish estates in their own right. Of the remainder Stone-by-Dartford was closely connected with the estate-centre at Darenth; Cuxton with that at Rochester; Stone-by-Faversham with that at Faversham; Stone in Bapchild with that at Milton Regis; Bredenstone and Maxton with that at Dover; Copstone with that at Otford; Lullingstone with that at Eynsford; Stone Grave with a territory probably based on Birling; and Stone in Saltwood perhaps with the *regio* based on Lympne. There is only one major exception to the association of names in 'stone' with early Jutish estate-centres, and that is the lost settlement of *Stone* in Cranbrook, in the heart of the Weald. The temptation to discuss this

5 Beyond the Jutes: preliminary considerations

interesting place at length must be resisted; here it is sufficient to note that it is associated with one of the very few significant archaeological complexes in the Weald, near the junction of two minor Roman roads, and close to a Mesolithic site.[65]

In many cases the archaeological context of these places, coupled with their situation on prehistoric routes like the Pilgrims' Way, and their association with other significant place-name elements,[66] suggests that they may also indicate an older stratum of occupation than that of the Roman period. It is unlikely that all of them do so;[67] but in places like Maidstone, Keston, Folkestone, Teston, Cuxton, and Copstone[68] there are grounds for believing that originally it was a megalithic structure of some kind that was referred to. In other counties some names of this type have long been recognized as referring to megaliths. In the East Riding, for example, the 'rood stone' from which Rudstone derives its name is a monolith of Bronze Age origin, and in Staffordshire the hundred-name of Cuttlestone may indicate a Neolithic site.[69] In south-eastern England the nine megaliths that still survive near Aylesford and Trottiscliffe – at Kits Coty, Stony Warren, the Coldrum Stones, the White Horse Stone, and elsewhere – have always seemed a curiously isolated group, connected rather with Ireland and Brittany than with neighbouring cultures.[70] A number of additional sites are known to have been destroyed in the last two centuries, moreover, and in built-up areas like Maidstone and Folkestone such structures are unlikely to have survived the vicissitudes of the last 1500 years. The possibility that the stone-names of Kent thus indicate a more extensive network of megalithic monuments than the nine that still remain is therefore a real one.[71] Several of the places in question are in the same neighbourhood as Aylesford and Trottiscliffe, and in this part of Kent it may be that prominent groups of stones associated with springhead chapels like Tottington and Cossington, and monoliths incorporated in mother-churches like St Mary's Lenham, also represent former megaliths rather than mere sarsens.[72]

The final point to note in connexion with these names in 'stone' is their association with early religious sites. Where they commemorate megalithic monuments, that association may obviously be of great antiquity; but there are also several places where they are associated with springs which became centres of Christian veneration. The church ruins at Stone-by-Faversham provide one example of this association, incorporating, as we have seen, part of a Romano-British mausoleum, and standing in the valley of the Oare stream, though nowadays some

PART TWO *The Foundations of Settlement*

way above the springhead. Stone in Bapchild furnishes another instance, where in the heavily-Romanized neighbourhood of Milton the *celde* of *Bacca* was one of the well-known holy springs of medieval Kent, with its chapel and shrine beside Watling Street.[73] Copstone in Otford provides a further instance, associated with major Roman remains and situated on the Pilgrims' Way by the spring later known as St Thomas's Well.[74] The most remarkable example is perhaps the Roman villa site at Lullingstone, where in the fourth century a Christian oratory was built directly over the sunken chamber devoted to the worship of local water-nymphs, and where pagan rites continued to flourish alongside those of Christianity.[75] What lends these places particular interest is the fact that the pre-Christian cults of Kent are also known to have been connected with water spirits, fertility rites, and the worship of springs and rivulets.[76] The celebrated Roman site at Springhead in Northfleet, with its seven pagan temples grouped around eight springs, is but the most notable instance of several where this association has come to light.[77] There seem to be several places in Kent, therefore, where names in 'stone' are probably indicators of what may be called 'religious continuity'; this is a point we shall return to in a later chapter.

6. SEMINAL SETTLEMENTS

In studying the origins of Kentish settlement in this chapter and the last, there are 40 or so especially prominent places that we seem to have been brought back to again and again by each line of enquiry.[78] These were more than merely 'primary' settlements in the usual sense of the word: they were peculiarly focal or 'seminal' places, in both the Jutish and the pre-Jutish periods. They were places, in short, where things always seemed to happen: places that seem to have attracted each successive wave of invaders, each successive development in the early history of the county: places where the historical arguments for continuity of occupation seem particularly cogent, perhaps as cogent as anywhere in England. Among them we find not only the more obvious archaeological centres such as Rochester, Dover, Reculver, and Lympne, where arguments for continuity might perhaps be expected. Scarcely less prominent are places like Maidstone and Aylesford in the Medway valley, Wrotham, Darenth, and Otford in West Kent, Wye, Lyminge, and Folkestone along the southern edge of the Downs, Northfleet, Faversham, and Milton Regis to the north of the Downs, or

5 Beyond the Jutes: preliminary considerations

Eastry, Sturry, Wingham, and Wickhambreaux beyond Canterbury, where at a superficial glance settlement may seem to be essentially English in origin.

Not all of these places are equally easy to identify; not all evince the full complement of primitive features; and not all are equally indisputable. Yet in each case a number of lines of argument converge upon them, and it is this *conjunction* of evidence that is significant. They tend, as we have seen, to bear primitive English name-forms, like Sturry and Eastry (*gē*), or in several cases names of pre-English origin, as at Lympne, Dover, Darenth, and Reculver. Virtually all of them are sited by rivers or major springheads, and most of them by recognized prehistoric routeways like Watling Street, the Pilgrims' Way, or the Greenway. Almost all are associated with more or less striking concentrations or complexes of archaeological evidence – not simply single finds – as at Faversham, Maidstone, and Milton Regis; and a number are well known as former Roman or Romano-British communities. In several cases they are specifically recorded as *villae regales*; many of them became *capita* of *regiones*; and in every case they are known to have been centres of early Jutish estates. At a later date, as we shall see in Chapter 8, minsters or mother-churches were associated with virtually all of them, and most of them became foci of the greater monastic manors of Christ Church, Rochester, St Augustine's, or St Martin's Dover. A substantial number eventually became centres of the early lathes of Kent, as at Aylesford, Eastry, Sturry, Hollingbourne, Milton, and Wye, or else were associated with the county's pre-Conquest meeting places, as at Maidstone and Folkestone. By the time of the Conquest, several of them had certainly developed into prescriptive or traditional markets, as at Maidstone, Milton, and Dartford, and ultimately almost all of them became market centres of some kind. The fact that these seminal settlements of Kent were situated, with very few exceptions, on the Foothills or in Holmesdale plainly points to these areas, and to no others, as the Original Lands of the people of Kent, both in the Jutish period and in that of their Romano-British predecessors.

PART THREE
THE EXPANSION OF SETTLEMENT

6

THE FIELD AND THE FOREST

1. THE EXPANSION OF SETTLEMENT, C.600–1050

In the last two chapters we have traced something of the pattern of primary settlement in Kent, and of its ultimate origins in the Romano-British world before the arrival of the Jutes. Our next task is to trace the outward expansion of settlement during the subsequent phases of Jutish colonization. In doing so we shall see how the wooded outback of the early *regiones* and estates was gradually reclaimed, and how the outline map of Kentish settlement was filled in, from one end of the county to the other, by some thousands of isolated hamlets and farmsteads. In many cases these farms had probably originated as seasonal shielings in the Old English period; the vast majority of them still survive as living settlements after something like a thousand years of continuous history.[1] Like much of the West Country and Wales, as a consequence, Kent is supremely a county of old and isolated farmsteads. In few other parts of England does so complete a primitive landscape of this kind survive, and in few does it furnish the historian of settlement with such abundant evidence.

In tracing this expansion of settlement, there are several lines of enquiry that need to be pursued. Those associated with the evolution of the church, following the introduction of Roman Christianity by St Augustine in 597, will be discussed in Part Four. In the present chapter we are concerned rather with the evidence of pre-Conquest land charters, of summer swine pastures, of woodland topography, and of forest nomenclature. For a number of reasons, not all of them obvious, these lines of enquiry tend to concentrate attention more particularly on the Downland region of the county, and in many ways this area holds the key not only to Kentish settlement history but also to the special character of early Kentish society.

PART THREE *The Expansion of Settlement*

The abundance of early Kentish charters is well known and is obviously of crucial importance for reconstructing a chronology of settlement. Altogether nearly 500 place-names are recorded in the 250 or so surviving charters, some 362 of which, as far as one can see, relate to specific settlements, and most of the rest to swine pastures or woods.[2] The only aspect of these names that needs to be discussed here is their distribution among the various settlement zones of the county. Systematic examination indicates once again that the Foothills and Holmesdale were indeed the Original Lands; but in this case it also indicates that, as the Old English period progressed, increasing numbers of places were appearing both on the Downs and on the central stretch of Chartland; while on the rest of the Chart, and in the Weald and Marshland, extraordinarily few permanent settlements, as distinct from summer pastures or shielings, were recorded before the Conquest.

Almost exactly half the 362 settlements were in fact situated in the Original Lands, which as we have seen comprised about one quarter of the county (see table 2).

Table 2. Settlement-names in pre-Conquest charters

No. of settlements recorded by	Original Lands		Downland		Chartland[a]		Weald[b]	Marshland[b]	Total
		%		%		%			
700	26	90	3	10	0				29
800	53	67	19	24	1	1		6	79
850	87	51	62	36	15	9	1	6	171
950	135	49	106	39	22	8	1	9	273
1066	184	51	129	36	32	9	7	10	362

[a] Almost entirely on the Central Chartland, between the Medway and the Stour.
[b] The figures for the Weald and Marshland are too small to yield significant percentages.

As the Old English period proceeded, the number of recorded places in these ancient areas steadily increased, but at the same time their percentage of all recorded names gradually declined as settlement elsewhere extended. Thus of the 29 places recorded before 700, 90 per cent were in the Original Lands, and of the 79 recorded before 800 nearly 70 per cent. By 1066, however, whilst the *number* of places in these areas had risen to 184, their proportion of the total had fallen to 51 per cent. On the Downland, by contrast, only three places of any description were recorded before the year 700, and only 19 before 800.

6   *The field and the forest*

Then during the next 50 years the Downland figure suddenly shot up to 62, or 36 per cent of all recorded names, and thereafter it continued to increase to a total of 129, though the percentage remained roughly constant at about a third, or a little more, of those recorded. On the Chartland, the relatively fertile central stretch between the Medway and the Stour followed a somewhat similar course of development to that of the Downs; but to the west of the Medway, where there was a good deal of stony heath and poor woodland, very few Chartland places were recorded until after the Conquest, though a few are known from other evidence to have existed. So far as the two remaining areas are concerned – the Weald and the Marsh – only one settlement was recorded before the year 950 in the whole of the Weald, and only nine in the Marshland. In these two zones together there were no more than 17 places recorded as settlements in all the pre-Conquest charters.

Now it is obvious that these early charters, though more numerous than in other counties, provide only a partial and in some ways haphazard coverage of Kent as a whole. No doubt many places existed for generations or even centuries before they were recorded. We certainly cannot say that by 1066 only seven places had come into existence in the Weald and only 32 on the Chartland. Quite probably most of the 62 Downland settlements recorded before 850 were already established by the beginning of the eighth century, if not before. Since most of the surviving charters relate to monastic estates, moreover, the extent of colonization on the Downs in particular is no doubt under-represented owing to the fact that comparatively little of that region came into the hands of the early monastic houses of Kent. Nevertheless, the *corpus* of 362 names is a substantial one, and is unlikely to give a wholly misleading picture of any one zone of settlement as compared with another. The conclusions it points to are broadly supported by other lines of evidence and can hardly be altogether fortuitous. They surely suggest relatively massive settlement at a very early period on the Foothills and in Holmesdale; substantial colonization of the Downland and central Chartland during the next phases of the Old English period; and a relatively empty countryside at that time, by and large, in the rest of the county.

2. FOREST AND FIELD

Next, we turn to the more intractable evidence of the *dens* or detached summer pastures of Kent, and the light that these shed upon early

PART THREE *The Expansion of Settlement*

settlement history. It has already been remarked that *denn* is a very common element in Kentish place-names, generally denoting 'a woodland pasture, especially for swine'.[3] In a typical Wealden parish like Biddenden we still find such characteristic farm-names as Hevenden, Ibornden, Lashenden, Omenden, Washenden, Standen, and Worsenden, all of which are recorded in thirteenth-century documents and must have developed from the old summer pastures. In the same parish there are also several lost *dens*, such as *Brickenden*, recorded in 1327, and a number of other places, like Rogley, Speldhurst, Stephurst, and Tryndhurst, which originated in the same way though they do not bear the familiar suffix.[4] The development of these *dens* or pastures in the forest areas of the county, and of the practice of transhumance associated with them, have already been mentioned and are wellknown characteristics of early Kentish society. There is abundant medieval and pre-Conquest evidence for their use in this way, not only in documentary sources, but in place-names like Somerden, or 'summer pasture', in the Wealden parish of Chiddingstone, or Summerlees (*lǣs*, 'pasture') in the Forest of Blean, and in those primitive droveways crossing the grain of the country from north to south which were discussed in Chapter 2. Such customary pastoral usages were no local peculiarity of Kent; they have long been acknowledged features of parts of the Highland Zone; and in recent years increasing evidence of their existence has been coming to light at various points in the Lowland Zone as well.[5] Nevertheless, since the early Kentish evidence is unusually abundant, systematic examination of it may be of more than local significance.

Owing chiefly to the labours of Edward Hasted in the eighteenth century, Robert Furley in the nineteenth, and J. K. Wallenberg and K. P. Witney in the twentieth, a list of nearly 700 *dens* or summer pastures has been compiled, and in all but a few cases the 'Upland' settlements to which they formerly appertained have also been traced.[6] These 700 or so *dens* present a number of problems of identification which must be briefly referred to. Many of them are difficult to identify with complete certainty, and until Mr Witney's recent study, *The Jutish Forest* (1976), many were wrongly located by older historians. A number of Mr Witney's identifications are necessarily tentative; but there can be no doubt that he has made more sense of the evidence as a whole. The problems of interpretation arise from the fact that the *dens* developed from the gradual subdivision of great tracts of forest generally thought to have once been common to the Kentish kingdom

6   The field and the forest

as a whole, so that the pastures themselves varied widely in extent, and probably in date of origin too.⁷ There can be no doubt, however, that the general pattern of the detached pastures is of great antiquity since large numbers of them are specifically referred to in pre-Conquest charters, about 100 of them by name. In view of these problems, although every effort has been made to avoid counting the same wood-pasture twice under different names, it is almost impossible in compiling statistics to be quite sure that one has avoided double-counting altogether. Yet since the majority of the *dens* still exist today as names of farms, hamlets, villages, towns, or woods, and since they still very clearly shape both the settlement pattern and the road system of Kent, they surely demand some attempt at systematic examination. Although the light they shed on early settlement history is in some respects difficult to interpret, they point to a number of striking conclusions, and raise questions that seem to be echoed in other parts of the country.

Before describing those conclusions in detail, a few general points about the nature of the *dens* must be made. The first to note is that, with comparatively few exceptions, they were wholly detached from the parental settlements from which they originated.⁸ These parental places were invariably situated in the Upland parts of the county, an expression which need not imply any great height above sea-level but which always indicates somewhere outside the Marshland and the Weald, or in other words north of the Chartland escarpment. The vast majority of the *dens* themselves were situated in the Weald, although there were also significant groups in Blean Forest and in a few places on the Downs and the Chart.⁹ They might be situated at almost any distance from the parental settlement, though the majority were between about 10 and 25 miles. Several of the *dens* of Teynham and Ospringe, for example, were in Headcorn, 14 or 15 miles away; those of Meopham in the Lowy of Tonbridge, 13 or 14 miles away; those of Frindsbury and Denton by Gravesend were also near Tonbridge, about 20 miles away; those of Bexley at Hever in Somerden hundred, 25 miles away; and those of the men of Thanet in Tenterden, more than 40 miles.¹⁰ Most of these places originated as pastures for swine, and are often specifically so described in early medieval and pre-Conquest records; but a number of place-names like Cowden and Oxenden here and there suggest other origins; and after the Conquest in particular there must have been an increasing shift away from swine towards cattle and sheep. So far as their nomenclature is concerned, the

PART THREE *The Expansion of Settlement*

majority actually terminate in the word *den*; but other elements may also be found, such as 'hurst' (*herst*, 'wood'), 'hay' (*(ge)hæg*, 'enclosure'), 'tigh' (*tēag*, 'enclosure'), 'hoath' (heath), and 'ridge'. In Kentish usage, as a consequence, such elements sometimes came to acquire a kind of subsidiary connotation as 'pasture', a point we shall return to in the following chapter.

So much for generalities: what are the conclusions which statistical examination of the evidence indicates? The chief point that needs to be discussed in the present chapter is the location of the Upland places to which the *dens* pertained. Curiously enough, although the summer pastures themselves have attracted a good deal of attention, and there is now a considerable body of literature on the Weald itself, very little attention of a systematic kind has been paid to the network of Upland places from which they originated. Yet the location of these places is highly significant since most of the *dens* remained attached to their original Upland communities throughout their history. Occasionally they were transferred to a new parental settlement as colonization proceeded, but save perhaps in the central stretch of Chartland that was evidently the exception rather than the rule.[11] The vast majority of the *dens*, moreover, were attached to major rather than minor settlements, and to places which in many cases acquired early minsters, like Faversham, Reculver, and Milton Regis. The status of these original Upland places as mother-communities thus sheds an important light on their antiquity, and their location upon both the settlement history of the Kentish kingdom and its ecclesiastical development.

When systematically examined, the distribution of the Upland communities to which the *dens* were attached is in fact a very striking one. Of the 676 *dens*, nearly three-quarters (74 per cent) pertained to places in the earliest-settled areas of the county, on the Foothills and in Holmesdale (see table 3). A further 14 per cent pertained to other early settlements on the central stretch of Chartland, such as Sutton Valence and Great Chart, which were not first-generation places but which may have been colonized from Holmesdale as early as the seventh century. In striking contrast with these areas, the later-settled parts of the Chartland exerted rights over only 6 per cent of the 676 *dens*, and the whole of the Downland area over a mere 2 per cent, or no more than 15 *dens* altogether. As we should expect, no *dens* were attached to communities in the Marshland or in other parts of the Weald. In summary, then, nearly 90 per cent of the *dens* altogether were established as detached pastures of very early settlements, on the Foothills, in

6   *The field and the forest*

Holmesdale, and in the old-settled part of the Chartland; whilst very few *dens*, a mere 8 per cent in all, were attached to places on the Downland, or in the later-settled areas of Chart.

Table 3. The *dens* or detached summer pastures

Dens pertaining to places in:	No.	%
Original Lands	497	74
Early Chartland	95	14
Late Chartland	41	6
Downland	15	2
Others	28	4
Total	676	100

These figures raise a number of thought-provoking questions, to some of which we shall return later, while to others the answer at present remains obscure. Their most striking feature is the contrast between the Original Lands, with rights in three-quarters of the *dens*, and the Downland, with rights in a mere 2 per cent. Although the colonization of the Downs occurred later than that of the Original Lands, it had certainly begun by the seventh century, so that it is remarkable that its people should have been denied almost all share in the resources of the Weald. In part that peculiarity is explained by the dominant role of the king and the early monastic houses in the original exploitation of the Weald; for most of the royal and monastic estates were situated in the Old Arable Lands or on the central stretches of the Chart, and not on the Downs.[12] In part, moreover, it is no doubt affected by the fact that the Downland itself had originated as a subsidiary pastoral zone, dependent on the Foothills, and may therefore be regarded as requiring no further pastureland. Yet it is doubtful if either of these circumstances offers an altogether adequate explanation. For by 1086 the Downland economy had in general become independent of the Foothills, and in most parts it seems to have been based primarily on vaccaries and sheep-farms rather than upon swine.[13] The possibility of acquiring rights in the Weald would surely, therefore, have offered a welcome addition to its own relatively meagre resources.

Whatever the explanation may be, the fact that the people of the Original Lands owned three-quarters of the county's 676 summer

PART THREE *The Expansion of Settlement*

pastures seems to suggest that their rights in the Weald originated before their daughter-settlements on the Downs had come into being; for otherwise the Downland communities would surely have obtained Wealden rights of their own. If this surmise is correct, those rights must have gone back in some form to the earlier phases of Jutish settlement. Since the people of the Original Lands had inherited so much from their Romano-British predecessors, it is also possible that they had inherited from them something of the tradition of transhumance and the first tentative exploitation of the Weald as a zone of detached pastureland.[14] However that may be, the evidence of the *dens* or summer pastures, like the evidence of pre-Conquest charters, and of each other line of argument, focuses attention once again on two matters. First, it re-emphasizes the distinctive place of the Foothills and Holmesdale as the Original Lands of the Kentish kingdom. Second, it points to the unique place of the Downland in the subsequent colonization of the county: and it is to this subject that we must now turn.

It is a curious fact that, although much has now been written on the Weald, no systematic study has yet been devoted to this other larger, older, and in many ways more interesting region of woodland pasture. If discussed at all, it is usually bracketed with the Old Arable Lands or Foothills; and yet, as all the evidence indicates, it was in every respect distinct from both the Foothills and the Weald. It differed from the Weald in that it was colonized from the seventh century onwards instead of the tenth or eleventh; in that it originated as outlying pasture and yet early became independent of the Foothills; in that its pastoralism seems to have been based predominantly on vaccaries and sheep-farms rather than on swine; and in its characteristic pattern of very small parishes, with their sparse population and distinctive manorial structure. It differed from the Foothills in that it was essentially a pastoral rather than an arable region; in that it was a relatively poor, intractable, and heavily wooded countryside; in that it attracted little or no original primary settlement and yields no definite evidence of continuity with the Roman period; in that it gave rise to no minsters but only daughter-churches and chapels;[15] in that relatively little of its land came into the hands of the original monastic houses of Kent; and in the fact that, though it early became independent of the Foothills, its people never acquired significant rights in the Weald. Up to a point, moreover, it differed from both Foothills and Weald in its nomenclature: in the relative frequency of names in 'wold', 'stead', 'lees' and 'minnis', for example, which are rare or unknown in the Weald, and in

6   *The field and the forest*

the comparative sparsity of those characteristically Wealden elements, *denn* and *herst*.[16] Although there are few elements that are wholly peculiar to the Downs, and few that are not represented there at all, the general *corpus* of Downland place-names forms an instructive contrast with that of other parts of the county. The very fact that it tends to be more varied than that of the Weald, and certainly less straightforward to interpret, points to some kind of fundamental difference between the two areas in terms of settlement origins and rural economy. Since at many points the evolution of the Downland sheds a certain light on the older wood-pasture lands of other counties, there seems an additional reason for devoting detailed attention to it.

3. THE TESTIMONY OF THE WOODS

For an understanding of the distinctive character of the Downland, and of how and why that character originated, we must return first of all to the river-estates discussed in Chapter 4, and more particularly to the group of territories lying between the Stour valley and the English Channel.[17] Towards the southern upland end of the Bourne territory, high on the Downs in the parish of Barham, there are still several large stretches of woodland, and among them one that bears the significant name of Walderchain. This word contains the same element, *wald*, that we find in Weald and in Wold, deriving from the Germanic *wald*, a forest or wood, so that Walderchain means 'the chine or ravine of the forest dwellers'. Now the interesting thing is that towards the southern end of every river-territory between the Stour valley and the coast there is evidence, in place-names and topography, of an outlying region of *wald*, or wold, or wood-pasture of this kind. Adjoining Walderchain to the east is Womenswold, the wold or *wald* of the estate based on Wingham. Beyond that is Sibertswold, and beyond Sibertswold Waldershare, meaning 'the boundary of the forest dwellers'. Altogether, in its various local forms – weald, wald, walt, wold, wheel, and wild – this word appears in some 15 place-names in this stretch of East Kent. In addition to the examples just mentioned, it is found at Waltham, Ringwould, East Studdal ('studwold'), West Studdal, Hammill (*hamel* + *wald*) in Woodnesborough, Waddling Wood (*wald* + *ing*) near Whitfield, perhaps Wildage and Wheelbarrow Town in Elham, and in the lost place-names of *Southwold* near Ringwould, *Wadling* or *Wolding* Wood near Ripple, and probably *Waldington* outside Canterbury.[18] These names reach for nearly 20 miles in a continuous arc of

PART THREE *The Expansion of Settlement*

country, from Waltham, the forest *hām*, near Wye on the west to Ringwould on the coastal cliff-tops south of Deal: whilst, north and south, the Downland forest once extended from the cliffs above Dover to within one mile of Canterbury.[19]

These circumstances take on particular significance when they are placed alongside the remarkable network of surviving woodland in this stretch of Downland country. Altogether nearly 300 woods are mentioned by name on the relevant 2½" Ordnance sheets and a further 835 are marked to which no name is attached, though many are known locally or recorded on the 6" Survey. Taken in conjunction with the settlement evidence of the area, the general distribution of these woods and their detailed local topography indicate that by and large they represent the last remnants of the original Downland forest, particularly to the west of the Dour valley, where about 700 of the total of 1,135 are to be found.[20] The larger stretches of woodland in this area are usually situated on the higher land of the clay-with-flints, and these often extend to more than 150 acres, as at Walderchain itself, or to several times that size, as at Covert Wood in Elham and Gorsley Wood in Bishopsbourne. In addition to these, there are some hundreds of long narrow shaws or hangers, winding irregularly along the flanks of the Downland combes, where the land is too steep to plough. Some of these shaws, as at Lodgelees Down in Denton and Fryarne Park in Stelling and Hardres, extend for nearly a couple of miles, though in places they are little more than 100 yards in width. Then, thirdly, there are some hundreds of smaller isolated copses in the area, and countless twisting shaves around the edges of the fields and along the local parish boundaries.

For an illustration of the extraordinary tapestry of surviving woodland to which these circumstances have given rise, the reader must be referred to the relevant maps (maps 7, 10, 14, and 16). In its complexity, so unlike anything to be found in regions of parliamentary enclosure like Leicestershire or Northamptonshire, it is clear that we have a profoundly ancient forest-landscape. For in almost every parish in the area – in Acrise, Wootton, and Denton, for example, in Stelling, Waltham, Barham, and Hardres – we see something of the same mosaic of small irregular fields, hemmed in by crooked shaws and shaves, that we also find in the Weald. In the latter area this mosaic has long been recognized as arising from piecemeal clearance in the medieval period, as the isolated forest farms endeavoured to reclaim, inch by inch, further pockets of marginal land from the wooded

6 The field and the forest

wilderness around them. On the Downland no comparable study of the surviving woodland evidence has yet been undertaken; but much may nevertheless be learned from systematic examination of local place-names and contemporary topography.

For this purpose we must extend our survey from the *wald* of East Kent alone to the Downland region as a whole. For while the word *wald* itself, which first alerted the present writer to the problem, rarely occurs to the west of the Stour valley,[21] the same broken, wooded landscape continues without a break to the Surrey border: in parishes like Stalisfield, Otterden, and Stockbury, for example, between the Stour and the Medway; or in Luddesdown, Meopham, and Ash-cum-Ridley between the Medway and the Darent (see map 7); or again in Halstead, Cudham, and Knockholt to the west of the Darent. Sometimes, as in the outlying lands of the *regio* of Milton Regis, the old coppices have now largely given way to cornfields or orchards; yet even there something of the same maze of woods and shaws may still be traced on the older Ordnance maps and in the surviving network of farmsteads, lanes, and boundaries. Throughout the 300,000 acres of Downland countryside, in short, we are confronted with a massive body of evidence indicating an old forest countryside moulded by individual assarting and piecemeal clearance. At many points this view is further confirmed by the findings of the botanists, who now recognize typical Downland species like the bluebell, wood anemone, and dog's mercury as valid indicators of ancient coppice.

If we turn to the place-name evidence of the area, we shall find that in origin this was no region of scattered woods and copses separated by open country, but more or less dense and continuous forest. In this connexion there are five types of place-name that need to be taken into consideration:

1. Those containing elements like *rede* and *lēah*, which indicate forest clearance or assarting;
2. Those referring to habitation sites and derived from woodland elements like *herst* and *grāf*;
3. Those of woods specifically recorded as such in medieval or pre-Conquest documents;
4. Those containing elements like *stede* and *denn*, which in Kentish usage indicate woodland pastures;
5. Those indicating the presence of forest animals.

If the whole *corpus* of names comprised in these five categories were

PART THREE *The Expansion of Settlement*

included, we should probably have more than 2,000 places to consider. For the purpose in hand, however, the survey needs to be restricted to names specifically recorded by Wallenberg[22] in medieval or pre-Conquest records, and indubitably indicating woodland or old wood-pasture. There are many hundreds of minor Downland names whose forms clearly point to medieval or Old English colonization, but which do not figure in the necessarily select range of sources, such as Assize Rolls and Feet of Fines, on which Wallenberg's work was based. In all probability the overwhelming majority of names in 'hurst', 'frith', 'snode', and 'holt', for example, are of medieval or pre-Conquest origin, though only 60 of them are actually recorded by Wallenberg.[23] Similarly, there are substantial numbers of place-names in 'hatch',

Table 4. Downland place-name elements[a]

1 Woodland clearance		2 Woodland settlements[b]		3 Ancient woods		4 Woodland pastures[c]		5 Woodland animals	
lēah, 'clearing'	70[d]	*wudu*, 'wood'	40	*wudu*, 'wood'	36	*stede* (stead)	42	*heort*, 'hart'	6
rede, 'clearing'	24	*herst*, 'wood'	27	*grāf*, 'grove'	7	*denn* (den)	40	*dēor*, 'deer'	6
stocc, 'tree trunk'	13	*grāf*, 'grove'	16	*fyrhth*, 'frith, wood'	6	*lǣs* (lees)	26	*bucc*, 'buck'	3
nīwe, 'new [land, etc.]'[e]	13	*holt*, 'holt, wood'	14	*wald*, 'forest'	7	*pearroc* (park, paddock)[k]	17	*brocc*, 'badger'	3
rod, 'clearing'	7	*wald*, 'forest'	13	*hōth*, '[wooded] heath'	4	*steall* (stall)	10	?*bera*, 'bear'	1
thwīt, 'cuttings, chips'		*fyrhth*, 'frith, wood'	7	*herst*, 'wood'	3	*swān* (herdsman)	7	*eofor*, 'wild boar'	1
bærnet, 'burnt clearing'	3	*snād*, 'detached wood'	4	*holt*, 'holt, wood'	2	(*ge*)*mænnes* (minnis)	7	3 other elements[m]	2
hīewet, 'place where trees are cut down'	2	*cēto*, 'wood, forest'	4	2 other elements[h]	2	*tēag* (tye, tigh)	6		
stubb, 'tree stump'	1	*hangra*, 'hanging wood'	3			(*ge*)*hæg, hægen* (a hay)	6		
	1	*hrīs*, 'brushwood'[f]	2			*stoc* (stock)	4		
		chastaignière, 'place of chestnut trees'	2			*fald* (fold)	2		
		hōth, '[wooded] heath'	2			7 other elements[l]	7		
		harad, 'wood'	2						
		6 other elements[g]	6						
All 9 elements		All 19 elements	134	All 9 elements	139	All 18 elements	67[j]	All 9 elements	174

6 The field and the forest

a 59 different elements are represented, of which there are 541 instances in all. The total number of *place-names* analysed is slightly below this figure since a few names, such as Ridley (*rede* + *lēah*), include more than one woodland element. Seven of the nine elements in column 3, it will be noted, also appear in column 2; the places represented in column 2, however, do not appear in column 3, so that the number of 'ancient woods' recorded is strictly speaking 206 (67 + 139). Names recorded in column 3 include only woods where there is *no settlement*.

b Only places known to have been *medieval settlements* are included; many of those rejected were probably of medieval origin.

c Only names certainly relating to *woodland* pastures are included. The connotation of the elements in this column in the Kentish context is discussed in the following chapter. The words in brackets represent merely the modern form of the element, not its meaning.

d In nine cases these relate to medieval settlements not discussed by Wallenberg, and early forms are needed.

e Only names indicating medieval woodland clearance are included.

f In both cases associated with *āc*, and meaning 'oak brushwood' or 'oak scrub'.

g Forest, *hǣs* ('brushwood'), *sceaga* ('shaw'), Acton ('oak farm'), Oakenpole ('oak fold'), Strood ('marshy land overgrown with brushwood'); in the last three cases topography indicates woodland settlements. 'Shaw' is a common element, but unlike 'hurst' and 'grove' can rarely be proved to relate to medieval *settlement*-names.

h Storth Oaks, Timberden ('timber valley').

j Probably, many of these related to settlements at one time; but specific evidence of settlement is lacking.

k Parks in the sense of enclosures for hunting or pleasure are excluded. In Kentish place-names, as in the West Country, 'park' frequently refers to a 'paddock'.

l Oxfrith ('ox wood'), Oxroad ('ox assart'), Challock ('calves' enclosure'), Hanslett's Forstal/Wood ('stallions' hill wood'), Swingfield ('swine field'), Sundridge in Bromley ('sundered pasture'), Sunderland in Lynsted (?'sundered land for pasture').

m Wolf, boar, badger.

'gate', 'shereway', 'forstal', 'warren', 'down', and the like which in Downland usage frequently indicate droveways or pastoral activity but which may also occur in other contexts; these names are therefore likewise excluded from the previous tabulation, though we shall need to reconsider them, along with others, in Chapter 7.[24] In limiting the evidence in this way it may seem that the lines have been drawn rather strictly; but we are still left with more than 500 names, and these provide ample evidence for the task in hand. Nearly 60 different elements are represented in these names, and these are classified in table 4. For convenience' sake brief interpretations of each element are

PART THREE *The Expansion of Settlement*

given, though these should not be regarded as more than summary notes.

Table 4 gives rise to a number of thought-provoking questions, to some of which we shall return in subsequent chapters. The elements relating to pastoral usage in column 4 form a particularly significant group and will be discussed more fully in turning to the rural economy of the area in Chapter 7. In the present context the most important point to note is the remarkable diversity of elements represented on the Downs, particularly when compared with those of a later-settled forest region like the Weald. Behind that diversity what we see is the highly localized and piecemeal character of Downland colonization, and the unusually lengthy period over which it extended, from the seventh century to the thirteenth or fourteenth. These circumstances have everywhere left a profound mark on Downland topography, moreover, and when related to surviving woodland evidence quite plainly demonstrate that the settlement of the area had originated through the gradual clearance of continuous forest. This may most clearly be illustrated by subjecting one or two limited stretches of Downland countryside to detailed scrutiny.

Along the crest of the Downs in West Kent, between the Medway valley and the Darent, where the prehistoric line of the Downland ridgeway divides Meopham and Luddesdown on the north from Trottiscliffe, Addington, Ryarsh, and Birling on the south, a continuous belt of ancient coppice-wood still extends for more than two miles: from Downs Wood on the west, through Great Wood, Admers Wood, and Hawsdown Wood, to Whitehorse Wood, Little Park Wood, and Daniel Chambers Wood on the east (see map 7). For Kent this is relatively high country, rising to 700 feet above sea-level, and even to a superficial observer it forms a striking contrast with the landscape of Holmesdale to the south, where the great arable fields of the Original Lands extend beyond the Pilgrims' Way. To the north of these woods, among the winding combes of the dip-slope, the continuation of the forest has everywhere been eaten into by piecemeal clearance; and this process has left a characteristic lacelike pattern of shaws, fields, and farmsteads, and a maze of narrow lanes and holloways. Take High Reed, or the 'high clearing' in Meopham, for example, just below the 600 foot contour: a settlement which is first recorded by Wallenberg in 1381, when it was probably already of some antiquity, and which is still surrounded by its irregular ring of coppice-lands known as Ridge Wood, Round Wood, Eight Acre Wood, Twelve Acre Wood, and

6   *The field and the forest*

Downs Wood. Or beyond these woods take the similar forest clearings of Woodlands and Culverstone (1381) to the west, Priestwood (1240) and David Street (1327) to the north, and Harvel (?939) and Boughurst Street (1200) to the east.[25] Throughout these boundary-lands of Luddesdown (939), Birling, and Meopham (788), in short, and throughout the lost parish of Dowde's Church (c.1100) between them, we find the same pattern of early medieval and pre-Conquest clearance, and the same fretted woodland countryside; much of it, though within 30 miles of London, still strangely beautiful, and strangely remote.

Some 40 or 50 miles to the east of Meopham, in the unfrequented upland country between Dover and Wye, the same pattern is repeated in the parishes of Acrise (first recorded in 1086), Swingfield (c.1100), Elham (1086), Denton (799), and Wootton (799) (see map 10). Here, in a nook or projection of Acrise, hemmed in by Elham, Denton, and Swingfield, Brandred or 'the burnt clearing' represents a pre-Conquest farm which must have been reclaimed by fire from the detached common waste of St Martin's Priory in Dover.[26] Like High Reed, Brandred is still surrounded by its chain of woods and shaws – Butchers Wood, Stockhill Wood, Biggin Wood, Stony Lane Wood, and Lad Wood – some 900 years after it was first recorded by name in Domesday Book. Beyond these woods we find once again a scattered nexus of isolated forest farms: at Selstead (first recorded in 1304), Stockham (1275), Smersole (1327), Foxholt (1254), Hoad Farm (1321), Ladwood (1240), Dreals (1348), Gatteridge (1304), and Tappington (1242–3). In many cases the settlement-names in this neighbourhood, like those in West Kent, also bear witness to the ultimate origins of these places in the reclamation of the *wald*. The name of Acrise, for example, means 'oak brushwood', that of Wootton 'wood farm', that of Gatteridge 'goat hurst', and that of Hoad Farm 'hoath' or 'heath'; while Stockham and Stockhill both contain the element *stocc*, or 'tree-stump', which is usually taken to indicate woodland clearance.

The Meopham and Acrise areas thus plainly illustrate something of the evocative topography of Downland colonization; but they are in no way untypical, and the same mingled network of winding shaws and solitary farmsteads recurs throughout the 60 or 70 miles of Downland countryside. It is found on the borders of Barham (799), Kingston (1172–3),[27] Stelling (1086), Elham (1086), and Upper Hardres (791),[28] for example; at Palmstead, first recorded about 767, Dane Farm (1240), Wildage (1292), South Lodge (?1313), Lynsore (845), and Farthingsole (see map 14). It is found once again in the outlying lands

133

PART THREE *The Expansion of Settlement*

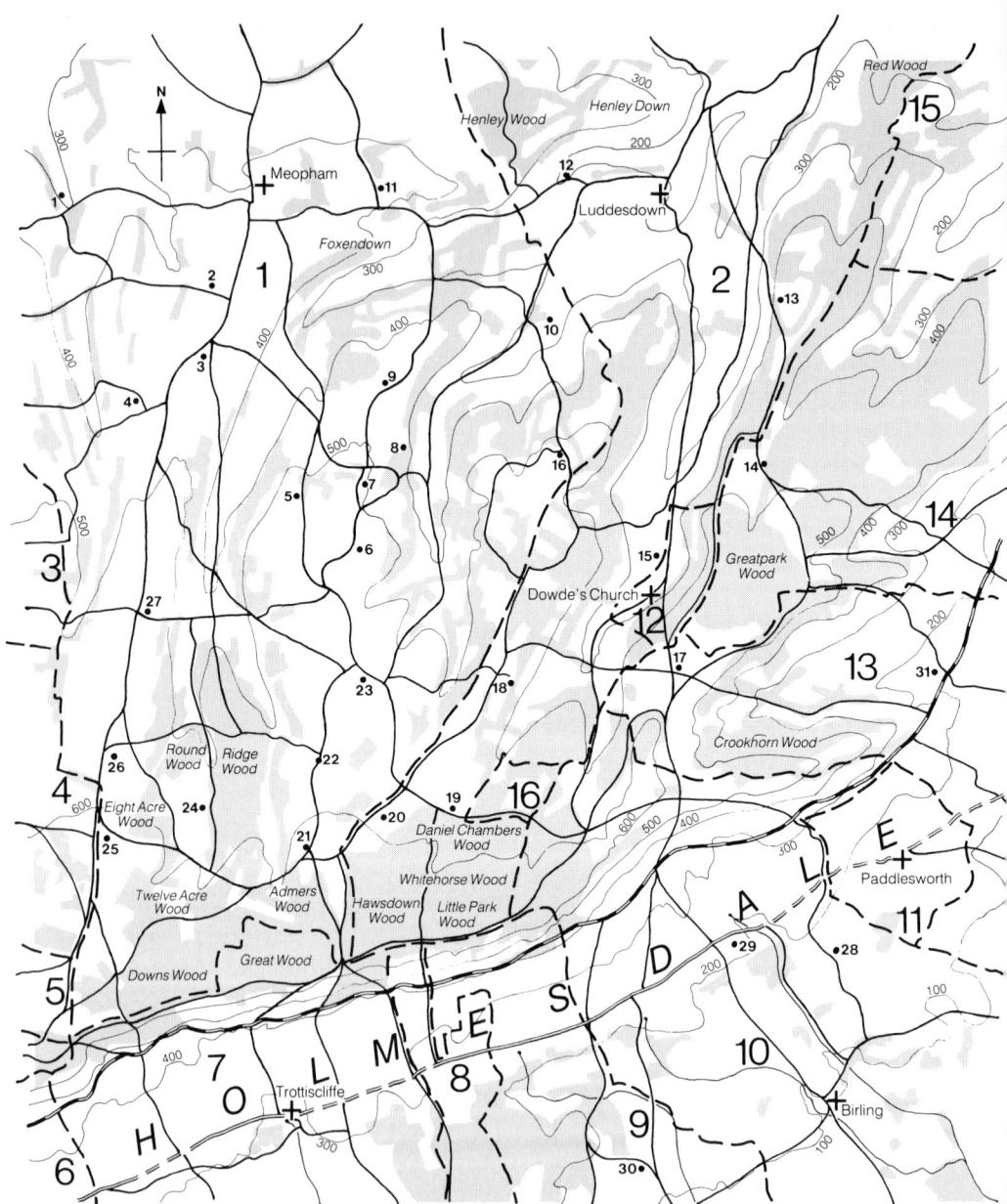

MAP 7. *Downland woods: Meopham and Luddesdown area* (based on the Ordnance Survey map with the permission of The Controller of Her Majesty's Stationery Office; Crown Copyright reserved)

6   *The field and the forest*

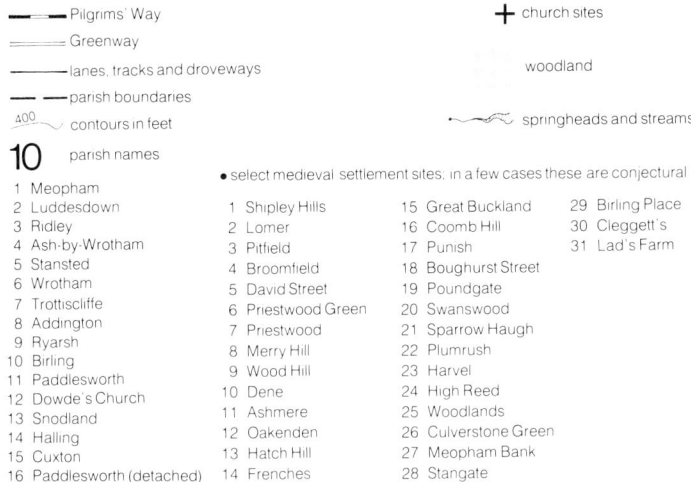

of Otterden (1086), Newnham (1177), and Doddington (c.1100), to the south of Faversham and Milton Regis, where Frith is first recorded in 1254, Monkston in 1202,[29] Seed in 1313, Frangbury in 1327, Sharsted in 1240, Slade in 1294, Hurst in 1262, Rigshill in 1270, and Longreach and Snode in undated documents of the thirteenth century (see map 16). In these areas, too, many of the local names bear witness to the ultimate origin of these settlements as forest clearings: at Hurst and Frith, for example, at Hardres or '[stony]wood', and at Snode or 'detached woodland'.

It is a curious fact that students of settlement have paid so little attention to the local topography of woodland in this country. In tracing the progress of colonization from parish to parish and farm to farm it is probably one of the least explored forms of historical evidence. In Kent it so happens that that evidence is exceptionally abundant, and when studied in conjunction with place-names, boundaries, and other topographical features, exceptionally informative. Yet there must be few parts of England where we have not something to learn from the testimony of the woods.

4. THE CHRONOLOGY OF DOWNLAND COLONIZATION

In the light of the evidence discussed hitherto, is it possible to assign a period of origin to the settlement of the Downland as a whole? It has already been pointed out that the process of forest clearance was a very gradual one; but is there any phase or period in Downland history when we can say that the basic outlines of settlement had been completed? In

PART THREE *The Expansion of Settlement*

analysing the charter evidence at the beginning of this chapter, we saw reason to believe that there was widespread colonization of the region during the Old English period, and that in this respect there was a marked contrast with the western Chartland, and the Weald, where very few settlements are recorded before the end of the eleventh century. The 129 places recorded in pre-Conquest charters form only a small minority of all Downland settlements, however, and the question still remains as to whether they can be regarded as typical. What proportion of the 3,000 or so farms and hamlets in the area had in fact been reclaimed from the *wald* by the time of the Conquest?

The answer to this question is complicated by the fact that in many cases Downland farms may have originated, like those of the Weald, as seasonal shielings, a point we shall return to in the following chapter. It is further complicated by the need to take account of the ecclesiastical and topographical evidence, and that is a subject that must await systematic investigation in the fourth and fifth parts of this book. Nevertheless, it is important at this stage to sum up our findings so far, and to reconstruct a tentative chronology of settlement before proceeding to a discussion of the Downland economy in the following chapter. In particular it is necessary to enquire what light the place-names and the woodland evidence discussed in this chapter may shed upon the phasing of colonization. In seeking to answer that question the typology of place-name elements recorded in pre-Conquest charters, though in other ways so revealing, is unfortunately too diverse to be of much assistance. Names in 'stead', 'down', 'dene', and 'hurst', for example, may have continued to be formed after the eleventh century as before, and evince no very distinctive pattern in this area so far as their period of origin is concerned. We are thus forced back upon other lines of enquiry.

The most fruitful approach to the problem is to subject a few limited stretches of Downland country to intensive scrutiny on the $2\frac{1}{2}''$ O.S. map, and to consider their nomenclature and period of settlement as a whole. If we take the 46 places mentioned in the last section of this chapter in the neighbourhoods of Meopham, Acrise, Stelling, and Doddington, and analyse them afresh according to their earliest recorded appearance, we find that 11 are first noted by Wallenberg in the fourteenth century, 16 in the thirteenth, 10 in the eleventh or twelfth, and 9 before the Conquest. Or if we take the 85 Downland names recorded by Wallenberg on a single sheet of the survey, that covering Elham (TR14), we find that 18 are first noted in the fourteenth

6   *The field and the forest*

century, 36 in the thirteenth, 9 in the eleventh or twelfth, and 13 before the Conquest, while a further 3 are late medieval foundations and 6 are of early medieval origin, though no precise date can be assigned to them.[30] If these two sets of figures are combined, it appears that 22 of the 131 places, or about 17 per cent, are recorded before the Conquest, and a further 15, or 11 per cent, in the eleventh century, while 81, or 62 per cent, are not recorded by Wallenberg until the thirteenth or fourteenth.[31]

These facts will bear thinking about. At first sight they may seem to suggest that Downland settlement was predominantly post-Conquest in origin. When the 131 places in question are followed up on the $2\frac{1}{2}''$ Ordnance sheets, however, it becomes apparent that this impression is misleading. For many of the names recorded before the Conquest are found to relate to quite obscure farmsteads, and not to major settlements. In a neighbourhood still densely wooded on the boundaries of Barham, Stelling, and Upper Hardres, for example, Lynsore is recorded in 845, Duskins in 824, Hardres in 791, and Palmstead in a charter of about 767.[32] In the neighbourhood of Elmsted, Waltham, and Hastingleigh, Holt and Hastingleigh are recorded in 993 x 996, Elmsted, Dean, and North Leigh in 811, Yockletts and Ittinge in 805, and Bodsham in a charter of about 690.[33] Neither of these areas is likely to be among the earliest-settled parts of the Downland; the parishes in question all originated as outlying chapelries in remote countryside; and in several cases they did not become fully independent of their mother-churches until the nineteenth century.[34] Yet in Elmsted alone, in the heart of this area, no fewer than six places appear in pre-Conquest charters, and of these Bodsham is actually recorded some 10 or 20 years before the minster-settlement of Lyminge, a few miles to the south-east.

There can be no real doubt, in fact, that a great deal of Downland settlement in Kent is much older than its earliest recorded appearance in the post-Conquest period would lead us to suppose. Even in some of the obscurest Downland valleys, isolated farmsteads like Bodsham and Palmstead were beginning to appear long before 1086. The number of places recorded in Old English charters clearly represents no more than a fraction of those that then existed, and this fact should not surprise us. No doubt many charters have failed to survive, and in an area of scattered settlement many isolated farmsteads are unlikely to be mentioned in such documents unless they also appear as boundary marks. On the Downs in particular, moreover, settlement is likely to be

PART THREE *The Expansion of Settlement*

under-recorded because relatively little of the area came into the hands of the early monastic houses of Kent. It is thus no surprise to find that by the eleventh century the overwhelming majority of Downland churches had already come into existence: and in this sense we may not unfairly say that the broad framework of Downland colonization was then largely complete.[35]

It is important, however, that the case for early clearance of the Downland forest should not be overstated. For while there can be little doubt that many places first recorded in the thirteenth or fourteenth century are of pre-Conquest origin, there can also be little doubt that a great deal of further clearance took place in succeeding centuries, in some areas as late as the eighteenth. In this connexion there are four groups of places whose names need to be taken into consideration. First, there are some hundreds of minor isolated settlements, as in other parts of Kent, whose names obviously derive from those of their early medieval owners. Sometimes, no doubt, names of this kind may have replaced older ones; but it is significant that they are found in virtually every parish in the region; and it seems unlikely that outlying places like Hault Farm in Petham, Dreals Farm in Elham, Digges Place in Barham, Youngs, Catts, and Cooks Farms in Lower Hardres, and Butts Farm, Dowles Farm, and Boormanhatch in Elmsted, were all rechristened in the twelfth or thirteenth century.[36] In many cases Wallenberg was able to identify the medieval families after whom these places were named: the Diggeses of Barham, for example, are recorded from 1254 onwards, the Hauts of Petham from about 1180, the Dreals or Thrals of Elham from 1348 to 1484, the Catts, Cooks, and Youngs of Hardres from the late thirteenth century, and the Boormans, Butts, and Dowles or Duls of Elmsted from about the same period. Second, there is a significant though of course smaller group of minor Downland settlements whose names are of French or partly French origin, and these must likewise have originated in the Anglo-Norman period: Paradise in Hartlip, for example, Beaux Aires or 'beau repaire' in Stockbury, Grandacre or 'great acre' in Waltham, Fredville or 'froide ville' in Nonington, and Kearsney or 'cressonnière', 'place where cress grows', in Temple Ewell.[37] Third, there are good grounds for believing that many of the fairly numerous Downland settlements in 'lees' and 'minnis', such as Staple Lees, Badlesmere Lees, Stelling Minnis, and Rhodes Minnis, did not originate until the late medieval or early modern period, when they often seem to have developed as squatters' communities on intercommonable pasturelands at a time of rising population.³⁸ Finally, there is a substantial group of Downland farmsteads bearing names of a satirical or quasi-humorous character, such as Starvecrow, Starveacre, Starvegoose, Kettlebender, Filchborough, Owl's Castle, Spider's Castle, Rat's Castle, Magpie Bottom, and the curiously frequent Heart's Delight, which are rarely recorded by Wallenberg, and which clearly refer to relatively late foundations.³⁹ Filchborough or Fitchborough, for example, is a deserted farm site on the borders of Crundale and Godmersham which means 'polecat's borough' and is not actually recorded until 1728.⁴⁰ It seems certain, therefore, that while the general framework of Downland colonization was already complete by the eleventh century, new farms continued to be carved out of the woods in substantial numbers until the time of the Black Death, while a final wave of settlement took place during the post-medieval period.

One final question relating to the chronology of settlement still remains to be answered: is it possible to discern any regional variation in the phasing of colonization as between the different stretches of Downland countryside? Without intensive investigation parish by parish in post-Conquest records, it is unwise to give a dogmatic answer to this question; but two tentative generalizations may nevertheless be advanced. First, there can be little doubt that colonization began very early in the area to the north-east of the Dour Valley, and that in this neighbourhood the landscape already wore the predominantly woodless appearance of today by the time of the Norman Conquest. It is the only extensive tract of Down that is not overlain with the intractable clay-with-flints, and in many places the woods which once extended as far north as Woodnesborough, and indeed almost to the walls of Canterbury, had by that time been largely cleared and turned over to cornland. In the outlying parts of Woodnesborough itself, for example, settlements like Ringleton, Buckland, and Hammill are recorded as separate estates or manors in Domesday Book: and of these Hammill at least had evidently been reclaimed from the forest, for its name means *hamel wald*, or 'broken wold'.⁴¹ For something like a thousand years, in fact, this stretch of the Downs has been celebrated as part of the great granary of Kent; but its nomenclature and topography bear ample witness to its ultimate origins in the clearance of the *wald*.⁴²

Second, it seems probable that early Downland settlement tends to be somewhat thinner on the ground towards the western end of the county. This impression must not be exaggerated, and in part it is perhaps due to the sparser early documentation of the diocese of

PART THREE *The Expansion of Settlement*

Rochester. Nevertheless, while there are certainly some very early Downland settlements to the west of the Medway, it is noteworthy that the parishes in this area tend to be substantially larger, as a rule, than those to the east. This circumstance does not in itself prove that they were settled later; but it is one of several indications that, like the parishes of the Weald, they were often more thinly populated at the time of their formation. On the Downs as a whole the medieval parish averaged about 1,500 acres in extent, and east of the Medway there are some like Bredhurst (602 acres), Bicknor (634), Barfreston (498), Chillenden (202), and Betteshanger (395), whose historic area was less than half that size. To the west of the Medway, by contrast, while small parishes may occasionally be found, as at Ridley (834 acres) and Nurstead (522), the historic area of Cobham extended to 3,056 acres, of Ash-by-Wrotham to 3,074, of Chelsfield to 3,378, of Meopham to 4,713, and of Cudham to nearly 6,000 acres.[43]

There can thus be no real doubt that Downland colonization in Kent in fact extended over a very lengthy period, and that it must be envisaged as involving a continuous process of reclamation from the seventh century to the thirteenth or fourteenth. Behind that lengthy process three dominant forces may be distinguished, each of which was of crucial importance in shaping the evolution of Kentish settlement and Kentish society. First, it was clearly determined in part by the sheer density and extent of the forest hinterland, and the physical problems of reclamation which that entailed upon a relatively sparse and primitive peasant population. Second, it was also in part determined by the custom of partible inheritance which, as population increased, necessarily occasioned continuous subdivision of property, and in consequence a continuous process of colonization. In this sense, partibility has always been one of the active principles behind Kentish settlement, accounting not only for its piecemeal character but also for its restless dynamism. In the very extent of the *wald* which had originally inhibited colonization, indeed, that dynamism found a land of opportunity for itself which may not unfairly be likened, on a miniature scale, to the American West of the nineteenth century. Third, this gradual yet dynamic process of settlement was also affected by the pastoral nature of the Downland economy, and the influence of that pastoralism on the dispersal of settlement and the rise of personal freedom. It is to the circumstances of that economy, and to the conditions behind the development of that 'freedom of the wold', that we turn next.

7

THE DOWNLAND ECONOMY

The evidence of early land-use on the Downs and the origins of the area as a pastoral region at one time dependent, like the Weald, on the Foothills and Holmesdale, form the subject of the present chapter. In the Weald itself these are relatively straightforward problems; for the *dens* are known to have originated, by and large, as summer swine pastures, while their dependence on the old Upland communities is amply documented in medieval sources. On the Downs, by contrast, there is little direct evidence of transhumance in the post-Conquest period, and we are driven back upon other lines of enquiry. For this purpose the place-names of the area provide the most obvious source, and these are examined in detail in the following section. The evidence of intercommonable pastureland associated with boundary settlement offers another line to pursue, and this is explored in the second section of this chapter. In the third section the dependent origins of the Downland economy are examined, and the evidence for transhumance associated with it; in the fourth, the indications of different types of pastoral usage in different localities are discussed; and in the last the gradual liberation of the region from the suzerainty of the old estate-centres of the Original Lands.

1. PASTORAL PLACE-NAMES

Downland place-names indicating old wood-pastures have already been alluded to in the previous chapter. There we saw that a total of 174 names of this kind were discussed by Wallenberg, and the real total must be several times that figure since he rarely recorded names of woods and covered only a minority of all known settlements. The 19 elements represented in these names, and their local connotation in the county, may be tabulated as shown in table 5.

In addition to these 18 elements specifically indicating pastoral usage, there are others which frequently do so, though that is not necessarily their primary meaning. Among the more important are those given in table 6.

The evidence of former pastoral usage to be found in the place-names of the Downs is thus varied and substantial. It is not possible to say

PART THREE *The Expansion of Settlement*

Table 5. Pastoral elements on the Downs: I

		Nos. recorded by Wallenberg
1.	*stede*, 'a stead, a place [utilized for pastoral purposes]'. Karl Inge Sandred suggested this as the usual interpretation after meticulous investigation in his *English Place-Names in -stead* (1963), 130–4, 166–75. In Kent, where the element is particularly common and is associated chiefly with the Downs, this interpretation is clearly correct.	42
2.	*denn*, 'a woodland pasture, especially for swine'.	40
3.	*lǣs*, 'lees, pasture'. In Kent this word generally refers to intercommonable woodland pasture on parish boundaries.	26
4.	*pearroc*, 'a park or paddock, a small enclosure [for pastoral purposes]'. Parks in the sense of enclosures for hunting or pleasure must of course be excluded. As in Devon, this term is common in minor place-names in Kent, where it often appears as 'parrock'.	17
5.	*steall*, 'a standing place, a stall for cattle'. This element is discussed more fully in the fourth section of this chapter.	10
6.	*swān*, 'a herdsman, a swineherd'.	7
7.	*(ge)mǣnnes*, 'minnis, commonland [utilized as pasture]'. In Kent this localized word always relates to intercommonable land on the boundary of two or more parishes. On the Downs, where it is most characteristic, it refers to old intercommonable upland forest (see Chapter 11, section 5.)	7
8.	*tēag*, 'a tye or tighe, a pastoral enclosure, a common pasture'. In Kent this word usually refers to smaller intercommonable tracts than 'minnis' and 'lees'.	6
9.	*(ge)hæg, hægen*, 'a hay, an enclosure [normally for pastoral purposes]'. In Kent this word does not usually refer to a hunting enclosure, as in Shropshire, Staffordshire, etc.	6
10.	*stoc*, 'a stock, a place (usually a vaccary)'. In Kent, as in Devon, topographical evidence supports Ekwall's view that this element generally indicates a cattle-farm, though that is not necessarily its significance elsewhere (*ODEPN*, 422; cf. *EPNE*, II, 154: see p. 168 *infra*).	4
11.	*fald*, 'a fold, a small enclosure for livestock'.	2
12.	Seven other elements, occurring once each.[1]	7
	Total	174

7 *The Downland economy*

Table 6. Pastoral elements on the Downs: II

1. *wald*, 'woodland, forest'. This element occurs at least 20 times on the Downs as a whole and in every case refers to the outlying woodland of the old river-estates. It always seems to indicate pasture, though there may be one or two cases where it retains its primary meaning of 'woodland'.

2. *grāf*, 'a grove, a wood'. Early Kentish wills sometimes refer to 'my grove of pasture', and Domesday Book records 'a small grove of twelve acres of pasture' under Hackington. Most of the 16 instances of the word recorded by Wallenberg on the Downs probably refer to pastures.

3. *herst*, 'a hurst, a wood'.[2] In the Weald 'hurst' came to acquire a secondary meaning as 'a woodland swine pasture', and many of the *dens* are specifically so called. It is probable that some at least of the 27 instances of the word recorded by Wallenberg on the Downs also bear this meaning.

4. *dūn*, 'down, hill'. Like *wald*, this word frequently refers to the outlying woodland-pastures of the old river- and springhead-estates, as at Kingsdown by Wrotham and Kingsdown by Faversham. It is a common element, however, and there are no doubt some places where it simply means 'hill'. Since the Downs are heavily wooded in Kent, it rarely refers to 'an expanse of open hill-country' as in other counties.[3]

5. *fore* + *steall*, 'forstal, place in front of [a farm house].' There are probably many cases where this common local word refers to a 'stock enclosure'; but the subject is a complex one and is discussed more fully in the fourth section of this chapter.

6. *hop*, 'a hope, a plot of enclosed land'. This is usually regarded as a specifically marshland element in Kent, where it is known to indicate 'sheep pasture'.[4] It also occurs in a number of places on the Downs, however, as at Hopton, Hoplands, Hope Farm, and the frequent Hope Wood; some of these probably indicate enclosures for sheep, though few are recorded by Wallenberg.[5]

7. *bǣr* or *bēr*, 'pasture, especially in woodland'. This element seems to be represented in several Downland place-names; but it is difficult to distinguish from *bær* ('bare'), *bere* and *bær* ('barley'), *bār* ('boar'), and *beorg* ('hill'). In several cases the names in question are not recorded by Wallenberg, and in others, such as Stockbury, contradictory explanations have been advanced. For these reasons it is not included in the first list given above. It is doubtful if it necessarily indicates a swine pasture on the Downs,[6] though it usually does so in the Weald.

8. *worð*, 'worth, an enclosure'. This is an uncommon element on the Downs, occurring only in a few subordinate settlements where topography suggests a 'stock enclosure'.

143

PART THREE *The Expansion of Settlement*

exactly how numerous such names may be altogether, since many are not recorded by Wallenberg, and those in the second group may not always denote pastureland. It is probably safe to say, however, that there are at least 1,000 names of this kind in the region as a whole. The significance of that figure, however tentative, becomes strikingly apparent when it is placed alongside the handful of names indicating other types of land use. References to the cultivation of wheat, for example, are found only two or three times: at Whiteacre in Waltham; probably at Whittakers Wood in Stockbury, though that may be of manorial origin; and perhaps at Grandacre in Waltham, which must indicate some kind of arable land.[7] Orchards are also recorded twice, at Appleton in Waldershare and Appleton in Ickham, and perhaps in a few names in *pirige*, though those seem to refer to wild or isolated pear trees rather than orchards.[8] References to arable husbandry may also be found at Barton in Crundale, Barton in Canterbury, the lost *Barton* in Barham, Supperton or 'south barton' in Wickhambreaux, Wingham Barton in Ash, Bush or *bere* + *ersc* ('barley stubble') in Cuxton, and the lost *Bereacre* or 'barley acre' in Bridge.[9] There are probably other places of the kind that the present writer has failed to note; but there can be no doubt that references to cultivation of any kind are rare on the Downs, or that where they occur, they often lie towards the northern edge of the region, as at Appleton in Ickham, Barton in Canterbury, Supperton in Wickhambreaux, and Wingham Barton in Ash. Even to the east of the Dour valley, where the landscape has long been largely given over to arable farming, there is remarkably little trace of cultivation in the early onomastic evidence. Elsewhere, the cornfields nowadays so characteristic of the Downland valleys are in general a relatively recent development.

2. BOUNDARY PASTURES

The nomenclature of the Downland is not the only evidence we have of its former pastoral status. One of the most curious features of the Kentish countryside is the number of settlements situated on parish boundaries, and there are strong grounds for believing that in many cases these also indicate early intercommonable pasture. The reasons for this interpretation are of some complexity, and it is important to recognize that not all boundary settlements arose in this way. Sometimes, as at Gravesend and at Greenstreet in Teynham, they originated as markets in the post-Conquest period; sometimes, as at

7 The Downland economy

Whitley Row and Brabourne Lees, as relatively late communities of smallholders, cottagers, or squatters. There can be little doubt, however, that many hundreds of them originated as isolated pasture-farms in an intercommonable countryside during the Old English period or shortly after the Conquest. If this view is correct, the subject clearly calls for further exploration in the present context.

Settlements on parish boundaries are not a peculiarity of Kent. They also occur in some parts of the Welsh Marches, and it is significant that they are usually associated with old woodland country or with zones of upland pasture. In Kent they seem to be substantially more numerous than elsewhere, however, and at one time they were certainly more so than today. Even now there are probably more than 1,500 places of the kind altogether, mostly situated on the Downs, on the Chart, or in the Weald, though they also occur in outlying places elsewhere. In the Weald, for example, we find them at Bassetts (recorded by Wallenberg in 1323), Scarletts, Basing, Gilridge (1202), Buckhurst (1232), Bramsells (1240), Mark Beech, and Horseshoe Green on the boundary of Cowden. On the Downs we find them at Great Shuttlesfield (838), Little Shuttlesfield, Rhodes Minnis (1327), Droveway House (1348), Wheelbarrow Town (?1278), South Lodge (?1313), Dane Farm (1240), Ladwood (1240), and two or three other places not named on the $2\frac{1}{2}''$ O.S. sheets, on the boundary of Elham. On the Foothills we find them at Perry Farm (1154/89), Twitham (1199), and Trapham (1270), on the outskirts of Wingham; and at Crixhall (1278), Summerfield (1275), and Creton Court in the neighbouring parish of Staple. In many cases settlements like these are situated at one side of the border in question; but there are also numerous places where parish boundaries pass through hamlets and farmyards; and not a few, as at Netters Hall in Benenden and Hawkhurst (1327), and Waldershare ('boundary of the forest dwellers') on the border of Coldred, where they cut straight through a farmhouse or manor house.

The reasons for believing that boundary settlements of this kind indicate old intercommonable pasture are not altogether obvious, and initially the present writer was slow to grasp them. Broadly speaking they are of three kinds. First, there is the onomastic evidence of the settlements and pastures themselves; second, the evidence of the divided manorial jurisdictions with which they are often associated; and third, the idiosyncratic topographical development of many of the parish boundaries involved. Before following up these three lines of enquiry in detail, it will be well to outline the general hypothesis to

PART THREE *The Expansion of Settlement*

which the facts themselves, taken as a whole, seem to point. In the first stage of development, as colonization spread outwards from the Original Lands into the *wald*, broad swathes of unappropriated woodland were apparently left uncolonized between one territory and another, and these came to be utilized not only as boundary lands or 'marks', but as intercommonable pastures.[10] Then, summer shielings and vaccaries must have been established in these common swathes or 'marks', and by the eighth century some of these were probably beginning to develop into permanent farmsteads, as at Shuttlesfield.[11] In the third stage, when it became necessary to define parochial boundaries more precisely, these shielings and farmsteads came to be utilized as convenient boundary-points in a kind of countryside where, as later perambulations show, it was often difficult to define a boundary beyond dispute.[12] Occasionally, it is clear, there were more ineluctable causes at work behind settlements of this kind; for to primitive people boundaries often tend to be objects of veneration or superstition, and in Kent there are certainly some places where they were associated with heathen sites or Christian crosses and shrines.[13] These cannot account for more than a minority of such places, however, and for the purpose in hand this generalized *schema* serves to account for the principal facts.

So far as the onomastic evidence is concerned, there are two types of place to take into account. First, there are many boundary settlements whose place-names still point to the colonization of woodland. Howt Green on the border of Bobbing and Milton Regis, for example, is recorded in 1278 and contains the element *holt*, 'a wood';[14] Kemsley Street (1198) on that of Detling and Bredhurst, contains the word *lēah*, 'a forest clearing'; Rhodes Minnis (1327) in Elham and Lyminge, *rod*, 'a clearing, an assart'; Wheelbarrow Town (?1278) in Elham and Stelling, *wald*, 'wood, forest'; Ladwood (1240) in Elham and Acrise, *wudu*, 'a wood'; Bargrove (1313) in Newington and Saltwood, *grāf*, 'a grove, a copse'; Buckhurst (1232) in Hever and Cowden, and Bredhurst (1240) on the edge of Boxley, *herst*, 'a wood'; while Twitham (1199) on the border of Wingham and Staple, and Twitton (1292) on that of Otford and Shoreham, probably contain the word *thwit*, which indicates 'cuttings, chips, shavings'.[15] These are but a few examples of many that might be cited; it is perhaps worth noting that names in 'hurst' are particularly common on parish boundaries in Kent, while those in 'grove' are almost always situated on a boundary or very close to one.[16] In many cases names like these are still associated with residual woodland of the kind described in Chapter 6.

7 The Downland economy

The second group of boundary names to take account of comprises those that specifically indicate pastoral usage. Prominent among these are the numerous Kentish places in 'minnis', 'lees', and 'tye'. Originally names of this kind seem always to have been associated with parish boundaries, and in most cases they still are at the present time: at Olantigh on the border of Crundale and Wye, for example, Tyehurst (on that of Chiddingstone and Edenbridge), and Grafty Green (Boughton Malherbe and Lenham); at Staple Lees (Wye and Hastingleigh), Badlesmere Lees (Badlesmere and Leaveland), and Boughton Lees (Boughton Aluph and Eastwell); and at Stelling Minnis (Stelling and Lyminge), Ewell Minnis (Temple Ewell and Alkham), and Rhodes Minnis (Lyminge and Elham). Nowadays such places are often associated with greens, heaths, or open spaces; but in origin there can be no doubt that they denoted common pastoral woodland, as their names, their situation, or their topography make sufficiently plain.[17] In one of the earliest recorded instances of the word 'minnis', a Canterbury charter of 839 specifically refers to a boundary mark as 'in commune silfa quod nos saxonicae *in gemennisse* dicimus': 'in the common wood which in the Saxon language we call *in gemennisse*', 'in the minnis'.[18] In other words, though as settlements places of this kind may be comparatively modern, as boundary pastures they are often of high antiquity. The connotation of the word 'minnis' in particular probably suggests that the higher reaches of the Downs originally formed a broad zone of common pasture exploited by relatively distant settlements, in much the same way as the Weald;[19] this is a point we shall return to in Chapter 11.

In turning to the evidence of divided manorial jurisdictions, with which so many boundary settlements in Kent are associated, it is the Wealden evidence that most clearly indicates their pastoral origins and needs to be examined first. In this area there are still many pasture-names in *denn* and *herst* to be found along parish boundaries,[20] and many of these are known to have been associated with pastoral units which once straddled the boundaries in question, and which subsequently came to form the basis of medieval manors, or of what were known in Kent as 'boroughs' (*borghi*). Of the *dens* of Charing, for instance, Comenden was partly in the parish of Frittenden and partly in Cranbrook, while Elmhurst was divided between Smarden and Egerton. Of those of Brook, Eldershurst was formed out of the wood of *Ægylbyrhtingahyrst*, which straddled the boundary of Tenterden and High Halden and is first recorded in a charter of 833 x 858. Similarly,

PART THREE *The Expansion of Settlement*

MAP 8. *Upland pastures of settlements on the Darent and Cray* (based on the Ordnance Survey map with the permission of The Controller of Her Majesty's Stationery Office; Crown Copyright reserved)

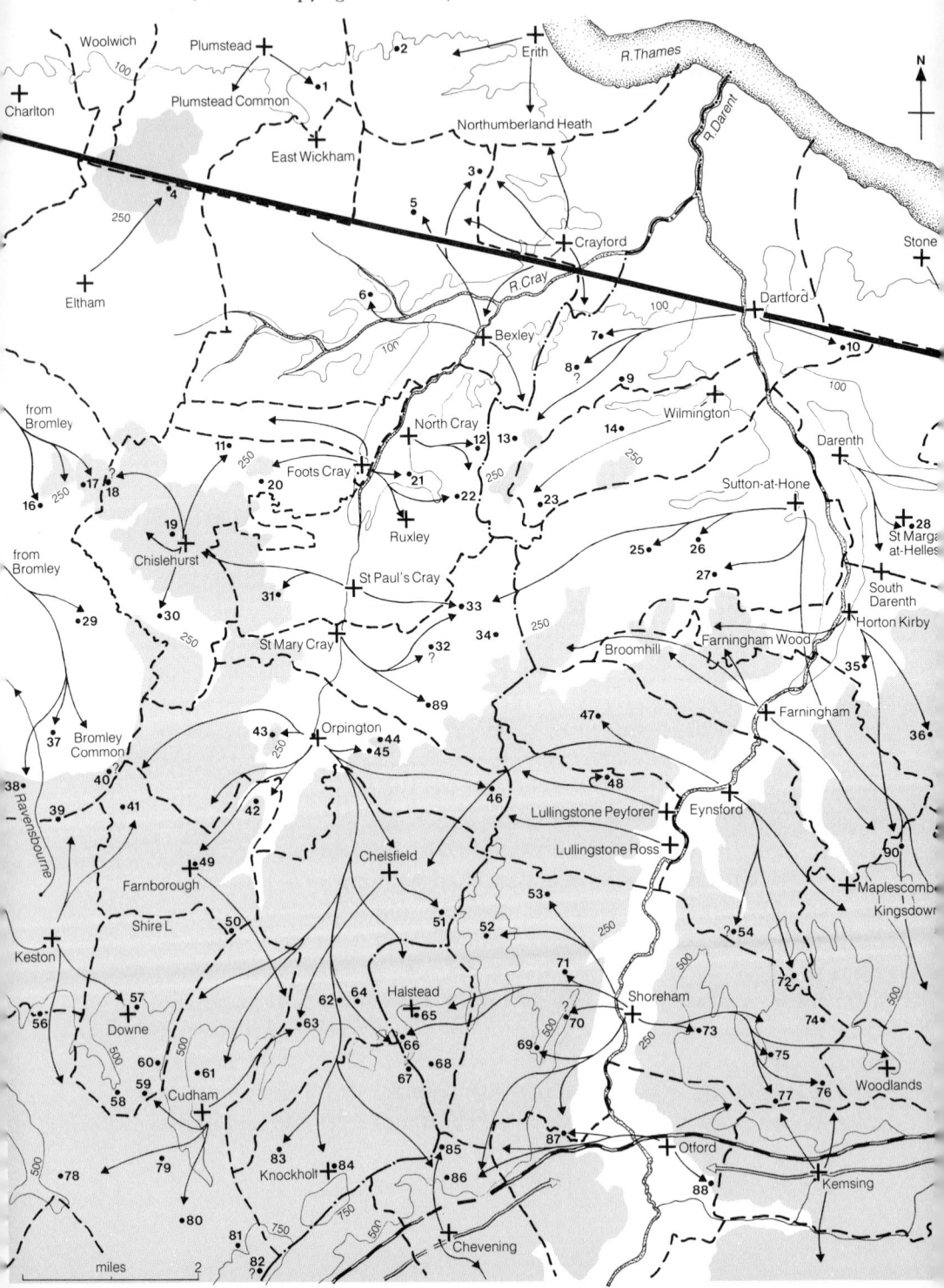

7 The Downland economy

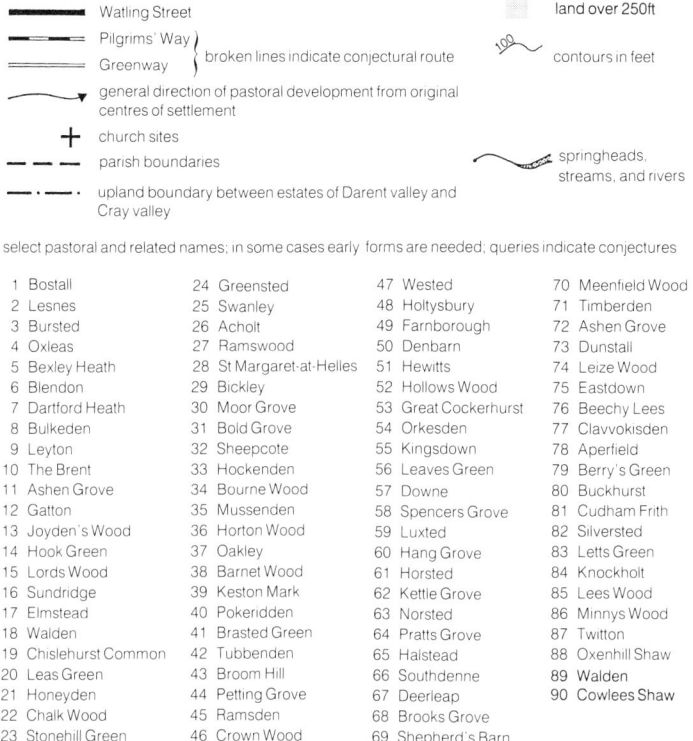

1	Bostall	24	Greensted	47	Wested	70	Meenfield Wood
2	Lesnes	25	Swanley	48	Holtysbury	71	Timberden
3	Bursted	26	Acholt	49	Farnborough	72	Ashen Grove
4	Oxleas	27	Ramswood	50	Denbarn	73	Dunstall
5	Bexley Heath	28	St Margaret-at-Helles	51	Hewitts	74	Leize Wood
6	Blendon	29	Bickley	52	Hollows Wood	75	Eastdown
7	Dartford Heath	30	Moor Grove	53	Great Cockerhurst	76	Beechy Lees
8	Bulkeden	31	Bold Grove	54	Orkesden	77	Clavvokisden
9	Leyton	32	Sheepcote	55	Kingsdown	78	Aperfield
10	The Brent	33	Hockenden	56	Leaves Green	79	Berry's Green
11	Ashen Grove	34	Bourne Wood	57	Downe	80	Buckhurst
12	Gatton	35	Mussenden	58	Spencers Grove	81	Cudham Frith
13	Joyden's Wood	36	Horton Wood	59	Luxted	82	Silversted
14	Hook Green	37	Oakley	60	Hang Grove	83	Letts Green
15	Lords Wood	38	Barnet Wood	61	Horsted	84	Knockholt
16	Sundridge	39	Keston Mark	62	Kettle Grove	85	Lees Wood
17	Elmstead	40	Pokeridden	63	Norsted	86	Minnys Wood
18	Walden	41	Brasted Green	64	Pratts Grove	87	Twitton
19	Chislehurst Common	42	Tubbenden	65	Halstead	88	Oxenhill Shaw
20	Leas Green	43	Broom Hill	66	Southdenne	89	**Walden**
21	Honeyden	44	Petting Grove	67	Deerleap	90	**Cowlees Shaw**
22	Chalk Wood	45	Ramsden	68	Brooks Grove		
23	Stonehill Green	46	Crown Wood	69	Shepherd's Barn		

the *den* of Aylesford known as Rugmer Hill was divided between the four parishes of Brenchley, Horsmonden, Yalding, and Hunton, and still survives as a farm-name near the Yalding boundary today.[21] Not all places of this kind became full-scale manors or boroughs, but many undoubtedly did so. Comenden, for example, developed into a manorial estate astride the borders of Frittenden and Cranbrook;[22] Rugmer Hill formed the basis of a borough which still comprised parts of Horsmonden and Yalding in Hasted's day, and was then still regarded as a detached part of the paramount manor of Aylesford, eight or nine miles to the north-east.[23]

In the Weald, therefore, there can be no doubt that divided manors and boroughs of this kind and the boundary settlements with which they are associated frequently originated in ancient pasture-rights. The interesting point to note, however, is that such divided jurisdictions were by no means a peculiarity of the Weald. Though their origins have not generally been recognized elsewhere, they are in fact equally characteristic of the Downs. There can be no doubt that they developed

PART THREE *The Expansion of Settlement*

from ancient pasture-rights in much the same way, moreover, since they are similarly associated with boundary settlements, and in many cases with place-names indicating pastoral usage. Take the stretch of upland *wald* between the Darent valley and the Cray valley, for example (see map 8). Here the manor of Hockenden, or 'Hoc's pasture',[24] was divided between the three parishes of St Mary Cray, St Paul's Cray, and Sutton-at-Hone, and between the old settlement-territories of the Cray people and the Darent people.[25] Three miles to the south-west of Hockenden, beyond the swine pastures of Walden and Ramsden, the demesnes of Tubbenden, or 'Tubba's pasture', lay partly in the parish of Farnborough and partly in that of Orpington.[26] Three miles to the south of Tubbenden, the manor of Norsted, or 'north pasture-place', lay partly in the parish of Chelsfield and partly in Farnborough and Cudham.[27] A mile or so to the east of Norsted, the boundary of Knockholt is described in a perambulation of 1463 as descending into 'the bottom of the vale down to Southdenne, and there in the midst of that Denne join the parishes of Chelsfield, Halstead, and [Kn]ockholt...'[28] Elsewhere on the Downs we find much the same kind of development: the manor of Selgrove near Faversham, for example, straddled the boundary of Preston and Sheldwich; the manor of Lidsing, in the wooded hill-country south of Gillingham, was divided between Gillingham, Chatham, and Wouldham;[29] the borough and estate of Twitham lay partly in the parish of Wingham and partly in that of Goodnestone;[30] the borough and manor of Tickenhurst, 'the young goats' wood', which lies between Heronden (*denn*) in Eastry and Hammill (*wald*) in Woodnesborough, was divided between the parishes of Northbourne and Knowlton. Throughout the old woodland countries of Kent, in short, the manorial structure was at many points moulded by circumstances of this kind. There were many parishes, moreover, which never developed a manorial structure of their own, but remained wholly divided between different external jurisdictions in this way. Near Maidstone, for example, most of Bearsted (?*bær* + *stede*, 'pasture stead') remained subordinate to Thurnham and Leeds throughout its history.[31]

In the light of these circumstances, the idiosyncratic topography of the parish boundaries often associated with settlements of this kind is worth noting. There are two points in this connexion that need to be mentioned. First, there are several places on the Downs where we find boundary settlements associated with a series of parishes whose outlying lands converge upon a single tract of upland forest. In places like

150

7 The Downland economy

this the parent communities themselves are eccentrically sited within their parishes, which generally extend long narrow fingers or tongues of dependent pastureland up into the woods. Once again the countryside between the Darent valley and the Cray furnishes good examples. Here, the parishes of Dartford and Wilmington still extend irregular outliers up into the *wald* of Joyden's Wood, some three or four miles from their eponymous church-settlements in the valley itself. Until the parish of Swanley was created in the nineteenth century, Sutton-at-Hone, Horton Kirby, and Farningham likewise reached up into this area, and beyond them Eynsford, Lullingstone, and Shoreham still march with the Cray valley parishes along the ridge. West of the ridge, the old boundaries have now been largely obliterated; but originally the outlying lands of Bexley, North Cray, Ruxley, St Paul's Cray, St Mary Cray, and Orpington all converged on this common upland forest. Something of the pastoral character of this forest has already been noted in discussing the names of Hockenden, Walden, Tubbenden, Norsted, and *Southdenne*. To these may be added places like Luxted (*loca + stede*, 'enclosed pasture'), Horsted (?'horse pasture'), Wested ('west pasture'), Ramsden (?'rams' pasture'), Swanley ('herdsman's clearing'), and perhaps the lost *Honeyden* and *Bulkeden* (?'bullocks' pasture'), together with several names in 'green', 'grove', and 'hurst'.[32] Originally the forest in this area once extended for something like ten miles in a continuous line, from Luxted near Downe in the south to Chalk Wood and Joyden's Wood itself near Dartford.

Second, there are also a number of places on the Downs where boundary settlements are associated with a striking network of interlocking parish bounds, somewhat in the form of the Greek key-pattern. One example of this kind of development may be found in the neighbourhood of Kemsley Street, on the border of Detling and Bredhurst, already referred to (see map 9). Here the outlying lands of Rainham, Hartlip, Stockbury, Thurnham, Detling, Boxley, Bredhurst, and the former chapelry of Lidsing are all interlocked with one another in this way, while the boundaries of the area are dotted with settlements like Dunn Street (recorded in 1535), Pollyfield (1240), Binbury (1214/19), Cockhill, Yelsted (1198), Beaux Aires (medieval, n.d.), Matts Hill (1343/4), Bredhurst (1240), and Kemsley Street itself (1198). Wherever we find this kind of development in Kent, it betokens an old

MAP 9 (*over*). *Downland boundaries between Rochester and Hollingbourne* (based on the Ordnance Survey map with the permission of The Controller of Her Majesty's Stationery Office; Crown Copyright reserved)

7 The Downland economy

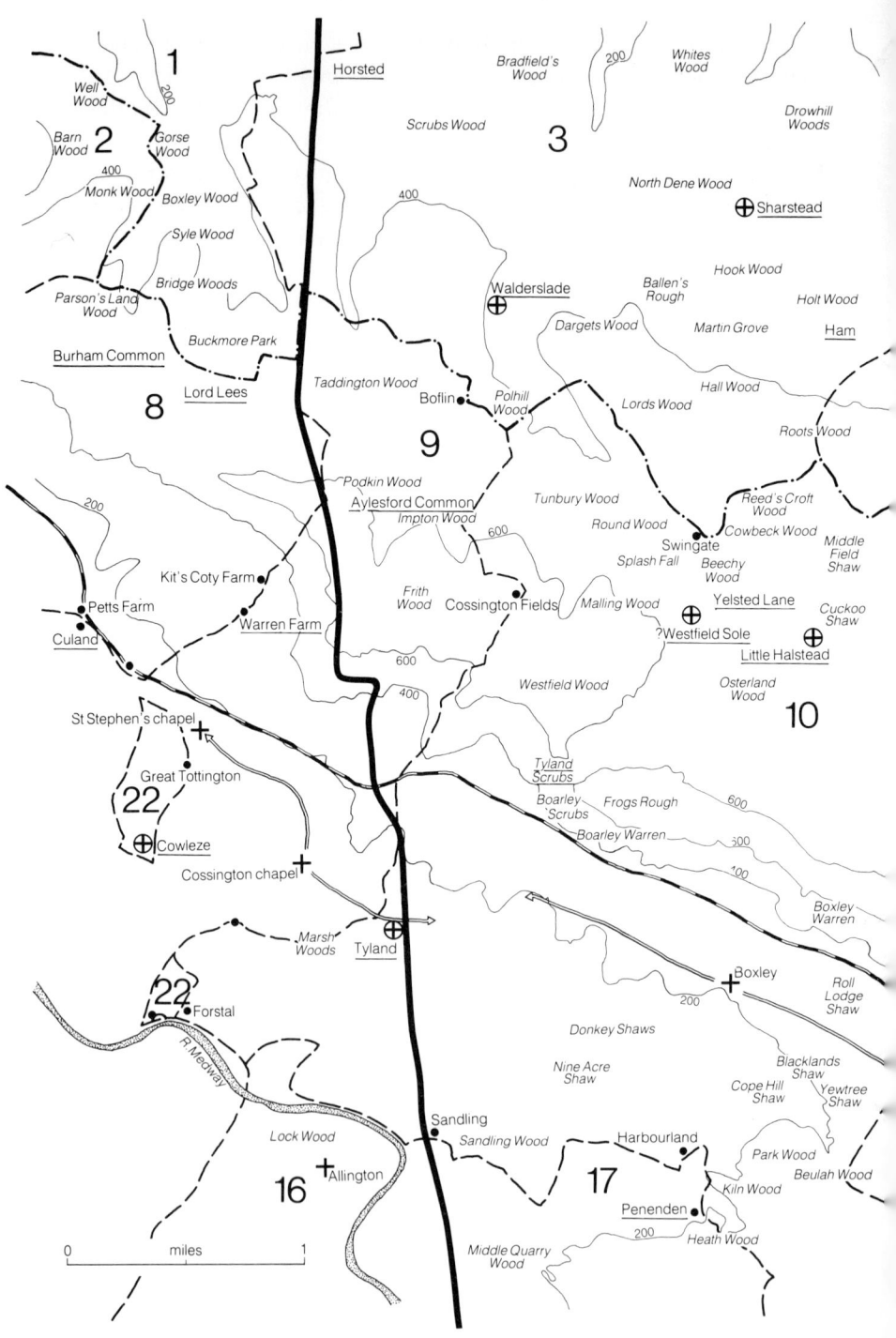

7 The Downland economy

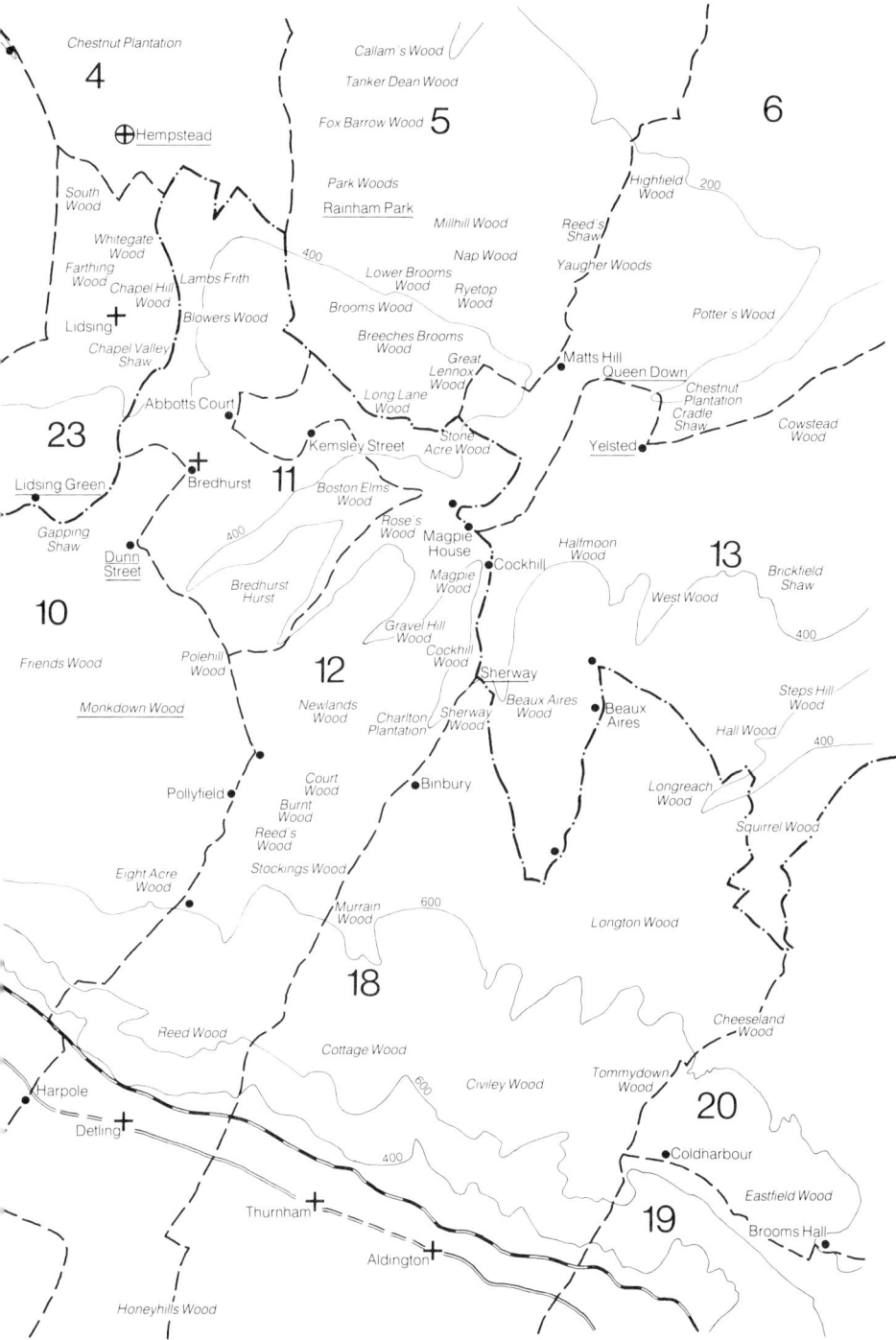

PART THREE *The Expansion of Settlement*

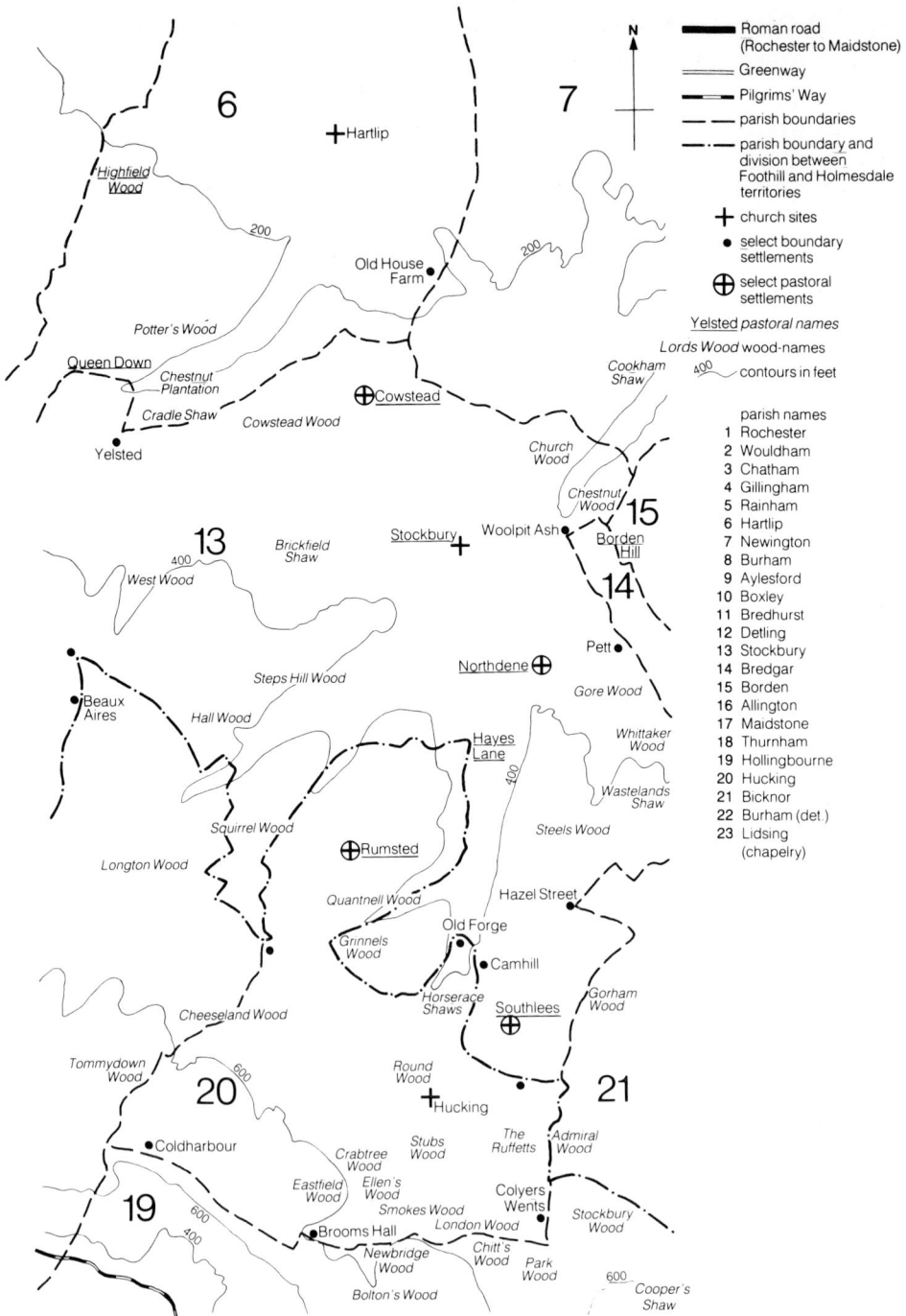

7 The Downland economy

intercommonable countryside at one time shared between different parishes and different *regiones* or estates. This is evident from the fact that it is always associated not only with boundary settlements, but also with ancient woodland, with pastoral place-names, and with indications of transhumance.[33] In the neighbourhood of Kemsley Street, for example, there are still nearly 40 woods specifically named on the $2\frac{1}{2}''$ O.S. map; names in 'park', 'down', 'stead', 'grove', 'hurst', and 'warren' are numerous; and the parish of Bredhurst itself originated as a detached pasture of Hollingbourne, some seven or eight miles to the south-east.[34]

There can thus be very little doubt that the boundary settlements of Kent frequently originated as forest pasture-farms. In many places they furnish substantial additional evidence for the pastoral origins of Downland colonization; in other parts of England such places would also be worth investigating with these possibilities in mind. Our next task must be to trace the relationship between this pastoral economy of the Downs on one hand and that of the mother-communities of the Original Lands on the other.

3. DEPENDENCE AND TRANSHUMANCE

The dependent origin of Downland settlement, and the custom of transhumance at many points associated with it, have already been alluded to more than once. What evidence is there, in fact, for the view that the economy of the Downs as a whole, like that of the Weald, was at one time dependent on the Original Lands? What proof have we that the colonization of the region was attributable to the seminal settlements of the Jutish *regiones* and estates?

At first sight the evidence may not seem very substantial. Something of the tentative beginnings of dependent settlement may be traced in the development of pasture-farms in the wooded outskirts of early minster-parishes on the Foothills. This has already been noted in the case of Twitham on the boundary of Wingham; it has likewise been observed in boundary settlements like Hammill (*hamel* + *wald*),[35] Tickenhurst (*ticcen* + *herst*), Denne Court (*denn*), and Heronden (*denn*) on the borders of Eastry and Woodnesborough.[36] Some further hints of the course of early colonization may be traced in the development of those long projecting spurs of outlying hill-pasture that appertained to parishes like Dartford and Wilmington; for such places are often the last remnants of a subordinate territory that never acquired an

PART THREE *The Expansion of Settlement*

independent life of its own. In a few places, moreover, there are definite indications of early pannage-rights on the Downs, such as those exercised by Longport near Canterbury in the neighbourhood of Stelling Minnis.[37] (In Chapter 11 this particular problem will be explored in more detail in examining the stretch of Downland country to the south of the *regio* based on Milton Regis.) Yet piecemeal evidence of this kind, though often of great interest, does not in itself perhaps amount to a conclusive argument for the dependent nature of the region as a whole. As a rule, in short, specific proof of subordination and transhumance is much sparser on the Downs than in the Weald, no doubt because in this area the shielings usually became independent farmsteads at an earlier period. Nevertheless, there are three ways in which the subordinate origins of Downland settlement, and the dependent status of its early economy, have left an indelible imprint behind them. They have left their mark in the ecclesiastical structure of the county, in the manorial structure, and in the basic character of Downland place-names. It is to these three subjects that we must turn for an understanding of the dependent origins of the region as a whole.

The early ecclesiastical evolution of the Kentish kingdom is a profoundly complex subject, and systematic investigation of it must await detailed discussion in the following chapter. In the present context the one point that needs to be noted is that Downland churches almost always originated as subordinate foundations of mother-churches situated on the Foothills or in Holmesdale. In the Weald, where similar conditions obtained, such dependent establishments are known to be associated with the subordinate nature of Wealden settlement. On the Downs churches usually originated at an earlier period than in the Weald, sometimes much earlier, but there too there can be no doubt that ecclesiastical dependence usually stemmed from similar causes. A few examples will serve to illustrate these points. Between Maidstone and Rainham the detached Downland chapelry of Bredhurst originated, as we have already seen, as a daughter of the mother-church at Hollingbourne in Holmesdale (see map 9). In the same stretch of country, the church of St Margaret at Hucking likewise originated as a Downland chapelry of Hollingbourne, while that of St Mary Magdalene at Lidsing was established by the mother-church of St Mary Magdalene at Gillingham.[38] On the hills overlooking the Darent valley both Wilmington and Kingsdown were established as chapelries of Sutton-at-Hone, and St Margaret-at-Helles and South Darenth as chapelries of Darenth (see map 8). West of the Darent, on

7 The Downland economy

the 725 foot contour, Knockholt developed as an upland chapelry of Orpington, which itself had probably been established as an early daughter-church of the minster at Crayford.[39] South of Canterbury, on the minnislands where the men of Longport had their pannage-rights, Stelling originated as a chapelry of Hardres, Hardres itself as a daughter of Nackington, and Nackington of an unidentified minster in the Stour valley, perhaps St Augustine's Abbey in Longport itself.[40] The evidence of subordination is not everywhere as straightforward as this; yet even where Downland parishes obtained complete freedom, some vestige of their former status often survived in local ecclesiastical customs. At East Langdon, near Deal, for instance, the medieval parishioners were bound to contribute to the repair of the mother-church at Northbourne: and since the manor of Northbourne claimed jurisdiction over part of the parish of Langdon, while both churches bear the unusual dedication of St Augustine, there can be little doubt that East Langdon had developed as a chapelry of St Augustine's minster at Northbourne.[41]

There are two further points in connexion with these dependent Downland churches that need to be noted. First, they were at one time substantially more numerous than they are now; for many failed to survive the demographic and economic decline of the later Middle Ages. In the estates based on the Darent valley, for example, though Wilmington and Kingsdown survived, Maplescombe, Woodlands, South Darenth, St Margaret-at-Helles, and Lullingstone Peyforer all disappeared (see map 8).[42] Similarly, in the upland parts of the Hoo peninsula, which in this respect formed an extension of the Downs, Merston, Lillechurch, Islingham, Bromhey, and Hoo St Margaret's failed to survive (see map 15).[43] Sometimes it was circumstances like these that gave rise to those outlying tongues or spurs of Downland pasture referred to earlier, as in the case of the lost chapelry of Ashdown in the parish of Lenham (see map 16). Second, where Downland parishes bear pastoral place-names, it is noteworthy that they are almost always known to have originated as subordinate chapelries. Of the eight Downland parishes in 'stead', for example, at least six certainly developed in this way: Lynsted as a daughter of Teynham, Stansted of Wrotham, Frinsted of Maidstone, Elmsted of Waltham, Milsted of Milton, and Nursted probably of Northfleet. Similarly of those in *denn* Borden is known to have been a dependency of Milton, Lydden of Folkestone, and Ashdown (*æsc* + *denn*) of Lenham;[44] of those in 'worth', Paddlesworth near Folkestone was a daughter of Lyminge,

PART THREE *The Expansion of Settlement*

Paddlesworth near Snodland of Birling, and the lost Trimworth, near Ashford, of Wye; of those in *dūn*, Downe was a daughter of Hayes, East Langdon probably of Northbourne, Kingsdown-by-Faversham of Milton, Kingsdown-by-Wrotham of Sutton, and Harbledown of an unidentified minster in the Stour valley. Elsewhere, we find Challock or *cealfa + loca*, 'calves' enclosure', originating as a chapel of Godmersham; Stockbury, or *stoc + bǣr* (?), as a chapel of Newington; Tunstall (*tūn + steall*, 'cattle stall') as a chapel of Milton: and so on.

The ecclesiastical evidence thus sheds an important light on the subordinate origins of Downland settlement.[45] Of the 200 or so churches in the region, at least half can be proved to have originated as dependent chapelries, and of those bearing pastoral place-names the proportion is more like four-fifths.[46] In every case, these dependent churches were subordinate to minsters situated on the Foothills or in Holmesdale, and in no case to churches situated elsewhere in the county. None of the Downland churches was itself a minster; and although some of them, like Waltham, Hardres, and Hayes, gave birth to subordinate chapelries of their own, as we shall see in the following chapter, only one, Stalisfield, seems to have founded a daughter-church outside the area.[47] These circumstances alone, quite apart from any other evidence, constitute a clear *prima facie* case for the ultimate dependence of Downland settlement upon the mother-communities of the Original Lands.

In turning to the manorial and borghal evidence, we find much to confirm that of ecclesiastical development, and much to amplify it.[48] For the rights of paramount manors in Kent often survived until a later period than those of minster churches, and hence enable us to identify many further subordinate settlements regarding which the ecclesiastical evidence is silent. In the neighbourhood of Northbourne, for example, where all the daughter-churches of St Augustine's minster except Sholden seem to have become independent by the early medieval period, the manor court of Northbourne was still claiming paramountcy over parts of Whitfield and West Langdon in Hasted's time, and still appointing borsholders to the manors of Little Mongeham, Martin in East Langdon, and part of Sutton-by-Dover, as well as to Sholden itself.[49] Such circumstances indicate that this stretch of Downland country was at one time dependent on Northbourne, and this suggestion is borne out by the local topography of the neighbourhood and by place-names like Sutton, Northbourne's 'south *tūn*' or southerly farm. Similarly, in the area between Chatham and Sit-

7 The Downland economy

tingbourne, where the churches of Hartlip, Rainham, Stockbury, Upchurch, and Lower Halstow all became independent of the minster at Newington during the early medieval period, the paramount manor of Milton Regis, from which Newington itself had originated, still claimed jurisdiction over the parishes of Hartlip, Rainham, Upchurch, and Halstow in the eighteenth century, and over parts of Stockbury and Newington as well.[50] Even where subordinate manors achieved virtual independence, some vestige of subordination of this kind often survived in local customs relating to quit-rents, profits of fairs, or the like. On the Chartland south of the Darent valley, for example, in the parish of Sevenoaks, the estates of Greatness, Bradbourne, *Clodhamer*, Brittains, and Rumsted were still paying small annual rents to the paramount manor of Otford in the sixteenth century, long after Sevenoaks itself had become independent of Otford and given birth to subordinate manors of its own at places like Bradbourne, Wickhurst, and Knole.[51] Both on the Chartland and on the Downs, circumstances like these point once again to the dependent origins of local settlement.

There is one further matter regarding the manorial structure of the county that should be noted in this connexion. This is the fact that there were once a number of places on the Downs, just as there were in the Weald, whose lands were wholly detached from the demesne lands of their paramount manors on the Foothills or in Holmesdale. In the Weald, discrete manorial estates of this kind have long been recognized as arising from the custom of transhumance. On the Downs there can be very little doubt that they likewise represent remnants of detached pastureland, though transhumance gave way to permanent settlement at an earlier period and is thus rarely recorded. One example of a detached Downland pasture of this kind has already been mentioned in connexion with Bredhurst, part of which was still subordinate to the paramount manor of Hollingbourne, seven or so miles to the southwest, in the eighteenth century. In the same stretch of country the evidence of detached-pasture rights south of Milton is especially significant and will be discussed in detail in Chapter 11. In East Kent, a few miles from Canterbury, we find another example, in this case associated with Reculver. Here the manor comprised not only the parent borough (*borgh*) of Reculver itself, but the Downland borough of Shottenden near Chilham, some 15 miles to the south-west, and the Chartland borough of Chelmington in Great Chart, nearly 30 miles away on the edge of the Weald.[52] In the neighbourhood of Shottenden both place-names and woodland topography distinctly point to former

PART THREE *The Expansion of Settlement*

pastoral usage: at Denne (*denn*), for instance, Shepherds Hill (*scēap* + *herst*), Sheldwich Lees (*lǣs*), Old Wives Lees (*eald* + *wudu* + *lǣs*), Grove (*grāf*), and Shottenden itself, the *dūn* or 'down pasture' of the men of Reculver.[53] Such examples might well be multiplied further; but perhaps the most interesting point to note is that they are usually associated with seminal places like Reculver, where the case for continuity between Roman and Jute is particularly cogent. In some parts of the Downs transhumance may thus reach back beyond the time of the Jutes to the twilight world of Celtic *Cantium*.

In turning to the onomastic evidence for Downland dependence there are two points that need to be taken into account. In the first place, there are a number of minor Downland place-names that probably point to early stock-droves. Few of these are recorded before the Conquest, and their interpretation is not without ambiguity, but there are four elements that call for discussion: 'drove' (*drāf*), 'hatch' (*hæc, hec*), 'gate' (*geat*), and 'shereway' or 'shireway'.[54] 'Drove' (or 'drift') is the most straightforward of the four and occurs in a number of places, such as Droveway in Lyminge (1348), though it may sometimes indicate no more than a medieval drove. Names in 'gate' and 'hatch' do not necessarily refer to droves; but in Kent they are numerous and are often found on trackways leading up on to the Downs or into the Blean, where they seem to denote 'pasturegates', as the local custom expressed it, or in other words rights of entry for common of herbage. This is probably the explanation of places like Bow Hatch in Chartham (1292), for example, *Hatch* in Chislet (1292), Hatch Spring in Hoath (1690), and Hatch Hill in Luddesdown (1537); or Bleangate in Chislet (1087), Ludgate on the border of Lynsted and Tonge (1338), and Dungate on the border of Rodmersham and Kingsdown (1591).[55] 'Shereway' or 'shireway' is a more difficult word to interpret, and in view of its local frequency really demands further investigation. It does not seem to be discussed by any of the standard authorities on place-names, and Wallenberg does not record it. According to White Kennett, in the seventeenth century, it signified a 'bridleway', and it was certainly still used in that sense by Hasted a century later.[56] Originally, however, the first element 'shire' or 'shere' probably derived from the Old English word *scīr*, so that a shereway really meant a 'district way'. If this surmise is correct, it seems likely that on the Downs the word at one time indicated a common stock-drove linking the mother-communities of the Original Lands with their upland pastures: for in Kent the word *scīr* is often associated with a tract of upland pasture, as at

7 The Downland economy

Higham Upshire, or marsh-pasture, as at Shirley Moor near Tenterden. Certainly this would account for the origin of names like Shereway Wood in Wormshill and Sherway Wood on the borders of Detling, Thurnham, and Stockbury; for both places are situated near old Downland droves, in the heart of the *wald*.

The second point to note about Downland place-names relates rather to their general character. In this connexion the outstanding fact is the preponderance of names derived from pastoral or topographical features. Taking the 3,000 or so place-names of the region as a whole, it is safe to say that at least three-quarters are of this kind, and less than one quarter specifically indicate habitation. Of the elements recorded in pre-Conquest charters,[57] as many as four-fifths are pastoral or topographical, and only 18 denote settlement, as table 7 shows. Towards the end of the Old English period a number of *ingas* names appeared on the Downs; but it is probably significant that only one of these is recorded before the Conquest, and that not until the tenth century.

These facts will bear thinking about. They may be interpreted in a variety of ways no doubt, and the specific circumstances behind the formation of individual place-names must in many respects remain elusive. Nevertheless, the preponderance of topographical and pastoral elements may well bear witness to the impact of a transhumant population upon a predominantly virgin countryside. In a land of isolated shielings, where society was essentially scattered and migrant in origin, it was necessarily the pastoral and topographical features of the landscape that the herdsman looked out for, season by season, in returning to the familiar droves. It was the particular combe, dene, dale, linch, down, hill, ridge, sole, mere, pool, or pett that remained in his memory: the particular wood, hurst, grove, holt, toll, *wald, harað, lēah, rod,* or *rydding*: the particular *den*, stead, fold, worth, hay, hope, *hamm*, lees, minnis, *bǣr, loca,* or cowland. It was from such elements as these, as a consequence, and from the beasts, the birds, the plants, and the trees of the forest – beech, oak, ash, elm, thorn, pear, apple, elder, maple, and so on – that the overwhelming majority of Downland farmsteads derived their names.

There can be no doubt, in short, that the pastoral economy of the Downs, like that of the Weald, was in origin a dependent one. Ecclesiastical, manorial, and onomastic evidence all bear witness to its initial exploitation by the mother-communities of the Original Lands, and to its ultimate origins in the primitive custom of transhumance. In

PART THREE *The Expansion of Settlement*

Table 7. Downland place-names: elements in pre-Conquest charters

Topography		Woodland		Pasture		Agriculture		Wild animals		Habitation	
down	9	*wald*	7	*stede*	11	land	6	*heort*	2	*tūn*	6
denu	7	*lēah*	6	*feld*	4					*hām*	3
beorg	4	wood	4	*(ge)hæg*	3					wickham	2
hlinc	4	*rod,rede*	3	*bær?*	3						
ing	3	hurst	2	*hamm*	2						
sole	3	oak	2	gate	2						
combe	2										
bourne	2										
mere	2										
stone	2										
other elements, each occurring once	18[a]		12[b]		10[c]		4[d]		2[e]		7[f]
Total	56		36		35		10		4		18

[a] *ceosol, wincel, scēat, sceorf, brigā,* ridge, *cropp,* hill, cliff, *wæl, swelgend, rōd, ōra, scylf, līm fīn, pett, scearu, scēad* ('boundary').
[b] holt, *haraδ,* grove, beech, elder, thorn, fern, apple tree, pear tree, ash, charcoal, *bryne.*
[c] cowland, *denn, loca,* worth, fold, rother, calf, horse, oxen, *steorf.*
[d] *campus, ersc,* hen, mill.
[e] *pur* (snipe), ?falcon.
[f] wick, *burh, ware, ingas, weard-setl, ?hӯscen, sceld.*

NB. One further element, *bidda* ('beggar') cannot be easily classified. The element *feld* should perhaps be included in Column 4 rather than Column 3. In a few other cases elements are difficult to classify with complete certainty; but they have been allocated in the table in the light of their local topography, and in the light of Wallenberg's comments on each name, as well as in respect of etymology.

Chapter 11 we shall find that the topographical evidence points in the same direction. Nevertheless, while there were many parallels between the Downs and the Weald, it is also clear that there were a number of fundamental contrasts. If the early Wealden economy was based predominantly upon pannage-rights, for what purposes, it must be asked, were the woodland pastures of the Downland exploited?

7   *The Downland economy*

4. PASTORAL USAGE

The outstanding contrast between the pastoral economy of the Downs and that of the Weald was undoubtedly its greater variety. In a sense it was this circumstance, in the last resort, that lay behind its more varied nomenclature. Nowhere on the Downs do we find anything like that concentration of names in *denn* and *herst* which is so distinctive of the Weald. Behind this diversity, what we also see is probably a less systematic process of exploitation, a more piecemeal movement of colonization. When the clearance of the Downs began, after all, the population of Kent was no doubt much sparser than in the tenth century, when the first permanent settlements appeared in the Weald, so that the urge behind reclamation was necessarily more localized and less intense. The lathal administration of the county, moreover, in so far as it already existed, was no doubt less fully developed, and hence less influential in its effect upon agrarian evolution. It must also be remembered that the Downland is a larger region than the Kentish section of the Weald, some 70 miles in length instead of 45, and one with a more diversified natural environment. In the Weald the prevalence of oak forest necessarily limited early exploitation largely to swine pastures, since cattle cannot be fed on oak-mast: it dries up their milk-yield and is liable to cause stoppage or miscarriage.[58] On the Downs, by contrast, though there were several areas where oakwoods and beech-woods yielded valuable pannage-rights, a more varied tree cover facilitated the development of a more varied economy. In addition to swine pastures, we find many place-names indicating vaccaries, as a consequence, and a number denoting pastures for oxen, sheep, horses, goats, and geese.[59] The frequency of names in *dēor* and *heort*, as at Deerton ('deer farm'), Dargate ('deer gate'), and Durlock ('deer enclosure') may suggest that in places the wild life of the region was likewise turned to account.[60] In the absence of other records relating to the pre-Conquest economy, it is thus the place-names of the Downs, once again, that provide the principal evidence of early land use. Only a limited number of elements is relevant in this context, since many of those discussed earlier, such as *lǣs, pearroc, tēag, wald,* and *dūn*, were not associated, as far as one can see, with any particular type of livestock husbandry.

So far as swine pastures are concerned, the chief element to take account of, as in the Weald, is *denn*. Apart from a few places where it is combined with 'oxen', and a few where early forms are conflicting or

PART THREE *The Expansion of Settlement*

where the precise situation is uncertain, there are about 35 Downland names in which this element appears. In addition, there are a few names in 'swine', 'hog', 'boar', and *eofor*,[61] and seven in *swān* or 'herdsman', probably meaning a swineherd, so that altogether there are about 45 or 50 names specifically indicating pastures for swine. These are modest numbers compared with the 600 or so recorded in the Weald; but the significant point to note is that they tend to occur in localized groups, suggesting that certain specific areas of the Downs were more particularly reserved for swine.

One prominent group is to be found between the Dour valley and the Little Stour, in the upland country where the parishes of Hawkinge, Alkham, Lydden, and Wootton converge upon Swingfield, or 'swine field' (see map 10).[62] Here we find Standen or 'stone + *denn*', Reinden ('roe + *denn*'), Densole ('miry pool + *denn*'), Fernden ('fern + *denn*'),[63] and Lydden (*hlēo*, 'shelter + *denn*'),* together with Pickleden‡ and Sladden,‡ for which early forms have not been found. In the same neighbourhood we also find Swanton in Lydden, Hogbrook‡ in Alkham, Everings[64] or *eofor + ingas* in Alkham, and an outlying swine pasture further north, at Dennehill in Womenswold. A second group of swine pastures is to be found north of Canterbury, in the Forest of Blean, which for this purpose may be regarded as an extension of the Downs. This area is known from other sources to have been widely utilized for this purpose in the pre-Conquest period by parishes like Wickhambreaux, Sturry, and Swalecliffe.[65] In a charter of 948, for example, Wickhambreaux is said to have had a *den* in *blean earnes hyrst*, or Blean Eagle's Wood, and the element *denn* is still found in this neighbourhood at places like Denly Hill in Hernhill, Bossenden in Dunkirk, and Ellenden and Thornden in Whitstable.[66] A third group of swine pastures occurs to the west of the Darent valley, in the outlying lands of the estate based on the River Cray, at Tubbenden, Hockenden, Walden, Ramsden,‡ Den Barn,‡ Pokeridden,‡ and the lost *Southdenne* in Knockholt, already referred to (see map 8).[67] Finally, between the Medway and the Stour, there is a more scattered group extending from Borden ('?boar + *denn*') to Otterden (?*Oter + ingas + denn*), and including Norton ('north + *denn*') in Stockbury, Swanton in Bredgar, Mordenden* in Hollingbourne, Hogshaw in Milsted, Borden‡ Wood in Doddington, Ashdown (*denn*) in Lenham, and Payden‡ in Wichling (see map 16).[68]

In addition to these places, it seems certain that at one time there were many further swine pastures on the Downs. In the Forest of Blean,

7 The Downland economy

names in *herst* as well as *denn* evidently bear this meaning,[69] and in the area around Stelling Minnis, where the men of Longport had their pannage-rights, it is noteworthy that the element *denn* does not actually occur at all. Nevertheless, though the evidence is obviously incomplete, it seems to point to two conclusions. First, it was in East Kent that the swine pastures of the Downs appear to have been most prominent. Owing to the geographical configuration of the county, this area was more restricted in its share of the Weald than the parts further west, as Mr Witney has shown:[70] and this circumstance, coupled with the fact that it was more thickly settled, necessitated the exploitation of swine pastures relatively close at hand. Second, it was in general the higher parts of the Downs, by and large, that seem to have been devoted to swine, while the areas nearer to the old estate-centres were utilized predominantly for other purposes. Naturally, there are local exceptions to this generalization, as in the case of a heavily-wooded parish like Borden near Milton; it seems unlikely, moreover, that any part of the Downs was ever limited to a single purpose. Nevertheless, it was chiefly in the outlying lands of the old estates and towards the crest of the hills that the swine pastures of the area were to be found. In Chapter 11 we shall see that these lands were at one time exploited on a communal basis, and by distant as well as neighbouring communities, in much the same way as the Weald. It was probably this circumstance that originally gave rise to the 'minnises' of places like Swingfield, Stelling, Ewell, and Minnetts Hill in Frinsted.

In turning to the Downland ox pastures, it is important to remember that historically speaking oxen have always played an important role in the Kentish economy. On the heavy clays of the Weald they were still ubiquitous for draught purposes in the mid-nineteenth century.[71] On the Downs they had long yielded pride of place to horses by that date; but the word 'oxen' itself appears in many minor place-names, and suggests that at one time they were usual in that region too. Wallenberg records seven instances of the word on the Downs: *oxa + fyrhðe*, 'ox wood', at Oxfrith in Boxley (1196); *oxa + rod*, 'ox clearing', at Oxroad in Elham (1242/3); *oxna + denn*, 'ox pasture', at Oxenden Wood in Adisham (1278) and Oxney Wood in Nonington (1278); and *oxna + (ge)hæg*, 'ox enclosure', at Oxenden Wood in Chelsfield (1270), Oxenhill Shaw in Otford (1278), and the parish of Oxney near Deal (1038–44). There are certainly other names in 'ox', moreover, which Wallenberg does not discuss, such as Oxenlees Wood in Crundale.

The most usual place-names indicating vaccaries on the Downs seem

PART THREE *The Expansion of Settlement*

MAP 10. *Downland farms and pastures: Alkham and Swingfield area* (based on the Ordnance Survey map with the permission of The Controller of Her Majesty's Stationery Office; Crown Copyright reserved)

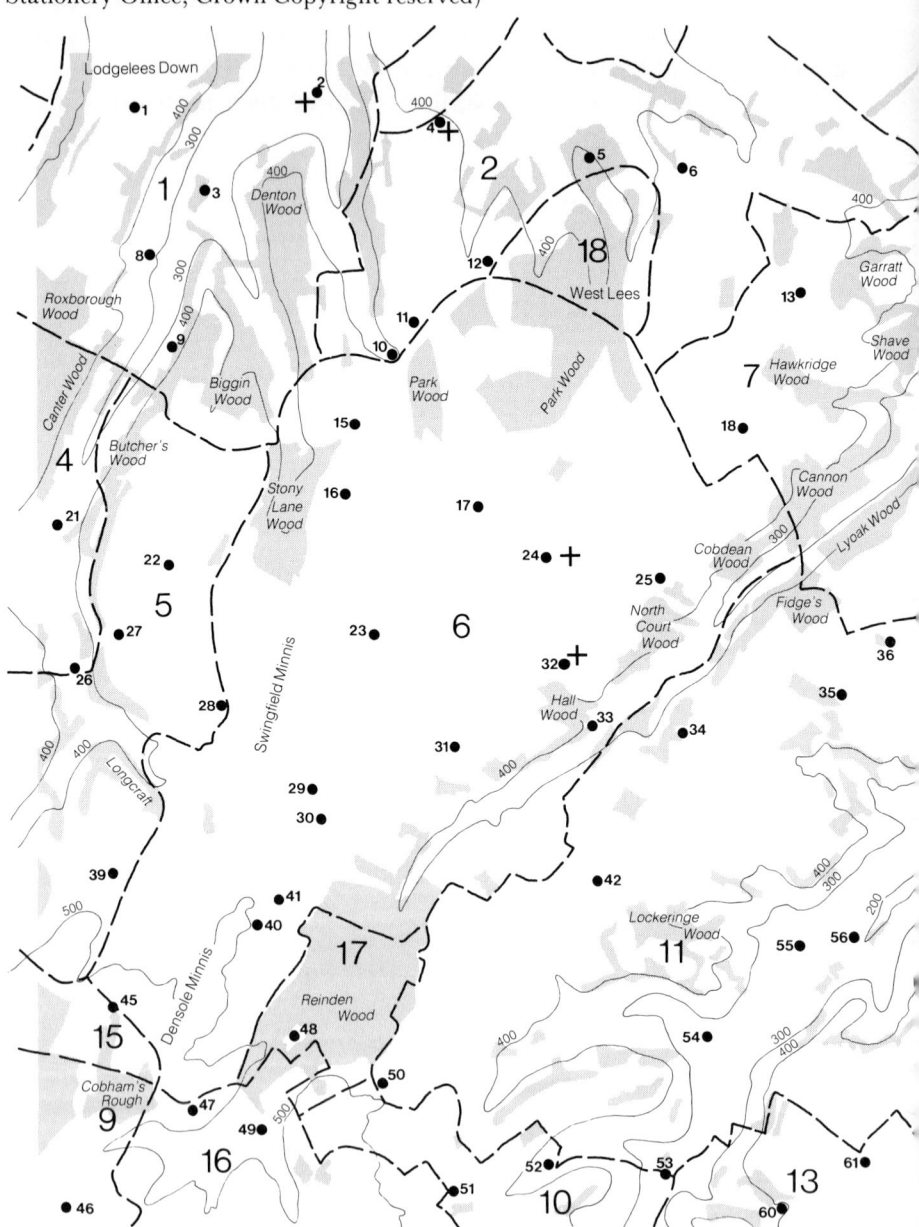

7 The Downland economy

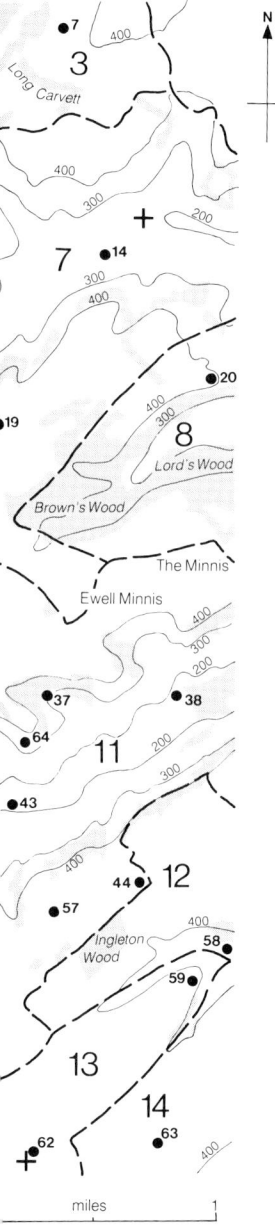

contours in feet
parish boundaries
woodland
+ church sites
● forest farms and pastures

1 Snodehill
2 Denton
3 Tappington
4 Wootton
5 Pickleden
6 Geddinge
7 Upton Wood
8 Gatteridge
9 Stockhill
10 un-named
11 un-named
12 Hill House
13 Wickham Bushes
14 Lydden
15 Selstead
16 Newlands
17 Stockham
18 Swanton
19 Langdon (?)
20 Cold Blow
21 Rakeshole
22 Brandred
23 Smersole
24 St Johns
25 North Court
26 Ladwood
27 Winterdown
28 Hoad
29 Great Foxholt
30 Little Foxholt
31 Boyington
32 Swingfield
33 Beards Hall
34 Ellinge
35 Chalksole Green
36 Chalksole
37 Sladden
38 Wolverton
39 Ridge
40 Densole
41 Little Densole
42 Everings
43 Hogbrook
44 Mount Ararat
45 Bush
46 Redsole
47 Pay Street
48 Reinden
49 Mudsole
50 Fernden
51 Cowgate
52 Upper Standen
53 Lower Standen
54 Drellingore
55 Upton
56 South Alkham
57 un-named
58 Poulton
59 Copt Hill
60 Hockley Sole
61 Tumble Tye
62 Capel-le-Ferne
63 West Hougham
64 Alkham

6 parish names
1 Denton
2 Wootton
3 Sibertswold
4 Elham
5 Acrise
6 Swingfield
7 Lydden (see also 18)
8 Temple Ewell
9 Paddlesworth
10 Hawkinge
11 Alkham
12 Poulton
13 Capel-le-Ferne
14 Hougham
15 Elham
16 Folkestone
17 extra-parochial tract
18 Lydden (detached area)

167

PART THREE *The Expansion of Settlement*

to be those in *steall*, 'stall', in the sense of 'cattle stall', 'standing place for cattle', and *stoc*, or 'stock', in the sense 'standing place [for livestock]', as in West Country names like Tawstock and Plymstock.[72] In later centuries the word 'wick' commonly came to be applied to dairies and cheesehouses in the Marshlands of Kent;[73] but on the Downs this is an unusual element, though it certainly refers to a vaccary at Sheldwich near Faversham and probably at Boyke ('boy + wick') in Elham. Of the 'stocks', the most prominent group is to be found on the lower reaches of the area near Milton Regis (see map 16). This includes Woodstock, Pitstock, Bistock, Pistock, and Stockbury, which are discussed in Chapter 11 in connexion with the *regio* based on Milton.[74] Elsewhere on the Downs, it is possible that a number of place-names thought to derive from *stocc*, 'tree-stump', are in fact from *stoc*; the two elements are often difficult to distinguish, and further local research on this point is needed.

Names in 'stall' are more numerous than those in *stoc* but they are also more problematical since they do not necessarily denote a dairy-farm. There can be little doubt that this is their meaning in places like Tunstall near Milton, Stalisfield above Charing, Mystole in Chartham, Dunstall in Shoreham, and Dunstall in Lenham.[75] But names in *borg* + *steall*, 'place of refuge, pathway up a steep hill', and *hām* + *steall*, 'homestall, farmyard', do not necessarily bear this significance. Both words occur in a number of places in Kent, and 'homestall' in particular remained a common local word for a 'farmstead' or 'farmyard' until relatively recent years.[76] The real problem in connexion with names in 'stall', however, arises with the much more numerous group of minor Kentish settlements known as 'forstals'.[77] This word is rarely found outside Kent and East Sussex, and its literal meaning seems to be *fore* + *steall*, a 'stall', 'enclosure', or 'standing place' in front of a farmhouse.[78] In Kent it is virtually confined to the pastoral areas of the county, particularly to the Weald and the Downs, and in origin it no doubt referred to an enclosure for livestock, often perhaps to a place where cattle were brought in to be milked. Beer-forstal in Elham, for example, specifically means either 'pasture forstal' or 'stall in front of a byre or cattle shed'.[79] The situation of a place like Mersham Forstal, amongst the water-meadows below the village of Mersham, also obviously denotes a subordinate dairy-farm. But the interpretation of the word is complicated by the fact that in later centuries it often came to be virtually synonymous in Kent with 'green'. Both on the Downs and in the Weald there are many parishes, such as

7 The Downland economy

Throwley near Faversham, where Hasted refers to houses and cottages 'built round the little greens or fostalls, of which there are several in different parts of the parish.'[80] It is likely, of course, that many of these 'forstals' or green-hamlets of Hasted's time had in fact developed from the subdivision of a farmholding through partible inheritance, and the consequent building of additional farmhouses or cottages round the original *fore steall* or farm-green. This seems to have happened in the parish of Throwley itself, indeed, at Throwley Forstal and Bell's Forstal, both of which lie towards the southern end of the parish, well away from the mother-settlement and the church. In such cases as these, the outlying forstals on the Downs no doubt often indicate early cattle-stations or vaccaries, and should certainly be noted in this context. Without detailed local research in medieval records, however, it would be hazardous to assume that they invariably do so.

There is one further place-name element on the Downs that needs to be discussed in connexion with dairy-farming, and that is the common local word *sol* or 'sole', meaning a 'miry pool'. At first sight it may seem strange, after all, that numerous places in a region largely devoid of streams should have been devoted to vaccaries. Some early Kentish place-names, such as Denwood or *Daneford* ('valley ford') in Crundale, show that there were once more streams in the area than there are now; but there can be no doubt that in historic times most Downland combes have always been dry valleys. It is this circumstance that lends special interest to the names in 'sole', since the overwhelming majority of them – about 90 per cent in all – are in fact to be found on the Downs.[81] In some cases, perhaps, these 'miry pools' may have been formed for drinking purposes; but in general drinking water in this area has for obvious reasons been obtained either from wells in the chalk, from roof-water, or from localized springs at the lip of the clay-with-flints. It seems more likely, in fact, that the Downland soles were originally constructed as stock-ponds, and that in many cases they may indicate early vaccaries. Some of them are certainly of great antiquity, such as Sole Street in Crundale, which is recorded in a charter of 824, and Brimsdale or *Brynnessole* in Eythorne, recorded in 944.[82] Altogether, there are probably about 100 names of this kind in the area as a whole, of which 27 are recorded by Wallenberg. In addition to these, there are also about 25 names in 'pool', 'mere', and *wǣl*, which often seem to bear much the same significance, and which in some cases are recorded equally early.

PART THREE *The Expansion of Settlement*

Though the evidence is in some respects not wholly conclusive, there can thus be very little doubt that vaccaries were among the most prominent features of the early Downland economy. They seem to have been particularly characteristic of the lower reaches of the dip-slope, no doubt because milch-kine cannot be driven far when in milk, and milk itself was difficult to transport for any distance. The earliest recorded instance of a vaccary was in fact on the borders of Faversham and Sheldwich, where a charter of 805 x 814 refers to the *Cinges culand*, 'quod nos possumus dicere pasturam vaccarum regis'.[83] The exact site of this 'king's cowland' is not known; but *Beuuestanuudan* in the same charter still survives in the name of Westwood Court in Sheldwich, within two miles of the estate-centre at Faversham itself. Later in the Old English period, cattle-stations of some kind were certainly appearing in some of the remoter parts of the Downland as well, as at Cowlees or *cu + lǣs*, 'cow pasture', on the borders of Farningham and Kingsdown. On the crest of the Downs above Westwell, indeed, the *cealfa + loca* or 'calves' enclosure' which gave Challock its name is recorded as early as 824, though that probably originated from Godmersham in the Stour valley.[84] Nevertheless, it seems to have been more usual for vaccaries to be sited relatively close to the estate-centres, as we shall see in Chapter 11 in reconstructing the *regio* of Milton.

Despite their overwhelming importance in later centuries, there are remarkably few place-names on the Downs referring to sheep. In the early fourteenth century Kent was the second most highly-assessed county in England in terms of wool production, surpassed only by Norfolk, which is substantially larger,[85] and there may have been something like 400,000 sheep in the county as a whole.[86] In these developments the Downland occupied a crucial position, as we saw in Chapter 2, and that position cannot have been a purely post-Conquest phenomenon. For something like a thousand years, in short, sheep-farming was the most important single industry in Kent, and yet there are only two early Downland place-names that unequivocally allude to it: Shepherds Hill in Sheldwich (*scēap + herst*, 'sheep wood'), already mentioned, and the lost *La Berchereye* in Chatham, a post-Conquest name derived from the Old French *bergerie*, 'habitation spécialement réservée aux bêtes ovines'.[87] To these we should perhaps add Hope in Hawkinge (1300), Hopton in Alkham (1477), and about a dozen other places called Hope Farm or Hope Wood, since *hop* or 'hope' may indicate an enclosure for sheep on the Downs, as it does in Romney Marsh.[88] Domesday Book supplies the names of two further sheep-

7 *The Downland economy*

stations, at Farningham and Wickhambreaux; but that seems to complete the evidence.[89]

Until the history of Kentish sheep-farming is written, it is perhaps useless to speculate on this relative paucity of early Downland evidence. It seems possible, however, that place-names in *stede* may in some cases refer to sheep-stations.[90] The point is not susceptible of actual proof; but the 'steads' are so characteristic of the Downland landscape that, in concluding this section, it seems appropriate to discuss them.[91] There are about 65 names of the kind in the county as a whole, and of these two-thirds are on the Downs. In several places they tend to occur in small groups, as in the vicinities of Stockbury and Cudham, and occasionally in the same neighbourhood as place-names in *denn*.[92] Except at Brasted, the element itself does not seem to be found in the Original Lands, and it never relates to a seminal settlement or a primary community.[93] In ten places it occurs in the name of a parish, but only in the case of subordinate parishes like Lynsted (a daughter of Teynham), Milsted (of Milton Regis), Stansted (of Wrotham), or Elmsted (of Waltham). On the other hand, though never belonging to the first phases of colonization, many of the Kentish 'steads' had probably come into existence well before the Conquest. In about a dozen cases they are recorded in ninth- or tenth-century charters; once, at Palmstead in Upper Hardres, in the eighth century; and perhaps once, at Bearsted, as early as 696, though that is a very doubtful example.[94]

Topographically, the Kentish evidence clearly bears out Grundy's view that 'the distribution of the place-names in stead in southern England shews that the *stede* was usually established on the patches of pasture-land in forest regions.'[95] Many of the Kentish 'steads' are thus found in relatively remote places among the woods; even in the eighteenth century Hasted could describe a settlement like Bursted in Bishopsbourne as 'in a lonely unfrequented situation, hardly known to anyone'.[96] In many cases they occupy marginal sites on the outskirts of the parish; sometimes they form an almost detached appendage to it, as at Rumsted in Hucking (see map 9); and frequently, as at Palmstead in Hardres, they are associated with those interlocking boundaries described earlier (see map 14). Their place-names, moreover, seem to support Sandred's view that in origin they were often pastures as such rather than occupation-sites.[97] Among the first elements represented in these names, *hām* (*hām* + *stede*, 'dwelling site') appears nine times, and other indications of human occupation, such as *burh* and *cēap*, eight

171

PART THREE *The Expansion of Settlement*

times.⁹⁸ But the overwhelming majority of first elements relate either to woodland clearance and pasture (13 times), or to natural environment and local situation (38 times). Hills, valleys, woods, brooks, birds, nettles, stony land, miry places, and above all wild trees like the oak, elm, beech, lime, pear, plum, nut, and apple: these are the elements that most frequently distinguish one 'stead' from another.⁹⁹ In this onomastic emphasis we can perhaps trace once again the imprint of the Downland herdsmen, as they ventured into a largely uncharted countryside: for the shepherd's life is often a solitary one, and one that necessarily develops a keen eye for topographical detail.

5. THE FREEDOM OF THE WOLD

The economy of the Downland was not moulded by matters of husbandry and environment alone. It must also have been affected by the structure of early Kentish society, by local customs of inheritance, and by forms of family organization. While these are matters of which we have little direct knowledge on the Downs in the pre-Conquest period, it would be simplistic to ignore them altogether. Traditionally, indeed, Kentish settlement has generally been explained in terms of the social and administrative structure of the lathes, and their origins in a supposedly immemorial 'folk-right'.¹⁰⁰ Although such an approach pays too little attention to the exigencies of a forest environment and to human response to it, the influence of social institutions should not be discounted merely because we know little about either their origins or their operation. So far as the Downs are concerned there is one fundamental matter in this connexion that needs to be considered. This is the gradual liberation of its farmsteads from the suzerainty of the old estate-centres of the Foothills and Holmesdale, and the eventual emergence of an independent and distinctive form of society in the region as a whole. Neither the origins of that independence nor its progress can be dated with any precision; we cannot chart the exact process by which the shielings or forest lodges of the Downs became permanent farmsteads; in this respect the analogous development of the Weald in the post-Conquest period affords little guidance, since it was influenced by a number of circumstances to which there seems to be no real parallel on the Downs.¹⁰¹ Nevertheless, the eventual development of an independent economy in the area is plain to see, and that development, it is fair to say, was ultimately implicit in the distinctive character of Downland colonization.

7 The Downland economy

If we turn to the evidence of Domesday Book, we find something of this distinctive economy delineated in the pattern of Downland landownership. By the eleventh century, it seems, the independence of the area was already far advanced, and a striking contrast had developed between the structure of landholding on the Downs on one hand and in the Original Lands on the other. The subject is a complex one and really demands fuller scrutiny than is possible here; but the essential

Table 8. Landownership in Kent, c.1086[a]

	Estates in the Original Lands[b]		Estates on the Downs		Total
Church and crown estates					
Crown[c]	9				9
Christ Church/Archbishop	31	⎫	3	⎫	34
Archbishop's Knights	1	⎪	3	⎪	4
Rochester Cathedral	2	⎬ 41	2	⎬ 21	4
St Augustine's Abbey	7	⎭	7	⎪	14
St Martin's Priory, Dover			6	⎭	6
Total	50 (82%)		21 (23%)		71
'Private' estates					
Odo, Bishop of Bayeux	9		62		71
Hamo de Crevequeur			3		3
Hugo de Montfort			2		2
Fulbert of Dover			1		1
Eustace, Count of Boulogne	1				1
Albert, the King's Chaplain	1				1
Unnamed owners			4		4
Total	11 (18%)		72 (77%)		83
Grand total	61 (100%)		93 (100%)		154

[a] In this table and table 9 the word estate is used to avoid the word 'manor' and its possibly misleading connotation in this context, but it should be stressed that these 'estates' are not equivalent to the early Jutish estates referred to elsewhere in this book.
[b] This column includes all 'seminal' and major primary settlements, which in most cases became the 'paramount' manors of later centuries. 'Subsequent' settlements in the outlying parts of the Foothills and Holmesdale have not been included. They accounted for a relatively small part of the Original Lands.
[c] One royal manor, that of Wye, had been granted to the Conqueror's new monastic foundation, Battle Abbey, by 1086.

PART THREE *The Expansion of Settlement*

outlines are not difficult to distinguish. Broadly speaking, Domesday gives a picture of landownership at two periods: the time immediately following the Norman Conquest, and the time of King Edward. For the purpose in hand it is the latter period that is the more important, but for an understanding of the pre-Conquest evidence it is necessary to examine that of the Domesday period first. The basic facts are summarized in table 8.

In considering these figures there are several preliminary qualifications that need to be borne in mind. First, the 'estates' or 'manors' represented in Domesday Book varied greatly in extent and wealth, and those on the Downs tended to be both smaller and poorer, sometimes much smaller and poorer, than those in the Original Lands.[102] Second, these contrasts of wealth were accentuated by the fact that extensive Wealden pastures were usually attached to estates in the latter areas, as we saw in Chapter 6, but very rarely to those on the Downs. Third, since the manorial estates of the Original Lands were essentially based on the old Jutish territories, a few of them, such as Milton Regis, still included substantial stretches of Downland of their own. Fourth, there are several places where Domesday under-represents the extent of ecclesiastical holdings, since subordinate estates are silently subsumed under the name of their paramount manor.[103] Finally, there are parts of Kent where the Domesday account seems suspiciously incomplete, and where unrecorded places which are known from other evidence to have existed are difficult to account for, since by no means all of them were subordinate settlements. The estates included in table 8 do not necessarily, therefore, represent the whole extent of the two regions under study.

Despite these problems of interpretation, the Domesday evidence is uniquely important in that it provides the earliest systematic survey of local landownership. When every allowance is made for its shortcomings, the contrast it reveals between the Original Lands and the Downland is altogether too striking to be ignored. While the figures in the table clearly cannot be adduced as a measure of relative wealth, they shed a dramatic light on the contrasting pattern of landholding as between one region and another. On the Foothills and in Holmesdale, it appears, more than four-fifths of the 61 estates recorded (82 per cent) were in the hands of the crown or the church, whereas less than one-fifth (18 per cent) were in the hands of 'private' individuals. Something like two-thirds of the 61, indeed, were in the hands of the church alone, and since these generally represented the richest and most extensive

7 The Downland economy

manors in the county, they give us some idea of the wealth of the early Kentish church, and of its massive role in the evolution of Kentish settlement. In turning to the structure of landownership on the Downs, by contrast, we find a very different picture. Here there were no recorded estates in the hands of the crown, and only 21, or 23 per cent of the total, in those of the church,[104] whereas 72, or not far short of four-fifths, were in 'private' possession. The most striking feature of the Downland, however, was the overwhelming dominance of Odo, Bishop of Bayeux; and since Odo's fief was a purely post-Conquest creation, without any historical unity, we must turn to the pre-Conquest figures for a real understanding of the area.

In reconstructing the pattern of landownership before the Conquest, it is not possible to make an exact comparison with that of the Domesday period. In the Original Lands no problem arises; the number of recorded estates is identical; but on the Downs there are several places where landowners in the time of King Edward are not named, and several where estates were split up into smaller units than in 1086, each held by different tenants. These problems are not sufficient to invalidate comparison altogether; but they necessitate a slightly different method of analysis, and they account for the fact that in table 9 there appear to be more Downland 'estates' in the time of King Edward than in 1086, though the actual area of land involved must have been somewhat smaller.

These figures present a number of points of interest. In the Original Lands, it seems clear, the dominance of church and crown at this time was even more striking than in 1086, and nearly 70 per cent of the area was in the hands of the church alone, whereas a mere 5 per cent was in 'private' possession. The most remarkable contrast, however, is to be found on the Downs. Here, in place of alien magnates like Odo of Bayeux and the de Montforts and de Crevequeurs, there was a multiplicity of relatively small and localized tenants who between them held more than 80 per cent of the 117 recorded estates. True, the situation is not quite so straightforward as at first sight appears. These estates varied greatly in scale, from whole parishes, as at Ash-by-Wrotham and West Wickham, down to mere fragments of a parish, as at Pising in East Langdon, which was itself split up amongst six separate individuals. Among the 65 recorded 'private' tenants, moreover, there were certainly some who held land elsewhere in the county, and a few who seem to have been relatively substantial. Yet the overwhelming majority of Downland owners, there can be no doubt,

PART THREE *The Expansion of Settlement*

Table 9. Landownership in Kent, TRE

	Estates in the Original Lands[a]	Estates on the Downs	Total
Church and crown estates			
Crown	10	1	11
Earl Godwin	4	1	5
Christ Church/Archbishop	33	6	39
Rochester Cathedral	2 }42	2 }20	4
St Augustine's Abbey	7	7	14
St Martin's Priory, Dover		5	5
Total	56 (92%)	22 (19%)	78

'Private' estates[b]	Original Lands[c]		Downs		Total	
	Tenants	Estates	Tenants[d]	Estates	Tenants	Estates
1 estate	3	3	41	41	44	44
2 estates	1	2	8	16	9	18
3 estates			3	9	3	9
4 estates			1	4	1	4
5 estates			2	10	2	10
6 estates			1	6	1	6
Unnamed owners			9	9	9	9
Total	4	5(8%)	65[e]	95(81%)	69	100
Grand total		61(100%)		117(100%)		178

[a] See table 8, notes a and b.
[b] i.e., held directly of the king.
[c] See table 8, notes a and b.
[d] Some tenants bearing the same name held widely scattered estates; in several cases these estates may in fact have belonged to different landowners bearing the same name.
[e] Assuming that the 9 unnamed owners represent 9 different individuals; this may not have been the case.

were relatively obscure local men, rarely possessing more than a couple of estates apiece, and in most cases only one, or merely part of one. Defective though the pre-Conquest evidence may be, in short, there can be no reasonable doubt that on the Downs there was a totally different structure of landownership in the time of King Edward from that of the Original Lands. In its remarkable fragmentation, and in the fact that it was so largely in lay hands, we see one of several historical signs that the Downland in general was not colonized under the auspices of the

7 The Downland economy

church or the crown direct, but by local landowners and peasants farming their own comparatively modest acres.[105] In many cases, perhaps, these men may have been ancestors of the obscure Saxon tenants recorded in Domesday Book, like Osward, Ailric, Edwin, Sired, and Sigar. Such was the old and deeply-rooted local world that was swept away to create Odo's vast, though temporary, inheritance. By 1086 two-thirds (63) of the 95 'private' Downland estates of King Edward's time had passed into the hands of the hated Norman bishop.

The evidence of Domesday provides the only means available for making a statistical comparison between the economy of the Downland and that of the Original Lands in the pre-Conquest period. The contrasts it brings to light relate to the very end of that period, it is true, and the historical processes that led up to them cannot now be charted in detail. Nevertheless, in a certain sense they were implicit in the basic circumstances of colonization, as has already been remarked. Our final task, therefore, is to identify these underlying circumstances, so far as possible, in the Downland area itself. There are five broad themes, or formative influences, that need to be distinguished. In discussing them we are venturing into a shadowy world, and a certain element of speculation and hypothesis is unavoidable if we are to draw the threads of the argument together.

In the first place, in the period before permanent colonization of the *wald* began, the Downs clearly formed a relatively poor and uninviting region. Yet just as in pre-industrial England a wooded or heathy district usually offered labourers a more comfortable living than a rich corn-growing country, so in the pre-Conquest period, as population expanded, the Downland doubtless offered a foothold to those in need of a living more readily than the Old Arable Lands in the hands of the church. Essentially, after all, it was an intercommonable countryside, and for that reason it was not so strictly parcelled out or minutely appropriated as the already densely settled lands of the Foothills and Holmesdale. Unrewarding though it might seem, and in most parts difficult to reclaim, there must have been a class of modest yet enterprising colonists to whom it appealed, and for whom its 300,000 wooded acres offered a means of establishing themselves on a more independent basis.

Second, as a consequence of its wooded, outlying character, the only way in which the Downland could be developed, in its early days, was as a pastoral region. In a primitive society livestock are more easily transported than crops, and for that reason if for no other the forest

PART THREE *The Expansion of Settlement*

outback of Kent, like that of other parts of England, tended to be devoted to pastoral purposes.[106] At first, and in places no doubt for centuries to come, this pastoral economy was essentially seasonal and migrant, and often based on transhumance from relatively distant communities.[107] As the herdsmen returned year by year to their forest lodges among the hills, however, something perhaps of that germ of individualism which is apt to develop in a region of scattered pasture-farms may have begun to undermine their dependence, and to weaken their links with the mother-communities of the Original Lands. At all events, their summer shielings began to develop into permanent farmsteads, and with the decline of communal control by the old estate-centres, their freedom was ultimately assured. By the early eleventh century they seem by and large to have already achieved it, and despite the landed upheaval of the Conquest, that freedom left a permanent mark upon medieval Downland society.

Third, in relation to both these matters, we must recall the development of boundary settlement. For if the *wald* as a whole was a land of herdsmen and pioneers, reclaiming their humble steads and shielings from the wilderness, those farms that came to be established in the outlying woodland swathes or 'marks' of so many Downland parishes represented only the final phase in a continuous process of reclamation which had already been under way for centuries. In other words, the society of the region as a whole developed essentially as a kind of 'boundary society', perpetually evolving on an irregular yet ever-advancing frontier. In this we can perhaps see a further sign of the origins of Downland freedom; for land on the outskirts of an estate is by its nature less closely controlled, less subject to vigilant scrutiny, than land near at hand. As in later centuries, the boundary settlements of the area thus necessarily encouraged the latent urge towards independence by the very fact that they afforded an opportunity for its development.

It is in this context that we need to take account of the tenurial structure of early Kentish society, and this is the fourth point to note. It seems to be generally agreed that there were three principal types of land in Kent: the lord's demesne, at the heart of the estate; the 'inland', which was tenant-land but which lay within the right of the lord and thus 'corresponded to the *terra villanorum* of the typical manor' of the Midlands; and the 'outland' or 'yokeland', which was 'the land of the Kentish peasantry *par excellence*, where the lord has no right of property, and tenure is by gavelkind, the ancient custom of Kent'.[108] It is with the outland or yokeland, where manorial services were much lighter than

7 The Downland economy

elsewhere,[109] that we are particularly concerned on the Downs. True, terms like 'outland' and 'inland' are technical or legal ones, referring to types of tenure and not to regions or *pays* as such. While there was a natural connexion between 'outland' and 'outlying land', moreover, there were also places in the Original Lands where these freer tenures obtained, no doubt because colonization had expanded first in the Original Lands before extending to the upland *wald*.[110] Nevertheless, the outland or yokeland was so profoundly characteristic of the Downs that in Hasted's time the manorial estates of the area were frequently known as 'yokes', while place-names in 'yoke' may still be found on the Downs today, and are particularly associated with parish boundaries.[111] The social significance of the yokeland is a point we shall return to in more detail in Chapter 11: here it is sufficient to point out that it clearly played a part in the development of Downland freedom.

Finally, the influence of gavelkind inheritance needs to be taken into consideration. Despite some rather positive assertions to the contrary,[112] the origin of partibility in Kent still remains mysterious. Was it common to pre-Conquest society in England as a whole? Was it introduced by the Jutes, as was once generally supposed? Was it a Romano-British custom? Was it part of the obscure Celtic legacy of pre-Roman *Cantium*? Or was it perhaps an evolutionary development, arising from localized and indigenous circumstances, as settlement advanced, and new pasturelands were taken in from the woods? These are questions that cannot at present be answered with certainty; yet although partibility was not formally recognized as the custom of Kent as a whole until after the Conquest, there can be no doubt of its antiquity. It was peculiarly characteristic of the outland or yokeland, moreover, which in many places was also specifically known as 'gavelland'.[113] As population increased, as a consequence, and as the need to provide for younger sons became more pressing, partibility became one of the dominant forces behind the expansion of Kentish settlement and the continuous evolution of new farmsteads. The curious local frequency of place-names in *boi(a)*, 'a boy, a young man, a servant', and the presence of names in *cild*, 'a child, a young man', may perhaps be consequences of it:[114] at Chilton in Alkham, for example, Chilton in Sittingbourne, Boyke in Elham ('boy + wick'), Bayford in Upchurch ('boy + worth'), Boyden Hill in Chislet ('boy + *tūn*'), Boyington Court in Swingfield, Boy Court in Ulcombe, Boyton Court in East Sutton, Bistock, or 'boy + stock', in Doddington, and so on. Such names are found only in the pastoral areas of the county, and they

179

PART THREE *The Expansion of Settlement*

may imply that the younger sons of the family were customarily employed as herdsmen while the eldest son retained control of the parental farm.[115]

Such perhaps were some of the circumstances behind the ultimate independence of the Downland economy, and the gradual evolution of the freedom of the wold. They imparted to that economy a certain toughness of character which in the long run proved peculiarly enduring. In one sense even the landed revolution of the Norman Conquest proved little more than an interlude in its inherent development. When Odo was disgraced, few of the Old English families of the area were restored to their inheritance; yet the structure of comparatively small estates was revived, and the striking contrast with the society of the Original Lands still remained. In the high medieval period, as a consequence, the Downs more than any other part of Kent became the great reservoir of the indigenous gentry of the county. Some of these gentry, like the Hardreses of Hardres and the Hodsolls of Hodsoll in Ash, remained rooted in their ancestral neighbourhood for seven or eight centuries.[116] Some, like the Oxindens of Oxinden in Nonington and the Honywoods of Honywood in Postling, migrated to other parts of the region as their fortunes rose.[117] Some, like the Filmers of *fugol + mere*, or 'bird pool', in Wichling, abandoned the humble forest lodges of their forebears altogether, and departed for grander houses like East Sutton Place.[118] Yet such changes as these, though often of profound importance individually, were no more than variations on a single theme. In contrast with Leicestershire, or the Fens, or Exmoor, in short, the Downland of Kent remained essentially an evolutionary region; it never became an area of over-mighty magnates, or great mansions, or parliamentary enclosure; fundamentally it was a land of unpretentious manor houses and lonely farmsteads, each growing up out of the ground it stood on, each constructed from its own landed resources, as successive generations adapted and added to the medieval core. In these thousands of isolated settlements of the region, and in the lacelike network of forest-lanes and coppice-woods in which so many of them lie embedded, we see a landscape that is still shaped, even in the twentieth century, by the circumstances of its original colonization, some 1300 years ago.

PART FOUR
THE ECCLESIASTICAL TESTIMONY

8

ECCLESIASTICAL DEVELOPMENT

1. THE CHURCH AND THE LANDSCAPE

It is probably true to say that the church has had a greater impact on the landscape and economy of Kent than any other human agency. Until recent generations its only rival in this respect has been the gentry community between the thirteenth or fourteenth century and the nineteenth. If the Roman colonization was the first major influence on local settlement, that of the church was undoubtedly the second, and to a remarkable extent it originally built upon Roman foundations. Most of the early minster churches were established in Romano-British communities, and Roman brickwork and parts of Roman structures are incorporated in perhaps more parish churches in Kent than in any other county. Little by little, as settlement itself extended into the *wald*, the influence of the church also extended, and eventually became more pervasive and more enduring than that of the Roman empire. That influence is still obvious even to a superficial eye in the 430 or so surviving medieval churches of the county, although these form little more than half the religious buildings – churches, chapels, monasteries, hospitals, friaries, colleges, chantries, and so on – that once existed. Despite the changes of the past century, moreover, the outlines of the ecclesiastical parishes of Kent are still embedded in those of its modern administrative divisions, and still largely based on those of a thousand years ago. The ecclesiastical evidence is thus of great importance for an understanding of the evolution of settlement.

The impact of the church on settlement is not of course a peculiarity of Kent. In varying degrees it has been felt in every part of England; but there are several reasons why in this area it has been unusually far-reaching. To begin with, the kingdom of Kent was the first in England to be converted to Roman Christianity, and its royal house was noted

PART FOUR *The Ecclesiastical Testimony*

not only for its devotion to the church, but for the number of its saints and the munificence of its grants to religious houses. Kent was the only county where two cathedrals were established, at Canterbury in 597 and Rochester in 601, and of these Canterbury has exercised a unique influence not only in England generally but in the development of its own diocese and county. It is some measure of that influence that there are more saints listed under Canterbury in *The Oxford Dictionary of Saints* (1978) than under any other ecclesiastical centre in England. Until the Reformation the county was further distinguished by the number of its monastic foundations, several of which were among the most ancient in England. Although most of these were both small and poor, St Augustine's, Rochester, Dover, Malling, Boxley, Faversham, and Leeds were all foundations of some standing, while the wealth and splendour of Christ Church were proverbial. Taken as a whole, therefore, the 40 or so abbeys and priories of Kent, the extent of their estates, and the hundreds of rectories and vicarages in their gift, bear striking testimony to that tradition of devotion for which the medieval county was noted. At the time of the Dissolution of the Monasteries, possibly something like two-fifths of the county had come into the hands of the church.[1]

The historic influence of the church has left its mark not only on the ecclesiastical and parochial structure of the county: it also gave rise to a remarkable number of Kentish place-names derived from the names of saints, churches, chapels, and wayside shrines or 'crouches'. In this connexion it is instructive to compare the Kentish evidence with that of a typical Midland county like Leicestershire. Apart from Misterton ('minster *tūn*), Buckminster ('Bucca's minster'), Wistow ('[St] Wistan's stow'), and three Kirbys or 'church villages', there are no Leicestershire parishes named after a church, a chapel, or a saint, and few names bearing any religious significance. In Kent, by contrast, there are more than 200 place-names of this kind, and at one time the number was at least twice that figure. In the Hoo peninsula, for example, most of the rural parishes originally bore no other name than that of their church, and were known as Hoo St Werburgh, St Mary's Hoo, Hoo Allhallows, High Halstow, St James-in-Grain, Hoo St Margaret's, and Lillechurch, though the last two of these have now disappeared.[2] In the Isle of Thanet the ancient parishes originated in much the same way and were called Minster-in-Thanet, St Peter-in-Thanet, St Lawrence-in-Thanet, St John's-in-Thanet, All Saints-in-Thanet, Woodchurch-in-Thanet, St Nicholas-at-Wade, and St Giles at

8   *Ecclesiastical development*

Sarre, most of which remain in use at the present day.³ Near Canterbury and in the Forest of Blean the same kind of local nomenclature was at one time to be found in the parish-names of St Stephen's, St Dunstan's, St Michael's, St Nicholas's, and St Cosmas and St Damian's, though the first two of these have now been absorbed into Canterbury. Elsewhere we find parishes bearing names like St Margaret-at-Cliffe, St Margaret-at-Helles, St Mary-in-the-Marsh, St Mary Cray, St Paul's Cray, St Martin's Pountney, and Minster-in-Sheppey, together with many whose names are derived from the word *cirice*, as at Eastchurch, Dymchurch, Newchurch, Dowde's Church, Upchurch, Ivychurch, and Cheriton.⁴ There are also some scores of medieval chapelries commemorated in names like Capel, Keppel, and Chapel, and in places like Blaise Wood, St Leonard's Tower, St Mary-at-the-Ness, St John's Jerusalem, St John's in Sevenoaks, and St John's in Swingfield. Finally, there is a substantial group of minor Kentish place-names derived from the Latin *crucis*, or 'crouch', as at Crouch in Selling, Horsnell's Crouch in Wrotham, Three Crutches in Frindsbury, and Pipsden Crouch, Skelcrouch, and St Margaret's Crouch in Hawkhurst.⁵ While it is not at present possible to construct a definitive list of these 'ecclesiastical' place-names of Kent as a whole, since we do not know how many have fallen into disuse, it is probably safe to say that at one time they numbered at least 400.

In the context of settlement history, these circumstances are of considerable significance. For the fact that such places originally bore no secular name, and in many cases have never acquired one, is a sign that they originated not as villages or hamlets but as churches, chapels, and wayside shrines. Their churches were not sited in established communities with names of their own, like the churches of Leicestershire, but as ecclesiastical centres of a nexus of scattered farms and dispersed hamlets, as in much of the West Country and Wales. In recent centuries places like St Lawrence-in-Thanet and St Peter-in-Thanet have come to be known as Ramsgate and Broadstairs; but originally these were merely the names of their outlying maritime hamlets. In much the same way a parish like St Cosmas-and-St Damian has gradually acquired its current name of Blean, or Cosmas-Blean, not from the name of a specific settlement, but from that of the surrounding forest; its neighbouring parishes of St Nicholas and St Michael acquired theirs of Harbledown from the name of *Herebeald's dūn* or 'hill', when the adjacent woods were grubbed up and assarted, probably in the twelfth century;⁶ St Mary Cray and St Paul's Cray

PART FOUR *The Ecclesiastical Testimony*

acquired theirs from their development as subdivisions of the old Cray river-territory; while Hoo St Werburgh, St Mary's Hoo, and St James-in-Grain acquired theirs from the regional name of the Hoo peninsula and its neighbouring Isle of Grain. In other words, none of these ecclesiastical names of Kent is strictly speaking a settlement-name or habitation-name in origin: in each ascertainable case the places themselves originally bore no other name than that of their church or chapel: and that for the simple reason that in an area of scattered settlement, whether in Kent, or Cornwall, or Wales, there was generally no central village where the church or chapel might be sited, or from which, as in Leicestershire, it might derive its name. In this respect places like Capel-le-Ferne and St Mary-in-the-Marsh in Kent are similar in topographical significance to those like Capel Curig in Wales or St Anthony-in-Roseland in Cornwall. What they point to is the role of the church in the colonization of the county, particularly in the reclamation of the *wald*, where the great majority of these places were situated.

It is in the light of these circumstances that the sequence of ecclesiastical foundation in Kent needs to be reconstructed. That process, which began with the coming of St Augustine, continued without a break for more than 600 years. By the thirteenth century or thereabouts, some 500 parishes had been formed, most of them with churches dating back to 1100 or beyond;[7] apart from an abortive attempt to divide the unwieldy territory of Wrotham in the Civil War period, no further parishes were created until the nineteenth century. Probably among the last to appear were Fairfield in Romney Marsh, Westenhanger near Hythe, and Capel-next-Tudeley near Tonbridge, whose churches were dedicated to St Thomas Becket and must have been built, or perhaps rebuilt, shortly after his martyrdom in 1170.[8] With the decline of population following the Black Death, and with the long-drawn-out depression of the later medieval economy, many Kentish churches entered on a period of decay, and by the seventeenth century probably fewer than 430 remained in regular use. The process of settlement recession lies outside the scope of this book, and in Kent it is a puzzling problem on which the evidence is contradictory and little research has yet been undertaken. Yet the fact that there were once many more parishes and churches than the 430 or so that have survived needs to be taken account of in reconstructing the early settlement history of the county. That so few were rebuilt, despite a certain revival of prosperity in the late fifteenth and sixteenth centuries, and despite the widespread rebuilding of chantries, chapels, church-towers, and

8 Ecclesiastical development

private houses at that time, bears witness to their marginal situation.[9] It is in Romney Marsh and the Downland that most of them are to be found, usually in rather remote places like Boardfield near Lenham, Monkston near Otterden, Dowde's Church near Meopham, Woodlands and Maplescombe near Wrotham, and Eastbridge, Orgarswick, Midley, Blackmanstone, and Hope All Saints in Romney Marsh.

The fact that the process of church formation in Kent extended over some 600 years, and spanned so lengthy a period of forest clearance and marshland reclamation, has left us with a wealth of evidence for reconstructing a relative chronology of church foundation. Since the churches of Kent usually originated in the wake of settlement, it also sheds a good deal of light on the course of colonization from parish to parish and *pays* to *pays*. There are many counties where medieval churches were more numerous than in Kent, both absolutely, as in Norfolk, Suffolk, Lincolnshire, Somerset, and Devon, and relatively speaking in counties like Leicestershire, Oxfordshire, Northamptonshire, Berkshire, and Rutland.[10] The comparative modesty of the ecclesiastical heritage of the county is one of several indications of its relatively modest ranking in terms of wealth in the early medieval period. Nevertheless, the evidence of ecclesiastical development is in several respects unusually abundant in Kent, and in some uniquely so. The survival of major early records like the *Domesday Monachorum of Christ Church* and the *Textus Roffensis* enables us to compile a more complete list of pre-Conquest churches than in most English counties, and in many cases to identify the original relationship between one parish church and another in the Old English period. In much of the county, moreover, the archaic structure of parochial organization survived largely intact into the early modern era, so that the sequence of minsters, mother-churches, daughter-churches, and chapelries can often be pieced together with unusual completeness.

In its broad outlines this ecclesiastical sequence did not greatly differ from that of other areas. In the legislation of Ethelred II and his Danish successors, English churches were classified under four main headings: 'head minsters' or cathedrals; 'ordinary minsters' or original mother-churches of a district; lesser parochial churches possessing graveyards; and 'field churches' built for recently established communities and not yet possessing the graveyard which entitled them to the burial fee called soul-scot.[11] Each of these categories may be distinguished in Kent, and one or two others in addition. First, there were the two cathedrals, or 'head minsters' of Ethelred's list. Second, there were the 'ordinary

PART FOUR *The Ecclesiastical Testimony*

minsters' or original mother-churches, which in Kent were often founded in the seventh century, and which were the ultimate ancestors of most other parish churches. Third, there were a number of churches, such as St Mary-in-Castro at Dover and St Martin's and St Pancras's outside Canterbury, which are known to date from the seventh century, though they did not become 'minsters' and do not seem to have given birth to subsidiary foundations. Fourth, there were many churches which were clearly 'mother-churches' in origin, each with its own daughters and dependent chapelries in later centuries, though they are nowhere specifically described as 'minsters', and in some cases are known to have once been dependent on other *monasteria*; these are described as 'secondary mother-churches' in this chapter. Fifth, and more numerous than all these groups together, there were the 'manorial' or originally semi-private churches built by thegns or noblemen on their 'bookland' estates, or in other words those that gradually developed into the lesser parochial churches of Ethelred's list. Finally, there were the 'forest' churches of the Weald, some of which may have originated in much the same way as the bookland churches, though their parishes were usually several times as extensive, and their status was in some respects dissimilar since they were often established by relatively distant minsters.

In addition to these major ecclesiastical sites in Kent, where full-scale parish churches eventually developed, there is also a substantial number of minor settlements where ecclesiastical development did not advance beyond the status of a chapel, a chantry, or a 'crouch'. Though relatively few of these chapels and chantries now survive in use, many may be tracked down in documents and on the ground, and since the great majority are associated with outlying farmsteads and remote woodland settlements, they provide further evidence of the continuing reclamation of the *wald* in the post-Conquest era. In many a Kentish manor house and hamlet, the urge to build a chapel of one's own, and to find a chaplain to serve one's family or neighbourhood, seems to have been well-nigh irresistible, so that by the time of the Reformation there were probably more than 300 chapels and chantries of this kind in the county as a whole. Of the crouches or crosses at one time so numerous in Kent,[12] not a single example seems to have survived the vicissitudes of the post-medieval centuries; but we should probably envisage them as wayside shrines of the kind still commonly met with in parts of Europe today.[13] In a sense they must have resembled the standing crosses erected at places where mass was offered before churches were

8 Ecclesiastical development

built, and many of the later parish churches of Kent probably originated in this way. The church of St James at Sheldwich, for example, dedicated as it is to a saint often associated with travellers, and oddly situated on its own parish boundary by the Faversham-Ashford road, must have originated as a wayside shrine. The chapels or churches of St John the Divine at Groombridge and St Nicholas and St John the Baptist at Sevenoaks were similarly sited by ancient droveways, and probably originated in the same way. No doubt the name of a settlement like Shrine Farm in Postling, by the prehistoric track leading from Lympne to Lyminge, marks a site of much the same kind, though in this case it did not develop into a church or chapel.[14]

This general *schema* of ecclesiastical development represents no more than an abstract picture, and it is important not to make it appear too systematic. The local realities of development were in practice complex, and many individual churches and chapels are difficult to classify. Since ecclesiastical foundation was an evolutionary process, moreover, its successive phases should not be thought of as rigidly distinct from one another, but as partially overlapping. On the Foothills of East Kent, for example, many 'bookland' churches are probably earlier in date than some of the secondary mother-churches in the western parts of the county. Nevertheless, as a guide to the evolution of settlement, it is important to keep the broad framework in mind. In the following sections, the distribution of each type of church and chapel, and its relationship to the evolution of settlement, will therefore be examined in detail. In the concluding section, the contrasting types of local community to which each kind of parish tended to give rise will be discussed.

2. MINSTERS AND PRIMARY MOTHER-CHURCHES

In reconstructing the sequence of church foundation in Kent there are a number of important early documentary sources that need to be taken into account. The oldest is King Wihtred's grant of privileges to the churches of Kent (696 x 716), which lists eight minsters in addition to the two cathedrals: Reculver, Dover, Folkestone, Lyminge, Minster-in-Sheppey, Minster-in-Thanet, Hoo St Werburgh, and an unidentified *Upminster*, which was most probably Monkton in Thanet (see map 11).[15] Wihtred's list is evidently not a complete one; it includes only one minster in the diocese of Rochester, that of Hoo, and it omits several of those in the diocese of Canterbury; but it is a uniquely interesting

PART FOUR *The Ecclesiastical Testimony*

MAP 11. *Minsters and mother-churches* (based on the Ordnance Survey map with the permission of The Controller of Her Majesty's Stationery Office; Crown Copyright reserved)

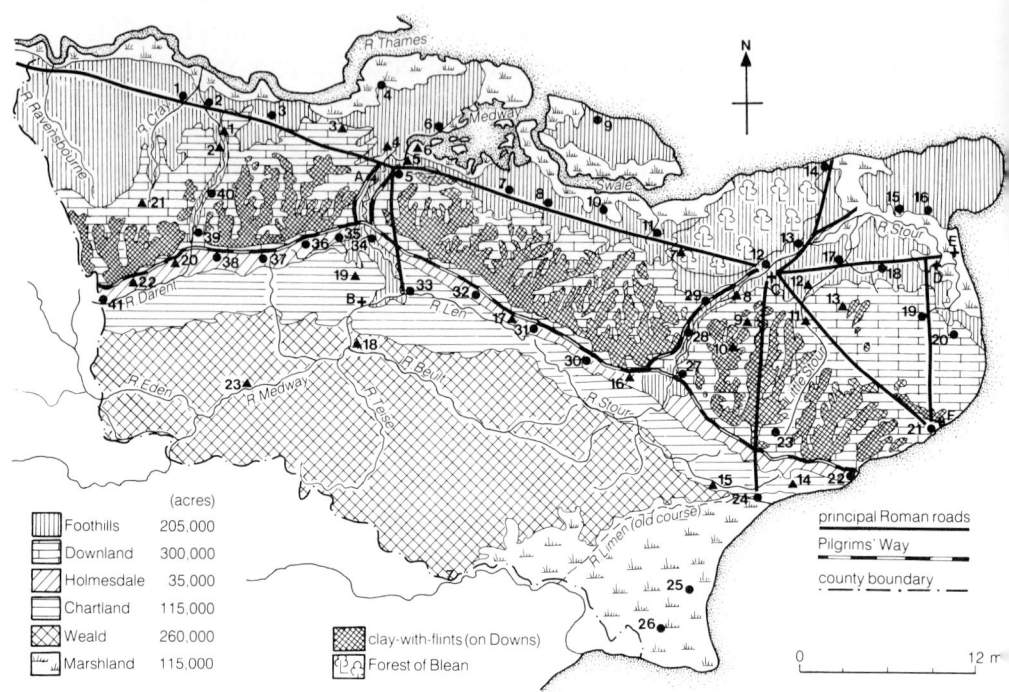

	(acres)
Foothills	205,000
Downland	300,000
Holmesdale	35,000
Chartland	115,000
Weald	260,000
Marshland	115,000

clay-with-flints (on Downs)
Forest of Blean

principal Roman roads
Pilgrims' Way
county boundary

0   12 m

● minsters and primary mother-churches

1 Crayford	21 Dover
2 Dartford	22 Folkestone
3 Northfleet	23 Lyminge
4 Cliffe-at-Hoo	24 Lympne
5 Rochester	25 Romney
6 Hoo St Werburgh	26 Lydd
7 Newington	27 Wye
8 Milton Regis	28 Godmersham
9 Minster-in-Sheppey	29 Chilham
10 Teynham	30 Charing
11 Faversham	31 Lenham
12 Canterbury	32 Hollingbourne
13 Sturry	33 Maidstone
14 Reculver	34 Aylesford
15 Monkton	35 Birling
16 Minster-in-Thanet	36 Trottiscliffe
17 Wickhambreaux	37 Wrotham
18 Wingham	38 Kemsing
19 Eastry	39 Shoreham
20 Northbourne	40 Eynsford
	41 Westerham

▲ secondary mother-churches

1 Darenth
2 Sutton-at-Hone
3 Shorne
4 Frindsbury
5 Chatham
6 Gillingham
7 Boughton-under-Blean
8 Chartham
9 Petham
10 Waltham
11 Bishopsbourne
12 Patrixbourne
13 Adisham
14 Saltwood
15 Aldington
16 Westwell
17 Harrietsham
18 Yalding
19 East Malling
20 Chevening
21 Orpington
22 Brasted
23 Tonbridge

+ other early churches mentioned in the text (select)

A Cuxton
B Teston
C Canterbury
  St Martin
  St Pancras
D Richborough
E Stonar
F Dover
  St Mary-in-Castro

188

8   *Ecclesiastical development*

document because of its early date. More difficult to interpret, but at the same time more revealing, is the ecclesiastical evidence of the *Domesday Monachorum of Christ Church*, relating to the diocese of Canterbury, and of the *Textus Roffensis*, relating to that of Rochester. Both these sources are roughly contemporaneous with Domesday Book, and are thought to incorporate evidence of pre-Conquest arrangements. Taken together, they show that there were many more churches in Kent at the time of the Conquest than are indicated in Domesday Book, and that most of the surviving parish churches were then already in existence, together with a number no longer extant. According to D. C. Douglas's calculation, the *Domesday Monachorum* alone records 212 churches, including several at places like Wolverton near Dover, Trimworth near Wye, and Ratling near Nonington, which have long since vanished and of which there is little other record.[16]

For tracing the course of ecclesiastical development, it is the well-known list of 'central' or 'head' churches in the *Domesday Monachorum*, with the numerous subsidiary churches attached to them, that forms the most important of these early records.[17] This list is divided into 12 sections, in one of which the name of the head church is omitted, and in one, that of Charing, the list of subordinate churches is incomplete, so that 11 head churches and 124 dependent ones are actually named: Dover St Martin, with 19 churches subordinate to it; Folkestone, with 10; Lympne, with 22; Lyminge, with 10; Milton Regis, with 10; Newington next Milton, with 7; Teynham, with 4; Wingham, with 6; Maidstone, with 17; Wye, with 8; Charing, with 1; and the unspecified minster, with 10.[18] The significance of this list, whose origins probably antedate the Conquest, has given rise to considerable debate; but in the main there is no reason to question D. C. Douglas's conclusion that it represents a list of early baptismal churches, or minsters, together with their daughter-foundations. In the present writer's view the idiosyncrasies of the list are a good deal more formidable than Professor Douglas seemed to suggest, however, and in this connexion there are three general points that ought to be made. First, it is not a complete list, either of the minsters or of the subsidiary churches of the diocese of Canterbury.[19] Second, despite Douglas's meticulous enquiry, a number of subsidiary churches cannot at present safely be identified, particularly where they are listed only by their dedications. Third, and most important, the list of minsters and subordinate churches can only be interpreted in the light of parochial topography and the ecclesiastical structure of subsequent centuries. These were not matters which

PART FOUR *The Ecclesiastical Testimony*

Douglas himself systematically investigated, and it does not seem to have occurred to him that the organization of the medieval church in Kent still incorporated the outlines of the old minster system. Nevertheless, despite the problems that beset its interpretation, the *Domesday Monachorum* is a profoundly important source for reconstructing the sequence of church foundation. In conjunction with Wihtred's list and other pre-Conquest records, it provides an essential starting-point from which to proceed to other lines of enquiry. In the following paragraphs we shall therefore first approach the problem with an examination of these early records. Then, in the light of what they tell us about the early Kentish minsters and the evolution of their dependent territories or 'minsterlands', an attempt will be made to identify the remaining mother-churches of the county.

Taken together, the pre-Conquest sources and the *Domesday Monachorum* record 21 Kentish *monasteria* or minsters: Rochester Cathedral and Hoo St Werburgh in the diocese of Rochester; and Canterbury Cathedral, St Augustine's Abbey, Dover St Martin, Folkestone St Mary, Maidstone St Mary,[20] Charing, Herne, Lyminge, Lympne, Milton Regis, Minster-in-Sheppey, Minster-in-Thanet, Newington next Milton, Reculver, Teynham, *Upminster*, Wingham, Wye, and the unnamed minster in the diocese of Canterbury. Of these 21 churches, Herne was never a minster in the sense of a mother-church, and for present purposes must be excluded;[21] the unnamed minster cannot definitely be identified and must also be excluded; and *Upminster* no longer exists as a place-name, though as already remarked it should probably be identified with Monkton in Thanet. This leaves us with a total of two cathedrals, St Augustine's own church at Canterbury, and 15 'ordinary minsters' recorded in early documents. The fact that only one of the 15 was in the diocese of Rochester is partly due to poorer documentation, and partly due to the relative sparsity of early settlement in the western parts of the county. It also seems possible, however, that originally Rochester Cathedral acted as the mother-church of its very small diocese as a whole in a way which was not paralleled in the diocese of Canterbury. Otherwise, all 15 'ordinary minsters' are marked by the same five or six basic characteristics. It is this circumstance that lends them special significance in studying the evolution of the early Kentish church, since it enables us to identify the remaining mother-churches of the county. What, then, are these identifying characteristics?

To begin with, all 15 recorded minsters were associated with ancient

8 *Ecclesiastical development*

royal estates, or estates granted by the crown to the church at a very early period, and not with the private 'bookland' estates of Kentish thegns or noblemen. In every ascertainable case, moreover, the church itself seems to have been sited in the estate-centre or the *villa regalis* of the territory in question; and with few exceptions the core or heartland of these territories remained in the hands of the church or the crown, as a major manorial estate, throughout the medieval period. Milton Regis, for example, was the site of a Jutish royal palace and the centre of a very extensive manorial territory, which remained in the king's hands until the seventeenth century. Wye is described as a *villa regalis* in a charter of 762 and formed the *caput* of another great royal estate, later granted by William the Conqueror to Battle Abbey in 1067.[22] Charing was given to Christ Church at so early a date that no record of the grant has survived, though it is known to have been restored to the cathedral in 799 after it had been temporarily wrested from it by King Offa. Lyminge formed the centre of a royal estate reputedly granted by King Eadbald to his sister St Ethelburga in 633 to enable her to found a minster. Reculver was granted by King Egbert to a priest named Bassa in 669 in order to establish a minster in the *villa regia* itself, and regranted to Christ Church three centuries later.[23] Very much the same pattern is to be found elsewhere in the county: at Dover, Folkestone, Maidstone, Lympne, Teynham, Wingham, Newington, Hoo St Werburgh, Minster-in-Sheppey, and Minster-in-Thanet.[24]

Then, all 15 recorded minsters are known from other evidence, as well as from the *Domesday Monachorum*, to have given birth to a number of daughter-churches, and in many cases to have exerted a certain authority over these dependent churches long after they had acquired parishes of their own in the medieval period. Charing, for example, gave birth to Pluckley, Little Chart, and the lost parish of Pevington, as well as to the solitary church listed under its authority at Egerton in the *Domesday Monachorum*. Maidstone still retained authority over the parishes of Detling and Loose in the nineteenth century, and also over the detached chapelry of Loddington, which between them represented the last remnants of its great minsterland of 17 parishes as recorded in the *Domesday Monachorum*.[25] Reculver is described in thirteenth-century documents as the mother-church of Herne, Hoath, St Nicholas-at-Wade, and All Saints-in-Thanet, and was still exacting certain carefully defined dues from these churches several centuries after they acquired parochial status in 1296.[26] In the Isle of Thanet, St Peter's (Broadstairs), St Lawrence's (Ramsgate), and St John's (Margate)

PART FOUR *The Ecclesiastical Testimony*

also acquired parishes of their own in the thirteenth century, yet still remained dependent chapelries of Minster at the time of the Dissolution of the Monasteries.[27] Very much the same conditions obtained in the remaining minsterlands: at Teynham and Wingham, for example, at Lyminge, Hoo St Werburgh, and Lympne.

In the third place, all 15 recorded minsters still retained unusually extensive parishes of their own after their daughter-parishes had been carved out of them. In the county as a whole, the 500 medieval parishes averaged a little over 2,000 acres in extent. As we should expect, they varied widely in size in different parts of Kent, from a mere 202 acres at Chillenden beyond Canterbury to more than 15,000 acres at Tonbridge, towards the western end of the Weald. More important than such extreme contrasts as these, however, is the average variation as between different *pays* and different types of parish. For this purpose they may be divided into three broad categories: those of motherchurches and minsters, those of their dependent or 'bookland' churches, and those of 'forest' churches in the Weald. These are only rough and ready categories; there are further significant variations both within each group and between the eastern, central, and western parts of the county; but for the topic in hand the threefold division will suffice. It was in the Weald, as in other late-settled forest regions, like parts of Essex and the Forest of Arden, that parishes tended to be largest, and the 52 Wealden parishes of Kent averaged almost 4,500 acres apiece. In the older-settled parts of the county, the minsterparishes came very close to those of the Weald in extent, and in the case of those under review averaged 4,340 acres.[28] It was the 300 or so subsequent or 'bookland' parishes that tended to be the smallest, and this was a circumstance that was directly connected with their bookland origins. Though in a few exceptional cases, such as Elham and Cudham, they extended to six thousand or so acres, their average size was no more than 1,570 acres, or roughly one-third that of the minsterparishes from which they had originated. These contrasts, it should be added, were not a regional peculiarity of the area, but were to be found in many parts of England. In Kent they were especially striking, however, and in conjunction with other lines of evidence they facilitate the identification of a number of additional minsters. We shall return to them, therefore, in the following section, and in connexion with the ecclesiastical topography of the county in Chapter 10.

Fourthly, all the 15 recorded minsters were established in those seminal settlements described in Chapter 5, where the evidence for

8   *Ecclesiastical development*

Romano-Jutish continuity is especially apparent. The point needs no labouring in connexion with St Augustine's earliest churches, at Canterbury and Rochester; yet it is scarcely less evident in many of the remaining places. At Dover, for example, the minster was sited in a Roman town, and Roman buildings have been found beneath both St Martin's and St Mary's, while St Mary-in-Castro adjoins the Roman *pharos* and stands within an Iron Age hill-fort.[29] At both Lympne and Reculver, the minster was sited in one of the Roman forts of the Saxon shore, and in both places there is also evidence of very early Jutish settlement.[30] At Milton Regis there was a Roman posting-station and the church is situated next to a Roman house – perhaps also within a Roman enclosure – while there is further evidence of very early Jutish occupation. At Maidstone there was a substantial Roman settlement, and Roman coin evidence has been discovered beneath the original site of St Mary's minster. At Lyminge there is a Roman building beneath the church and an early Jutish cemetery nearby; and at Wingham, Newington, Hoo St Werburgh, Minster-in-Thanet, and Minster-in-Sheppey there is also evidence of Roman settlement.[31] Only at Wye, Charing, and Teynham is there no clear proof as yet of pre-Jutish occupation in the immediate vicinity of the church: and even there Romano-British or Iron Age remains have come to light elsewhere in the parish. It seems clear, then, that the Kentish minsters were as a rule deliberately established in former Romano-British communities. Since most if not all of them date back to the seventh century, and since all were planted in Jutish estate-centres that by then were already of some antiquity, they tend to reinforce the arguments for Romano-Jutish continuity.

Finally, all these recorded minsters of Kent tend to be associated with a similar spectrum of topographical characteristics. This is a complex subject, and one which is of fundamental importance in reconstructing their dependent territories, so that we shall return to it in more detail in Chapters 10 and 11; but the salient points may be briefly summarized here. First, they are for the most part prominently sited on river banks or by major springheads, or in one or two cases in dominating defensive positions, as at Lympne and Minster-in-Sheppey. Second, their place-names either incorporate the word 'minster' itself or else tend to be markedly primitive in character, in some cases deriving from a Celtic root, as at Dover, Reculver, and Lympne, and in others from significant early English elements, as at Lyminge (*gē*, 'district' or *regio*) and Wye (*wīg*, 'heathen temple'). Third, when the

193

PART FOUR *The Ecclesiastical Testimony*

boundary of the original minsterland is reconstructed, it is often found to describe a continuous line or ring around the whole territory, and to delimit a more or less coherent group of parishes focused on the mother-church. Fourth, the dedication pattern of these mother-churches is clearly a distinctive one, most of them being associated with St Mary, St Martin, the Holy Trinity, or St Peter and St Paul, or with local saints like St Mildred, St Eanswythe, and St Ethelburga.[32] Fifth, in many cases Roman building materials are incorporated in the church structure, sometimes on a substantial scale as at Reculver. In this connexion Reculver is additionally instructive in view of the early cross that formerly stood within the church itself, in front of the high altar. The remains of this cross are now preserved in the crypt of Canterbury Cathedral, and perhaps suggest that such celebrated crosses as that at Bewcastle in Cumberland were at one time not so much a regional peculiarity of the Border counties as is sometimes supposed.[33]

With these characteristics in mind, it is possible to identify by analogy most of the remaining primary mother-churches of Kent. They may be divided into two broad categories. The first group comprises 15 churches whose status may be regarded as virtually certain: Shoreham, Wrotham, Northfleet, Aylesford, Crayford, and Dartford in the diocese of Rochester; Faversham, Eastry, Sturry, Lydd, Northbourne, and Wickhambreaux in the diocese of Canterbury; and two additional churches in the neighbourhood of Canterbury itself, whose identity is not certain, though they are known to have given birth to Nackington, Hardres, and Stelling to the south of the city and the Blean Forest parishes to the west.[34] The second group comprises 12 further foundations, whose status as mother-churches is undoubted, but which at one time may have been dependent on other churches, though the evidence is not conclusive. These comprise Trottiscliffe, Westerham, Cliffe-at-Hoo, Kemsing, Birling, and Eynsford in the diocese of Rochester; and Romney, Monkton, Chilham, Godmersham, Lenham, and Hollingbourne in that of Canterbury (see map 11).[35]

Though not all these 26 additional mother-churches display the full range of distinguishing characteristics, and the differences between the two groups should not be forgotten, they bear a strong family resemblance and are best discussed together. Like the recorded minsters, all 26 were situated in the Original Lands, and almost all in seminal settlements with distinct evidence of pre-Jutish occupation. In all cases the minsterland seems to have been based on an early royal or ecclesiastical estate, and in most the mother-church was sited in the

8 Ecclesiastical development

caput or *villa regalis* of the estate. Where it was not, as at Shoreham, it was nevertheless closely connected with the administrative *caput*, which in that case was situated in the adjacent parish of Otford (see map 13). All 26 churches, moreover, can be shown to have given birth to subsidiary parishes and chapelries of their own, and in many cases they still exerted authority over their dependent churches in later centuries. All of them except Trottiscliffe also had unusually extensive parishes, averaging more than 4,000 acres apiece, or roughly the same size as those of the recorded minsters discussed above.[36] Topographically, as we should expect from the diversity of their local environment, there was rather more variation between them; but in this respect too they displayed a marked similarity. So far as their origins are concerned, it seems unlikely that they all date from the same very early period as the recorded minsters; but there can be no real doubt that mother-churches like Faversham, Eastry, Aylesford, Crayford, Northfleet, Sturry, and Lydd are of great antiquity, quite possibly dating from the first or second generation of Augustinian Christianity.

This account of the primary mother-churches of Kent leaves a number of important problems in the original ecclesiastical development of the county unresolved. As already remarked, there are some very ancient churches which do not seem to have been minsters themselves, yet which cannot readily be fitted into other minsterlands: Richborough and Stonar near Sandwich, for example; St Martin's and St Pancras near Canterbury; and St Mary-in-Castro on the cliffs above Dover. Between Yalding and Rochester there is a group of early churches on the Medway whose origins are equally difficult to identify: Teston and East Barming above Maidstone, for instance, and Cuxton and Burham between Maidstone and Rochester. In each of these places the church is associated with a Romano-British settlement and, like other early baptismal churches, sited on the river bank; yet in most respects there is little further sign of 'minster' status.[37] Nevertheless, while enigmas and eccentricities remain, the general bearing of the early ecclesiastical evidence on the question of settlement is plain enough. When St Augustine landed in 597, he established his first three churches in the Roman towns of Canterbury and Rochester. Others followed quickly in old Roman centres like Dover, Reculver, and Lympne; in native Romano-British settlements like Faversham, Maidstone, and Milton Regis; and in early Jutish communities with some kind of pre-Jutish history, such as Lyminge, Chilham, Wingham, Eastry, Sturry, Folkestone, and Wye. Altogether, including the two

PART FOUR *The Ecclesiastical Testimony*

cathedrals and St Augustine's Abbey, some 29 or 30 churches of this kind may be identified in the diocese of Canterbury, and a further 14 in the diocese of Rochester. Virtually all of these were situated on the Foothills or in Holmesdale, and almost all in Jutish estate-centres or *villae regales*. There were none in the Weald, none on the Downs or the Chart, and none except Lydd and Romney in the Marshland. The absence of early mother-churches from these areas is one of several indications that, when St Augustine landed, they had not yet been widely colonized by the Jutes, although in places no doubt they were already being exploited as summer pasturelands.

The foundation of these 43 or 44 mother-churches firmly set the pattern in Kent for the future development of the church. Ultimately, most of the remaining churches of the county were descended from them, and in numerous cases they retained some token of authority over their daughter-foundations for many centuries to come. The fact that they were generally established in places that were already focal points of *regiones* or estates not only underlines the contemporary status of these places themselves, moreover, but emphasizes the original impetus behind church foundation. At this initial stage, that impetus stemmed from the royal house itself in alliance with the ecclesiastical leaders. Since the old *regiones* or estates were either retained in the king's hands, as at Milton Regis, or granted out to the new minsters themselves, as at Reculver, Lyminge, and Minster-in-Thanet, it was almost inevitable that they should also come to form the basis of the new minsterlands. Ecclesiastically, as well as agriculturally and administratively, the centres of these territories were thus indeed seminal places.

3. SECONDARY AND 'BOOKLAND' CHURCHES

The secondary mother-churches of Kent that followed these primitive foundations are often more difficult to identify, and are not always easy to differentiate from the minsters themselves. In a few cases those discussed in this section should perhaps be included in that category; but they lacked several of the major distinguishing marks, and their dependent territories were substantially smaller than those of the original minsters. That they were not simply 'manorial' churches, on the other hand, is generally evident from the unusual size of their parishes,[38] from their local topography, and from their rights over manorial churches in later centuries. So far as the period of foundation

8   *Ecclesiastical development*

is concerned, there seems to have been a good deal of variation in different parts of the county, according to local circumstances. In heavily settled areas some of them may have been established by the early eighth century, but in newly colonized places like Tonbridge probably not until the ninth or tenth, or in other words later than some of the early bookland churches elsewhere in the county.

For these reasons it is difficult to compile a definitive list of secondary mother-churches; but it is important to recognize their distinctive status and as far as possible to identify them. Altogether, 23 definite examples have been traced, though in all probability the real number is somewhat greater. These 23 fall into two groups. The first comprises 13 churches which are known to have given birth to subsidiary foundations and are not known to have been dependent on other minsters, though they are very unlikely to have been minsters themselves. These include Brasted, Chevening, Chatham, Gillingham, and Shorne in the diocese of Rochester; and Chartham, Petham, Waltham, Adisham, Aldington, Saltwood, Harrietsham, and Westwell in the diocese of Canterbury (see map 11). The second group comprises 10 churches which certainly once formed part of another minsterland, yet which eventually became independent and gave birth to subsidiary churches and chapels of their own. These include Patrixbourne, Bishopsbourne, and Boughton-under-Blean in the diocese of Canterbury; and Frindsbury, Orpington, Darenth, East Malling, Sutton-at-Hone, Yalding, and Tonbridge in that of Rochester. Of these, Darenth and Sutton-at-Hone had originated as daughter-churches of Dartford, Boughton-under-Blean of Faversham, Orpington of Crayford, Frindsbury probably of Rochester, Malling of Aylesford, and the two Bourne parishes of Wickhambreaux.

Taken as a whole, these 23 secondary mother-churches point to a significant development in the early settlement history of Kent. Eleven of them, like the minsters, are situated in the Original Lands, and in several cases in seminal communities like Westwell that closely resemble those of the early *monasteria*. The remaining 12 are not situated in places of this kind, but in areas of subsequent colonization, or on the borderland between the old lands and the new. As such, they bear witness to the tentative movement of settlement away from the Original Lands, and the beginnings of permanent colonization in the *wald*. Boughton, Patrixbourne, Frindsbury, and Shorne, for example, lie partly on the Foothills and partly on the Downs; Aldington, Yalding, and Saltwood on the borders of the Stone Hills or Chartland; Petham,

PART FOUR *The Ecclesiastical Testimony*

Waltham, Bishopsbourne, and Orpington on the Downs themselves; and Tonbridge, which may have been the last of the 12 to be established, on an important river-crossing in the Weald.

As has been remarked, the dependent territories of these secondary churches were in general substantially smaller than those of the minsters, and in most cases they gave birth to many fewer subsidiary foundations. Orpington seems to have been unusual in the number of subordinate churches it gave rise to: at Knockholt and St Mary Cray, probably also at Hayes and Downe, and perhaps at Cudham.[39] Elsewhere such circumstances would generally suggest that the church in question was perhaps a primary mother-church; but since Orpington had originated in the outlying *wald* of the Cray river-estate, it was probably still dependent on the minster of St Paulinus at Crayford when it was first recorded, as *Cray Ewelme* (*cræges æuuelme* or 'river-spring'), in 798 (see map 8).[40] More typical of the secondary churches than Orpington were those like Chevening, Waltham, Gillingham, and Sutton-at-Hone, with only two or three dependent churches and chapels. Chevening, for example, seems to have given birth to only two daughters, at Sundridge on the Chartland and at Chiddingstone in the Weald, both of which later became independent parishes. Sutton-at-Hone likewise gave birth to two churches, at Wilmington on its northern boundary, and at West Kingsdown on the wooded crest of the Downs, five or six miles to the south. Gillingham eventually established four subordinate chapelries in its outlying pastures, at Lidsing, Twydal, Grange, and St James-in-Grain, though in this case only St James became fully parochial and only Lidsing acquired its own tithing.[41] Similarly, in the remote Downland country beyond Wye, Waltham established four subordinate chapels of its own, at Elmsted, Wadenhall, Ashenfield, and Deane, of which only Elmsted graduated to parochial status. Very much the same pattern of limited development is found at most of the remaining places; at Harrietsham, Saltwood, Aldington, Petham, and Chartham in the diocese of Canterbury, and at Frindsbury, Darenth, Yalding, Shorne, and East Malling in that of Rochester, none of which seem to have given birth to more than two or three subsidiary foundations.

It was the 'manorial' or 'bookland' churches of Kent, founded in the outlying territories of the minsters and mother-churches, that formed the most numerous group, and that still account for most of the surviving medieval churches of the county.[42] Originally almost all the churches of the Downland and the Chartland were of this kind,

8   *Ecclesiastical development*

together with most of those in the subsidiary parishes of the Foothills and the Marsh, and many whose parishes straddle the boundary between one region and another. Not all 'manorial' churches were founded on the private bookland of substantial thegns and noblemen; many seem to have been established by comparatively minor landowners; and a number were set up on royal or monastic estates, as names like Kingsdown and Monkston in Otterden indicate. Yet in a sense it was their individual, 'private', or 'proprietary' status that was their hallmark, just as royal status had been the hallmark of the original minsters. In their foundation, in fact, what we are really witnessing is the gradual break-up of the old river-estates, with the conversion of their outlying *wald* and marshland, little by little, into permanent farms, and the establishment of settled farmsteads or 'manor houses' in place of seasonal shielings. It was never more than a small minority of the thousands of outlying farmsteads that acquired churches of this kind; yet eventually it was a very large number, many more than have survived as parish churches until today, and by the thirteenth century at least 300. As we shall see in the following section, moreover, many 'bookland' settlements that did not acquire parish churches of their own nevertheless, at a later date, acquired chapels or chantries.

It was in the early-colonized *wald* or upland forests that the bookland churches of Kent were most numerous. All along the Downs they are to be found, as a consequence, nearly 200 of them in all, amongst the woods and combes of that great arc of chalkland countryside lying between the Surrey border and the Channel (see map 12). Or take the wooded belt of the Quarry Hills between Maidstone and Ashford, where by the tenth or eleventh century the mother-churches of Holmesdale had carved out some 20 new parishes and chapelries in their forest-pastures on the Chart: Loose, Otham, Linton, Loddington, Bearsted, and Boughton Monchelsea in the minsterland of Maidstone; Leeds, Langley, Broomfield, Sutton Valence, East Sutton, and Chart Sutton in that of Hollingbourne; Egerton, Pevington, Pluckley, and Little Chart in that of Charing; Ulcombe and Boughton Malherbe in the outlying lands of Harrietsham and Lenham; and Hothfield and perhaps Great Chart in those of Westwell.[43] Although there were often important differences of detail between churches of this kind, particularly in their period of origin, the essential point to grasp is the

MAP 12 (*over*). *Ecclesiastical development in Mid-Kent* (based on the Ordnance Survey map with the permission of The Controller of Her Majesty's Stationery Office; Crown Copyright reserved)

PART FOUR *The Ecclesiastical Testimony*

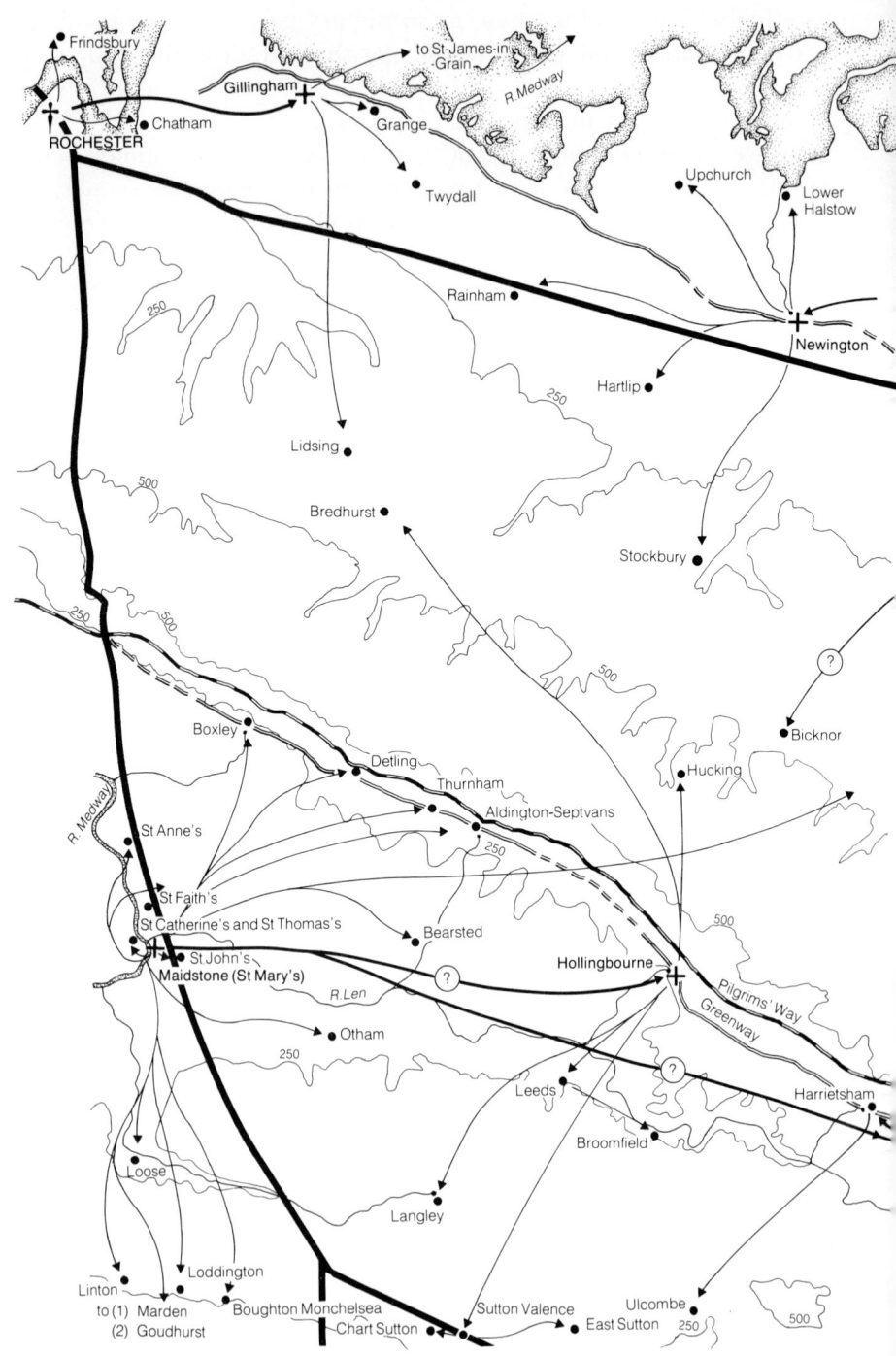

8 *Ecclesiastical development*

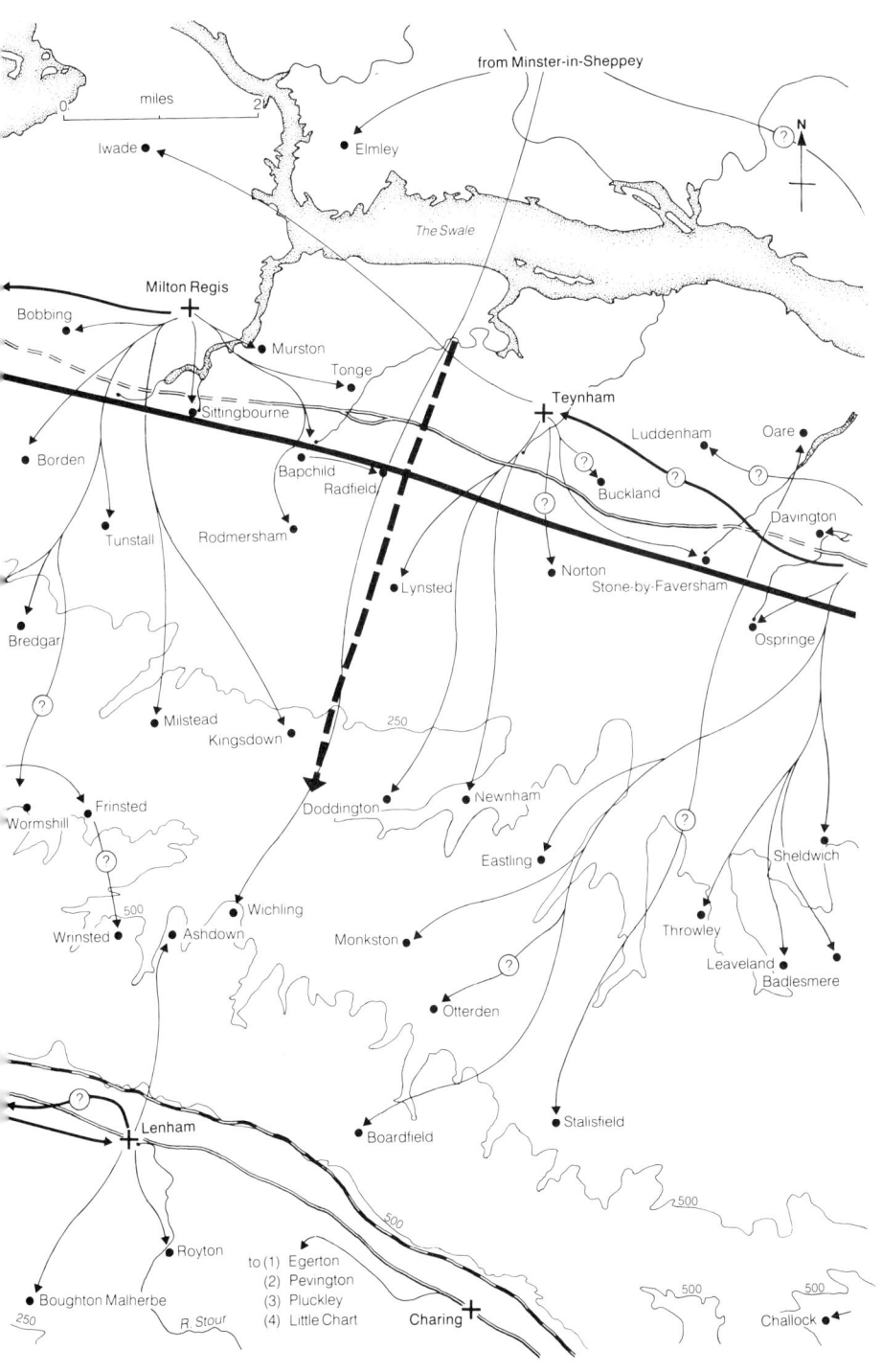

PART FOUR *The Ecclesiastical Testimony*

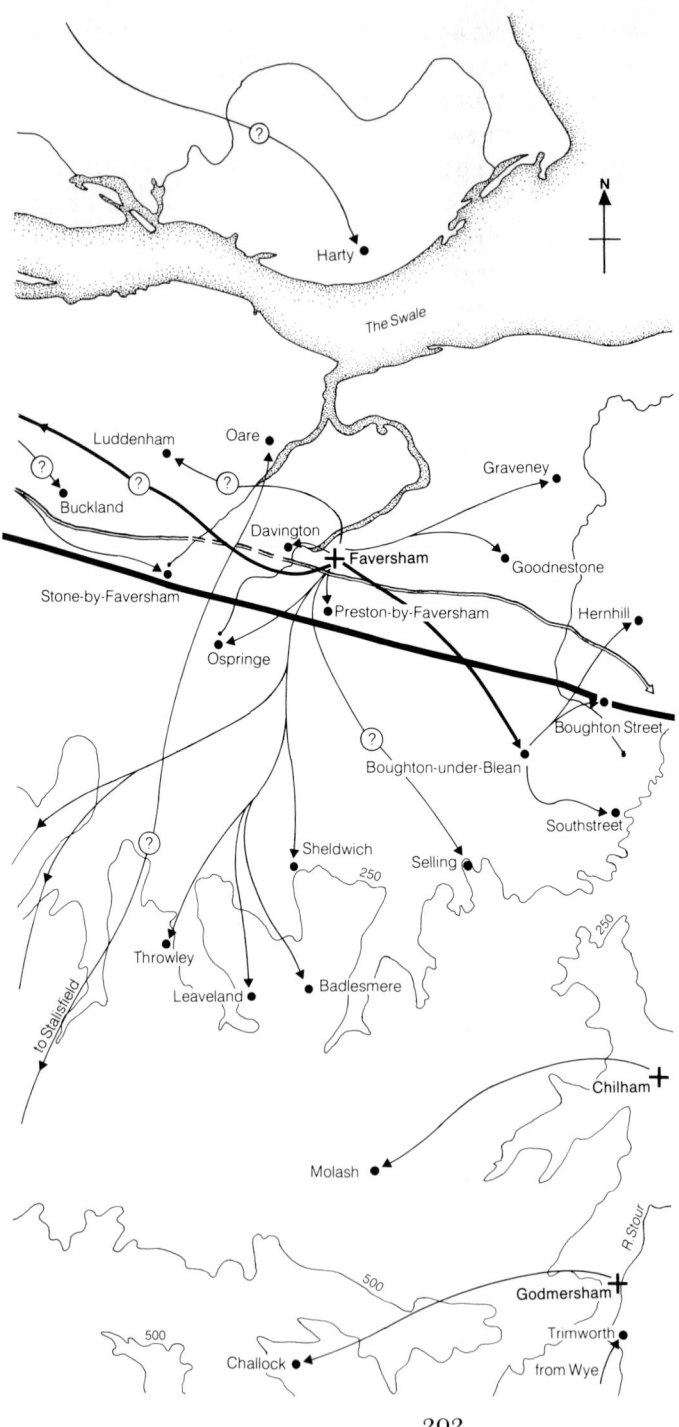

8 Ecclesiastical development

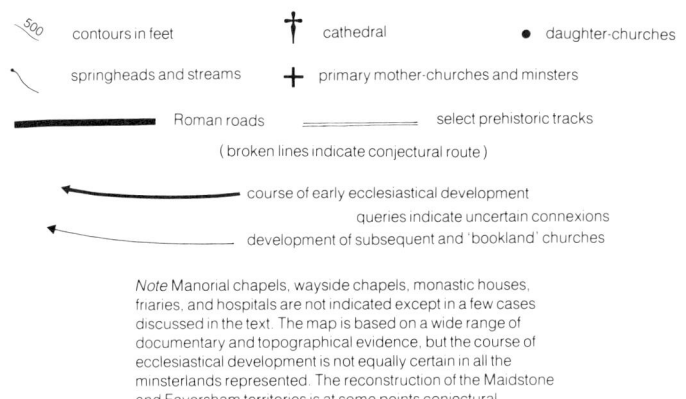

Note Manorial chapels, wayside chapels, monastic houses, friaries, and hospitals are not indicated except in a few cases discussed in the text. The map is based on a wide range of documentary and topographical evidence, but the course of ecclesiastical development is not equally certain in all the minsterlands represented. The reconstruction of the Maidstone and Faversham territories is at some points conjectural.

pronounced family likeness that marked them off as a group from the minsters and mother-churches of the Original Lands. One of the most striking points in that resemblance is the fact that their parishes, as already remarked, were on average only one-third as large as those of the minsters, rarely exceeding 2,000 acres in extent, and in many cases covering less than 1,000.

It was these bookland churches that also gave rise to most of the Kentish parishes specifically named after churches or saints. Names like St Margaret-at-Cliffe, St Nicholas-at-Wade, St Mary's Hoo, and St Cosmas-and-St Damian-in-the-Blean almost invariably relate to places of this kind, and not to mother-churches or minsters. Names like Dymchurch, *Blacemannescirce*, *Ordgarescirce*, and *Ælsiescirce* in the diocese of Canterbury, or Lillechurch, Dowde's Church, *Ordmærescirce*, and *Deremannescirce* in that of Rochester, allude to the names of early owners or founders, and indicate their proprietary interest in the original church. Both *Ælsiescirce* and *Blacemannescirce*, for instance, may have come into existence about the time of Edward the Confessor, when according to Domesday Book they were held by Ælsi and Blaceman.[44] In some cases the suffix *cirice* or 'church' was subsequently altered or abandoned, occasionally as early as the eleventh century, so that such places are often now known by names like Blackmanstone and Orgarswick. At Dymchurch and other places, however, the original name still survives to indicate the early proprietor. In other words, these churches were not founded in old-established places with historic names of their own, like the minsters of the Original Lands, but in the scattered settlements and newly established farmsteads characteristic

PART FOUR *The Ecclesiastical Testimony*

of pastoral colonization. Where they occur we thus see the local evolution of the church going hand in hand with the local evolution of settlement, and with the reclamation of the *wald* or the marsh.

It is also for such reasons as these that the manorial churches of Kent are so often found standing alone, attended merely by their manor house or 'court lodge'. Such isolated churches and lodges still survive in great numbers, especially on the Downs and the Chart: at Badlesmere, Stalisfield, Challock, Hucking, and Boughton Aluph in the diocese of Canterbury, for example: at Ridley, Nursted, Lullingstone, Luddesdown, and Offham in that of Rochester: their very names have a kind of homely poetry about them. Sometimes the original estate has subsequently been divided into a number of separate farms, each with its own lodge and forstal, as at Egerton and Luddesdown. Sometimes the original settlement has expanded to become a small village, with groups of later cottages and other buildings around the forstal or green, as at Eastling and Milsted. Sometimes the court lodge has developed into a mansion with a park, as at Lullingstone Castle and Otterden Place. Occasionally it has disappeared altogether, and left the church standing quite alone, as at Wichling and Crundale. And once, but once only in Kent, at Mereworth, the church itself was moved and rebuilt outside the park, in the early eighteenth century. Whatever the subsequent history of these places may be, however, their origins were everywhere identical, and in many cases the pattern has survived unchanged until the present day. Where it has been altered, what we now see is not a shrunken village, as it would be in the Midlands, but a later accretion around the original elemental core. As we move back in time, we find these accretions gradually dissolving away and leaving the primitive unit, the manor house and its attendant chapel, standing alone. It is this circumstance that makes places like Lullingstone, in its lovely Downland valley, or Otterden on its wooded ridge, so intensely historic. Despite all the changes of later centuries, despite the rebuilding of the medieval manor house and the enrichment of the family church with armorial tombs, the basic Jutish association that has shaped their history is still there unaltered, a thousand years old.

With the establishment of the last of these manorial churches in the twelfth or early thirteenth century, and the gradual definition of their territories, the period of parish formation in Kent virtually came to an end. Not all of them had by that date become fully independent; for many if not most still owed some kind of fealty to their mother-church or minster, and many did not acquire a completely separate life until the Victorian era. Nevertheless, except in parts of the Weald, and in a few wooded or marshy spots elsewhere, the parochial structure we know today seems to have been almost complete by the thirteenth century. Even in the Weald, which was apparently still thinly settled at that time, many parish churches are recorded in the *Textus Roffensis* or the *Domesday Monachorum* of c.1100, although probably most of them were then recent foundations. In wooded or heathy districts, it is true, the practice of intercommoning at times precluded precise lines of demarcation between them, and in some areas intercommoning survived until after the end of the Middle Ages.[45] More than 70 of the 500 medieval parish churches of the county subsequently disappeared, moreover, leaving their parishes to be split up among their surviving neighbours. Nevertheless, in a general way, the historic parish boundaries of Kent must also have been broadly marked out by the twelfth or thirteenth century, and in many places before, if only because the tithe system necessitated some kind of subdivision.[46] At many points they went back far beyond the Norman Conquest, and at places like Bexley they were identical with the boundaries of Anglo-Saxon estates.[47]

4. CHAPEL AND CHANTRY

No systematic survey of the post-Conquest chapels and chantries of Kent has ever been undertaken, and their history raises many problems that cannot at present be answered. In some respects they carried a stage further the tradition of the bookland church; but since relatively few of them graduated to full parochial status, and not all originated as manorial chapels, they need to be investigated in their own right. In many parishes their bearing on the evolution of medieval settlement is significant.

Though some scores of these chapels still survive, either wholly or in ruins, few have remained in active use, and no very reliable estimate can be given of their original numbers. A search through 95 parishes has yielded a total of 151, however, and there can be no doubt that at one time they were more numerous than is commonly realized. The ever-vigilant Hasted recorded 115 of these 151; yet there were many that he failed to discover, and that are known only through local place-names, surviving remains, or casual documentary allusions. In the neighbourhood of Sevenoaks, for example, he does not mention the medieval chapels at Knole and Ightham Mote; the chapel at St Clere in

PART FOUR *The Ecclesiastical Testimony*

Ightham, which was founded or re-founded in Charles I's reign; the chapel at Cory Yokes in Knockholt recorded in a perambulation of 1463; or the medieval chapel at Bradbourne, which was reconsecrated in 1614 and mentioned in a baptismal record as late as 1645. Elsewhere, minor place-names like Capel in Horsmonden, Capel in Petham, Keppel in Chatham, Capel Farm in Warehorne, Capel Hill in Eastchurch, Chapel Wood in Hartley, Chapel House in Ospringe, Chapel Bottom in St John's-in-Thanet, Chapel Valley in Gillingham, Chapel Farm in Newchurch, Chantry Farm in Headcorn, and Dane Chantry in Petham also commemorate the sites of former chapels and chantries.[48] Altogether, there may well have been more than 300 places of this kind in Kent on the eve of the Black Death.

Their origins were very varied. Some were erected at roadsides, especially along the Canterbury road, like those of the Holy Trinity at Boughton Street and St Nicholas at Ospringe, where mass was offered for the safety and good success of passengers. Some were erected at isolated spots along the coast for the benefit of fishermen and seafarers, like those of St Mary at Dungeness, St Rumwold and St Botolph at Folkestone, Our Lady of Pity at Broadstairs, and St Nicholas at Newington-next-Hythe. Some were founded, or perhaps refounded, as preceptories, like those of St John's at Swingfield Minnis and St John's Jerusalem at Sutton-at-Hone. Some were built as chapels to monastic granges, like those of St Augustine's Abbey at Salmestone and Durlock in Thanet.[49] Some were associated with holy wells, like St Edith's at Kemsing, St Anne's at Maidstone, St Blaise's at Bromley, and the springhead chapel at Bapchild. Some marked sites of particular local sanctity, like the oratory at Ebbsfleet where St Mildred was supposed to have landed from France and left her footprint in the rock. Some originated as hermitages, like St James's Chapel on the cliffs at Reculver and that of Leland's 'industrious man' at Richborough.[50] A considerable number were founded or refounded in connexion with medieval hospitals, like St Nicholas's in Harbledown, St James's in Tonge, St Peter's in Maidstone, St John the Baptist's in Sevenoaks, the Maisons Dieu in Dover and Ospringe, and St Bartholomew's in Sandwich, Chatham, Hythe, and Buckland-by-Dover.[51] By far the largest number, however, perhaps as many as two-thirds in all, originated as manorial chapels, very much as the manorial churches had originated before them. In many cases, therefore, they indicate a further stage in that gradual, individual colonization of the outlying *wald* or wood-pasture which had begun five or six centuries earlier.

8   *Ecclesiastical development*

Many of them were remotely situated as a consequence, towards the edge of the parish, sometimes on the boundary itself, as at Cory Yokes near Knockholt Pound or St Lawrence of Longsole near Aylesford.[52] Of the three manorial chapels in Petham, on the Downs south of Canterbury, Swarling lay a mile and a half to the north of the church, Capel a mile and a half to the west, and Dane Chantry a mile and a half to the south: all of them in the forested outskirts of the parish, and Capel still remarkably isolated among its pheasant-haunted woods. In the next parish of Waltham, or 'forest *hām*', the chapels at Ashenfield, Wadenhall, and Dean were nearly two miles from the church, and that at Elmsted more than three. In the 11,000 acre parish of Wrotham, Stansted was two miles from the parish church, Comp nearly three miles, and Plaxtol and Old Soar more than four miles. In a number of cases the dedications of these buildings also emphasize their woodland origins, as at St Leonard's in Malling and St Blaise's in Mereworth Woods, where the patron saint was one whose name was often associated with forest settlements (see map 13).

The origins of these chapels were thus very varied; but there were three general characteristics in the economy of the county that tended to encourage their development and that need to be taken account of in the context of colonization. Probably the most important factor was the scattered nature of local settlement and the fact that so many farmsteads lay remote from the parish church. In seeking to establish a new chapel or to extend the rights of an old one, these circumstances were frequently adduced by local people and manorial lords. In 1303, for example, Sir John Malmeyns of Malmaynes Hall in Stoke at Hoo petitioned the abbot of Boxley 'that as he was, on account of his house being situated at such a distance from the parish church, often prevented from attending divine service there, he might be enabled to build an oratory, for himself and his family, on his own estate, and might have a priest to celebrate divine services in it.' His petition was granted, provided that no prejudice accrued to the church of Stoke or to Boxley Abbey, the monastic impropriator.[53] A century earlier the inhabitants of Betburgh or Bid Bridge, a Wealden hamlet of Leigh, claimed that they were 'much incommoded by the length and badness of the way to Leigh, and the inundation that frequently happened', and petitioned for a priest to celebrate in their chapel on Sundays, festivals, 'and such other days as they used to go to the church of Leigh'. They were not in fact much more than a mile from the church, but in wintertime that might be a formidable distance on the Wealden

PART FOUR *The Ecclesiastical Testimony*

MAP 13. *Evolution of the minsterlands: Shoreham, Wrotham, and Aylesford* (based on the Ordnance Survey map with the permission of The Controller of Her Majesty's Stationery Office; Crown Copyright reserved)

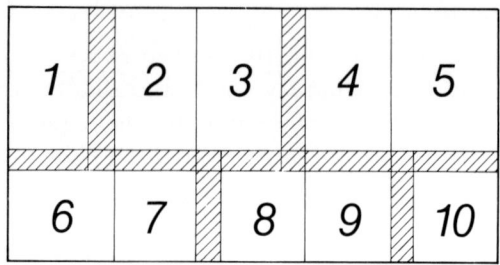

Note The chart to the left indicates the make-up of map 13 over the subsequent pages.

▬▬▬	minsterland boundaries
— — —	parish boundaries
✠ (circled)	minster churches
✠	other mother-churches
⊕	daughter-churches with parochial rights
+	chapels-of-ease (or of similar status) without parochial rights
⊕ (small)	manorial and other comparable chapels
+ (small)	crouches and crosses (queries indicate uncertain status)
◇	British church site (pre-Augustinian)
✕	abbeys, friaries
□	commandery
☆	holy wells (recorded examples only are shown)
—·—►	course of ecclesiastical sequence: primary phase
—··—►	course of ecclesiastical sequence: subsequent and secondary phases
—(?)—	indicates an element of uncertainty in ecclesiastical sequence
- - - -►	hypothetical but unsubstantiated ecclesiastical connexion
⌇600⌇	contours in feet (the 200′ contour is omitted)
～►～	springheads, streams and rivers
▬▬▬▬	select prehistoric tracks
—·—·—	droveways mentioned in text
··—··—	other likely droveways
··········	other forest lanes and tracks

} broken lines indicate conjectural routes

to Preston ⊕	related churches or chapels off the map
CHEVENING	parish names
Cory Yokes	names of chapels, crouches, crosses, and minor settlements
St Botolph	dedications
SEAL CHART	names of Chartland woods, heaths etc. (select)

0 — miles — 2

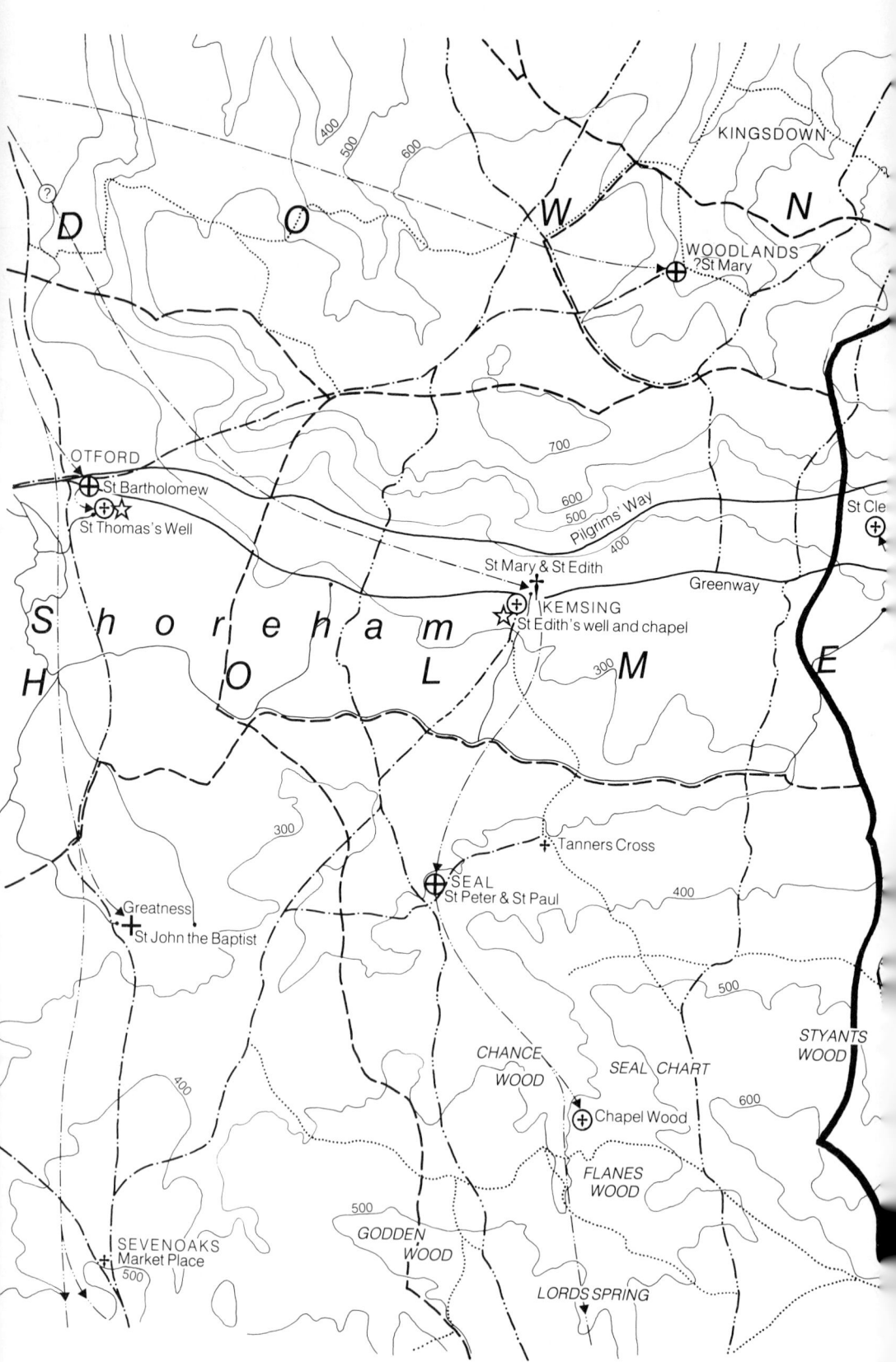

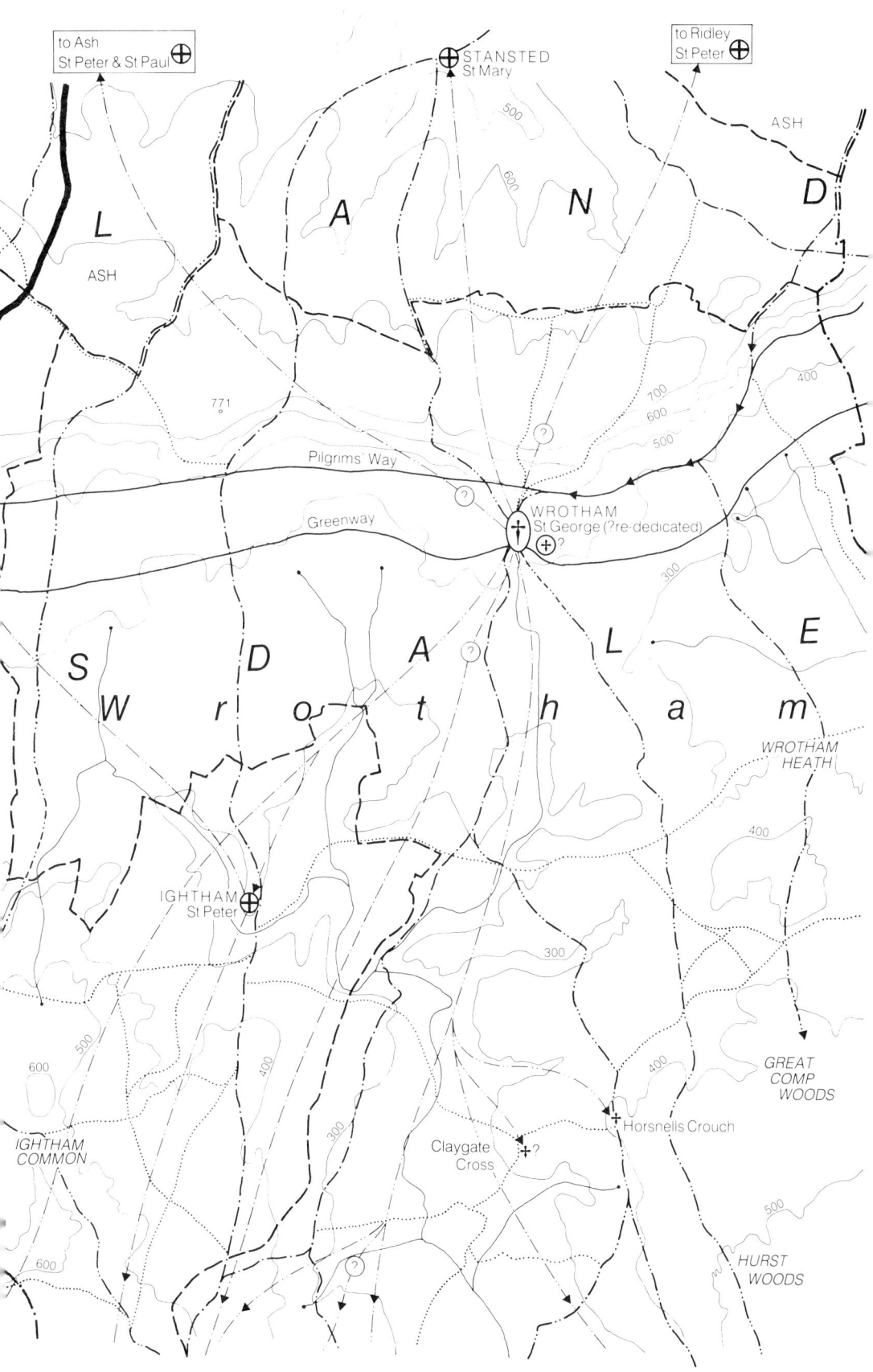

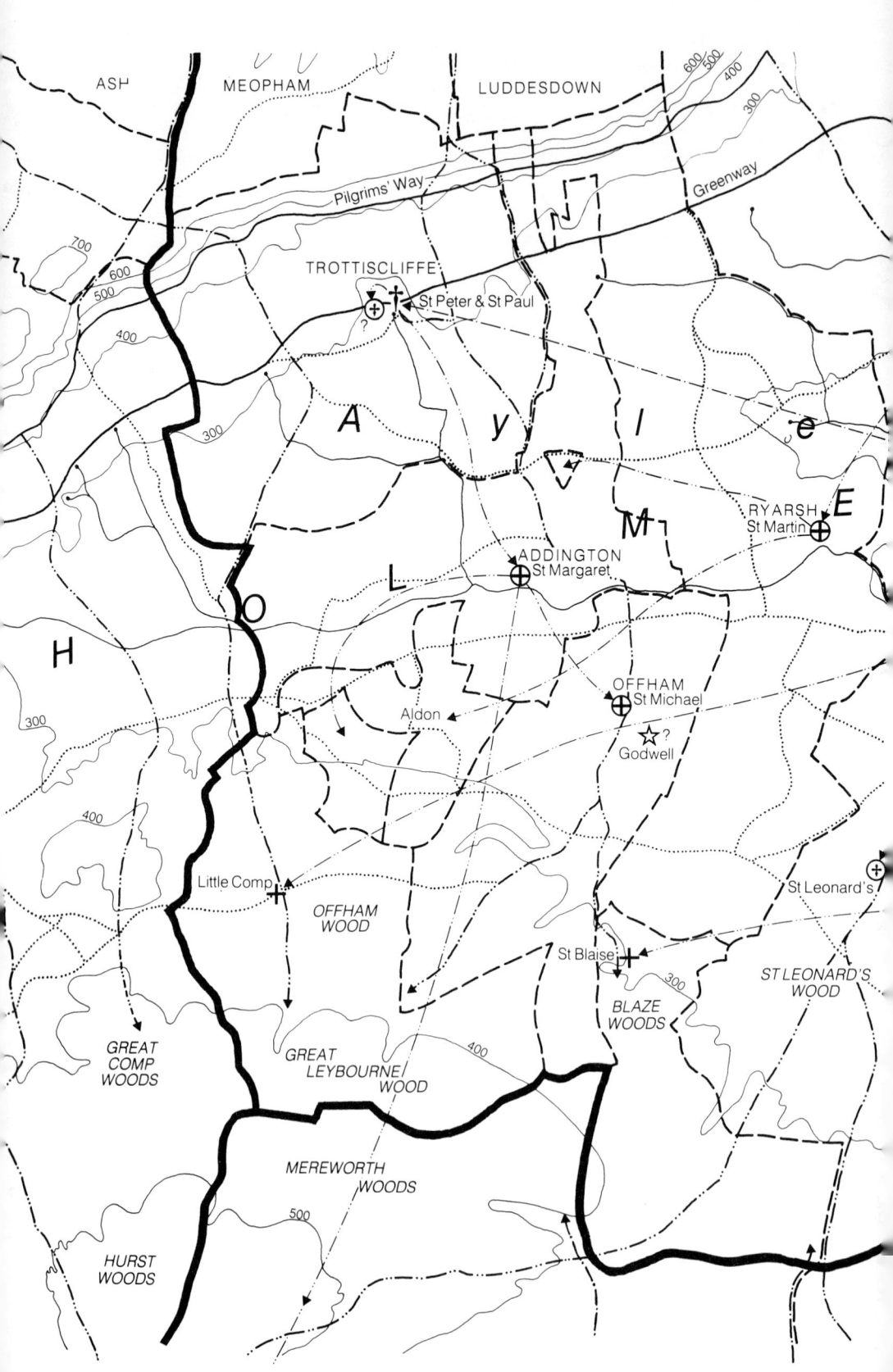

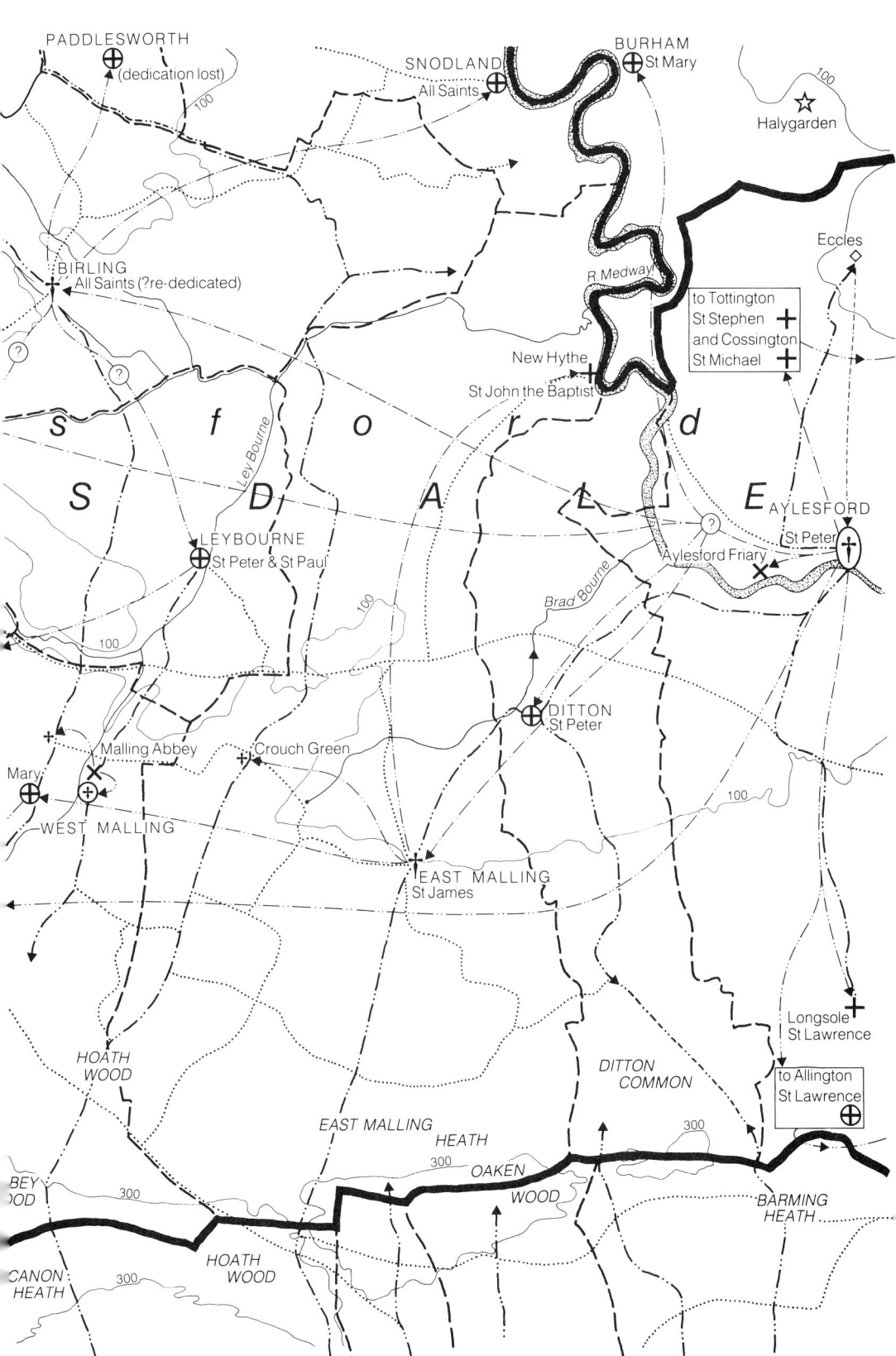

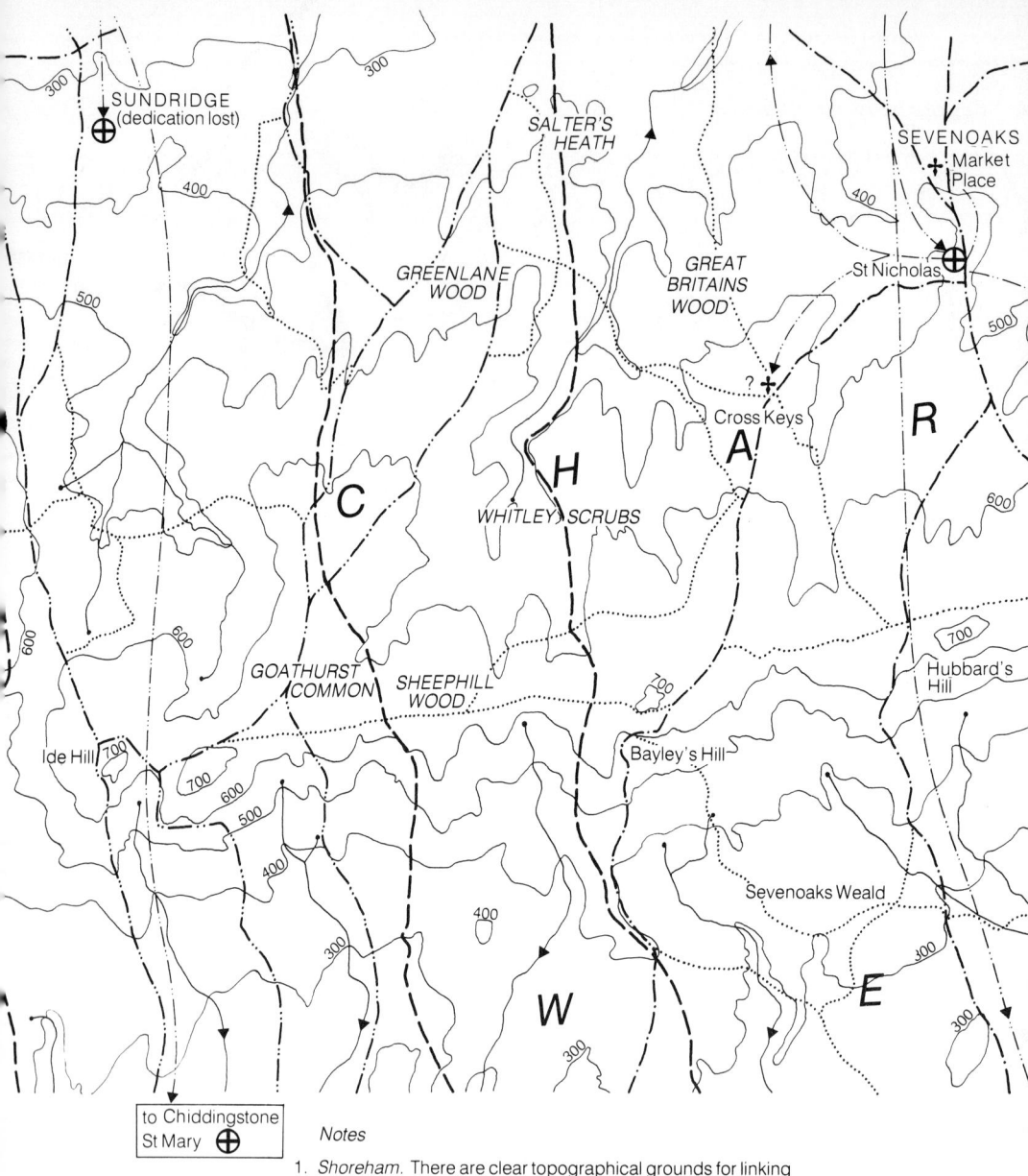

Notes

1. *Shoreham.* There are clear topographical grounds for linking Kemsing with Shoreham, though no documentary proof survives. Chevening may rather have been associated with Westerham, but on balance the link with Shoreham is more likely.

2. *Wrotham.* (i) Hasted records Shipbourne as a chapelry of Tonbridge; but Tonbridge itself may have originated as a daughter-church of Wrotham, and there are other grounds for linking Shipbourne with Wrotham originally.

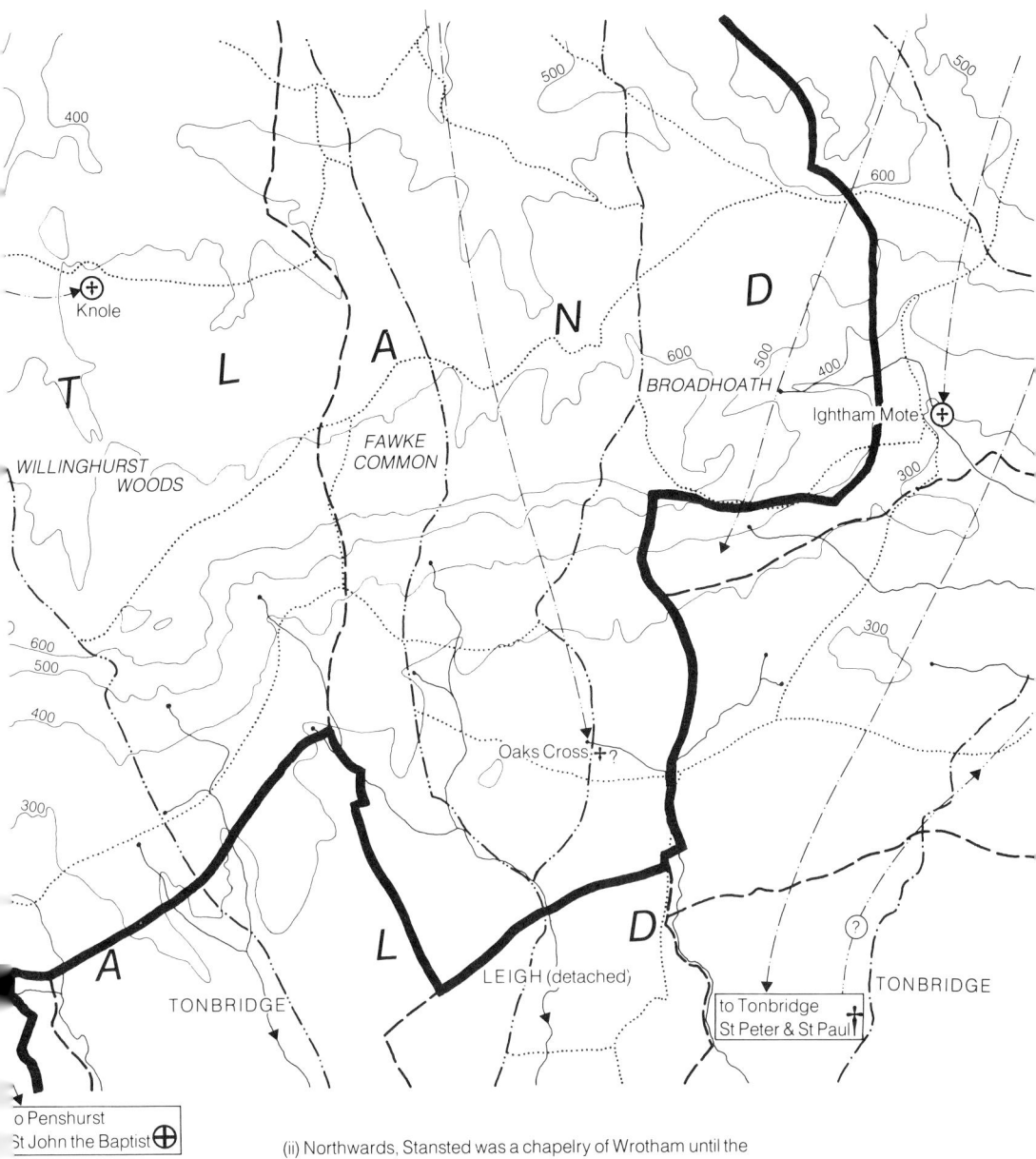

(ii) Northwards, Stansted was a chapelry of Wrotham until the nineteenth century. The boundary topography of the area, and the curious way that the U-shaped parish of Ash surrounds Stansted on all sides except the south, strongly suggest that Ash and its daughter-church of Ridley also originated from Wrotham, though there is no documentary proof of their connexion. West of the Darent valley, the parish of Cudham provides a close parallel with Ash, almost surrounding that of Downe except on its northern side. Both these localities probably represent Downland 'minnises' of the kind described in Chapter 11.

(iii) The dedication of Wrotham to St George is unlikely to be the original one for a minster. The fact that its daughter-churches of Ightham and Ridley were dedicated to St Peter, and those of Tonbridge and Ash to St Peter with St Paul, hints that Wrotham may have originally been associated with St Peter and St Paul (like the neighbouring mother churches of Shoreham and Trottiscliffe) or with St Peter alone (as at Aylesford). Dedications to St Peter, with or without St Paul, were particularly popular in the diocese of Rochester.

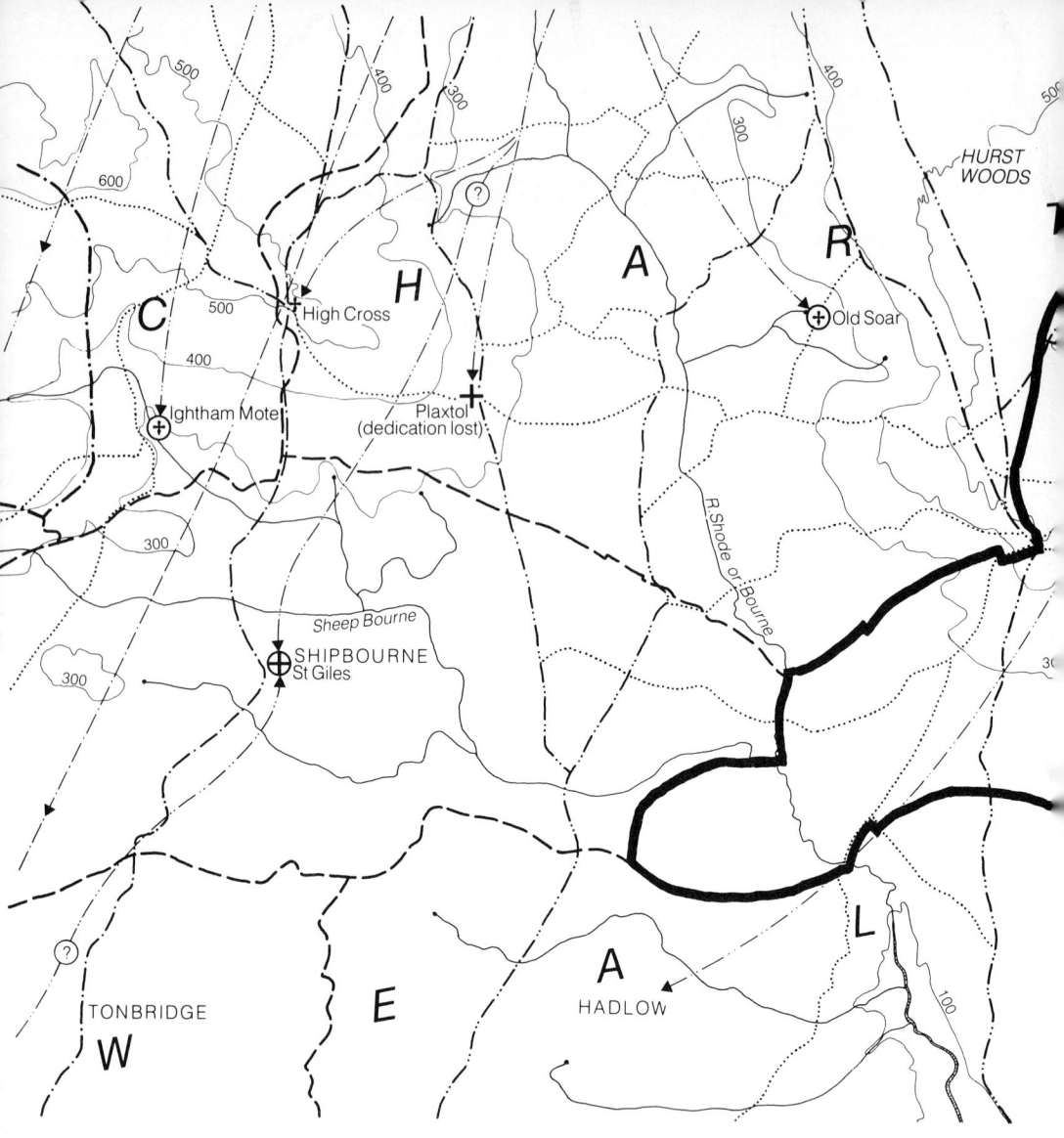

3. *Aylesford.* Documentary evidence for the development of Aylesford is more sketchy than for Wrotham or Shoreham; but when examined in the light of the tithe maps, it plainly suggests the broad reconstruction outlined here, though some important steps in the ecclesiastical development of the minsterland remain unsubstantiated. The fact that the detached chapelry of St Blaise remained a dependent hamlet of Aylesford at the time of the Tithe Survey, while Little Comp (with Great Leybourne Wood) still pertained to Leybourne, and Aldon to Ryarsh, indicates that the area as a whole has originated from Aylesford, and that in this case development moved predominantly from east to west rather than from north to south, as at Shoreham and Wrotham.

What lends this reconstruction interest is the further association of Aylesford with the British church-site at Eccles, and the fact that all the nine surviving megaliths of Kent are to be found in its minsterland, near Aylesford itself in the east, and near Trottiscliffe and Addington in the west. It is possible, therefore, that the Aylesford territory represents a far more ancient religious unit than that of the Augustinian minster of St Peter.

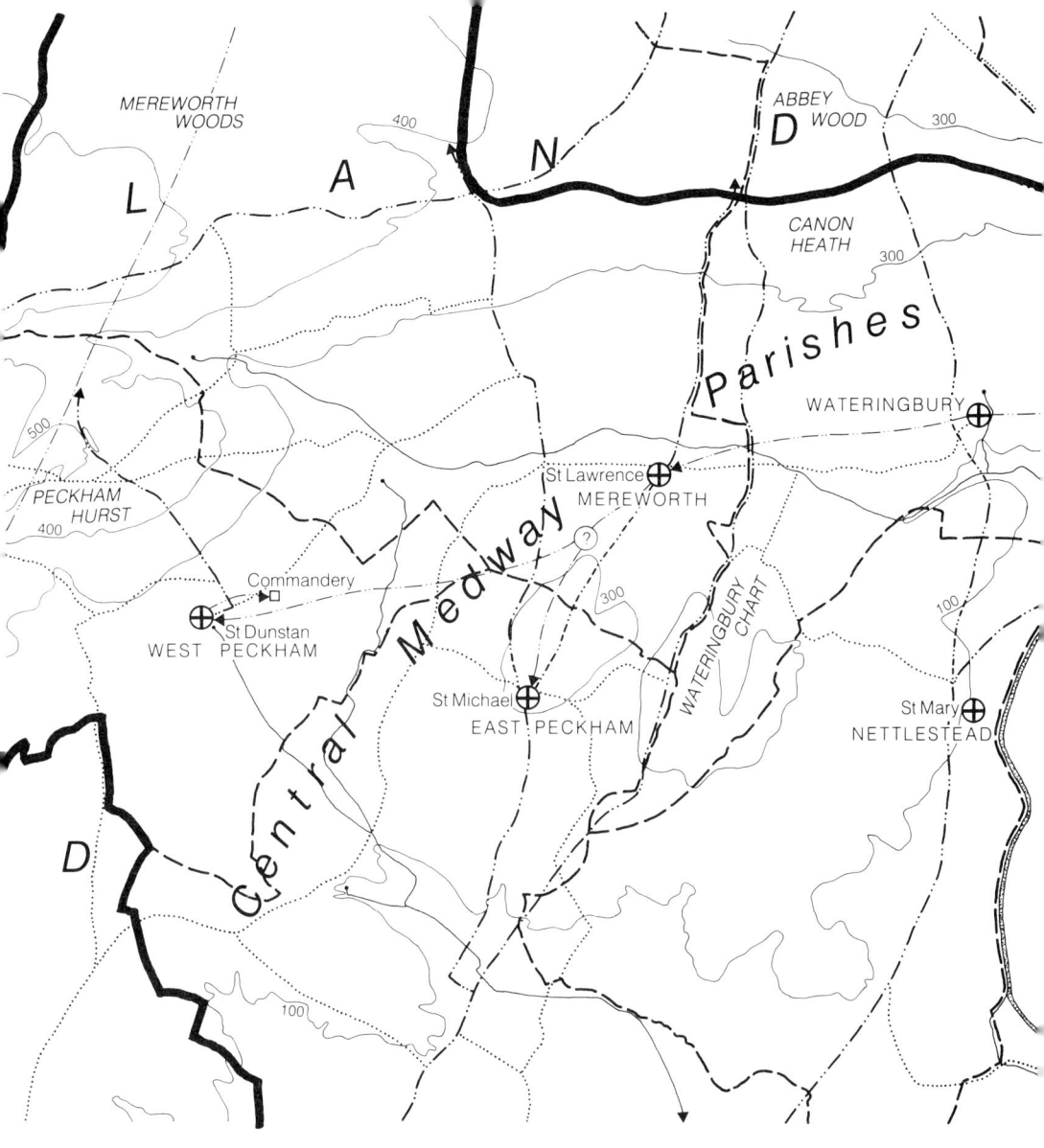

4. *Central Medway Parishes.* The origins and inter-relationships of this group of parishes remain obscure. They cannot have originated from Maidstone, as might at first seem likely, since that was in a different diocese (Canterbury). There is no clear evidence to connect them with Aylesford, however, and in terms of settlement-history they must have originated from the Medway valley, on their southern edge, not from the Chartland to the north. On the other hand, the rectory of Hadlow was in some sense subordinate to Addington (H, IV, 548).

The Chartland here formed an extensive intercommonable district between the Aylesford estate and the central Medway parishes. The bounds of Addington, Aldon, Offham, Ryarsh, Little Comp, Mereworth, and St Blaise provide a classic example of those 'interlocking boundaries' so characteristic of intercommonable areas in Kent. Much of the Chartland hereabouts remained virtually uninhabited at the time of the Tithe Survey; in many places it is still densely wooded.

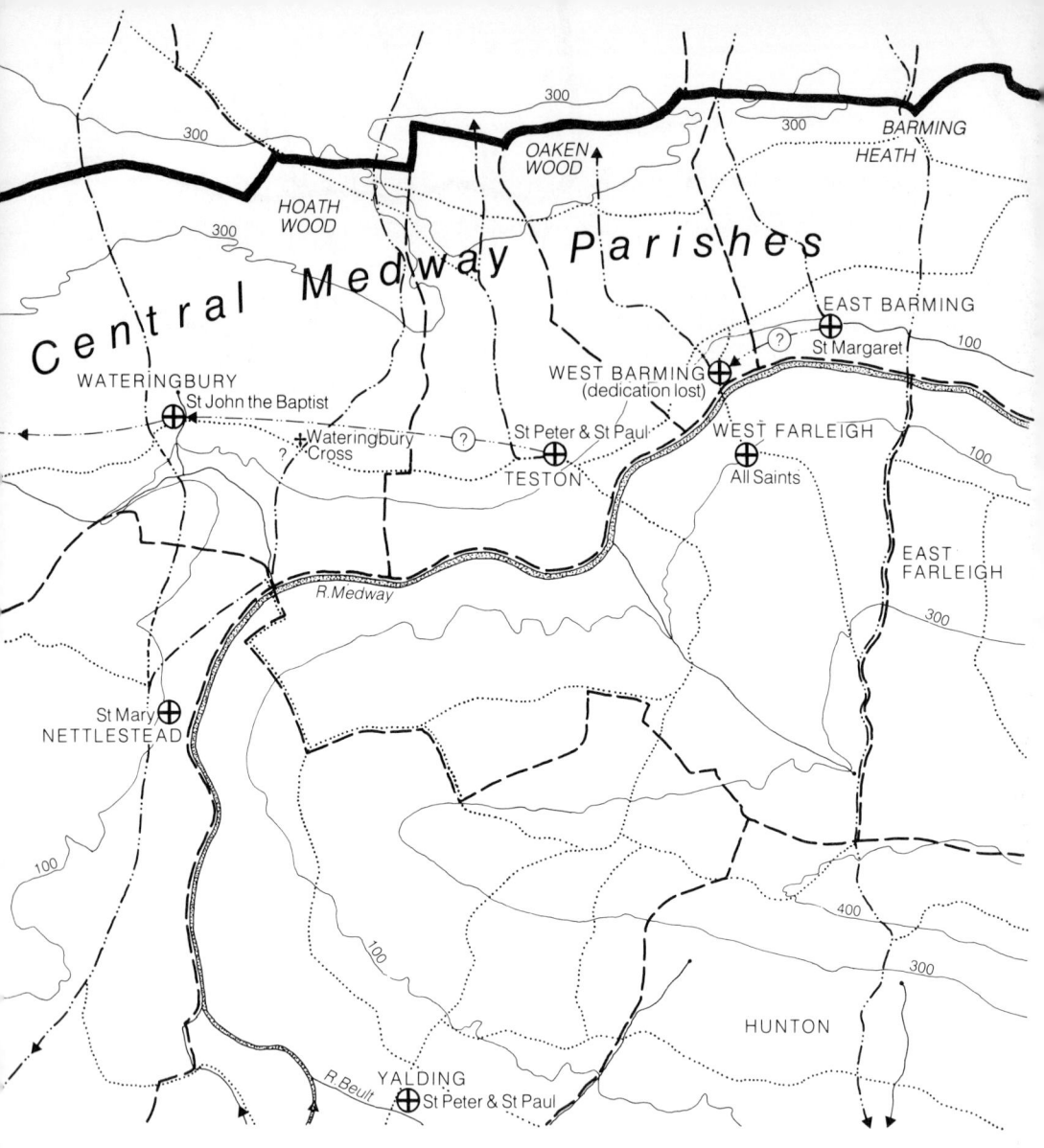

5. All medieval parish churches are marked on the map, including those like Woodlands and West Barming no longer extant. All subsidiary ecclesiastical sites are also marked, so far as they are known, but there are probably further manorial chapels and crouches (perhaps substantially more) still awaiting discovery.

6. Parish boundaries have been reconstructed principally from the Tithe Index sheets, the 2½" O.S. sheets, and the boundary marks (trees, stubs, stones, etc.) recorded on the latter. In general current boundaries closely follow those of the Tithe Survey, except that detached parts of parishes have now generally been amalgamated with neighbouring territories.

8 *Ecclesiastical development*

claylands, and they were granted both a chaplain of their own and the right to all tithes and offerings arising in the hamlet.[54] Towards the end of Henry VI's reign, in the great Wealden parish of Cranbrook, John Lawless founded and endowed a new chapel at Milkhouse, about two miles from the parish church, 'as well for the benefit of the inhabitants of this eastern part of the parish, who in the depth of winter could not get to church, as for the receiving the alms [*sic*] and offering up prayers for the welfare of travellers passing this way'.[55] As late as 1614 Sir Ralph Bosville obtained permission to reconsecrate the disused medieval chapel at Bradbourne specifically on the ground that his manor house was 'a mile at least from the parish church of Sevenoaks' – it was in fact nearly two miles – so that he and his household could not easily repair 'to the said parish church for almost all the winter and in [*sic*] other rainy and stormy days.'[56]

Probably as a result of these conditions many of the outlying manorial chapels of Kent gradually came to serve a wider community than that of the manorial household alone, and as population increased to develop a kind of quasi-parochial function.[57] The process of transition may be seen taking place at Dene in St John's-in-Thanet, for example, where the original oratory was built by Sir Henry de Sandwich about 1230 for his own household, yet gradually 'not only the lord of that manor and his family, but the inhabitants of Twenties, Vincents, and Fleet likewise' resorted to it.[58] In places like Dene the church was under constant pressure to upgrade manorial chapels to the status of chantries, 'free chapels', 'great chapels', 'district chapels', or chapels-of-ease to the mother-church. Little by little such places often underwent a gradual metamorphosis, as a consequence, until by the fourteenth or fifteenth century they varied in status from tiny chambers in a private house at one end of the scale, such as may still be seen at Hever Castle, to substantial detached buildings with their own burial grounds and baptismal rights at the other. Many still remained purely private, of course, and many still formed part of the manor house itself; yet substantial numbers exercised burial rights, and in some cases acquired separate tithings or parishes, though few became entirely independent.

The varied ecclesiastical status that developed in this way may be illustrated from many parts of the county. In the minster-parish of Northbourne near Deal, for example, both Sholden and Cottington became chapels-of-ease to the mother-church, each with its own tithing, although Cottington eventually disappeared while Sholden

PART FOUR *The Ecclesiastical Testimony*

acquired a small subsidiary parish of its own and is still in use today. In the neighbouring minster-parish of Eastry, Worth and Shingleton likewise became chapels-of-ease to the mother-church, though in this case Shingleton disappeared and Worth later became a subordinate parish.[59] In the Stour valley, of two apparently similar foundations, Milton Septvans early acquired a minute parish of its own, extending to a mere 403 acres, whilst its neighbour Horton Parva, though possessed of 'more than ordinary privileges', never became independent of the church of Chartham and eventually lost its ecclesiastical status altogether.[60] In the Downland parish of Waltham, Ashenfield, Wadenhall, and Dean never seem to have advanced beyond the manorial stage and have long since disappeared, whilst Elmsted, as we have seen, ultimately obtained parochial rights of its own and in the nineteenth century became wholly independent.[61] In the minster-parish of Wrotham, in West Kent, Old Soar and St Clere seem to have remained purely manorial; Stansted became a distinct though still dependent chapelry, with burial and baptismal rights, but no separate tithing; Plaxtol a chapel-of-ease to Wrotham, with a burial ground but neither baptismal rights nor tithing; Comp a detached chapel-of-ease to another parish, that of Leybourne, on whose glebe it had been erected; whilst Horsnell's Crouch seems to have remained a shrine or mass-centre, without any permanent building.[62]

Dispersal of settlement was thus one important factor behind the proliferation of outlying chapels in Kent, and their location often points to the continuing expansion of settlement in the post-Conquest period. It would be misleading, however, to suggest that this was the only circumstance behind their foundation. A further factor of great importance was the gradual emergence of a new social order in the county, that of the independent manorial gentry. Although the complex economic and agrarian forces behind this development lie outside the scope of this book, no account of medieval settlement would be complete without some reference to it. In Kent, as in Devon, it was the formative generations between 1150 and 1350 that witnessed the origin of many of these ancient indigenous gentry. It was then that families like the Twysdens and Oxindens, the Northwoods and Honywoods, the Derings, Engehams, Hardreses, Harfleetes, Culpepers, and many others like them, first began to emerge from their obscurity, often taking their surnames from the outlying settlements whence they arose: the Twysdens from Twyssenden in Goudhurst, for instance, the Hardreses from Hardres near Canterbury, the Engehams from Engeham in Woodchurch, and the Honywoods from Honywood in Postling.[63] As they ascended in the social scale and in many cases married into the Anglo-Norman families of the county, as they gradually succeeded to the local influence of those families, and frequently to their ancestral estates, it was not unnatural that their ecclesiastical aspirations should also undergo something of a metamorphosis. For some of them the right to a manorial chapel was perhaps as much a matter of dynastic pride, as much a symbol of the expansion of their households and estates, as of mere distance from the parish church. Like the private chapels and chantries added to many Kentish parish churches at this time[64] – and in few counties are they more numerous or more striking – the manorial chapels of Kent thus bear vivid testimony to the rise of the indigenous gentry of the shire, and their impact upon local settlement. Eventually it was they who were destined to succeed to the age-old influence of the church itself, and to dominate the governing classes of the county until the eighteenth and nineteenth centuries.

The third and final factor to note behind the foundation of outlying chapels and chantries is a more elusive one: and that is the presence of a certain wayward individualism in the religious temperament of the county. There was often a quasi-illicit element in their origins, indeed, and in some cases they were certainly established before the grant of an official licence. It was not until 1194, for example, that the abbot of St Augustine's granted Richard de Garwynton the right to have the divine office celebrated in his manor house at Garrington in Littlebourne: yet his private chapel there was certainly in existence several years earlier, and perhaps as early as the end of the eleventh century.[65] Even where the origins of such places were perfectly lawful, moreover, an element of inconformity sometimes crept in, and a tendency to press individual rights beyond their legal limits. In 1300 complaint was made to the abbey of St Augustine, for example, that Henry Thorne of Thorne in Thanet was causing 'mass to be publicly said in his private oratory, or chapel ... at this his manor of Thorne ... to the prejudice of the mother-church [of Minster] and the ill example of others; and he accordingly was inhibited from so doing in future by the archbishop's letters to the vicar of Minster.'[66] The right to an oratory of one's own necessarily perhaps encouraged a certain independence of mind; the fact that such places often lay remote from the rectorial eye made it more difficult to enforce ecclesiastical order than in Midland parishes, where everyone lived under the shadow of the church. It was these same circumstances that in later centuries often encouraged the

PART FOUR *The Ecclesiastical Testimony*

development of Protestant Nonconformity in Kent, at remote woodland spots like Yelsted in Stockbury, Ebenezer in Stelling, and Omenden Green in the Weald. Though there were obviously profound differences of *mentalité* between the old traditions and the new, yet in both developments there was something of the same restless individualism, something of the same dislike of being organized into any rigid local community, and of accepting any of the constraints of the manorial village, which so often seems to have characterized Kentish society. In the development of the outlying chapels and chantries of the medieval period, in short, what we see is not only the advance of settlement itself, but the influence of that 'freedom of the wold' which was referred to in Chapter 7.

5. CONTRASTING COMMUNITIES

By the high medieval period, before the decline of the fourteenth century set in, some 500 parishes and parish churches had thus been established in Kent, of which rather more than 400 still survive today. Of these 500, probably 43 or 44 were minsters or primary mother-churches, at least 23 were secondary mother-churches, 52 were Wealden 'forest' churches, and about 40 were churches of small urban parishes in towns like Canterbury, Dover, Sandwich, and Rochester. Of the remaining 340, probably 300 or more were 'manorial' or 'bookland' foundations, principally situated on the Downland or Chartland, though in places in the Original Lands and the Marshlands too. In addition to these parish churches, there were at least 300 non-parochial chapels, of which the great majority antedated the Black Death, though a number are not actually recorded until the later medieval period and some were certainly late foundations. For the study of early settlement, it is the contrast between the minsters and mother-churches on one hand, and the manorial or bookland churches on the other that is the salient fact to bear in mind. The peculiarities of Wealden and urban parishes are equally instructive in their own context; but in differentiating between landscapes of continuity and landscapes of colonization, it is the former distinction that is the crucial one. It is a distinction, moreover, that not only lies at the root of Kentish settlement history, but that also gave rise to far-reaching contrasts in the rural economy and social structure of the county. In concluding this chapter these contrasts ought to be briefly explored, therefore, before turning to the subject of church-dedications in Chapter 9.

8 *Ecclesiastical development*

Numerically, it was the bookland churches that formed the most substantial group, probably accounting for quite 60 per cent of the 500 medieval parish churches of Kent, whereas the 67 minsters and mother-churches accounted for only 13 or 14 per cent. The relative importance of the two groups also needs to be seen, however, in relation to the extent of their parishes, and the scale of their respective wealth. As we have seen, the minster-parishes averaged rather more than 4,300 acres in extent, the secondary mother-parishes nearly 3,500 acres, and the Wealden parishes about 4,500, whereas those of bookland churches extended, on average, to less than 1,600 acres. For some of the minsters and secondary mother-churches, it is not possible to reconstruct the original area; but if these are excluded, together with minor urban churches and those of uncertain status, we arrive at the figures given in table 10.[67]

Table 10. Church typology and parish size

	Numbers	Average extent of parish	Total extent of parishes	Total extent as percentage of county area	
Minster churches	38	4,341	164,951	15.9	
Secondary mother-churches	22	3,450	75,903	7.3	23.2
Wealden forest churches	52	4,459	231,866	22.3	
Bookland churches	c.300	c.1,570	c.471,000	c.45.3	
Total	412		c.944,000	c.90.8+	

When the relative extent of the parish is taken into account, the minsters and mother-churches of Kent thus represent at least 23 per cent of the county area rather than 13 or 14 per cent, and perhaps (if we had figures for all of them) nearly 30 per cent, whereas the bookland churches account for only 45 per cent.

So far as wealth is concerned, it is obviously impossible to construct realistic figures for the period of parish formation;[68] but something may perhaps be learned from the relative wealth of each region in later centuries. In the early modern period Downland rents often seem to have been only one-third or one-half as high as those in the mother-communities of the Original Lands; and if these figures have any validity for earlier centuries, they suggest that the latter were two or three times as wealthy, acre for acre, as the former. Since they were also on average nearly three times as extensive, the mother-parishes of Kent must generally have been quite six or eight times as wealthy as the typical bookland parish. In other words, though the latter were four or five times as numerous as the former (300:67), their total wealth was greatly inferior, perhaps amounting to no more than three-fifths of that of the 67 mother-parishes as a whole. Clearly these figures cannot be regarded as genuine statistics; but intrinsically they are not implausible. Every other line of evidence also points to the relative poverty of the Downs and the Chart and the relative wealth of the Foothills and Holmesdale, where the minsters and mother-churches were mostly situated. Some of the bookland parishes were also situated in these areas; but these were never more than a small minority of the total, and against this fact must be set the additional wealth accruing to the mother-parishes from their rights in the Weald. On the whole, in short, the contrast between the mother-communities and the bookland communities is likely to have been at least as great in the settlement period as in the seventeenth or eighteenth century.

At first sight it may seem paradoxical, perhaps, that the richer lands of Kent should thus give rise to the larger parishes, and that the structure of ecclesiastical development, far from equalizing the disparity, should actually accentuate it.[69] In reality this contrast was the logical outcome of contrasts in territorial organization. For the mother-churches, as we have seen, had almost all originated as royal or monastic foundations, so that their parishes necessarily represented the territories of powerful landed magnates: whereas the bookland churches were essentially subordinate foundations, established for the most part by laymen whose estates were rarely comparable with those of the crown or the church.[70] From the beginnings of settlement, as a consequence, there was a great gulf fixed between these two types of local community in Kent: a gulf not only of scale and of fortune but of rural economy and social structure too. The contrasts it gave rise to formed some of the most deeply-rooted and enduring features of Kentish society for more than a thousand years. They were still very apparent when Edward Hasted took up his pen in the eighteenth century, and their consequences may yet be traced in the Kentish landscape of the present day.

9

CHURCH-DEDICATIONS

Ever since Frances Arnold-Forster wrote her monumental work in the 1890s, the historical interest of English church-dedications and their local and regional variety have been widely recognized. Yet while it is generally admitted that certain dedications tend to be characteristic of certain periods, and that some are associated with very early churches, or even with pre-Christian sites, there has been little systematic attempt to reconstruct a relative chronology of the subject, either in England generally or in most English counties. Rarely has it received the same searching scrutiny as the study of place-names, for example, or Anglo-Saxon charters. Yet the dedications of English churches provide a substantial body of evidence which it ought to be possible to interpret, and which ought to be of some use to the student of English settlement. In the present chapter an attempt will be made to reconstruct a chronology for Kent as a whole, and to see what light the general pattern of dedications sheds on the progress of settlement.

1. THE EVIDENCE AND ITS PROBLEMS

To avoid merely subjective conclusions, a methodical approach to the evidence is essential. Where dedications are concerned, there is a place for intuitive judgment; many of the more arresting aspects of the subject can only be solved in this way; in tracing the topographical significance of a dedication, indeed, there is no substitute for a noticing eye. Yet in a field of study where some rather positive assertions have sometimes been advanced, it is also necessary to test intuition by objective standards. For this purpose a substantial *corpus* of evidence is needed, and this chapter is based on an analysis of some 540 Kentish dedications altogether. Statistical investigation may seem inappropriate in a subject of this kind; but in Kent at least it brings to light a number of striking contrasts between the early dedication-pattern of the county and that of its later churches and chapels. With these contrasts in mind it is then possible to proceed to other lines of enquiry, and to place intuitive judgments in perspective.

The problems involved in analysing the evidence are of three kinds. In the first place, how complete is it? In Kent there are only four

PART FOUR *The Ecclesiastical Testimony*

surviving churches whose dedications are unknown: Sundridge, Keston, Elmstone, and Plaxtol. This is a negligible figure compared with that for some counties; and although there are many vanished churches and chapels whose dedications cannot now be traced, most of these were late or minor foundations and not major churches. The surviving evidence is ample, therefore, for reaching valid conclusions, and if the lost dedications were known to us, they would probably reinforce the conclusions advanced here rather than undermine them.[1] A more serious problem arises in connexion with the dedications of subsidiary chantries and altars destroyed at the time of the Reformation. No systematic search for these has yet been made in Kent; but in many churches it is plain that they were numerous. At Minster-in-Thanet, for instance, there were altars to St James, St Anne, and the Holy Trinity; at St John's-in-Thanet to St Anne, St George, and St John; at St Peter-in-Thanet to St James, St Margaret, and St Mary of Pity; and at St Lawrence-in-Thanet to St James, St Catherine, St Thomas, and the Holy Trinity. In the great Marshland church of Lydd, there were lights and altars to St James, St Mildred, St Catherine, St Barbara, St Anthony, St Nicholas, St George, St John, St Peter, Our Lady, Our Lady of Pity, Allhallows, and the Holy Trinity.[2] In most cases subsidiary altars like these were probably of post-Conquest origin and have no direct bearing on ecclesiastical foundation or the origins of settlement as such. Yet a systematic survey would no doubt enable us to trace the development of local and regional cults more precisely than is at present possible. It is noteworthy, for example, that in four of these five maritime churches there was an altar to St James, a patron saint of travellers, while those to St Mildred, St Margaret, and St Anne likewise fit into a recognizable regional pattern.

The second problem relates to the authenticity of the surviving dedications: how far can we be certain that these date back to the origin of the churches in question? There are several places where the old appellations are known to have been altered, usually in consequence of a change in ecclesiastical status. At Maidstone, for example, St Mary's minster was rededicated to All Saints when rebuilt as a collegiate foundation by Archbishop Courtenay in 1395, and the chapel of St Thomas and St Catherine across the river was reconsecrated to St Peter when converted into a hospital for poor travellers by Archbishop Boniface in 1261.[3] There are also several early Kentish churches where a change of dedication must be suspected, though no specific record of it has come to light. At Wrotham, for instance, it is unlikely that St

9 Church-dedications

George was the original patron of the minster, since his cult was predominantly a post-Conquest development, though his name was known to the Old English church.[4] Similarly at Lydd, Birling, and Hollingbourne the dedication to All Saints, like that at Maidstone, may not be original; for elsewhere in Kent it always indicates a late foundation, and at Lydd and Hollingbourne the annual fair was held not on All Saints day, as we should normally expect, but on the festivals of St Anacletus and St Anne.[5] Except where a change of status was involved, however, there are grounds for believing that the great majority of Kentish dedications go back to the early medieval period and in all probability beyond. Very few seem to have been altered at the time of the Reformation;[6] in most cases they are recorded in medieval wills or other early documents; and in a significant number in the *Domesday Monachorum* or in pre-Conquest sources. Further confirmation is afforded by the fact that ancient fairs and wakes are often known to have been held on the patronal festivals of the parish churches in question. Where a change has occurred, moreover, the original dedication often survives alongside the new one, giving rise to such double ascriptions as St Mary and St Eanswythe at Folkestone, St Mary and St Ethelburga at Lyminge, and St Mary and the Holy Cross at Milsted.

Taken as a whole, therefore, the surviving *corpus* of Kentish dedications is certainly worth investigating and table 11 lists all those that have been traced. In interpreting the table caution is necessary since it makes no distinction between the various types of ecclesiastical building to which the 62 dedications refer. About three-quarters relate to parish churches; the rest to a wide variety of buildings, such as monastic houses, hospitals, chapels, chantries, and so on. In some cases, such as St Margaret and All Saints, all the dedications in question relate to parish churches; but in others, like St John the Baptist and St Bartholomew, a substantial proportion relate to hospitals, chapels, preceptories, and the like. For comparative purposes, the figures for England as a whole are also given. These indicate significant differences in the relative popularity of a number of dedications as between Kent and the rest of the country. St Mary, as we should expect, was everywhere pre-eminent; but St Martin, St Nicholas, St Margaret, St Mary Magdalene, and St Peter and St Paul were all more widely venerated in Kent than in England generally, whereas St Andrew, St Michael, St Peter (alone), All Saints, and the Holy Trinity were all more frequent elsewhere. As we should also expect, there are several saints peculiarly associated with the county,

PART FOUR *The Ecclesiastical Testimony*

such as St Augustine, St Mildred, St Dunstan, and St Alphege, whose local dedications form a major proportion of the total.

The third problem in interpreting church-dedications is of a different kind, and demands more detailed discussion. This is the fact that, while many patron saints were predominantly associated with certain phases of church foundation, their adoption was also influenced by other

Table 11. Dedications in Kent and in England Generally

		Kent[a]		All England[b]	
		Nos.	%	Nos.	$\frac{1}{20}$[c]
1	St Mary	120	22.2	2,094	105
2	St Peter & St Paul	39	7.2	280	14
3	All Saints	37	6.9	1,097	55
4	St Nicholas	34	6.3	393	20
5	St John the Baptist	28[d]	5.2	458	23
6	St Margaret	22	4.1	239	12
7	St Peter	21	3.9	760	38
8	St Martin	18	3.3	159	8
9	St Michael	18	3.3	623	31
10	St James	17	3.2	339	17
11	St Mary Magdalene	13	2.4	175	9
12	St Lawrence (of Rome)	11	2.0	226	11
13	St Bartholomew	10	1.8	151	8
14	Holy Trinity	9	1.7	242	12
15	St Augustine	7	1.3	28	1
16	St George	7	1.3	111	6
17	St Mildred	7	1.3	6[g]	
18	St Giles	7	1.3	147	7
19	St Andrew	7	1.3	595	30
20	St Thomas Becket	7[e]	1.3	72	4
21	St Botolph	6	1.1	61	3
22	Holy Cross	6	1.1	75	4
23	St Catherine	6	1.1	58	3
24	St Clement	5		36	2
25	St Dunstan	5	2.8	20	1
26	St Leonard	5		160	8
27	St Edmund the King	4	1.5	56	3
28	St Stephen	4		40	2
29	St Anthony	3		4	
30	St Radegund	3		4	
31	St Alphege	3	3.3	5	
32	St Rumwold	3		7	
33	St Gregory	3		30	1
34	St John the Evangelist	3		109	5

9 Church-dedications

35	St Paulinus	2		5	
36	St Pancras	2		6	
37	St Cosmas & St Damian	2		3	
38	St Helen	2		120	6
39	St Eanswythe	2	3.7	2	
40	St Blaise	2		4	
41	St Anne	2		33	2
42	St Crispin & St Crispinian	2		0[g]	
43	St Paul	2		29	1
44	St Thomas the Apostle	2		30	1
45	St Saviour	1		9	
46	St Bertha	1		0[g]	
47	St Eadburga	1		1	
48	St Edith of Kemsing	1		0[g]	
49	St Ethelburga of Lyminge	1		0[g]	
50	St Faith	1		24	1
51	Holy Innocents	1		5	
52	St Lawrence of Canterbury (?)	1		0[g]	
53	St Luke	1	3.2	18	1
54	St Matthew	1		25	1
55	St Oswald	1		57	3
56	St Sepulchre	1		4	
57	St Sexburga	1		1	
58	St Vincent	1		5	
59	St Werburga	1		10	
60	All Souls	1		3	
61	Corpus Christi	1		1[g]	
62	Christ Church	1		6	
	Others			1,039	52
	Dedication unknown	4[f]	0.7	534	27
	Total	540	100.0	10,834	

[a] *For Kent* all dedications that have been traced are tabulated, including those of lost churches, hospitals, monastic houses, preceptories, friaries, chapels, and chantries, where these are known. (Dedications of chantries, etc., within churches are not included.) Where churches are dedicated to more than one saint (as Folkestone to St Mary and St Eanswythe), each saint is listed separately, except in the case of the joint-dedications of St Peter and St Paul, St Cosmas and St Damian, and St Crispin and St Crispinian. In a few special cases local cults have also been included, as of St Crispin and St Crispinian at Faversham and Lydd, though these did not involve the formal dedication of the church in question. The total number of churches represented in Kent is thus somewhat lower than the number of dedications. No dedication is included, however, unless it is related to an ecclesiastical building; those of wells, for example, such as St Eustace's Well at Wye, are not represented in the table unless a well-chapel has also been traced.

PART FOUR *The Ecclesiastical Testimony*

ᵇ *For England* as a whole, the figures are based on A-F, III, 1–26, 'Statistical Summary of Dedications'. I have included all those there listed as 'Ancient: Pre-Reformation', together with all pre-Reformation 'Double Dedications' and 'Triple and Fourfold Dedications'. All post-medieval figures are excluded, together with those of 'Chapelries: Period doubtful'. The figures for England as a whole are thus not strictly comparable with those for Kent. While Miss Arnold-Forster's research was remarkably thorough, there are substantial numbers of chapels, hospitals, and lost churches which she did not trace. In many cases these can only be discovered through intensive local research, for example into the dedications of many hundreds of churches of lost villages that have come to light since she wrote in the 1890s. This circumstance explains why in a few cases figures are given for Kent, while there is a lower figure or no corresponding one for England.

ᶜ The total for Kent is almost exactly one-twentieth of the total for England, as reconstructed from A-F. To indicate the relative popularity of each dedication in Kent and in England respectively, the figures for England are therefore divided by 20 in this column (except where there are fewer than 15 dedications).

ᵈ A few of these may possibly relate to St John the Evangelist. One, Doddington, is to the Beheading of John the Baptist.

ᵉ Two or three of these may possibly refer to St Thomas the Apostle.

ᶠ Sundridge, Plaxtol, Keston, Elmstone. This does not include the lost dedications of *lost* churches and chapels; such a figure would in fact be very difficult to reconstruct since the full number of lost chapels is unknown. Arnold-Forster's figure of 534 unknown dedications for England generally includes those of such lost churches as she was aware of. Since she wrote, however, some hundreds of further lost churches have been discovered, and in some counties a number of lost dedications have subsequently been traced. It is not at present possible, therefore, to give figures of lost dedications for England and for Kent that are strictly comparable. But there can be no doubt that so far as surviving churches are concerned the Kentish figure is much smaller than that for many counties. A-F, II, 524, gives figures of 29 for Yorkshire, 37 for Sussex, nearly 50 for Dorset, and 60 for Devon, while in Somerset and Essex there were apparently about as many as in Sussex.

ᵍ In these cases Frances Arnold-Forster's coverage is incomplete: see notes a and b above.

circumstances which often cut across any direct relationship between dedication and date. Broadly speaking, these modifying circumstances were of four kinds. In the first place, certain groups of appellations arose through the ramifications of royal or monastic estates, or through some other tenurial or customary connexion. Of the six parish churches dedicated to St Augustine, for example, all were situated on ancient territories of St Augustine's Abbey, with the possible exception of Richborough.⁷ Of those to St Mildred, that at Tenterden owed its

9 Church-dedications

origin to Tenterden's links with St Mildred's minster in the Isle of Thanet. Of the two to St Eanswythe, that at Brenzett probably originated through a similar connexion with St Eanswythe's minster at Folkestone.[8]

Secondly, many Kentish churches owed their dedications to the evolution of local or regional cults, and these were often associated with the patron saints of certain very early churches. This occurred in the case of those dedicated to St Martin, for instance, the patron saint of the oldest church in the county, at Canterbury, and of nearly 20 other Kentish churches, as well as many subsidiary chapels and altars. It also occurred in the case of St Margaret, the patroness of at least 22 parish churches, as well as of many local lights, altars, and crouches. It likewise helps to explain the exceptional frequency of dedications to St Peter and St Paul (39), the original patrons of St Augustine's Abbey. Where dedications are associated with local cults like these, they may originate in almost any period between the seventh century and the fourteenth, though in many cases they tend to be early; we shall return to them later in this chapter.

In the third place, a number of Kentish churches and chapels seem to have been deliberately given the same dedication as their mother-churches or minsters. In the Darent valley, for instance, the mother-church of St Martin at Eynsford gave birth to a subsidiary church at Chelsfield which was likewise dedicated to St Martin. Further down the same valley, the mother-church of St Margaret at Darenth gave birth to an upland chapelry at St Margaret-at-Helles, or 'St Margaret-on-the-Hills'. On the Medway estuary, the mother-church of St Mary Magdalene at Gillingham founded a chapelry in its outlying woodland at Lidsing, which was also dedicated to St Mary Magdalene. In the Cray valley, the minster of St Paulinus at Crayford created a new church of St Paulinus at St Paul's Cray, the only other church to bear this dedication in southern England.[9] In the Stour valley, it seems likely that Thanington gave birth in much the same way to the small neighbouring parish of Milton; for both churches are dedicated to St Nicholas, and their parish boundaries indicate that Milton was carved out of Thanington's territory. Elsewhere the connexion may not be so straightforward as this; yet on closer inspection it often becomes apparent that some kind of link once existed. At West Kingsdown, for instance, the dedication to St Edmund the King seems at first sight to bear no relation to that of its mother-church of St John the Baptist at Sutton-at-Hone. Yet at an earlier period Sutton itself had originated as

PART FOUR *The Ecclesiastical Testimony*

the 'south *tūn*' of Dartford, and the minster at Dartford certainly gave birth to another chapelry of St Edmund, on the heathland known as Dartford Brent. Since Kingsdown, Sutton, and Dartford originally formed part of the same royal estate, based on Darenth, there was always a close connexion between them; and since St Edmund is an unusual dedication in Kent, it seems possible that Dartford had created both chapelries before Sutton-at-Hone became independent of it.[10] While in a sense this kind of development tends to complicate the task of reconstructing a chronology, it is often of interest to the student of settlement in tracing the ecclesiastical origin of the churches in question.

Finally, it is important to remember that certain patron saints were associated with specialized cults that had no connexion with the origins of settlement as such. Several of these cults are of considerable importance in their own right, and a few ought to be briefly mentioned at this point. Churches dedicated to St Faith and St Giles, for example, were frequently associated with fairs, both in Kent and in other counties. There were notable fairs of St Faith at Norwich and at Maidstone, for instance. There were notable fairs of St Giles at Winchester and Northampton, and in Kent five of the seven parish churches dedicated to St Giles – at Shipbourne, Farnborough, Kingston, Sarre, and Tonge – were likewise associated with fairs. The name of St Bartholomew was also sometimes connected with major fairs, as at Dover and of course in London;[11] but his special concern was with poor travellers and with rites of healing, as at Otford and Bobbing, and at several hospitals bearing his name in Chatham, Sandwich, Saltwood, Buckland by Dover, and again in London.[12] Both St Mary and St Anne were frequently connected with holy wells and fertility customs, and this association probably goes some way towards explaining the unusual number of early springhead churches dedicated to the Virgin, a point we shall return to in Chapter 10.[13]

One further group of dedications of this kind which is of particular interest in Kent comprises those associated with fishermen and mariners. Medieval fishing communities often tended to be 'superstitious', it seems, just as in the nineteenth century they often tended to be Evangelical and 'fundamentalist': there was something in the harshness and uncertainty of their lives, no doubt, that tended to encourage direct belief in the supernatural. In Kent, as in other maritime counties, the unusual popularity of St Nicholas, the patron saint of mariners, is in part attributable to these circumstances; for eleven of the

9 Church-dedications

34 churches bearing his name were on tidal water, and a further eight within three miles of it.[14] In all probability similar circumstances account for seven of the 17 churches and chapels dedicated to St James, at Cooling, Dover, Elmley, Grain, Sandwich, Warden, and Reculver, and four of the five dedicated to St Clement, at Sandwich, Rochester, Leysdown, and Old Romney; for St James was a patron saint of travellers, and St Clement of ships and lighthouses. There were many more localized cults in the maritime parishes of the county, moreover: of St Rumwold and St Botolph at Folkestone, for example, Our Lady of Pity at Broadstairs, and St Mary and St Barbara at Lydd. At Folkestone the last relics of the old custom of 'Rumbald Night', as it was called, lingered on into Hasted's time; at Broadstairs the image of Our Lady 'was held in such veneration that the ships as they sailed by this place used to lower their topsails to salute it'.[15]

In reconstructing a chronology of church-dedications, there are thus several complicating factors to be borne in mind. The relationship between the dedication of a church and the period of its foundation is not always straightforward, and some of the commonest appellations, like St Mary the Virgin and St Peter and St Paul, may occur in any period from the seventh century onwards. The importance of relics and the impact of translation must likewise be remembered, though in general we know little about such matters in the period when most dedications originate. Nevertheless, there is no doubt that a broad distinction can be drawn in Kent between the general pattern of early dedications, taken as a whole, and that of subsequent[16] and secondary churches. Except in the case of post-Conquest saints and obviously French ascriptions like St Leonard, St Blaise, and St Faith, it is not generally possible to draw a further distinction between the dedications of 'subsequent' churches and those of the post-Conquest period; for by 1100 the overwhelming majority of parish churches had already come into existence.[17] For the purpose of dating the 500 or so churches under discussion, there are two means available. The first involves analysis of all those known to have originated as minsters and mother-churches on one hand, or as their daughter-churches and dependent chapels on the other, as described in Chapter 8. The second involves the analysis of churches and dedications in relation to *pays*, according to the general period of settlement and ecclesiastical foundation in each area. Broadly speaking these two approaches confirm one another, and, with the reservations mentioned above, indicate a more or less coherent pattern in the county as a whole. In the following pages the dedications of Kent

PART FOUR *The Ecclesiastical Testimony*

will first be examined in relation to settlement zones or *pays*; in subsequent sections a more detailed investigation will be attempted of each category.

2. DEDICATIONS AND *PAYS*

In examining dedications in relation to *pays*, it is necessary to restrict the survey to those churches that can be so classified more or less unequivocally. There are certain groups, therefore, that need to be excluded:

1. Churches whose dedications are obviously influenced by other factors than the period of colonization of the area in question: for example, some of those associated with St Nicholas and St Bartholomew, and some whose dedications derive from those of their mother-churches;

2. The churches of certain areas where settlement is too varied or uncertain in origin to assign any definite date to the dedications of the area generally: these include much of the Downland east of the Dour valley, much of Romney Marsh and the Isle of Thanet, and most of the Chartland east of the Stour valley;

3. Some churches on the Foothills and in Holmesdale, such as Bobbing, Murston, and Otford, that are known to have originated as subordinate chapelries, and in consequence shed no light on the original dedication pattern of these otherwise early *pays*;

4. Churches on the borderland of one zone of settlement and another;[18]

5. Some urban churches in places like Dover and Canterbury whose period of origin is doubtful;

6. A few churches for which the evidence of origin is otherwise inconclusive.

This leaves us with a total of 320 dedications whose period of origin may be classified according to *pays* with some degree of confidence: 61 on the Foothills, 34 in Holmesdale, 25 elsewhere in the Original Lands, 110 on the Downland, 41 on the Chartland, 39 in the Weald, and 10 in the Forest of Blean. In point of fact there were differences of some interest within some of these areas; on the Downland and Chartland, in particular, the range of dedications tended to be more primitive towards the east of the county than towards the west. For the purpose in hand, however, the broad regional division will suffice. The dedications of the Original Lands are best examined as a single group, moreover, since they were clearly marked by a certain coherence throughout;[19] the

9 Church-dedications

Table 12. Dedications and *pays*
(47 different appellations in all are represented)

Original Lands (29 appellations)		Downland (31 appellations)		Chartland and Blean (18 appellations)		Weald (17 appellations)	
St Mary	48	St Mary	17	St Nicholas	7	St Mary	10
St Peter & St Paul	16	St John the Baptist	8	St Mary	6	All Saints	5
St Martin	10	St Peter & St Paul	7	St Michael	5	St Peter & St Paul	4
St Peter	5	St Margaret	7	All Saints	5	St Michael	3
St Margaret	5	All Saints	7	St Lawrence	4	St Peter	2
St Augustine	4	St Nicholas	6	St Margaret	4	St Margaret	2
Holy Trinity	3	St Mary Magdalene	6	St John the Baptist	3	St John the Baptist	2
St Botolph	3	St Peter	5	St Peter & St Paul	2	St Lawrence	2
St Clement	3	St James	5	St Peter	2		
All Saints[a]	3	St Giles	5	St James	2		
St Andrew	2	St Michael	5	Holy Cross	2		
		St Bartholomew	4				
		St Lawrence	4				
		St Martin	3				
		St George	2				
		Holy Cross	2				
		St Catherine	2				
Occurring once each	18[b]	Occurring once each	14[c]	Occurring once each	7[d]	Occurring once each	9[e]
		Not known	1	Not known	2		
Totals	120		110		51		39

[a] Probably re-dedications (Hollingbourne, Birling, Lydd).
[b] Holy Innocents, St George, St Gregory, Christ Church, St Paulinus, St Helen, St Pancras, St Eanswythe, St Mary Magdalene (possibly a re-dedication: Gillingham), St Lawrence of Canterbury (?), St Werburgh, St John the Evangelist, St Vincent, St Ethelburga, St Stephen, St Sexburga, St Mildred, St Nicholas (possibly a re-dedication: Sturry).
[c] St Paulinus, St Botolph, St Pancras, St Andrew, St Stephen, St Mildred, St Oswald, St Anthony, St Radegund, St Dunstan, St Cosmas & St Damian, St Leonard, St Edmund the King, St Blaise.
[d] St Martin, St Giles, St Dunstan, St Cosmas & St Damian, St Leonard, St Blaise, St Alphege.
[e] St Martin, St George, St Mary Magdalene, St John the Evangelist, St Mildred, St Nicholas, St Dunstan, St Leonard, St Thomas Becket.

PART FOUR *The Ecclesiastical Testimony*

small number of churches in the Forest of Blean may appropriately be bracketed with those of the Chartland, with which they had much in common. Table 12 presents a breakdown of these 320 dedications. The problem of assigning a period of origin to the remaining 220 is one that we shall return to later in this chapter.

There are three predominant characteristics brought to light by this tabulation. The first is the distinctive pattern of early dedications in the Original Lands, a point we shall return to in the following section. The second is the fact that, in a general way, the later the period of settlement, the more its range of dedications tended to depart from that of the Original Lands. In the Weald this generalization does not altogether hold good, chiefly perhaps because churches like Tenterden and Goudhurst adopted the patron saints of their distant mother-churches in the Original Lands, at Minster, Maidstone, and other early ecclesiastical centres. But broadly speaking it appears to be true, so

Table 13. Dedications in the Original Lands and the Wilderness parishes[a]

(A) Original Lands			(B) Wilderness parishes			Total of (A) and (B)		
29 Appellations	Nos.	%	32 Appellations	Nos.	%	47 Appellations	Nos.	%
1. St Mary	48	40.0	St Mary	33	16.5	St Mary	81	25.3
2. St Peter and St Paul	16	13.3	All Saints	17	8.5	St Peter and St Paul	29	9.1
3. St Martin	10	8.3	St Nicholas[e]	14	7.0	All Saints	20	6.3
4. St Peter	5	4.2	St Peter and St Paul	13	6.5	St Margaret	18	5.6
5. St Margaret	5	4.2	St Margaret	13	6.5	St Martin	15	4.7
6. St Augustine	4	3.3	St John the Baptist[f]	13	6.5	St Nicholas	15	4.7
7. Holy Trinity	3	2.5	St Michael	13	6.5	St Peter	14	4.4
8. St Botolph[b]	3	2.5	St Lawrence	10	5.0	St John the Baptist[f]	13	4.1
9. St Clement	3	2.5	St Peter	9	4.5	St Michael[j]	13	4.1
10. All Saints[c]	3	2.5	St James	7	3.5	St Lawrence[j]	10	3.1
11. St Andrew[b]	2	1.7	St Mary Magdalene[e]	7	3.5	St Mary Magdalene	8	2.5
12.			St Giles	6	3.0	St James[j]	7	2.2
13.			St Martin	5	2.5	St Giles[j]	6	1.9
14.			St Bartholomew	4	2.0	St George	4	1.2
15.			Holy Cross	4	2.0	St Augustine[k]	4	1.3
16.			St George[e]	3	1.5	St Botolph	4	1.3
17.			St Leonard	3	1.5	St Bartholomew	4	1.2
18.			St Dunstan	3	1.5	Holy Cross[j]	4	1.3
19.			St Mildred[e]	2	1.0	Holy Trinity[k]	3	0.9
20.			St Catherine	2	1.0	St Andrew	3	0.9

9 Church-dedications

21.			St Cosmas & St Damian	2	1.0	St Mildred	3	0.9
22.			St Blaise	2	1.0	St Clement[k]	3	0.9
23.						St Leonard[j]	3	0.9
24.						St Dunstan[j]	3	0.9
25.						St Paulinus	2	0.6
26.						St Pancras	2	0.6
27.						St John the Evangelist	2	0.6
28.						St Stephen	2	0.6
29.						St Catherine[j]	2	0.6
30.						St Cosmas & St Damian[j]	2	0.6
31.						St Blaise[j]	2	0.6
	Occurring once each, including 8 also occurring in Wilderness parishes[d]	18	15.0	Occurring once each,[g] including 6 also occurring in Original Lands	12	6.0	Occurring once each[l]	16	5.0
				Not known[h]	3	1.5	Not known[h]	3	0.9
Totals		120	100.0		200	100.0		321	100.0

[a] (1) Dedications occurring more than once in both the Original Lands and the Wilderness parishes are printed in italics.
(2) Where churches are dedicated to more than one saint (as Folkestone to St Mary and St Eanswythe), both dedications are taken into account. The figures also include the dedications of some lost churches, hospitals, chapels, and monastic houses, and in a few cases associations as well as formal dedications, as of St Crispin and St Crispinian at Faversham and Lydd.
[b] Occurring once also in the Wilderness parishes.
[c] Probably re-dedications.
[d] Holy Innocents, St Gregory, Christ Church, St Helen, St Eanswythe, St Lawrence of Canterbury (?), St Werburgh, St Vincent, St Ethelburga, St Sexburga, St George, St Paulinus, St Pancras, St Mary Magdalene, St John the Evangelist, St Stephen, St Mildred, St Nicholas, of which the last eight also occur in the Wilderness parishes.
[e] Occurring once also in the Original Lands.
[f] One of these churches, Doddington, was dedicated to the Beheading of John the Baptist.
[g] St Oswald, St Anthony, St Radegund, St Edmund the King, St Alphege, St Thomas Becket, St Paulinus, St Botolph, St Pancras, St Andrew, St John the Evangelist, St Stephen, of which the last six also occur in the Original Lands.
[h] Sundridge, Plaxtol, Keston.
[j] Dedication confined to the Wilderness parishes.
[k] Dedication confined to the Original Lands.
[l] In the Original Lands: Holy Innocents, St Gregory, Christ Church, St Helen, St Eanswythe, St Lawrence of Canterbury (?), St Werburga, St Vincent, St Ethelburga, and St Sexburga. In the Wilderness parishes: St Oswald, St Anthony, St Radegund, St Edmund the King, St Alphege, and St Thomas Becket.

PART FOUR *The Ecclesiastical Testimony*

that on the whole the dedications of the Chartland differ more radically from those of the Original Lands than do those of the Downs, and those in the west of the county more radically than those in the east. Taking the Blean and the Chartland together, indeed, dedications to St Mary and to St Peter and St Paul were actually less numerous than those to St Nicholas, and if the earlier churches in these areas were excluded, such as Sutton Valence and Great Chart, probably neither of the former would be represented more than twice or thrice.[20]

The third point to note is that, despite these differences, the outstanding contrast is that between the Original Lands on one hand, and the Downland, Chartland, Weald, and Blean, taken together, on the other. What characterized all these latter areas, as we have seen in earlier chapters, was the fact that, when St Augustine landed, they were still predominantly regions of woodland, forest, or heath, where permanent colonization by the English had in most parts scarcely begun. While it is important not to minimize the differences between these areas or to imply that their resources were then wholly unexploited, it is nevertheless legitimate to regard them collectively as the 'Wilderness' areas of the county at that time. In none of them were minsters or early mother-churches established, and in all the story of ecclesiastical evolution is essentially that of the foundation of daughter-churches in a subordinate countryside. To illustrate this contrast more clearly, the evidence for the Wilderness areas as a whole is combined in table 13 and placed alongside that of the Original Lands.

In this table, too, there are three general points to take into account. The first is that, out of a total of 47 different appellations, only 15 or 16 are common to both the Original Lands and the Wilderness areas, and only five (or perhaps six) occur more than once in both types of countryside: St Mary, St Martin, St Margaret, St Peter, and St Peter and St Paul.[21] Taken as a whole, therefore, the range of dedications in these contrasting zones is remarkably dissimilar. The second point to note is that, as ecclesiastical foundation extended into the wild, dedications to the three dominant patron saints of the early Kentish church tended to diminish: those to St Mary from 40 per cent of the total in the Original Lands to 16.5 per cent in the Wilderness parishes, those to St Peter and St Paul from 13.3 per cent to 6.5 per cent, and those to St Martin from 8.3 per cent to 2.5 per cent: or in other words from about 62 per cent to 25 per cent, if taken together. The third point to note is the lengthy list of patron saints whose names are rarely found at any point in the Original Lands and in most cases are almost entirely

9 *Church-dedications*

confined to the Wilderness areas of the county:[22] All Saints (which occurs 17 times), St Nicholas (14), St John the Baptist (13), St Michael (13), St Lawrence (10), St James (7), St Mary Magdalene (7), St Giles (6), St Bartholomew (4), Holy Cross (4), St Leonard (3), and St Dunstan (3). Together with a few other dedications occurring once or twice, such as St Blaise, St Edmund, St Radegund, St Oswald, and St Cosmas and St Damian, these appellations account for nearly 60 per cent of the Wilderness churches of Kent, yet in the Original Lands they are virtually unrepresented. The general pattern of dedications in each of these contrasting zones of settlement thus clearly merits more detailed investigation.

3. EARLY DEDICATIONS

The dedications of early Kentish churches fall into three groups. The first comprises those of the 50 or so native or 'indigenous' saints of the county; the second those of five saints who seem to have been especially popular in the early Kentish church, though they were not of local origin; the third comprises a number of very rare or unique dedications, most of which, in Kent, are peculiar, or almost peculiar, to very early churches. Altogether there were about 80 primary churches associated with these three groups of saints, including minsters, mother-churches, and early independent foundations like St Mary-in-Castro at Dover. In many cases the buildings in question were also associated with holy wells or springs, a topic we shall return to in the following chapter, and with a network of pre-Christian sites and regional cults ultimately centred on Canterbury, a matter discussed in the following section. At these points the evidence thus seems to hint at the possibility of an older stratum in the religious history of the county underlying that of the Augustinian church.

The indigenous saints of Kent consist of two groups: those of the royal house, and those associated with Canterbury and Rochester as ecclesiastical centres. Of the former, the earliest were St Ethelbert and his wife Bertha, who received St Augustine and his missionaries into Kent in 597.[23] From Ethelbert's stock, in the words of the *Catalogus Sanctorum Pausantium in Anglia*, there arose 'a numerous and holy race, which shines with virtue through the whole world'.[24] Many of the descendants of Ethelbert and Bertha married into other Anglo-Saxon dynasties, or were born elsewhere in England; but among those more particularly venerated in Kent itself were St Eanswythe (d. c.640), St

PART FOUR *The Ecclesiastical Testimony*

Ethelbricht (d.640/670), St Ethelred (d.640/670), St Ethelburga of Lyminge (d.647), St Ercongota (d. c.660), St Mildred (d. c.700), St Sexburga (d. c.700), St Ermengild (d. c.700), St Ermenburga (d. c.700), St Werburga (d. c.700), St Eanflæd (d. c.704), St Ermengitha (d.?), St Mildgyth (seventh century), St Edburga (d.751), and St Edith of Kemsing.[25] At least 11 primary churches were associated with these saints of the royal house,[26] all but one of them minsters, and several of them with more than one saint: Minster-in-Sheppey, for example, with St Sexburga and St Ermengild, and Minster-in-Thanet with St Mildred, St Edburga, St Ermenburga, and St Mildgyth.

Among the 30 saints associated with the two cathedral cities there were 23 archbishops of Canterbury who were canonized, two bishops of Rochester, two abbots of St Augustine's, and two other figures: Queen Bertha's chaplain St Liudhard (d. c.603), and St William of Rochester, a Scottish baker who was murdered in that city in 1201 and buried in the cathedral. A number of these saints were late Old English or post-Conquest figures and are not strictly relevant to the present discussion; but they are included here because their cults, like those preceding them, were associated with very early churches. The two canonized abbots of St Augustine's were St Peter of Canterbury (d.607) and St Adrian (d.709/10); the two bishops of Rochester were St Paulinus (d.644)[27] and St Ithamar (d. c.660); and the early archbishops of Canterbury included St Augustine (d. c.604), St Lawrence (d.619), St Mellitus (d.624), St Justus (d.627), St Honorius (d.653), St Deusdedit (d. c.664), St Theodore (d.690), St Berhtwald (d.731), St Nothelm (d.739), St Tatwine (d.741), St Bregwine (d.764), and St Jaenbeorht (d.792). Among the later archbishops to be canonized were St Dunstan (d.988), St Alphege (d.1012), St Anselm (d.1109), and St Thomas Becket (d.1170), to all of whom churches or chapels were also dedicated; to these we should perhaps add Robert Winchelsea (d.1313), who was not canonized but whose shrine was widely venerated in Kent down to the time of the Reformation.[28] Ten primary churches, seven or eight of which were minsters, were associated with the early saints of Canterbury and Rochester, while at least 29 churches altogether were associated with these 'ecclesiastical' saints. At Canterbury itself there were numerous shrines and altars in their honour, both in Christ Church and in St Augustine's Abbey.

The five non-local saints whose names were especially popular in the early Kentish church were St Martin, St Margaret, St Mary the Virgin, and St Peter and St Paul. Dedications to these saints were in no way

9 Church-dedications

peculiar to Kent; but as already remarked they were notably more common there than in England generally. Altogether, they accounted for nearly 200 churches in the county as a whole, those to St Margaret representing one-tenth of the total for England, those to St Martin one-ninth, and those to St Peter and St Paul one-seventh. Of the primary churches under discussion, six were dedicated to St Margaret, six to St Peter and St Paul, eight to St Martin, and 22 to St Mary;[29] of these at least 24 were minsters. The special Kentish preoccupation with St Margaret and St Mary is a point we shall return to below in discussing dedications to women. The local cult of St Martin no doubt arose from his patronage of St Martin's Canterbury, a Romano-British building restored by St Liudhard for Queen Bertha's use on her marriage to Ethelbert (c.588), and probably dedicated to the Frankish saint before the arrival of St Augustine.[30] The popularity of St Peter and St Paul must likewise have developed from the dedication of one of the earliest Kentish churches, that of St Augustine's own monastic house in Canterbury.

The locally rare or unique dedications with which most of the remaining primary churches of Kent were associated are 16 in number: St Pancras, St Anacletus, St Gregory, St Pelagius, St Vincent, St Stephen, St Andrew, St Rumwold (or Rumbald), St Botolph, St Helen, St John the Divine,[31] St Anthony the Martyr, St Crispin and St Crispinian, Christ Church, Holy Trinity, and Holy Innocents. Rare dedications are not necessarily early, and not all of these are rare in other parts of England; but in Kent they were restricted to an exceptionally limited number of early foundations, not more than 23 altogether. Only a few of these can be discussed within the limits of this chapter; but the following examples illustrate the unusual circumstances with which dedications of this kind are often associated.

1. Holy Trinity. There are only three ancient churches in Kent dedicated to the Trinity – Canterbury Cathedral, Milton Regis, and Dartford – and the fact that all three were minsters is remarkable. In some counties this was not an uncommon appellation; but in Kent it was not given to any ordinary parish church, the six remaining dedications all relating to late medieval chapels or hospitals. Is it possible that it was regarded as in some sense too lofty for common use in the early Kentish church? It is noteworthy that of the additional dedications of Canterbury Cathedral, St Saviour occurs only once elsewhere in Kent, at Faversham Abbey after the Conquest, and Christ Church is unique.[32]

2. *St Andrew*. The fact that there are only five churches in Kent associated with St Andrew is likewise remarkable, since elsewhere this is one of the commonest English dedications, occurring nearly 600 times. It is the more striking in that two of the early mother-churches in the county were so dedicated – Rochester Cathedral and Wickhambreaux – no doubt because St Andrew was the patron saint of St Augustine's own monastic house in Rome. Yet just as Christ Church remained unique in the diocese of Canterbury, so St Andrew remained unique in that of Rochester. At Wickhambreaux it is perhaps significant that the two adjacent churches of Littlebourne and Ickham, both of which were probably early daughters of Wickham, were also given dedications unique among Kentish parish churches: St Vincent and St John the Divine.

3. St Gregory. This dedication, too, was given to only one parish church, the minster of St Martin and St Gregory at Wye.[33] The point is of special interest because the name of Wye means 'heathen temple' and St Gregory is known to have advised St Augustine not to destroy heathen temples but to reconsecrate them for Christian purposes. The original church at Wye may well have been one of the temples St Gregory was referring to. The name of the place itself, coupled with its early development as a *villa regalis* and minster-settlement and its situation at an important route junction on the Pilgrims' Way, no doubt suggests that Wye was a pagan shrine of more than ordinary significance. The fact that Alkham, another early Kentish church possibly occupying a pagan site, also bears a very rare dedication, St Anthony the Martyr, is perhaps worth noting in this connexion. Alkham was not a minster and is unlikely to be as early as Wye; but its name may mean '*hām* by a heathen temple', and St Anthony was particularly celebrated for his dialectical skill in disputing with the heathen.[34]

4. St Helen. Of the two Kentish churches at one time associated with St Helen, that at Canterbury has long since disappeared, but Cliffe-at-Hoo survives and is one of the finest churches in the diocese of Rochester. The topographical connotation of minster-dedications is generally worth investigating, and that at Cliffe is no exception. For this was a Romano-British military settlement in origin, associated with the garrison at Rochester, situated at the terminus of a Roman road, and still perhaps retaining traces of centuriation in its field-system. Since it was also associated with an early Jutish burial ground, the arguments for continuity seem particularly strong at Cliffe, and it

9   *Church-dedications*

may be that the dedication to St Helen harks back, as in similar circumstances in Yorkshire, Lancashire, and Lincolnshire, to the Celtic Elen, the goddess of armies and roads.[35] In view of the unusual rarity of this dedication in Kent, it may be significant that St Helen's Canterbury was likewise situated on a Roman road and within a Roman military community. It is also worth noting that Cliffe seems to have been associated with another enigmatic patron saint, St Pelagius, whose identity remains a mystery.[36]

5. Holy Innocents, St Pancras, and St Rumwold. These three dedications all refer to child-saints. The first two were given to two of the earliest churches in the county, at Adisham and in Canterbury, and all three are extremely rare in England generally. Like the minster at Wye, the church of St Pancras at Canterbury is said to have been a heathen temple in origin, and to have been the first church in England dedicated by St Augustine. Frances Arnold-Forster was no doubt right in rejecting Dean Stanley's picturesque notion that this circumstance harked back to the story of Pope Gregory and the English slave-boys in the Roman forum;[37] yet there is some reason to think that there may have been a deliberate *cultus* of child saints in the early Kentish church. St Pancras was also associated with another early church, in the earthworks at Coldred, though not so early as that at Canterbury, and St Rumwold with the early minster-settlement at Folkestone as well as with later churches at Boxley and Bonnington. In one respect the most interesting of these child-dedications is that of the Holy Innocents at Adisham; for Adisham may have been one of the first estates granted to Canterbury Cathedral, reputedly by King Eadbald in 616, and its church does not seem to have been subordinated to any mother-church or minster.[38] The settlement structure of the parish is unusual, moreover, and the fact that its liberties became the basis for many subsequent Christ Church estates clearly places it in an exceptional category.[39] On several counts, indeed, the historical development of Adisham and its medieval economy would repay detailed investigation.

4. EARLY CULTS AND CULT CENTRES

These early dedications of Kent raise many points of interest; they also pose a number of unresolved problems. Several of the saints in question are difficult to identify, and the legends associated with them cannot always be reconciled with traditionally accepted facts. The St Edith who is said to have been born at Kemsing, and who 'wrought many

PART FOUR *The Ecclesiastical Testimony*

miracles for such as applied to her for relief there, cannot well be identified with her Wessex and Mercian namesakes, of Wilton and Polesworth.⁴⁰ Quite why St Rumwold, the legendary Mercian saint who cried out 'Christianus sum' as he was born, and expired in the odour of sanctity three days later, came to be specially venerated in Kent it is impossible to say. Neither is it possible to say why the third-century Roman martyrs St Crispin and St Crispinian were believed to have lived at Faversham, where their house was still an object of veneration in the seventeenth century, and to have been shipwrecked and buried at Lydd, where a great mound of stones was regarded as their tomb.⁴¹ Such problems as these cannot be pursued here; but in the context of early settlement history there are three general matters that need to be discussed.

The first is the fact that so many of these early dedications of Kent are associated with pre-Christian sites. To some extent this is due no doubt to the planting of early churches in places of Romano-British origin; yet at many points local circumstances seem to suggest that there is more behind the association than that. In numerous cases the churches in question are situated either within or directly adjacent to Roman buildings and reconstructed from their remains.⁴² A number of them seem to have originated as heathen temples, as we have seen, and many are also associated, as at Cliffe, with heathen burial grounds. At Canterbury, for example, St Martin's, St Pancras's, and Christ Church are all said to have been pre-Augustinian structures in origin; at Dover the minster of St Martin stood on the site of a Roman building and near a Jutish burial ground; at Lyminge the minster of St Ethelburga was built on the foundations of a Roman house and near a Jutish burial ground; at Wye that of St Martin and St Gregory probably originated as a heathen temple and is similarly associated with a Jutish burial ground; at Lydd settlement also extends back into the Roman period and the church itself may just possibly have originated as a Roman basilica. Elsewhere, something of the same pattern is repeated, though not necessarily in every detail: at St Mary's Faversham, for example, St Mary's Eastry, Holy Trinity Dartford, Holy Trinity Milton Regis, St Martin's Eynsford, St Martin's Romney, St Margaret's Darenth, St Margaret's High Halstow, St Margaret's Rainham, St Augustine's Stonar, St Augustine's Richborough, St Paulinus' Crayford, St Werburga's Hoo, St Mary and St Mildred's Minster-in-Thanet, St Mary and St Eanswythe's Folkestone, and St Mary and St Sexburga's Minster-in-Sheppey.⁴³

9 Church-dedications

The second point to note is the fact that virtually all these primary churches are linked together by a striking network of prehistoric tracks and Roman roads. Once again this is partly dictated by their location in Romano-Jutish settlements; yet in this respect, too, local circumstances often seem to indicate that there is more behind the association than that. In Holmesdale, for example, the Greenway passes not only through the British church-site at Eccles but directly through the churchyards of a long line of primary churches at the foot of the Downs: St Botolph's Chevening, for example, St Mary and St Edith's Kemsing, St George's Wrotham, St Peter and St Paul's Trottiscliffe, St Mary's Burham, All Saints' Hollingbourne, St Mary's Lenham, St Peter and St Paul's Charing, St Mary's Westwell, St Martin and St Gregory's Wye, St Mary's Brabourne, St Martin's Cheriton, and St Mary and St Eanswythe's Folkstone.[44] Similarly, on the Foothills, Watling Street and its prehistoric predecessor provided a direct link between St Augustine's Richborough, St Andrew's Wickhambreaux, Christ Church Canterbury, St Mary's Faversham, Holy Trinity Milton, St Mary's Newington, St Andrew's Rochester, Holy Trinity Dartford, and St Botolph's Crayford, in several cases once again originally passing through the churchyard. Elsewhere, on the network of subsidiary Roman roads and ancient ridgeways branching off Watling Street, we find St Martin's Eynsford, St Margaret's Darenth, St Helen's Cliffe, St Margaret's High Halstow, St Mary's Maidstone, St Mary's Chilham, St Lawrence's Godmersham, St Mary's Reculver, St Mary's Wingham, St Mary's Woodnesborough, St Mary's Eastry: and so on. At a number of these places, such as Dartford, Lenham, and Charing, it seems that the church must actually have been built on the course of the roadway itself. Beneath the whole complex of early Christian centres associated with these saints, in short, there seems to be a distinct system of prehistoric roads and tracks, and there is some reason to think that the use of these routes as 'pilgrim-ways' goes back beyond the Christian era. Their frequent association with holy wells and springs is possibly significant in this connexion and is discussed in Chapter 10.

The third topic demands fuller investigation, and that is the remarkable number of early Kentish churches dedicated to women. If all the 540 historic dedications of the county are taken into consideration, it appears that 184 or 34 per cent relate to women saints, and 294 or 54 per cent to men. If the survey is confined to parish churches alone, the proportion rises to 40 per cent (or 165) dedicated to women and drops to 51 per cent (or 214) dedicated to men. These figures may be compared with those for Leicestershire given in table 14, where it appears that only 22 per cent of all parish churches were dedicated to women in comparison with 57 per cent to men. In other words, the latter were two and a half times as numerous as the former in Leicestershire (154:60), whereas in Kent they outnumbered them by less than one-third (214:165). It was in the early phases of church foundation that the preponderance of dedications to women saints in Kent was especially remarkable. Of the primary churches under discussion probably as many as 40 (or 51 per cent) were originally dedicated to women and only 31 (or 39 per cent) to men.[45] Statistics are a crude yardstick in this connexion, but it seems evident that there was a notable preoccupation with women's cults in the early Kentish church. That preoccupation was particularly striking in the case of St Mary the Virgin, St Margaret, and the women saints of the royal house; these three groups will therefore bear further scrutiny.

In almost all parts of England dedications to St Mary form the most numerous single group, as already remarked, and Leicestershire is unusual in that those to All Saints almost equal them (40:44). In Kent, however, where they are three times as numerous as those to any other saint and account for nearly a quarter of all the churches in the shire, the pre-eminence of St Mary is exceptional. In the primary phases of ecclesiastical foundation, at least 22 churches out of a total of about 80 were dedicated to the Virgin, or three times as many as those to St Mary's nearest rival, St Martin, and four times as many as those to St Peter and St Paul, the second most popular dedication in the county. Among these early foundations many of the most prominent minsters were to be found, moreover, such as Faversham, Folkestone, Maidstone, Eastry, Lyminge, Reculver, Wingham, Minster-in-Sheppey, and Minster-in-Thanet.[46]

Table 14. Dedications in Kent and in Leicestershire[a]

1. Men	Kent	Leicestershire		Kent	Leicestershire
(A) *General*	%	%			
St Peter & St Paul	39(7.2)	3(1.1)	St George	7(1.3)	0
St Nicholas	34(6.3)	10(3.7)	St Giles	7(1.3)	4(1.5)
St John the Baptist	28(5.2)	18(6.7)	St Andrew	7(1.3)	13(4.8)
St Peter	21(3.9)	32(11.9)	St Botolph	6(1.1)	3(1.1)
St Martin	18(3.3)	4(1.5)	St Clement	5	0
St Michael	18(3.3)	22(8.1)	St Leonard	5	4(1.5)
St James	17(3.2)	8(3.0)	St Edmund the King	4	0
St Lawrence of Rome	11(2.0)	1	St Stephen	4	0
St Bartholomew	10(1.8)	5(1.9)	St Anthony	3	0
			St Rumwold	3	0

9 Church-dedications

1. Men (contd.)	Kent	Leicestershire
(A) *General* (contd.)	%	%
St Gregory	3	0
St John the Divine	3	1
St Pancras	2	0
St Cosmas & St Damian	2	0
St Blaise	2	0
St Crispin & St Crispinian	2	0
St Paul	2	0
St Thomas the Apostle	2	0
St Luke	2	4(1.5)
St Matthew	1	1
St Denis	1	6(2.2)
St Cuthbert	0	2
Others, occurring once each	2[b]	7[c]
Total	269	148
(B) *Local to Kent or Leics.*		
St Augustine	7(1.3)	0
St Thomas Becket	7(1.3)	4(1.5)
St Dunstan	5	0
St Alphege	3	0
St Paulinus	2	0
St Lawrence of Canterbury(?)	1	0
St Wistan	0	2
Total	25	6
Total men	294(54.4)	154(57.0)

2. Women	Kent	Leicestershire
(A) *General*	%	%
St Mary	120(22.2)	44(16.3)
St Margaret	22(4.1)	3
St Mary Magdalene	13(2.4)	5(1.9)
St Catherine	6(1.1)	2
St Radegund	3	0
St Helen	2	5(1.9)
St Anne[d]	2	0
St Faith	1	0
Total	169	59

2. Women (contd.)	Kent	Leicestershire
(B) *Local to Kent or Leics.*	%	%
St Mildred	7(1.3)	0
St Eanswythe	2	0
St Bertha	1	0
St Edburga	1	0
St Edith	1	?1
St Ethelburga of Lyminge	1	0
St Sexburga	1	0
St Werburga	1	0
Total	15	1
Total women	184(34.1)	60(22.2)

3. General	Kent	Leicestershire
	%	%
All Saints	37(6.9)	40(14.8)
Holy Trinity	9(1.7)	5(1.9)
Holy Cross	6(1.1)	2
Holy Innocents	1	0
St Saviour	1	0
All Souls	1	0
Corpus Christi	1	0
St Sepulchre	1	0
Christ Church	1	0
Total	58(10.7)	47(17.4)

4. *Unknown*	4	9
Grand total	540(100.0)	270(100.0)

[a] The Leicestershire figures relate to parish churches only, and are thus not strictly comparable with those for Kent; those for chapels, etc., are not available.
[b] St Vincent, St Oswald.
[c] St Philip, St Edward, St Swithin, St Wilfred, St Remigius, St Egelwine, St Guthlac.
[d] Also many lights to St Anne in Kentish churches.

PART FOUR *The Ecclesiastical Testimony*

Of the 22 churches dedicated to St Margaret, White Kennett remarked in the seventeenth century that she was 'a saint of great veneration in Kent, there being very many churches dedicated to her...'[47] In saying so he was specifically referring to his patron's church, St Margaret's Hothfield; but he must also have been recalling the legends and traditions of his childhood; for his father was vicar of Postling near Hythe and he himself was born at Dover, not far from St Margaret-at-Cliffe. One telling circumstance in support of his comment is the fact that in both parishes bearing names in *hālig* or 'holy' – High Halstow and Lower Halstow – the church is dedicated to St Margaret.[48] Several other Kentish churches bearing this dedication are associated with pre-Christian sites, moreover: Darenth and East Barming, for instance, with Roman cremations and cemeteries, and Addington with an important group of Neolithic chamber tombs and with Bronze Age and Roman remains.[49] Like the churches dedicated to St Mary, therefore, some of those to St Margaret seem to have a distinct bearing on early Kentish settlement, though apart from Darenth it is doubtful if any of them were mother-churches in the strict sense of the term, and her name remained popular in the Wilderness areas.

Of the 17 saints of the royal house mentioned earlier, 14 were women, and once again we find them predominantly associated with major primary foundations: St Ethelburga with Lyminge, St Eanswythe with Folkstone, St Edith with Kemsing, St Werburga with Hoo, St Mildgyth with Eastry, St Sexburga and St Ermengild with Minster-in-Sheppey, St Bertha with St Augustine's Abbey, and St Mildred, St Edburga, and St Ermenburga with Minster-in-Thanet. In most cases very little is known about the cults of these dynastic saints of Kent; but Dr Rollason's recent work has shown the extraordinary local popularity of St Mildred. When Minster-in-Thanet was destroyed by the Danes in 1011, both St Augustine's Abbey and St Gregory's Priory claimed to have obtained possession of her body. Whichever claim was correct, many miracles were wrought at St Mildred's shrine in St Augustine's, and according to William of Malmesbury, 'although almost every corner of that monastery is filled with the bodies of saints of great name and merit ... yet no one is there more revered, more loved, or more gratefully remembered' than she.[50]

There can be very little doubt, therefore, that there was a distinctive emphasis in the early Kentish church on cults associated with women saints. The fact that so many of the churches in question are not only of great antiquity in themselves but are associated with Romano-British settlements, and with centres of heathen worship, gives some ground for believing that this emphasis may have ultimately stemmed from pre-Christian traditions. The frequent association of these places with holy wells and springs later connected with rites of healing and fertility, and with saints like St Anne, the patroness of barren women, lends further support to this hypothesis; for the pre-Christian cults of Kent were also based on fertility customs and the worship of female water-spirits. In the development of this regional tradition one place in particular stands out: Maidstone, the 'stone of the maidens'. For here, not only was the minster church dedicated to St Mary; many of the medieval townsmen's houses were adorned with emblems of the Virgin; two of the four medieval chapelries in the borough were dedicated to virgin saints, St Catherine and St Faith; the chapel and wells of St Anne were probably associated, as in other towns, with fertility customs; and the place-name itself suggests that these customs and traditions may have originated in the pre-Christian era.

Behind the whole network of early church-dedications in Kent we must envisage a widespread tradition of local pilgrimage, originating with the death of St Augustine at the beginning of the seventh century, and continuing without a break for more than 900 years. In this connotation the pilgrimage to Canterbury later associated with the name of Becket needs to be seen not simply as a national or international development, but as the culmination of a massive regional movement which had been bringing pilgrims to Canterbury from many parts of Kent for more than five centuries before Becket's death. It was this tradition that linked the nexus of localized cult-centres together, moreover, based on places like Rochester, Maidstone, Folkestone, Lyminge, Eastry, Kemsing, Reculver, Minster-in-Thanet, Minster-in-Sheppey, and Hoo St Werburgh, and ultimately united them with Canterbury. In other words Canterbury was not simply the political capital of the Kentish kingdom and the seat of the archbishop, but the focal point of a whole galaxy of indigenous cults and local devotional customs.[51] The veritable constellation of shrines to be found from the earliest days in St Augustine's Abbey, where St Ethelbert, St Bertha, and all the early archbishops were buried, was particularly remarkable. At many points these cults were based on pre-Christian religious centres like Aylesford, Maidstone, and Wye, moreover, and it may be that they inherited more than has yet been recognized from the pagan world.

PART FOUR *The Ecclesiastical Testimony*

5. THE CHURCH IN THE WILDERNESS

There are many parts of Kent where the pattern of Wilderness dedications was in its way no less distinctive than that of the early churches of the county. The dedications of the Chartland churches, for example, contrast strikingly with those of their mother-churches in Holmesdale. Between the Surrey border at Westerham and the Stour valley at Wye, there were 19 mother-churches strung out along the springs at the foot of the Downs; and of these, seven were dedicated to St Mary, four to St Peter and St Paul, three to St Martin, two to All Saints, and one each to St Botolph, St Edith, St Gregory, St Peter, and St George.[52] So far as All Saints and St George are concerned, it is unlikely that these were the original ascriptions, as has already been remarked; but there is no reason to suspect the status of the remainder. Of the 41 churches and chapels to which these minsters gave birth on the Chartland, by contrast, at least 29 were dedicated to saints whose names are scarcely represented amongst the original dedications of Holmesdale: six to St Nicholas, at Leeds, Linton, Otham, Pluckley, Boughton Monchelsea, and Sevenoaks; four to St Margaret, at Broomfield, Hothfield, Addington, and East Barming; three to St Michael, at Offham, Chart Sutton, and East Peckham; three to St John the Baptist, at Sevenoaks, Wateringbury, and New Hythe; three to St Lawrence, at Mereworth, Longsole, and Allington; three to All Saints, at Ulcombe, West Farleigh, and Loose; two to St James, at Egerton and East Malling; and one each to St Giles at Shipbourne, St Dunstan at West Peckham, St Leonard at West Malling, St Blaise in Mereworth Woods, and the Holy Cross at Bearsted. Of the remaining Chartland churches, six were dedicated to St Mary, two to St Peter and St Paul, and two to St Peter alone, while in two cases the original dedication is unknown.[53] Of these, however, it is noteworthy that St Peter's at Ditton was probably given its dedication by the mother-church of St Peter at Aylesford, while three of the churches dedicated to St Mary – at Sutton Valence, West Malling, and Great Chart – were relatively early foundations despite their Chartland situation.[54] In other words, at least three-quarters of the late Old English and post-Conquest churches of the Chartland bear dedications that are not represented among the mother-churches of Holmesdale.

In the equivalent Wilderness areas on the Downs, the same striking contrast is repeated. Of the 77 surviving Downland churches between the Surrey border and the Stour valley, all but 24 (or nearly 70 per cent)

9 Church-dedications

bear dedications that are scarcely found at all amongst those of their mother-churches on the Foothills. Seven of them are dedicated to St John the Baptist; five each to St Mary Magdalene, St Margaret, and All Saints; four each to St Nicholas, St Michael, and St Giles; three each to St Lawrence and St James; two each to St Catherine, St Bartholomew, and St George; and one each to St Dunstan, St Leonard, St Edmund, St Blaise, St Cosmas and St Damian, and the Holy Cross. Most of the remainder are dedicated to St Mary (10) or to St Peter and St Paul (6); but as on the Chartland, several of these, as at Eastling (St Mary), Milsted (St Mary and the Holy Cross), and Lynsted (St Peter and St Paul), are likely to be relatively early foundations. In this area, too, therefore, we find the same distinctively localized pattern, the same varied range of patron saints, and the same absence of most of the indigenous cults of the early Kentish church, except that of St Margaret.

That the churches bearing these dedications were indeed relatively late foundations, and almost invariably subordinate in origin, is also apparent from their antecedents. Of the 34 churches in Kent dedicated to St Nicholas, for example – the third most popular saint in the county – all save Sturry seem to have been subordinate establishments, probably dating from the late Old English or post-Conquest periods: and Sturry, like All Saints, Maidstone, may be a re-dedication.[55] Ashby-Sandwich, for example, is known to have originated as a daughter-church of Wingham, Boughton Malherbe of Lenham, Pluckley of Charing, Leeds of Hollingbourne, Southfleet of Northfleet, Strood of Frindsbury, Deptford of Greenwich, Sevenoaks of Shoreham, Sholden of Northbourne, Rodmersham of Milton Regis, St Nicholas-at-Wade of Reculver, Woodchurch-in-Thanet of Minster, Otham and Linton of Maidstone, Hythe of Saltwood and Lympne, New Romney of Old Romney, Buckland of Teynham or Faversham, and Milton on Stour most likely of Thanington.[56] In other cases we cannot be so certain of the identity of the mother church; but Oxney, Ringwould, and Chislehurst are all typical subordinate parishes on the Downland; Harbledown was certainly a subordinate parish in the Forest of Blean;[57] Sandhurst is a late forest parish in the Weald, first recorded about 1100; Newington-next-Hythe is also a relatively late parish first recorded in Domesday Book; while none of the three remaining churches of St Nicholas – in Canterbury, Rochester, and Plumstead – is likely to belong to the primary phases of ecclesiastical development.

Exactly the same pattern also occurs in the case of churches

PART FOUR *The Ecclesiastical Testimony*

dedicated to St Michael, St James, and St John the Baptist. Of the 18 associated with St Michael, probably all save perhaps Cuxton were subordinate foundations; of the 17 associated with St James all save East Malling; and of the 28 associated with St John the Baptist all save perhaps Halling.[58] Certainly none of the 63 was a primary foundation, and although St John's Harrietsham and St John's Sutton-at-Hone eventually gave birth to daughters of their own, both had originated as dependent churches themselves, of Lenham and Dartford respectively. The same story is repeated yet again in the case of dedications to St Bartholomew, St Leonard, St Blaise, St Giles, St Catherine, St Lawrence, St Dunstan, St Edmund, St Cosmas and St Damian, and the Holy Cross. Of the 59 Kentish churches and chapels bearing these dedications, none was a primary foundation except St Lawrence's Godmersham: and that was perhaps associated with St Lawrence of Canterbury rather than with St Lawrence of Rome.[59] The overwhelming majority of the 122 churches discussed in this paragraph can in fact be shown to have originated as dependent chapelries in the late Old English period or shortly after the Conquest.

Why was it that there were so many dedications in Kent thus largely confined to subsidiary churches, and especially to those in the Wilderness areas? Why was it that the dedication pattern of these woodland regions was so distinctive? Was it simply the consequence of a change in ecclesiastical fashion, as settlement advanced and the old indigenous cults began to wane, or were there more fundamental causes at work? That fashion and popularity affected it, and the rise of novel cults like those of St Dunstan, St Alphege, and St Thomas Becket, there can of course be no doubt. Yet the great majority of Wilderness dedications reverted to the early saints of the Christian church, like St John the Baptist, St Mary Magdalene, and St Nicholas. The immediate circumstances behind individual dedications are of course largely unknown to us; yet if we turn to the legends and traditions associated with saints like these, we often find a certain appropriateness to a Wilderness environment. St John the Baptist, for example, was pre-eminently the saint of the Wilderness, where he lived among the beasts, we are told, and fed upon locusts and wild honey. St Michael, too, the archangel who slaughtered the Beast in the Book of Revelation, was widely connected with apparitions on remote hill-tops, so that his churches are often found in commanding positions, as at Hawkinge and Chart Sutton, overlooking the *wald*. Other Wilderness saints, like St Leonard, were in origin specifically connected with regions of unreclaimed woodland;[60]

9 *Church-dedications*

or like St Blaise with the blessing of sick and wounded creatures in the wild; or like St Anthony with a strange ascendancy over savage beasts; or like St Cosmas and St Damian, with the healing of sick and injured livestock. Others again were associated with roads and tracks, and with the protection of wayfarers: St Nicholas, for example, with drovers and travellers generally, as well as with mariners; St James with travellers and pilgrims, and hence with wayside churches and hospitals; and St Bartholomew with hospitals for indigent wayfarers, and with rites of healing generally. In many cases it is further noteworthy that saints like these were believed to have lived the solitary life of the desert hermit: St Anthony, for example, in the deserts of Egypt and the Red Sea; St Leonard in the forest of Noblac in France; St Giles near the mouth of the Rhone, not far from Nîmes; and St Mary Magdalene, quite apocryphally, in the recesses of the Maritime Alps.[61]

In the pattern of Wilderness dedications, in short, what we probably see is the characteristic response of a pastoral people to the reclamation of a wooded, inhospitable countryside. As the summer shielings of the herdsmen developed into permanent farms, as churches and chapels began to appear alongside the old droveways, it was but natural that they should be placed under the patronage of those saints who seemed most able to protect them in a hostile environment. There are many places as a consequence where the place-names and the topography of these churches still bear witness to their origins in the reclamation of the forest: at St Bartholomew's Waltham and St Nicholas's Ringwould, for example, which contain the element *wald*; at St Nicholas's Pluckley and St James's Elmley (*lēah*); at St James's Elmsted and Holy Cross Bearsted (*stede*); at Holy Cross Hoath ('heath') and St Lawrence's Otterden (*denn*); at St Lawrence's Hawkhurst, St Leonard's Falconhurst, St Nicholas's Sandhurst, and St John the Baptist's Penshurst (*herst*): and so on. Otherwise the one general point worth noting in connexion with these later dedications of Kent is their frequent association with landing-places and hithes: eleven times, as remarked earlier, in the case of St Nicholas, five times in those of St John the Baptist and St James, twice in that of St Michael, and once or twice in those of St Leonard and St Giles.[62] In the late Old English port of New Romney, St Nicholas, St Michael, and St John the Baptist were all at one time represented, and in that of Hythe, which originated through the silting up of the Limen at Lympne, St Nicholas, St Michael, St John the Baptist, and St Leonard.[63] As the clearance of the *wald* itself proceeded, there was thus a subsidiary development of settlement

253

PART FOUR *The Ecclesiastical Testimony*

alongside navigable waters in Kent; in all probability, indeed, there was a direct connexion between the two movements.

6. TOWARDS A CHRONOLOGY

While it is important not to oversimplify the interpretation of church-dedications, and it is unwise to take them out of context, there are many places where, in the reconstruction of settlement, they lend supporting

Table 15. Dedications: a tentative chronology

1[a]		2		3		4		5	
St Augustine	7	St Mary	120	St Margaret	22	All Saints[d]	37	St Anthony	3
St Paulinus	2	St Peter &		St Clement	5	St Nicholas	34	St Rumwold	3
St Pancras	2	St Paul	39			St John the		St John the	
St Helen	2	St Peter	21			Baptist	28	Evangelist	3
St Eanswythe	2	St Martin	18			St Michael	18	St Anne	2
St Crispin &		Holy Trinity	9			St James	17	St Paul	2
St Crispinian	2	St Mildred	7			St Mary		St Thomas	
St Bertha	1	St Andrew	7			Magdalene	13	the Apostle	2
St Edburga	1	St Botolph	6			St Lawrence		St Luke	1
St Edith	1	St Stephen	4			of Rome	11	St Matthew	1
St Ethelburga	1	?St Gregory[c]	3			St Bartholo-		St Saviour	1[e]
Holy Inno-						mew	10		
cents	1					St George	7		
?St Lawrence of						St Giles	7		
Canterbury[b]	1					St Thomas Becket	7		
St Sexburga	1					Holy Cross	6		
St Vincent	1					St Catherine	6		
St Werburga	1					St Dunstan	5		
Christ Church	1					St Leonard	5		
						St Edmund	4		
						St Radegund	3		
						St Alphege	3		
						St Cosmas & St Damian	2		
						St Blaise	2		
						St Faith	1		
						St Oswald	1		
						St Sepulchre	1		
						All Souls	1		
						Corpus Christi	1		
Totals: 16	27	10	234	2	27	25	230	9	18

9 Church-dedications

Note: In four cases the dedication is not known; the grand total is 540. The basis of the table is as in table 11. The first column lists those that, as far as can be seen, relate only to minsters or other early churches; the second, those that relate to both minsters and churches of subsequent periods; the third, those that relate to both early and late churches, but not to minsters; the fourth, those that invariably, or almost invariably, refer to late Old English or post-Conquest churches; and the fifth, those whose period of origin is often uncertain, but which in some cases may refer to quite early churches, though not to minsters.

[a] It is possible that one or two of the dedications in this column (e.g. St Eanswythe's, Brenzett) are late Old English.
[b] Godmersham. But this may be dedicated to St Lawrence of Rome.
[c] The minster at Wye is dedicated to St Martin and St Gregory; but St Gregory may be a later addition.
[d] Assuming that Birling, Hollingbourne, and Lydd, like All Saints Maidstone, are re-dedications. Otherwise All Saints should be in column 2. But the great majority of All Saints dedications are certainly late, and there are no indisputable cases of early churches bearing this dedication.
[e] Faversham Abbey; St Saviour is also sometimes given as an alternative dedication of Christ Church, Canterbury – the two are of course in a sense the same.

evidence to other lines of enquiry. To sum up the argument, it may be useful therefore to classify the 62 different dedications found in Kent into tentative categories, according to their period of origin, and this is done in table 15. The classification in this table should not be regarded as more than a provisional one; an element of uncertainty is unavoidable in any attempt to categorize the dedications of more than 500 buildings, and a margin of error must be allowed for. It should also be remembered that the table relates strictly to recorded *dedications*, not to churches as such, so that where re-dedication has taken place but has not been traced it will not provide a reliable guide to the origin of the church in question. Nevertheless, in its broad outlines it can probably be accepted with reasonable confidence. What are the main conclusions it indicates?

In the first column, the principal point to note is the prominence of the Old Saxon saints of the county. Except in the case of St Mildred (see column 2), such dedications almost invariably indicate very early churches in Kent, though only occasionally can they represent the original appellation.[61] In most cases these churches were minsters; but even where they were not, they are sometimes thought to date back to the seventh century, as at St Augustine's Richborough, and in all cases

PART FOUR *The Ecclesiastical Testimony*

they probably antedate the ninth. After the primary phases of ecclesiastical foundation very few local churches were dedicated to the dynastic saints of Kent apart from St Mildred, though their cults remained notable features of the area – as in the case of St Edith of Kemsing – until the end of the medieval period.

In the second column the principal dedications to take note of are those of St Mary, St Martin, and St Peter and St Paul, who between them, as we have seen, accounted for more than 60 per cent of all the early churches in the Original Lands. While their patronage extended to churches of all periods, moreover, even to late Wealden foundations like St Martin's Ashurst and St Mary's chapel in Pembury churchyard, they were more characteristic of early churches generally than of those in the Wilderness. Of the remaining dedications in this column, that of St Peter (alone) also calls for a brief comment. Of the churches so dedicated in Kent, it is noteworthy that only one, that at Aylesford, was a minster, and that the rest, unlike those dedicated to St Peter with St Paul, were almost all relatively late foundations, either in the Weald at places like Hever and Pembury, or in subordinate parishes elsewhere, such as Bredhurst, Molash, Oare, Bridge, Ridley, and St Peter-in-Thanet. Except at Aylesford, indeed, it is probable that St Peter alone, as distinct from St Peter with St Paul, should generally be regarded as a late dedication in Kent, though in this respect the local evidence does not seem to be typical of other counties.

The dedications listed in the fourth column may be divided into three different groups. The first comprises those that obviously originate towards the end of the Old English period or after the Conquest: St Thomas Becket (d.1180), St Dunstan (d.988), St Edmund (d.869), St Alphege (d.1012), and St Oswald (d.961). Some of these may possibly represent re-dedications; but there is no real reason to suspect their authenticity, and all the 20 churches involved are likely to be relatively late ones. The second group comprises 14 dedications that in Kent always, or almost always, seem to be late in origin, and are sometimes generally so regarded elsewhere in England, though the case is not always self-evident: St Michael, St Bartholomew, St George, St Giles, Holy Cross, St Catherine, St Leonard, St Radegund, St Cosmas and St Damian, St Blaise, St Faith, St Sepulchre, All Souls, and Corpus Christi. Except in the case of St George's Wrotham and perhaps St Michael's Cuxton, it is unlikely that any of the 70 Kentish churches and chapels bearing these dedications antedate the late Old English period, and in many cases they are post-Conquest foundations.[65] The third

9   *Church-dedications*

group comprises the 130 churches dedicated to All Saints, St John the Baptist, St James, St Mary Magdalene, St Lawrence, and St Nicholas. In a sense this is the most interesting group of the three; for at first sight there is no very obvious reason why these dedications should not have been given to early churches, and in other counties they sometimes were. Yet in Kent, with the possible exceptions of All Saints' Lydd, All Saints' Hollingbourne, St Nicholas's Sturry, and St Mary Magdalene's Monkton,[66] they were never given to primary churches, and as far as we can see they rarely antedate the late Old English period. We cannot be so positive on this point as in the case of the first two groups of churches: the cults of All Saints, St John the Baptist, and St Mary Magdalene may indeed have originated rather earlier than those of St Lawrence, St Nicholas, and St James. Certainly churches like St John's Harrietsham and St Mary Magdalene's Gillingham must have been relatively early, since they were mother-churches (though not minsters) in the Original Lands. Yet of the 130 Kentish churches bearing these six dedications not more than 13 or 14, and probably many fewer, are likely to have been founded before the late Old English period, and in several cases, as at Sturry, Hollingbourne, Monkton, and Lydd we must suspect a re-dedication. Of the remainder, the great majority, as we have seen, are to be found in the Wilderness areas of the county, and in most cases they are known to have originated as subordinate chapelries. There can be no real question, in short, that in Kent at least these are almost invariably late appellations.

It seems not unreasonable to claim that church-dedications shed a certain light on the evolution of settlement as well as on the evolution of the church. The patterns observed in Kent may not everywhere be so clearly delineated, and this is a subject where every region is likely to be marked by characteristics of its own. In Leicestershire there is at many points a broad similarity to Kent; but, as we have seen, dedications to St Martin and to St Peter and St Paul are decidedly less numerous, those to St Andrew and All Saints more numerous, and those to specifically local saints comparatively insignificant. Some of the circumstances behind these contrasts are not far to seek; but their significance for the student of settlement can only be fully understood by systematic scrutiny of the Leicestershire setting.

Yet if the subject itself raises many questions that cannot at present be answered, it also raises many points that are worth pondering. Is it merely a coincidence, for example, that all the four Kentish parish churches dedicated to St Botolph – at Northfleet, Chevening, Lulling-

PART FOUR *The Ecclesiastical Testimony*

stone, and Ruxley – occur within a few miles of one another, though they were never part of the same ecclesiastical territory; or does it indicate some kind of obscure link, some localized cult perhaps, whose origins now elude us? Or again is it merely a coincidence that in the stretch of countryside between Folkestone, Aldington, and Wye, where the origins of settlement are in some ways strangely enigmatic, 11 parish churches out of a total of 21 are dedicated to the Virgin and a further three to St Martin and St Peter and St Paul? Or does it in fact suggest that in this favoured area, so warmly sheltered by the Downs, and so well watered by the headsprings of the Stour, settlement was substantially earlier than on the less hospitable Chartland further west? Such questions as these cannot be answered by a study of dedications alone; they can only be investigated in the light of other kinds of evidence. But they illustrate some of the countless curious problems that the subject itself brings to light, and that sometimes may be more important than we know.

PART FIVE
TOPOGRAPHICAL RECONSTRUCTION

10

TOPOGRAPHICAL METHOD: ANALYSIS

1. THE EVIDENCE AND ITS PROBLEMS

Topography, or the historic interpretation of the landscape evidence, is a subject of great importance to the student of settlement, and it is also a fascinating subject in its own right. As yet, however, it has received relatively little systematic investigation over the country as a whole, and scientifically speaking it is still in its infancy. For that reason, while it can be fully understood only by intensive examination of individual places, it is necessary to outline some of the basic methods and characteristics of the subject, so far as settlement is concerned, before turning to the reconstruction of a specific area in Chapter 11. In describing these characteristics, there are several types of evidence that need to be taken into consideration, although there are few places where all will be available. Among the more important are the evidence of settlement direction, settlement patterns, woodland clearance, lanes and droveways, pastoral usage, certain types of place-name, territorial relationship, parish boundaries, church siting, holy wells and springs, church structures, and church-dedications. Of these, dedications have been discussed in Chapter 9, woodland clearance in Chapter 6, and pastoral evidence in Chapter 7. Much has also been said on place-names, and only a few specialized points need be added here. In the present chapter we are rather concerned with the remaining aspects of the subject, and in this connexion there are four general points that need to be made at the outset.

In the first place, it must be stressed that in matters of topography there are few universal rules, and that generally speaking such facts as we have are in the nature of signposts or pointers rather than absolute proofs. In other words, topography is an inductive science, like detective work, and a matter of devising the best possible hypothesis to account for all the known facts. For that reason it is usually risky to argue dogmatically from a single topographical feature, taken in

PART FIVE *Topographical Reconstruction*

isolation, since identical features may have very different origins. As far as possible, it is essential to follow up every available line of argument before advancing conclusions, and then to try and strike a balance of probabilities between them. That is why questions of topography can be fully understood only by intensive examination of individual places, taking all the known circumstances into consideration, and arguing analogically by comparison with other places of the same type, or in the same kind of countryside.

For example, it is common in Kent to find early churches sited on river banks; but we cannot argue that a church on a river bank is necessarily an early one without further investigation. If its parish is a small one, as at Teston on the Medway or Milton on the Stour, it is in general unlikely to be early. If, however, it bears an early place-name and is associated with a Romano-British site, or if there is evidence that a number of subsidiary churches or chapels were at one time attached to it, it may nevertheless be an early church, despite the smallness of its parish. If, in addition, it is associated with a paramount manor, or bears a double dedication to St Mary and a local saint, it is very probably an early foundation. If, on the other hand, it bears a single dedication and is not known either to have been a Romano-British site or to have claimed over other churches, it is unlikely to be early. Even in a county where the topographical evidence is as abundant as in Kent, therefore, we are likely to find many places where it is difficult to interpret, or where it points to conflicting conclusions. Whereas the church of Milton-on-Stour is in fact a relatively straightforward case of a late manorial foundation, despite its riverine site, at Teston we are faced with a more difficult problem. Its tiny parish of 520 acres seems at first sight to point to a late Old English origin, and there is certainly no record that it was a minster or that it gave birth to subordinate churches of its own. On the other hand, there is no proof that it was ever subordinated to any other church; its dedication to St Peter and St Paul is often an early one; it is situated in an area of very early Jutish settlement and associated with a Romano-British villa site; its place-name is one of the primitive Kentish names in *stone*, whose first element may possibly derive from a Celtic stream-name cognate with the Hampshire River Test.[1] In other words, the evidence at Teston is conflicting, and it is significant that it is equally problematic at a number of neighbouring places in this section of the Medway valley. On the whole, it seems probable that it was an early 'manorial' foundation which, in this fertile and populous area, acquired its

10 Topographical method: analysis

independence at a relatively remote period, perhaps as early as the eighth century. It is possible, however, that it had always been independent, and for the present we must keep an open mind.

In the second place, it has often been stressed in the course of this book that ecclesiastical development and the evolution of settlement went hand in hand in Kent, so that the gradual break-up of the 'minsterlands' or early ecclesiastical territories into their constituent parishes sheds a good deal of light on the progress of colonization as well. For this reason, there is a sense in which Kentish topography is peculiarly concerned with the reconstruction of *ecclesiastical* development and with the interpretation of the parochial structure. Much of the evidence for this view has already been discussed, and much will come to light in the course of this chapter and the next; but there are several basic points that should be mentioned here. To begin with, owing to the fact that the Kentish minsters were generally royal or monastic foundations associated with early Jutish estate-centres, it was almost inevitable that their dependent territories should usually come to be based on those of the old estates and *regiones*. The fact that the paramount manors of Kent were likewise based on these territories while the evolution of the manors often followed much the same course as that of the minsterlands, lends further support to this hypothesis. Indeed, the very circumstance that the Wealden swine pastures were generally attached to paramount minster-settlements, and not to subordinate places on the Downs, as we saw in Chapter 6, indicates the supremacy of the paramount places in terms of settlement-origins as well as ecclesiastical development.[2] Naturally, the correlation between church foundation and the structure of settlement was not everywhere exact, and in coming to form the basis of new territorial units some of the early Jutish *regiones* underwent something of a metamorphosis. At Milton Regis, for example, an unusually extensive royal estate was eventually divided into two distinct minsterlands, based on Milton and Newington respectively, though the original unity of the area was still preserved in the medieval manor and hundred of Milton.[3] Nevertheless, owing to the early establishment of Christianity in Kent, there can be no doubt that ecclesiastical development usually followed in the wake of colonization, and that owing to the abundance of early evidence, it can often be pieced together more fully there than elsewhere. Since the rural landscape has been less subject to revolutionary changes than in many counties, moreover, patient attention to the *minutiae* of parochial topography enables us to solve a number of

PART FIVE *Topographical Reconstruction*

basic problems which elsewhere remain largely unanswered. In the following discussion, therefore, the ecclesiastical evidence will figure prominently.

Thirdly, it must be emphasized that this chapter is based on the Kentish evidence alone, and that its conclusions do not necessarily hold good in other areas. The topographical development of the county has obviously been affected by such matters as the scattered nature of local settlement and the late survival of local woodland in a way that is not equally apparent in all parts of the country. Nevertheless, some of the seeming peculiarities of Kent are more frequently echoed elsewhere than may be supposed, even in clearly dissimilar regions. The siting of churches like Sheldwich, Patrixbourne, and Foot's Cray on the parish boundaries of their mother-communities, for example, is not a purely local characteristic, but is also found at places like Little Staughton in Huntingdonshire and Throapham in South Yorkshire.[4] Similarly, the long narrow strip-parishes of places like Brasted and Sundridge in West Kent are also found in other scarpland areas, and in counties like Buckinghamshire and Wiltshire are more striking than in Kent. Though great caution is needed in extrapolating from the Kentish evidence, there can be no doubt, therefore, that at many points it sheds light on parochial development elsewhere. This is a field where there is urgent need for more comparative regional study.

Fourthly, it is important to note that even within Kent some of the topographical characteristics advanced here are not universally valid. In the Weald, in particular, parochial topography has in some ways been moulded by very different circumstances from those that operated elsewhere in the county, and is usually less informative about the progress and direction of settlement. Since this is also a characteristic of several other areas of secondary settlement, such as the Forest of Arden, it seems pertinent at this stage to enquire why this should be so. Why is it that in the primary and subsequent areas of settlement – Holmesdale, the Foothills, the Downs, and much of the Chartland – the peculiar relationship of churches with parish boundaries, the distinctive shape of many individual parishes, and the topographical interconnexion between one parish and another, are more revealing than in areas of predominantly secondary settlement like the Weald? In the latter region, there can be no doubt that the apparently meaningless form of many parishes – meaningless, that is, in terms of topographical development, though not of course in other respects – is partly occasioned, as in Arden, by the size of the parishes in question; but there were also more fundamental circumstances at work. Broadly speaking, these circumstances were of two kinds, and since the area is not discussed in detail in this chapter, it may be useful to mention them at this point.

It should be remembered, to begin with, that the Weald was essentially a region of *detached* pasture, where settlement was moulded by the practice of transhumance, and usually originated from relatively distant places on the Foothills and in Holmesdale. In other words, it was not generally colonized by *neighbouring* communities, anxious to extend their own local territory by pressing their boundaries further into the adjacent forest. Its colonization arose rather through the establishment of numerous scattered *dens* or shielings in the heart of the forest, and the ultimate evolution of these summer pastures into permanent, yet still isolated, farms. For these reasons, the settlement of the Weald did not proceed regularly from parish to parish, in a more or less consistent progression, as it tended to do elsewhere. When churches came to be set up, therefore, they were not necessarily established in the earliest settlement of the parish, near the boundary of the mother-church, as they frequently were on the Downs or the Chart, but rather in some convenient spot (or so we may suppose) for the scattered population of the parish as a whole. The Wealden churches, as a consequence, are rarely so eccentrically sited as those elsewhere, and rarely indicate the direction from which colonization originated. Their parish boundaries, moreover, were not drawn by mother-churches nearby, anxious to press their rights as close to their daughter-chapelries as possible, but by relatively distant minsters, sometimes situated more than 20 miles away. In many cases, no doubt, these boundaries were based on the traditional limits of a group of *dens* or swine pastures, and for this reason they bore little relation to the progress of permanent settlement or the local evolution of the church.

In the second place, when the churches of the Weald began to be established towards the end of the Old English period, it seems possible that the original minster-system, based on a central church whose priests served a wide tract of country, was already passing away. By that time many of the 'bookland' churches of Kent were already ancient, with priests or chaplains of their own, and a measure of parochial independence. If this surmise is correct, it suggests that the parishes of the Weald may never have been so closely integrated into the minster-system as the bookland parishes of earlier centuries. Since their territories were detached and rarely continuous with those of the

PART FIVE *Topographical Reconstruction*

original minsterlands, moreover, it can never have been so easy for the mother-churches of Holmesdale and the Foothills to exercise supremacy over them as over their daughter-settlements nearby, on the Downs and the Chart. Whereas in the ecclesiastical topography of the latter areas, therefore, we can often trace the gradual break-up, step by step, of more or less compact ecclesiastical territories based on early Jutish estates, in the detached parishes of the Weald we can rarely do so, and in this respect their topography is correspondingly less informative to the historian of settlement.

2. SETTLEMENT DIRECTION AND PLACE-NAMES

The evidence of settlement itself provides us with two lines of topographical enquiry. The first relates to the general direction or movement of colonization and the light that church foundation sheds upon this process. Owing to the fact that the minsters dated from a very early phase of Jutish settlement, ecclesiastical development usually tended to move in a southerly or south-westerly direction, as we have seen, from the Original Lands on the Foothills up on to the Downs, and from the minsters of Holmesdale up on to the Chart. Beyond these areas it subsequently moved further south into the Weald and Romney Marsh. Naturally there are exceptions to these broad generalizations. The most important occur along the northern side of the county, where parishes with a good deal of wet low-lying marsh like Stodmarsh, Ash-by-Wingham, and Worth lie to the north or east of their minsters, which in these cases were situated at Wickhambreaux, Wingham, and Eastry. There are also exceptions in the neighbourhood of Blean Forest, where parishes like Swalecliffe, Herne, Hoath, and Harble-down were subordinate to mother-churches to the south and east, at Sturry, Reculver, and other early centres. In Holmesdale, moreover, there are a few places where minsters gave birth to woodland chapelries on the Downs to the north: at Stansted, for instance, which originated from Wrotham, and at Hucking and Bredhurst, which originated from Hollingbourne. In cases like these, however, there are more or less obvious agrarian reasons for exceptions to the general rule. Such developments as that of Oare near Faversham, where a Marshland church seems to have originated as a chapelry of Stalisfield on the remote Downland to the south-east, are by contrast quite exceptional. Only in the extreme east of the county, near Eastry and Northbourne, do some of the more eccentric relationships between one church and another suggest a radically different pattern, perhaps in this primitive area arising from pre-Augustinian circumstances.

The general movement of church foundation in a southerly or south-westerly direction in the wake of settlement in this way may be illustrated at many places. Westerham, for instance, at the westerly end of Holmesdale, gave birth as we have seen to a southerly chapelry at Edenbridge; its neighbour Brasted to a southerly church at Hever; Chevening to churches at Sundridge and Chiddingstone; Shoreham to Otford, Sevenoaks, St John's (Greatness), and Penshurst; and Kemsing to a subsidiary foundation at Seal. The same pattern continues all along Holmesdale to the east, with the establishment of outlying churches and chapels on the Chartland by such mother-churches as Wrotham, Trottiscliffe, Aylesford, Maidstone, Hollingbourne, Harrietsham, Lenham, and Charing (see map 13). Linton, Loose, and Boughton Monchelsea, for example, developed as daughter-churches of Maidstone; Sutton Valence, East Sutton, and Chart Sutton of Hollingbourne; and Egerton, Pevington, Pluckley, and Little Chart of Charing. In much the same way, on the Downland of East Kent, Nonington, Goodnestone, and Womenswold originated as southerly chapelries of Wingham; Nackington, Lower Hardres, Upper Hardres, and Stelling as chapelries of a minster in the Stour valley; and Throwley, Eastling, Leaveland, Sheldwich, Badlesmere, and other places as daughter-churches of Faversham (see map 12). Wherever we find a mother-church or minster, in short, the first direction in which to look for its subordinate foundations is generally to the south or southwest. The mother-church itself will thus often be found lying on the northern side of its territory, and quite eccentrically within its own minsterland. In Milton Regis the minster stands little more than a mile from the northern boundary of the area, yet seven miles from its southern border, towards the crest of the Downs.

The second line of enquiry relates to place-name evidence, and in this connexion there are four groups of names that call for discussion: those indicating heathen sites, those indicating Christian sites, those arising from territorial subdivision, and those relating to orientation. Of the first of these there may be as many as 20 examples in Kent. Several of these are of very doubtful significance; but in view of the fact that heathen temples were sometimes rededicated for Christian purposes, we might expect some of them to have become early ecclesiastical centres. There are a few places, such as Wye (*wīg, wēoh*, 'idol', etc.), where this is known to have happened, and a few where

PART FIVE *Topographical Reconstruction*

minor heathen-names are associated with early churches nearby: Hillborough (*hālig* + *beorg*, 'holy barrow'), for example, with the minster at Reculver; Ospringe (? *ōs* + spring, ? 'god's spring') with that at Faversham; Shalmesford ('shambles ford', possibly meaning 'place of animal sacrifice') with that at Chilham; and *Schamele* and *Gadshill* in Sittingbourne ('shamble' and 'god's hill') with that at Milton Regis. In most cases, however, the heathen place-names of Kent bear remarkably little relationship to early Christian sites, and bear out Dr Margaret Gelling's view that such names may often be comparatively late in origin. Several of them relate to remote places on the Downs or in the Weald, such as Greenacre ('Grim's acre') in Elham, and in these cases, though affording instructive evidence of heathen survival in the forest outback, they tell us nothing about the origins of early churches. In this connexion, the lost *Kyrsmondenn* or 'Christian man's pasture' in Wittersham is of some interest, since it is not recorded until 1253–4 and suggests that Christianity may sometimes have been very slow to penetrate the deeper recesses of the Weald.[5]

Of the specifically Christian place-names of Kent, the vast majority, as we have seen, are derived from the names of churches, chapels, or patron saints, and relate to subsequent or secondary settlements like Dymchurch, Capel-le-Ferne, and St Mary-in-the-Marsh. There is also a small but significant group of very early ecclesiastical names, however, of which the most interesting is Eccles in Aylesford. This is the only south-eastern example of the well-known British word for a Christian community or a church, and although Eccles itself did not become an Augustinian minster, its close association with that at Aylesford is suggestive.[6] Its great Roman villa, its situation on the Greenway, its proximity to the Medway megaliths, and its connexion with the Pilgrims' Way, plainly imply a far earlier origin for the development of Aylesford and its vicinity as a religious centre. Apart from Eccles, the most obvious early Christian place-names are those of the two surviving Minsters, in Sheppey and Thanet, to which we should add the *Reculfmynster* (Reculver) of the Anglo-Saxon Chronicle, together with *Limining mynster* (Lyminge) and the unidentified *Upmynster* (?Monkton) of King Wihtred's grant. It is also worth remarking that at least five Kentish minsters are adjoined by subsidiary settlements called Preston, or 'priest's *tūn*', probably indicating the farm originally allotted to the support of the monastic clergy: Preston in Shoreham, Preston in Aylesford, Preston by Faversham, Preston by Wingham, and Preston near Minster-in-Thanet. It is possible that the lost

10 *Topographical method: analysis*

Presteshelle in Maidstone, near St Peter's church in the West Borough, may have borne much the same significance.[7]

Names indicating orientation, or the subdivision of a larger territory, are obviously worth noting in the context of topographical development. Where parish-names occur in groups or pairs, as at Great and Little Mongeham, Old and New Romney, Upper and Lower Hardres, East and West Malling, or Littlebourne, Patrixbourne, Bekesbourne, and Bishopsbourne, they almost always indicate the subdivision of an older territory (see map 4). Similarly, names like Sutton, Eastchurch, and Southfleet generally indicate places lying to the east or south of the church or settlement giving birth to them.[8] Eastchurch, for example, originated as the 'easterly church' of Minster-in-Sheppey; Southfleet as the southern church of St Botolph's minster at Fleet, or Northfleet; Sutton-by-Dover as the 'south farm' and southerly church of Northbourne; Sutton-at-Hone as a southerly development of Dartford; and Sutton Valence as a southerly daughter of Hollingbourne which eventually gave birth to a subordinate chapel of its own, known as East Sutton or 'east south *tūn*' (see map 5).[9] In cases like these the churches in question generally formed part of the same minsterland, and the minsterland itself was usually based on an older *regio* or estate.

3. LANES AND DROVEWAYS

Roads and tracks of all kinds probably have more to tell us about the evolution of settlement than has yet been recognized. Reconstruction of the Roman road-system of this country has been revolutionized in recent years through the detective work of scholars like Ivan Margary; but post-Roman roads have not yet been subjected to the same systematic scrutiny, and their topography is possibly one of the least understood aspects of landscape history. In an old-enclosed county like Kent the evidence is particularly abundant, though adequate interpretation of it demands more extended treatment than is possible in this book. Something has already been said about Roman roads and prehistoric tracks, of their crucial part in the development of seminal settlement, and their role as primitive pilgrim-ways. Here we are rather concerned with post-Roman roads, and with what these may have to tell us about the progress of subsequent and secondary colonization.

Like many areas of scattered settlement, Kent is pre-eminently a county of lanes, and broadly speaking these lanes have a twofold origin. In virtually every part of the county, but particularly in the Weald and

PART FIVE *Topographical Reconstruction*

on the Downs and the Chart, they must often have arisen as local forest footpaths trodden out between one pasture or farmstead and another during the Old English period or after the Conquest (see maps 7 and 16). In places they incorporate stretches of prehistoric trackway or minor Roman roads; but there can be little doubt that the veritable maze of lanes and holloways in these areas has originated by and large through the piecemeal clearance of a heavily wooded countryside. The narrowness of these lanes, their twisting courses, their lack of verges, and the fact that they are so often sunk beneath the surface of the land – sometimes by as much as 15 or 20 feet where they descend a hillside – are typical signs of early-colonized woodland, and are echoed in other forest areas like parts of Shropshire and the West Country. In broken wooded countryside of this kind, foot-passengers tend to follow the easiest course rather than the most direct one, and are readily turned aside by natural obstacles like steep slopes, fallen trees, and boggy places. When trunk routes eventually developed, they arose through the amalgamation of localized lanes and footpaths like these, and this accounts for many of the more sinuous major roads of Kent today. The frustrated motorist between Tunbridge Wells and Ashford may at least take heart that in this respect the restless twentieth century has not yet been able to obliterate the imprint of the pre-Conquest peasant.

Not all the lanes of Kent have originated as localized forest footpaths, however; many have developed as relatively long-distance droveways between the mother-settlements of the Original Lands and their forest-pastures on the Downs or in the Weald. It is this circumstance, as we saw in Chapter 2, that lies behind their tendency to run across the grain of the county from north to south. The main droveway of the estate based on Otford in West Kent is an instructive example of this kind of development, leading from the Darent valley at Shoreham through Otford itself, across Holmesdale, and then by way of Sevenoaks and Hubbard's Hill to the swine pastures of the Otford Weald in the neighbourhood of Penshurst and Chiddingstone.[10] The topography of the parish of Sevenoaks in particular sheds a good deal of light on the evolution of this droveway and is worth describing in detail (see map 13).

The origins of Sevenoaks as an urban settlement are not documented, but they probably go back to the later generations of the Old English period. It was not a 'primary town' in the sense of an old *caput*; but archaeological evidence indicates a pre-Conquest market at this point, and the fact that this market was a prescriptive or traditional

10 Topographical method: analysis

one, and never acquired a formal charter from the crown, tends to confirm its Old English origin. As an outlying Chartland settlement of the Otford estate, Sevenoaks is not actually recorded until the *Textus Roffensis* in the eleventh century; but in the present context its place-name is a particularly suggestive one. In England it is unique; but it has several parallels on the continent, and Dr Margaret Gelling has suggested that names of this type may have a folkloric significance.[11] The original settlement must have arisen at some noted meeting-place by seven oak trees, and there are grounds for believing that it was the meeting-place of the Hundred of Codsheath.[12] This was one of the relatively few Kentish hundreds based on a Jutish estate, and its meeting-place must have been situated on heathland, or in other words on the Chart. In addition to Sevenoaks itself, it included the parishes of Shoreham, Otford, Halstead, Kemsing, Seal, Sundridge, Woodlands, and part of Chevening, and the routes leading southwards from these places still converge upon Sevenoaks market place. That this market developed as the commercial centre of the estate is further attested by the fact that it was the main droveway itself – the Otford road and not the London road – that became the High Street and market place of the town, while the London road was a subsidiary track branching off it.[13] Though Sevenoaks is only 25 miles from the capital, its origins were essentially dictated by the local needs of the estate and its herdsmen in this way, and not by metropolitan impact. The name of the hundred may also help to explain the unusual situation of the town, some 500 feet up on a windswept ridgeway.[14] The first element of Codsheath has not been satisfactorily explained, but if its earliest recorded form *Godehede* in 1178–9 means 'god's heath', it may suggest that Sevenoaks originated not only as a hundredal market but as a centre of heathen worship in the forest outback.[15] That would go some way towards explaining its own place-name, moreover, with its possible folklore connotation.[16]

There is one further topographical clue that is often worth following up in reconstructing the course of the droveways, and that is the ecclesiastical dedications with which they tend to be associated. In this connexion the Otford Droveway once again provides an instructive example. The mother-church of the area was situated at Shoreham, towards its northern edge, and characteristically dedicated to St Peter and St Paul. The patron saints of the droveway churches themselves, however, were all associated with the protection of travellers. Shoreham's first dependent chapelry, at Otford, was dedicated to St Bar-

PART FIVE *Topographical Reconstruction*

tholomew; its second, at Greatness on the edge of the Chart, to St John the Baptist; its third, in the town of Sevenoaks itself, to St Nicholas; and its last, where the droveway terminated at Penshurst, once again to St John the Baptist. At Sevenoaks the origins of St Nicholas as a wayside shrine on the course of the drove are still plain to see in its striking position directly abutting on the High Street. At St John's, in the same parish, the pre-Conquest chapel recorded in the *Textus Roffensis* was later refounded as a hospital and failed to survive the Reformation; but like St Nicholas it also originated as a wayside shrine, adjoining the droveway at the foot of St John's Hill.

There are many other parts of Kent where droveway churches and chapels are directly associated in this way with the protection of wayfarers or herdsmen; dedications to saints like St Nicholas, St James, St Giles, St Lawrence, St Leonard, St Michael, St Mary Magdalene, and St John the Baptist are particularly characteristic of them. On the Downland route leading southward from Faversham, for example, Sheldwich is dedicated to St James, Badlesmere to St Leonard, Leaveland to St Lawrence, and Challock to St Cosmas and St Damian (see map 12). Elsewhere on this stretch of the Downs, Bicknor is associated with St James, Wormshill with St Giles, Rodmersham with St Nicholas, Hartlip with St Michael, Otterden with St Lawrence, Stockbury and Lidsing with St Mary Magdalene, and Bredgar, Tunstall, and Doddington with St John the Baptist.[17] On the Chartland to the south of this area something of the same pattern is repeated in the churches of St James at Egerton, St Michael at Chart Sutton, and St Nicholas at Leeds, Pluckley, Linton, Otham, and Boughton Malherbe (see map 5). In all these cases except Badlesmere and Leaveland it is noteworthy that the church or chapel immediately adjoins the droveway, as at Sevenoaks and Greatness, and probably originated as a wayside shrine or crouch. Not all droveway churches bear dedications of this kind; St Mary, St Peter, and All Saints are also represented; yet there are many places where church-dedications add confirmation to other lines of enquiry and facilitate the reconstruction of the droves.

4. TERRITORIAL RELATIONSHIP

Historically speaking the territorial and administrative subdivisions of Kent are remarkably diverse, ranging from extensive lathes at one end of the scale, through hundreds, honours, 'lowies', baronies, and halimotes, down to 'boroughs', *loghi*, 'tithings', 'precincts', 'villes', 'towns', 'districts', 'dens', manors, parishes, and chapelries.[18] The lathes have already been referred to in Chapter 1, the *dens* and their parental settlements on the Upland in Chapter 6, and the boroughs or *borghi* in Chapter 7. Some of the remaining units, such as honours and baronies, developed relatively late and usually arose through territorial reorganization after the Conquest; in most cases they have little to tell us about settlement as such. Others, like 'tithings', 'districts', and 'precincts', were of only localized importance in Kent, and though often worth noting in the settlement context, need not be discussed in detail. Here we are rather concerned with the hundredal, parochial, and manorial structure of the county.

The 66 hundreds of Kent have generally been regarded as alien rather than indigenous institutions, and in most cases they bore little or no relationship to the evolution of settlement. There are several places, however, where they closely corresponded with early minsterlands and seem to have incorporated primitive Jutish *regiones* or estates. This has already been noted in the case of Codsheath hundred, which was based on the Otford territory. It is also apparent in the neighbouring territory of Wrotham, where the minsterland comprised Ightham, Wrotham, Stansted, Plaxtol, and perhaps Shipbourne, an area which was almost identical with the original hundred of Wrotham (see map 13).[19] Similarly, between the Thames and the Medway, both the hundred and the minsterland of Hoo comprised the parishes of Hoo St Werburgh, Hoo Allhallows, St Mary's Hoo, Stoke at Hoo, High Halstow, and the lost parish of Hoo St Margaret.[20] Perhaps the most instructive example of a minsterland associated with a hundred in this way is that of Milton Regis, and this is a case we shall return to in Chapter 11. There are several other places where hundreds incorporated early estates or minsterlands, moreover, if only in a partial and fragmentary form. Nevertheless, it is the manorial and ecclesiastical structure of the county that usually supplies the most important territorial clues to follow up in reconstructing the original Jutish *regiones* of Kent. There are many places where the last relics of these *regiones* still survived in the archaic ecclesiastical and manorial framework of the eighteenth and nineteenth centuries. It is this circumstance that makes the evidence of Edward Hasted so important, with his interest in primitive jurisdictions, and in the relationship between one church and another, and one manor and another, in his own time.

The survival of early ecclesiastical jurisdictions into relatively recent generations is no peculiarity of Kent; to some extent it is found in

PART FIVE *Topographical Reconstruction*

almost every English county. In general it endured longest perhaps in the later-settled parts of the country, particularly in moorland areas, and over much of the more thinly populated parts of the Highland Zone it may be described as the norm. In the more densely settled Midland counties parish churches often became independent at a relatively early period; yet even in Leicestershire, where they were as thick on the ground as anywhere, the six daughter-foundations of Melton Mowbray – Welby, Sysonby, Freeby, Thorpe Arnold, Eye Kettleby, and Burton Lazars – did not become fully autonomous until the nineteenth century.[21] In Kent there was a good deal of variation in this respect between the different parts of the county, according to local diversities of settlement and agrarian potential. Most of the minsterland dependent on Milton Regis, for example, was situated on relatively fertile soils and settled early, so that all its 11 mainland chapelries except Rodmersham apparently became independent parishes before Henry II's reign, some of them perhaps before the Conquest. In several cases, indeed, it is only because they are recorded as dependencies of Milton in the *Domesday Monachorum* that we can be certain of their original status. In poorer areas, by contrast, and in districts with a good deal of dense woodland or infertile chart, ecclesiastical development was often arrested at some stage, and the primitive pattern of subordination survived almost unaltered for many centuries. In the minsterland of Wrotham only one of the outlying churches and chapels became fully independent before the nineteenth century, that of Ightham, and several failed to survive the medieval period (see map 13). In the Weald there are a few places, like Groombridge and Smallhythe, where chapelries have remained subordinate down to the present day. In all probability the pattern that we see in cases of 'arrested development' like these characterized the greater part of Kent at the time of the Conquest, so that they provide an instructive model to bear in mind in seeking to elucidate the development of territories like Milton, which were broken up at an earlier period.

In most cases, the break-up of the Kentish minsterlands into separate parishes began much earlier than at Wrotham, though perhaps not often so early as on a great royal estate like Milton. It is difficult to suggest any general pattern to which the date and manner of their break-up tended to conform, however; obviously it was everywhere affected by the varying proclivities of local landlords and ecclesiastics; and the fundamental point to grasp is its highly localized idiosyncrasy. At Wingham, for example, of the six dependent churches listed in the *Domesday Monachorum*, Ash and Nonington became independent parishes on the foundation of Wingham College in 1286; Womenswold also became independent at that time, but was later resubordinated, on this occasion to Nonington; Ratling disappeared altogether and was absorbed into Nonington; and Walmestone also disappeared and was re-absorbed into Wingham. In addition to these, a new chapelry of Wingham was founded after the Conquest at Goodnestone which, like Ash and Nonington, became a separate parish in 1286; and two other new chapels were founded in the 7,000-acre parish of Ash itself, at Fleet and Overland, though these never became independent churches and have long since disappeared (see map 5).[22] Or take the great minsterland of Maidstone, which at one time may have comprised as many as 17 parishes and reached as far as Goudhurst on the Sussex border. In this case only the two neighbouring parishes of Detling and Loose still remained subordinate to the motherchurch in Hasted's time, and of all the vast dependent area to the south – some 35,000 acres in extent – only one small fragment failed to acquire a life of its own, the detached chapelry of Loddington, some five miles from the town (see map 5). The fact that Loddington still formed part of the parish of Maidstone as late as the 1880s, though wholly separated from it by Loose and Boughton Monchelsea, is an interesting sign of the original extension of the minsterland in this direction a thousand years earlier.[23]

The evidence of manorial jurisdiction often confirms and supplements that of ecclesiastical development. It is relatively rare in Kent, it is true, to find that precise correlation between manor and parish which characterized much of the Midlands, and in places the whole system of 'paramount' and 'subordinate' manors seems confused and baffling. Yet in fact the development of the former in the Original Lands, and of the latter in the outlying pastures of the Downland, Chartland, Weald, and Marsh, was the logical consequence of the custom of transhumance, as we have seen, and of varying local agrarian conditions at the time of colonization. Broadly speaking it arose from the fact that, when the seasonal shielings in the outlying wood-pastures developed into permanent farms, with a separate life of their own, the parent communities of the Original Lands still retained some measure of authority over them. In a general way, therefore, and despite numerous exceptions in detail, the manorial structure of Kent closely reflected the evolution of settlement: and since ecclesiastical development normally followed colonization, it often illuminates the sequence

PART FIVE *Topographical Reconstruction*

of church foundation as well. Although, with the passage of time, much of the original framework was gradually obscured or obliterated, its outlines survived more completely than in many counties, and at some points more completely than those of the primitive Kentish church.

In the Isle of Thanet, for instance, where the parish of St Peter finally became independent of the mother-church of Minster about the time of the Dissolution, the manor of Minster continued to claim paramountcy over most of the parish in Hasted's day, and still exacted 'a certain rent called Pennygavel' from its landholders. Similarly at Wingham, although the subordinate chapelries of Goodnestone, Nonington, Womenswold, and Ash became independent parishes in 1286, the manor of Wingham continued to claim over most of their territory five centuries later.[24] Again, at Milton Regis, the manorial structure likewise continued to incorporate the original relationship, indicating that places like Tunstall, Bobbing, Sittingbourne, and other parishes in the hundred were at one time ecclesiastical as well as manorial offshoots of Milton, as we shall see in Chapter 11.[25] Not all examples of manorial relationship are as well authenticated as these; in some parts of Kent, such as the neighbourhood of Eastry and Northbourne already referred to, the whole tangled skein is impossible to unravel with certainty without more detailed research into medieval records. Yet in a general way the manorial evidence often adds striking confirmation to other lines of argument. Used with caution and common sense, it enables us to add many an additional piece to the settlement puzzle.

5. THE PAROCHIAL UNIT

The parish itself offers three points for consideration in tracing the evolution of settlement: its relative extent, the position of the church in relation to its boundaries, and the topography of the boundaries themselves. The varying scale of the Kentish parish has already been referred to in Chapter 8. There we saw that the minster-parishes averaged some 4,340 acres in extent, those of secondary mother-churches 3,450 acres, those of manorial or 'bookland' churches, 1,570 acres, and those of the Wealden 'forest' churches nearly 4,460 acres. Topographically, the principal point to note is that the minster-parishes were nearly three times as large, on the average, as those of 'bookland' or subsequent status. Averages, of course, tell only part of the story. A few minster-parishes, such as Wye, extended to 7,000 acres, and in the freakish cases of Wrotham and Lydd to 11,000 or

10 Topographical method: analysis

12,000, whereas in the more populous and fertile areas there were some, like Milton Regis, that covered less than 3,000 acres. The territories of subsequent or manorial churches also varied widely in extent, from the 200 or 300 acres of Chillenden and Bircholt in East Kent to the freakish 5,925 acres of Cudham, in poor Downland country on the Surrey border.[26] Nevertheless, in almost every case the minster-parishes of Kent tended to be several times as large as their daughters, and this is the crucial point to take into account. At 2,560 acres Milton was almost twice the average size of its daughters; at 4,580 Maidstone was nearly three times their average size; and at 7,350 Wye was more than four times. As a rule it was only the forest parishes of the Weald or the Blean that tended to be larger than those of their mother-churches, no doubt because of their sparse population at the time of foundation.

Some of the chief reasons for these contrasts in parochial scale are not far to seek. In giving birth to a daughter, and in carving out a parish for it, the mother-church was in the stronger bargaining position of the two; and with that reverence for material advantage which generally characterized the medieval church, she ceded as little of her own territory as possible. In the outlying manorial settlement, moreover, there was normally only a single priest or chaplain to support in place of the quasi-monastic establishment of the parent body. Where we find a small rural parish, as a consequence, it is likely to be that of a subsequent or manorial foundation, and not that of a minster. The two obvious exceptions to this general rule are Trottiscliffe and Reculver; but in the latter case, like a number of other churches on the north coast of Kent, the minster has lost much of its original territory to the sea. In other counties there may well be more variation in this respect, and in moorland, fenland, or forest regions, subordinate parishes, as in the Weald of Kent, were often substantially larger than those of their mother-churches. Yet there are certainly many places elsewhere, such as Wimborne Minster in Dorset, Luton in Bedfordshire, and Melton Mowbray and Bottesford in Leicestershire, where the original extent of the mother-parish was several times that of its daughter-churches and chapels.

When we turn to the siting of the parish church in relation to its boundaries, we are at once struck in Kent by the strangely eccentric position of many local churches.[27] This is a characteristic sign of old woodland country in many areas; but the fact that it is more frequent in Kent than in the heartlands of England is significant. In the subsequent or 'manorial' parishes of the county it is particularly common, and

PART FIVE *Topographical Reconstruction*

ultimately there are two circumstances behind it. Partly it arises from the scattered nature of local settlement and the germ of individualism inherent in a pastoral and transhumant society, so that the ecclesiastical unit and the agrarian unit rarely became precisely coterminous as they often did in the Midlands. In origin, as we have seen, the Kentish parish usually arose from the subdivision of a minsterland based on an early Jutish estate, so that groups of parishes frequently represent old *regiones* or estates, but individual parishes rarely consist of those closely integrated agrarian units characteristic of the Midlands, with their fields, their husbandry, and their social institutions centred on a single settlement, with the church at its heart. In most cases, therefore, when parish churches were built, they were established near one of a number of isolated farmsteads; and since woodland clearance proceeded in a piecemeal fashion, that farmstead was usually one of the older settlements of the parish, near the boundary of the mother-community. For this reason the topographical situation of the church is often an important indicator in Kent of the direction from which local colonization originated.

Behind these developments what we also see is once again the bargaining power of the mother-church. There are many places where it has clearly pressed its own territorial claims as far as possible, often to within a few hundred yards of its daughter-chapels, and occasionally, as at Sheldwich, Patrixbourne, and Bridge, virtually to the wall of the churchyard. There are also many places where the daughter-community itself has stretched its claims as far as possible, and pressed close against its own daughters, situated further out into the *wald*. What seems to have happened in cases like the latter is that, when the original settlement founded a new colony in its outlying pasture, it at first left a good deal of uninhabited woodland beyond it, either as commonland over which both mother and daughter exercised certain joint rights, or else as unappropriated waste. Then, at a later stage, either the parent settlement, or sometimes the subsidiary one, gave birth to yet another colony, situated further out into the *wald*, and the daughter-church pressed its own boundary-claims as close to the new establishment as possible. In the common-field areas of England, where farmsteads were usually sited in the church-village, such eccentric arrangements would have been highly inconvenient, and must at times have necessitated a journey of some miles to the outlying lands of the village. The churches of the Midlands, as a consequence, are more frequently – though by no means always – sited towards the centre of the parish. Where they are not, it is noteworthy that they are often associated with old woodland country, as in much of Huntingdonshire and north Bedfordshire, or with the subdivision of an older territorial unit, as at Hemingford Abbots and Hemingford Grey.[28] But in Kent, where the farmsteads generally stood alone in their own fields, an eccentric site did not greatly matter from the agrarian standpoint, though it often meant that the farmer was two or three miles from his parish church. It was this circumstance, as we saw in Chapter 8, that gave rise to many of the outlying chapels of the county.

Many instances of this kind of eccentric siting might be mentioned, but in the limits of this chapter four examples must suffice. In Holmesdale, to cite an instance in West Kent, when Kemsing gave birth to a daughter at Seal (*sele*, 'hall') on the edge of its Chartland, the new church was barely half a mile from the Kemsing boundary yet nearly five miles from its own boundary beyond Under River, which had formerly marked the southern limit of Kemsing (see map 13).[29] Further east in Holmesdale, Addington gave birth in much the same way to Offham, whose church stands only 400 yards from the Addington border yet $1\frac{1}{2}$ miles from its own outlying land in the wild countryside of Mereworth Woods.[30] In Mereworth, which was settled from the Medway valley rather than Holmesdale, the original church stood little more than 300 yards from the borders of Wateringbury, yet two miles from its own outskirts, where it marched with Offham, Ryarsh, and West Malling. In this case, a further woodland chapelry was ultimately established, almost at the point where these four parishes met, and dedicated to a saint often associated with forest areas, St Blaise. The chapel itself has long since vanished; but its site is still commemorated in the name of Blaise Wood.

Towards the eastern end of the county, much the same kind of development occurred in the Stour valley, reaching southwards up into the Downs along the line of Stone Street. Here the sequence of parish formation seems to have begun in Canterbury and proceeded *via* Nackington, Lower Hardres, and Upper Hardres, to Stelling and Stelling Minnis. In each case the subsidiary church was built relatively close to the parental boundary yet remote from its own southern extremity in the poor wooded outback known as the *hardz*. Upper Hardres, for example, is only 500 yards from the border of Lower Hardres, yet two miles from that of Stelling; Stelling is 500 yards from that of Upper Hardres, yet two miles from its own outlying pastures on Stelling Minnis. Eventually the Minnis itself was split off and formed

PART FIVE *Topographical Reconstruction*

into a tiny civil parish of its own, ostensibly to bring some semblance of order to a lawless neighbourhood. 'A barren, dreary country, covered with flints, and enveloped among woods', says Hasted characteristically of the *harad*, or 'stony, forested ground', that gave this countryside its name.[31] Nowadays, with its sombre woods and hidden combes, it has acquired a charm for us that people of earlier centuries rarely appreciated; its natural sterility, moreover, has to some extent been ameliorated by modern methods of cultivation. Yet even today the strange relics of its unenclosed minnis, the scattered cottages and old garden-plots taken out of the heath, the great stretches of woodland surrounding it at Atchester, Fryarne, and Upper Hardres, and the presence of woodland place-names still bear witness to its primitive forest origins (see map 14).

6. PARISH BOUNDARIES

The topography of parish boundaries is a subject of the utmost importance for the study of settlement. There are many places where they have now been subjected to local alteration; yet in most rural parts of Kent those marked on the older Ordnance sheets still follow their historic courses with only minor variations. For many centuries the collection of tithes and parish rates and the development of local government created a vested interest in continuity, and there are several ways in which the general antiquity of parish boundaries may be tested. In most places they still broadly follow the course recorded on the tithe index sheets of the 1840s, before substantial revision had begun to take place. On the $2\frac{1}{2}''$ and $6''$ maps they are often marked by boundary stones, or by posts, trees, or stubs, whose origins probably antedate the first general cartographic record of bounds in the early nineteenth century, which rendered such landmarks largely obsolete. There are also numerous records of boundary perambulations in past centuries, some of which are more or less readily accessible in print, such as that of Knockholt in 1463.[32] In addition, there are many hundreds of farms and hamlets in Kent that are actually sited on parish boundaries, as we saw in Chapter 7, and in numerous cases early records and the forms of their place-names, as at Marley ('boundary clearing') and Waldershare ('boundary of the forest-dwellers'), indicate that these have been so situated for many centuries, sometimes, as at Shuttlesfield near Elham, since before the Conquest. Finally, of the many thousands of minor place-names and woodland-names in the

10 *Topographical method: analysis*

county, the overwhelming majority are still to be found within the same parishes as those under which they appear in early modern or medieval records. This circumstance does not in itself prove that the *boundaries* of these parishes follow precisely the same course as in the medieval period; but since many of the names in question are situated near the edge of the parish, it does indicate a general correlation between the medieval parishes of the county and those of the nineteenth century.

There are three important qualifications that need to be mentioned, however, before accepting the antiquity of surviving parish boundaries. In the neighbourhood of Kentish towns they have often been altered substantially, as in other counties, and sometimes wholly obliterated, in recent generations. In the more sparsely settled areas the smaller rural parishes have sometimes been amalgamated, so that the original division, as at Nackington and Lower Hardres near Canterbury, or Goodnestone, Chillenden, and Knowlton near Wingham, is not now marked on the $2\frac{1}{2}''$ O.S. sheets, though it is traceable on the tithe index sheets. And thirdly there were at one time many outliers or detached portions of Kentish parishes, and in all but a few cases these have now been incorporated into neighbouring territories. Most of these outliers are not difficult to track down, however; many of them are recorded by Hasted; and their boundaries are usually marked on the tithe index. Despite the fact that in many cases we must be prepared to find minor local variations, there can thus be no doubt that the parish boundaries of Kent provide a massive and truly fascinating body of topographical evidence for the elucidation of settlement. At many points, as Professor Du Boulay has pointed out in the case of Bexley, they coincide with the boundaries of Anglo-Saxon estates as recorded in pre-Conquest charters: such is the ability of even the humblest English institutions to survive, in some form or another, the unending changes of the centuries.[33]

What, then, can these boundaries tell us about Kentish settlement and the evolution of the Kentish church? There are five principal aspects of this subject that need to be mentioned. To begin with, there are several places where groups of parishes originally forming a complete minsterland still constitute a coherent unity on the $2\frac{1}{2}''$ O.S. map. One striking case already referred to is that of Hollingbourne, with its seven adjacent daughters of Hucking, Leeds, Broomfield, Langley, Chart Sutton, Sutton Valence, and East Sutton.[34] Except at Langley, the boundary of this area still forms a single continuous line or ring around the old minsterland, while those of its constituent parishes

PART FIVE *Topographical Reconstruction*

abut upon it, forming a T-junction, without passing through it. Only on the southern edge of the area is the boundary noticeably jagged or irregular, and this irregularity is a characteristic feature of the minster-lands of Holmesdale and the Chart wherever they merge into the common pastures of the Weald. There are few universal rules in matters of local topography; but where we find a series of parish boundaries abutting on those of another parish without passing through them in this way, there is a *prima facie* case that the latter form the more ancient line of demarcation. Another striking instance of the same topographical phenomenon, though no longer marked on the Ordnance Sheets, is that of Crayford and its eight daughter-parishes of Bexley, North Cray, Foot's Cray, Chislehurst, Ruxley, St Paul's Cray, St Mary Cray, and Orpington (see map 8).

In the second place, where minster churches are situated on the banks of major rivers, it is noteworthy that their parish boundaries usually extend on both sides of the stream, whereas those of their subordinate parishes very rarely do so. In the early-settled stretch of the Medway valley below Yalding, both Maidstone and Aylesford thus straddle the river, whereas in every other case the Medway forms the parish boundary: at Nettlestead, Wateringbury, Teston, Barming, Allington, Ditton, East Malling, Snodland, Halling, and Cuxton on the west bank; and at Yalding, West Farleigh, East Farleigh, Boxley, Burham, and Wouldham on the east (see maps 5 and 13). So far as Kent is concerned, it is perhaps only on the Medway that we can be certain of the significance of this phenomenon; on the Stour it may be affected by other circumstances, and on the Thames there are no minster churches. At both Maidstone and Aylesford, however, there can be no doubt that it is a sign of the antiquity of the community, not only as a minster-settlement, but as the *caput* of an early Jutish estate. Wherever a minster-parish straddles a major river in this way, there is thus a *prima facie* case that it represents the last remnant of a pre-Christian territory; in the cases of Maidstone and Aylesford that territory may well be of Romano-British origin.

Thirdly, there are several places, as we have seen in an earlier chapter, where the original territory of the mother-church was clearly very long and narrow, and at some subsequent date was divided in two across its centre. At Westerham, which is only two miles in width and yet once extended for nine miles along the Surrey border, the southern or Wealden half, Edenbridge, remained a dependent chapelry of Westerham until the nineteenth century. At Brasted, the next parish eastwards, there is no record of when Hever, the southern half of the territory, was given a separate life; but its original relationship with Brasted is apparent not only by analogy with Westerham, but from the evidence of the boundary, and from the fact that Brasted held outlying land in Hever, known as Brastedlands, about a mile north of Hever Castle. In much the same way, to the east of Brasted, the long narrow territories of Sundridge and Chevening were divided to form the separate Wealden parish of Chiddingstone, though here again there is no specific record of when the division took place. Further east, beyond Maidstone, the southern half of Harrietsham was split off to form Ulcombe; and across the Downs, near Faversham, that of Teynham was divided to form Lynsted and Doddington.[35] In all these cases the subsequent boundary dividing the mother-church from its daughter abuts on the older one, without passing through it, just as at Hollingbourne.

The existence of long narrow strip-parishes like these has often been commented upon in other areas, such as the Wiltshire Downs, the Chiltern Hills, and east Cambridgeshire. They are especially characteristic of the chalk and greensand scarplands, although the case of Teynham, which is on the dip-slope of the Downs, shows that they may also be found in other situations. Their obvious inconvenience from the agrarian point of view has usually been explained as an attempt to provide each farmer or community with a fair share of the good land and poor land of the area, and in many places this explanation is no doubt true enough. The fact that they tend to occur in groups or blocks, however, as in the case of Westerham and Brasted, suggests that ecclesiastically they often originated through the subdivision of an older, larger territory which at one time comprised the whole block of parishes.[36] So far as the West Kent group is concerned, there is reason to think that Brasted and Hever once formed a single territory subordinate to Westerham.[37] The evidence is not conclusive; but the fact that Westerham was roughly twice as large as Brasted, which is nowhere much more than a mile in width yet originally extended for nine or ten miles in length, is significant in this connexion: for in such circumstances the older parish often tends to be the larger one.

The fourth topographical peculiarity of many Kentish parishes is the irregularity of their boundaries. The compact ecclesiastical territories characteristic of the Midlands may occasionally be found, but they are comparatively unusual. Where they occur, it is worth noting that they are often associated either with minsters or with early independent

PART FIVE *Topographical Reconstruction*

churches like Westwell and Adisham. In recent generations, these irregularities have sometimes been modified; yet even now many parishes, such as Sheldwich near Faversham, Langley near Maidstone (see map 5), and Stone-by-Dartford, are extraordinarily contorted in form, with long projections and outlying tongues of land that to modern eyes seem wholly irrational. There must always be good historical reasons for such peculiarities, however, for in this sense primitive people are never irrational. Sometimes, no doubt, they are due to the fact that the Kentish parish consisted of a loose network of independent farms, each standing in its own fields, rather than a communally-organized society centred on a single village. But generally speaking there can be little doubt that they represent remnants of old common woodland and communal pasture. They frequently arose, in short, through the gradual subdivision of the outlying *wald* between neighbouring farms and parishes, as population increased from the late Old English period onwards, and colonization pressed ever further into the unappropriated waste. In many cases they are thus still associated with substantial stretches of woodland, as well as with characteristic woodland names, and with those crooked shaws and shaves around the

MAP 14. *Interlocking boundaries near Elham* (based on the Ordnance Survey map with the permission of The Controller of Her Majesty's Stationery Office; Crown Copyright reserved)

contours in feet — — — parish boundaries   woodland

• select medieval settlements; queries indicate conjectures   4 parish names

1 Stelling Lodge	20 Yewtree Farm	1 Upper Hardres
2 Bossingham	21 Highchimney Farm	2 Kingston
3 Lynsore Bottom	22 Fryarne Park	3 Barham
4 Reeds	23 South Lodge	4 Elham
5 Little Duskins	24 Abbotswood	5 Stelling
6 Duskins	25 Farthingsole	6 Lyminge
7 Horsehead	26 Wildage	7 Elmsted
8 Ham	27 Fir Tree Farm	8 Stelling Minnis (extra-parochial area)
9 Kingswood	28 Charcoal Farm	
10 Lynsore Court	29 Redoak	
11 Clambercrown	30 Bladbean	
12 Great Palmstead	31 Wingmore	
13 Little Palmstead	32 Worldswonder Farm	
14 Dane Farm	33 Greenacre	
15 Butts Farm	34 Jacques Court	
16 Mead Farm	35 Droveway House	
17 Prim Farm	36 Wheelbarrow Town	
18 Chapel Farm	37 Eastleigh Court	
19 Coxsole Farm	38 Parkgate	

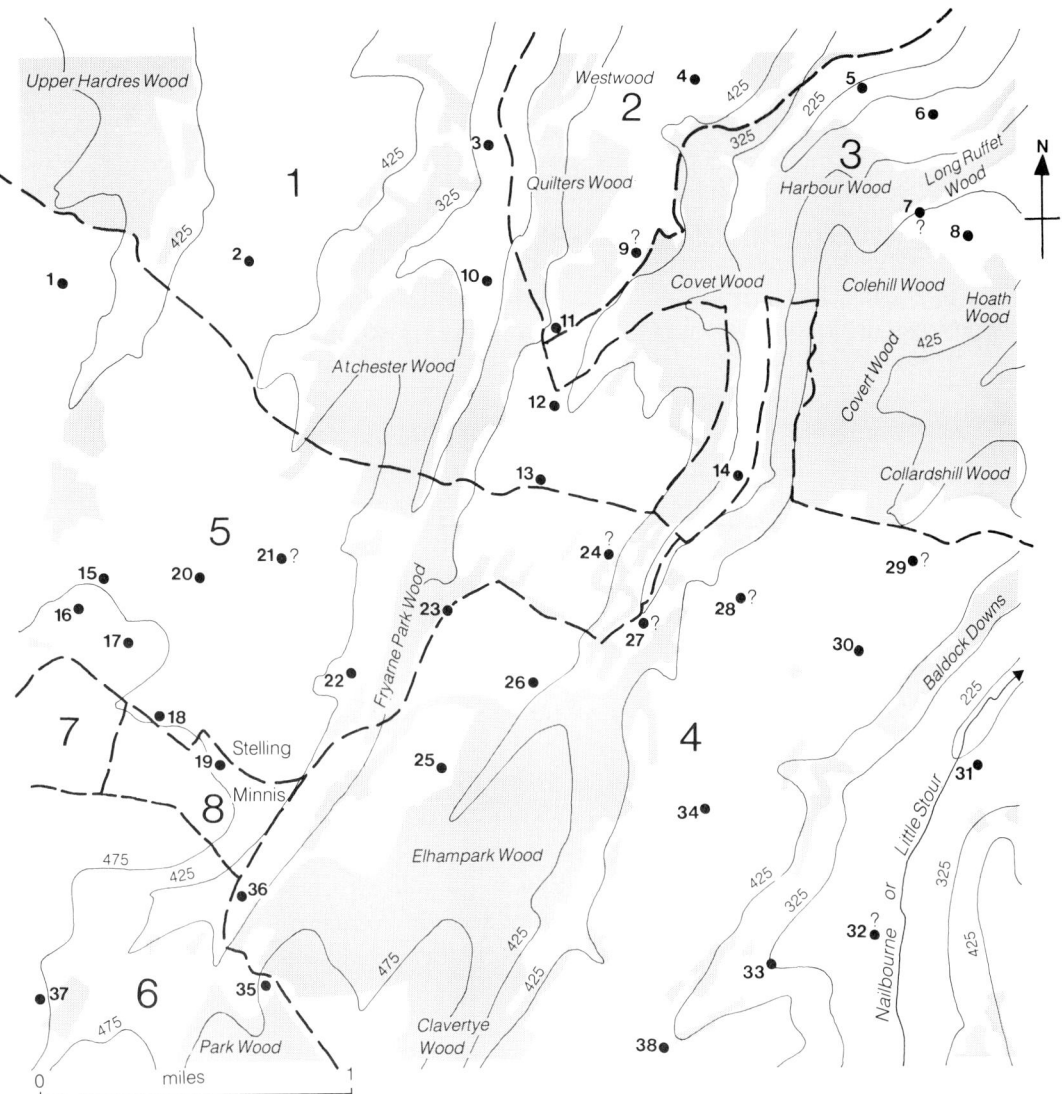

edges of the fields which in Kent often betoken old assarts. In an area already referred to on the borders of Alkham, Hawkinge, Acrise ('oak brush-wood'), Wootton ('wood farm'), and Swingfield ('swine *feld*'), for instance, we find names like Stockhill Wood, Biggin Wood, Butcher's Wood, Stonylane Wood, Ladwood, and Cobham's Rough (i.e. 'scrub'), and long sickle-shaped shaws like those at Longcraft on the edge of Acrise (see map 10). In this same area we also find many pastoral place-names, such as Densole Minnis and Swingfield Minnis (*gemǣnnes*), Fernden, Reinden, and Standen (*denn*),[38] Winterdown (*dūn*), Selstead (*stede*), Park Wood (*pearroc*), Hoad Farm ('hoath'), and West Lees (*lǣs*). Other place-names in the neighbourhood, such as Brandred ('burnt clearing'), Stockhill, and Stockham (*stocc* + *hamm*,

PART FIVE *Topographical Reconstruction*

'[tree]-stump enclosure'), point to early woodland clearance. It was the origin of areas like these as common pastureland, moreover, that in later centuries often gave rise to a certain ambiguity in their legal status. Even in James I's reign conflicting rights over them were still giving rise to lawsuits and to special commissions and depositions in the Exchequer; in a few places, indeed, the boundary was not finally settled until the nineteenth century.

A careful study of these outlying appendages of the Kentish parish is thus of singular interest for an understanding of local settlement-history. In some cases, as we saw in Chapter 7, the boundaries of five or six parishes may be found intricately interlocked with one another, in the form of the Greek key pattern (see map 9). In the steep Downland combes between Hythe and Canterbury, in an area still densely wooded, the outlying lands of Elham, Barham, Kingston, Stelling, and Upper Hardres are all interlocked in this way, and names like Wildage, Palmstead, Elhampark, Fryarne Park, and King's Wood are significantly numerous (see map 14). On the Downs south of Milton Regis, the outlying parts of Rodmersham, Milsted, Sittingbourne, Tunstall, and Bredgar provide another striking series of interlocking bounds, as we shall see in more detail in Chapter 11. Wherever we find a boundary pattern of this kind in Kent, it seems to indicate the subdivision of old common woodland in such a way as to give each parish or group of farms a more or less carefully proportioned share in its varied resources.

Finally, there are still many localities where the bounds of a whole series of parishes converge upon a single stretch of woodland, or on some outlying ridge of *wald*. We have already noted this phenomenon in the upland country between the Darent valley and the Cray (see map 8), and a further example is to be found in the Hoo peninsula, between the Medway estuary and the Thames. In this area most of the churches lie close to the springline on either side of the watershed, but each parish extends a long finger or tongue of land up on to the wooded ridge or *hōh* which gave the area its name and which rises to about 400 feet near Shorne Ridgeway (see map 15). Shorne, Chalk, Denton, Cobham, Strood, Frindsbury, Higham, and the lost parish of *Merston* all converge in this way on a tract of woodland in the west; and Cliffe, Cooling,

MAP 15. *The Hoo Peninsula: pastoral development* (based on the Ordnance Survey map with the permission of The Controller of Her Majesty's Stationery Office; Crown Copyright reserved)

10 Topographical method: analysis

- ⌢ contours in feet
- ∿ rivers, streams, creeks, coastline
- —··—··— hundredal boundaries (coincidental with parish boundaries)
- — — — parish and chapelry boundaries
- ······· edge of marshland
- ──── direction of pastoral development
- ──── Roman roads and likely prehistoric trackways ▬▬▬ Watling Street
- – – – – routes converging on High Halstow broken lines indicate conjectural route
- ✞⊕ minsters
- ✞ other mother-churches
- ⊕ other parish churches
- ✛ chapels-of-ease or of similar status without parochial rights
- ⊕ manorial chapels
- ✚ crouches and crosses
- ✗ priories and hospitals
- MILTON parish names
- *Denton Marshes* marshland pastures; queries indicate conjectural location
- ● W.Filborough select minor settlement-names related to pastures
- Three Crouches minor ecclesiastical sites

Shamel etc. are hundredal names

Upland pastures and woodlands; queries indicate conjectural location

1 West Wood	27 Chilton Hills Wood
2 ?Raynehurst and Timberwood	28 Starmore Wood
3 Clay Lane Wood	29 Court Wood
4 Henhurst	30 Great Crabbles Wood
5 Winstead Hill	31 Gadshill
6 Dark Sallows	32 Peartree Wood
7 Battle Wood	33 Higham Upshire
8 Ashenbank Wood	34 Cole Wood
9 Haydon ['heath + *dūn*']	35 Broad Oak Wood
10 Shorne Wood	36 Great Wood
11 Randall Heath	37 Clay Pond Wood
12 Brummelhill Wood	38 Temple Wood
13 Harts Hill	39 Hangman's Shaw
14 Ifield ['yew + *feld*']	40 Head Barn Wood
15 Randall Wood	41 Magpie Shaw
16 Woodlands	42 Ranscombe
17 Shorne Ridgeway	43 Merrals Shaw
18 Puckle Hill	44 Longhoes Wood
19 Brewers Wood	45 Swyre's Shaw
20 Winterham Hill	46 Purty's Shaw
21 Lodge Wood	47 Borstal
22 Horwood Grove	48 Rede Court
23 Green	49 Broom Hill
24 Beckley Hill	50 Brompton
25 ?Haselden	51 Dallywood
26 Gore Green	52 Stonehouse

10 Topographical method: analysis

53 Sole Street
54 Wainscot *alias* Parlabiens Yoke
55 Oak Street
56 Sandy Hill
57 Lee Green
58 Haven Street ['heath hill']
59 Haven Street Wood
60 Stone House Wood
61 Bingham Roughs
62 Little Oakleigh
63 Great Oakleigh
64 Cliffe Common
65 ?Northope

66 ?Southwould
67 Cliffe Wood
68 Ratly Hills Wood
69 Great Chattenden Wood
70 Chattenden Rough
71 Round Top Wood
72 Berry Court Wood
73 Rough Shaw
74 Lodge Hill Wood
75 Wybornes Wood
76 North Wood
77 Fisher's Wood
78 Huggin's Wood

79 Cart Wood
80 Deangate Wood
81 Timberwood
82 Chattenden
83 Rams Bottom Wood
84 Hoo Common
85 Woodland Park
86 Cockham Wood
87 Brompton
88 Rams Green
89 Newlands

Notes

1. All the parish churches in the hundred of Hoo originated as daughters of Hoo St Werburgh: St Mary's Hoo, High Halstow, Allhallows Hoo, Stoke, and Hoo St Margaret's. A small but unidentified part of Cobham parish also formed a detached portion of this hundred.

2. Ecclesiastical development in the hundred of Shamwell is more difficult to reconstruct. Shorne was the mother-church of Merston, Cobham, St Catherine's, probably Chalk, and possibly Denton. Frindsbury was the mother-church of Strood, and possibly also of Islingham and Bromhey; but if Hasted is right in saying (III, 540) that there was no church at Frindsbury when Gundulph became Bishop of Rochester after the Conquest, Bromhey must have antedated it, since it is recorded in the *Textus Roffensis*, and possibly Islingham also (cf. H, III, 528), though the parochial status of these two churches remains doubtful. The most important church in the hundred was the minster at Cliffe, which certainly gave birth to West Cliffe, probably to Cooling, Higham, and Lillechurch, and possibly also to Shorne.

3. The number of lost parishes and chapelries in this part of Kent is noteworthy: among them Hoo St Margaret's, St Catherine's, Merston, Lillechurch, Islingham, Bromhey, West Cliffe, Grange, and more recently Denton. Only at Grange, Denton, and Bromhey are their boundaries now recoverable.

4. The meeting-place of Shamwell Hundred is not known, but since the hundred was appendant to the manor of Shorne (H, III, 447), it must probably be sought for in Shorne, perhaps where the Hoo ridgeway joined Watling Street, near the holy well later associated with St Thomas, or perhaps at Gadshill, near the Shorne/Higham boundary. The name of Shamwell, from *sceamol*, 'shambles', possibly indicates a heathen site, as in other places in Kent where it occurs in a rural context of this kind.

5. Parish boundaries have been reconstructed principally from the Tithe Index sheets, the 2½″ O.S. sheets, and the boundary marks (trees, stubs, stones, etc.) recorded on the latter.

Note The chart below indicates the make-up of map 15 over the subsequent pages.

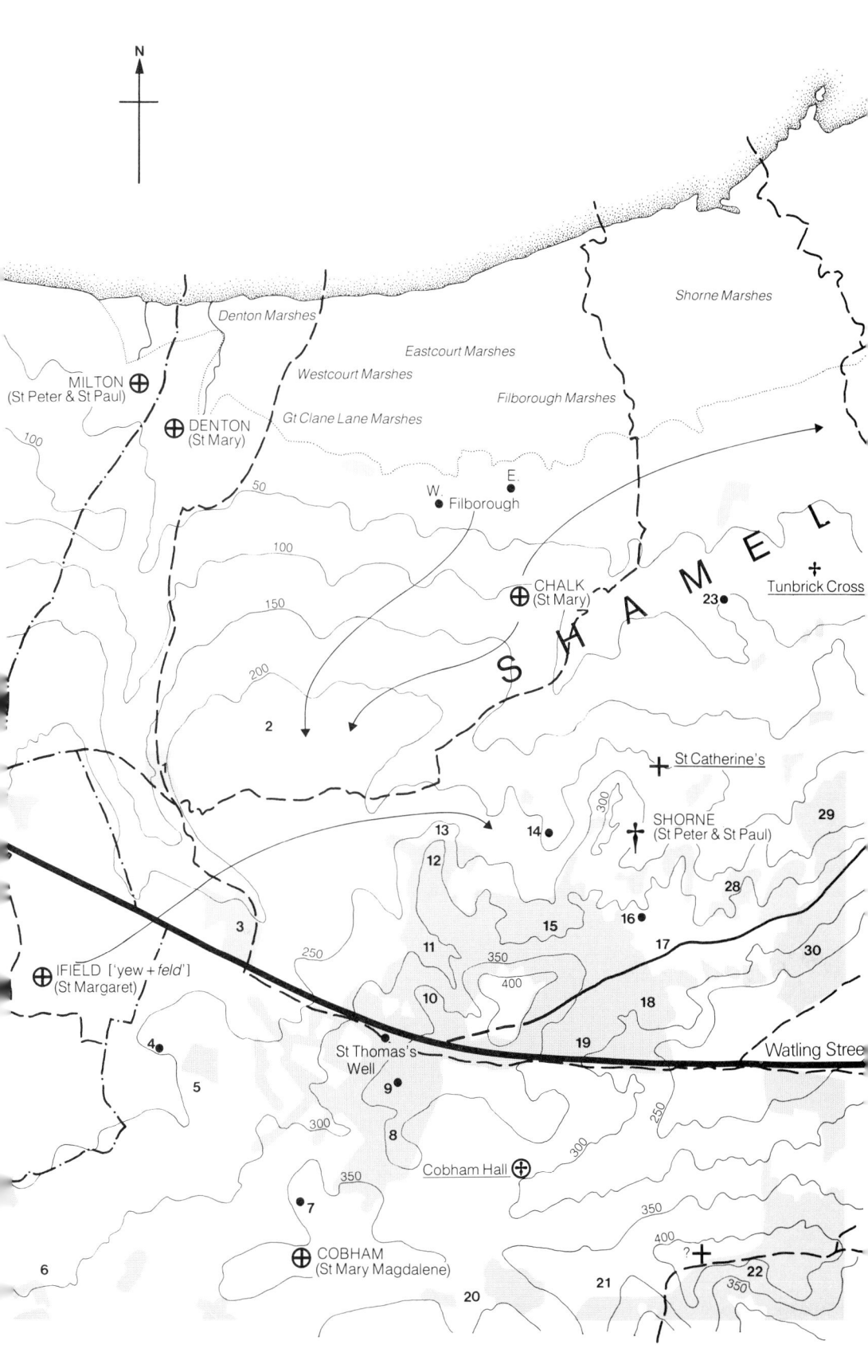

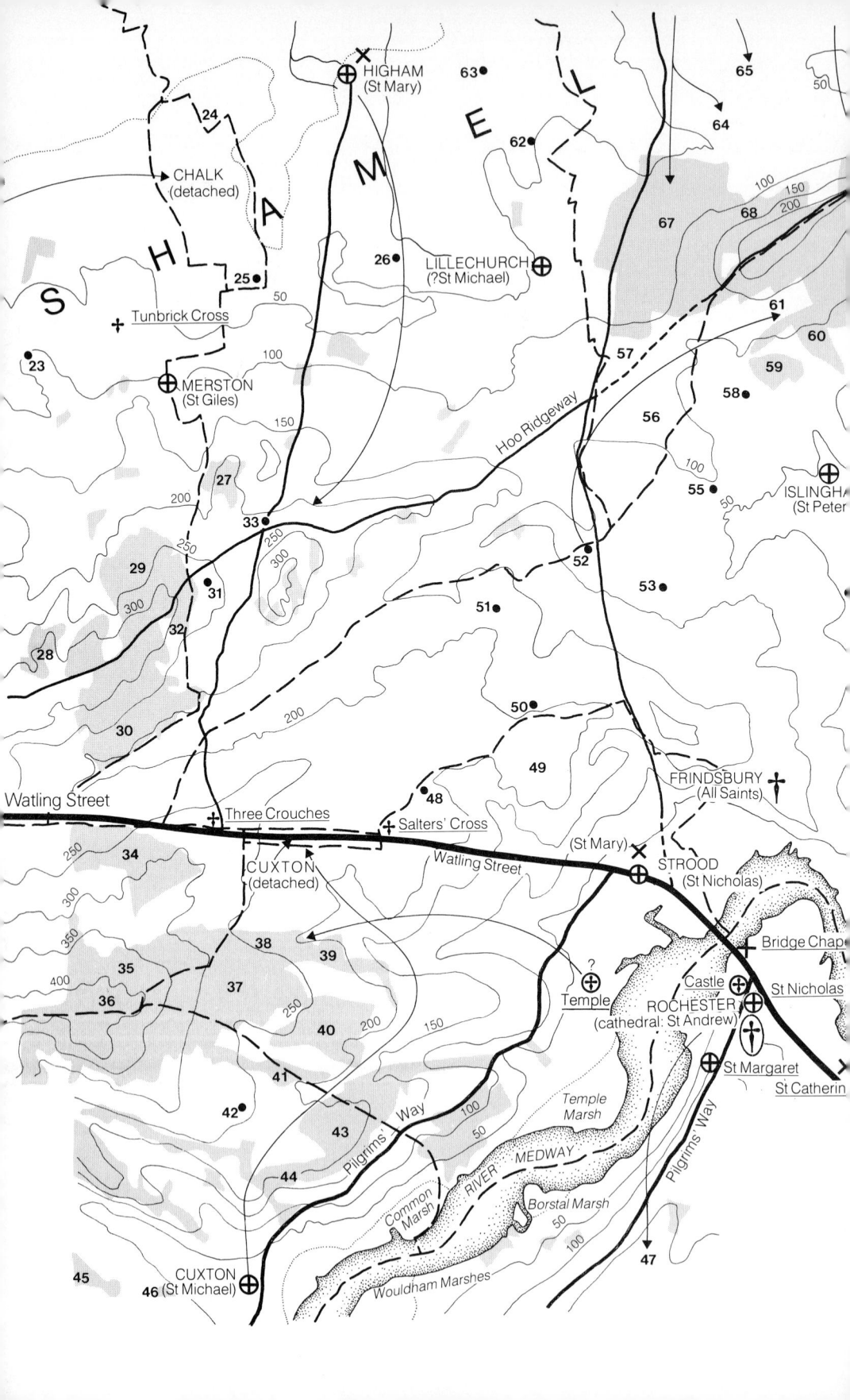

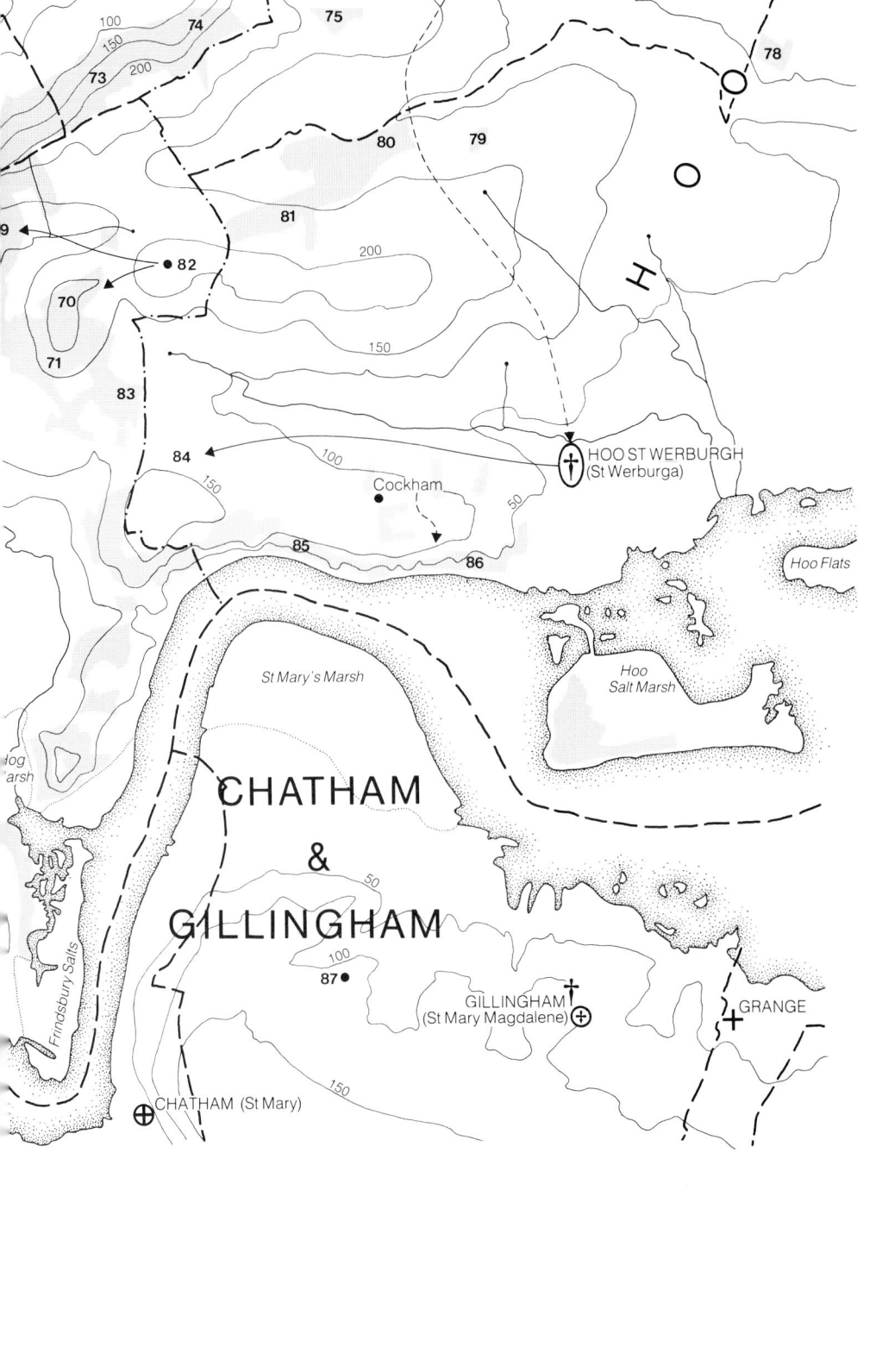

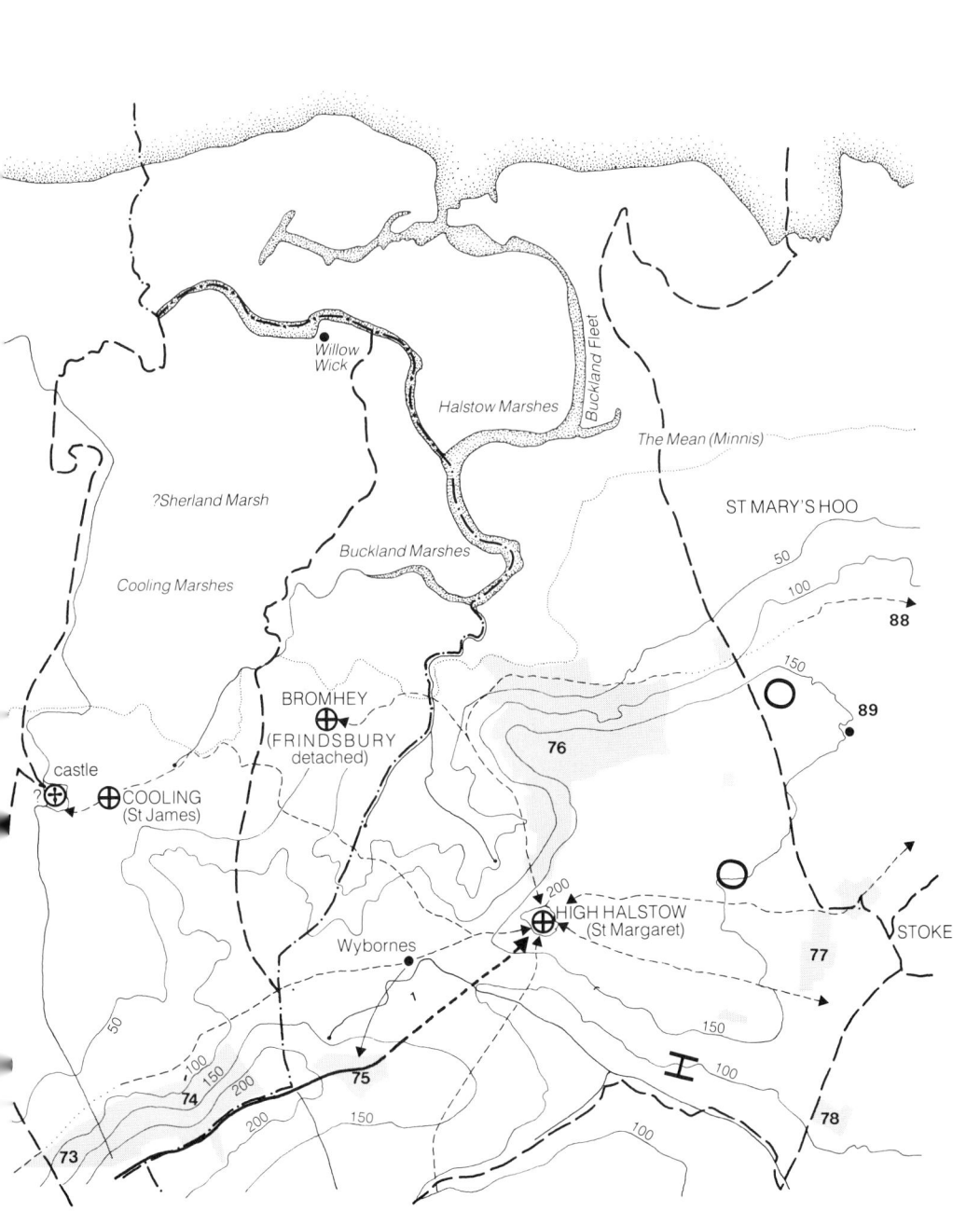

PART FIVE *Topographical Reconstruction*

Halstow, Hoo St Werburgh, and the lost Islingham, Lillechurch, and Bromhey on the woods of Chattenden, Lodge Hill, and Ratly Hills to the east. At one time the whole area was evidently known as 'the upland *scīr* or district', a name which still survives in that of Higham Upshire, and which once had its marshland counterpart in Sherland Marsh, 'the marsh of the shire land', in Cooling. Before the coming of the English, the Celtic peoples must have called this upland region the *cēto* or 'forest'; and this element too is one that still survives, at Chattenden Farm and Great Chattenden Wood in Frindsbury, reappearing as we have seen in the name of Chatham and other places on the further side of the Medway. The gradual colonization of the district is indicated by many of its minor place-names, such as Oakleigh (*lēah*), Rede Court (*rede*), and Lee Green (*lēah*), which point to clearances in the woods; Magpie Shaw and Rough Shaw, which mark the sites of medieval assarting; and Bromhey ('broom enclosure') and Brompton ('broom farm'), which recall the sandy soils and poor natural vegetation of the early wood-heath farms.[39]

Few people nowadays would think of the Hoo peninsula as a romantic region, though beyond Frindsbury it still wears something of the forlorn strangeness that Dickens described in *Great Expectations*. Yet to the settlement historian its landscape is a wonderfully revealing document. Its place-names and its boundaries tell us not only about the evolution of settlement in the Augustinian era. At several points they also seem to hint at something beyond Christianity, at the heathen bedrock beneath the Christian soil. The ancient ridgeway dividing the peninsula, which still survives as Shorne Ridgeway (1250) and as a lane in Higham Upshire, and which reappears as the parish boundary between Frindsbury, Cooling, Cliffe, and Hoo St Werburgh, is evidently a route of primitive religious significance. Exactly where its course originated is uncertain; but it must have left Watling Street somewhere in the hundred of Shamwell, a name possibly indicating a 'place of animal sacrifice', and close to the holy well later dedicated to St Thomas of Canterbury. It then passed by Puckle Hill (?'demon hill'), a Romano-British burial place in Great Crabbles Wood, and Godshill, or 'god's hill', perhaps indicating a further heathen site in the locality.[40] Finally, it led on for a further six miles through the woods of Chattenden to High Halstow, where several tracks converge on what was once the 'holy stow' of Hoo, on its commanding promontory overlooking St Werburga's minster, down by the Medway.

10   *Topographical method: analysis*

7. THE CHURCH AND ITS SITUATION

Both the structure of the parish church and its geographical situation are worth taking account of in tracing the sequence of settlement. Though most Kentish churches, like those of other counties, were largely rebuilt after the Conquest, they raise two points of general significance in this connexion. First, though sometimes of doubtful date and uninspiring architecturally, the Saxon remains of the county are often instructive archaeologically. Of the remains at Lydd, for example, John Newman remarks: 'the nearest parallel in size and plan is the fifth-century Romano-British church excavated at Silchester. The masonry shews none of the knowledge of Roman building techniques so evident in the early seventh-century churches at Canterbury. Indeed Lydd stands quite apart from Augustinian importations'. In the light of Lydd's origins as a Romano-British settlement and its isolation from other Romanized parts of the county, this judgment is of considerable historic interest.[41] When the first Teutonic settlers arrived, it may still in fact have been an island; for its name *hlid* is said to mean 'slope' or 'hillside', and in this flat country that can only have referred to the original seashore facing the mainland. In view of Lydd's importance as a minster-community, and its association with early Roman saints like St Anacletus, St Crispin, and St Crispinian, the architecture of the church may thus point to a pre-Augustinian foundation. It may be, indeed, that the structural development of the minster churches of Kent as a group would repay detailed investigation on a comparative basis.

Second, owing to the fact that the early churches of the county were usually established in places ultimately antedating the Jutish invasions, Roman brickwork appears in perhaps more churches in Kent than in any other county. In several instances, such as the ruins of Reculver, it is employed extensively. In a number of places, such as St Martin's and St Pancras's near Canterbury, and the original minster of St Martin at Dover, the building itself is said to have been a Romano-British or at least pre-Augustinian structure.[42] In view of Pope Gregory's instructions to St Augustine not to destroy heathen temples but rather to convert them to Christian uses, such origins are not incredible. Where we find Roman bricks employed, they are almost always associated with early ecclesiastical buildings, and in most cases with mother-churches, as at Northfleet, Eynsford, Reculver, Minster-in-Sheppey, and Minster-in-Thanet. The fact that they are not found at

PART FIVE *Topographical Reconstruction*

all in Wealden[43] or Chartland churches, and very rarely in those of the Downland, is certainly significant in the context of continuity. On the other hand, the fact that Roman work of some kind occurs in a number of quite minor churches in the Original Lands, such as Stourmouth and Stone-by-Faversham, suggests that in some places the process of creating subordinate churches in Kent may have begun at a very early period. At Richborough and St Mary-in-Castro at Dover, it is possible that the original foundation dated back to the seventh century.[44]

So far as the situation of the parish church is concerned, there are two groups of buildings calling for comment. The first comprises the substantial number situated on hill-tops. In view of the fact that such churches elsewhere are often thought to be of great antiquity, the point is of some importance. Places like Oldbury in Gloucestershire, Breedon in Leicestershire, Naseby and Brixworth in Northamptonshire, and Wednesbury and Wolverhampton in Staffordshire are certainly ancient, and in several cases stand within or adjacent to Iron Age hill-forts. In Kent there are a number of churches that appear to be associated with early sites of this kind. Some, like Woodnesborough, and probably Addington and Bidborough, adjoin prehistoric barrows or burial mounds.[45] A few, like Coldred, occupy massive earthworks, and bear early dedications like St Pancras. A few, like High Halstow, bear obviously significant place-names and may be of pre-Christian origin. One at least, St Mary-in-Castro at Dover, stands in an Iron Age hill-fort, and two, at Lympne and Reculver, in Roman forts. It is also possible that early hill-top churches in commanding positions like Chilham and Minster-in-Sheppey occupy prehistoric military sites, though as yet unidentified. Certainly Kenardington, on the old cliff-line overlooking Romney Marsh, stands in the remains of a fort, perhaps dating only from the Danish invasions, but perhaps very much older. Even in the heart of the Weald we find a place like Goudhurst, or 'battle-wood', whose striking situation and suggestive place-name may perhaps indicate a vanished hill-fort, as at Castle Hill a few miles away.[46] Then what is one to make of that remarkable line of ten parish churches strung out along the rim of the Stone Hills, between Linton and Pluckley, with their dramatic views over the Weald? Were they intended merely as landmarks for the Wealden herdsmen, or had some of them, such as Sutton Valence with its Norman Castle, an older history as defensive outposts of the fertile springlands of Holmesdale?

Such examples as these are clearly worth pondering in connexion with early settlement. At places like Woodnesborough, Lympne, and Minster-in-Sheppey the situation of the church seems particularly suggestive. Yet the great majority of hill-top churches are associated with the later-settled parts of the county, and in most cases there can be very little doubt that they are relatively late foundations. Many of those on the Downs and the Chart are known to have originated as subordinate chapels, as we have seen, and bear typically late dedications like All Saints, St Nicholas, St Michael, St James, and St John the Baptist. Of the dozen or so dedicated to St Michael, for instance, all save perhaps Cuxton originated as subsidiary churches, either in the late Old English period or shortly after the Conquest: four on the Downs, three on the Chart, three in the Weald, and two in the Blean. In other words there is little reason to think that the hill-top churches of Kent are in general associated with the 'high places' of the heathen world. Occasionally the possibility of a defensive origin should not be ruled out, and if manorial churches developed from the quasi-defensive structure of the lord's hall, as has sometimes been argued, this may explain the extraordinarily massive early towers of 'bookland' churches like Leeds. In most cases, however, it seems more likely that they originated through the need for a prominent landmark in a heavily forested countryside. Their dedications and their frequent association with droveways tend to confirm this view.

The second group of buildings calling for discussion comprises those on the banks of rivers and springs. Such a position is not of course peculiar to Kent; many of the earliest churches of Cambridgeshire are to be found by the Cam or Granta, and of Bedfordshire and Huntingdonshire on the Ouse or its tributaries, as at Hemingford, Tempsford, and Eynesbury. Yet the long line of early Kentish churches situated beside rivers and springheads is certainly remarkable: Wickhambreaux, Littlebourne, Patrixbourne, and Lyminge on the banks of the Little Stour, for instance; Sturry, Fordwich, Canterbury, Chartham, and Godmersham on those of the Great Stour; Cuxton, Wouldham, Halling, Burham, Aylesford, and Maidstone on the Medway; Dartford, Darenth, Horton Kirby, Eynsford, and Lullingstone on the Darent; and so on.[47] On the Thames, by contrast, it is noteworthy that there is not a single early foundation on the Kentish side, a circumstance that is due not only to the extent of the marshes, but to the fact that settlement rarely originated from the Thames itself, though occasionally, as at Northfleet, from its minor tributaries. Neither are there any on the Medway above Yalding, where the flood-plain of the

PART FIVE *Topographical Reconstruction*

river widens out into the Weald and primary settlement came to an abrupt halt. Sometimes it must have been the rite of baptism that lay behind the location of churches like these; in places it was no doubt affected by their association with early Jutish estate-centres; yet there are grounds for suspecting an older tradition behind it, perhaps stemming from the pagan cults of the county and their links with local water-spirits.[48] This seems to be suggested by the association of early churches with holy wells and springs, and it is to this subject that we must finally direct our attention.

8. HOLY WELLS AND SPRINGS

In contrast with some counties, Kent has paid strangely little attention to its holy wells and springs, and most of them are now no longer remembered. The subject is a difficult one, which raises as many questions as it answers, and in the present state of knowledge it is important that the evidence should not be overstated. A few holy wells, however, have been venerated until quite recent generations, and a number may still be traced without much difficulty. The healing properties of St Thomas's Well at Otford were acknowledged into the present century, when children were sent to bathe their grazes there, and hop-pickers took bottles of its waters back to London at the end of the season. In the neighbouring parish of Kemsing the perennial waters of St Edith's Well were likewise venerated into the early twentieth century, when they were still considered locally to provide a cure for bad eyes. Other noted springs and waters included St Ethelburga's Well by the church at Lyminge, St Anne's Wells at Springfield in Maidstone, Our Lady's Well at Dover, St Thomas's Watering in Frindsbury, St Thomas's Well by Watling Street in Cobham, St Eanswythe's Water in the Bail at Folkestone, St Augustine's Well at Ebbsfleet in Thanet, St Eustace's Well at Withersdane in Wye, and the former pilgrims' well in the crypt of Canterbury Cathedral.[49] A number of other holy springs may be recognized by their place-names or by some other local characteristic. The church at Hollingbourne is situated by springs that at one time were probably associated with St Anne, like those at Maidstone a few miles away.[50] In several cases names in *hālig* also indicate places of this kind, as at Holywell Shaw on the boundary of Brasted and Westerham; Holywell in Folkestone, near prehistoric sites at the foot of the Downs; and Holywell in Upchurch, near the boundary of Lower Halstow. The ancient religious site at

Hawley, or 'holy clearing', in Sutton-at-Hone likewise seems to have been associated with a chapel and a spring. The well at *Halygarden* in Burham is said to have been 'highly reverenced by the common people for the virtues and sanctity which they attributed to it, to which they made pilgrimages from all the neighbouring parts'.[51]

The significant fact to note about these wells is their association with early centres like Canterbury, Maidstone, Lyminge, Folkestone, Wye, Otford, Kemsing, Hollingbourne, Halstow, Burham, Westerham, and Sutton-at-Hone. For this reason it is interesting to find that many other early Kentish churches are situated by springheads, though we must not assume that all these were objects of veneration, and in most cases proof of sanctity needs further investigation. Otford and Kemsing are by no means the only churches associated with springs near the Pilgrims' Way, for instance: there is a long line of others extending from Chevening near Sevenoaks to Postling and Newington near Folkestone. The mother-church of St Mary at Lenham, for example, virtually adjoins the source of the Great Stour at Streetwell, perhaps a suggestive place-name. That of St Mary and St Radegund at Postling adjoins the headwaters of the East Stour, 'which comes out of the rock [above the church], at five or six spout-holes big enough to receive a man's hand,' providing 'a constant fountain, which never fails in the driest seasons.' The mother-church of St Peter and St Paul at Charing is similarly situated by the copious springhead that probably gave the place its name. At Stowting the same primitive name-forming suffix, *-ing*, is associated with another early church at the source of a stream.[52] Further examples include Trottiscliffe, Boxley, Westwell, and Eastwell near the Pilgrims' Way; Newington, Teynham, Stone, Faversham, and Preston near Watling Street; Wateringbury and East Malling by springs eventually flowing into the Medway; Orpington at the source of the River Cray; and Alkham and Temple Ewell near the two head-springs of the Dour. In some cases this association may be due to nothing more than the siting of churches in estate-centres; yet the fact that many of the springs in question rise immediately beside the church, or in the churchyard itself, suggests that there may also be other circumstances behind it.[53]

In addition to wells and springs associated with pre-Conquest churches like these, there is a further group where churches or chapels are not recorded until after the Conquest, although in some cases the well-cults may have been very much older. Sometimes these chapels eventually acquired burial rights and became full parish churches, as at

PART FIVE *Topographical Reconstruction*

St Leonard's Hythe, St Mary's Langley, and St Michael's Sittingbourne. In other places they were later re-founded as hospitals, as at St John's Chapel by Greatness Springs in Sevenoaks, St Nicholas's Chapel by the Prince's Well in Harbledown, and the chapel of St Bartholomew's Hospital at Sandwich. Others again never graduated beyond the stage of an oratory or chantry, and so remained until they were dissolved at the Reformation. St Leonard's Chapel in West Malling, for instance, was probably founded by Gundulf, the first Norman bishop of Rochester. The oratory at St Blaise's Well in Bromley, a mineral spring near the episcopal palace, was founded by another Norman bishop of Rochester. The founder of the springhead oratory at Bapchild is not known, but it was certainly in existence by the twelfth century, and in this case the well-cult may be much older, for Bapchild is recorded as *Baccancelde*, or 'Bacca's spring', in a charter of 696 x 716.[54]

The connexion of early Kentish churches with holy wells and springs does not necessarily, of course, imply that these places were centres of religious cults before the advent of Christianity. The fact, however, that in several cases the springs are known to have been associated with local fertility customs and rites of healing suggests that this is sometimes a possibility that should not be ruled out. At Kemsing, for instance, the image of St Edith is said to have been 'greatly frequented for the singular benefits she daily dispensed in preserving corn and grain from blasting, mildew, and other harm incident to it.' At Otford, in addition to the popular veneration for St Thomas's Well, there was a notable cult of St Bartholomew, 'a saint of great credit here for the gift of curing barrenness in women, which caused great resort of people to his image and shrine in this church. . .' At Maidstone the springs of St Anne must also have been associated with fertility customs; for St Anne was the patron saint of barren women and was associated with similar customs at Malvern, Buxton, Nottingham, and elsewhere.[55] At Wye the water of St Eustace's Well was believed to be 'endowed by such miraculous power that by it all diseases were cured.'[56] Detailed investigation of other notable wells, such as St Thomas's in Cobham, St Eanswythe's at Folkestone, St Augustine's at Ebbsfleet, and St Ethelburga's at Lyminge, might bring similar local customs to light. The fact that the medieval hospitals of Kent, for lepers and other sick and aged folk, were likewise usually associated with wells and springs is noteworthy in this connexion.[57]

There are several places, moreover, where the topographical connotation of early springhead churches seems to confirm these hints of a pre-Christian origin. At Lullingstone, as we have seen, a Christian chapel was built directly over the pagan cult-room of the Roman villa with its springs devoted to the worship of local water-nymphs.[58] At Stone-by-Faversham, the ruins of the springhead church incorporated part of a fourth-century Romano-British mausoleum, and the place-name itself may denote a lost megalithic structure. At Bapchild the springhead chapel appears to have been associated with a Roman cremation site, a Belgic pottery site, and another place-name in 'stone'. At Springfield in Maidstone the chapel of St Anne was situated by a Roman road and close to the site of a Roman villa. At Otford the waters of St Thomas's Well supplied the neighbouring Roman villa many centuries before legend first associated them with St Thomas Becket.[59] At Milton Regis the *caput* of the Jutish estate was associated not only with a major Romano-British settlement, but with a springhead church near the lost settlement of *Godshill*, a springhead hospital at *Puckeshall* (possibly meaning 'demons' corner'), and a springhead chapel at *Shamwell* (perhaps indicating a 'place of animal sacrifice').[60] The most celebrated pagan cult-centre of Kent, at Springhead or *Vagniacae*, with its seven temples grouped around a concourse of eight springs, does not seem to have developed into a Christian shrine: yet only a short distance down the same stream or *flēot* a mother-church was established at Northfleet.[61]

Such circumstances as these are worth pondering. If archaeologists are right in believing that the native cults of Kent were all associated with fertility and healing, and with the worship of female water-spirits, one is inclined to think there may be some significance behind them.[62] The fact that three out of four early springhead churches were dedicated to female saints is perhaps worth noting in this connexion and may confirm these suspicions of a pre-Christian stratum. The evidence seems particularly telling in the case of Maidstone, with its medieval *cultus* of virgin saints, its doubly significant place-name, its numerous indications of a pre-Christian past, and its link by way of the Pilgrims' Way and the Greenway both with the Medway megaliths and with a long line of other springhead minsters at the foot of the Downs. It is just possible that Maidstone formed a kind of regional focus for the pagan spring-cults of Kent, as Penenden Heath on the edge of the town formed the meeting-place for the early Jutish kingdom. This is no more than speculation; but taking the evidence as a whole, there seems to be a *prima facie* case of 'religious continuity' in Kent which merits further

PART FIVE *Topographical Reconstruction*

investigation when the network of holy wells and springs has been reconstructed as a whole.[63]

9. CONCLUSION

There are many aspects of topographical reconstruction that have not been touched on in this chapter, and many which demand more detailed scrutiny. Little has been said about the evidence of agrarian evolution, for example, though in Kent at least land usage varied greatly from parish to parish, according to type of settlement and period of colonization. Little has been said about the topography of field-systems, though this is a matter that was everywhere affected by the evolution of agriculture, and often has much to tell us about the origins of settlement.[64] Little has been said about the distinctive forms of social organization to which different types of parish tended to give rise, though this is a topic we shall return to in Chapter 11, and one for which every topographer needs to develop a noticing eye. More might certainly be said about the topography of parish boundaries; but that is a subject which really demands a volume to itself. Enough has been said, however, to indicate some of the main lines of argument available in seeking to reconstruct the topography of colonization.

In conclusion it ought to be emphasized once again that in topographical matters there are few universal principles, so that every available pointer needs to be taken into consideration. The early churches of Kent were not always sited on the banks of rivers or springs. The minsterlands were not always based on the old Jutish estates. Their boundaries did not always describe a coherent area, or necessarily form a single continuous territory. Ecclesiastical evolution did not always follow in the wake of settlement, and settlement itself did not everywhere proceed in the same southerly or south-westerly direction. Manorial development does not necessarily follow the same course as ecclesiastical foundation, and in places there were paramount manors like Otford that ecclesiastically were no more than chapelries. Daughter-churches were not invariably to be found near the boundary of their mother-communities, and their territories are not in all cases less extensive than those of their parents. The original relationship between one parish and another cannot everywhere be elucidated by a study of its boundaries, and occasionally, as at Lyminge and Elham, the topography of those bounds may at first sight seem strangely eccentric.[65] Nevertheless, the limitations of the subject do not

10 Topographical method: analysis

invalidate the case for a systematic approach to topographical investigation; its complexities and enigmas, indeed, often serve to indicate further lines of enquiry. In the following chapter an attempt will be made to draw the threads together by tracing the evolution of a single territory in the round.

11

THE LANDS OF MILTON REGIS: SYNTHESIS

During the course of this book the names of many of the old estate-centres of Kent have been mentioned, and in several cases the evolution of their territories has been discussed in some detail. To illustrate the complexity of the evidence, however, and the wealth of all it can teach us, it is necessary to reconstruct an individual territory in depth. By so doing, we see not only how the evolution of settlement and the evolution of the church went hand in hand, but also how the evidence of documents, place-names, dedications, parish boundaries, church-siting, ecclesiastical relationship, manorial dependence, woodland survival, and so forth, may be combined to reconstruct the territory as a whole. Such a reconstruction necessarily depends on microscopic examination of countless topographical details, and individually such *minutiae* may at first sight seem trivial. Yet when taken together and interpreted in the light of settlement origins elsewhere, they enable us to unravel the secrets of local colonization in a way that is not otherwise possible.

For this purpose the *regio* dependent upon Milton Regis has been chosen (see map 16). It cannot be claimed that Milton was altogether typical, or that the pattern found elsewhere can necessarily be recreated with the same wealth of detail. In some areas the daughter-parishes were larger than at Milton; in some the territory itself was less extensive; in some, manorial chapels were more numerous; in some the basic agrarian structure was different; and in some, as at Wrotham, the final break-up of the territory came several centuries later. Everywhere, in fact, we find great diversity, and that diversity is an essential point to bear in mind in reconstructing the origins of settlement. With patience, however, many other territories may also be reconstituted, in whole or in part: and in each we find something of the same complexity as at Milton, something of the same intractable mass of human and environmental reality, and embedded in that mass something of the same imprint of an earlier world.

MAP 16. *The lands of Milton Regis* (based on the Ordnance Survey map with the permission of The Controller of Her Majesty's Stationery Office; Crown Copyright reserved)

11   The lands of Milton Regis: synthesis

- 500 ⌣ contours in feet
- — — — parish boundaries, based on Tithe Index sheets
- —·—·— boundary of Milton's territory after detachment of Newington
- —··—··— division between Milton's territory and the Minnis
- —···—···— boundary with Iwade, jurisdiction over which was shared by Milton and Teynham
- .... edge of marshland
- springheads, streams, rivers, creeks, coastline
- ▬▬▬ Roman roads and prehistoric tracks; broken lines indicate conjectural route
- ——— other surviving ancient lanes and tracks recorded on first edition O.S.
- ⊕ minsters and primary mother-churches
- † secondary mother-churches
- ⊕ other parish churches
- ✚ chapels-of-ease or of similar status without parochial rights
- ⊕ manorial chapels (select)
- ✚ crouches and crosses (select)
- ✕ hospitals
- BOBBING   parish names

■ 65   settlements and farmsteads of woodland/pastoral origin; only recorded medieval sites are marked (place-names are given only where significant in this context)

1 Gore Wood	31 Bowl Reed	61 Tickham
2 Wentwood	32 Woodgate	62 Rumsted
3 Grange	33 Wood Street	63 Pond Farm
4 Boxted	34 Eyhorne Hatch	64 Icknor
5 Oak Hill	35 Chestnut Street	65 Hazel Street
6 Chinkwell Wood	36 Riddles	66 Beltsgreen
7 Keycol Hill	37 Sutton Baron	67 Southlees
8 Cutnell	38 Grove End	68 Colyers Wents
9 Cambray	39 Oakwood	69 Swanton
10 Little Norwood	40 Fulston	70 Swanton Street
11 Howt Green	41 Chilton	71 Bedmonton
12 Coleshall	42 Highsted Forstal	72 Park
13 Great Grovehurst	43 Woodstock	73 Horsalls
14 Foxgrove	44 Pistock	74 Deans Hill [$d\bar{u}n$ + $(ge)sella$]
15 Kemsley	45 Broadoak Forstal	75 Norwood
16 Bayford	46 Newbury	76 Baxon
17 Wildfoots [$wald$?]	47 Pitstock	77 Yokes Court
18 Bax	48 Rodmersham Green	78 Newage
19 Hempstead	49 Upper Rodmersham	79 Marley
20 Ricklands Wood	50 Little Newbury	80 Boldrewood
21 Chesley	51 Ludgate	81 Marley Farm
22 Danaway	52 Scuttington	82 Lea Farm
23 Cowstead	53 Dully	83 Woodside Green
24 Hill Green	54 Harwood	84 Broom Hill
25 Nettlested	55 Little Dully	85 Wichling Green
26 Stockbury	56 Claxfield	86 Dungate
27 South Green	57 Sunderland	87 Hole Street
28 Norton Green ['north $denn$']	58 ?Batteries	88 Little Sharsted
29 Deans Hill [$d\bar{u}n$ + $(ge)sella$]	59 Cambridge [?$b\bar{e}r$]	89 Homestall
30 Manns Place	60 ?Bogle	90 Bistock

PART FIVE *Topographical Reconstruction*

91 Down Court	100 Greet	109 Little Brisley
92 Sharsted	101 ?Road	110 Eyhorne Green
93 Frangbury	102 Slade	111 Harpswood
94 Seed	103 Payden	112 Greenway Court
95 Sandhurst	104 Warren Street	113 Greenway Forstal
96 Little Frith	105 Hurst	114 Sandhurst
97 Newlands	106 Longreach	115 Keycol Farm
98 Frith	107 Little Snoad	116 Gotteridge
99 Snoad Farm	108 ?Redborough	117 Wrinsted
		118 Wood Street

Broom Downs   names of woodlands/pastures mentioned in the text or otherwise significant of woodland/pasture (names of individual woods are generally omitted unless significant in this connexion; some parish-names, such as Borden, also indicate woodland/pastures)

Milton Regis ●   other settlement-names

▓   woodland (based on the 2½" O.S. sheets, augmented from the first edition 1" O.S.; in some parts of this area further clearance has been substantial over the past 150 years, and the latter source is not always sufficiently precise to admit reconstruction of the historic pattern in every detail)

ᵀᵀᵀᵀᵀᵀᵀ   edge of Downland escarpment (c.610 – 630ft in this area)

0 ————— miles ————— 1

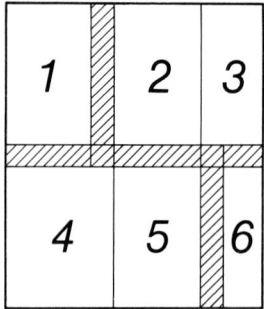

Note The chart to the left indicates the make-up of map 16 over the subsequent pages.

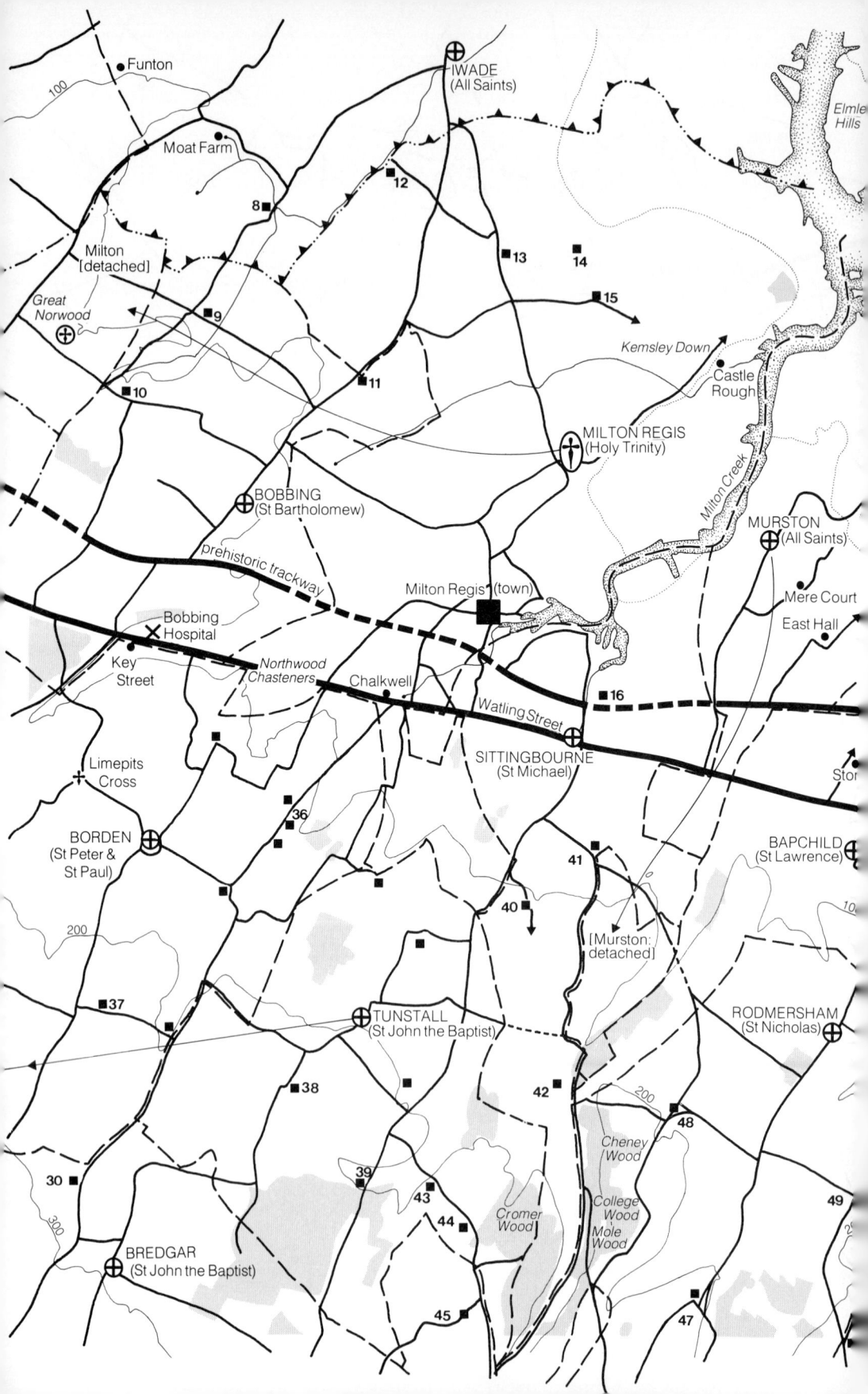

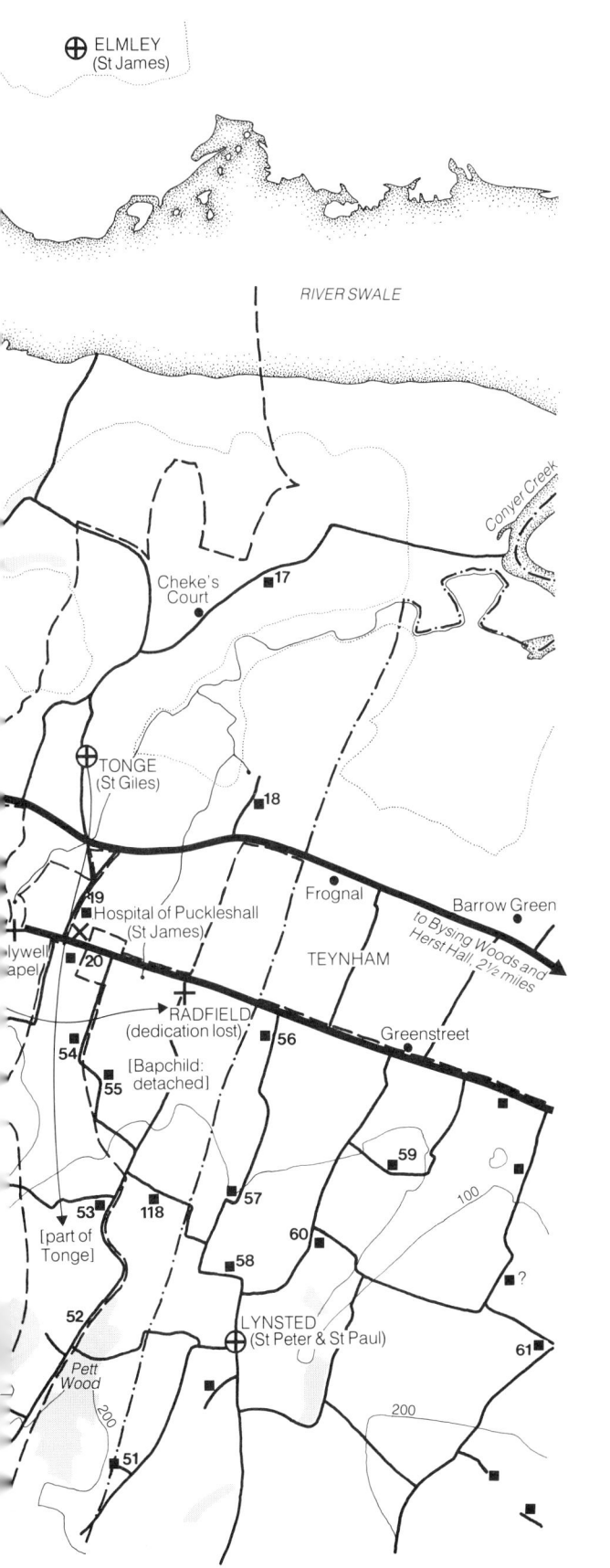

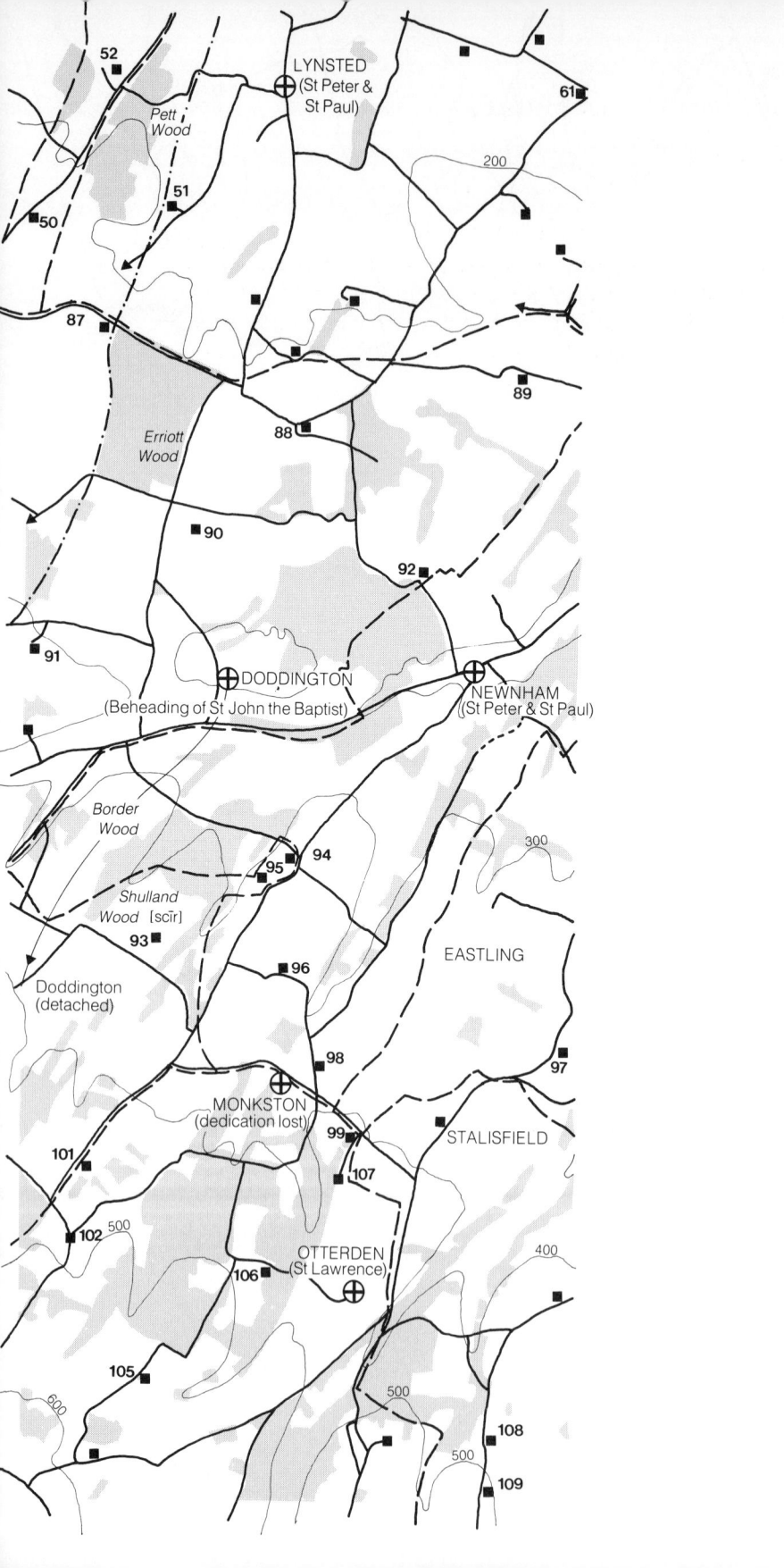

11 The lands of Milton Regis: synthesis

I. *REGIO* AND MINSTERLAND

Milton Regis stands at the centre of the Foothill country of Kent, some 40 miles from the capital, and roughly equidistant between London and Dover. As we have seen in an earlier chapter, it was certainly a place of Romano-British origin, if indeed it does not date back to Bronze Age or Neolithic times.[1] Like other primary settlements in this stretch of the Original Lands – Chatham, Gillingham, Newington, Teynham, and Faversham furnish other examples – it lies a short distance to the north of the Roman road, in a gently undulating countryside between the Street and the Swale. The principal settlement is situated at the point where the springs gush out at the foot of the Downland valleys, giving rise to the tidal inlet of Milton Creek; the minster church stands in an isolated position, about a mile to the north of the springs; and the old town of Milton, with its fifteenth-century court-house, at the head of the creek, by a lane that is thought to be the prehistoric predecessor of the Roman road. Like many early settlements in Kent, Milton is thus situated at the junction of the Foothills and the Marsh, in a neighbourhood largely devoid of attraction to modern eyes. The rapid growth of Sittingbourne alongside Watling Street, and the development of nineteenth-century brickfields and twentieth-century paper mills, cannot be said to have added to its charms. Yet historically speaking, with its locally fertile soils and its proximity to a sheltered harbour, it was natural that it should attract successive waves of colonists and invaders, until last of all the predatory Danes of the ninth century established their fortress a mile or so to the north-east at Castle Rough.[2]

In view of its Romano-British origins, Milton is the kind of place, in Kent at least, that we should expect to become a 'king's town' or *villa regalis*, and in fact it also acquired a palace of the Kentish royal house. Its place-name, *middel tūn* or 'central *tūn*', is one that was appropriate to the *caput* of a major royal estate, and one that reappears in connexion with several other minster churches, such as Melton Mowbray in Leicestershire, though it may not have been the original name.[3] The royal estate on which the minsterland was based had developed as one of the springhead territories of Kent, and it was this estate that later formed the basis of the great hundredal manor of Milton. At the time of the Conquest, the manor of Milton was one of the most valuable in the county, according to Domesday Book worth £200 a year in the time of King Edward. So wealthy a territory was not to be lightly granted

PART FIVE *Topographical Reconstruction*

of Kent, and at Teynham its origins go back to Henry VIII's reign. The great chestnut woods of the Stockbury valley which once extended for five or six miles between Thurnham and Bobbing, and which gave their name to Chestnut Street in Borden, are now largely confined as a consequence to Thurnham and Stockbury itself, which lay outside Milton's immediate territory. Only in the two southernmost parishes, Milsted and Kingsdown, are the woodlands still predominant: and there even today they amount to several hundred acres, the last relics of the prehistoric *wald* to survive in the Milton neighbourhood.

Nevertheless, although this district has in some respects been subjected to more revolutionary change than is usual in the rural parts of Kent, the visual impact of the past is still very apparent. To take place-names alone, Wallenberg discusses almost 80 local names in the 12 parishes under discussion, while the $2\frac{1}{2}''$ O.S. maps record a further 120 which, to judge from their name-forms, must also be of medieval or pre-Conquest origin. In these 200 places, almost all of which still survive, we have an invaluable *corpus* of localized topographical detail. Some of the apparently modern features of the area, such as its big fields and the frequent absence of hedgerows, are in many places of considerable antiquity and are not due to modern clearance, as they would be in the East Midlands, but to the local value of the land in a county not generally notable for its fertility.[11] Despite the gradual extension of fruit-growing, moreover, the forest lanes still sinuate their historic way between the orchards; the farmsteads of the area still occupy their Saxon or medieval sites; their place-names are mostly recorded in twelfth or thirteenth-century documents, as at Highsted (1197), Fulston (1197), Swanton (1204), and Deans Hill (1225); and in many cases, as at Grovehurst (1312), Grove End (1278), Woodstock (1212), and Hogshaw (1357), they tell their own story of woodland reclamation.[12] When interpreted in the light of early maps, parish boundaries, church siting, and manorial relationship, such evidences enable us to trace the gradual clearance of the wood-pastures of the estate with unusual completeness.

The 12 parishes under discussion fall into four groups. Milton and its two immediate neighbours, Murston and Sittingbourne, composed the heartland of the area, both ecclesiastically and territorially, although parochially the two latter were among the last places to be created. To the south and west of Milton, Tunstall, Bobbing, Bredgar, and Borden formed part of the outlying lands of the territory, and were almost entirely reclaimed from the Downland forest. To the east, Tonge,

314

11 The lands of Milton Regis: synthesis

1. *REGIO* AND MINSTERLAND

Milton Regis stands at the centre of the Foothill country of Kent, some 40 miles from the capital, and roughly equidistant between London and Dover. As we have seen in an earlier chapter, it was certainly a place of Romano-British origin, if indeed it does not date back to Bronze Age or Neolithic times.[1] Like other primary settlements in this stretch of the Original Lands – Chatham, Gillingham, Newington, Teynham, and Faversham furnish other examples – it lies a short distance to the north of the Roman road, in a gently undulating countryside between the Street and the Swale. The principal settlement is situated at the point where the springs gush out at the foot of the Downland valleys, giving rise to the tidal inlet of Milton Creek; the minster church stands in an isolated position, about a mile to the north of the springs; and the old town of Milton, with its fifteenth-century court-house, at the head of the creek, by a lane that is thought to be the prehistoric predecessor of the Roman road. Like many early settlements in Kent, Milton is thus situated at the junction of the Foothills and the Marsh, in a neighbourhood largely devoid of attraction to modern eyes. The rapid growth of Sittingbourne alongside Watling Street, and the development of nineteenth-century brickfields and twentieth-century paper mills, cannot be said to have added to its charms. Yet historically speaking, with its locally fertile soils and its proximity to a sheltered harbour, it was natural that it should attract successive waves of colonists and invaders, until last of all the predatory Danes of the ninth century established their fortress a mile or so to the north-east at Castle Rough.[2]

In view of its Romano-British origins, Milton is the kind of place, in Kent at least, that we should expect to become a 'king's town' or *villa regalis*, and in fact it also acquired a palace of the Kentish royal house. Its place-name, *middel tūn* or 'central *tūn*', is one that was appropriate to the *caput* of a major royal estate, and one that reappears in connexion with several other minster churches, such as Melton Mowbray in Leicestershire, though it may not have been the original name.[3] The royal estate on which the minsterland was based had developed as one of the springhead territories of Kent, and it was this estate that later formed the basis of the great hundredal manor of Milton. At the time of the Conquest, the manor of Milton was one of the most valuable in the county, according to Domesday Book worth £200 a year in the time of King Edward. So wealthy a territory was not to be lightly granted away, and it was not until the seventeenth century that the crown parted with an estate which had been in its hands for more than a thousand years.[4]

Situated as it was at the administrative heart of this *regio*, it was almost inevitable that Milton should also become the site of an early minster. It may be, indeed, that it was one of the first to be established in the county. Part of the surviving structure dates back to the Saxon period, and John Newman has suggested that the church's unusually lofty proportions must also be of Saxon origin. As we saw in Chapter 6, it adjoins the site of a Roman house, and stands within an enclosure that is also thought by some archaeologists to be of Romano-British origin.[5] Its dedication to the Holy Trinity is one that it shares with only one other parish church in the county, the minster at Dartford, and it may be significant that, just as Dartford stands on the Roman road midway between the two 'head minsters' of Rochester and St Paul's, so Milton stands midway between Rochester and Canterbury.

Originally, the territory dependent upon this church seems to have comprised the whole of the royal *regio*; but as the *Domesday Monachorum* indicates, a second minster was subsequently established at Newington, and the western half of the area, extending to about 15,000 acres and comprising the parishes of Newington, Upchurch, Rainham, Hartlip, Stockbury, and Lower Halstow, was then detached from Milton and subordinated to the new church.[6] The fact that Newington lies on the edge of its minsterland, near the Milton boundary, whilst at the same time it remained part of the royal hundred and manor of Milton, is a suggestive reminder of its original status. It may possibly have been the change in its ecclesiastical fortunes that led to the abandonment of the old name and the substitution in its place of Newington or 'new *tūn*', a name which is not in fact recorded until Domesday Book.[7]

After Newington had been severed from it, the Milton minsterland still extended to more than 17,000 acres, and it is this area that forms the main subject of the present study. The 12 parishes into which it was eventually divided formed a compact territory on either side of Milton, some five miles broad and seven or eight miles from north to south, reaching from the tidal waters of the Swale, across Watling Street, and up into the wooded Downland valleys around Milsted and Bredgar. All of these parishes lay to the south, the south-east, or the south-west of the mother-church, so that Milton itself was characteristically situated on the northernmost edge of its territory. Seven of the 11 subordinate

11 The lands of Milton Regis: synthesis

churches are recorded as dependencies of Milton in the *Domesday Monachorum*: Tonge, Bapchild, Rodmersham, Milsted, Bredgar, Tunstall, and Bobbing. To these the same source also adds Eastchurch, Leysdown, and an unidentifiable 'Northcip' in Sheppey; but these had in fact originated from Sheppey Minster, and were probably linked with Milton only as a temporary expedient following the Danish raids of the ninth century, so that they are not included in the present study.[8] The four remaining churches – Sittingbourne, Murston, Borden, and Kingsdown – had apparently not yet been created when the *Domesday Monachorum* list was drawn up in the eleventh century; neither had the chapelry of Radfield, a detached part of Bapchild parish beyond Tonge. None of these places is mentioned in Domesday Book or in the *Domesday Monachorum*; their names are not recorded before the end of the twelfth century;[9] and three of them – Sittingbourne, Kingsdown, and Murston – bear typically late dedications, to St Michael, St Catherine, and St John the Baptist. Beyond this area, on the higher Downland to the south, the influence of Milton also extended over parts of Bicknor, Wormshill, Frinsted, Wichling, Stockbury, and Ashdown.[10] Ecclesiastically, none of these places originated from Milton alone, and they do not seem to have ever been under its sole jurisdiction. But the significance of their ambiguous connexion with the old minster and *villa regalis* is a point of considerable interest which we shall return to in the fifth section of this chapter.

Nowadays, it is difficult to believe that when the mother-church of Milton was founded, perhaps soon after 600, most of this territory still formed part of the *cēto*, or Forest of Blean, which had once extended from Canterbury to the Hoo peninsula. Despite its heavily Romanized environment and despite the Roman road passing through it, Milton was then still a comparatively isolated place, with the forest coming down to its borders along the southern side of Watling Street, and extending well to the north of the Street on either side of the original settlement. Even in Hasted's time the woods still remained extensive in several of the parishes lying to the south, and in places came down to the road itself in Bobbing, Bapchild, and Milton. By that date, however, the great bulk of the woodland had long since been cleared and cultivated; the characteristic process of more recent centuries, of converting old coppice and arable to orchard, was already under way; and nowadays more than half the land in Bobbing, Borden, Bredgar, Rodmersham, Bapchild, and Tonge is given over to fruit-growing. The Milton area is in fact the oldest of the five major fruit-growing districts

PART FIVE *Topographical Reconstruction*

of Kent, and at Teynham its origins go back to Henry VIII's reign. The great chestnut woods of the Stockbury valley which once extended for five or six miles between Thurnham and Bobbing, and which gave their name to Chestnut Street in Borden, are now largely confined as a consequence to Thurnham and Stockbury itself, which lay outside Milton's immediate territory. Only in the two southernmost parishes, Milsted and Kingsdown, are the woodlands still predominant: and there even today they amount to several hundred acres, the last relics of the prehistoric *wald* to survive in the Milton neighbourhood.

Nevertheless, although this district has in some respects been subjected to more revolutionary change than is usual in the rural parts of Kent, the visual impact of the past is still very apparent. To take place-names alone, Wallenberg discusses almost 80 local names in the 12 parishes under discussion, while the $2\frac{1}{2}''$ O.S. maps record a further 120 which, to judge from their name-forms, must also be of medieval or pre-Conquest origin. In these 200 places, almost all of which still survive, we have an invaluable *corpus* of localized topographical detail. Some of the apparently modern features of the area, such as its big fields and the frequent absence of hedgerows, are in many places of considerable antiquity and are not due to modern clearance, as they would be in the East Midlands, but to the local value of the land in a county not generally notable for its fertility.[11] Despite the gradual extension of fruit-growing, moreover, the forest lanes still sinuate their historic way between the orchards; the farmsteads of the area still occupy their Saxon or medieval sites; their place-names are mostly recorded in twelfth or thirteenth-century documents, as at Highsted (1197), Fulston (1197), Swanton (1204), and Deans Hill (1225); and in many cases, as at Grovehurst (1312), Grove End (1278), Woodstock (1212), and Hogshaw (1357), they tell their own story of woodland reclamation.[12] When interpreted in the light of early maps, parish boundaries, church siting, and manorial relationship, such evidences enable us to trace the gradual clearance of the wood-pastures of the estate with unusual completeness.

The 12 parishes under discussion fall into four groups. Milton and its two immediate neighbours, Murston and Sittingbourne, composed the heartland of the area, both ecclesiastically and territorially, although parochially the two latter were among the last places to be created. To the south and west of Milton, Tunstall, Bobbing, Bredgar, and Borden formed part of the outlying lands of the territory, and were almost entirely reclaimed from the Downland forest. To the east, Tonge,

11 The lands of Milton Regis: synthesis

Bapchild, Radfield, and Rodmersham likewise originated as outlying settlements, partly reclaimed from the forest and in part from the Swale marshlands. Finally, on the southern edge of the area, Milsted and Kingsdown also developed as woodland places; but in these cases the relationship with the rest of the territory was a somewhat special one. Milsted and its development as the common 'milk-stead' or vaccary of the estate will be discussed below. The small parish of Kingsdown, covering only 705 acres, arose through the relationship of the 'king's *dūn*' with the 'king's *tūn*' of Milton, and stands in a class by itself as the royal pastureland of the territory: just as Kingsdown-by-Wrotham formed the royal pastureland of the Darenth estate, and Kingsdown by Walmer of that based on Northbourne. The evolution of the first of these four groups of parishes will be described in the following section, and that of the second and third groups in sections 3 and 4.

2. THE HEARTLAND

Until Murston and Sittingbourne were carved out of it in the twelfth century, the parish of Milton must have extended to about 5,000 acres and was by far the largest in the area. Nowadays, the three parishes have been reunited and we can see once again something of their original relationship. Symmetrically grouped around Milton Creek, they still form a coherent whole, with Murston, the *mōres tūn* or 'moor farm' of Milton, in the marshes, and Sittingbourne its adjacent woodland pasture on gently rising ground to the south-east. The boundaries of several neighbouring parishes, moreover, such as Bapchild and Rodmersham, run up to the old Milton border without passing through it, a telling sign of their subsequent origin. So far as Murston and Sittingbourne themselves are concerned, the chief clues to their ecclesiastical origins are to be found in their topography, and in the fact that in the medieval period they were subordinate manors of Milton. The boundary of the mother-parish originally came close to their churches,[13] and they themselves were almost surrounded by Tonge, Bapchild, Rodmersham, Tunstall, and Bobbing, which are listed as subordinate churches of Milton in the *Domesday Monachorum*. There can be no doubt, therefore, that ecclesiastically they both originated from Milton, though they are not mentioned in the *Domesday Monachorum*, and there is no documentary proof of the fact.

Nowadays, Sittingbourne is so heavily built up, and like many Foothill settlements so devoid of trees, that it is difficult to visualize it as

PART FIVE *Topographical Reconstruction*

at one time a predominantly woodland community. Yet there can be no doubt that such was its origin, or that this circumstance shaped its manorial and ecclesiastical history. Until it was granted a market charter by Queen Elizabeth and began to develop into an independent town in its own right, it is clear that mother and daughter represented complementary but contrasting types of parish. Milton, as we have seen, was a typically large and primitive 'community' foundation, with its minster church at the heart of a great *regio* and hundredal manor which at one time extended over more than 20 parishes, and with a *port* (or market) and portreeve probably dating from before the Conquest.[14] Sittingbourne, by contrast, was a typically small 'bookland' parish of less than 1,000 acres, split up into the three microscopic sub-manors of Bayford, Chilton, and Fulston. Its church, like those of other parishes in the *wald*, was also a characteristic 'manorial' establishment, dedicated to St Michael,[15] in which the owners of these three sub-manors each had their own independent chancel, for whose upkeep they were individually responsible. Like many manorial churches of Kent, it was filled with armorial glass in the later Middle Ages, and when it was destroyed by fire in 1762, the families in question for a time prevented its rebuilding by refusing to contribute their customary share of the expense. By that date, however, Sittingbourne had become a thriving market centre, with its great coaching inns strung out along the Dover road – the Rose and the George pre-eminent among them – and eventually the townsmen were able to rebuild the church out of their own resources.[16] The fact that they did so symbolized a fundamental change in the social structure and economic status of the parish; but that change must not be read back into the humble origins of Sittingbourne as a forest community. Essentially, it was due to the revival of inland trade in Queen Elizabeth's reign, and the rapid development of carrying and coaching between London, Canterbury, and Dover in the two following centuries.

Until Murston and Sittingbourne were formed, it is clear from the topographical evidence that Milton still retained extensive woods and pastures of its own, despite the creation of eight or nine other parishes in its outlying *wald*. Beyond Bobbing, there was a detached part of the parish significantly known as Great Norwood. On the low hills to the north of the church we find such characteristic woodland names as Grovehurst (1312), Foxgrove, Howt Green (*holt*, 1278), and Kemsley (*lēah*, 1410), though the area is now virtually treeless.[17] To the west, the chestnut woods of Stockbury came down to Milton itself, where the

11 The lands of Milton Regis: synthesis

name of Northwood Chasteners (1214) survived as Chestnut Street in Borden, a mile or so to the west.[18] To the south, in the upland part of Sittingbourne, a remarkable tongue or corridor of land stretches past Highsted, or 'high [pasture]place' (1197), between Tunstall and Rodmersham, alongside a droveway representing Milton's ancient route to its outlying cattle pastures in the woods of Milsted (c.1100).[19] The historic boundaries in this area were so arranged that seven or eight parishes had independent access to these common pastures at Milsted, and to the woodlands on either side of the common drove. In the same stretch of Downland there are indications of other cattle stations, moreover, for example at Pitstock in Rodmersham (1254), Bistock in Doddington (1270), Woodstock and Pistock in Tunstall, and Stockbury near Newington (1086), in each of which the element *stoc* probably indicates a dairy farm, as at Tawstock and Plymstock in Devon.[20] It seems probable, as we saw in Chapter 7, that much of this middle-Downland country of Kent was at one time turned over to vaccaries or stock-farms, just as the Weald of Andred was utilized as swine pasture. Finally, we may note that in Cromer Wood, Birch Wood, Bassiline Wood, Conchers Wood, Hadler Hook, Cheney Wood, and Duke's Shaw, some of the woodland names of the Highsted cattle drove still survive: and to these, early maps add many others of a similar kind.

Six or seven miles to the east of the estate, in Bysing Woods near Faversham, Milton had further outlying, or rather detached, pasture-lands in the Forest of Blean.[21] In Hasted's time there was still a detached portion of Murston known as Herst or Herst Hall in these woods, and before Murston was created this area must have appertained to the mother-settlement of Milton itself.[22] The fact that Herst was in the same neighbourhood as the lost *Chetham* and was directly linked to Milton by the prehistoric track running parallel to Watling Street, is therefore of considerable interest. It may suggest that, before the Weald of Andred began to be systematically exploited, it was primarily to the Blean that Milton looked for its swine pastures. It may also indicate that the connexion of Milton with Blean dates back beyond the coming of the Jutes, to that twilight world of which the landscape in this area offers so many a tantalizing glimpse.

3. OUTLYING LANDS TO THE EAST

The first new parishes to be formed after Milton itself, some centuries probably before Murston and Sittingbourne, were most likely Tonge and Bapchild, which form a unity with Rodmersham to the east of the mother-church. That all three originated from Milton is evident from the *Domesday Monachorum*, where they are listed among its dependent churches. All three were also within the *regio* and hundred of Milton; the ancient St Lawrence's Fair at Bapchild appertained to the manor of Milton; and in Rodmersham the mother-church retained her burial rights until long after the Conquest.[23] In Tonge, moreover, the parish church is sited within a few hundred yards of the old Milton boundary,[24] yet three miles from its own outlying bounds at Newbury (1342) and Hole Street. In Rodmersham the church is likewise situated near the northern boundary of the parish, yet more than two miles from its southern border in Mintching Wood (1268). Finally, it is noteworthy that all three churches bear late Old English dedications: St Nicholas at Rodmersham, St Lawrence at Bapchild, and St Giles at Tonge.

These three places did not originate at the same time, however, and the evidence for their relative antiquity is of some interest. At first sight, it may seem that Tonge was the earliest, since its church lies to the north of the Roman road, like other early churches in this stretch of country, whereas that at Bapchild lies a short distance to the south, near the Tonge parish boundary. On the modern map, moreover, the remarkable topography of Tonge, with its long narrow tongue or arm of land stretching up on to the Downs and embracing both Bapchild and Rodmersham, seems to suggest that the two latter parishes were carved out of its outlying forest-pastures. There are grounds for believing, however, that it was Bapchild that was the first parish to be created on this side of the estate, and that Tonge as well as Rodmersham was formed from its outlying territory. The place-name of Bapchild, *Baccancelde*, is recorded in one of the oldest Kentish charters, dating from 696 x 716;[25] with its primitive well-cult, 'Bacca's spring' may possibly have formed the early religious centre of the estate, before the coming of St Augustine.[26] In this area, moreover, where parish boundaries have been substantially altered, it is essential to base our reconstruction on those known to Hasted and recorded on the tithe index sheets: and these show that the eastern side of what is now the parish of Tonge then formed a separate chapelry, based on Radfield, and that Radfield itself was a detached part of the parish of Bapchild. In other words the upland arm of Tonge was historically no more than a narrow corridor of land 300 or 400 yards in width, tightly sandwiched between the two parts of Bapchild.[27] The parish boundaries of the area are extra-

11 The lands of Milton Regis: synthesis

ordinarily contorted in form, even by Kentish standards, and some of their ramifications are difficult to account for; but these circumstances almost certainly imply that it was Bapchild that was the original foundation, and that Tonge was established as a subsidiary settlement in its outlying marsh, though given access to the communal forest pastures on the Downs to the south.

On this eastern side of the estate, there can be very little doubt, indeed, that virtually the whole area lying to the south of Watling Street was originally carved out of the Downland forest. Both Rodmersham and Radfield, it is plain, were in some sense dependencies of Bapchild. Now that so much of the area has been converted to orchards, its old woodland character is not at first sight apparent; yet it is still evident in the narrow winding lanes and minor place-names of the neighbourhood, such as Wood Street, Erriott Wood, Pettwood (1252), Picklands Wood, Golden Wood, College Wood, Dully, Pitstock (1254), and Dungate (1591). At Radfield itself (1254) the woods certainly extended to Watling Street, if not beyond it, for its name means *rod* + *feld* or clearing field; and in the Highsted valley they still came down to the Street in the eighteenth century.[28] Even now there are a few remnants of the forest left at Cheney Hill (1489), Spittal Wood, and Mintching Wood ('the nuns' wood', 1268),[29] and along the parish boundary of Tonge, between Scuttington (1220) and Upper Rodmersham. In Kent, as in other counties, residual woodland often tends to survive longest on parish boundaries in this way.

One of the most interesting features on this side of the territory has yet to be mentioned, and that is its eastern boundary. For several miles this border runs practically dead straight and at right angles to Watling Street, between Tonge, Radfield, and Kingsdown on one side, and Doddington, Teynham, and Lynsted on the other. Its alignment seems to be picked up again in Sheppey on the other side of the Swale, though a little further to the west, in the straight parish boundary between Elmley, Eastchurch, and Minster. There can be no doubt that this border is an ancient one, for it is recorded on the tithe index sheets and at many points it is marked by boundary stones on the $2\frac{1}{2}''$ O.S. map. The most likely explanation is that it follows the course of an abandoned Roman road or droveway connecting the marshes of the *regio* with the uplands to the south, and perhaps at one time continuing across the Swale to the uplands of Sheppey. Nowadays, the Swale is three-quarters of a mile wide at this point and no road can continue across it; but in the Roman period, as is evident from the pottery kilns of the Medway estuary, these tidal flats were for the most part dry land, so that the crossing to Sheppey was relatively short and easy. We find the same use of a Roman road as a boundary line in the countryside south of Canterbury, where Stone Street still divides the territory of Petham, Waltham, and Elmsted from that of Nackington, Lower Hardres, and Stelling.

This eastern boundary of Tonge and Radfield was the dividing line not merely between two groups of parishes, moreover, but between two minsterlands and two *regiones*.[30] The exact course of development to the east is obscure; but there was certainly a mother-church at Teynham, with subsidiary chapels at Lynsted, Doddington, Stone, Norton, and Newnham; and there is reason to think that this Teynham territory may once have formed part of the *regio* based on Faversham, just as Newington formed part of that based on Milton Regis.[31] If this reconstruction is correct, the eastern boundary of Tonge may have marked the division not only between two minsterlands and two estates, but between two Romano-British territories, respectively based on *Durolevum* or Faversham and the Roman station at Milton.[32] At this point, therefore, the ecclesiastical topography of Kent perhaps affords another momentary glimpse into the Romano-British world beyond the Jutes.

4. OUTLYING LANDS TO THE WEST

On the western and southern sides of the territory a somewhat similar development to that of Tonge, Radfield, and Rodmersham took place at Tunstall, Bobbing, Bredgar, and Borden. That all four places originated as woodland chapelries of Milton there can be no doubt. All were in the hundred of Milton; their churches are eccentrically sited towards the Milton side of their parishes; the first three are listed as its dependent churches in the *Domesday Monachorum*; over the last three its manor claimed paramountcy; and in three cases their churches bear the characteristic Wilderness dedications of St John the Baptist (at Tunstall and Bredgar) and St Bartholomew (at Bobbing). There are also other indications that they originated from Milton, such as the fact that the profits of Bobbing Fair belonged to the lord of Milton manor, and the tithes of Bobbing church to St Augustine's Abbey 'in right of their church of Middleton'.[33]

The earliest of the four places to develop was Tunstall. It is the only one recorded in Domesday Book, when it was already a well-

11 The lands of Milton Regis: synthesis

established settlement. Like Tonge, moreover, and in contrast with other places in the area, it early became a separate manor independent of Milton.[34] The fact that its own manor extended beyond the parish bounds, and claimed over parts of Bredgar, Borden, and Bicknor, also suggests that it originated before those places.[35] Nevertheless, as at Tonge, its ultimate subordination to Milton is sufficiently plain; for though it ceased at an early date to acknowledge the paramountcy of the parent manor, its own claims over Borden and Bredgar remained subsidiary to those of Milton,[36] and it always remained a member of the Hundred of Milton. The name Tunstall, moreover, probably indicates that it originated as the outlying *stall* of the *tūn* of Milton, or in other words that it was one of the vaccaries of the original estate. This suggestion is further supported by the minor place-names of the parish, such as Woodstock and Pistock, which, as we have seen, likewise indicate cattle stations. The word *tūn steall* also occurs at several points in the north of England, in names like Heptonstall in the West Riding, which was probably a vaccary of Hebden, and at places like Rawtenstall, Saltonstall, and Whittonstall.[37] Its appearance in Kent is therefore a point of some interest.

The three remaining parishes on the western side of the territory developed in what was then densely wooded countryside bordering Newington. In Hasted's time the woods which had given their name to Northwood Chasteners (*chastaignières*),[38] still extended to the Roman road in this area, and well beyond it in Bobbing. At one time, as early maps and place-name evidence show, they covered the whole of Bobbing and Borden, probably most of Bredgar, and as we have already seen the western side of Milton itself. The administrative centre of the forest manor of Northwood Chasteners was in fact situated in Milton, but its territory extended as far as Chestnut Street in Borden, a mile to the west, Chestnut Wood in Stockbury, three miles to the southwest, and Great Norwood beyond Bobbing, two or three miles to the north-west.

Although all three places thus developed in the woodland, they were not identical in character or in date of origin. Their development reveals a significant progression from the small manorial *wald* (or Downland) type of parish at Bobbing to the later, larger, freer kind of territory more characteristic of secondary settlement at Borden. Bobbing was the first of the three to develop. The fact that its manor, like that of Tunstall, claimed over part of Bredgar suggests that it originated before Bredgar, whilst Borden is not recorded at all until the end of

PART FIVE *Topographical Reconstruction*

the twelfth century. Nevertheless, though Bobbing is an *-ing* or *ingas* place-name and lies to the north of the Roman road, it may not have originated until relatively late in the Old English period. Its soils are in general poor, with a good deal of sand and gravel on the higher land. It is not sited on the springline like other places north of the road, but on a low projecting spur of Down rising to about 200 feet above the marsh at Keycol Hill. Unlike Tunstall, moreover, it never became independent of the paramount manor of Milton, and probably for that reason it is not separately recorded in Domesday Book.[39] In most respects, in short, Bobbing more closely resembles the late Old English parishes of the Downland to the south than other places north of the road, such as Milton, Teynham, and Newington. The whole of the parish was at one time typical *wald* or wood-pasture; even on its northerly side, where there is now scarcely a tree to be seen, we still find such tell-tale names as Little Norwood, Howt Green, and Cambray (1278), whose second element is *bær*, 'pasture'.[40]

Bredgar or 'broad gore' ('triangular plot of land') was also a wood-pasture parish, and in Hasted's time, though long since cleared of wood, it was still for the most part pastoral.[41] It lies on the southern uplands of the estate, and in its outlying lands beyond Swanton the *wald* rises to some 500 feet above sea level. Yet here we find one significant difference from Bobbing. There was never a *manor* of Bredgar, as there was of Bobbing, and authority over the parish was in consequence divided between the three external manors of Milton, Bobbing, and Tunstall. A series of small subsidiary or 'reputed' manors developed, at Baxon, Swanton, Manns, and Butters; but these were never true manors in the historic sense of the term. Like so many of the 'reputed' manors of Kent, they were little more than woodland farms or minuscule gentry estates. Of the history of Butters virtually nothing is known; Swanton, as its name indicates, originated as a *swānatūn* or herdsman's farm; Manns is not recorded before 1377, and is characteristically described by Hasted as an 'estate . . . which was formerly accounted a manor;' while Baxon was apparently divided into two parts, one called 'Baxon or Cromps', and the other 'the manor or yoke of Peter Dodswell, *alias* Baxon'.[42] In other words, Bredgar developed as a typical agglomeration of scattered woodland farms in the outlying forest-pastures of the estate, where manorial organization, in so far as it ever truly existed, was typically feeble and fragmented. The significance of the term 'yoke' in this context is a point that we shall return to in a moment.

11 The lands of Milton Regis: synthesis

The last of the four woodland parishes to the west, Borden, was probably also the last to be created. Since it originated too late to be recorded in the *Domesday Monachorum*, we have no direct documentary proof that it formed part of the Milton territory. Its origins are nevertheless sufficiently evident, from the siting of its church near the Milton boundary; from the fact that Milton claimed manorial paramountcy over it;[43] from its position as part of the Northwood *chastaignières*; and from the remarkable way that Bobbing, Milton, Tunstall, and Bredgar embrace its territory on all sides except the west.

Owing to its post-Conquest origin as a woodland parish, and perhaps owing to other more obscure reasons, Borden in some ways more closely resembled the detached pastoral parishes of the Weald than the older pastoral parishes of the Downland or *wald*. For one thing, though not large by Wealden standards, at 2,150 acres it was substantially larger than any other parish in the Milton territory apart from Milton itself. Its place-name, moreover, may well mean *bārdenn* or 'boar pasture'; its second element is certainly the term *denn*, which is relatively rare on the Downs but which is so frequent among the swine pastures of the Weald.[44] Its whole landed structure, in fact, carried a stage further that relative freedom from manorial control that we have noted at Bredgar; and in this respect, too, it more closely resembled the characteristic Wealden pattern than that of the Downs. Like Bredgar, it developed no manor of its own under the paramountcy of Milton; and although some kind of quasi-manorial structure evolved at Sutton Baron, its 'south farm', Borden never became a parish of significant landowners, or manorial squires, like many Downland parishes.[45] Essentially, from its origins until Hasted's time, it seems to have remained a classic parish of small, independent landholders, very much as the Weald remained the classic area of yeomen landholders. In this connexion, the evolution of Borden raises a problem of general importance in Kentish settlement history, and one which, in concluding this section, it will be well to explore more fully.

One of the terms that we find recurring repeatedly in the landed development of Borden is the word 'yoke' or 'yokeland'. This is a term that is found in the outlying parts of many early Kentish estates and ultimately it derives from the Latin *jugum*, signifying 'a measure of land'. As such, it is obviously of some historical interest, and its fiscal and agrarian import has given rise to occasional scholarly debate. For the purpose in hand it is not necessary to pursue this debate in detail; but it is necessary to consider the topographical significance of the

PART FIVE *Topographical Reconstruction*

expression. In this connexion, it should be noted that it still survives in a considerable number of minor Kentish place-names, such as Yotes Court in Mereworth, Yoakes Court in Old Romney, York Farm in Gillingham, and Yokes Court in Frinsted, a short distance to the south of Borden.[46] In the eighteenth century it was a good deal more common than today, particularly in the stretch of Downland under discussion, where Hasted tells us that 'upon these hills the small manors are frequently called yokes,' and that 'the several estates held of the manor of Milton are in the [court] rolls of it in general called *yokes*.'[47] By his time the significance of the term had clearly undergone something of a metamorphosis, and his interpretation of it as a 'small manor' should not be taken at its face value. Nevertheless, while the connotation of the word itself may have changed, with the gradual evolution of Kentish society, it still pointed to an essential feature of local settlement, and in this connexion there are three matters to take into account.

In the first place, in the sense in which it eventually developed, the term 'yoke' always seems to refer to minor, outlying places, and not to paramount manors or to important settlements in the Old Arable Lands. Generally speaking, it indicates places that had originated as pastoral settlements in the *wald* – 'upon the hills' in Hasted's expression – or occasionally in the marsh; and in many cases these settlements are situated on parish boundaries, as at Yokes in Frinsted, or towards the edge of the parish, as at Yotes in Mereworth. In the second place, although, as Hasted implies, the yokes often came to be thought of as small manors, they were not in fact manors in origin, or in any true feudal sense. Sometimes, as at Sutton Baron, they developed a kind of quasi-manorial court; but in reality they bore little resemblance to the classic manors of Kent or of other areas. They must rather be thought of as small landed properties that had probably never been burdened with much in the way of seigneurial dues, and that at a relatively early date, as a consequence, became virtually freehold properties.

Thirdly, in the late medieval and early modern period, when they had already achieved freehold status, many of these estates gave rise to a kind of very localized *gentillâtre*, or class of obscure 'yokeland' gentry. In Borden itself, for example, we find families like the Seagers described as holding 'the Yoke of Corbett', the Allens as holding 'the Yoke of Boxfield', the Generys as holding 'the Yoke of Woodstreet', and a number of similar families, such as the Napletons, the Barrows, the Matsons, and the Plots of Sutton Baron, the local ancestors of Robert Plot the historian.[48] In economic status, as their surviving houses

11 *The lands of Milton Regis: synthesis*

suggest, these families must often have been virtually indistinguishable from the independent yeomen of the Weald, and they certainly cannot be thought of as squires in even the humblest sense of the term. Despite its rather grand-sounding name, the family home of the Plots, for example, is nothing more than a substantial farmhouse of the local type nowadays known, rather misleadingly, as a 'Wealden'. Yet socially speaking, there was clearly some kind of distinction in the minds of contemporaries, though its precise nature is now difficult to identify. Many of the families in question bore arms and were intensely conscious of their armigerous status; they frequently married among the acknowledged gentry of the county, and were clearly scrupulous in respect of their own family relationships. For the student of settlement, in short, they indicate a distinctive type of local community, and that, in the present context, is the essential point to grasp. In this sense, the social structure of the English parish may often supply an important clue to its origins as a settlement, and in the case of Borden those origins evidently stemmed, in the last resort, from the evolution of the parish as a forest society.

5. THE MINNIS

Beyond these parishes, in the valleys to the south, lies a stretch of country reaching up to the crest of the Downs, over which jurisdiction was shared or divided between Milton Regis and other royal and ecclesiastical centres. Though none of the parishes in the area can be proved to have originated from Milton alone, it is significant that neither can any of them be attributed exclusively to other minsters: they form, in short, a kind of no man's land in terms of ecclesiastical origins. Coupled with the fact that most of the parishes in question have always straddled the boundary between different hundreds, and between different legal and administrative jurisdictions, the obscurity of their origins raises an important problem of Kentish history. It is one that we also find in other parts of the upper Downland, moreover, as at Denton and Wootton north of Folkestone, where jurisdiction was divided in much the same way between the hundreds of Eastry and Kinghamford, and between the territories of the Eastry people and the Bourne people.[49] The most likely explanation of these circumstances is that much of the higher Downland of Kent, like the Weald of Andred and the western Chartland, was at some remote period common to several different estates. No single territory could lay claim to exclusive

PART FIVE *Topographical Reconstruction*

rights in it, so that when it eventually came to be divided, and the boundary finally fixed, the jurisdiction over each parish was split up between the various territories or communities laying claim to its resources. What makes the area south of Milton peculiarly interesting in this connexion is that here there are indisputable indications that such common rights once existed, and that some of the communities that claimed them were situated as much as 15 miles away. In other words, originally it was not merely a pastoral area for places adjacent, but a substantial district of *detached* pasture, like the Weald or the Blean. Quite clearly, then, we have an unusual problem here, and one that is worth further investigation.

The parishes in the area today comprise Stockbury, Bicknor, Wormshill, Frinsted, and Wichling. To these must be added the long stretch or tongue of Downland lying between Wichling and Frinsted, which has for centuries formed an outlying part of Lenham parish, but which seems to have once been a separate chapelry or parish of itself, probably centred on Ashdown. There is also some reason to think that there was once a further church at Wrinsted, which is now part of Frinsted parish, so that originally there were six or seven parishes and chapelries in the area as a whole.[50] Nowadays, with its lonely combes and ever-changing skies, it is an area of great natural beauty; but in terms of agrarian potential it has always been a relatively poor and densely wooded upland district, and it was this fact no doubt that gave rise to its use as common pasture. As late as Hasted's day it still wore an aspect of rustic poverty, and the farmland in parishes like Wormshill was let for as little as 5s. or 6s. an acre, or less than a third as much as the rich 'roundtilt' lands in the neighbourhood of Milton itself. At that time Hasted described Wormshill, for example, as a 'parish so obscurely situated, and of so little thoroughfare, as hardly to be known': its hills so steep, its soil so flinty, and its aspect so bleak and exposed to the north, that the very trees refused to grow to any size. Of other parishes in the area he makes much the same comments, and at Bicknor gives a characteristic description of the rector's house as a mere hovel or shed 'built against the north side of the church ... a miserable habitation even for the poorest cottager to dwell in'.[51] In such an area it is not surprising to find most of the parish churches dedicated to typical Wilderness saints like St Giles, St Dunstan, St Mary Magdalene, and St James.

Something of the complexity of the ancient common rights over these parishes and chapelries is suggested by the elaborate network of

11 The lands of Milton Regis: synthesis

jurisdictions to which they were subjected in later centuries, and which probably fossilized a very ancient pattern of customary claims. Five of the six parishes were divided not only between two different paramount manors and two hundreds, but between two different lathes, and between the two different historic divisions of the county, East Kent and West Kent.[52] Bicknor, Stockbury, Frinsted, and Wormshill all lay partly in Eyhorne Hundred and the Lathe of Aylesford in West Kent, and partly in Milton Hundred and the Lathe of Scraye in East Kent. Ashdown also was divided in much the same way between the Hundreds of Eyhorne and Calehill, and between the Lathes of Aylesford and Shepway.[53] The sixth place, Wichling, lay entirely within the Lathe of Aylesford and the Hundred of Eyhorne; but originally it too must have straddled some important boundary, since the earliest forms of the name are *Winchelesmere* or 'Winchele's boundary', the form *Winchelinges* not being recorded until the thirteenth century.[54] It seems possible, in fact, that the boundary here referred to was a continuation of the Romano-British line dividing Teynham and Radfield, which would have passed close to Wichling church.

In the case of Ashdown, Wichling, Frinsted, and Wormshill, the local network of common rights was particularly complex. In this area, in addition to Milton and Hollingbourne, we find Leeds, Lenham, Teynham, Maidstone, Ospringe, Bobbing, Newington, Minster-in-Sheppey, and Boughton Malherbe all laying claim to certain rights. Ashdown, for example, was not only the *æsc denn* or 'ash pasture' of Lenham; its pastureland was also made use of by the peoples of Teynham and Ospringe, some six or seven miles to the north-east. This is indicated by the fact that Timbold Hill, on its northern side, probably means the 'fold [or stock enclosure] of the Teynham people', while the important droveway leading from Ospringe to the Weald by way of Syndale, or 'the great valley', passes through the centre of Ashdown, and gave Ospringe rights in the neighbouring pastures of Wrinsted.[55] In Wichling, too, it is probable that Teynham claimed certain common rights; and in this case Minster-in-Sheppey, 13 or 14 miles to the north, may also have done so, since Wichling church seems to have originated as a detached chapelry of Minster.[56]

In Wormshill, as many as four other places in addition to Milton and Hollingbourne appear to have exercised rights: Bobbing and Newington, five or six miles to the north; Boughton Malherbe, six or seven miles to the south; and Ospringe, eight or nine miles to the east. This is suggested by the fact that the manor of Wormshill was anciently an

PART FIVE *Topographical Reconstruction*

'appendage' of the manor of Boughton Malherbe, which itself was a dependency of Ospringe; whilst Bedmonton in Wormshill was partly in the manor of Newington, and partly in the manor of Bobbing. In this case there may also be a significant antithesis between the two historic divisions of the parish: for whereas Wormshill or '?Woden's hill' itself, on its remoter southern side, may indicate a place of heathen worship, Bedmonton or *gebedmann* + *tūn*, the 'priest's or worshipper's farm', which lies to the north, probably indicates a Christian community settled from Milton.[57] In Domesday Book and the *Domesday Monachorum* the parish of Wormshill is actually given the alternative place-name of *Godeselle* or 'God's Hill', so that at one time, we may suppose, these remote upland pastures of 'Woden's Hill' or 'God's Hill' may have straddled the boundary not only between two lathes, two *regiones*, and two minsterlands, but also between the old religion and the new. It seems possible indeed that much of the upland *wald* of Kent should thus be envisaged as offering a natural area of refuge for an ancient culture at bay.

It is the evidence of Frinsted, probably meaning 'fenced-in stead' or pasture, that lets us into the ultimate secret of this upland *wald*.[58] For here, at some 600 feet above sea level, near the crest of the Downs, we find the significant place-name of Minnetts Hill. This represents the local word 'minnis' or *gemǣnnes*, 'land held in common', which is found in many places along the higher reaches of the Downs, and which indicates common pastureland on the boundary of a group of parishes.[59] In several cases these boundaries are associated with the kind of quirky interlocking pattern referred to in the last chapter, and Minnetts Hill itself forms a narrow tongue of land between Hollingbourne, Harrietsham, Lenham, and Wormshill. In view of these circumstances it is particularly interesting to find that the common rights over Frinsted seem to have been exercised by a whole constellation of widely scattered communities. Wrinsted, or 'stallions' pasture', for example, near the boundary of Frinsted and Ashdown, was held, as already remarked, of the manor of Ospringe, seven miles to the northeast; Yokes Court, on the same boundary, was held of the Honour of Leeds, six or seven miles to the south-west; a further part of the parish, around the church, was subordinate to Maidstone, some ten miles to the west; while Minnetts Hill itself was under the jurisdiction of Whorne's Place in Cuxton, as much as 15 miles away, on the other side of the Medway, opposite Rochester.[60]

These facts will bear thinking about. Once they are rightly under-

11 The lands of Milton Regis: synthesis

stood, the whole boundary here, along the ridge of the Downs, between the dip-slope parishes to the north and the Holmesdale parishes to the south, seems to take on a new significance. When we recollect that this was a major dividing line, not only between different parishes but between different lathes, different *regiones*, and different minsterlands, it is surely a remarkable one. For whereas to the west of the Darent valley the equivalent boundary generally follows a regular, clear-cut course along the Downland ridgeway, which offered the one obvious line of demarcation in a densely wooded countryside, in *this* area, between the Medway and the Stour, there is no regularity in the boundary whatsoever. For the whole of its course of 20 miles and more in a direct line between Rochester and Wye, it is characterized, mile after mile, by the same kind of erratic indentations as at Minnetts Hill, the same irregularity of outline as we have already noted in the estates based on Holmesdale where they merge into the common pastures of the Weald (see map 9). That these irregularities originated in the same way as at Minnetts Hill is plainly indicated, moreover, by local place-names and local topography. For along much of its length this Downland boundary is still bordered by old woodland, and on either side of the woods it is thickly studded with minor place-names indicating former commonland and former pastoral usage. Altogether, some 50 names of this type are marked on the $2\frac{1}{2}''$ Ordnance maps, and a thorough search of older cartographic evidence and original documents, parish by parish, would no doubt bring many others to light. The word *lǣs*, for example, occurs three times, *denn* six times, *stede* eight times, *dūn* four times, 'common' four times, *wald* twice, *pearroc* thrice, and *lēah*, *rede*, and *rod* – probably indicating pastoral clearings – at least 12 times. In addition to these places, there are other suggestive names, such as Lade or Sheplade on the Downland ridgeway in Lenham, which means 'sheep-way', and Shereway, which occurs twice, in Wormshill and in Stockbury, and which probably indicates old stock droves.

The nomenclature and topography of this fascinating upland boundary is therefore of great historical interest. None of the place-names in themselves actually prove that the common rights in question were exerted by distant or detached communities, and in some cases those rights were no doubt of purely local significance. But the claims of settlements like Whorne's Place over Minnetts Hill, or of Maidstone over Frinsted, were by no means freakish exceptions. At Wichling, Ashdown, and Wormshill we have already noted the rights of relatively distant communities like Ospringe, Teynham, Minster, Newington,

PART FIVE *Topographical Reconstruction*

and Boughton Malherbe, and this same pattern is repeated at many places further west. At Bredhurst ('board wood' or 'broad wood'), for example, the detached chapelry founded by Hollingbourne arose from similar circumstances and is associated with the same kind of interlocking boundaries as at Minnetts Hill.[61] Two miles beyond Bredhurst, in the upland parts of Boxley, Malling Wood probably represents a detached pasture of the *Meallingas* or Malling folk, seven miles away on the other side of the Medway. Beyond Malling Wood, the nomenclature and the topography of Burham Common, Aylesford Common, Wouldham Common, Buckmore Park, Walderslade (*wald* + *slæd*), and Lord Lees indicate an extensive tract of intercommonable pasture, where the outlying woods of Burham, Wouldham, Aylesford, Rochester, and Chatham (*cēto* + *hām*) meet, some 600 feet above sea level. Beyond Burham Common itself, in a nook or projection of Rochester which is still heavily wooded, the name of Boxley Wood perhaps represents a further detached pasture, of Boxley, some four or five miles from its parent-settlement in Holmesdale.

The development of the Milton *gemǣnnes* is thus of more than purely local significance: it sheds a vivid light on the early evolution of the Downland as a whole. West of the Darent valley, where the boundary between the Foothill *regiones* and those of Holmesdale follows the ridgeway, the evidence is not at first sight so obvious; but between the Darent and the Medway (see map 7), and to the east of the Stour valley, we find the same kind of erratic boundary development and the same telling pattern of local place-names as in the area discussed above. In the remote upland country between Canterbury, Dover, and Wye there can be very little doubt that these circumstances explain the recurrence of the word *gemǣnnes* at places like Rhodes Minnis, Stelling Minnis, Swingfield Minnis, River Minnis, Densole Minnis, and Ewell Minnis (see maps 10 and 14). The marked resemblance of the boundary topography in these areas to that of the Holmesdale territories wherever they merge into the common pastures of the Weald is also plainly significant in this context. It is possible, moreover, that the striking network of detached pastoral claims in the area south of Milton goes some way towards elucidating the strangely discrete structure of the very early estates of East Kent, beyond Canterbury, already referred to.[62] If that supposition is correct, it suggests that the original exploitation of the Downland pastures of Kent may ultimately go back beyond the Jutes, and perhaps stems from Romano-British tradition.

11 *The lands of Milton Regis: synthesis*

6. CONCLUSION

The story of the Milton estate has been described at some length in order to illustrate both the complexity behind the reconstruction of such areas and the varied range of problems that topographical detective work of this kind may be expected to illuminate. The evidence of the local landscape is more complex, and often more tricky to interpret, than popular generalization has sometimes led us to suppose; but it is also, there can be no doubt, a far more revealing document than has yet been realized. In the limits of this book it has not been possible to trace the evolution of more than a single territory in detail; but sufficient evidence has been collected for other areas to facilitate, in many cases, a comparable reconstruction. From this it is plain that, while each territory was in some degree distinctive, and in some respects each raises different problems, there are certain basic features common to most of the Kentish *regiones* and estates which, in conclusion, it will be well to point out.

In the first place, in reconstructing the Milton territory, we have found the evolution of the minsterland closely interwoven with that of the royal estate, and based on the same Romano-British community. It was not at all points identical with it, and perhaps we should not expect precise correlation between estate and minsterland. If only because at the time of the conversion so much of the Kentish kingdom was still uncolonized forest, the boundaries of the royal estates must in places have remained somewhat indeterminate, and marked rather by broad swathes of woodland, such as still survive along many parish boundaries today, rather than by exact lines of demarcation. And yet, because the original ecclesiastical structure of Kent was largely determined by the crown, and because the minsters themselves were generally associated with the royal estate-centres, the development of the minsterlands was necessarily shaped, by and large, by the old estate pattern. The fact that these centres had usually originated as Romano-British settlements, moreover, suggests that the estates and minsterlands sometimes incorporated far older territories than those of the Jutish invaders. This suggestion is not susceptible of absolute proof, and on this point it is particularly important not to press the evidence beyond what it will bear. Yet here and there, as in the Romano-British boundary between Teynham and Tonge, or the link between Milton and its detached pastures at *Chetham*, there seem to be hints and vestiges of a more ancient territorial organization.

PART FIVE *Topographical Reconstruction*

In the second place, at Milton itself the *regio* eventually came to form the basis, as we have seen, of two ecclesiastical territories, centred respectively on Milton and Newington: and this also is a circumstance that recurs elsewhere. To the east of Milton there are grounds for thinking that the unusually small minsterland of Teynham[63] at one time formed part of the Faversham territory, as already remarked, and it may be that other small territories, based on places like Kemsing, Chevening, Trottiscliffe, Birling, Lenham, and Harrietsham, originated in much the same way. At present there is no actual proof that these areas arose through the subdivision of a larger territory; but the comparative modesty of their scale, only at Chevening amounting to more than 10,000 acres, clearly calls for some explanation, and intensive local investigation might bring conclusive evidence of subdivision to light. At Maidstone there can be little doubt that Hollingbourne at one time formed part of the original minsterland, since it was still recorded as a dependency of Maidstone in the *Domesday Monachorum* of the eleventh century, though by that date it had already given birth to eight daughter-churches of its own, and seems to have given its name to one of the Kentish lathes.[64]

Finally, in discussing the varied origins and topography of the parishes dependent upon Milton, we have also glimpsed something of the different types of community to which those origins gave rise: and this diversity is likewise characteristic of other territories. Such places as Tonge, Bobbing, Bredgar, Borden, Wormshill, Frinsted, Sittingbourne, and Milton itself not only originated during different phases of settlement, but also represent more or less distinct kinds of local society. Naturally, their subsequent history was not determined solely by their origins as settlements: the evolution of Sittingbourne in particular, and its metamorphosis from an obscure woodland community into a busy 'thoroughfare town' by the early modern period, illustrates how profoundly such places might be affected by extraneous circumstances. Yet in many cases there can be no doubt that the origins of settlements like these gave a decisive twist or bias to their subsequent history, and an historic character that was still apparent in the contrasting communities of the area in the eighteenth and nineteenth centuries. For that reason, if for no other, the study of topography can never be wholly divorced in England from the study of social structure and rural economy: in endeavouring to unravel the evolution of the landscape, we must always keep an eye on the evolution of the local society that moulded it.

12

LANDSCAPE AND SETTLEMENT IN ENGLAND

1. PARALLELS AND CONTRASTS

Originally it was intended to conclude this book by pointing out the parallels between Kent and other areas and outlining a more general view of the origins of English settlement. In writing, however, I have become increasingly conscious of the complexity of the evidence, and of the need for more thorough local and regional investigation before drawing broad conclusions. Where settlement is concerned it is all too easy to advance glib generalizations without adequately recognizing the diversity of the English landscape. Even in the sixteenth and seventeenth centuries there were great regional contrasts in the rural economy of this country: why should we suppose that these were any less pronounced before 1086? In the Danelaw counties, and in the Highland Zone of England in particular, there are many problems of settlement history to which there is no parallel in Kent, and to which the techniques employed in this book may be of limited relevance. Yet while there are dangers in extrapolating from the Kentish evidence, some assessment of its general significance, however tentative, ought perhaps to be attempted.

The first point to consider is the extent to which the distinctive features of Kentish settlement in fact set the county apart, as has often been argued, from other regions of England. In other words, just how untypical was it? Taken together there can be no doubt that these features gave rise to an unusual society and went far to shape the unique Law and Custom of Kent as it came to be codified after the Conquest. When examined individually, however, it becomes plain that none of them was peculiar to the county; it was rather their *conjunction* that was unusual. The absence of common fields, the dispersal of settlement, the prevalence of woodland, the sudden contrasts between one type of country and another, the predominance of pasture, the development of transhumance, and the peculiarities of Kentish custom were all echoed more or less distinctly elsewhere, though there was no other county where they all seem to have characterized the community as a whole. A brief discussion of each

12 *Landscape and settlement in England*

point in turn may thus serve to place the Kentish evidence in perspective.

1. *The absence of common fields*

Kent is one of the few counties where no definite evidence of communally organized field-systems has yet come to light; yet there are many counties where communal arrangements were far from universal, and many where the classical or 'Midland' pattern never developed or tended to disintegrate towards the edge of the common-field zone. In much of the West Country, East Anglia, and the Pennines, for example, no common fields have yet come to light; in east Cambridgeshire the field-systems of the Suffolk-border parishes were often quite eccentric; in Staffordshire recent work confirms H. L. Gray's view that outside the Trent valley irregular systems likewise prevailed; in much of Shropshire communal organization was rudimentary, and fields were based on small hamlets rather than villages, so that enclosure often occurred very early: and so on in other areas.[1] The absence of communal organization in Kent was unusual in its universality, but it was thus by no means unparalleled. It was particularly characteristic of the old-settled coppice countrysides of England, and the Kentish evidence may shed light on the development of these areas generally.

2. *The dispersal of settlement*

The absence of nucleation marks a further broad distinction between Kent and the common-field counties. Yet there can be little doubt that scattered settlement has always been characteristic of other parts of England, both in Highland and in Lowland areas: in much of Sussex, Essex, Suffolk, Cornwall, Devon, and Westmorland, for example, and in the Welsh Marches, the Lake District, and the Pennines. Even in the Midlands there are some areas, such as north Bedfordshire, north Warwickshire, and west Cambridgeshire, where nucleation is less clearly developed than in the classic common-field zones, and where outlying farmsteads and place-names still bear witness to the origins of these areas as early-colonized woodland. There may be many places, therefore, where the eccentricities associated with Kentish settlement would be worth bearing in mind in investigating these districts, and where up to a point they probably indicate similarities of rural economy. It is noteworthy, for example, that dispersal seems to be particularly characteristic of pastoral countrysides, both in woodland and in moorland regions.

3. The prevalence of woodland

The fact that so much densely wooded country survived into the post-Conquest period in Kent sets it apart not only from the common-field areas but from much of East Anglia; coupled with a sparser or more slowly expanding population, it also entailed an exceptionally lengthy period of colonization. That so many Kentish farms and hamlets thus did not originate until after the Conquest, not only in the Weald but on the Downs and the Chart, points to a fundamental contrast between the rural economy of Kent and that of areas like these, where the woods had been largely cleared and colonization virtually completed by the time of Domesday. Yet it is important to recognize that in this respect, too, Kentish experience was not unique. It was echoed not only in the neighbouring forest counties of Sussex and Surrey, but in areas as diverse as Staffordshire, Westmorland, Furness, Essex, the Welsh Marches, and the Forest of Arden. The further parallel between the evolution of the *wald* or Downland of Kent and that of other early-colonized woodlands or 'wolds' is a topic we shall return to later in this chapter.

4. Contrasting countrysides

It was the extent of woodland and marsh that also lay behind those dramatic contrasts between advanced civilization along Roman roads and very primitive conditions natural to fen and deep wood which Nellie Neilson singled out as one of the hallmarks of medieval Kentish society. The early ecclesiastical development of the county and the relative abundance of pre-Conquest documentation have given rise to a misleading impression that by the eleventh century its economy was exceptionally prosperous and advanced.[2] While the Original Lands must have been thickly settled at that time, however, at least three-quarters of Kent needs to be envisaged as both sparsely inhabited and relatively poor and backward by the standards of East Anglia or the Midlands. The modesty of its early architectural heritage and the fact that there were more than 20 counties where medieval parish churches were thicker on the ground bear witness to this comparatively humble status. That so much of the county was thus extensively rather than intensively exploited until well into the medieval period was a circumstance of great importance in the evolution of early Kentish society; it explains much that seems backward or eccentric in its customary institutions, and it obviously distinguishes it, by and large, from the

English heartlands. Nevertheless, the sharply contrasted countrysides of Kent were not without numerous parallels elsewhere; they were certainly echoed in counties like Gloucestershire, Sussex, and Warwickshire, for example, and in Yorkshire, Shropshire, Devonshire, Somerset, and County Durham. In this respect too, therefore, the Kentish evidence may be expected to shed some light on the evolution of other areas.

5. Pasture and transhumance

The pastoralism of early Kentish society and the development of transhumance were natural concomitants of these contrasting countrysides, with their diverse agrarian potential; for pasture is the most obvious primary use to which uncleared woodland may be put before population pressure necessitates an extension of the arable. Yet although the early Kentish evidence for pasture and transhumance, both documentary and topographical, happens to be uniquely abundant, there can be no doubt that similar customs once obtained in other parts of the country. Even in the centre of England Mr W. J. Ford and Dr Della Hooke have demonstrated that they played a major role in the settlement history of the West Midlands;[3] there may be many areas where topographical evidence such as these scholars have exploited still awaits investigation, although documentation of the kind found in Kent may remain far to seek. In Essex, for example, the outlying appurtenances of the pre-Conquest manor of Havering, at Leyton and Loughton in the neighbourhood of Epping Forest, quite probably represent remnants of detached wood-pasture. In Staffordshire the appendages of major river-valley manors in the pre-Conquest period may have originated in much the same way as those of paramount manors like Milton Regis in Kent.[4] There are probably many parts of England where hints and vestiges of this kind would be worth following up in the light of local topography, and with the analogy of Kent in mind.

6. The law and custom of Kent

Originally, therefore, many of the distinctive features of early Kentish society were not so freakish or eccentric as they appear to be in later centuries. There are a number of ways in which, as we move backward in time, the parallels in other areas tend to increase rather than diminish. That does not mean that Kentish custom and the customs of these areas were identical; for even if no other influences were at work, local diversities of environment and variations in the scale of the landscape must have entailed certain fundamental distinctions. But it does seem to hint, up to a point, at a partial community of custom between the basis of settlement in Kent and in some other parts of England. The ultimate circumstances behind this community of custom and the reasons for its belated survival in Kent raise difficult questions which cannot be pursued here; but there is still much to be said for the tentative explanation advanced by Nellie Neilson in the 1920s. As it came to be codified after the Conquest, she believed, the Law of Kent incorporated a:

> whole accretion of custom representing, it would seem, an early stage in social and agrarian arrangements ... which was once probably in existence throughout England, before the unifying and consolidating manorial arrangements [associated with feudalism] had built up another type of rural economy. The earlier system with its later modifications and developments survived with such clearness and vigour in Kent because that county was sufficiently united and conscious of its own identity to force from the courts [after the Conquest] the recognition of customs already partly crystallized, and thereby to oppose them to the common law arrangements. Elsewhere than in Kent the remnants of the gafol paying arrangements of earlier days remain only as exceptions, not as the definite and recognized customs of the county.[5]

It is probably going too far to suggest that the customs associated with Kent once obtained throughout the country; yet since Dr Neilson wrote much has come to light to support her hypothesis and to suggest at least a partial parallel with Kent, not only in regard of pastoralism and transhumance, but also in regard of such matters as partible inheritance and administrative organization.[6]

The extent of unreclaimed forest and marsh already referred to was undoubtedly a further factor in the belated survival of the customary framework of early Kentish society. In the late Old English period the people of the Original Lands could still turn to a vast reservoir of largely untapped resources in these areas, so that in Kent there was never the same pressure of population to convert a transhumant structure of colonization into a common-field system as there often was in the Danelaw counties and the Midlands. It was the increasing exploitation of these parts of Kent after the Conquest that eventually transformed a relatively poor and backward community, by and large, into one of the wealthier regions of England; but intensive exploitation of this kind must not be read back into the period of settlement itself. The consequent survival of a more primitive framework of society is what makes the Kentish evidence so illuminating in turning to other parts of England where early documentation is less abundant and where the economy was transformed at an earlier period. With that evidence in mind, there are many places where the much barer landscapes of areas like Leicestershire seem to take on a new meaning, though they do not exactly repeat the experience of Kent.

If the Kentish evidence is thus of more than local import, what are the main characteristics to bear in mind in turning to other parts of England? There are three matters that should perhaps be discussed in this connexion: the relationship between period of settlement and type of countryside or *pays*; the general significance of those areas here described as 'landscapes of continuity'; and the significance of those described as 'landscapes of colonization'.

2. SETTLEMENT AND *PAYS*

In Kent the relationship between type of countryside and period of settlement is in general a close one. In other counties the link may be less pronounced, the structure of *pays* may be more complex, and the landscape very different in scale; yet there are probably many areas where the association is worth following up. For this purpose there are several different types of English landscape that need to be distinguished; but before turning to these we must enquire what basic qualities differentiate one type of *pays* from another. In many ways it is considerations of geology and soil type that are paramount; yet essentially it is a whole range of local circumstances, operating together, that mould the character of an area as a settlement zone: land forms, altitude, contours, fertility, water supply, cultivability, woodland cover, drainage, aspect, shelter, rainfall, warmth, accessibility, proximity to river or sea-coast, and so on. Few areas are likely to combine every advantage in this respect; in most cases the period of settlement and the kind of landscape and community it gives rise to are the result of compromise – sometimes, as in marshland areas, a fluctuating and uneasy compromise – between the colonist and his environment. In Kent itself the early-colonized Foothill country was well placed in so far as it was fertile, accessible, readily cultivated, well supplied with springs, relatively sunny, and blessed with adequate though not excessive rainfall. In other respects, such as its bleak northerly aspect, its bitter winters and belated springs, it was less favoured; but the advantages were sufficient to outweigh the drawbacks and in many places attract settlement and cultivation from before the Roman conquest. That does not mean that the evolution of settlement is determined simply by environmental circumstance; but it does mean that it is the consequence of lengthy and persistent human effort in response to widely varying natural problems and natural resources. When the foundation of settlement has been laid, the society that arises upon it will itself gradually become part of the environment, moreover, sometimes accentuating the character of the *pays*, and sometimes modifying or transforming it. It was the social environment of wood-pasture countries like Arden and the Weald, for example, quite as much as their natural qualities, that eventually gave rise to local by-employments and in much of the Arden country ultimately created an industrial region.

In reconstructing the evolution of settlement, there are perhaps seven or eight dominant types of country that need to be broadly distinguished: field, forest, heath, fell, fen, marsh, down, and *wald*. These categories are only rough and ready ones; they must not all be thought of as rigid in their boundaries or unchanging over the centuries, and a number of further subdivisions might obviously be suggested. There are marked differences as well as resemblances between the fell or moorland countries of the Pennines, the Lake District, the North York Moors, and Dartmoor, for example. There are also major differences between the arable or fielden countrysides of Somerset, Warwickshire, Essex, the Border shires, and the Welsh Marches. In Kent and Sussex the High Weald is in some ways very unlike the Low Weald, and in places little more than sandy heath, though in general both districts may be regarded as classic forest. There are also many places where parishes or townships overlap regional boundaries, and even in fielden areas like the Vale of Aylesbury comprise a mixture of ancient arable lands and outlying woodland, giving rise to very diverse patterns of settlement in the same neighbourhood. The suggestion that different types of country tend to be colonized in different periods, moreover, should not be taken to imply that all settlements in those areas originated at the same time. In regions of scattered settlement in particular, as we have seen in Kent, farms and hamlets even in the same parish often originated in different periods, as woodland clearance or marshland reclamation proceeded and as population pressure dictated. Nevertheless, it is often possible to distinguish a *characteristic* period of settlement in each kind of *pays*, a period when colonization tended to originate. When every exception has been admitted, the Kentish evidence still points to a basic distinction, by and large, between areas of continuity and areas of colonization.

In arguing analogically from the Kentish evidence, however, there are two basic qualifications that must be remembered. First, we cannot always assume, as we sometimes can in Kent, that areas of 'subsequent' or 'secondary' settlement were necessarily virgin territories, never previously occupied. There are now many parts of England where 'rescue' archaeology has brought evidence of substantial settlement to light in areas of this kind during the Romano-British period. In Nottinghamshire, for example, Sherwood Forest seems to have been one such region, so that although in certain ways it resembled the Weald – it was after all the 'shire wood' – it was also in some sense basically dissimilar. Second, great sensitivity is needed in spotting those local *nuances* of landscape and topography that so often distinguish two apparently similar districts. In the Chilterns, for example, we find a landscape that in some ways closely resembled the Kentish Downland; yet the evolution of the area was also shaped by the development of early trunk routes like Watling Street, and by the establishment of major river-estates at places like Luton, in a way to which there was no parallel on the Downs of Kent.

Yet despite these qualifications the basic distinctions found in Kent are worth bearing in mind in turning to other parts of England. The fact that early river-estates and seminal communities like those of Kent also appear in counties as diverse as Warwickshire, Hampshire, Yorkshire, Gloucestershire, Lincolnshire, Bedfordshire, Essex, and Devon suggests that the fundamental contrast between areas of continuity and areas of colonization is no regional peculiarity. That does not mean that all English settlement originated in this way, or that the contrast is everywhere as sharply delineated as in Kent; in counties like Leicestershire and Bedfordshire, after all, the local *pays* are less distinct and smaller in scale, and in this context differences of scale necessarily entail differences of kind. Yet there are many parts of England where the evidence of early settlement points to an elaborate mosaic of interlocking rural economies, as in Kent, though the character and extent of those economies varied greatly from region to region.

12 *Landscape and settlement in England*

3. LANDSCAPES OF CONTINUITY

The word 'continuity' has intentionally been used in a broad sense in this book; but in discussing 'landscapes of continuity' it is important to recognize that it has a threefold significance. It may refer to continuity of *population*, to continuity of *occupation*, or to continuity of *territorial organization*. Nowadays, probably most scholars would admit to some degree of continuity in the first sense of the term; it is the second and third senses that more frequently feature in contemporary debate. Though these two senses are connected, the continuous occupation of a settlement site does not necessarily imply continuity in the territorial organization behind it, so that the problems at issue need to be considered separately.

In reconstructing the network of early Jutish estates in Kent we have noted many striking indications of continuity in the second sense of the term: in the survival of Celtic place-names, for example, in their connexion with early estate-centres, in the archaeological complexes of the Original Lands, in the magnetic influence of the seminal settlements, in the siting of minster-churches, in their association with holy wells and pre-Christian cult centres, and so on. By plotting the distribution of these territories on the map, it has also become clear that there were distinct zones of continuity as well as continuous occupation of the estate-centres themselves. The question must therefore arise as to how far the pattern of Romano-British settlement as a whole is likely to have survived in these areas, and how far the present network of early medieval farmsteads represents a pre-Jutish structure of settlement. In other parts of England the impression is sometimes given that the outlines of Iron Age colonization may still be traced, in the contemporary pattern of isolated farms and hamlets, virtually intact. In Kent there may be some parts of the Original Lands where this is true; there is evidence of continuous occupation at a number of minor places like Great Grovehurst, near Milton Regis; there can be little doubt that excavation will bring further examples of this kind to light; and there is almost certainly more continuity in the detail of the landscape than has yet been recognized.[7] On our present knowledge, however, it is important that the case for continuity of occupation should not be overstated. Though it is probably more striking in Kent than in many counties, we should never forget the evolutionary nature of English settlement, or the fact that no landscape is likely to survive the vicissitudes of two millennia without fundamental alteration: demographic changes alone entail some degree of metamorphosis. Even in the Original Lands there are outlying farmsteads that do not seem to have been established until the end of the Old English period or after the Conquest. Neither in Kent nor in other counties, moreover, is there any reason to suppose that dispersal of settlement in itself necessarily points to a primitive landscape or to a Celtic tradition of farming, though it may sometimes of course be associated with it.

The extent to which the early Jutish estates of Kent may incorporate an older system of territorial organization as well as an older pattern of settlement is a more difficult question, and one to which the answer is necessarily tentative. The existence of the seminal settlements and the nature of their dependent territories obviously suggest more than mere continuity of occupation; the evident coexistence of British and Germanic populations at these places must also hint at some degree of continuity in their social organization. Nevertheless, in this respect too it is important not to press the evidence too far. There are several considerations that seem to point to the modification of an older system, and its piecemeal adaptation by the Jutes, rather than outright and widespread survival. The demographic decline at the end of the Roman period and the virtual desertion of a major settlement like Canterbury must have entailed some changes in the framework of agrarian society in the area. The consequent recession of settlement and the extension of secondary woodland following the Roman withdrawal, though perhaps less apparent in Kent than in some areas, must also have involved a certain reorganization in the structure of Romano-British estates. Perhaps the most telling pointer in this connexion, however, is to be found in the diversity of the early Jutish estates themselves. There were major differences, as we have seen, between those based on places like Darenth, Wrotham, Milton, and Eastry; there are parts of Kent, such as the lower Medway valley and the stretch of Holmesdale beyond Wye, where the original pattern remains uncertain; there are some areas, such as the vicinity of Lydd, where it is possible that estates of this kind never developed; and it is not altogether easy to account for the anomalous status of a place like Lyminge, five miles from its eponymous river and from the original *caput* at Lympne, yet clearly the centre of an early territory itself, and certainly based on a Romano-British community. In its earliest phases, in short, the pattern of Jutish estates that we actually find in Kent does not seem to indicate a systematic organization inherited from the Roman world, but to a loose association of rural territories whose local origins were highly amorphous, and whose structure only gradually approximated to a common form. In parts of East Kent Romano-British estates may have been taken over more or less intact; elsewhere perhaps only the nucleus of Imperial organization survived in the structure of the early Jutish territories.

If we consider the subsequent history of Kentish territorial development these considerations should not surprise us. In the organization of the Domesday lathes, for example, there can be little doubt that we see more or less definite outlines of early Jutish estates, whereas the 66 hundreds of Kent represent later institutions almost certainly imposed from without. Yet behind this broad abstraction what we actually find is a local administrative situation of great historical complexity. In place of the 40 or so estates there were probably only nine or ten lathes, so that the latter can only have arisen through the gradual fusion of the former; amongst the 66 hundreds, by contrast, there were certainly several, such as Milton, Wrotham, Codsheath, Faversham, and Hoo, that incorporated early Jutish territories more or less complete. If the relationship between medieval administrative units and those of the pre-Conquest period was thus partial and haphazard, is it likely that the Jutish territories themselves corresponded any more systematically with the landed organization of the Roman empire?[8]

In writing this book I have gradually come to feel that the case for continuity is easy to overstate and more complex than appears. In Kent it has been possible to reconstruct the basic outlines of the subject and to identify definite zones of continuity as well as individual communities. In other counties there are clear examples of seminal settlements like those found in Kent; in Leicestershire Charles Phythian-Adams has traced substantial indications of continuity in the estate based on Claybrooke; elsewhere Glanville Jones and others see an extensive nexus of discrete estates surviving from the Romano-British era.[9] The degree to which these settlements and estates may also indicate entire 'landscapes of continuity', however, is a problem of great complexity which must be left to other scholars to investigate. In some areas we cannot expect a definite answer; but it is my hope that the techniques exploited in this book may be of some assistance to those working elsewhere.

4. LANDSCAPES OF COLONIZATION

In turning to the 'landscapes of colonization', it is the areas of subsequent or intermediate settlement that demand special comment, and particularly the early-colonized upland forests. Historians, archaeologists, and place-name scholars have now devoted much attention to identifying areas of very primitive settlement; quite a substantial literature also exists on the evolution of the post-Conquest forests. But the solution to many problems in settlement history probably lies in turning more attention to these enigmatic zones of early-colonized *wald* or woodland-pasture, and it is here that the evidence of the Kentish Downland is so illuminating. In most areas of this kind settlement seems to have begun relatively early in the Saxon period, and in many cases to have been more or less complete by the time of Domesday Book. In contrast with the old fielden areas, however, they often seem to have been predominantly regions of colonization, not continuity, or in some cases recolonization of secondary woodland originally cleared in the Romano-British period. Amongst them one thinks of areas like the Cotswolds and the Chilterns, for example, the Leicestershire Wolds, the west Cambridgeshire Wold, the Kesteven uplands, the Bromswold of Bedfordshire, Huntingdonshire, and Northamptonshire, the upland country bordering Essex, Cambridgeshire, and Suffolk, and the south Leicestershire uplands overlooking the Welland valley.[10]

Precise parallels with Kent are not likely to be found in any of these regions; there are few areas, moreover, where the progress of subsequent settlement can be reconstructed with the same wealth of early documentation or topographical detail. Apart from the Cotswolds, they are substantially smaller than the Kentish Downland, and in some ways their early society was no doubt dissimilar. In most districts there are evidences of common-field settlement which are not found in Kent; in west Cambridgeshire and Northamptonshire much of the old wood-pasture landscape seems to have gradually been assimilated to that of the common-field zones around it. Yet beneath these differences there is an underlying resemblance that tends to become more pronounced as we move backward in time. In this context the Downland region of Kent represents a remarkable survival of a kind of landscape that was once more widespread than is generally realized, though elsewhere it was often cleared more completely than in Kent and largely reclaimed at an earlier period.

It is on the Chilterns perhaps that the parallels with Kent are most pronounced. In the river valleys, as we have seen, early settlements tended to develop at places like Luton; but much of the area was capped with clay and densely wooded, as in Kent, and the local settlement pattern is markedly more dispersed than in the Midlands generally. Minor place-names are numerous, as a consequence, and many of these are probably significant in the context of early woodland-pasture. It has long been recognized that names in *hōh* or 'hoo', for example, are particularly characteristic of the area, though their exact significance has never been adequately explained. They are especially common in the Bedfordshire and Hertfordshire stretch of the Chilterns, as at Luton Hoo, Lilley Hoo, and Offley Hoo. Literally, the word *hōh* simply means a 'ridge' or 'spur of land'; but topographical and historical inspection suggests that in this area (though not necessarily elsewhere) it often indicates an outlying woodland-pasture. The immediate environment of these names, their subordinate character, their situation on the more intractable clayland, the survival of woodland in their vicinity today, their association with names in 'ley', 'grove', 'stead', and 'green', together with the analogical argument from the Kentish evidence, distinctly seem to point to this interpretation. Between Hitchin, Luton, and Harpenden, for instance, where *hōh* is found in at least ten place-names, it is associated with 13 names in 'ley', 8 in 'grove', 3 in 'stead', and 19 in 'green', though some of the latter may be relatively modern.[11] In this area, therefore, we find some marked parallels with the Kentish Downland.

In Leicestershire the evidence is at first sight less revealing. The county is one of the least well-wooded in England, and one that was most affected by parliamentary enclosure in the eighteenth century. On the Wolds themselves names like Dalby Wolds and Burton-on-the-Wolds may indicate no more than the 'elevated stretch of open country' which is usually taken to be a secondary meaning of the word.[12] At places like Waltham, Wymeswold, and Prestwold, however, *wald* can hardly bear this signification, since these names are recorded in Domesday Book, and Waltham itself – nearly 600 feet up in the heart of the area – probably indicates old royal forest. Though there are few minor names to help us and the topographical evidence is too complex to discuss here, there is a *prima facie* case that the Leicestershire Wolds may have been at one time extensively wooded, like the equally bare *wald* country of East Kent beyond the Dour valley.

In other parts of Leicestershire there can be no doubt that many parishes formerly possessed their own outlying stretch of *wald* or woodland, often called a 'holt', and usually situated on the higher land towards the edge of the parish. Normally this word is taken to indicate an isolated wood, and that is certainly its usual connotation today. There are grounds for believing, however, that some of the Leicestershire 'holts' represent the last remnants of continuous belts of woodland, or minor 'wolds', along the watersheds or ridges between neighbouring parishes and river valleys, like the woods of the Hoo peninsula in Kent.[13] The word 'holt' still survives in a considerable number of places, and although some of these look like modern fox- or game-coverts, they are often replantings of ancient woodland. To the north-east of Leicester, for example, we find Barkby Holt on the edge of Barkby, Beeby, and South Croxton, and in this case the word actually appears in some medieval records as *wolt* and *wold*.[14] It is also found at many places in south Leicestershire, as at Walton Holt, 550 feet above sea-level in the parish of Kimcote. In this instance only a trained eye can now discern evidence of former woodland; but local place-names indicate its existence and suggest that it once extended into the nearby parishes of Mowsley (*lēah*), Laughton (*lēac* + *tūn*), and Gumley (*lēah*).[15] In all probability this belt of wooded countryside originally extended in a continuous arc along the watershed between the Welland and the Soar; its last relics may still be seen on the steep slopes of Laughton Hills, near the Northamptonshire border. A further example of a Leicestershire 'holt' is Nevill Holt, to the east of Market Harborough, with its great medieval manor house on a ridge overlooking the Welland valley. Nevill Holt originated as an outlying chapelry of Medbourne, the early estate-centre in the valley below, and formed part of what was once another substantial stretch of upland forest. To the north it still adjoins Horninghold, 'the *wald* of the Horningas', and to the south-east Drayton (*dræg* + *tūn*) and Bringhurst, 'the wood of Bryni's people'. In this district we certainly have an early-settled forest, for Horninghold and several of its neighbouring settlements are recorded in Domesday Book.[16] Originally this stretch of *wald* may have extended in a more or less continuous line through Cranoe (*hōh*) towards Gumley and Mowsley. In that case it would have linked up with Walton Holt, 15 miles away to the south-west, at the further end of the Welland watershed. There may always have been a breach in the woods between Cranoe and Gumley, however, where the hills dip down at Langton and the road to Leicester cuts through them, since no woodland place-names now survive in this vicinity.

The place-names of these upland *wald* areas of the Midlands raise many points of interest. They vary considerably from one district to another, and some of them, like the Chiltern 'hoos', are markedly localized in their distribution. There are a few, however, that appear repeatedly in different areas, such as Drayton, Hardwick, Shipton, Shipley, Leighton (*lēac*), Caldecote, and other names in *cot*. None of these names is confined to the Midlands, and they are not associated only with early-colonized *wald*. Nevertheless, they have a certain regional typicality and frequently indicate settlements originating in the pre-Conquest period. Drayton is a particularly interesting name in this connexion. Along with the related names of Draycott and Draydon, it occurs in at least 50 places in England, more than 30 of them in the Midland counties.[17] Its root meaning is that of a place where something is dragged or drawn, and it sometimes relates to a place where boats were drawn up or dragged over a narrow neck of land. But it is also especially characteristic of old woodland country, and here it seems to refer to a 'dray', or a way along which timber is dragged from a forest. This was the meaning which the word still retained in Somerset in the seventeenth century, as Thomas Gerard pointed out in relation to Draycote in his *Description of the County of Somerset* in 1633.[18] Ten miles south of the Leicestershire Drayton the name recurs at Draughton in Northamptonshire, on the edge of Rockingham Forest, and in the same neighbourhood as Old (*wald*), Walgrave (*wald* + *grāf*, 'grove'), Cransley, Mawsley, Pytchley (*lēah*), Thorpe Underwood, and other woodland names. It is also found in the west Cambridgeshire Wold, at Dry Drayton, of which the original name was *Walddraitton*,[19] and where the 'dray' probably still survives in the present lane leading up through the village. Like the *wald* of south Leicestershire, both these areas must have been colonized well before the Conquest; for most of their place-names are recorded in Domesday Book, and a few in tenth-century charters.

The topography of these regions of upland *wald* is equally instructive. In some areas, like the borders of Suffolk, Essex, Hertfordshire, and Cambridgeshire, we find marked parallels with the old coppice-country of the Kentish Downland, with its scattered woods, small parishes, twisting lanes and isolated hamlets and farmsteads. There are many places where indications of early-colonized forest-pasture still survive in local droveways, moreover, or in drays like the track leading up through Dry Drayton.[20] In east Leicestershire, for example, the parish of Barkby retained its Woodgate Way until the seventeenth century,[21] and a series of narrow tracks still leads up from the valley of the Wreake to the upland *wald* around Tilton, Halstead, Somerby, Withcote, and Owston, sometimes followed by parish boundaries, as at

Ridgemere Lane between Barkby and Queniborough. Even where the landscape was largely transformed at the time of enclosure, as in the southern tip of Leicestershire, it is striking to observe how the boundaries of places like Swinford, Shawell, Cotesbach, Lutterworth, Gilmorton (*mōr*), Kimcote (*cot*), North Kilworth, South Kilworth, Westrill, and Starmore all converge on those of their mother-church of Misterton, or 'minster + *tūn*', though they have long since ceased to acknowledge any subordination.[22] There can be little doubt that the field-systems of these areas also have much to teach us about the topographical development of subsequent settlement. The irregularities of the 'woodland systems' of the West Midlands have been discussed by Brian Roberts,[23] and the tendency of field-patterns to become eccentric towards the edge of common-field zones was referred to earlier in this chapter. Some of the place-names of areas like these, such as Hardwick ('herd farm'), Shipton ('sheep farm'), and Caldecote ('cold cottage or stock-shelter'), are obviously significant in this connexion, since they indicate settlements that must have originated as isolated farms rather than as common-field villages; it may be that the field-systems which eventually developed at such places would be worth tracing back to their earlier phases on a comparative basis. Finally, there are certainly some areas of this kind where the pattern of church-dedications tends to repeat that of the Wilderness parishes of Kent, and thus confirm the evidence of local topography. Of the 28 surviving churches in the upland *wald* of south Leicestershire, for example, four are dedicated to St Nicholas, four to St John the Baptist, four to St Michael, three each to St Peter and St Andrew, two each to All Saints, St Mary, St Helen, and St Denis, and one each to St Luke and St Giles: a pattern closely reminiscent of that of Kent, though with obvious local inflexions.

5. THE COMMUNITIES OF ENGLAND

The contrasting types of countryside we have been considering in this chapter lie at the roots of all English history. England is one of the most varied countries in the world in its landscape, and in that diversity we see something of the diversity of colonization itself. In exploring the origins of settlement, as a consequence, whether in place-names, in pre-Conquest charters, in archaeological remains, in ecclesiastical development, in territorial relationship, in church-dedications, in woodland topography, or in other ways, each line of argument necessarily brings us back, in the last resort, to the evidence of the landscape – the only record we possess, in so many ways, of the language of settlement.

In these contrasting countrysides what we also see, moreover, is something of the diversity of the historic communities of England. We have already noted that diversity in the evolution of the *regio* of Milton Regis, with its mingled elements of transformation and tradition: at Milton itself a Romano-Jutish community which through all its varied phases continued to act as a focus of local economic activity; at Ashdown, Swanton, and Sutton Baron places which have remained isolated farmsteads ever since they were carved out of the Downland forest, perhaps a thousand years ago; yet at Sittingbourne a medieval woodland settlement which was reborn as a thoroughfare town in the sixteenth century, and again as a minor industrial community in the nineteenth.

In the origins and contrasting development of places like these, humble though they may seem, we have a kind of allegory of English provincial life. Sympathetically understood, their history has as much to tell us about the England that we love as Flora Thompson's Lark Rise, or W. G. Hoskins's Wigston Magna, or George Eliot's Middlemarch. Behind it, in an unending chain, we must visualize the countless unrecorded acts of individual colonists and peasants: generation after generation clearing the woods, creating farms, tilling the fields, tending their flocks, building their houses, raising their families. These were the men who laid the real foundations of England; the landscape itself is their memorial, and its inscription our greatest historical treasure.

ABBREVIATIONS

Note   Places of publication are given only for works published outside the United Kingdom. In abbreviating less frequently cited periodical titles, commonly accepted abbreviations such as *J.* for *Journal*, *Rev.* for *Review*, have been used. Other abbreviations are listed below.

AC	*Archaeologia Cantiana*
A-F	Frances Arnold-Forster, *Studies in Church-Dedications, or England's Patron Saints* (3 vols., 1899)
AHR	*The Agricultural History Review*
ASC	P. H. Sawyer, *Anglo-Saxon Charters: an Annotated List and Bibliography* (1968)
Copley	Gordon J. Copley, *An Archaeology of South-East England: a Study in Continuity* (1958)
DB	Domesday Book
DM	*The Domesday Monachorum of Christ Church Canterbury*, ed. David C. Douglas (1944)
EPNE	A. H. Smith, *English Place-Name Elements* (English Place-Name Society, XXV and XXVI, 1956)
Furley	Robert Furley, *A History of the Weald of Kent, with an Outline of the Early History of the County* (2 vols., 1871, 1874)
H	Edward Hasted, *The History and Topographical Survey of the County of Kent* (12 vols.; 3rd edn, 1972, a reprint of 2nd edn, 1797–1801)
Jessup	Ronald Jessup, *South-East England* (Ancient Peoples and Places Series, 1970)
Jolliffe	J. E. A. Jolliffe, *Pre-Feudal England: the Jutes* (2nd edn, 1962, a reprint of 1st edn, 1933)
KPN	J. K. Wallenberg, *Kentish Place-Names: a Topographical and Etymological Study of the Place-name Material in Kentish Charters dated before the Conquest* (1931)
Newman, *EK*, *WK*	John Newman, *North East and East Kent*, and *West Kent and the Weald* (The Buildings of England, 1969).
ODEPN	Eilert Ekwall, *The Concise Oxford Dictionary of English Place-Names* (3rd edn, with corrections, 1951)
ODS	David Hugh Farmer, *The Oxford Dictionary of Saints* (1978)
OE	Old English
OED	*The Oxford English Dictionary*
ON	Old Norse
O.S.	Ordnance Survey
PNK	J. K. Wallenberg, *The Place-Names of Kent* (1934)

Abbreviations

Sandred	Karl Inge Sandred, *English Place-Names in -Stead* (1963)
TR	*Textus Roffensis: Rochester Cathedral Library Manuscript A.3.5*, 2 vols., ed. Peter Sawyer (Early English Manuscripts in Facsimile, 1957 and 1962)
VCH	Victoria County History
Ward	Gordon Ward, *Sevenoaks Essays* (1931)
Witney	K. P. Witney, *The Jutish Forest: a Study of the Weald of Kent from 450 A.D. to 1380 A.D.* (1976)

NOTES

PREFACE

1. For the authenticity and dating of these charters, see Ch. 6, n. 2.
2. I should add that some of the topics discussed in Chapters 2, 3, 4 and 6 received preliminary investigation in the following articles: 'The making of the agrarian landscape of Kent', *AC*, XCII (1977); 'River and wold: reflections on the historical origin of regions and *pays*', *J. Historical Geography*, III (1979); 'Place-names and *pays*: the Kentish evidence', *Nomina*, III (1979). The two former articles are reprinted in my volume *Landscape and Community in England*, published by the Hambledon Press (1985).

I PROBLEMS AND APPROACHES

1. Perhaps with a population of as much as 4–6 million: cf. A. R. Birley, in *Times Literary Supplement*, 6 Nov. 1981, 1305.
2. P. H. Sawyer (ed.), *Medieval Settlement: Continuity and Change* (1976), 1, 2. The quotation from Professor H. R. Loyn is from *Anglo-Saxon England and the Norman Conquest* (1962), 36. Professor Sawyer's point that many Wealden churches unrecorded in DB are evidenced in *TR* and *DM* was also made by Hasted in the eighteenth century and by Douglas in his edition of *DM*.
3. Roman farm sites on the Downs usually seem to have been occupied for limited periods and then abandoned, so that they are not relevant to continuity.
4. W. J. Ford, 'Some settlement patterns in the central region of the Warwickshire Avon', in Sawyer, *op. cit.*, 274–94; Della Hooke, 'Pre-Conquest estates in the west Midlands: preliminary thoughts', *J. Historical Geography*, VIII.iii (1982), 227–44; Della Hooke, 'The Anglo-Saxon landscape', in *Field and Forest*, ed. T. R. Slater and P. J. Jarvis (1982), 79–103.
5. As when working on *The Agrarian History of England and Wales*, IV, 1500–1640 (1967), ed. Joan Thirsk, Chs. VII and VIII.
6. Many Kentish wood-names of the early modern period are recorded in medieval or pre-Conquest sources.
7. Neither does that for a county like Staffordshire: cf. VCH, *Staffs.*, VI (1979), 'Medieval agriculture' and 'Agriculture, 1500–1793'. The widespread evidence of post-Conquest assarting in counties like Essex must also be borne in mind: cf. VCH, *Essex*, VII.
8. Jolliffe, 73–97.
9. Helen Cam, *Liberties and Communities in Medieval England* (1963 reprint), 103; their development from *regiones* was also Jolliffe's view (Jolliffe, 46).
10. 'Pre-feudal Scotland: shires and thanes', in G. W. S. Barrow, *The Kingdom of the Scots* (1973), 7–68.
11. Jolliffe, 40–8.
12. According to Jolliffe, 46, the word 'lathe' is only once recorded in pre-conquest Charters. In this connexion too much has been read into the word

ware in early Kentish records. Though sometimes associated with lathal units, as in *Wiwarawic* ('*wīc* of the Wye people'), or with regions, as in *Cantware* ('people of Kent'), it need not be so, as the case of Waldershare shows. It occurs in other counties, as at Ridware (Staffs.) and Clewer (Berks.), and its basic meaning is simply 'dwellers'.

13. It is not possible to give a fully definitive list of such centres. But the certain and virtually certain examples include the following, though the real total was larger, perhaps significantly so: Rochester, Faversham, Milton Regis, Folkestone, Maidstone, Lympne, Lyminge, Aylesford, Eastry, Sturry, Wye, Hollingbourne, Dartford/Darenth, Crayford, Otford, Reculver, Dover, and Canterbury.

14. Witney, Ch. 2; H. M. Chadwick, *Studies on Anglo-Saxon Institutions* (1963 reprint), 252; Jolliffe, 46, also pointed out that the 'lathes grow smaller as we go backward in time'; but he seems to have visualized a total of only 12 or 13 (*ibid.*, 48, 65).

15. F. M. Stenton, *Anglo-Saxon England* (1971 edn), 293; Chadwick, *op. cit.*, *passim*; Cam, *op. cit.*, essays V and VI.

16. Jolliffe; *DM*, Introduction. Both seem to me to have arrived at some mistaken views of Kentish settlement and society through failing to recognize a clear distinction between village and parish, and between hamlet, parish, and farm. Jolliffe (see especially 1–19, and Ch. 11) made much of an allegedly 'hamlet' countryside in his four south-eastern counties, and even of a 'hamlet system' of organization (*ibid.*, 81), without realizing that, in Kent at least, his 'hamlets' were generally isolated farms. In fairness to Jolliffe and Douglas it must be said that when they wrote the historical study of the landscape was in its infancy.

17. The figure of 12,000 probably understates the real abundance of topographical evidence: for the single manor of Wrotham (admittedly a large one) nearly 900 field- and place-names are recorded in a rental of 1495: J. L. Semple, 'The Manor of Wrotham in the early sixteenth century' (dissertation for Diploma in Local History, University of Kent at Canterbury, 1982), 2.

18. As, for example, in Margaret Gelling, 'English place-names derived from the compound *wīchām*', *Medieval Archaeology*, XI (1967), 87–104; J. McN. Dodgson, 'The significance of the distribution of English place-names in -ingas, -inga- in south-east England', *Medieval Archaeology*, X (1966), 1–29.

19. Professor F. R. H. Du Boulay aptly describes them as the 'Old Arable Lands' in *The Lordship of Canterbury: an Essay in Medieval Society* (1966).

2 LANDSCAPE AND ECONOMY

1. Cf. *KPN*, 181, and *EPNE*, II, 99, *scēad*. Wallenberg wrongly associated Shuttlesfield with the Nailbourne, which is more than a mile distant.
2. H. C. Darby, *A New Historical Geography of England* (1973), 386.
3. For the seventeenth-century community, see my *Community of Kent and the Great Rebellion, 1640–60* (1966).
4. Estimates of historic county areas vary considerably. The chief variable apparently relates to saltings, tidal marshes, embanked islets, etc.; if these

are excluded, Somerset and Hants. (including the Isle of Wight) were also slightly larger than Kent.
5. There are no early settlements on the Dover branch, but several on the main route between Canterbury and Richborough. The London-Maidstone-Folkestone road is a rationalization of local lanes during the turnpike era; until then the London-Maidstone route ran *via* Rochester. The London-Sevenoaks-Hastings road seems to have developed as a main road with the rise of the Sussex Cinque Ports, but it did not become a post-road until the seventeenth century.
6. R. E. Glasscock's map of the distribution of lay wealth in Kent in 1334, in *AC*, LXXX (1965), 64.
7. As for instance in F. W. Maitland, *Domesday Book and Beyond* (1960 edn), 530, 537.
8. Its assessment for the Fifteenth in 1225 works out at 16s. per square mile, a figure exceeded by those for Norfolk, Suffolk, Lincs., Rutland, Northants., Beds., Bucks., Middx., Berks., Oxon., and Glos. In 1334 it was surpassed by Norfolk, Cambs., Hunts., Northants., Beds., Oxon., Berks., Rutland, Middx., and Glos. The validity of these assessments is of course fraught with difficulties: in so far as the Cinque Ports were excluded the figure for Kent is understated; in so far as the county was nearer the centre of government, it was probably over-assessed in relation to remoter counties where the government was less well-informed.
9. In the subsidies of the 1520s a larger area of Kent was taxed at 40s. and more per square mile than of any other county; in the Civil War it ranked with Norfolk, Suffolk, Essex, and Devon; but in the 1650s its assessment was drastically reduced. By 1707, in terms of wealth per square mile, it had fallen back into ninth place, behind Middx., Surrey, Herts., Bucks., Beds., Berks., Essex, and Oxon.: Darby, *op. cit.*, 196, 308; Alan Everitt, *Change in the Provinces: the Seventeenth Century* (1969), 16–17, 54.
10. Dr Glasscock's map in Darby, *op. cit.*, 139, suggests that in 1334 the coastal plain of north-east Kent was several times as wealthy as the Weald, and more than six times as wealthy as the south-east corner of the county.
11. G. H. Garrad, *A Survey of the Agriculture of Kent* (1954), 1–2, 209, 95.
12. *Ibid.*, and Ch. 11 *infra*.
13. William Marshall, *The Review and Abstract of the County Reports to the Board of Agriculture*, v (1818), 435–6: 'the idol of the men of Kent', Marshall called it.
14. Based on 1961 acreages: judged by those of 1801 Kent would still have been tenth (1:3·2), but Surrey would have taken the place of Cheshire next above it.
15. Darby, *op. cit.*, 306–7; Alan Everitt, 'The making of the agrarian landscape of Kent', *AC*, XCII (1977), 28 and n.
16. With an average parish size of 2,493 acres in 1861 Kent ranked 22nd among English counties, and was surpassed by: Leics. (1,482 acres); Oxon. (1,613); Notts. (1,765); Suffolk (1,802); Norfolk (1,820); Berks. (1,888); Northants. (1,916); Rutland (2,038); Warwicks. (2,088); Som. (2,116); Beds. (2,158); Worcs. (2,206); Dorset (2,218); Glos. (2,218); Mon. (2,274);

Derbys. (2,344); E. Riding (2,366); Herts. (2,371); Bucks. (2,395); Lincs. (2,429); Herefs. (2,470). But these figures take no account of lost or new parishes, and the relationship with early wealth is a very rough one.
17. F. W. Jessup, *A History of Kent* (1958), 52.
18. Garrad, *op. cit.*, 198. Sussex has 14·6% under wood, Surrey 14·1%, Hants. 12·2%, Kent 10·1%, and England generally 5·7%.
19. H, VI, 169–70.
20. *PNK*, 244, 255.
21. Witney, 61 sqq.; Jolliffe, 50 sqq.
22. This meaning is not recorded in *EPNE* and seems peculiar to Kent.
23. H, VI, 4, VII, 333; 'A survey of the parish of Ash', by T. Fulljames, 1792 (in hands of Rev. Allen of Ash).
24. H, VI, 169–70; there are still extensive woods in parts of Stockbury.
25. H, VI, 4, V, 586; *PNK*, 208.
26. As comparison of early O.S. sheets with those of the Malling area today shows.
27. DB normally records only pannage-rights in Kent. Its account is thus largely limited to oak and beech woods, and in many parishes surviving place-names and woodland topography suggest serious understatement.
28. Furley, I, 164, where 'the wood called Rip' is The Ripe at Lydd (*KPN*, 37); cf. also *PNK*, 483, 484. A miniature holly-forest still survives at the Holmstone.
29. G. A. Cooke, *Topographical and Statistical Description of the County of Kent* (n.d., c.1820), 273.
30. H, X, 225.
31. *KPN*, 308; *ODEPN*, 93; *EPNE*, I, 92; for *Chetham*, which Wallenberg does not record, see H, VI, 499.
32. For the name of Blean see Ch. 5, n.30.
33. In 1299 Edward I required 17 guides to take him from Dover to Chichester and back to Canterbury, spending 16 days on the journey: Furley, II, 256.
34. As in Staffs.: VCH, *Staffs.*, VI (1979), 12.
35. Furley, II, 715; *PNK*, 295. Milch-cattle cannot be fed off mast.
36. Garrad, *op. cit.*, 199. Only 9 per cent is 'high forest'.
37. Under the old system of management, 3,000–4,000 hop-poles were needed for each acre, so that when the hop acreage was at its maximum (c.45,000 acres) in the nineteenth century about 150 million poles were utilized each year: Garrad, *op. cit.*, 95, 99.
38. Oliver Rackham, *Trees and Woodland in the British Landscape* (1976), and *Ancient Woodland: its History, Vegetation, and uses in England* (1980).
39. Darby, *op. cit.*, 686.
40. *The National Gazetteer of Great Britain and Ireland* (1868), XII, Appendix, 4.
41. *The Imperial Gazetteer of England and Wales* (1870), I, 205.
42. *National Gazetteer, loc. cit.*
43. R. J. P. Kain, 'Tithe surveys and the study of land occupation', *Local Historian*, XII (1976), 88; cf. also Cooke, *op. cit.*, 47.
44. H, VI, 276, 272; Cooke, *op. cit.*, 42. Upland Sheppey was poor breeding-land.

45. Cooke, *op. cit.*, 47–53; Kain, *loc. cit.*
46. P. J. Bowden, *The Wool Trade in Tudor and Stuart England* (1962), 40; Furley, II, 341–2.
47. R. A. L. Smith, *Canterbury Cathedral Priory* (1943), 152–3. There was an average of 337 sheep on Christ Church manors in Kent (10,770 on 24 manors, and none on 8), and there were 1,100+ manors in the county. Since manors varied greatly in size and wealth, no great weight can be attached to the above figure of 400,000; but it may represent the order of magnitude involved. The Christ Church manors were very large ones, but the figures relate only to demesne.
48. *KPN*, 21, 24.
49. Cf. N. Neilson (ed.), *The Cartulary and Terrier of the Priory of Bilsington, Kent* (1928), 24–5.
50. Partible inheritance, the best-known characteristic of the Custom of Kent, remained general until well into the nineteenth century; it was not abolished in law until 1926.
51. *EPNE*, I, 80.
52. Cf. H, VII, 3–4.
53. There are 62 in Smarden, for example, a medium-sized Wealden parish of 5,386 acres; even in Thanet there were 35 'hamlets or knots of houses' in the 2,930-acre parish of St Peter in the eighteenth century: *Kentish Traveller's Companion* (1779), 189.
54. A. R. H. Baker and R. A. Butlin (eds.), *Studies of Field Systems in the British Isles* (1973), Ch. ix.
55. For example Meitzen, cited in Maitland, *op. cit.*, 537n. Maitland regarded Meitzen's views as 'interesting though hazardous'; they are worth reconsidering.
56. In this context the parallels between the Kentish Downland and the chalk country of east Cambridgeshire and the Chilterns should be noted. The latter display marked differences from classic common-field areas and are often characterized by small hamlets and isolated farms; both were early-colonized woodland zones, capped with boulder clay or clay-with-flints, and relatively poorly endowed: cf. Margaret Spufford, *Contrasting Communities* (1974), 32.
57. Since this was written visits to Wales have led me to feel that resemblances between early Welsh and early Kentish development may be more substantial than is generally suspected. These need not be due to common 'Celtic' or other 'racial' influences. Both areas, after all, were basically *forest* countries over much of their surface, even in historic times: the possibility of a comparable response to similar environmental conditions of this kind might repay further consideration. Jolliffe long ago (3, 63 *et passim*) saw parallels in the early society of the two areas.
58. See my remarks in *AC*, XCII (1977), 10n.
59. The view is now gaining ground, however, that Midland villages may often have originated as 'polyfocal' settlements; if that is correct, the contrast with Kent, though still valid, is less pronounced.

3 REGIONS AND *PAYS*

1. But for the topographical significance of the boundary between East and West Kent see Ch. 11, section 5.
2. G. H. Garrad, *A Survey of the Agriculture of Kent* (1954), 1–2; William Marshall, *The Review and Abstract of the County Reports to the Board of Agriculture*, V (1818), 413.
3. In the *Kentish Gazette* for January 1979, Mr John Boyle of Canterbury argued that Hasted's topographical descriptions were written by a 'ghost', not by Hasted himself. Since Hasted was in prison when his second edition appeared, this is a theoretical possibility, though it is equally likely that he drew on his own notes and intimate personal knowledge of each parish, together with information supplied by local incumbents and others; alternatively, of course, a 'research assistant' may have been employed. The articles are not footnoted and the author produces no contemporary evidence for his belief, which was apparently unknown to some of Hasted's most intimate friends. The alleged stylistic differences between the 'topographical' and 'historical' sections of the work represent a personal opinion which does not square with the facts. Broadly speaking, the descriptions tally with other lines of evidence, whether Hasted wrote them or not, though like any source of the kind they should not be regarded as infallible.
4. H, VI, 123, regarding Bapchild; for other roundtilt parishes see H, VI, 134, 290–1, 532.
5. H, IX, 300, VI, 438. 'Cludgy' or 'cledgy' is the local word for the sticky Downland clay: see *OED*, *sub* 'cledge', 'cledgy'.
6. H, VIII, 118.
7. The name of Holmesdale is not discussed by Wallenberg (or apparently any other place-name scholar), no doubt because as a district, not a settlement, it does not figure in Wallenberg's select medieval sources. My earliest reference to it is in William Lambarde, *A Perambulation of Kent* (1970 reprint), 468–9, c.1570, when it was evidently an ancient name, referring to the whole valley from Reigate to the Medway. Earlier forms are needed before an etymology can be suggested; it is still in use in the area.
8. H, III, 159, 51.
9. For Hothfield Common see H, VII, 515–16. Brabourne Lees is a late eighteenth-century squatters' settlement, typically situated on common land on a parish boundary; Godden Green is first definitely recorded in 1516: *PNK*, 64.
10. *Ex inf.* the late J. B. Stonebridge. Porteus, bishop of London, purchased a small property here. It was these circumstances that led to the building of Ide Hill church at Porteus's instance c.1805 (*The Imperial Gazetteer of England and Wales* (1870), III, 1035), the first of many new Anglican chapels of the kind to be built in rural Kent: it was rebuilt in 1865–6. For the similar backwoods character of Blean Forest, see P. G. Rogers, *Battle in Bossenden Wood* (1961); this likewise resulted in a new church, at Dunkirk, in 1840.
11. H, VII, 91, 173, 221. In 1743, despite an unusually dry summer, it took Sir

Notes

Edward Filmer of East Sutton Place five hours to travel 20 miles to his manor court at Hoathly in Lamberhurst: Furley, II, 729–30.

12. Cf. Hasted's comments on Orlestone (H, VIII, 361), High Halden (H, VII, 220), and Capel (H, V, 193–4).
13. Jolliffe, 54 sqq.
14. Cf. F. R. H. Du Boulay, 'Denns, droving and danger', *AC*, LXXVI (1961), 75–87; Witney, Ch. vii; there is also much incidental information in Furley.
15. The late seventeenth-century chapels at Tunbridge Wells and Deal were not parochial.
16. But not all of it: cf. N. P. Brooks, 'Romney Marsh in the early Middle Ages', in *The Evolution of Marshland Landscapes*, Oxford University Department for External Studies (1979), 74–92. For convenience' sake I have included Walland Marsh in Romney Marsh in this book.
17. There are acute practical difficulties in tracing early Marshland settlement. In North Kent it is often impossible in contemporary documents to distinguish between the marshland part of a parish and its upland; much of the area colonized in Roman times, moreover, is now a wilderness of oazes and saltings.
18. H, VIII, 423, VI, 25.
19. H, VIII, 415, 259, 423, VI, 144, 290–1.
20. H, VIII, 469, 379, 270, 400, 266, 415.
21. H, VIII, 258–9, 423.
22. H, VIII, 265, 476, 283, 379.
23. H, VI, 26–7.
24. H, VIII, 470, 476, 382, 389.
25. H, VI, 204, regarding Iwade; for Romney Marsh cf. H, VIII, 270, 423, 469, 476.
26. G. A. Cooke, *Topographical and Statistical Description of the County of Kent* (n.d., c.1820), 47.
27. R. J. P. Kain, 'Tithe surveys and the study of land occupation', *Local Historian*, XII (1976), 88–92; cf. Cooke, *op. cit.*, 48–9; R. A. L. Smith, *Canterbury Cathedral Priory* (1943); *ASC*, 453. The charter allegedly of 616 x 618 relating to Burmarsh (*KPN*, 269–70) is spurious: cf. *ASC*, 350.
28. Joan Thirsk (ed.), *The Agrarian History of England and Wales*, IV, *1500–1640* (1967), 410 (the Foothills are here described as the 'Lower Downland').
29. H, VIII, 258, 415, 270, 272, X, 249.
30. H, VIII, 258, X, 222, 250.
31. H, VI, 290, 204, 144, VIII, 472.
32. Kain, *op. cit.*, shows that the association of the Marshes with upland farms, which entailed this draining away of wealth, still formed an essential feature of the marshland economy in the mid-nineteenth century.
33. H, VIII, 469–70, 266; cf. H, X, 250, for similar conditions in Sarre.
34. H, VIII, 382, 422.
35. H, VI, 36; *Annals of a Fishing Village*, ed. J. A. Owen (1892): see, for example, pp. 83, 94, 105, 128, 209–14. The author, Denham Jordan, wrote under the pseudonym 'A Son of the Marshes'; Milton was disguised as

Marshton and Sittingbourne as Standbeck.

36. N. Neilson (ed.), *The Cartulary and Terrier of the Priory of Bilsington, Kent* (1928), 2.
37. For two important studies, see Peter Clark, 'The migrant in Kentish towns, 1580–1640', in *Crisis and Order in English Towns, 1500–1700*, ed. P. Clark and P. Slack (1972); A. F. Butcher, 'The origins of Romney freemen, 1433–1523', *Economic History Review*, 2nd ser., XXVII (1974), 16–27.

4 THE JUTISH BASIS

1. For England as a whole *ODEPN* records 64 examples of 'east *tūn*', 57 of 'west *tūn*', 46, of 'north *tūn*', and 59 of 'south *tūn*'. I owe these figures to Dr Margaret Gelling.
2. During the Interregnum Stansted and Plaxtol were detached from Wrotham and formed into separate parishes, but this arrangement was annulled at the Restoration.
3. H, IX, 470–1, 475, records anchors and other maritime evidence found at Charlton.
4. The Stair or wharf (H, V, 178) at Hadlow is recorded in 1327 (*PNK*, 178). This use of the word 'stair' is not evidenced in *OED* until 1517; *EPNE* omits it.
5. Early Downland settlements were probably fed by local springs at the lip of the clay-with-flints, or perhaps by roof-water. When the clay 'saucers' were pierced, the springs disappeared and wells became necessary; many Downland wells are more than 200 feet deep and their excavation through solid chalk rock no doubt postdates the early settlements.
6. W. G. Hoskins and H. P. R. Finberg, *Devonshire Studies* (1952), 302–5.
7. Margaret Gelling, *The Place-Names of Berkshire*, Part III (English Place-Name Society, LI, 1976), 820–2; T. R. Slater, 'More on the wolds', *J. Historical Geography*, V (1979), 213–18.
8. Alan Everitt, 'River and wold: reflections on the historical origin of regions and *pays*', *J. Historical Geography*, III (1977), 5 and n.
9. For Meon I am indebted to Dr C. R. Hart, who also mentions the case of Wylye, Wilts. Since the above account was written two major studies of early estates in the West Midlands have been published by Dr Della Hooke: see Ch. 1, n. 4.
10. Alan Everitt, 'The primary towns of England', *Local Historian*, XI (1975), 263–77.
11. It is often said that manorialization was 'weak' in Kent; but it was not weak in the paramount manors, and the subject generally needs more thorough investigation. Many manorial courts were still held in the late eighteenth century.
12. *KPN*, 83–4. *Cray Ewelme* survived as Newell in Orpington.
13. Lymbridge Green was closely related to Lympne, but cf. *PNK*, 429.
14. Or possibly 'marsh [river]': A. L. F. Rivet and Colin Smith, *The Place-Names of Roman Britain* (1979), 387.
15. But some Devonshire place-names derived from Celtic river-names, such as the Clysts, did not acquire the suffix *tūn*.

16. South Darenth, St Margaret-at-Helles, and Maplescombe lost their parochial status in the late medieval period; North Darenth is now known as Darenth.
17. Twenty-two names in 'wood', one in 'hurst', one in 'grove', one in 'rough' (i.e., scrub), and two in 'shaw' are marked on the 2½" O.S. map, and many unnamed woods.
18. In this neighbourhood Tubbenden, Ramsden, Hockenden, and perhaps Denbarn and Pokeridden (for which early forms are needed) also contain the pastoral element *denn*.
19. Everitt, 'River and wold', 8 and n.
20. Jolliffe and Witney both argued that east Surrey once formed part of Kent, and it was certainly at one period under the authority of the Kentish crown; but the subject is a difficult one and cannot be pursued here.
21. *KPN*, 227; H, III, 162.
22. Except where the estate merges into the Weald, where the boundaries are characteristically irregular.
23. Cf. pp. 279–80.
24. Everitt, 'River and wold', 8–10.
25. *KPN*, 21. The name Stour itself seems originally to have applied only to the Great Stour.
26. As remarked earlier, the Canterbury-Richborough road is studded with early English settlement sites, whereas on the branch to Dover there are probably none. The *tumuli* on Barham Down and the fact that Barham is recorded in 799 have led to the erroneous belief that Barham itself is very early; in fact it is significantly sited just off the Dover road, and is a typical subsequent settlement on relatively infertile Downland.
27. Margaret Gelling, 'English place-names derived from the compound *wīchām*', *Medieval Archaeology*, xi (1967), 87–104; Ickham is from *iuga*, 'yoke'.
28. Everitt, 'River and wold', 9 and n.
29. At a later date there seems to have been a royal residence at Kingston (*English Historical Documents*, I, no. 129); but it is a minor upland settlement with a characteristically small strip-parish, and stands in apposition to the adjacent Charlton or 'ceorls' farm' in Bishopsbourne. For names in *ceorl* see H. P. R. Finberg, *Lucerna* (1964), 144–60; Charlton in Bishopsbourne should be added to those discussed there.
30. See Ch. 10, section 5.
31. *KPN*, 158.
32. Everitt, 'River and wold', 10–17.
33. *KPN*, 5–7; H, IX, 68–78 *passim*, 86, 101; cf. also H, VIII, 518–20.
34. Copley, 274.
35. Jolliffe's *Pre-Feudal England: the Jutes* was primarily based on the evidence for the lathe of Wye.
36. See Ch. 5, section 5. The view sometimes advanced that the name of Maidstone derives from the river has not found general acceptance: cf. *KPN*, 306. The derivation from *mægð* must also be regarded as dubious: cf. M. Gelling, W. F. H. Nicolaisen, and M. Richards, *The Names of Towns and Cities in Britain* (1970), 132.

Notes

37. E.g., Eastry, Northbourne, and Westerham.
38. For the Milton Regis territory see Ch. 11.
39. Alan Everitt, *Ways and Means in Local History* (1971), 14, 15.
40. At Hollingbourne, as at several Kentish places in 'bourne' (e.g., Patrixbourne), the prefix may have been added later for purposes of distinction; this would explain the presence of *ingas* (if such it is) in a first-generation settlement. Perhaps for similar reasons, Bourne near Dover was renamed River after the Conquest: *PNK*, 563.
41. Everitt, *Ways and Means*, 16.
42. *Ibid.*, 15. Lenham also had Downland pastures, at Ashdown (*æsc* + *denn*).
43. *KPN*, 142–4; *ODEPN*, 91. At Kemsing Wallenberg apparently thought the name referred to a hill; but a hill in this area would not be sufficiently distinctive. All these *-ing-* names of Kent are associated with notable springs, and at Kemsing it is obviously the springs near the church, later associated with St Edith, that are referred to.
44. See Ch. 10, section 4.
45. For the early 'problem-names' involved, see Ch. 5, section 4.
46. The prominence of *hām* in early habitative names is also well known elsewhere: see Margaret Gelling, *Signposts to the Past* (1978), 112sqq.
47. See Ch. 1, section 3. There is a clear parallel between these ancient 'royal/ecclesiastical' estates of Kent and the ancient 'composite estates' which have been identified in Staffordshire. These consisted of a manor with attached berewicks and appendages, and were likewise held by king, earl, or bishop; they were distinct from the 'small unitary estates' associated with later Staffordshire settlement, which evidently parallel the 'subsequent' territories of the Kentish Downland discussed in Chs. 6 and 7: cf. H. R. Loyn, *Anglo-Saxon England and the Norman Conquest* (1962), 342, citing C. F. Slade in VCH, *Staffs.*, IV, 9–10.

5 BEYOND THE JUTES

1. Margaret Gelling, *Signposts to the Past* (1978), 11–12.
2. *EPNE*, I, 80; Kenneth Jackson, *Language and History in Early Britain* (1953), 600–1.
3. If estimates of a Romano-British population of 4–6 million now being cited are valid (cf. A. R. Birley, in *Times Literary Supplement*, 6 Nov. 1981, 1305), the decline must have been drastic indeed in view of an apparently substantial increase in the late OE period, before DB was compiled.
4. But it is vital to remember that the existence of a Romano-British farm in a given parish, or even several farms, does not prove that the landscape *generally* in that neighbourhood was cleared and settled; this obvious point is too frequently forgotten in settlement studies. In the parish of Goudhurst today there are 82 settlement sites and colonization extends back for a thousand years, yet there are still about 1,000 acres of woodland devoid of habitation.
5. As in laying drains, excavating for buildings, etc.
6. I have drawn principally on the following: (1) G. J. Copley, *Archaeology of South-East England: a Study in Continuity* (1958; particularly the county gazet-

Notes

teer for Kent, pp. 271–83); (2) Sites recorded on the 60 2½" O.S. sheets for Kent; (3) Ronald Jessup, *South-East England* (1970); (4) Articles and reports in *Archaeologia Cantiana*, particularly the more recent volumes; (5) John Newman, *North East and East Kent, West Kent and the Weald* (1969). Copley included the former Kentish parishes of Charlton, Eltham, Greenwich, Lewisham, Plumstead, and Woolwich under London. He did not include minor finds, as of a single implement or the like, so that his gazetteer covers only 'major' finds. I have excluded his references to Roman roads from the above figures, and his questionable coverage of 'significant' place-names. For the present purpose, Jutish finds have also been excluded from the above figures: these add a further 110 or so sites, 82 of which are on the Foothills and 12 in Holmesdale: many of these refer to early (pre-Christian) cemeteries and are, of course, taken into account elsewhere in this book.

7. This point cannot be too strongly emphasized. The practice of producing small-scale distribution maps based on the blank outline of a whole region or county, on which sites are unrelated to other types of topographical feature, is virtually useless for tracing the evolution of settlement. In Kent such an outline distribution map of Romano-British sites would seem to indicate extensive colonization in most of the county; when the places in question are plotted in detail on the 2½" O.S. sheets, it becomes quite plain that three-quarters of the county was largely bare of settlement in the Roman period so far as current evidence indicates. It is the *immediate* context of the site that matters.

8. The precise figures are as follows: Foothills 302, Downland 62, Holmesdale 37, Chartland 32, Weald 13, Marshland 36, total 482. The apparently low figure for Holmesdale is, of course, in part due to its smaller scale (35,000 acres, or about one-sixth the size of the Foothills).

9. In the Iron Age, 60% of the total; Belgic era, 75%; Romano-British, 70%; Jutish, 80%. No great significance should be attached to these figures; the lower percentage in the Iron Age is chiefly occasioned by the number of hill-forts on the Chartland.

10. The paucity of Romano-British evidence on the Downs in particular, which has often aroused comment in the past when comparing the region with other chalklands like Salisbury Plain (cf. Copley, 139; Jessup, 188), should thus probably be taken to indicate a real contrast of settlement and economy in the Roman period. O. G. S. Crawford remarked (*Archaeology in the Field* (1953), 94) that, though Celtic fields were found almost everywhere on the southern Downland, 'most surprisingly none have been found in Kent, where cultivation must have been intensive and is mentioned by Julius Caesar'. This is based on a misconception: Caesar traversed the northern edge of the Foothills and probably did not penetrate into the Downland of Kent.

11. *Ex inf.* T. Tatton-Brown; but rural settlement probably continued in the neighbourhood of Canterbury.

12. To save needless repetition, facts readily traceable in Copley (especially in the county gazetteer, 271–83) or on the 2½" O.S. maps are not individually referenced in the following account unless otherwise stated.

13. Jessup, 184. There is a Roman cremation site at Welling and Roman brick is used in Erith church, near Crayford.
14. First bishop of York, and subsequently of Rochester until his death in 644. A cult of St Paulinus developed at both Rochester and Canterbury: *ODS*, 318–19.
15. Baston is also a stone-name: see *infra*, pp. 113–15.
16. Jessup, 189.
17. For this Wickham, which has come to light since Margaret Gelling's article in *Medieval Archaeology*, XI (1967), 87–104, see Ward, 96; F. R. H. Du Boulay, *The Lordship of Canterbury* (1966), 20. Five of the six sites are in Otford.
18. Jessup, 193–4. This is not to be confused with Ebbsfleet near Minster-in-Thanet.
19. *Ibid.*, 35.
20. See n. 11, *supra*.
21. Jessup, 165.
22. That is, the *church* site, which is nearly always the crucial point to note in reconstructing early Kentish settlement. The present village of Ospringe is a medieval street-migration, no doubt due to the pilgrim traffic.
23. Copley, 131, 153, 278, 280; Jessup, 88–93, 197–8. Some of these sites are described as at or near Sittingbourne; but Sittingbourne is a late settlement and originally they were in Milton.
24. Copley, 278.
25. Jessup, 88sqq.
26. Copley, 174. There are other early settlements, such as Sturry and Sarre, where evidence of 'English' settlement before 500 has come to light: *ibid.*, 163.
27. *Ibid.*, based on assessment of the archaeological evidence.
28. Unless otherwise stated, the interpretation of place-names in the rest of this chapter is based principally on *KPN*, *PNK*, and *EPNE*; facts readily traceable in these sources are not generally referenced individually. Other basic works consulted include Kenneth Cameron and Margaret Gelling (eds.), *Place-Name Evidence for the Anglo-Saxon Invasion and Scandinavian Settlement* (1975); Margaret Gelling, *Signposts to the Past* (1978); articles in *Nomina*, *The English Place-Name Society Journal*, and *Medieval Archaeology*. Since this is not a linguistic study, I have not discussed philological problems unless these seem crucial to the argument; what I have devoted particular attention to is the topographical aspect of place-name evidence.
29. A. Mawer, *Problems of Place-Name Study* (1929), Ch. i; for an opposite view see Colin Smith, 'The survival of British toponymy', *Nomina*, IV (1980), 27–40.
30. Andred was originally the name of a place, generally identified with Pevensey in Sussex (*ODEPN*, 9). The suggestion of Ekwall (*ODEPN*, 46) and Wallenberg (*KPN*, 357–8) that the name of Blean may derive from a Germanic word meaning 'coarse cloth, rug' does not sound convincing; the form Blee, which seems to support it, is not recorded until Chaucer's reference to it in the fourteenth century; the form Blean, by contrast is

recorded consistently from 724 (*KPN*, 33, 61–3). Forest-names are often very ancient, and the names in *cēto, caito* in this region of Kent raise the possibility than Blean may be of pre-English origin, though it does not seem to be Celtic.

31. Wallenberg mentions river-names only in connexion with settlement-names. Most stream-names in Kent have not been studied, and those of minor rivers like the Beult, Bewle, and Shode have not been explained.
32. The Limen was still so known in the medieval period (Furley, II, 37). For *Colne*, see *PNK*, 509–10; for *Sarre*, *KPN*, 43, *PNK*, 599; for *Daven*, discussion *infra*, p. 112. Other Celtic or pre-English river and stream-names in Kent include: *Avon* (Eden), for which see *PNK*, 90, *KPN*, 137, and Eilert Ekwall, *English River-Names* (1928), 22–3; *Loddon* (Teise), *PNK*, 170; *Humber*, a stream in Erith, *PNK*, 30–1; and possibly the Kennet or Kent in Hawkhurst, now known as the Kent Ditch – it is on the county boundary – though Kennet seems to be the old form (H, VII, 145, 158). Wallenberg (*PNK*, 222) hesitated to accept *Carey* as the root of Caring in Leeds, on the Len; he did not know that the same name recurs in the lost *Caring* in Maidstone (H, IV, 266), where the Len joins the Medway; this seems to confirm derivation from *Carey* as a river-name. The current names Len, Teise, Rother, and Eden are early-modern back-formations. In a few cases the above names need further investigation before they can be finally accepted.
33. The distribution is as follows: Foothills 7, Downland 21, Holmesdale 4, Chartland 5, Weald 13, uncertain 1+. *Dūn* ('down') is likewise an English loan-word from the British and is common in Kent, but again mostly in minor or subsequent settlements, no doubt bearing no Celtic significance. *Torr* probably occurs once, at Torry or Torre Hill in Lenham, but early forms are needed. Dr Gelling tells me that *dūn* must have been borrowed by the Germanic peoples before migration to Britain.
34. Their relationship to the estate-centres resembled that of names in *wealh*.
35. Unless the lost *Briogoningwara* in Cuxton was on the Downs (*KPN*, 226).
36. But the proximity of these two names is interesting, since Frittenden is one of the few Wealden parishes where Roman pottery has been found and Roman brick is perhaps used in the church: Copley, 275.
37. So *ODEPN*, but not Wallenberg. *Cefn* is topographically apt, and a pre-English root would not be surprising at this point on the Pilgrims' Way.
38. Charles Thomas, *Christianity in Roman Britain to A.D.500* (1981), 263.
39. *KPN*, 212, tentatively suggests a Celtic origin for the first element of Keston; but an OE personal name is more likely.
40. *KPN*, 225–6; *ODEPN*, 371; A. L. F. Rivet and Colin Smith, *The Place-Names of Roman Britain* (1979), 348; but cf. Gelling, *Signposts*, 56.
41. It was attached to Swalecliffe as a swine-pasture; see Ch. 7, n. 65.
42. *PNK*, 556.
43. *KPN*, 298–9; *ODEPN*, 470, 471.
44. *Limen* may mean 'marsh [river]' rather than 'elm [river]': Rivet and Smith, *op. cit.*, 387. For Walton by Folkestone and Walmer see Kenneth Cameron, 'The meaning and significance of Old English *walh* in English place-

names', *English Place-Name Society Journal*, XII (1979–80), 1–46, especially 42, 45. For Walton in Eastry see *KPN*, 299; this is not recorded before 1302 but there seems no real reason to question its authenticity. Wales in Chilham and Walmer Hill in Chislet, however, though both associated with early Jutish parent-settlements, are probably of manorial origin.
45. See pp. 194–5, *infra*.
46. To these Chevening should be added if its first element is not from *cefn*. For Kemsing, Charing, and Stowting see Ch. 4, pp. 88–9, and n. 43.
47. *ODEPN*, 167; M. Gelling, W. F. H. Nicolaisen, and M. Richards, *The Names of Towns and Cities in Britain* (1970), 94.
48. *EPNE*, I, 163.
49. *KPN*, 117.
50. Jessup, 189; this also confirms Dr Margaret Gelling's suggestion (*loc. cit.*) as to the origins of Faversham.
51. Copley, 152–3, 174, 206, 275.
52. *Ibid.*, 163.
53. It is described as *oppidum regis* when first recorded in 811: *KPN*, 29.
54. *PNK*, 280–4. Wallenberg objected to a Celtic root because the stream is insignificant; but it is now known that quite obscure streams sometimes bear Celtic names. His alternative suggestion, *denu* + *tūn*, is unacceptable since Davington is on a pronounced hill-top above the stream.
55. *KPN*, 148; *PNK*, 289–90; *ODEPN*, 335; cf. also *EPNE*, II, 56. In a personal communication Dr Gelling tells me that she doubts whether the second element is 'spring' in the sense 'source of a stream'; it may be 'spring' in the sense of 'copse', though Ospringe is at a springhead.
56. Copley, 152–3, 174, 275.
57. Gelling, *Signposts*, 67–76; *Medieval Archaeology*, XI (1967), 87–104.
58. Also Stone in Warehorne, Stone-by-Dartford, Stone in Thanet, Stone in Bapchild, Stone in Buckland-by-Faversham, Stone in Newington, Stone in Saltwood, Stone in Cranbrook, and perhaps Stone in Beckenham, though this is not recorded by Wallenberg before the eighteenth century.
59. Also Maidstone, Axtane, and Baston. Wallenberg did not discuss Bredenstone; but Breden, or more correctly Bredon (H, IX, 501, 525), is the name of the hill on which the Roman pharos or Bredon Stone stood, and is presumably a doublet of Bredon (Worcs.) and Breedon (Leics.), from British *brigā*, 'hill', + OE *dūn*, 'hill'.
60. Cf. Stone Street in East Kent, in Maidstone, in Cranbrook, in Gravesend, in Seal, and in parts of 'Watling' Street.
61. Copley, 225, 144, 281; H, IX, 525; Newman, *WK*, 528.
62. Jessup, 35; Copley, 274; Newman, *EK*, 452.
63. Jessup, 198, 167, 190; Kent County Local History Committee, Minutes, 29 Nov. 1974; Copley, 276, 277, 139, 278.
64. Maxton is on the Roman road from Dover to Folkestone and close to a Roman pottery site at Farthingloe; Teston adjoins a Roman house (Copley, 281); Copstone is near several Roman sites and the lost *Combe* and Wickham in Otford (B. Philp, *Excavations in West Kent, 1960–70* (1973), map showing Wickham Field); Stone-by-Dartford is in a heavily Romanized

locality, with a Belgic settlement near the church and an Iron Age settlement near Stone Castle (Copley, 281; Newman, *WK*, 527–8); Stone in Thanet stood near a Roman settlement and in a locality thickly strewn with Neolithic, Iron Age, Belgic, Roman, and Jutish remains; Stone in Saltwood (a more doubtful case) is probably on a minor Roman road between Roman sites at Saltwood and Beachborough; Stone in Newington-next-Hythe seems to have stood on the Roman paved way from Hythe to Stone Street, which was still visible in Hasted's time (H, VIII, 219); Stone Abbage in Pluckley is on the lost Roman road from Maidstone to Lympne (Ivan D. Margary, *Roman Ways in the Weald* (1965), 232). For Lullingstone Wallenberg prefers *tūn*; the early *stān* forms recorded in the eleventh century he interprets as an attempt to distinguish the two adjacent settlements bearing this name (*PNK*, 46–7); but these places were already distinguished by their suffixes Peyforer and Ross by the eleventh century, so that further distinction was needless. Keston, Baston, and Cuxton, as well as Copstone, are near names in *wīchām*.

65. Copley, 274; cf. H, VII, 100. It gives rise to the surviving Stone Street in Cranbrook town, which apparently led to *Stone*.
66. As at Folkestone (*folc*), Maidstone, Bredenstone, etc.: see Ch. 5, pp. 113–14 and n. 59.
67. In places they may refer to Roman milestones like that found at Southfleet in the eighteenth century: H, II, 422–3.
68. *PNK*, 59–61: some early forms of Copstone suggest identity with Copplestone in Devon, which denotes a tall standing stone: *EPNE*, I, 106–7.
69. K. J. Allison, *The East Riding of Yorkshire Landscape* (1976), 52–3; D. M. Palliser, *The Staffordshire Landscape* (1976), 36, 51.
70. Jessup, 95, 111–12; A. Hadrian Allcroft, *The Circle and the Cross: a Study in Continuity*, I (1927), 48.
71. Especially perhaps at Maidstone, in view of its first element (*mægd*, 'maiden' or perhaps 'folk, people'), its proximity to the Aylesford megaliths and the prehistoric meeting-place of Kent at Penenden Heath, and its division into the three boroughs of Week (*wīc*), Westree, and Stone.
72. Jessup, 101–2; Copley, 272, 277. But caution is needed here: natural sarsens are also frequent in the Aylesford area.
73. *PNK*, 242; Copley, 272, 281 (*sub* Tonge).
74. *Ibid.*, 279; *PNK*, 59–61.
75. Jessup, 186, 196–7.
76. *Ibid.*, 195. See Ch. 10, section 8.
77. Jessup, 193.
78. In assessing the case for continuity in this chapter, it has been necessary to summarize a massive volume of evidence accumulated for Kent as a whole, of which only a fraction is cited here. Such an approach inevitably obscures the import of individual places, such as Faversham, Maidstone, and Milton Regis, which need to be reconstructed in the round, as in Ch. 11. Nevertheless, it is essential to regard such communities as examples of a distinct type or species of settlement, rather than as isolated or freakish instances, and in consequence to study them in their regional setting.

Notes

6 THE FIELD AND THE FOREST

1. The problem of water supply on the chalk (see Ch. 4, n. 5) has tended to anchor individual settlements in a single place.
2. Wallenberg discusses about 250 charters and related documents in *KPN*. A few of these, particularly for the earlier period, are certainly spurious, and some others are of doubtful authenticity or are incorrectly dated, though the great majority are genuine. The indispensable guide to these matters is *ASC*. I have rejected all charters certainly regarded as spurious, though these may sometimes contain early name-forms; I have followed Professor Sawyer's dating in *ASC*, though he rarely suggests substantial emendations of Wallenberg's. Where authenticity is doubtful, I have been guided by what appears to be the burden of authoritative opinion as far as I am able to judge; in a few cases I may have erred on the side of inclusiveness, but not sufficiently to affect my general conclusions.
3. It may represent the OE *denn*, meaning 'a den, a wild beast's lair, a pit': *EPNE*, I, 129.
4. *PNK*, 331–4.
5. Notably in Warwickshire: see W. J. Ford, 'Some settlement-patterns in the central region of the Warwickshire Avon', in P. H. Sawyer (ed.), *Medieval Settlement: Continuity and Change* (1976), 274–94; cf. also Della Hooke, 'The Anglo-Saxon landscape' in *Field and Forest*, ed. T. R. Slater and P. J. Jarvis (1982), 79–103. For transhumance in Kent generally see Witney; F. R. H. Du Boulay, 'Denns, droving and danger', *AC*, LXXVI (1961), 75sqq. P. H. Reaney, 'Place-names and early settlement in Kent', *ibid.*, 58–74, needs amendment in the light of Witney.
6. H, I-IX, *passim*; Furley, particularly II, 827–36; Witney, particularly Part II. The exact number is 676 on my reckoning.
7. According to N. Neilson (ed.), *The Cartulary and Terrier of the Priory of Bilsington, Kent* (1928), 3sqq., common rights were being limited to specific areas as early as the eighth century. A general distinction existed between the 'great *dens*' and 'small *dens*'; in DB, for example, Dartford had three 'great' and eight 'small' *dens*.
8. Exceptions occur mainly along the foot of the Stone Hills, where Chartland settlements like Boughton Malherbe had their *dens*.
9. E.g., Shenden, Wickenden, and the lost *Orkesden* near Sevenoaks (Ward, 291); and Hockenden, Walden, Ramsden, and Tubbenden near Orpington. The Downland *dens* were generally attached to places on the Foothills, and those on the Chart to places in Holmesdale; they are too few to affect the statistical argument of this chapter.
10. Furley, II, 711; *KPN*, 245, 135; H, III, 474–5; P. H. Reaney, *The Origin of English Place-Names* (1960), 130.
11. It seems to have happened, for example, at Boughton Malherbe: Witney, 251–2.
12. This latter circumstance helps to explain the relatively large number of *dens* attached to Chartland places. For the royal and monastic origins of estates in the Old Arable Lands see pp. 90–2 and n. 47, *supra*.

13. See Ch. 7, section 4.
14. Jessup, 52–3, 60, suggests on the basis of the archaeological evidence that transhumance may go back to Mesolithic times; but he is referring to the Weald as a whole, not the Weald of Kent as such.
15. See Ch. 8.
16. Of the 206 places on the Downs bearing woodland names recorded by Wallenberg, 30 bear names in 'hurst', but in the Weald this element occurs at least 200 times.
17. This paragraph and the next are based on Alan Everitt, 'River and wold: reflections on the historical origin of regions and *pays*', *J. Historical Geography*, III (1977), 10sqq.
18. *Wald* may also be represented in Garrington in Ickham, if that place is identifiable with *Garwaldingtune*; but this is doubtful. It may recur in Old Downs near Sutton-by-Dover, and in Old Bottom near St Margaret-at-Cliffe; but early forms are needed. *Waldington* has come to my notice since compiling the list in 'River and wold', *loc. cit.*; *KPN*, 164, gives a different interpretation of it, but the topographical context suggests a *wald* name. Some of these areas of *wald* may at one time have been intercommoned by neighbouring estates; the fact that Ickham had detached lands in Womenswold suggests former rights.
19. As *Waldington* and other names immediately south of Canterbury, such as Ridlands (*rede*, 'a clearing'), indicate.
20. East of the Dour the straight boundaries of some woods suggest plantation, but they often bear early-recorded names.
21. It recurs in Walderslade in Chatham and Walden in St Mary Cray, and in an Elizabethan boundary perambulation of Wye in such phrases as 'the wolde beeche': PRO, E134, 30/31 Eliz., M11. I am indebted to Dr F. Lansberry for this reference.
22. Together with a few recorded by other scholars, or in medieval records not discussed by Wallenberg.
23. 'Hurst' 30 times, 'holt' 16 times, 'frith' 10 times, and 'snode' 4 times. No criticism of Wallenberg's work is here intended, of course.
24. See Ch. 7, sections 1 and 3.
25. Culverstone = *culfre* + *sol*, 'dove pool'; the identification of Harvel with the charter-name of 939 is dubious, but the settlement is an old one.
26. H, VIII, 114–15.
27. So *KPN*, 315; but H, IX, 341, shows that Kingston is recorded in a grant by the Conqueror.
28. The reference in 791 may be to Lower Hardres, or more probably to the whole of Hardres before its subdivision.
29. The name of this lost church site survives in Mountain Wood nearby.
30. A further 85 places on this sheet are not recorded by Wallenberg; in a few cases the above dates are drawn from other sources. Only Downland settlements have been included; springline settlements like Lyminge are omitted.
31. The percentages for the two sets of figures do not agree precisely, but the differences are largely fortuitous.

Notes

32. Jumping Downs in this area may be recorded in 799 (*KPN*, 85), but identification is doubtful.
33. The identification of Ittinge and Holt is uncertain, and Leigh may be East rather than North Leigh.
34. Elmsted, for example, originated as a daughter of Waltham (itself probably a daughter of Petham), Stelling of Hardres (itself a daughter of Nackington), and Barham of Bishopsbourne (itself a daughter of Patrixbourne).
35. It may be urged that many Wealden churches also are recorded by 1100; but in this connexion it is significant that in most Wealden parishes no place-names are recorded before the Conquest, whereas in a remote Downland parish like Elmsted six of the 20 settlements are so recorded. On the Downs, moreover, churches were more than three times as numerous as in the Weald.
36. Particularly since most of them still retain these names unaltered today.
37. The second element in Grandacre is the English *æcer*; the medieval form of Fredville is derived from 'freide ville'. Most names of this kind seem to be first recorded in the thirteenth century; Paradise is not discussed by Wallenberg, but cf. H, VI, 16.
38. Occasionally not until the eighteenth century, as at Brabourne Lees. As a rule, settlements in 'row', 'green', and 'common' are also of late medieval or early modern origin in Kent; but these are more frequent on the Chart. It should be noted that such elements do not in themselves imply habitation.
39. As building evidence often suggests.
40. *PNK*, 383. I owe this explanation to Mr J. McN. Dodgson, who also tells me that Kettlebender is a jocular name for a tinker. Some of these quasi-humorous names may not have originated till the Napoleonic Wars, when numbers of new farms were established on marginal lands in Kent as population rose.
41. H, X, 130, 132–3, 136.
42. Everitt, 'River and wold', 10sqq. The Woodnesborough neighbourhood cannot now be regarded as part of the Downs; but in places like Durlock ('deer enclosure') in Ash the *wald* originally extended across and indeed beyond it.
43. The largest Downland parish, Elham (6,599 acres) is in East Kent; but this is in the valley of the Little Stour, and must be regarded as exceptional.

7 THE DOWNLAND ECONOMY

1. Challock ('calves' enclosure'); Oxfrith ('ox wood'); Oxroad, ('ox assart'); Hanslett's Forstal (*hengest* + *hyll*, 'stallions' hill'); Swingfield ('swine field'); Sundridge in Bromley (*sundor* + *edisc*, 'sundered pasture'); Sunderland in Lynsted (?'sundered land', i.e., probably for pastoral purposes).
2. There is nothing in Kent to support the suggestion in *EPNE*, I, 276, that *herst* may mean 'hillock'. It has often been said that it is especially characteristic of the High Weald; actually the element is equally distributed between High Weald and Low Weald, and often occurs in low-lying places.
3. *EPNE*, I, 138.

4. N. Neilson (ed.), *The Cartulary and Terrier of the Priory of Bilsington, Kent* (1928), 56 and n.; the Black Book of St Augustine is cited for 325 sheep in '10 hopes'. See also R. A. L. Smith, *Canterbury Cathedral Priory: a Study in Monastic Administration* (1943), 186 and n., for this usage in Thanet.
5. *PNK*, 450, records Hope Farm in Hawkinge (1300) and suggests *hop*, 'piece of enclosed land in the midst of waste land' as its origin.
6. Despite *ODEPN*, 423 (Stockbury); *EPNE*, I, 16.
7. *PNK*, 552, 231, 551.
8. *PNK*, 585, 521. *Pirige* is much more common in Kent than *æppel*. Wallenberg records nine examples, and there are many others; generally it occurs in the simplex form as Perry, but also as Periton, Palmsted, etc.
9. *KPN*, 174; *PNK*, 382, 553, 527–8, 114, 541; H, IX, 288.
10. In the nineteenth century, J. M. Kemble evolved an ingenious theory, based on Germanic analogy, of the development of the Weald in general as a 'mark', with its own Mark Court or 'Court of Dens' at Aldington, which he regarded as a kind of 'folk parliament'. Furley (I, x–xii, 57–8, II, 731–42) was no doubt right in demolishing this theory; Aldington with its 44 *dens* was merely one of many paramount manors with such rights; but there may well be something in Kemble's ideas on the development of a communal 'mark', or region of boundary woodland left between settlements or estates, though the case is too complex to argue here.
11. The first element, *scēad*, indicates a boundary (cf. *PNK*, 436, and *EPNE*, II, 99); the place is apparently recorded in 838 (*KPN*, 180), and Great and Little Shuttlesfield stand on either side of the Lyminge-Elham boundary. The second element may be a further indication of arable husbandry.
12. In a perambulation of Otford in 1794, no fewer than 70 boundary marks are named (Ward, 213); cf. also the Knockholt perambulation of 1463 (*ibid.*, 211), and the sixteenth-century Wye perambulation which describes one mark as 'a twisted beech marked with a pair of spectacles' (PRO, E134.30/31 Eliz., M11).
13. See Ch. 8, pp. 186–7 and n. 13.
14. *PNK*, 243. Unless otherwise stated the facts in this and subsequent paragraphs are based on *PNK* and *KPN*.
15. Wheelbarrow Town is a medieval farmstead, but Wallenberg's identification of it with *Wealdingworth* seems uncertain, though both places are in the same hundred (*PNK*, 436); for Twitham and Twitton, see *EPNE*, II, 221–2.
16. E.g., Grove Court in Chislet, Grove in Wickhambreaux, Grove in Sellindge, Grove in Woodnesborough, Great Grovehurst in Milton Regis, Grove in Sheldwich, Selgrove in Faversham/Sheldwich, Gravesend, and several Grove Ends. These are all recorded medieval or pre-Conquest settlements.
17. For the continuing importance of common rights in these minnises cf. H, VIII, 121–2, regarding Colonel Dixwell's case against the Commonwealth government on behalf of the commoners of Swingfield Minnis.
18. *KPN*, 181–2. Professor G. W. S. Barrow suggests that 'saxonicae' is used in excessive erudition for 'saxonice'.

Notes

19. 'Minnis' occurs only three times outside the Downs: at Minnis Bay in Birchington, The Mean in High Halstow/St Mary's Hoo, and Worth Minnis.
20. As at Tilden on the Benenden/Hawkhurst boundary; Holden and Copden on that of Biddenden/Cranbrook; Dockenden and Chittenden on that of Benenden/Cranbrook.
21. Witney, 259, 263, 229; *KPN*, 170, 172.
22. H, VII, 115. Hasted does not refer to the part in Cranbrook; but it survives in Camden Hill and Camden Park in that parish; the meaning is 'combe + *denn*'.
23. H, V, 311, 154, 156.
24. Or perhaps 'hook + *ing* + *denn*': *PNK*, 20.
25. H, II, 119.
26. H, II, 50; *PNK*, 26. Formally the last element of Tubbenden may be *denu*, 'valley'; but in view of other pastures nearby, *denn* seems more likely.
27. H, II, 91; *PNK*, 16.
28. Quoted in Ward, 211; *Southdenne* no longer exists; Knockholt is *āc* + *holt*.
29. H, VI, 493, IV, 211, 241.
30. Comparison of H, IX, 191, 224, 230, 234, and 241 suggests this; Hasted seems to imply Twitham borough was wholly in Wingham; part of it was, but in 1286 Alanus de Twitham held lands 'in Goodnestone, at Twitham' (*ibid.*, 230). For Twitham, see n. 15 *supra*.
31. H, IX, 593, V, 506. Bearsted is usually identified with the *Berkamystede* recorded in a charter of 696, and interpreted as 'homestead on a hill' (*KPN*, 18; *ODEPN*, 31; Sandred, 210; cf. *EPNE*, I, 29). But the identification cannot be correct. Bearsted is not on a hill; it is not otherwise definitely recorded before 1226; and the early forms cited in *KPN* do not tally with that of 696. The context suggests that it originated as a common pasture of Leeds and Thurnham in the later OE period, rather than as a seventh century settlement. Wihtred's charter of 696 is dated from *Berkamystede*, but it does not refer to land there and the place itself may not be in Kent; alternatively it may be a lost Kentish settlement.
32. Most of these interpretations are based on *PNK* and *KPN*. Horsted is not recorded by Wallenberg, but appears on the first edition O.S. and is now represented by Hostye. Ramsden is not recorded by Wallenberg, and may rather mean 'raven's *denn*'. *Honeyden* was near the present Cray Hall; its second element may be *denu*. *Bulkeden* was in Dartford, but its site is uncertain; it too may be a *denu* name: *PNK*, 19, 33. In such areas boundary settlements are often found on ridgeways dividing early estates – e.g., *Clavvokisden* was on the Downland ridgeway dividing Kemsing and Shoreham: Ward, 225.
33. For this development in the Milton Regis area, see Ch. 11, section 5.
34. Hollingbourne still claimed manorial rights over part of Bredhurst in the eighteenth century, and the rector of Hollingbourne was patron of the living: H, V, 585, 590.
35. *PNK*, 587–8.
36. In such heavily Romanized parts of Kent, is there perhaps an older pattern

behind cases like these? Professor S. Applebaum points out that Carolingian estates sometimes perpetuated a Roman tenurial structure of 'estate-centres surrounded by rings of peripheral holdings (*mansi*)': 'The pattern of settlement in Roman Britain', *AHR*, XI (1963), 2. The possibility may be worth exploring in Kent; but names like Twitham and Tickenhurst imply woodland clearance in the *English* period.

37. Furley, II, 743 n.
38. H, V, 476, IV, 243; the chapel at Lidsing no longer exists.
39. H, II, 362, 373, 381, 524, 82.
40. H, VIII, 95. Nackington appears as a subordinate church in *DM*; the mother-church is not named, but manorial and topographical evidence suggests it was in the Stour valley, and Staplegate outside Canterbury was in Nackington: H, IX, 293.
41. H, IX, 550, 557, where 1696 is an error for 1396: cf. 603.
42. H, II, 550; Lullingstone Peyforer, near the Roman villa, was united with Lullingstone Ross in 1412.
43. For Bromhey see H, III, 535.
44. For Ashdown see Ch. 11, section 5; for Lydden, *DM*, 78. *ODEPN* derives Lydden from *denn*; *PNK*, 452, prefers *denu*.
45. Detached portions of parishes often indicate former pasture. Luddenham, for example, had 22 acres detached south-east of Faversham, and a further 32 between Goodnestone and Boughton on the edge of Blean Forest: H, VI, 386–7. For the detached land of Murston and Milton at Herst Hall (H, VI, 145), see Ch. 11, section 2. Sometimes, as at Herst Hall and Uplees (H, VI, 387), it was these circumstances that encouraged boundary settlement.
46. These figures relate to proven cases only; a dependent origin is likely in all cases.
47. A chapel-of-ease at Oare: H, VI, 384.
48. The structure of 'honours' and 'baronies' is rarely significant in Kent in this connexion, and bears little relation to older territories: cf. Ch. 10, section 4.
49. H, IX, 604, 394, 401, 579, 550, 558, 605. 'Borsholders' were officers of the 'boroughs' (*borghi*) of Kent.
50. H, VI, 17, 6, 27, 36, 47; H, V, 572. They are recorded as dependent churches of Newington in *DM*, 78, but not in the medieval evidence cited by Hasted. Upchurch and Halstow are on the Foothills and in the Marsh, not on the Downs.
51. Ward, 226–7; H, III, 91, 82, 62. Ward's identification of some of the other estates here is doubtful.
52. It also had marshland boroughs at Stourmouth, about five miles to the south.
53. Not all these pastures appertained to Reculver itself; the area as a whole was also intercommoned by Chilham, Chartham, Selling, Sheldwich, and Boughton-under-Blean, in whose outland it was situated.
54. Other names in 'way' are also sometimes significant, as at Shepway ('sheep way') in Lympne and in Maidstone.
55. According to Philipott, cited by Furley, I, 390, Bleangate Hundred derived

its name from 'the way to the Blean or [? for] common of herbage'. After the Conquest Faversham Abbey received rents known as 'gate-silver' in respect of 'nine gates leading to the said Blean . . .' This common local word sometimes came by extension to imply a 'track' in Kent; but it derives from OE *geat*, not ON *gata*.

56. Furley, I, 412n., quoting White Kennett, *Parochial Antiquities attempted in the History of Ambrosden, Burcester, and other parts in the Counties of Oxford and Bucks. A Glossary to explain the original words and phrases* (1695); H, VI, 26, 396. The shereway at Sheldwich known as Selgrave Lane or the Portway (H, VI, 494) may be prehistoric.
57. I.e., in names relating to *settlements*; if those relating to woods or pastures as such were included, the topographical proportion would of course be much greater.
58. Cf. George Sturt, *A Farmer's Life* (1922), 73.
59. Horses are indicated, for example, in Studdal in Mongeham, Hanslett's Forstal in Ospringe, Horselees in Boughton-under-Blean, and perhaps in Stud Hill in Herne, Wrinsted in Frinsted, Horsted in Chatham, and Horsted near Orpington; goats in Tickenhurst in Northbourne and Gatteridge in Denton; and geese in Goss Hall in Ash-by-Wingham.
60. The creation of medieval deer-parks is another matter.
61. Perhaps referring to the wild boar (cf. *EPNE*, I, 153–4); but in the Swingfield ('swine field') area it occurs among names referring to swine-pasture.
62. There are difficulties on the Downs in distinguishing names in *denn* from those in *denu*; those in which *denu* may be represented are asterisked. Names not recorded by Wallenberg and for which early forms are needed are marked‡.
63. Now Fernfield.
64. Now Everden.
65. Swalecliffe's lost pasture of *Chathurst* is identified in *KPN*, 308, with *Chetterste at Merestune*, recorded in the thirteenth century. If this is correct, *Merestune* cannot be Merston near Shorne, as *KPN* suggests, since Shorne is near Gravesend. Swalecliffe's other links were with Sturry, Hernehurst, and Shoart in Hackington, in the Blean area.
66. *KPN*, 277–8.
67. Swanley, 'swineherd's clearing', is also in this area, but on the Darent side of the watershed.
68. Other, more isolated, Downland *dens* include: Heronden in Eastry, Denne in Woodnesborough, Denne in Chilham, Lavington in Wye, and Oakenden in Luddesdown.
69. Cf. the lost *dens* of *Earnesherst* and *Chathurst*.
70. Witney, 76 *et passim*.
71. Cf. Michael Winstanley, *Life in Kent at the Turn of the Century* (1978), Ch. III, 'Oxen'. But in north-east Kent horses may have been used for draught purposes as early as the seventh century; Stodmarsh, 'stud marsh', is recorded in a charter of 675: *KPN*, 9.
72. *EPNE*, II, 154; *ODEPN*, 422; see p. 142, *supra*. For Devonshire examples see W. G. Hoskins and H. P. R. Finberg, *Devonshire Studies* (1952), 302–4.

73. *AC*, LXVI (1953), 144–5; cf. also Kenneth Cameron, *English Place-Names* (1963), 147–8.
74. Stockbury is wrongly interpreted in *ODEPN*, 423, and *EPNE*, I, 302, as 'the *bær* or swine-pasture of the people at Stoke'. Stoke is 20 miles from Stockbury and there was never any connexion between the two places. In *EPNE*, II, 155, a different interpretation is suggested: 'the *burh* of the people of a *stoc*'. There is a motte-and-bailey site at Stockbury; but on topographical grounds *stoc* + *ingas* + *bær* seems a more likely explanation.
75. 'Dunstall' seems to have also occurred elsewhere in Kent, for example in Wrotham: cf. J. L. Semple, 'The Manor of Wrotham in the early sixteenth century' (dissertation for Diploma in Local History, University of Kent at Canterbury, 1982), 25 *et passim*.
76. *KPN*, 50–1; *PNK*, 224; *EPNE*, I, 42, 231–2; Sandred, 68.
77. There is a short note on this word and on 'homestall', 'tunstall', and 'borstal', by Gordon Ward in *AC*, LXXVI (1961), 207–9; his apparent belief that such places were used for tethering visitors' horses cannot be taken seriously.
78. *EPNE*, I, 184. Or is it possible that it was in some way connected with the 'forelands' and 'forelanders', i.e. holders of more recent clearances in the forest, as described by Professor F. R. H. Du Boulay in *The Lordship of Canterbury* (1966; e.g., 135n., 165, etc.) and *AC*, LXXVI (1961), 82? The word does not seem to be recorded before the Conquest; my earliest reference is in 1119, when Robert de Crevequer granted the canons of Leeds 'the forstal, which was before their gate' in the foundation charter of the priory: H, V, 491–2.
79. *PNK*, 431.
80. H, VI, 446. 'Fostall' represents a common dialect pronunciation.
81. The rest are mostly on the Chart at places like Longsole in Aylesford. This distribution is influenced no doubt by the heavy capping of clay-with-flints on the Downs; but the absence of *sol* on the claylands of the Weald (where ponds are common), the Gault, and the Blean shows that the distribution is not purely environmental in origin.
82. *KPN*, 146–7, 150, 263–4.
83. *KPN*, 106; see also *KPN*, 140, and discussion of these names under a related but dubious charter dated to 699, *KPN*, 27–8. Wallenberg identified the 'king's cowland' with the lost Kingsland in Faversham hundred.
84. *KPN*, 146; but the church site is below the crest.
85. Furley, II, 341–2.
86. Cf. Ch. 2, n. 47. No great weight should, however, be attached to this figure.
87. *PNK*, 295, 127. 'Sheep hurst' probably indicates the feeding of sheep off the browse.
88. *PNK*, 450, 441. Hopton in Alkham is not recorded until 1477 unless Wallenberg's tentative but unlikely identification of it with Upton (1327) is accepted; in that case it is not from *hop*.
89. Furley, I, 255; the Wickhambreaux reference may not relate to the Downland part of the parish. Domesday in any case makes little of sheep com-

pared with swine; there are only two other references for Kent, at Higham and Cliffe-at-Hoo. Other Downland sheep-names, such as Sheepcote in St Mary Cray, are not recorded by Wallenberg and may be relatively modern.

90. But not in all: Horsted probably means 'stud-farm'; Milsted indicates a 'milking place'; Tunstead (Lancs.) was also a vaccary (*EPNE*, II, 199); in Sweden *stad* means dairy farm (Sandred, 127).
91. I hope to write on this topic more fully elsewhere; the evidence is complex, and only a brief summary is possible here. Linguistically, Sandred's study is definitive; topographically, more remains to be said, and his views on the antiquity of south-eastern names in 'stead' (Sandred, 14, 174–5) need modification. I have traced about 10 further 'steads' in Kent which he does not record, though for several of these early forms are needed.
92. Cowsted, Nettlested, Yelsted, and Rumsted near Stockbury; Norsted, Luxted, Horsted, Halstead, and perhaps Silversted near Cudham. The latter are in the same neighbourhood as Tubbenden, Walden, Hockenden, etc., discussed earlier.
93. At Highsted in Chislet there is evidence of Iron Age, Romano-British, and perhaps early Anglo-Saxon settlement: *AC*, XCII (1976), 236–8. But this is on the former edge of the Blean and may represent Jutish recolonization of secondary woodland rather than continuity of occupation.
94. See n. 31, *supra*.
95. Cited by Sandred, 134.
96. H, IX, 330.
97. See, for example, Sandred, 174–5.
98. The *hām* + *stede* names are usually the earliest recorded in Kent. The total number of elements represented is 72, since some names contain more than one.
99. Trees occur 15 times (pear 4 times); birds 3; vegetation 4 (nettles 3); type of ground (stony, etc.) 4; situation (north, high, etc.) 6; hills, valleys, streams 6; forest clearings 3 (?5); pasture 7; cultivation once, at Whetsted, first recorded as a swine-pasture.
100. Cf. Jolliffe, 39, 71 *et passim*.
101. Such as the Wealden timber-rights of great monastic houses like Christ Church.
102. See Ch. 4, pp. 90–2 and n. 47, *supra*.
103. Knockholt and Downe, for example, are probably thus included under Orpington.
104. Most of these were in the early-colonized Downland east of the Dour valley, at places like Whitfield, East Langdon, Little Mongeham, Guston, and St Margaret-at-Cliffe; this distribution further emphasizes the role of the church in early Kentish settlement.
105. One tenant is actually described as a villein. Cf. Ch. 4, pp. 90–2 and n. 47, *supra*.
106. As in Yorkshire and Shropshire. At Myddle the outlying woodlands (still known as 'out grounds' in the early seventeenth century) were divided up into predominantly freeholder townships. Dr Hey believes they may have originated as dependent dairy farms like the 'booths', 'stalls', and 'wicks'

elsewhere, and suggests a parallel with the outlying parts of parishes on the Pennine foothills in south Yorkshire: *An English Rural Community* (1974), 21–31. There is clearly a parallel here with the 'stalls', 'steads', and 'stocks' of Downland parishes in Kent.

107. See Ch. 11, section 5.
108. Jolliffe, 17–18; Smith, *op. cit.*, 120; cf. Witney, 158, 172–3; Furley, II, 413, regarding the 'free yokes' of Wye. See also Du Boulay, *Lordship of Canterbury*, 122–5, for yokes, jugation, *loghi*, etc.
109. Smith, *op. cit.*, 120, described it as 'the traditional area of an immemorially free peasantry', perhaps over-enthusiastically.
110. As at Chevening (H, III, 107), Shoreham (H, III, 3), Northbourne (H, IX, 585–6), and Otford (Ward, 95): such yokes were in the *outlying* parts the Original Lands, as at Twitton on the Otford boundary.
111. E.g., Yokes Court in Frinsted. They are also characteristic of the Chart: Leeds was divided into six yokes (H, V, 490).
112. As in Jolliffe, 39. The fact that it remained the custom of the whole region, as in Wales, not merely of isolated areas or places, is to be noted. There is a brief but useful account of gavelkind in Kent, pointing out its partial parallels with Celtic tribal custom, in H. R. Loyn, *Anglo-Saxon England and the Norman Conquest* (1962), 185–6.
113. Smith, *op. cit.*, 120; cf. also Du Boulay, *Lordship of Canterbury*, 306–7, for 'gavelkind yokelands' of Otford in 1388.
114. *PNK*, 264; Wallenberg records a dozen or so, and there are certainly others. For the possible significance of names in *cild* see Jolliffe, 27.
115. The fact that Bistock, Bayford, and Boyke specifically denote vaccaries is noteworthy.
116. H, IX, 305–6, II, 468. Hasted was wrong in believing the Hodsolls gave their name to Hodsoll: the place-name is recorded in 1198 (*PNK*, 37). The Hardreses are said to have held land in Hardres as early as 1080.
117. H, IX, 251, VIII, 37–8, 215; *PNK*, 456–7. The Oxindens eventually moved to Deane in Wingham, the Honywoods to Evington in Elmsted.
118. *PNK*, 239; H, V, 378–9. They must have left *fugol + mere*, before Edward II, when they are recorded at Herst in Otterden nearby; their original farm is lost, but is represented by Filmer Wood in Wichling.

8 ECCLESIASTICAL DEVELOPMENT

1. Peter Clark, *English Provincial Society from the Reformation to the Revolution: Religion, Politics and Society in Kent 1500–1640* (1977), 6.
2. For St Margaret's see *PNK*, 121n. Lillechurch survives as a farm-name.
3. For St Giles see H, X, 248.
4. This type of place-name was once much more numerous in Kent; 11 of the 22 churches attached to Lympne in *DM*, 78, bore names like *Ordgarescirce* (now Orgarswick) and *Blacemannescirce* (now Blackmanstone).
5. Furley, II, 499 n.; H, VII, 145.
6. The parish church of St Nicholas was refounded as a leper hospital by Lanfranc c.1084; it was then known as 'the hospital of the forest, or wood of

Blean' (H, IX, 12, 16; cf. Newman, *EK*, 326); the name Harbledown is not recorded until 1175.
7. The vast majority are recorded in *DM*, *TR*, or DB.
8. All three were chapelries; but Capel is basically a Norman structure.
9. More than 100 church towers were rebuilt in this period, and there are probably more surviving farmhouses of the time in Kent than in any other county.
10. See Ch. 2, n. 16.
11. H. P. R. Finberg, *The Formation of England, 550–1042* (1974), 209.
12. Often now written as 'cross'; but early references usually show that a 'crouch', and not a mere cross-roads, is referred to.
13. My earliest reference to a wayside cross in Kent is in the 'Liber de Hyda' of 993 (for 996; cited in Furley, I, 144), regarding the bounds of Nackington. Such crosses were often associated with boundaries (cf. Furley, II, 4), and evidently sometimes 'held in great reverence' (cf. H, X, 229, for those on the Minster-Birchington road).
14. *PNK*, 457; Wallenberg's suggestion that it referred to a building 'resembling' a shrine seems pointless.
15. *KPN*, 21–2. Minster-in-Thanet is called Southminster; *Upminster* is also called Northminster in 943 (*KPN*, 258–9) and according to Wallenberg was near Southminster, so that it must have been in Thanet. Douglas tentatively identified it with St Peter-in-Thanet (*DM*, 11 and n.), but this was certainly only a chapelry of Minster. A charter of 748 (*ASC*, 94) refers specifically to *two* minsters in Thanet: that of 'St Mary' (Minster itself), and that of 'St Peter and St Paul'. Monkton is the only other recorded mother-church in Thanet; it was an ancient possession of Christ Church; though it lies only 50 feet above sea-level, that is 'up' in relation to Minster; and though the church itself is west-north-west of Minster, the land north of Minster was in Monkton's territory. The suggestion that it was the second minster is perhaps further confirmed by a charter of c.761 granting to the abbess 'of St Peter's Minster, Thanet' remission of toll on two ships at Fordwich and Sarre (*ASC*, 78), since Sarre was a daughter-church of Monkton. In that case the present dedication of Monkton to St Mary Magdalene cannot be the original one; it is an unlikely dedication for a minster (see Ch. 9), though there is no record that it was altered.
16. *DM*, 15; but the problems of identification make one question so positive a figure. I identify *Wulfereston* (*DM*, 78) with Wolverton, since *PNK*, 442, shows that the first element of Wolverton is *Wulfhere*. For the pre-Conquest significance of churches in the *Textus Roffensis* see Gordon Ward, 'The list of Saxon churches in the Textus Roffensis', *AC*, XLIV (1932), 39–59, especially 54sqq.
17. *DM*, 78–9.
18. Douglas's tentative identification of the last with Eastry is manifestly incorrect. The dependent churches in question do not in fact form a coherent group and may not have been subordinate to any single minster; several are remote from Eastry.
19. It omits more than 70 churches mentioned elsewhere in *DM*, and such

well-evidenced minsters as Faversham, Eastry, Sheppey, Thanet, and Reculver.
20. Re-dedicated to All Saints when re-founded as a collegiate church by Archbishop Courtenay in 1395.
21. It was a chapelry of Reculver, in the Forest of Blean: H, IX, 92–4.
22. H, VI, 175, VII, 345; *KPN*, 45–6, 182.
23. *ASC*, 110–11; Newman, *EK*, 361, 414; H, VII, 432, VIII, 82, IX, 115–16.
24. For Dover see H, IX, 478–9, 507sqq.; Folkestone, H, VIII, 154; Maidstone, H, IV, 285; Lympne, H, VIII, 288–98 *passim*; Teynham, H, VI, 284; Wingham, H, IX, 226; Newington (part of the Milton *regio*), H, VI, 47; Hoo, H, IV, 3; Sheppey, H, VI, 217–18; Thanet, H, X, 268. Hasted's dating of charters cannot of course always be accepted. See also *KPN* and *ASC, passim*, for discussion of relevant charter evidence; also Newman, *EK* and *WK*, under places mentioned in the text.
25. H, IV, 320–1, 357–8, 363–4.
26. H, IX, 92–4, 96, 100, 123, X, 226, 238, 245. The lost All Saints originated as a chapelry of St Nicholas-at-Wade, and hence as a 'granddaughter' of Reculver.
27. H, X, 288, 352, 374–5, 403–4. Minster also claimed over Stonar: H, X, 414.
28. This relates to the 14 'rural' minster parishes only: the original area of the 'urban' minster-parishes in Canterbury, Rochester, and Dover cannot be recovered. The real average was rather higher than 4,340 acres, since Reculver had lost much of its land to the sea by the time its area was first recorded (at 1,214 acres).
29. Newman, *EK*, 274–6. St Martin le Grand was the original minster (*DM*, 9 and n.); but St Mary-in-Castro and probably St Mary's in the town are also of seventh-century origin.
30. Copley, 174, 276, 277–8; Jessup, 200.
31. Copley, 163, 174, 278, 277, 282, 276; Jessup, 167.
32. See Ch. 9, section 3.
33. Newman, *EK*, 188–9. Names like Stonecrouch in Goudhurst (*PNK*, 311) and Stone Cross in Seal (Ward, 145) no doubt indicate former crosses of stone; but these were probably of post-Conquest origin.
34. The latter was associated with the Westgate or *Estursete regio*; one of the two may have been St Augustine's Abbey.
35. *DM*, 79, lists Hollingbourne as a dependent church of Maidstone; if it in fact formed part of the Maidstone minsterland, it early became independent, since it gave birth to eight daughter-churches of its own, one or two of which may have existed in the eighth century. For Monkton see n. 15, *supra*.
36. 4,004 acres excluding the freakish parish of Lydd (12,000 acres); 4,340 acres including Lydd. The 1,155-acre parish of Trottiscliffe is an interesting exception.
37. There are also puzzle-churches like Stone-by-Faversham, which incorporates part of a Romano-British pagan mausoleum: Newman, *EK*, 452. The possibility that there were other (unrecorded) pre-Augustinian churches in Kent, in addition to that at Canterbury, must likewise be borne in mind.

Notes

38. They averaged 3,450 acres, or more than twice the size of the average 'bookland' parish.
39. H, II, 109, 82. The manor of Orpington Magna claimed over Hayes and Downe as well as over Knockholt and St Mary Cray (H, II, 98); Downe was subordinate to Hayes, but the rector of Orpington was patron of Hayes and possessed the parsonage of Downe in right of his rectory (H, II, 58). There were also 'free chapels' at Aperfield in Cudham and Crofton in Orpington; the latter may once have been parochial (H, II, 69, 101, 103); there was a further chapel at Cory Yokes in Knockholt (Ward, 211). These circumstances illustrate the complexity behind some of these secondary ecclesiastical units.
40. *KPN*, 84. The name survived as Newell, at the river-head near the church.
41. Lidsing was a chapel-of-ease; Grange and Twydall were founded or perhaps refounded in the late medieval period (H, IV, 235, 237). The fact that Henry I in his 22nd year gave the rectory of Gillingham, 'with the chapels, tithes, and other appurtenances belonging to it', to Minster-in-Sheppey (H, IV, 246) suggests that more than one chapel already existed, and the tithe index sheets show that Grange possessed a distinct territory of its own.
42. I use the word 'bookland' to describe these churches generically; we cannot of course prove that all were established on land actually held by 'book'.
43. Bearsted is not wholly on the Chart; Hollingbourne also gave birth to Hucking and Bredhurst on the Downs to the north; Pevington disappeared in the sixteenth century (H, VII, 473); the DM evidence (*DM*, 79) may imply that Westwell (with Hothfield and Great Chart?) was once dependent on Wye.
44. *DM*, 13, 78; H, IV, 20.
45. The Mean or minnis between High Halstow and St Mary's Hoo was still 'indefinitely divided' as late as 1870: *The Imperial Gazetteer of England and Wales* (1870), III, 844.
46. A document of 855 quoted in Furley, II, 815, shows that 'manorial' churches and tithes in manorial hands were already usual by that date; but the provenance of the document is not stated. The word 'parish' first appears in the seventh century in the earliest life of St Cuthbert: F. M. Stenton, *Anglo-Saxon England* (1971 edn), 148.
47. F. R. H. Du Boulay, *The Lordship of Canterbury* (1966), 126. Cf. D. J. Bonney, 'Early boundaries and estates in southern England', in P. H. Sawyer (ed.), *Medieval Settlement: Continuity and Change* (1976), 72–82.
48. Newman, *WK*, 336; Ward, 211, 120; R. Ogley (ed.), *Lady Boswell's School, 1675–1975* (1976), 9; H, X, 339, VI, 500; *PNK*, 214. At Ightham Mote there is also a Tudor chapel.
49. H, VII, 18, VI, 500, VIII, 438, 172, 209, 123–4, X, 365, 278; Newman, *EK*, 369–70. Durlock, St John's Jerusalem, St John's Swingfield, and Our Lady's Broadstairs survive.
50. A-F, I, 494, II, 361; H, IX, 113, 216.
51. For Harbledown, see H, IX, 16; Tonge, H, VI, 135; Maidstone, Newman, *WK*, 384; Sevenoaks, H, III, 104; Dover, H, IX, 535; Ospringe, H, VI,

521–2; Sandwich, H, X, 185–6; Chatham, H, IV, 215; Hythe, H, VIII, 246; Buckland, H, IX, 466. At Harbledown, Maidstone, Sevenoaks, and probably elsewhere, the chapel antedated the hospital.
52. Ward, 211; H, IV, 441.
53. H, IV, 40.
54. H, III, 273–4. This has been wrongly identified with Bidborough; but Bidborough was a rectory in its own right, not a chapel of Leigh. Betburgh is no doubt the bridge called *Bittebregge* referred to in H, III, 266, which still survives as Bid Bridge and is otherwise recorded in 1353 (*PNK*, 85).
55. H, VII, 103–4; now known as Sissinghurst and rebuilt in 1837–8.
56. Ogley, *loc. cit.*
57. Many, for example, exercised more or less limited burial rights: e.g., St Edmund the Martyr, Dartford (H, II, 326–7); St Nicholas, Harbledown (H, IX, 16); the Maison Dieu, Ospringe (H, VI, 522); Preston in Shoreham (H, III, 4); and St Peter's Maidstone. At Maidstone and Ospringe the burial-rights *antedated* the hospital.
58. H, X, 314, implies that it was built for the local population, but pp. 338–9 make plain its manorial origins.
59. H, IX, 602–3, 609, 610, X, 106, 117.
60. H, IX, 28–32, VII, 312–15. Horton had all the privileges of the mother church except burial rights.
61. H, IX, 322, 326.
62. These facts illustrate the ambiguous status of many such chapels in Kent. Hasted lists Stansted as a separate parish, but though it had its own district and its own distinct boundaries, it was actually a mere chapelry of Wrotham; its curate was appointed by the rector of Wrotham, who received all the tithes (H, V, 1–5, 27). Plaxtol, by contrast, had no clearly defined district; its curate received no *de jure* maintenance from Wrotham, but depended, like a Dissenting minister, on local bequests and *ex gratia* donations for a living. The place-name itself, moreover, refers only to a hamlet, not to a tithing or borough (*borgh*); when the late medieval chapel was rebuilt in 1648–9, it was paid for by the inhabitants of the boroughs of Hale and Roughway. Hasted may well be right in suggesting that before Plaxtol chapel was built, the inhabitants of this area resorted to the manorial chapel at Old Soar: H, V, 22–6; Newman, *WK*, 443–4. On the tithe index sheets Comp is marked as a detached part of Leyborne parish; but for its former association with Wrotham see H, V, 22.
63. H, VIII, 215, and cf. *PNK*, 456–7; the Honywoods still held this farm in Hasted's time.
64. Sometimes these were detached buildings in the churchyard: cf. H, VIII, 325 (Aldington), X, 117 (Eastry), VI, 525 (Ospringe), and V, 271–2 (Pembury). That at Eastry was dedicated to Our Lady and may not have been manorial. Generally, however, they were built to the north or south of the chancel, as in other counties, and attached to particular manorial estates. At Milsted, for example, the south chapel pertained to Higham Court, c.2m. away, and the north to Milsted Court Lodge, *alias* Hogshaw, near the church.

Notes

65. H, IX, 153; *DM*, 79. And were the burial rights spasmodically exercised at such obscure manorial chapels as the Bucklands' at Preston in Shoreham (H, III, 4) in fact legitimate?
66. H, X, 183; this chapel still survives. For a late medieval example see Furley, II, 445–6, regarding Roger Harlackenden of Harlackenden in Woodchurch.
67. Those excluded are as follows: (a) 8 parishes of minsters and mother-churches whose original extent cannot safely be reconstructed; (b) c.40 small urban parishes in Canterbury, Rochester, Dover, etc.; (c) c.40 parishes whose status is uncertain, or whose original extent cannot now be ascertained. The two very large mother-parishes of Lydd (12,000 acres) and Tonbridge (15,000 acres) have also been excluded to avoid distorting the average.
68. The DB evidence cannot be used for this purpose in Kent, since it is based on manors which were not necessarily coincident with parishes and included substantial detached areas, particularly in the Weald.
69. Except in the Weald where, as explained earlier, different circumstances operated.
70. Cf. pp. 90–2 and n. 47, *supra*.

9 CHURCH-DEDICATIONS

1. Those of lost churches that are known tend to follow the same pattern as dedications of surviving churches. In England as a whole 666 dedications were lost when A-F wrote (III, 452–7); some of these have since been recovered.
2. H, X, 286, 351, 371, 401, VIII, 437. At All Saints Staplehurst the number was even greater and included lights to St Catherine, St Christopher, St Erasmus, St James, St Margaret, St Nicholas, St George, St John the Baptist, St Mary Magdalene, St Anthony, St Loye, St Appollonius, St Blaise, St Clement, Holy Cross, St Michael, St Stephen, and St Peter: Anita Thompson, 'Family and society in Staplehurst, 1450–1660' (dissertation for Diploma in Local History, University of Kent at Canterbury, 1982), 6.
3. H, IV, 308–9; Newman, *WK*, 381. Gravesend St Mary's was rededicated to St George when rebuilt in 1731–3 following destruction by fire: H, III, 333.
4. *ODS*, 166. Most Kentish churches dedicated to St George existed by the eleventh century.
5. In towns dedications to All Saints are sometimes associated with the development of a new market, as at Northampton and Stamford. Fairs are often associated with patronal festivals; where they are not they sometimes indicate a former dedication. The mother-church of Monkton in Thanet may also have been rededicated: see Ch. 8, n. 15, *supra*.
6. Rochester Cathedral was rededicated to St Mary, but the original ascription to St Andrew was the one that survived.
7. Brookland, East Langdon, Northbourne, Richborough, Stonar, and Snave: H, VIII, 384, 395–6, IX, 550, 584, X, 414. Historically Richborough was

partly in Stonar and partly in Ash, and hence divided between St Augustine's and Christ Church: H, IX, 216–17, 193, X, 408, 414.
8. Brenzett was a 'limb' of Newington next Folkestone: H, VIII, 389.
9. H, II, 381–2, IV, 243; A-F, III, 436.
10. H, II, 321, 326–7. Probably this was one of the chapels of Dartford recorded in DB, which also indicates that the significantly named Hawley ('holy clearing') in Sutton originally formed part of Dartford: H, II, 294–5. There was a church of St Edmund in Canterbury and a chapel in Dover: Newman, *EK*, 287.
11. There was a chapel of St Bartholomew on the site of the Dover fair: H, IX, 516.
12. Those at Chatham and Sandwich still exist; for Otford see H, III, 29–30; for Saltwood, H, VIII, 228, 246; for Buckland, H, IX, 466–7. At Bobbing the hospital was at Key Street (H, VI, 193), but there was probably some connexion with the church of St Bartholomew.
13. There were also lights of St Anne in many Kentish churches.
14. Buckland by Faversham, Oxney, Sholden, Woodchurch-in-Thanet, Ospringe (a lost chapel), Newington next Folkestone, Blackwose or Canons Court in Newington, and a seashore chapel also at Newington. Elsewhere in Kent St Nicholas was particularly associated with droveways (see Ch. 10, section 3), and the chapel at Ospringe was specifically connected with 'the safety and good success of passengers' on Watling Street: H, VI, 500.
15. H, VIII, 438, 175, X, 365; A-F, I, 172–3. The proliferation of lights and altars at Lydd referred to earlier should be noted in this connexion; St Barbara, for example, was a protectress against thunder and lightning.
16. That is, OE but not primary foundations.
17. But the late medieval period saw a revival in dedications to the Holy Trinity: six of the total of nine in Kent were of this period, though none was parochial.
18. Where the church settlement is clearly within a certain zone, it is so classified here, though its parish may extend into other zones; Wye, for example, is classified under the Original Lands, though its parish included stretches of Downland.
19. But there are some interesting contrasts: for example, St Martin occurs only once on the Foothills (at Canterbury) but six times in Holmesdale, while St Augustine, St Margaret, and the Holy Trinity are not found in Holmesdale.
20. St Mary, and St Peter and St Paul, are not in fact represented in the Blean.
21. The lower figure is the correct one if the dedications to All Saints are not original.
22. That is, so far as the 320 dedications under discussion are concerned.
23. Bertha is not listed in *ODS*, but is described as a saint in A-F.
24. Quoted in *ODS*, 137; there is an account of the royal saints of Kent in A-F, II, 352–63.
25. No Kentish churches were actually dedicated to St Eanflæd and St Ercongota; for St Ermengitha see H, X, 271. St Edith's dates are not known; she is said to have been born at Kemsing, so that it seems difficult

Notes

to identify her with St Edith of Wilton (d. 984), as in *ODS*, 120. In addition to the church of St Mary and St Edith at Kemsing, there was a chapel in her honour by St Edith's Well and an image in the churchyard (H, III, 46; cf. bequest referred to in Ward, 202). No other Kentish church is associated with her name, but Ide Hill, c.7 miles distant, is first recorded as *Edythehell* in the thirteenth century (*PNK*, 70).

26. At least 20 churches in all were associated with them, and probably many more if subsidiary altars are included.
27. The former bishop of York, who returned to Kent as bishop of Rochester, where he was buried, and where (as at Canterbury) there was a cult in his honour: *ODS*, 318–19.
28. Furley, II, 304–5. The cult of Archbishop Winchelsea, especially among the poor of Kent, illustrates the continuing magnetism of Canterbury as a local pilgrimage centre; it occasioned the destruction of his shrine at the Reformation.
29. There were six churches of St Mary in Canterbury; the above figure includes only that founded by King Eadbald c.618 (Newman, *EK*, 222); three others may have been early foundations.
30. *ODS*, 136, 248.
31. In Kent, as elsewhere, virtually all dedications to St John relate to the Baptist; Ickham is the only parish church dedicated to the Evangelist, though there are two non-parochial chapels of post-Conquest origin, at Groombridge and (formerly) Sissinghurst.
32. Professor G. W. S. Barrow tells me that Holy Trinity was also an early dedication in Scotland. The episcopal see of Brechin and that of Moray (antedating the cathedral eventually fixed at Elgin) were both so dedicated. So too were several churches in the lower Tay valley region, including Dunkeld, Scone, Cupar, and St Andrews (parish church, not cathedral), which were almost certainly early foundations. He also points out that 'Holy Trinity' and 'Christ Church' seem in some sense to be regarded as equivalent, as at Dunfermline (a daughter-house of Canterbury) and at Christchurch in Hampshire.
33. The original dedication was presumably to St Martin, but as at other minsters the secondary dedication probably came into use at a very early date. Norman Scarfe (*The Suffolk Landscape* (1972), 103–4) points out that dedications to St Gregory relate to early churches in Suffolk.
34. *ODS*, 20; *ODEPN*, 6. But the derivation of the first element in Alkham from *ealh*, 'heathen temple', is questioned by Dr Margaret Gelling in 'Further thoughts on pagan place-names', in *Place-Name Evidence for the Anglo-Saxon Invasion and Scandinavian Settlements*, ed. Kenneth Cameron (1975), 103, 106. Only three other English parish churches were dedicated to St Anthony, at Byker, Cartmel Fell, and in London (A-F, III, 339); but in Kent there were also chapels associated with his name at Lydd and Westenhanger House: H, VIII, 65.
35. Cf. D. G. Hey, *The Making of South Yorkshire* (1979), 84–5. St Helen does not usually bear this signification elsewhere. Perhaps, after all, her association with the emperor Constantius and his son by her, Constantine, is sufficient

to account for her presence at Cliffe. For centuriation see Jessup, 169.
36. The fair at Cliffe was known as St Pelagius's Fair. No such saint seems to be recorded, though Pope Gregory's predecessor was so named (*ODS*, 177). In some accounts St Margaret of Antioch, commemorated in High Halstow nearby, is said to have originally been named Pelagia; is there a link here?
37. A-F, I, 169.
38. H, IX, 181. The charter supposedly of 616 is probably spurious (*ASC*, 443–4); but the fact that the 'liberties of Adisham' became the basis for other early estates of Christ Church implies that it belonged to the cathedral from a remote period.
39. It is the parish most nearly resembling the nucleated parishes of the Midlands; according to Hasted (IX, 180), it also had 'open common fields', though these no doubt were of the local not the Midland type; and at the Conquest it was reputedly 'a hundred within itself' (*ibid*.).
40. See n. 25 *supra*.
41. They were said to have fled to Faversham at a time of persecution and set up as shoemakers in Preston Street; their altar still exists in St Mary's church (*ODS*, 93). Their association with Lydd (H, VIII, 423–4; A-F, I, 145) should probably be connected with the early isolation of the place and the proliferation of local cults there.
42. Where no other source is given, the following account is based principally on Copley: see Ch. 5, section 2.
43. Newman, *EK*, 166, 362n.; Jessup, 23, 165; H, IX, 216–17. Though not formally dedicated to St Mildred, Minster-in-Thanet was universally associated with her, and the manor of Minster is recorded under her name in DB: H, X, 272.
44. Beyond Brabourne the course is less clear, but it seems to have terminated at Folkestone.
45. Assuming that All Saints Hollingbourne was originally dedicated to St Anne or St Mary and that four of the six churches of St Mary in Canterbury were early foundations.
46. These should be distinguished from churches like Boxley Abbey, Ashurst, and Gillingham, where notable cults developed at a later period: H, V, 279, IV, 246.
47. White Kennett, *Parochial Antiquities . . . of Ambrosden, Burcester and other adjacent parts in the counties of Oxford and Buckinghamshire* (1818), II, 303. The number is in fact greater in Norfolk (50) and Lincs. (30), where churches are more numerous; but in Kent St Margaret was also associated with many subsidiary chapels and altars, and with places like St Margaret's Crouch in Hawkhurst.
48. At Lower Halstow there is evidence of Roman occupation; both places were probably pre-Christian religious sites.
49. Jessup, 103–8.
50. A-F, II, 363; *ODS*, 279–80; *DNB*, *s.v.* St Mildred. Newman, *EK*, 361, says her remains were moved once more, in 1085, to Lyminge. For the cult of St Mildred see D. W. Rollason, *The Mildrith Legend: a Study in Early Medieval Hagiography in England* (1982).

Notes

51. The remarkable cult of Robert Winchelsea, which continued at Canterbury down to the Reformation though he was never canonized, may in a sense be regarded as the culmination of these regional cults: see n. 28, *supra*.
52. Wye and Kemsing have double dedications.
53. Sundridge and Plaxtol.
54. Malling is recorded in 942–6, Sutton Valence in 814, and Great Chart in 762: *KPN*, 252, 126, 45–6.
55. The evidence of dependence in this and subsequent paragraphs is based mainly on *DM* and H, supplemented by local histories where necessary. In a few cases it rests on reconstruction of individual minsterlands based partly on topographical evidence, as at Milton Regis (see Ch. 11). Some of the churches mentioned were chapels rather than full parish churches.
56. Hythe originated as a daughter of Saltwood, which itself was a daughter of Lympne. Parish boundaries suggest Buckland originated from Faversham; but it lies between Teynham and Stone, which is listed as a daughter of Teynham in *DM*.
57. St Nicholas is the dedication of the hospital chapel, but originally this was parochial: H, IX, 16.
58. East Malling seems to have been a secondary mother-church originating from Aylesford.
59. Dedications to St Lawrence of Rome are sometimes associated with Roman roads, and this may be the explanation of Godmersham, on the lost route from Canterbury to Ashford. But in Kent their most notable characteristic is their association with late OE churches, especially those on droveways (see Ch. 10, section 3); the fact that Godmersham was the mother-church of an early Christ Church estate (H, VII, 321) thus sets it apart from other churches of St Lawrence. That churches so dedicated elsewhere are on Roman roads does not necessarily indicate an early origin; it may arise from growth of traffic in the late OE or post-Conquest period.
60. Cf. A-F, II, 111.
61. *ODS*, 19–20, 244, 173, 270; cf. also A-F, II, 68sqq. for St Anthony.
62. St John the Baptist at New Hythe, Smallhythe, New Romney, Halling, and Erith ('gravel hithe'); St James at Elmley, Cooling (*via* Buckland Fleet and the Thames), Warden, Reculver, and Grain; St Michael at Hythe and New Romney; St Leonard at Hythe and Deal; and St Giles at Sarre and Tonge. At Deal and Tonge the church itself is not actually on tidal water.
63. Only St Leonard survives at Hythe, and St Nicholas at New Romney, by the quay once known as St Nicholas' Quay: Furley, II, 770. St Leonard was also the patron saint of captives and prisoners of war.
64. The saint in question was often the founder or an early abbess whose name was subsequently added to that of the original patron.
65. Dedications to the Holy Cross, St Radegund, St Cosmas and St Damian, St Blaise, St Faith, St Sepulchre, All Souls, and Corpus Christi are probably all post-Conquest.
66. Monkton may originally have been dedicated to St Peter and St Paul: see Ch. 8, n. 15, *supra*.

10 TOPOGRAPHICAL METHOD: ANALYSIS

1. *PNK*, 166–7.
2. See Ch. 6, section 1.
3. The hundred also included Sheppey and Elmley; it is doubtful if these two islands formed part of the estate of Milton.
4. David Hey, *The Making of South Yorkshire* (1979), 39–40, 84.
5. *PNK*, 489–90; no doubt it was not a new settlement at that date.
6. Charles Thomas, *Christianity in Roman Britain to A.D.500* (1981), 268.
7. H, IV, 307.
8. But not at a place like Westerham, the 'westerly *hām*' of the Darent valley.
9. H, V, 383 implies that East Sutton was subordinated to Sutton Valence at the request of Leeds Priory; in fact it is recorded in DB before the priory was founded.
10. H, III, 229; the pastures were in Somerden ('summer pasture') hundred.
11. M. Gelling, W. F. H. Nicolaisen, and M. Richards, *The Names of Towns and Cities in Britain* (1970), 169. The place-name is recorded in the List of Churches in *TR*; for the dating of this list and its probable pre-Conquest basis, see Gordon Ward, 'The list of Saxon Churches in the Textus Roffensis', *AC*, XLIV (1932), 54–9.
12. Hundreds are often named after trees as meeting-places (*EPNE*, II, 186); a meeting-place by seven oak trees would thus not be unusual.
13. At Tonbridge, significantly, the London road was likewise subsidiary to the High Street.
14. It is very rare to find a town sited on a hill-top in the pre-Conquest period, though other examples include Shaftesbury and Brill, both also on Greensand outcrops. These early heath-towns of England would perhaps repay comparative study.
15. *PNK*, 52. There would thus be a parallel between Codsheath and possible heathen sites like Gadshill in Higham, and Wormshill *alias* Godshill near Milton; 'Godshill' is the DB and *TR* form of Wormshill, which has been interpreted as 'Woden's hill' (*PNK*, 240), though this is questioned in Gelling, 'Further thoughts on pagan place-names', in *Place-Name Evidence for the Anglo-Saxon Invasion and Scandinavian Settlements*, Eight Studies collected by Kenneth Cameron (English Place-Name Society, 1975), 112.
16. In this context it is worth noting that 'heathen' is probably cognate with 'heath': *EPNE*, I, 220.
17. Strictly, Doddington is dedicated to the Beheading of John the Baptist.
18. 'Town' was used in Kent to mean 'township'; 'tithing' normally denotes an ecclesiastical 'tithery', not a secular unit or 'township'.
19. H, V, 52, describes Shipbourne as a chapelry of Tonbridge; but Tonbridge was a late secondary mother-church, not a minster, and may itself have originated from Wrotham. It seems likely that Ridley and Ash were also originally dependent on Wrotham.
20. H, IV, 2, 13–14; for Hoo St Margaret see *PNK*, 121n.
21. W. G. Hoskins, *Leicestershire: an Illustrated Essay on the History of the Landscape* (1957), 7; *The Imperial Gazetteer of England and Wales* (1870), IV, 312.

Notes

22. *DM*, 79; H, IX, 222, 260, 266, 232–4, 249, 212, 195. Ratling possibly still existed in 1286, when it formed one of the prebends of Wingham College; the ruins of Overland but not Fleet survived until Hasted's time.
23. *DM*, 79; H, IV, 357–8, 363–4, 320–1; Kelly's *Directory of Kent* (1882 edn), 345. Wallenberg's association on linguistic grounds of Loddington with Loddenden in Staplehurst (*PNK*, 138) provides further evidence of Maidstone's extension to the south. Loose is not recorded in *DM*, 79.
24. H, X, 375, 359 (St Peter's); H, IX, 193, 222 (Ash); H, IX, 242, 249 (Goodnestone); H, IX, 252, 260 (Nonington); H, IX, 263, 266 (Womenswold).
25. H, VI, 99, 194, 155; cf. also H, VI, 2–4, 171–2, for the correlation of the manor and hundred of Milton, in which these parishes lay.
26. But there was an outlying chapel in Cudham, at Aperfield.
27. But not often in the minster-parishes or in the Weald, where different circumstances operated, as explained earlier.
28. Midland churches on river-banks forming boundaries, as at Eaton Socon (Beds.), are also often eccentric.
29. Seal Chart was originally known as Kemsing Chart: Ward, 86–7.
30. That Addington gave birth to Offham is suggested by topography and by the fact that Addington once claimed over Hadlow, beyond Offham: in 1287 the rector of Hadlow still paid 18d. p.a. to the rector of Addington in token of this subservience: H, IV, 548. Addington itself had originated from Trottiscliffe.
31. H, IX, 291; Kelly, *op. cit.*, 511.
32. Ward, 211–12. For the origins of the parochial system as such, perhaps as early as the seventh century, see H. R. Loyn, *Anglo-Saxon England and the Norman Conquest* (1962), 245. Professor Loyn is not of course arguing that parish boundaries are generally of this date.
33. F. R. H. Du Boulay, *The Lordship of Canterbury* (1966), 126. See also Geoffrey Hewlett's reconstruction of the Otford boundary in *AHR*, XXI (1973), 94–110. The boundary of Godmersham has been reconstructed in detail by Mr J. McN. Dodgson, and I am much indebted to him for taking me and parties of students round it on several occasions. There is no authoritative study yet available of the Kentish charter-bounds as a whole. While isolated *individual* points may be recognized topographically without undue difficulty, it must be stressed that the reconstruction of any boundary *in toto* demands very intensive scrutiny on the ground, on large-scale maps, and in early perambulations and other records. No such systematic reconstruction of the numerous bounds recorded for Kent has been possible for this book, and I have necessarily depended on the work of others. There is a complete list of the surviving charter-bounds for Kent in P. R. Kitson, *Studies in Anglo-Saxon Charter Boundaries* (Ph.D. thesis, University of Cambridge, 1982), 182sqq.
34. An eighth daughter-parish, Bredhurst, was detached.
35. H, VI, 306, 314–15; *DM*, 79.
36. For Berks. examples see Margaret Gelling, *Signposts to the Past* (1978), 192, 194.

37. In Hasted's time the hundred of Westerham still comprised Westerham, Edenbridge, and part of Brasted and Cowden (H, III, 158). At an early date, probably for the creation of a borough and market, part of Brasted (including the church) had been split off to form the Ville and Borough [?*burh*, not *borgh*] of Brasted (cf. Maurice Beresford and H. P. R. Finberg, *English Medieval Boroughs: a Handlist* (1973), 128). Originally the whole parish had probably been in Westerham hundred, together with Edenbridge and part of Cowden.
38. Densole (*denn* + *sol*) appears as Densole Minnis in 1539/40 (*PNK*, 455); for Fernden (now Fernfield) see *PNK*, 440–1; it may be *dūn*, not *denn*.
39. *PNK*, 113; *KPN*, 57. Oakleigh is recorded in 774: *KPN*, 53–4 and n.
40. *PNK*, 111, 118. The meeting-place of Shamwell hundred is not known but it may have been near St Thomas's Well or at Gadshill, a name which recurs along with another *Shamwell* in Sittingbourne (formerly Milton). For Shamwell (*sceamol*, 'shamble') as 'a place where animals . . . were killed as a sacrifice to the god worshipped on Gadshill', see *PNK*, 371–2, 107.
41. Newman, *WK*, 376; Copley, 277.
42. A-F, I, 169; *DM*, 9n.; Newman, *EK*, 232–3.
43. Except possibly at Frittenden: Copley, 275.
44. Newman, *EK*, 417.
45. H. P. R. Finberg, *Gloucestershire: an Illustrated Essay on the History of the Landscape* (1955), 38; D. M. Palliser, *The Staffordshire Landscape* (1976), 53; Trevor Rowley, *The Shropshire Landscape* (1972), 81; Copley, 194; *PNK*, 184.
46. *AC*, LXXXIV (1969), 79; Copley, 183; *PNK*, 306. Roman occupation has been found beneath Chilham Castle.
47. Is there a link here with the widespread survival in England of Celtic river-names?
48. Jessup, 195.
49. *Cantium*, v.iii (1973), 50; H, III, 32, 526, and map facing 303; H, VIII, 174; Walter Jerrold, *Highways and Byways in Kent* (1907), 35, 358; *ex inf.* Canon D. Ingram Hill. St Eanswythe's Water was strictly speaking an aqueduct, believed to flow miraculously uphill from its source in Bredmer Wood.
50. Hollingbourne Fair was held on the feast of St Anne: H, V, 463.
51. Several of these springs and wells are on boundaries. In the Lower Halstow neighbourhood, in addition to Holywell, there are six other well-names: Wardwell, Libbetwell, Chinkwell, Chalkwell, Wellfield, and Funton or 'fountain': H, IV, 409, 427, VI, 64; see also $2\frac{1}{2}''$ O.S. map and tithe index map.
52. Cf. H, V, 417, 418, VIII, 211; for Kemsing and Charing see Ch. 4, n. 43, and relevant text.
53. Many springhead churches and chapels are now above the springline owing to the fall in the water-table, especially on the Downland dipslope. In Hasted's time the Dour, for example, rose at Drellingore in Alkham: H, VIII, 134.
54. For Hythe, see H, VIII, 249–50; Sittingbourne, H, VI, 153; St John's Greatness, Ward, 14–16, 87–8; Harbledown, H, IX, 15–16; St Leonard's Malling, H, IV, 519–20, 523, 529, and Newman, *WK*, 579–80; St Blaise's

Notes

Bromley, A-F, I, 494; Bapchild, H, VI, 128–9, *PNK*, 242, and *KPN*, 21–2, 24.
55. H, III, 46, 29–30. There were also lights of St Anne in many Kentish churches; she was believed to have given birth to the Virgin Mary in her old age.
56. H, VII, 342.
57. E.g., St Nicholas's Harbledown, St Bartholomew's Sandwich, St John's Sevenoaks, and St James's Sittingbourne.
58. Jessup, 185–6, 196; Newman, *WK*, 373–4.
59. Newman, *EK*, 452; Copley, 272; Ward, 127–30; H, III, 24.
60. H, VI, 135; *PNK*, 265–6, 371. After the Conquest, when Sittingbourne was carved out of Milton, *Godshill* and *Shamwell* were included in the new parish; *Puckeshall* seems to have been in Tonge, which had been formed out of Milton at an earlier date. The above interpretation of *Puckeshall* and *Shamwell* is only one of several possibilities.
61. Jessup, 193.
62. *Ibid.*, 195.
63. Since final revision of this section in the summer of 1984, I have become more sceptical of the significance of holy wells and springs. There *is* a case for further investigation; but it has to be admitted that there are few places where we can be certain that well-cults antedated the Conquest. – *Author's note, September 1985.*
64. It is noteworthy, for example, that common-field systems often tend to become eccentric towards the edge of a *pays*, as in the east Cambs. hundred of Radfield: cf. VCH, *Cambs.*, VI (1978), 165 *et passim*. See also H. S. A. Fox, 'Approaches to the adoption of the Midland system', in *The Origins of Open-Field Agriculture*, ed. Trevor Rowley, 1981.
65. Taken alone, they seem to imply that Lyminge was carved out of Elham; actually Elham was a relatively late parish – it is not recorded until DB and is probably a *hamm*, not a *hām* – whereas Lyminge was an early minster.

11 THE LANDS OF MILTON REGIS: SYNTHESIS

1. Copley, 278.
2. H, VI, 167, 154, 164–5; Copley, 180.
3. H, VI, 171. 'Middleton' is of course a common place-name and does not always indicate a minster-settlement. In a personal communication Dr Margaret Gelling doubts if *middel tūn* can have been the original name of the Kentish *caput*, since the element *tūn* seems unlikely to occur as early as c.600; she queries if Milton can previously have been named after the *Sidingeburn*, which later gave its name to Sittingbourne. The idea is attractive, since so many estates derived their names from the word 'bourne'; but the name *Sidingeburn* is not actually recorded before 1200.
4. It was usually granted to successive queens as part of their dowry, or to other members of the royal house, who 'procured many exemptions and privileges' for the town, most of which it still retained in Hasted's day: H, VI, 172–3. For the early development of the lathe of Milton, see Jolliffe, 64–5 *et passim*.

Notes

5. Newman, *EK*, 375; Copley, 278.
6. Cf. *DM*, 78, which also lists Minster-in-Sheppey and an unidentified Newchurch under Newington. Minster's subordination was probably of recent origin, following its destruction during the Danish raids; Gordon Ward's identification of Newchurch with Borden (*ibid.*, n.) is incorrect, since Borden was a daughter of Milton.
7. *PNK*, 259.
8. The islands of Sheppey and Elmley were also included in the Hundred of Milton.
9. Kingsdown may be recorded as the name of a pasture in 850 (*KPN*, 191); but the charter recording it is dubious and the absence of any further record before 1182 suggests there may have been no permanent settlement or church. Borden is first recorded in 1177, Murston in 1198, Sittingbourne in 1200, and Radfield in 1254.
10. For convenience' sake the outlying part of Lenham parish, between Frinsted and Wichling, is referred to in this chapter as Ashdown, the name of its central farm near Chapel Wood, which probably marks the site of a former chapel. Milton's rights also extended over part of Iwade to the north, but the church was a chapelry of Teynham.
11. Around Milton and Bapchild it was typical 'roundtilt' land, i.e. land under continuous tilth, with no fallow: cf. H, VI, 123.
12. Dates of place-names mentioned in this chapter are normally based on the earliest reference in *PNK* or *KPN*. In some cases Wallenberg's identification is necessarily tentative; many settlements he does not record are no doubt of medieval or pre-Conquest origin.
13. Murston old church stood near the creek, opposite that of Milton.
14. H, VI, 3–4, 165, 166.
15. There may, of course, have been an earlier springhead shrine here, as at Bapchild, though there is no record of it. There may also have been a medieval market at Sittingbourne.
16. H, VI, 160–1.
17. Howt Green is on the boundary of Bobbing. Places mentioned in this chapter which are not recorded on the $2\frac{1}{2}''$ O.S. sheets have been located from earlier maps, such as the O.S. first edition, the tithe index sheets, Andrews and Dury's map of Kent (1769), and those in Hasted.
18. See H, VI, 177, for Northwood Chasteners, and cf. H, VI, 169–70, 171. It is marked as Chestnut Street to the west of Chalkwell (in Milton: H, VI, 164) by Andrews and Dury, who also mark Chestnut Street in Borden. The woodland for pannage of 220 hogs recorded in DB may have been in this area or in the Weald: H, VI, 172.
19. *PNK*, 253–4. It was from Highsted that the family-name of the Hasteds ultimately derived. A similar tongue of land stretched southwards from Maidstone towards Linton and probably had the same purpose.
20. Cf. *EPNE*, II, 154; W. G. Hoskins and H. P. R. Finberg, *Devonshire Studies* (1952), 302–4. Pitstock in Rodmersham and Pistock in Tunstall have confusingly been regarded as the same place; the O.S. first edition and Andrews and Dury make it plain they were distinct. The $2\frac{1}{2}''$ O.S. map adds

Notes

to the confusion by describing Woodstock as 'on the site of Pitstock'. Though H, VI, 94, says that the name of Pitstock or Pistock in Tunstall had recently been changed to Woodstock, *PNK*, 263–4, 272, makes it clear that Woodstock is an early name, first recorded in 1202.

21. That is, in what was then part of the Blean woodland, though historically the term is confined to the area east of Faversham.
22. H, VI, 145, 149.
23. H, VI, 3–4, 125, 117, 122, 191.
24. I.e., before Murston and Sittingbourne were carved out of it.
25. *KPN*, 21, 24. But the authenticity of the charter is not beyond doubt: cf. *ASC*, 76–7.
26. It was also where King Wihtred held his great council (H, VI, 123–4); the archaeological evidence associated with Stone and Hempsted should likewise be noted.
27. Tonge probably derives from *twang*, 'spit of land', or *tang*, 'tongs', perhaps referring to land in the fork of one of the streams in this neighbourhood: cf. *EPNE*, II, 176, 199; *ODEPN*, 455.
28. Dully probably derives from *lēah*; for Dungate, 'the gate to the down' on the border of Kingsdown, see *PNK*, 263; for Radfield see the tithe index map, Andrews and Dury's map, *PNK*, 242, and H, VI, 128–9.
29. *PNK*, 252, and cf. 286, 354 for the same element elsewhere.
30. Boundaries following Roman roads are not necessarily early, but those dividing early *regiones* and minsterlands in this way are in a different category from the late boundaries discussed by Margaret Gelling in *Signposts to the Past* (1978), 195.
31. Doddington and Stone are listed as subordinate churches of Teynham in *DM*, 79, and Doddington, Stone, and Lynsted (which lies between Teynham and Doddington) in H, VI, 294. Topographical evidence suggests that Norton, Newnham, and possibly Buckland should be added to these. Norton and Buckland lie between Stone and Teynham, and their churches are close to the Teynham boundary; boundaries also suggest that Newnham ('new-*hām*', 1177) went with them – it is sandwiched between the two parts of Doddington – and here there may have been a link with the manor of Newnham in Lynsted (H, VI, 298). In addition there was a detached chapelry of Teynham at Iwade (H, VI, 294), in which Milton likewise claimed rights.
32. Copley, 131–2, describes it as at Sittingbourne, but originally it was in Milton.
33. H, VI, 194, 202.
34. Hasted avoids saying that Milton claimed paramountcy over either place; that Tunstall was in some sense originally subordinate to Milton, however, is clear from H, VI, 99. The fact that Bobbing and Bredgar are omitted from DB but recorded in *DM* probably arises from their subordination to Milton.
35. H, VI, 92.
36. Cf. H, VI, 99, where Milton is said to claim over Bredgar parish 'as do the subordinate manors of Tunstall and Bobbing over some part of it.'

37. *EPNE*, II, 198, and cf. 142–3.
38. *PNK*, 255, and cf. 244.
39. H, VI, 192, 194.
40. *PNK*, 243. The first element is doubtful.
41. H, VI, 98.
42. H, VI, 99, 100, 101, 573.
43. H, VI, 69; the court baron of Tunstall also claimed over part of it: H, VI, 92.
44. *PNK*, 243–4.
45. Hasted (VI, 69) thought Sutton Baron derived its suffix from a court baron; but *PNK*, 245, shows that it probably means Sutton-in-Borden.
46. Cf. *KPN*, 113 (where Yoakes Court is placed in New Romney); *PNK*, 130.
47. H, V, 573, VI, 570.
48. H, VI, 74–5, 77, 78, 572 *et passim*; cf. Jolliffe, 26–7, for the yokes of Wye, whose names went back to Henry III.
49. H, IX, 328, 364, 369.
50. Cf. H, V, 556; for Ashdown see n. 10 *supra*.
51. H, V, 561–2, 568–9; cf. H, VI, 123.
52. The origin of these divisions is a difficult problem that cannot be pursued here, but like some of the hundreds they seem to have incorporated boundaries of older territorial units. They did not correspond to diocesan divisions; but they were based on the ancient county meeting-places of Canterbury and Maidstone (Penenden Heath).
53. There is some uncertainty here: the parish of Lenham was divided into East Lenham in Calehill hundred and Shepway lathe in East Kent, and West Lenham in Eyhorne hundred and Aylesford lathe in West Kent. The main settlement in Ashdown was apparently in West Lenham, but Syndale in Ashdown was in East Lenham.
54. *ODEPN*, 491–2; *PNK*, 238. The alternative sense, 'Winchele's pool', is less likely on topographical grounds.
55. *ODEPN*, 442; H, V, 556. Wrinsted itself is in Frinsted, but its territory at one time overlapped into Ashdown; Wrinsted Wood is still divided between Ashdown and Frinsted.
56. It was among Minster's possessions in 18 Edward III: H, V, 553.
57. *PNK*, 240, and cf. 197. Bedmonton belonged to St Augustine's Abbey. But the derivation of Wormshill is uncertain: see Ch. 10, n. 15, *supra*.
58. *ODEPN*, 179; but cf. *PNK*, 210–11.
59. In places these boundaries were not finally settled until recent generations.
60. H, V, 558, 554; *DM*, 79, lists Frinsted as a dependent church of Maidstone. The name of Whorne's Place dates from the fifteenth century, but as a manorial estate it was much older.
61. *PNK*, 208.
62. See pp. 264–5, *supra*.
63. Probably about 10,000 acres excluding the detached marshland chapelry of Iwade, which was divided between Teynham and Milton.
64. *DM*, 79; Witney, 32. It may also be significant that there was a cult of St Anne in both places.

Notes

12 LANDSCAPE AND SETTLEMENT IN ENGLAND

1. Cf. VCH, *Essex*, VII (1978), *passim*; VCH, *Staffs.*, VI (1979), 58–9; VCH, *Shropshire*, VIII (1968), *passim*; Brian Roberts, 'Field systems in the West Midlands', in A. R. H. Baker and R. A. Butlin (eds.), *Studies of Field Systems in the British Isles* (1973).
2. N. Neilson (ed.), *The Cartulary and Terrier of the Priory of Bilsington, Kent* (1928), 2. The extent of early documentation in Kent is chiefly due to the early and unbroken history of Canterbury and Rochester as major ecclesiastical centres.
3. W. J. Ford, 'Some settlement patterns in the central region of the Warwickshire Avon', in P. H. Sawyer (ed.), *Medieval Settlement: Continuity and Change* (1976); Della Hooke, 'Pre-Conquest estates in the west Midlands: preliminary thoughts', *J. Historical Geography*, VIII.iii (1982), 227–44. As in Kent, it was evidently the survival of extensive woodland that occasioned transhumance.
4. VCH, *Essex*, VII (1978), 11; VCH, *Staffs.*, VI (1979), 1.
5. Neilson, *op. cit.*, 24–5.
6. Cf. G. W. S. Barrow, *The Kingdom of the Scots* (1973), 7–68.
7. A *caveat* should be registered here, however, against too ready an identification of medieval parish boundaries with those of Anglo-Saxon/Romano-British estates. In this connexion it is vital to distinguish between boundaries indicating the *outer* edge of an estate and those of its internal subdivisions. In parishes like Murston and Sittingbourne, for example, entirely surrounded as they were by other parishes of the Milton territory and probably not originating until after the Conquest, there can be no connexion with the territorial units of Roman *Cantium*.
8. In the reform of local government in 1888 and in 1974 we find just the same intermingling of new units and old – a significant parallel.
9. Charles Phythian-Adams, *Continuity, Fields, and Fission: the Making of a Midland Parish* (1978); G. R. J. Jones, 'The multiple estate as a model framework for tracing early stages in the evolution of rural settlement', in *L'Habitat et les Paysages Ruraux d'Europe*, ed. F. Dussart (Les Congrès et Colloques de l'Université de Liège, LVIII, 1971), 251–67; G. R. J. Jones, 'Historical geography and our landed heritage', *University of Leeds Rev.*, XIX (1976), 53–78.
10. Cf. Della Hooke, 'Early Cotswold woodland', *J. Historical Geography*, IV (1978), 333–41; Alan Everitt, 'The Wolds once more', *ibid.*, V (1979), 67–71.
11. These figures are based on the 1" O.S. map; the 2½" sheets might add further examples.
12. *EPNE*, II, 240.
13. 'Holt' referred to an extensive tract of woodland, once used as common pasture, in the Forest of Buckholt on the Downs of East Kent: cf. Neilson, *op. cit.*, 4, 6.
14. *Ex inf.* Mrs Suella Postles.
15. For *lēac-tūn* as a woodland name see Everitt, *op. cit.*, 69 and n.

Notes

16. Blaston, Hallaton, Stockerston, and Easton are also recorded in DB: Nevill Holt, Drayton, and Bringhurst are not but may have been subsumed under Medbourne.
17. For a discussion of these names see *EPNE*, I, 134–6.
18. E. H. Bates, ed., *The Particular Description of the County of Somerset drawn up by Thomas Gerard of Trent, 1633* (Somerset Record Society, XV, 1909), 180–1. I am much indebted to Dr H. S. A. Fox for this reference, which confirms A. H. Smith's conjecture in *EPNE*, I, 135.
19. *Ibid.*, II, 242.
20. In parts of the Chilterns there are numerous tracks crossing the grain of the country like the Downland droveways in Kent.
21. *Ex inf.* Mrs Suella Postles.
22. *Cot* also occurs in Cotes de Val, a detached part of Kimcote in this area.
23. Roberts, *op. cit.*

INDEX

Note The following conventions have been used in compiling this index.

Place-names on the maps have been indexed and are indicated by italic figures; where names appear as part of a numbered key rather than on the map itself, the index reference is to the page on which the number appears, not the key. Counties have not been given for obviously Kentish place-names. The following abbreviations have been employed:

archaeol.	archaeological	m.ch.	mother-church
archit.	architecture	Neo.	Neolithic
b.	boundary	OL	Original Lands
cath.	cathedral	p.b.	parish boundaries
ch.	church	r.	river
ch. at	church at place indexed	rems.	remains
ch. of	church or chapel belonging to place indexed but situated elsewhere	Rom.	Roman
		R-B	Romano-British
		St	saint
chp.	chapel	sec. m.ch.	secondary mother-church
Conq.	Conquest (Norman)	settle.	settlement
dau. ch.	daughter-church	subord.	subordinate
Jut.	Jutish		
med.	medieval		

abbeys, 182
Abbey Wood, *213*
Abbotswood, Stelling, *283*
Abbotts Court, *153*
Acholt, *148*
Acrise, 128, 136, 146, *166*, 283; manor house, 20; name, 133
Addington, 132, *134*, 277; ch. of St Margaret, *212*, 250; Neo. chamber tombs, 248, 294
Admers Wood, 132, *134*
administration, 92, 337–8; evidence for units of, 10; relationship between med. and pre-Conq. units of, 343; *see also* institutions, jurisdiction
administrative sub-divisions of Kent, 270–4
Adisham, 48, *80*, 90, 165; estate granted to Canterbury Cath., 243; sec. m.ch., *188*, 197, Holy Innocents, 243, 282
Admiral Wood, *154*
Adrian, St, 240
Ægylbyrhtingahyrst, 147
Ælsiescirce, 205
æsc denn, 'ash pasture', 327
Afon Crai, Brecon, 75
agrarian conditions, 273; evidence, 300; organization, 74; potential, 272, 336; structure, 45
agriculture, 32; products, 66
air photography, 1, 95
Aldington-Septvans, *153*, 198, *200*, 258; sec. m.ch., *188*, 197
Aldon, *212*

Alkham, 147, 164, 166–7, 283, 297; ch. of St Anthony the Martyr, 242
Allhallows altar dedication, 226
Allington, *152*, 280; ch. of St Lawrence, *213*, 250
All Saints church dedications, 226, 227, 239, 246, 250, 251, 257, 295, 348
All Saints-in-Thanet, 182, 191
All Souls church dedications, 256
Alphege, St, 227, 240, 252, 256
altars, 226, 240; destruction of, 226; subsidiary, 226, 227
American War of Independence, 20
Anacletus, St, 227, 241, 293
Andrew, St, 227, 241, 242, 257, 348
Anglesey, 24
Anglo-Norman, 138, 221
Anglo-Saxon Chronicle, 266; invasion, 4; period, 40, 41, 54; settlement, 1
animals, 252; badger, 32; bears, 32; boars, 32; calf, 162; deer, 32; forest, 129, 161; otters, 32; pine-marten, 32; wild cats, 32; wolves, 32
Anne, St, 226, 227, 232, 249
Anselm, St, 240
Anthony, St, 226, 242, 253; the Martyr, 241
Aperfield, *148*
Appledore, 58
Appleton in Ickham, 144; in Waldershare, 144
arable farming, 32, 144; lands, 23, 50, 66, 68, 70, 313, 336, 339

395

archaeology, 6, 10, 93–5; evidence of, 96–103, 105, 112, 117; remains, 114, 348, 293; 'rescue', 1, 95, 340; sites, 95, 106, *110*, 115, 116
archbishops, 56, 226
architecture, *see under* buildings, churches, houses
Arden, Forest of, Warcs., 6, 19, 41, 192, 262, 335, 339
Ash, 144, 180; ch. of St Peter & St Paul, *211*
Ashburton, Devon, 73, 74, 82
Ash-by-Sandwich, 251
Ash-by-Wingham, 58, *81*, 264, 273, 274
Ash-by-Wrotham, 28, *134*, 140, 175
Ash-cum-Ridley, 129
Ashdown in Lenham, *85*, 157, 164, *201*, *309*, 313, 326, 328, 329, 349; ash pasture, 327
Ashenbank Wood, Cobham, *287*
Ashenfield, 198, 207, 220
Ashen Grove, *148*
Ashford, 53, 70, 199, 268
Ashmere, *134*
Ashurst, 29; ch. of St Martin, 256
assart, 146, 283
assarting, 25, 27, 129; medieval, 53, 297
Atchester, 278; Atchester Wood, *283*
Augustine, St, 92, 119, 184, 193, 195, 196, 228, 230, 238, 239, 240, 241, 242, 243, 249, 293, 318; St Augustine's Abbey, Canterbury, 182, 190, 196, 221, 231, 240, 248, 249, 320; estates of, 173, 176, 230; monastic manors, 117
Aylesbury, Vale of, 339
Aylesford, 76, *84*, 106, 108, 116, 149, *152*, *188*, 197, 249, 295, 330; early 'estate' at, 86, 380; ch. of St Lawrence of Longsole, 207, *213*; primary m.ch. of St Peter, 194, 195, *213*, 250, 256, 265; prehistoric rems., 100, 115; Rom. rems., 100, 108
Aylesford Common, *152*; Friary, *213*; lathe of, 177, 327

Bacca, 116
Baccancelde (Bapchild), 298, 318
Badlesmere, 147, *201*, 204; St Leonard, dau. ch. of Faversham, 265, 270; Badlesmere Lees, 128, 147
bǣr/bēr, 143, 161, 162, 322
bærnet, 130
Baldock Downs, *283*
Ballen's Rough, *152*
Bapchild, 59, *201*, 313, 315; ch. of St Lawrence, *306*; springhead chp. at, 206, 298, 299; St Lawrence's Fair, 318
baptism, 296; record, 206; rights, 219, 220
bār, 143
Barbara, St, 226, 233
bārdenn, 323
Barfreston, *80*, 140
Bargrove, 146
Barham, *80*, 82, 127, 128, 133, 137, 138
Barkby Holt, Leics., 346
barley, 144

Barming, 280; Barming Heath, *213*
Barnet Wood, *148*
Barn Wood, *152*
baronies, 270, 271
Barrow Green, *110*, 307
barrows, prehistoric, 294
Bartholomew, St, 227, 232, 234, 239, 251, 252, 253, 256, 320
Barton in Crundale, 144; in Barham, 144; in Canterbury, 144
Basing, 145
Bassetts, 145
Bassiline Wood, *309*, 317
Baston, 114
Batteries, *307*
Battle Abbey, 173, 191
Battle Wood, *287*
Bax, *307*
Baxon, *309*, 322
Bayford in Upchurch, 179, *306*, 322
Bayley's Hill, *214*
Beards Hall, Swingfield, *166*
Bearsted, *36*, *84*, 86, 150, 199, *200*; ch. of Holy Cross, 250, 253
Beaux Aires, Stockbury, 138, 151, *153*; Beaux Aires Wood, *153*
Beckley Hill, *288*
Bede, the Venerable, 23
Bedfordshire, 21, 73, 277, 295, 340, 345; north, 334
Bedgebury Forest, 54
Bedmonton, Wormshill, *308*, 328
Beechy Lees, *148*; Beechy Wood, *152*
Beerforstal, Elham, 168
Bekesbourne, 79, *80*, 82, 267
Belgae, 96, 97, 98, 99, 100, 101, 102, 113; Belgic cemetery, 108; cremations, 100; rems., 114, 299
Bell's Forstal, Throwley, 168
Beltsgreen, *308*
Benenden, 54, 145
beorg, 91, 143, 162, 266
bera, 130
bere, 33, 143
Bereacre, Bridge, 144
bergerie, 170
Berkshire, 47, 185; Berkshire Downs, 78
Berry Court, *290*; Berry Court Wood, *288*
Berry's Green, *148*
Bertha, Queen and St, 239, 241, 248, 249
Betburgh, Leigh, 207
Betteshanger, *81*, 140
Beulah Wood, *152*
Beuuestanuudan, Sheldwich, 170
Bewcastle Cross, Cumb., 194
Bewley Bar, 37
Bexley, 75, 123, *148*, 151, 205, 279, 280; Bexley Heath, *148*
Bickley, *148*
Bicknor, *36*, 140, 154, 200, 313, 321, 326, 327; ch. of St James, 270, 308
Bidborough, 294
Bid Bridge, *see* Betburgh
Biddenden, 40, 106, 122

Biggin Wood, 133, *166*, 283
Billerica, 105, 107
Binbury, 151, *153*
Bingham Roughs, *288*
Bircholt, 275
Birch Wood, 309, 317
birds, 172; falcon, 162; forest, 161; geese, 32, 163
Birling, 132, 133, *134*, 158; primary m.ch. All Saints, *188*, 194, *213*, 277; territory based on, 114
Birling Place, *134*
Bishopsbourne, 80, 82–3, 107, 128, 171, 198, 267; sec. m.ch., *188*, 197
Bistock, Doddington, 168, 179, *309*, 317
Blacemannescirce, 203
Black Charles, 52
Black Death, 71, 139, 184, 206, 222
Blackhall, 52
Blacklands Shaw, *152*
Blackmanstone, Romney Marsh, 61, 185, 203
Bladbean, Elham, *283*
Blaise, St, 233, 239, 250, 251, 253, 256, 277
Blaise Wood, 183, 277
Blaze Woods, *212*
Blean, 183; ch. of St-Cosmas-and-St-Damian-in-the-Blean, 183, 203
Blean Eagle's Wood, 164
Blean Forest, 29–30, 34, 46, 52, 65, *76*, 86, 101, 107, 109, *111*, 112, 122, 183, *188*, 295, 313, 326; ch. dedications in, 234–8; *dens* in, 123; name, 104; parishes in, 194, 251, 264, forest-parishes, 275; pasturelands of Milton Regis in, 317; swine pasture, 164–5; trackways, 160
Bleangate, Chislet, 160
Blendon, *148*
Blindgrooms, Shadoxhurst, 55
Blowers Wood, *153*
'boar' names, 164
Boardfield, nr Lenham, 185, *201*
Boarley Scrubs, *152*; Boarley Warren, 27, *152*
Bobbing, 146, *201*, 232, 274, 313, 314, 315, 316, 327, 332; ch. of St Bartholomew, *306*, 320; manor, 322, 328; parish, 321; subord. chp. of Milton Regis, 234, 320
Bobbing Fair, 320; Hospital, *305*
Bodsham, 137
Boflin, *152*
Bogle, *307*
boi(a), 179
Bold Grove, *148*
Boldrewood, *309*
Bolton's Wood, *154*
Bonnington, 243
Boormanhatch, Elmstead, 138
Borden, *154*, 157, 165, *201*, 313, 314, 321, 332; chestnut woods, 26, 28; ch. of St Peter & St Paul, *305*; gentry of, 324; parish, 323–5; swine pastures, 164; woodland chapelly of Milton Regis, 320; yokeland, 323

Borden Hill, *154*, *305*; Borden Wood, in Doddington, 164, *309*
Border Counties, 18, 194, 339
Borough Green, 40
'boroughs' (*borghi*), 12, 74, 159, 270, 271; evidence for, 158; marsh, 58; upland, 52; Wealden, 52, 147, 149
borsholders, 158
Borstal, *288*; Borstal Marsh, *288*
Bossenden, Dunkirk, 164
Bostall, *148*
Boston Elms Wood, *153*
Bosville, Sir Ralph, 219
botanists, 129
Botolph, St, 206, 233, 241, 250, 257, 267
Bottesford, Leics., 275
Boughton Aluph, 147, 204
Boughton Lees, 147
Boughton Malherbe, *85*, 147, 199, *201*, 327, 330; chartland pastures, 89; dau. ch. of Lenham, 251, St Nicholas, 270; manor, 328
Boughton Monchelsea, 51, *84*, 199, *200*, 273; ch. of St Nicholas, 250; dau. ch. of Maidstone, 265; hill-fort at, 86, 100
Boughton Street, 40, *202*; chp. of Holy Trinity, 206
Boughton-under-Blean, sec. m.ch., *188*; dau. ch. of Faversham, 197, *202*
Boughurst Street, 133
boundaries, 12, 13, 88, 129, 292; Anglo-Saxon, 279; antiquity of p.b., 27–8, 84; chs. on p.b., 187, 197, 199, 206, 234, 262–3, 275–6, 277–8, 280; common pastureland on p.b., 147, 328–9; estate b., *80*, *81*, *84–5*, 205, 331; farms/hamlets on, 278; interlocking p.b., 157, 171, 284, 328–9, 330; irregularity of p.b., 281–2, 328; p.b., 2, 14, 16, 20, 75, *80*, *81*, 93, 128, 142, 144–6, 150, 179, 206, 259, 262, 263, 278–92, 302, 314, 315, 318, 331, 347; regional b., 3–4; rivers as p.b., 280; settles. on p.b., 324; topography of, 145, 150, 274, 278–300; woodland on p.b., 319
boundary, disputes, 284; Downland, 329; erratic development of, 330; marks, 26, 137, 146, 147, 178; perambulations, 278; R-B, 331; Rom. road as, 319–20; stones, 278, 319; upland, 328–30
'bourne' names, 82, 90, 162
Bourne, r. estate, 79–82, 127; parishes, 197; territory of B. people, 325
Bournemouth, Hants, 32
Bourne Wood, *148*
Bow Hatch, Chartham, 160
Bowland, 6
Bowl Reed, *305*
Boy Court, Ulcombe, 179
Boyden Hill, Chislet, 179
Boyington, Swingfield, *166*, 179
Boyke, Elham, 168, 179
Boyton Court, East Sutton, 179
Boxley, *84*, 86, 87, 146, 151, *152*, 165; dau.

Boxley – *contd.*
  ch. of Maidstone, 182, *200*, 297; detached pasture of, 330; St Rumwold, 243
Boxley Abbey, 207, 280; Boxley Warren, 27, *152*; Boxley Wood, *152*, 330
Boxted, *305*
Brabourne, 106; St Mary's, 245; Brabourne Lees, 40, 52, 145
Bradbourne, 159; chp. at, 206, *209*, 219
Bradfield's Wood, *152*
Bramsells, 145
Brandred, Acrise, 133, *166*, 283
Brasted, 79, 171, 262, 265, 280–1; sec. m.ch., *188*, 197
Brasted Green, *148*; Brasted Chart, 50, 51
Brastedlands, 281
Breach, *305*
Bredenstone, Dover, 114
Bredgar, *154*, 164, *201*, 284, 312–14, 322, 332; ch. of St John the Baptist, 270, *305*, 320
Bredhurst, 28, *84*, 140, 146, 151, *153*; ch. of St Peter, 256; detached chapelry, 88, 156, *200*, 264, 330; detached pastures of Hollingbourne, 155, 159
Bredhurst Hurst, *153*
Breeches Brooms Wood, 153
Breedon, Leics., 294
Bregwine, St, 240
Brehtwald, St, 240
Brenchley, 149
Brenzett, ch. of St Eanswythe, *231*
Brickenden, Biddenden, 106, 122
brickfields, 311
Brickfield Shaw, *153*
Bridge, *80*, 82–3, 144, 276; ch. of St Peter, 256
Bridge Woods, *152*
bridleway, 160
brigā, 106, 162
Brimsdale, Eythorne, 169
Bringhurst, Leics., 346
Briogoningwara, 106
Brittany, 115
Brixworth, Northants., 294
Broadhoath, 215
Broad Oak Forstal, *306*; Broad Oak Wood, *288*
brocc, 130
Bromley, St Blaise's Well, 206, 298; Bromley Common, *148*
Brompton, Frindsbury, *288*, 292
Brompton, Gillingham, *289*
Bromswold, Beds., 344
Bronze Age, 98, 99, 114, 115, 248
Brook, 147
Brookland, 62, 64
brooks, 172
Brooks Grove, *148*
Broomfield, 36, *84*, 88, 199, *200*, 279, *308*; ch. of St Margaret, 250
Broomhill, *148*
Broom Hill, *148*, *288*, *309*
Broom Street, *111*

Brooms Hall, *154*
Brooms Wood, *153*
Brown's Wood, Temple Ewell, *167*
browse (foliage), 31
Brummelhill Wood, *287*
bryne, 162
Brynnessole, Eythorne, 169
bucc, 130
Buckhurst, 145, 146, *148*
Buckinghamshire, 6, 21, 22, 262
Buckland, 139, *201*; dau. ch. at, 251; R-B site, *110*; Buckland Marshes, *291*
Buckland-by-Dover, ch. of St Bartholomew, 206, 232
Buckminster, Leics., 182
Buckmore Park, *152*, 330
buildings, 55, 63–4; ecclesiastical, 293; timber-framed, 26, 40; *see also* churches, houses
Bulkeden, *148*, 151
Bunker's Hill, 20
burh, 162, 171
Burham, *152*, 195, 280, 295, 297, 330; ch. of St Mary, 213, 245; *Halygarden*, well in, *213*, 297; Burham Common, *152*, 330
burial: cremation, 100, *110*, *111*; grounds, Jut., 20, 102, 103, *110*, heathen, 244, Rom., 99, 102, *110*, and Saxon, 77, 103; fee (soul-scot), 185; mounds, 294; rights, 219, 220, 297, 318; sites, pre-Christian, 14
Burmarsh, 58, 59, 60, 61
burna, 74, 91
Burnt Wood, *153*
Bursted, Bishopsbourne, *148*, 171
Burton-on-the-Wolds, Leics., 345
Bush, Cuxton, 144; Bush, Elham, *166*
Butchers Wood, 133, 283
Butters, 322
Butts Farm, Elmsted, 138; Butts Farm, Stelling, 283
Buxton, Derbys., 298
Bysing Woods, Faversham, 317

Caernarvon, 25
Caesar, Julius, 23
Caldecote, *347*, 348
Calehill, Hundred of, 327
Callam's Wood, *153*, *305*
Calne, Wilts., 73, 74
Cambray, *306*, 322
Cambridge (Kent), *307*
Cambridgeshire, 30, 31, 32, 48, 281, 295, 344, 347; east, 334; west, 334; wold, 344, 347
Camhill, *154*
campus, 113, 162
Canon Heath, *213*
Cannon Wood, Lydden, *166*
Canterbury, 18, 20, 21, 22, 28, 29, 40, 41, 43, *45*, 58, 65, *76*, *80*, 83, 96, 97, 104, 107, 117, 128, 139, 144, 156, 157, 159, 164, 182, 183, *188*, 192, 193, 195, 222, 234, 251, 277, 279, 284, 295, 297, 312, 313, 320, 330; archaeol. rems., 100; archbishops,

canonized, 240; charters of, 147; churches in: St Helen, 242–3; St Martin, 231, 241; St Martin & St Pancras, 186, *188*, 195, 244; St Mary in Castro, 186; St Pancras, 243; cults at, 239, 240, 249; desertion at end of Rom. period, 97, 342; diocese of 187, 189, 196, 198, 203, 204; early Jut. estate, 107; monastic houses of, 62, 63; pilgrimages to, 249; saints, 182, 240; *see also* St Augustine's Abbey, Christ Church Cathedral
Canter Wood, Elham, *166*
Cantion/Cantium, 7
Cantware, 7, 104
Capel, 183
Capel, Horsmonden, 206
Capel, Petham, 206, 207
Capel Curig, Wales, 184
Capel Farm, Warehorne, 206
Capel Hill, Eastchurch, 206
Capel-le-Ferne, *166*–7, 184, 266
Capel-next-Tudeley, Tonbridge, 184
caput, capita, 9, 40, 72, 74, 75, 86, 100, 107, 117, 191, 195, 268, 280, 311; *see also* estate-centres, *regiones* and *villae regales*
Carey, r. *see* Len. r.
Caring, 106
Cart Wood, *289*
carvett, 27
Castle Hill, 294
Castle Rough, *306*, 311
cathedrals, 182, 185, 196
Catherine, St, 226, 236, 249, 251, 252, 256, 313
cattle, 31, 123, 163, 168
cattle stations, 169, 170, 317
Catts Farm, Lower Hardres, 138
cealfa, 158, 170
cēap, 171
cefn, 106
celde, 91, 116
Celtic/Celts, 5, 7, 160; evidence, 17, 39, 108; goddess Elen, 243; peoples, 97, 103, 292; place-names, 17, 20, 103, 104, 108, 193; speaking, 95, 105; stream-name, 260; traditions, 41–2, 114, 179, 343
cemeteries, 96; Belgic, 100; Jut., 98, 100; Rom., 100, 101, 106, *111*, 248
centuriation, 99, 242
ceosol, 162
cēto, 29, 65, 106, 130, 292, 313, 330
Chalk, 284, *287*
Chalksole, Alkham, *166*; Chalksole Green, *166*
Chalkwell, *306*
Chalk Wood, *148*, 151
Challock, 28, 158, 170, *201*; isolated ch. of St Cosmas & St Damian, 204, 270
chamber tombs, 248
chancels, 316
Chance Wood, *210*
Channel, English, 25, 47, 70, 83, 127, 199
chantries, 181, 186, 199, 205–6, 219, 221,
222, 227, 296; rebuilding of, 184; destruction, 226
Chantry Farm, Headcorn, 206
Chapel, 183
Chapel Bottom, St John's-in-Thanet, 206
Chapel Farm, Newchurch, 206; Chapel Farm, Stelling, *283*
Chapel Hill Wood, *153*
Chapel House, Ospringe, 206
chapelries, 12, 79, 137, 151, 156–7, 158, 183, 186, 191, 195, 198, 199, 220, 231, 232, 249, 264, 265, 271, 313, 326; dependent, 252, 269, 273, 280; detached, 273, 326, 327; mainland, 272, outlying, 346; subord., 234, 257, 263, 272; upland, 231; woodland, 264, 320
chapels, 15, 78, 116, 126, 158, 181, 182, 183, 184, 186–7, 198, 199, 204, 205–22, 227, 231, 241, 253, 266, 273, 297; daughter, 276; dependent, 232, 233, 267; droveway, 270; -of-ease, 219, 220; manorial, 206–7, 219, 220, 221; names in, 206; non-parochial, 222; origins of, 206–7; outlying, 220, 222, 265, 277; pre-Conquest, 270; quasi-parochial function, 219; rebuilding of, 184; springhead, 115, 206; subord., 267, 295; subsidiary, 320; woodland, 277
Chapel Valley, Gillingham, 206
Chapel Valley Shaw, *153*
Chapel Wood, *210*; Chapel Wood, Ashdown, *309*; Chapel Wood, Hartley, 206
chaplain, 219, 275
charcoal, 162
Charcoal Farm, Elham, *283*
Charing, 49, 76, 88, 89, 102, 108, 168, 191, 193, 199, *201*, 251; dau. chs., 265; *dens* of, 147; m.ch. of St Peter & St Paul, *188*, 189, 245, 297
Charlton, *148*; Charlton Plantation, *153*
Charnwood, Leics., 6
Chart, 50; *and see* Chartland
charters, 34, 54, 135; borough, 74; early, 120, 121, 318; market, 316; pre-Conquest, 41, 58, 69, 74, 78, 86, 89, 119, 120, 121, 123, 126, 130, 147, 161, 164, 169, 170, 171, 191, 279, 347, 348
Chartham, 160, 168, 197, 220, 295; sec. m.ch., *188*
Chartland, 6, 23, 24, 28, 29, 44, *45*, 49–52, 61, 64, 68, 70, 76, 79, *84*–*5*, 86, 96, 97, 105, 159, *188*, 204, 224, 262, 264, 268–9, 277; escarpment, 50, 52, 123; churches on, 51, 197, 198, 222, 238, 265, 270, 294; common land, 51; dedications, 234, 236, 250; *dens* on, 124–5; droveways in, 39; lanes in, 267–8; outlying pastures, 88, 89, 273; parishes, 51; settle. of, 41, 51–2, 65–6, 70, 120, 121, 145, 238, 258, 335; western, 136, 325; wooded, 72; wood-pastures, 66
Chart Sutton, 50–1, *84*, 99, 199, *200*; ch. of St Michael, 250, 252, 270; dau. ch. of Hollingbourne, 265, 279
chastaignière, 26, 130, 321

Chatham, 29, 46, 65, 106, 107, 150, *152*, 158, 170, 198, *200*, *289*, 292, 311, 330; Jut. estate-centre, 101, 107; hospital of St Bartholomew, 206, 232; sec. m.ch. of St Mary at, *188*, 197
Chathurst (Swalecliffe), 30, 106
Chattenden, 29, 106, *289*, 292; Chattenden Farm, 292; Chattenden Rough, *289*
cheesehouses, 168
Cheeseland Wood, *153*
Chelmington, 159
Chelsfield, 78, 140, *148*, 150, 165; ch. of St Martin, 231
Cheney Wood, *306*, 317, 319
Cheriton, 183; ch. of St Martin, 245
Cheshire, 24
Chesley, *305*
Chestnut Plantation, *153*
Chestnut Street, Borden, *305*, 314, 316, 321
Chestnut Wood, *154*; in Stockbury, 321
Chetham, in Ospringe, 30, 106, *110*, 112, 113, 317, 331
Chetney, in Iwade, 30, 106
Chevening, 49, 76, 79, 106, *148*, 197, 198, 265, 269, 281, 297, 332; sec. m.ch., *188*; ch. of St Botolph, *209*, 245, 257
Chichester, 7
Chiddingstone, 37, 79, 113, 122, 147, 198, 268; ch. of St Mary, *214*, 265; Wealden parish, 281; Chiddingstone Hoath, 27
Chilham, 40, 47, *76*, 86, 109, 159, 194, 195, *202*, 266, 294; archaeol. rems., 101; castle, 86, 101; ch. of St Mary, 245
Chillenden, *80*, 140, 192, 275, 279
Chilterns, 6, 21, 281, 340, 344–5; 'hoos' on, 345, 346
Chilton, Alkham, 179, *188*; Chilton, Sittingbourne, 179, *306*, 316
Chilton Hills Wood, *288*
Chinkwell Wood, *305*
Chislehurst, *148*, 251, 280; Chislehurst Common, *148*
Chislet, 86, 101, 109, 160, 179; 'droves' on, 58
Chitt's Wood, *154*
Christianity, 49, 93, 109, 261, 266; Augustinian, 195, 292; centres of, 245; Roman, 119, veneration of springs, 115
Christ Church Cathedral, Canterbury, 182, 190, 240, 242, 244, 245; crypt, 194; pilgrims' well in, 296; dedications of, 241; estates of, 61, 173, 176, 191, 243; manors of, 34, 117
church(es), 12, 13, 14, 55, 57, 77, 86, 100, *110*, 169, 181–7, 231, 232, 233, 250, 252, 253, 263, 266, 267, 316; archit., 293–4; associated with wells/springs, 296–300; Augustinian, 107, 193, 195, 239; autonomous, 272; baptismal, 189, 195; 'bookland', 186, 187, 192, 196, 198–205, 200–2, 222, 223, 224, 263, 295; British, *213*, 245; colonization of *wald*, 184; chronology of development, 185–7, 196, 204, 257; daughter-, 15, 126, 156–8, 185, 186, 189, 191, 192, 196, 197, 231, 233, 238, 251, 265, 267, 272, 281, *332*; dependent, 189, 252, 320; dependent territories of, 190, 191, 193, 194, 195, 198, see also minsterlands; Downland, 138, 156, 157, 198, 250–1, 294; droveway, 269, 270; early foundations, 226, 231, 238–46, 248, 250, 251, 255, 256, 260, 274, 293, 294, 295, 296, 297; family monuments in, 64, 204; 'field', 185; forest, 186, 192, 222, 253; foundation, 15, 190, 196–7, 224, 233, 261, 264, 265; founders, 203, 221–2, 224; grants of privileges to, 182, 187; head, 189; hill-top, 294–5; independent, 282; isolated, 12, 42; later foundations, 222, 224, 233, 238, 251, 256, 257, 260, 274, see also subord. and subsidiary; lost or vanished, 157, 219, 220, 226, 273, 275; manorial, 186, 196, 198–205, 222, 260, 275, 295, 316; maritime, 226, 232–3; Marshland, 62, 199, 264; medieval, 181, 190, 198, 205, 335; minster-, 14, 75, 92, 113, 158, 181, 185–6, 222, 223, *293*, 316, 341, *also see under* minsters; mother, 51, 79, 93, 98, 108, 109, 115, 117, 137, 156, 157, 185–6, 187–96, 198, 219, 222, 223, 231, 233, 234, 236, 239, 248, 250, 251, 257, 263–4, 265, 269, 273, 275, 276, 280, 281, 243, 297, 313, 318, 348; Old English, 227, 231; outlying, 265; owners of, 203; parish, 18, 42, 51, 56, 64, 78, 100, 102, 114, 181, 205, 207, 221, 222, 223, 227, 231, 257, 258, 263, 272, 276, 297; pre-Augustinian sites, 244; pre-Conquest, 185; primary, 239, 240, 241, 245, 246; private, 199; on river banks, 193, 195, 260, 286; ruins, 114, 115; Saxon, 57, 99, 293, 312; sec. mother-, 186, 187, *188*, 196–8, 223, 233, 274; sites, 14, 75, 78, springhead, 299; structures, 259, 293–5; subord., 251, 252, 294, 312–13, 315; subsidiary, 276, 277, 295; towers, 184, 295; typology, 223; Weald, 223, 263, 294; Wilderness, 250–5; -yards, 18, 108, 185, 245, 276, 297; *see also* boundaries, parish, *and* dedications, church
Church Wood, *154*
cille, 91
cirice, 183, 203
Civiley Wood, *153*
claims, detached pastoral, 327, 330; manorial, 321, 323; on resources, 326; settles., 329–30
Clambercrown, *283*
Clavertye Wood, *283*
Clavvokisden, 148
Claybrooke, Leics., estates based on, 343
Claygate Cross, Wrotham, *211*
Clay Lane Wood, *287*
Clay Pond Wood, *288*
Claxfield, *307*
clearance of land, 3, 25, 129, 132, 133; *and see* colonization
Cleggett's, *134*
clergy, 266, 275

clif, 91
cliff, 162
Cliffe-at-Hoo, 76, 284, 290, 292; estate-centre, 99; heathen burial ground, 244; m.ch., *188*, 194; ch. of St Helen, 242–3, 245
Cliffe Common, *288*; Cliffe Marshes, *290*; Cliffe Wood, *288*
Clodhamer, 159
cloth, 55
clothiers, 67
Cobdean Wood, Swingfield, *166*
Cobham, 90, 140, 284, *287*; St Thomas's Well, *287*, 292, 296, 298
Cobham's Rough, Paddlesworth, *166*, 283
Cockham, *289*; Cockham Wood, *289*
Codsheath, Hundred of, 269, 343
coin evidence, 193; hoards, 96, 100
Colchester, 22
Cold Blow, Temple Ewell, *167*
Coldharbour, 37, *153*
Coldred, 80, 145; ch. of St Pancras, 243; earthworks at, 294
Coldrum Stones, Trottiscliffe, 17, 115
Colehill Wood, *283*
Coleshall, *306*
Cole Wood, *288*
Collardshill Wood, *283*
colleges, 181, 226
College Wood, *306*, 319
Colne, r., 105
colonists, 11, 349
colonization, 2, 4, 6, 7, 12, 23, 30, 43, 44, 51, 54, 69, 70, 71, 72, 74, 75, 89, 92, 97, 103, 113, 116, 140, 146, 171, 180, 206–7, 234, 263, 273, 302; areas of, 340; direction of, 276; diversity of, 348; Iron Age survival, 341; long period of c. in Kent, 335; medieval, 20, 130; pastoral, 204; pre-Conquest, 20, 130; progress of, 261, 264, 282; role of church in, 184; subsequent, 197, 267; transhumant structure of, 337; zones of, 69
'combe', 105, 161, 162
Combe, 105, 106, 107
combes, 47, 50, 78, 199, 278
Combwell, 105
Comenden, 147; manorial estate, 149
Commandery, 217
'common', 329
common(s), 12, 20, 51, 71; land, 326–9; waste, 133
Common Marsh, *288*
communities, cottager, 52, 145; daughter, 88; historic c. of England, 349; industrial, 40, 349; mother, 124, 232, 262; neighbouring, 263; parent, 151; primary, 54, 69; riverine, 90; R-B, 117, 342; seminal, 113, 197, 340; smallholder, 145; springhead, 90; squatter, 138–9, 145
Comp, 207; chapel-of-ease, 220
Compton Census, 61
Conchers Wood, *309*, 317
Conquest, Norman, 9, 20, 21, 24, 29, 38, 41, 54, 55, 69, 117, 139, 160, 174, 178, 180, 189, 311; *see also* post- *and* pre-Conquest continuity, 1, 65, 92, 97, 116, 278; areas of 340; of occupation, 341–3; religious, 116, 299–300; Rom.-Jut., 65, 74, 78, 87, 90, 93–5, 100, 102, 103, 105, 112, 113, 160, 193, 349; zones of, 341, 343
Cookham Shaw, *154*
Cooks Farm, Lower Hardres, 138
Cooling, 284, 291, 292; ch. of St James, 233; Cooling Marshes, *291*
Coomb Hill, 134
Coopers Shaw, *154*
Cope Hill Shaw
coppice, 27, 28, 31, 129, 180, 313, 334; ancient, 132; country, 347
copse, 12, 19, 27, 53, 128, 146
Copt Hill, Capel-le-Ferne, *167*
cornland, 32, 43, 46, 61, 129, 144
Cornwall, 4–5, 42, 64, 184, 334
Corpus Christi dedications, 256
Cosmas, St, & St Damian, 239, 251, 252, 253, 256, 270
Cosmas-Blean, *see* Blean
Cossington, 115; chp., *152*; ch. of St Michael, 213; Cossington Fields, 152
cot, names in, 347, 348
Cotswolds, 344
cottages, 169, 204, 278; cottagers, 71
Cottage Wood, *153*
Cotesbach, Leics., 348
Cottington, 219
Countless Stones, 100
countryside, exploitation of, 1, 3; fertile, 46, 49–50; forest, 52, 53, 129, 295; old settled coppice, 334; pastoral, 334; types of, 338–40, 348–9, infertile, 48–9, 50–1; wooded, 52–3, 126, 268; *see also pays*
Court Wood, *153*, 287
Covert Wood, Elham, 128
Covet Wood, Elham, *283*
Cowbeck Wood, *152*
Cowden, 31, 79, 123, 145, 146
Cowgate, Hawkinge, *166*
cowland, 161, 162
Cowlees Shaw, *148*
Cowleze, *152*
cows, 32
Cowstead, *154*, 305; Cowstead Wood, *153*
Coxsole Farm, Stelling Minnis, *283*
Crabtree Wood, *154*
Cradle Shaw, *153*
craeges aeuuelme, 198
crafts, 40
Cranbrook, 53–4, 56, 147, 149, *219*
Cranoe, Leics., 346
Cransley, Northants., 347
Cray, r., 17, 75, 76, 77, 78, 97, 105, 106, *148*–9, 284, 297; estate based on, 75, 164, 198; valley, 72, 75, 150, 151, 231
Cray Ewelme, 75, 198
Crayford, 75, *76*, 97, 99, *148*, 157, 194; archaeol. rems., 98; ch. of St Paulinus, 198, 231, 244; minster, 194

Crediton, Devon, 74
Creedy, r., Devon, 73
Creton Court, Staple, 145
Crispin, St, & St Crispinian, 241, 244, 293
Crixhall, 145
Crockham Hill, 51
Cromer Wood, *305*, *317*
Crookham Wood, *134*
cropp, 162
crosses, 146, 186–7, *209–18*
Crosskeys, Sevenoaks, *214*
Crouch, Selling, 183
Crouch Green, East Malling, *213*
'crouches', 182, 183, 186, *209–18*, 231, 270
crouco, 107
Crown Wood, *148*
crucis, 183
Crundale, 139, 144, 147, 165, 169, 204
cu, 170
Cuckoo Shaw, *152*
Cudham, 21, 129, 140, *148*, 150, 171, 192, 198, 275; Cudham Frith, *148*
Culand, *152*
Cullompton, 74
Culm. r., Devon, 73
cults, 244–5, 249; centred on Canterbury, 239, 249; child, 243; development of, 226, 252; fairs, 232; female, 246–9; fertility, 116, 232, 249, 299; local and regional, 226, 231, 257; pagan, 296, 299; pre-Christian, 116, 239, 244, 249, 298–300, 341; religious, 16; saints, 227, 232; seafarers, 232–3; springs, 299; springhead, 232, 297–8; water spirits, 299–300; well, 92, 116, 232, 297–8, 318
Culverstone, 133; Culverstone Green, 37, *134*
customs, fertility, 232, 249, 298; local, 159
Cutnell, *306*
Cuttlestone, Staffs., 115
Cuxton, Rochester, 90, 99, 106, 113, 114, 115, *134*, 144, 280; Rom. rems., 100; ch. at, *188*, 195; ch. of St Michael, 252, 256, *288*, 295
cysse, 114

dairies, 168
Dalby Wolds, Leics., 345
dale, 161
Dallywood, *288*
Danaway, *305*
Dane Chantry, Petham, 206, 207
Dane Farm, 133, 145, *283*
Daneford, Crundale, 169
Danelaw counties, 337
Danes, 248, 311; Danish invasions, 294, 313
Daniel Chambers Wood, 132, *134*
Darent, r., 17, 46, 47, 70, 71, 88, 105, 129, 132, *148–9*, 295; valley, 22, 77, 78, 79, 98, 99, 150, 151, 156, 159, 164, 231, 268, 284, 329, 330
Darenth, *76*, 77, 82, 86, 87, 106, 114, 117, *148*, 156, *188*, 197, 232, 295; ch. of St Margaret, 231, 244, 245, 248; people of,
78; territory of, 77–8, 82, 83, 98–9, 114, 315, 342
Dargate, 163
Dargets Wood, *152*
Dark Sallows, *287*
Dart, r., 77
Dartford, *45*, 46, 72, *76*, 77, 78, 79, 82, 98, 99, 103, 117, *148*, 151, 155, *188*, 194, 197, 232, 252, 267, 295; Holy Trinity minster at, 232, 241, 244, 245, 312
Dartford Brent, chp. of St Edmund, 232
Dartford Heath, *148*
Dartmoor, 25, 339
daven/dafn, 112
Daven, r., (Fishbourne stream in Faversham), 105, 112
Davenham, 112
Davenport, 112
David Street, 133, *134*
Davington, 109, *110*, 112, 113, *201*
Deane, 198
Deal, 30, 41, 46, *81*, 107, 128, 157
Dean, Waltham, 137, 207, 220
Deangate Wood, *289*
Deans Hill, *305*, *308*, 314
dedications, church, 14, 15–16, 93, 222, 225–58, 259, 270, 302, 348; assoc. with landing places, 253–4; assoc. with pre-Christian sites, 244, 249; changes in, 226; chronology of, 225, 233, 254–5; destroyed, 226; early, 225, 233, 236, 239–43, 294; evidence of, 225–7; founder, 203; indigenous/native saints, 239–40, 260; late OE, 318; later, 225, 253, 254–5, 295; Leics. upland *wald*, 348; m.ch., 194; non-local, 240–1; Original Lands, 234–9; owner, 203; pattern, 225; *pays*, 235; popularity, 227–8; popular saints, 239; rare, 239, 241–3, 312; re-dedications, 226, 227, 251, 257; saints, 226–8, 270; tables of, 228–30, 235, 236–7, 246–7; unknown, 226; Wilderness parish, 236–9, 248, 250–4, 320, 326; women, 245–9
Deerleap, *148*
Deerton, 163
Deerton Street, *110*
demography, 67–8, 341–2
den, denn(s), 33, 34–5, 54, 121–6, 127, 129, 130, 141, 142, 143, 147, 149, 157, 160, 161, 162, 163–4, 165, 171, 253, 263, 271, 283, 323, 329
Den Barn, *148*, 164
'dene', 136, 161
Dene, Meopham, *134*; Dene, St. John's-in-Thanet, 219
Denge, 58; Denge Wood, 58
Dengemarsh, 58
Denis, St, 348
Denly Hill, Hernhill, 164
Denne, 160; Denne Court, 155
Dennehill, 164
Densole, Swingfield, *166*; Densole Minnis, Swingfield, *166*, 283, 330
Denton, 20, *80*, 82, 128, 133, *166*, 284, 325;

ch. of St Mary, *287*; Denton Marshes, *287*;
  Denton Wood, *166*
Denton by Gravesend, 123
denu, 162
Denwood, Crundale, 169
dēor, 130, 163
Deptford, 21, 22, 251
Deremannescirce, 203
Dering family, 220
Derventio, 106
Detling, 36, *84*, 86, 146, 151, *153*, 161, 191;
  ch. under Maidstone, 191, *200*, 273;
  interlocking p.b., 151; Rom. rems. at, 102,
  108
Deusdedit, St, 240
Devon, 4, 5, 11, 21, 25, 33, 42, 73, 76, 342,
  185, 334, 336, 340; r. estates in, 73
Digges Place, Barham, 138
dikes, 60
'districts', 271
Ditton, 250, 280; ch. of St Peter, *213*; Ditton
  Common, *213*
documentary evidence, 11, 51, 107, 123, 261,
  274, 278, 302, 336, 344; early modern,
  279; ecclesiastical, 185, 187, 189;
  medieval, 129, 130, 141, 227, 279, 314,
  346; post-Conquest, 139; pre-Conquest,
  129, 130, 190, 227, 335; wills, 227
Doddington, 135, 136, 164, 179, *201*, 281,
  309, *317*, *319*; ch. of the Beheading of St
  John the Baptist, 270, *310*; subsid. chp.,
  320
Domesday Book, 9, 16, 30, 55, 59, 74, *83*,
  133, 139, 143, 170, 173, 177, 189, 203,
  251, 311–12, 313, 320, 322, 328, 335, 344,
  345, 346, 347; evidence of, 1, 29, 31, 174
Domesday Monachorum of Christ Church,
  51, 59, 185, 189, 190, 191, 205, 227, 272,
  273, 312, 313, 315, 318, 320, 328, 382
Donkey Shaws, *152*
Dorset, 17, 47, 73; r. estates in, 73
Dour, r., 17, 71, 75–6, 77, 105, 297; valley,
  128, 139, 144, 164, 234, 345
Dover, 21, 33, 43, *45*, 47, 72, 75, 76, 77, *83*,
  86, 87, 102, 103, 105, 107, 114, 116, 117,
  133, 189, 195, 222, 232, 234, 248, 311,
  330; castle, 17; estate-centre, 144; ch. of St
  James, 233; Maison Dieu, 206; St Mary-
  in-Castro, 186, *188*, 193, 195, 239, 294;
  minster (St Martin), 187, *188*, 190, 191,
  193, 244, 293; Our Lady's Well, 296;
  Priory of St Martin's, 117, 133, 181, 189,
  193, and estates of, 173, 176; Rom. rems.
  at, 77, 102, 107, 114, 193
Dowde's Church, 133, *134*, 183, 185, 203
Dowles Farm, Elmsted, 138
down, 131, 136, 162, 339; names in, 155
Down Court, *309*
Downe, 21, 75, 78, *148*, 151, 158, 198
Downland, 19, 23, 24, 27, 29, 33, 36, 39, 41,
  42, 44, *45*, 45–9, 51, 56, 61, 65, 66, 67, 75,
  76, 78, *84–5*, 96, 97, 119, 127–80, 185, *188*,
  198, 222, 234, 238, 251, 264, 265, 273,
  275, 313, 317, 340, 344–5; clearance of,

48, 139, 140, 163, 318; colonization of, 48,
  49, 132, 133, 135–40, 155, 172, 177;
  combes, 76, 128, 284; coppice country,
  347–8; *dens* on, 124–5; droves, 160–1;
  ecclesiastical, 136, 161; economy, 15, 47,
  49, 125, 132, 140, 141–7, dependent on
  OL, 155–6, 162; escarpment, 35, 36, 37;
  evolution of, 49, 127, 180, 330, 335;
  flowers, 129; forest, 15, 20, 25, 128, 138,
  314, 319, 349; 'freedom', 177–9, 180, 222;
  landownership, 173–7; landscape, 171,
  180, 344; ox pastures, 165; parishes, 323;
  pastoral origins, 155; pasture, 34, 159,
  162, 330; place-names, 126–7, 129–39,
  141–4, 146–7, 147–9, 151, 155, 157–8,
  160–2; rents, 223–4; ridgeway, 77, 79, 86,
  88, 132, 329, 331; route, 270; settle., 49,
  65, 70, 120–1, 128, 132, 135–40, 156, 158,
  161, 169; settle. dependent on OL, 155,
  156, 157, 160; sheep, 170–1; society, 172,
  178; swine pastures, 163–5, upper
  Downland, 325; vaccaries, 165, 168–71;
  valleys, 28, 87, 137, 144, 204, 311, 312;
  woods, 14, 25–7, 72, 129, 312
Downs, 6, 17, 27, 28, 31, 35, 36, 42, 44, 46,
  50, 70, 74, 77, 82, 83, 87, 88, 98, 105, 107,
  116, 120, 123, 126, 127, 132, 141, 143,
  145; colonization on, 121, 137–8, 335;
  cultivation rare on, 144; foot of, 245, 250;
  North, 22, *36*; parishes on, 140, 322;
  South, 30, 78
Downs Wood, 132, 133, *134*
dræg, 346
drāf, 160
drainage, 59; channels ('sewers'), 60; clay-
  pipe, 29, 53; ditches, 60
Draughton, Northants., 347
'dray', 347
Draycott, 347
Draydon, 347
Drayton, Leics., 346, 347
Dreals Farm, Elham, 133, 138
Drellingore, Alkham, *166*
'the Drove', 36
drovedens, 70
drovers, 253
droves, 34, 38, 160, 161, 317; stock, 160,
  329
Droveway House, Stelling, 145, *283*
droveways, 16, 36–7, 39, 43, 75, 122, 131,
  160, 187, *209–18*, 253, 259, 267–70, 317,
  318, 347; assoc. with ecclesiastical
  dedications, 269–70, 295; Marshland, 58;
  Otford, 269–70; *see also* lanes, roads, tracks
Drowhill Woods, *152*
Dry Drayton, Cambs., 347
Dubris, 77, 107
Duke's Shaw, *309*, 317
Dully, *307*, *319*
dūn, names in, 20, 78, 143, 158, 160, 163,
  283, 329; 'king's *dun*', 315
Dungate, 160, *309*, *319*
Dungeness, 60; chp. of St Mary, 206
Dunn Street, 151, *153*

flēot, 91
fold, 142, 161, 162
folk-lore, 269
Folkestone, 43, 49, 50, 70, 76, 88, 117, 157, *166*, 249, 258; dau. ch. of, 189; early Jut. estate, 107, 116, 195; minster at, 187, *188*, 231, 243; St Eanswythe, 231, 248, Holywell, 296; St Mary, 190, 191, 227, & St Eanswythe, 244, 245, 246; St Eanswythe Water in the Bail, 296, 298; Rom. rems., 102, 114, 115; St Rumwold, 243, & St Botolph, 206, 233
Folkestone Warren, 47
Foothills, 28, 32, 41, 44, *45*, 45–7, 55, 56, 61, 66–7, 68, 72, 76, 100, 101, 106–7, 109, 120, 126, 141, 145, 155, 159, 174, 177, 187, *188*, 197, 199, 224, 245, 263, 311; communities, 54, 58; *dens on*, 124–5; early settle. in, 46, 65, 70, 97, 117, 121, 262, 338; estate-centres, 172; m.chs. on, 156, 158, 196, 234, 251, 264; pasture on Downland, 51; R-B occupation, 96, 117, 121, 262; *and see* Original Lands
footpaths, forest, 268
Foot's Cray, 75, *148*, 262, 280
'ford', 90, 91
Fordwich, *80*, 295
fore+steall, 143, 168
forest, 2, 25, 29, 30, 52, 56, 122–3, 129, 172, 238, 263, 268, 269, 275, 319, 339, 344; animals, 129, 130; clearance of, 1, 25, 52, 55, 66, 67, 129, 132, 135, 140, 185, 315; clearings, 89, 122, 135, 146; Downland, 15, 25–7; dwellers, 127; early colonized, 344, 346; common upland, 150, 151, 199, 346; intercommonable upland, 142; nomenclature, 119, 151; origins, 278; pasture, 30–1, 86, 171, 199, 268, 319, 322, 347; pasture farms, 155; royal, 345; uncolonized, 331, 337
Forest Counties, 4
Forstal, *152*
forstals, 12, 131, 143, 168–9, 204
forts, *see* hill-forts and forts, Roman
Fox Barrow Wood, *153*
Foxendown, *134*
Foxgrove, *306*, 316
Foxholt, 133
France, 253
Frangbury, 135, *309*
Fredville, Nonington, 138
freeholders, 52
Frenches, *134*
friaries, 181
Friends Wood, *153*
Frindsbury, 30, 113, 123, 183, 197, 198, *200*, 284, 292; ch. of All Saints, *288*; sec. m.ch. *188*; subord ch. at Strood, 251; St Thomas' Watering, 296; Frindsbury Salts, *289*
Frinsted, 36, *85*, 157, 165, *201*, 313, 326, 327, 329, 332; ch. of St Dunstan, 309
frith, 26, 27, 130
Frith, 135, *310*; Frith Wood, *152*

Frittenden, 106, 147, 149
Frognal, *307*
Frogs Rough, *152*
fruit-growing, *see* farming
Fryarne Park, Stelling, 128, 278, *283*, 284; Fryarne Park Wood, *283*
Fulston, *306*, 314, 316
Funton, *305*
Furness, 335
fyrhth, 130, 165

Gadshill, *288*, 292; *Gadshill*, Sittingbourne, 266
Gapping Shaw, *153*
gardens, 278; hop, 23
Garratt Wood, Lydden, *166*
Garrington, Littlebourne, *80*, 221
Garwynton, Richard de, 221
gate, 131, 160, 162
Gatteridge, *80*, 133, *166*
Gatton, *148*
gavelkind, 178–9; inheritance, 179–80
gē (territory), 77, 83, 91, 107, 117, 193
geat, 160
gebedmann+tūn, 328
Geddinge, Wootton, *166*
(ge)mǣnnes, 20, 130, 142, 283, 328, 330
gentry, 63, 180, 181; indigenous, 220–1; manorial, 56, 220–1; 'yokeland', 324–5
geology, 338; alluvial deposits, 44; Chalk, 44, 199, 281; Gault Clay, 44, 49; Kentish Ragstone, 50, 88; Limestone, 50; London Clay, 43, 44; Lower Greensand, 44, 49; Thanet Beds, 44; Upper Greensand, 44, 49, 281; Wealden Clay, 44; Wealden Sandstone, 44
George, St, 226, 250, 251, 256
Giles, St, 232, 239, 250, 251, 252, 253, 256, 270, 318, 326, 348
Gillingham, 41, 101, 150, *153*, *200*, 206, 311; sec. m.ch., 156, *188*, 197, St Mary Magdalene, 231, 257; subord. chps. of, 198, *289*
Gilmorton, Leics., 348
Gilridge, 145
glass, armorial, 316
Gloucestershire, 24, 336, 340
Goathurst Common, *214*
goats, 32, 163
Godden Green, 52; Godden Wood, *210*
Godehede, 269
Godeselle, 328
Godmersham, 76, 139, 158, 170; m. ch., *188*, 194, St Lawrence, 245, 252; chp. of, *202*; by river, 86, 295
Godshill, Milton Regis, 299
Godwell, Offham, 212
Godwin, Earl, 176
Golden Wood, *319*
Goodnestone, *80*, *111*, 150; chapelry at, *202*, 265, 273, 274, 279
Gore Green, *288*; Gore Wood, *154*, *305*
Gorham Wood, *154*
Gorse Wood, *152*

406

Gorsley Wood, Bishopsbourne, 128
Gossy Hill, 309
Gotteridge, *308*
Goudhurst, 29, 40, 56, 87, *200*, 220, 236, 273, 294
government, local, 278
grāf, 129, 130, 143, 146, 160, 347
Grafty Green, 147
Grain, Isle of, 184; St James, 233
Grandacre, Waltham, 138, 344
Grange, 198, *200*, *289*, *305*
granges, monastic, 206
Gravel Hill Wood, *153*
Graveney, *111*, *202*
Gravesend, 22, 46, 123, 144
graveyards, 185
graziers, 33, 67
Great Barksore, *305*
Great Britains Wood, *214*
Great Buckland, *134*
Great Chart, Ashford, 51, 124, 159, 199, 238
Great Chattenden Wood, *289*, 292
Great Clane Lane Marshes, *287*
Great Cockerhurst, *148*
Great Comp Woods, *211*
Great Crabbles Wood, *287*, 292
Great Foxholt, Swingfield, *166*
Great Grovehurst, 102, *306*; continuous occupation, 341
Great Lennox Wood, *153*
Great Leybourne Wood, *212*
Great Mongeham, *81*, 267
Greatness, 159, 265; St John the Baptist, *209*; chp. by droveway, 270
Great Norwood, 305, 316, 321
Great Oakleigh, *288*, 292
Great Palmstead, *283*
Greatpark Wood, *134*
Great Shuttlesfield, 145
Great Tottington, *152*
Great Wood, 132, *134*
'green' names, 345
Green, *288*
Greenacre, Elham, 266, *283*
Greenlane Wood, *214*
greens, 12, 147, 151, 168, 204
Greensted, *148*
Greenstreet, Teynham, 144, *307*
Greenway, 49, *84–5*, 87, 88, 106, 108, 117, *134*, *152–3*, *200–1*, *209*, *210*, *148–9*, *211*, *212*, 245, 266, 299, *308*
Greenway Court, *308*; Greenway Forstal, *308*
Greenwich, 22, 37, 38, 251
Greet, *309*
Gregory, Pope, 242, 243, 293
Gregory, St, 235, 241, 242, 248, 250
'Grim's Acre', 266
Grinnels Wood, *154*
Groombridge, chp. of St John the Divine, 187, 272
grove, 27
grove names, 143, 146, 151, 155, 161, 162, 345
Grove, 160

Grove End, *306*, 314
Grovehurst, 30, 102, 314, 316
Gumley, Leics., 346
Gundulf, Bishop of Rochester, 298
Guston, *81*
gwy, 106

habitation-sites, 129
Hackington, 143
Hadler's Hook, *309*, 317
Hadlow, *216*; Hadlow Stair, 72
hæc, 160
(ge)*hæg*, 124, 130, 142, 162, 165
Halfmoon Wood, *153*
hālig, 248, 266, 296
halimotes, 270
Halling, *134*, 280, 295; ch. of St John the Baptist, 252
Hall Wood, Chatham, *152*, *153*; Hall Wood, Swingfield, *166*
Halstead, 79, 129, *148*; ch. of St Margaret, *209*, 269; Halstead, Leics., 347
Halstow Marshes, *291*
Halygarden Well, Burham, *213*, 297
hām names, 20, 91, 109, 162, 171, 207
Ham, *81*, *152*; Ham, Stockbury, *283*
hamlets, 12, 41, 48, 53, 56, 70, 71, 72, 119, 123, 136, 145, 186, 207, 219, 334, 335, 339; dispersed, 183; green, 40; heathland, 52; isolated, 347
hamm names, 20, 89, 161, 162, 283
Hammill, *81*, 127, 139, 150, 155
Hampshire, 4, 25, 32, 53, 73, 340
Ham Street, Orlestone, 40
hanger, 27
Hang Grove, *148*
hangra, 130
Hangman's Shaw, *288*
harad, harað, 130, 161, 162, 278
Harbledown, 158, 183; ch. of St Michael, 183; ch. of St Nicholas, 183, 206, 298; Prince's Well, 298; subord. parish, 251, 264
harbour, 311
Harbourland, *152*
Harbour Wood, *283*
Hardres (Lower and Upper), 128, 135, 137, 157, 158, 194, 220; *see also* separate entries
Hardres family of Hardres, 180, 220
Hardwick, 347
hardz, 277
Harpenden, Herts., 345
Harpole, *153*
Harpswood, *308*
Harrietsham, 36, 76, *85*, 89, 197, 199, 281, 328, 332; sec. m.ch., *188*, 198, St John the Baptist, 252, 257, *308*; subord. chps. of, *200*, 265
hart, 162
Hartley, 206
Hartlip, 138, 151, *154*, 159, 312; dau. ch. of St Michael at, *200*, 270, *305*
Harts Hill, *287*
Harty, Isle of, 29, 33, *202*

Harvel, 133, *134*
Harwood, *307*
Haselden, *288*
Hastingleigh, 137, 147
Hatch, Chislet, 160
Hatch Hill, Luddesdown, *134*, 160; Hatch Spring, Hoath, 160
Hault Farm, Petham, 138
havens, 78
Haven Street, *288*; Haven Street Wood, *288*
Havering, Essex, 336
Hawes Wood, *305*
Hawkhurst, 29, 145, 183; ch. of St Lawrence, 253
Hawkinge, 164, *166*, 170, 283; ch. of St Michael, 252
Hawkridge Wood, Lydden, *166*
Hawley, 297
Hawsdown Wood, 132, *134*
'hay', 124, 161
Haydon, *287*
Hayes, 98, 158, 198; Hayes Lane, *154*
Hazel Street, *154*, *308*
Head Barn Wood, *288*
Headcorn, 37, 123, 206
healing, 232, 253, 296, 298
heathland, 2, 88, 232, 269; heaths, 12, 16, 121, 124, 147, 238, 253, 278, 339; wood-heath, 292
Heath Wood, *152*
Hearth Tax, 22, 23
Hebden, Yorks., 321
Helen, St, 241, 242–3, 348
Hemingford Abbots, Hemingford Grey, Hunts., 277
Hempstead, *153*, *307*
hen, 162
Henhurst, *287*
Henley Down, *134*; Henley Wood, *134*
Henry II, 272
Henry VIII, 314
heort, 130, 162, 163
Heptonstall, Yorks., 321
herdsmen, 142, 161, 164, 172, 178, 180, 270
Herebeald's dūn, 183
Herefordshire, 24
hermitages, 206
hermits, desert, 253
Herne, 86, 190, 191, 264
Hernhill, *111*, 164, *202*
Heronden, 150, 155
herst, hurst, 26–7, 124, 127, 129, 130, 143, 146, 147, 160, 161, 162, 163, 165, 170 253
Herst, 317
Hertfordshire, 5, 21, 22, 345, 347
Hebenden, 122
Hever, 79, 123, 146; ch. of St Peter at, 256; separate parish, 265, 281
Hever Castle, 281; chp. in, 219
Hewitts, *148*
hīewet, 130
Higham, 284, *288*; Higham Marshes, *290*; Higham Upshire, 161, *288*, 292
Highchimney Farm, Stelling, *283*

High Cross, 37, *216*
Highfield Wood, *153*
High Halden, 54, 147
High Halstow, 182, 271, 292, 294, 297; ch. of St Margaret, 244, 245, 248, *291*
highland, 2
Highland Zone, 4, 5, 122, 272, 334
Highlands, Woodchurch, 55
High Reed, Meopham, 132, 133, *134*
Highsted, 314, 317, 319; Highsted Forstal, *306*
Hillborough, 266
hill-country, 150
hill-forts, 17, 51, 78, 79, 86, 98, 99, 100, 193, 294
Hill Green, *305*; Hill Hoath, 27; Hill House, Wootton, *166*
hills, 12, 47, 89, 143, 161, 162, 165, 172; hill-top, 86, 252
Histon, Cambs., 18
Hitchin, Herts., 345
hithes, 87, 253
hlēo, 164
hlid, 91, 293
hlinc, 162
Hoad Farm, Acrise, 133, *166*, 283
hoath, 27, 124, 283
Hoath, 160, 191, 264; ch. of Holy Cross, 253; Hoath Wood, *213*, *283*
Hockenden, *148*, 150, 151, 164
Hock Green, *148*
Hockley Sole, Capel-le-Ferne, *166*
Hodsoll family of Hodsoll in Ash, 180
'hog', 164
Hogbrook, Alkham, 164, *167*
Hog Marsh, *289*
Hog's Back, 47
Hogshaw, Milsted, 164, 314; Hogshaw Wood, *309*
hōh, 91, 284, 345, 346
Holborough, 100
Hole Street, *309*, 319
Hollingbourne, 36, 49, 108, *153*, 164, 264, 279–80, 281; bookland chs. of, 199, *200*; detached pastures of, 155, 156, 159, 327, 328, 330; dau. chs., 251, 265, 267; early lathe, 117, 332; Jut. estate, 76, *84*, 102; Maidstone minsterlands, 332; primary m.ch., *188*, 194, All Saints, 227, 245, 257, 296, 297, *308*; springhead estate, 88, 89; interlocking p.b., 328
holloways, 26, 36, 39, 47, 132, 268
Hollows Wood, *148*
Holmesdale, 41, 44, *45*, 49–50, 55, 66, 68, 70, 72, *76*, 87, 88, 89, 90, 106, 120, 126, 132, *134*, 141, 159, 172, 174, 177, *188*, 224, 234, 262, 263, 268, 277, 294, 329, 330; Chartland pastures of, 66; continuity in, 97; *dens* in, 124; early settle. in 24, 49, 51, 65, 70, 108, 117, 121; estate/manors in, 159, 172; Jut. estates in, 84–5, 88, 342; m.ch., 156, 158, 196, 199, 245, 250, 264; problem names, 108–9; R-B occupation, 96; springline, 49, 88, 102; Wealden

pastures of, 54; *see also* Original Lands
Holmstone, Lydd, 60
holt, 130, 146, 161, 162, 316
'holt' (in Leics.), 345–6
Holt, 137; Holt Wood, *152*
Holtysbury, *148*
Holwood, 17; Holwood Park, 98
Holy Cross dedications, 227, 238, 239, 250, 251, 256
Holy Innocents dedications, 235, 241, 243
Holy Trinity dedications, 194, 235, 226, 241, 312
Holywell, Folkestone, 296; Holywell, Upchurch, 296, *305*; Holywell Chapel, *307*; Holywell Shaw, Brasted, 296
Homestall, *310*
homestalls, 168
Honeyden, *148*, 151
Honeyhills Wood, *153*
Honorius, St, 240
honours, 270, 271
Honywood, Postling, 221; Honywood family of Postling, 180, 220, 221
Hoo Allhallows, 182, 271
Hoo Common, *298*; Hoo Flats, *298*; Hoo Ridgeway, *287–8*; Hoo Salt Marsh, *289*
Hoo, Hundred of, 21, 64, 271, 343
Hoo peninsula, 28, *45*, 99, 157, 182, 184, 284, 292, 313; woods on, 345
Hoo St Margaret, 157, 182, 271
Hoo St Werburgh, *76*, 106, 182, 184, 191, 248, 249; archaeol. rems. at, 107, 244; estate centre, 99; minster, 187; *188*, 190, 192, 271, *289*, 292; Rom. rems., 193
Hook Wood, *152*
hop, hope, 143, 161, 170
Hope, Hawkinge, 170
Hope All Saints, Romney Marsh, 59, 61, 185
Hope Farm, 143, 170; Hope Wood, 143, 170
hop gardens, 23, 25, 46, 53, 68; growing, 53; pickers, 296; poles, 26, 31
Hoplands, 143
Horninghold, Leics., 346
Horsalls, *308*
horse, 162, 163, 165; pack, 37
Horsehead, *283*
Horserace Shaws, *154*
Horseshoe Green, Cowden, 145
Horsham, *305*
Horsmonden, 149, 206
Horsnell's Crouch, Wrotham, 183, 211, 220
Horsted, *148*, 151, *152*
Horton Kirby, 77, *148*, 151, 295
Horton Parva, 220
Horton Wood, *148*
Horwood Grove, *287*
hospitals, 206, 226, 227, 232, 241, 253, 270, 298
hōth, 130
Hothfield, 199, 250; ch. of St Margaret, 248; Hothfield Bogs, 51; Hothfield Common, 51, 52
Hougham, 167

houses, 169; court, 311; manor, 145, 180, 204, 219; med., 346; monastic, 62, 63, 66, 125, 126, 138, 227, 242; rebuilding of private, 184–5; religious, 182; 'Wealden', 325; yeoman's, 55
Howt Green, 145, *306*, 316, 322
hrīs, 130
Hubbard's Hill, *214*, 268
Hucking, *36*, *84*, 88, *153*, 171, 204; dau. ch of St Margaret, 156, *200*, 264, 279, 308
Huggin's Wood, *289*
Hulberry, 78, 99
humber/amber, 'river', 106
hundreds, 261, 270–1; Calehill, 327; Codsheath, 269, 271, 343; Eastry & Kinghamford, 325; Faversham, 343; Hoo, 21, 64, 271, 343; imposed, 343; incorporating early Jut. territories, 343; incorporating estates/minsterlands, 271; Milton Regis, 311, 312, 343; shared jurisdictions, 325, 327, 328; teritorial units, 75; Wrotham, 271, 343
Huntingdonshire, 277, 295, 344
Hunton, 149, *218*
'hurst' names, 124, 130, 136, 151, 155
hurst, *see* herst
Hurst, 135, *309*; Hurst Hill, *305*; Hurst Woods, *211*
?hȳscen, 162
Hythe, 50, 60, 184, 248, 251, 253, 284; chs. of St Leonard, 298, St Bartholomew, 206

Ibornden, 122
Ickham, *80*, 82, 101; ch. at, 242
Icknor, *308*
Ide Hill, Sundridge, 52, *214*
Ifield, *287*
Ightham, 37, 271, 272; ch. of St Peter, *211*; Ightham Common, *211*; Ightham Mote, 205, *215*
immigrants, 112
immigration (within Kent), 68
Impton Wood, *152*
industry, 41; cloth, 55; iron, 67, 112; quarrying, 50; sheep-farming, 170–1
ing names, 89, 91, 162, 322
ingas, 14, 161, 162, 322
Ingleton, Poulton, *167*
inheritance, 172; partible 140, 179, 337, *see also* gavelkind
inns, coaching, 316
institutions, 10–11; development of, 10
intercommoning/intercommonable, *see* pasture, common
Ireland, 115
Iron Age, 51, 78, 79, 95, 96, 98, 99, 100, 101, 102, 193, 294; finds, 100; pottery, 9, 100, 101; rems., 114, 193
iron masters, 67; -stone, 112; working, 112
Islingham, 157, 288, 292
Ithamar, St, 240
Ittinge, 137
Ivychurch, 59, 62, 183
Iwade, 62, *201*; ch. of All Saints, *306*

Jacques Court, Elham, 283
Jaenbeorht, St, 240
James I, 284
James, St, 226, 233, 238, 239, 250, 251, 252, 253, 257, 270, 295, 326
Jenkeys, Shadoxhurst, 55
John the Baptist, St, 226, 227, 239, 250, 251, 252, 253, 257, 270, 295, 313, 320, 348
John the Divine, St, 241, 242
Joyden's Wood, *148*, 151
Julliberries Grave, 101
jurisdiction, ecclesiastical, 275–6; hundredal, 327; manorial, 145, 147–8, 274, 327; territorial, 327
Justus, St, 240
Jutes, 7, 65, 97, 104, 105, 119, 160, 317, 330
Jutish burial ground, 20, 98, 101, 102, *110*, *111*, 242, 244; cemetery, 98, 100, 113, 193; colonization, 108, 119, 196; diversity of early Jut. estates, 342; estates/territories, 9, 72, 74–5, *76*, 78, *84–5*, 90, 95, 96, 98, 99, 100, 101, 107, 117, 155, 174, 264, 269, 271, 276, 280, 299, 341, 342, 343; estate-centres, 101, 102, 105, 106, 114, 193, 196, 261, 296; inheritance, 179, 204; invaders, 331; kingdom, 34, 54, 299; occupation, 104, 126, 293; period, 30, 39, 76, 77, 107, 116, 117; places, 107; pre-Jut., 86, 101, 116, 194, 293; *regiones*, 271; rems., 100; royal palace, 191; settlers/communities, 10, 71, 74, 95, 102, 193, 195; summer pastures, 53
Jutland, 7

kartr (Norwegian), *see* Chart
Kearsney, Temple Ewell, 138
Kemsing, *76*, 79, 88, 89, 108, *148*, 249, 269, 332; dau. ch. of, 265, 277; primary m.ch. of, *188*, 194, St Mary & St Edith, *210*, 245; Rom. occupation nr, 99, 102; springs at, 49, 297; well and chapel of St Edith, 206, 255, 296, 298
Kemsing Chart, 88
Kemsley, *306*, 316; Kemsley Down, *153*, *305*; Kemsley Street, 146, 151, 155
Kenardington, 294
Kennington, 102
Kent/Kentish: British names in, 103; Celtic names in, 5, 7, 17, 103–7; chalk country of, 28, 47–9; characteristics of, 25; church, 93, 174–5, 187, *188*, 190, 204, 226, 238, 243, 274, 279; Christianity, 15–16, 57, 181–2, 261; coastal plain, 24; community, 87, 224; comparision with other parts of Britain, 18–19, 23–5, 40–1, 185, 228–9, 246–7, 262, 271–2, 275, 276–7, 281, 294, 295, 333–48; countryside, 17–20, 43, 67, 336; East K., 10, 20, 22, 43, 83, 107, 127, 129, 159, 165, 187, 265, 275, 327, 330, 345; economy, 30, 34, 38–9, 43, 49, 165, 335; English settle. of, 1, 6, 7, 8, 90, 103; environment, 43; evolution of settle., 11–12, 14, 22, 32, 39–42, 55, 70, 89, 105, 140, 175, 179, 279, 337; exploitation of forest and marsh, 337–8; formation of indigenous gentry, 220; fruit-growing areas, 313–14; 'Garden of England', 23–4; geological structure of, 27, 43–4, *see also under* soils; history, 28, 30, 38–9, 40, 63, 65, 66, 75, 116, 119; history *not* affected by proximity to London, 21–2, 68; impact of church on economy and landscape, 181–7; industry, 170; institutions, 11, 117, 270–8, 335–6; Kingdom of, 8, 22, 124, 126, 156, 181–2, 249, 331, 335; kings, 11, 125, 181–2, 196, 311; Law and Custom, 38–9, 140, 172, 178–9, 333, 336–8; legal system, 38, 140, 178–9; map of settle. in, 119; maritime, 232–3; med., 116, 335; monastic houses, 121, 137; North coast, 275; peasantry, 178–9; prehistoric meeting-places, 87, 117, 229; 'problem names', 103, 168; regional divisions, 3–6, 43–5; relative poverty of med. K., 335; religious history, 239; road system, 21, 35–9; settle. history of, 54–5, 59, 65, 66, 68, 113, 123, 124, 172, 222, 223, *see also under* settlement; sheep-farming, 171, and wool production, 170; society, 23, 42, 119, 122, 140, 172, 178, 222, 224, 324, 336–8, evolution of, 12, 38–9, 56–7, 179–80, 335, survival of framework of, 337–8; territorial development, 343; territorial and administrative sub-divisions, 270–4; Teutonic peoples/settles., 90, 108; Vale of, 53; wealth of, 22–4, 224, 338; W. Kent, 10, 16, 27, 43, 50, 77, 106, 116, 132, 133, 220, 262, 268, 277, 281, 327; wills, 143
Kentings, 104
Keppel, 183, 206
Kesteven uplands, Lincs., 344
Keston, 74, *76*, 97, 98, 114, 115, *148*, 226; Keston Common, 98; Keston Mark, *148*
Kettlebender, 138
Kettle Grove, *148*
Kettleshill, Under River, 36
Keycol Farm, *305*; Keycol Hill, *305*, 322
Key Street, *305*; Key Street Wood, *305*
Kiln Wood, *152*
Kimcote, Leics., 18, 348
Kinghamford, 325
Kingsdown-by-Faversham, 78, 143, 158, 160, 199, 201, *309*, 313, 314, 315, 319
Kingsdown by Walmer, 315
Kingsdown-by-Wrotham, 77–8, 82, 143, *148*, 156, 157, 158, 170, 198, 232, 315; ch. of St Edmund the King, 231
Kingston, *80*, 82, 133, *283*, 284; ch. and fair of St Giles, 232
King's Wood, 284
Kingswood, *283*
Kirby, Leics., 182
Kits Coty, 100, 115; Kits Coty Farm, *152*
Knockholt, 75, 129, *148*, 150, 157, 164, 198, 278; ch. of St Catherine, 209; chp. at Cory Yokes, 206, 207, *209*
Knole, 52, 159, 205, *215*
Knowlton, *81*, 150, 279

Kyrsmondenn, Wittersham, 266

La Berchereye, Chatham, 170
Lac Léman, Switzerland, 77
Lade, 329; Lade Wood, *309*
Lad's Farm, *134*
Lad Wood, 133
Ladwood, Elham, 133, 145, 146, *166*, 283
l*ǣ*s, 122, 130, 142, 160, 163, 170, 283, 329, *and see* 'lees'
Lake District, 53, 334, 339
Lamberhurst, 29
Lambs Frith, *153*
Lancashire, 4, 21, 24, 243
land, arable, 339; boundary, 133, 146; demesne, 159; 178; enclosed, 143; inland or tenant, 178; measure of, 323; names in, 162; Original or Old Arable, *see* Original Lands; outlying, 150, 151, 165, 179, 199, 276, 277, 322; outland or yokeland, 178–9, *see also* yokeland; stony, 172
landholders, 323
landing-places, 57, 253
landlords, 272; absentee, 62, 63; upland, 55–6
landowners, 199; names of c.1086, 173
landownership, 173–7; church, 173–7, 182, crown, 173–7; 'private', 173–7
landscape, continuity and changes, 341; and economy, 17–42; English, 1, 3–4, 5; evidence, 7, 11–12, 17, 18, 30, 39, 224; of evolution, 3, 11, 332; forest, 128, 259, 349; as historical document, 3, 11–12, 317, 349; history, 267; pastoral and topographical features, 161; primitive, 119, 342; rural, 261–2; Scandinavian, 5; shaped by colonization, 180; of sixteenth/early seventeenth cents., 2–3; and society, 6–13
landscapes of colonization, 2, 3, 5, 15, 222, 343–8; of continuity, 1–2, 5, 15, 222, 341–3
lanes, 12, 13, 16, 19, 38, 47, 48, 129, 132, 259, 267–70, 311, 319; forest, 53, 180, *209–18*, 314; sunken, 36; twisting, 347; *see also* droveways, roads, tracks
Langdon, 167, *and see* East Langdon, West Langdon
Langley, *36*, *84*, 88, 199, *200*, 279, 282; ch. of St Mary, 298
Lashenden, 122
lathes, 7–11, 86, 92, 117, 270, 327, 328, 329, 332; administration, 163, 172; linked to Jut. estates, 343; origin of, 8, 9–10
Laughton, Leics., 346; Laughton Hills, Leics., 346
Lawless, John, 219
Lawrence, St, 239, 240, 250, 251, 252, 257, 270, 318
lawsuits, 284
lēac, 346, 347
Lea Farm, *309*
lēah names, 20, 88, 129, 130, 146, 161, 162, 253, 292, 316, 329, 346, 347
Leas Green, *148*

Leaveland, 147, *201*, 265, 270
Leaves Green, *148*
Leeds, *36*, *84*, 88, 106, 150, 327, 328; dau. ch. at, 199, *200*, 251, 279, 295, St Nicholas, 250, 270
Leeds Castle, *84*, *308*; Priory, 182
Lee Green, *288*, 292
'lees' (*lǣs*), 33, 126, 138, 142, 147, 161
Lees Rough Wood, *309*
Leicestershire, 12, 23, 30, 42, 65, 128, 180, 182, 183, 184, 185, 246, 257, 272, 338, 340, 345; South Leics. uplands, 344, 347
Leigh, 207, *215*
Leighton, 34
Leize Wood, *148*
Len, r., *36*, 37, 105, 106
Lenham, *36*, 40, 49, 76, *85*, 88, 89, 102, 108, 157, 164, 185, 199, *309*, 326, 327, 328, 329, 332; dau. ch. of, 251, 252, 265; m.ch., *188*, 194, *201*; St Mary, 115, 245, 297
Leonard, St, 233, 250, 251, 252, 253, 256, 270
Lesnes, *148*
Letts Green, *148*
Lewisham, 37, 38
'ley' names, 345
Leybourne, ch. of St Peter & St Paul, *213*, 220
Leysdown, ch. of St Clement, 233, 313
Leyton, *148*
Leyton & Loughton, Essex, 336
Libbetwell, *305*
Lidsing, 150, 151, *153*; subord. chp. at, 198, 200, St Mary Magdalene, 156, 231, 270; Lidsing Green, *153*
lighthouse, 114, 193, 233
Lillechurch, 157, 182, 203, 292; ch. of St Michael, *288*
Lilley Hoo, Herts., 345
limen, 107
Limen, r., 77, 105, 114; silting up, 253
Limepits Cross, *305*
lim fin, 162
Liminig mynster, 266
linch, 161
Lincolnshire, 21, 33, 34, 73, 185, 243, 340; Wolds, 19
Linton, *84*, 86, 294; dau. ch. at, 199, *200*, 251, 265, St Nicholas, 250, 270
Little Brisley, 310
Littlebourne, 79, 80, 82, 221, 267, 295; ch. at, 242
Little Chart, Ashford, 51, 89, 191; dau. ch. at, 199, *201*, 265
Little Comp, *212*
Little Densole, Swingfield, *166*
Little Dully, *307*
Little Duskins, *283*
Little Foxholt, Swingfield, *166*
Little Frith, *310*
Little Halstead, *152*
Little Mongeham, *82*, 158, 267
Little Newbury, *307*
Little Norwood, *305*, 322

411

Owston, Leics., 347
ox, 113
oxa, 165
oxen, 24, 32, 53, 162, 163, 165
Oxenden, 32, *80*, 123, 165; Oxenden, Adisham, *80*, 165
Oxenhill Shaw, Otford, *148*, 165
Oxenhoath, 32
Oxenlees Wood, Crundale, 165
Oxfordshire, 6, 73, 185
Oxfrith, Boxley, 165
Oxinden, Nonington, 180; Oxinden family, 180, 220
Oxleas, *148*
oxna, 165
Oxney, 33, 54, *81*, 165, 251
Oxney Wood, Nonington, 165
Oxroad, Elham, 165

packhorses, 37
paddock, 142
Paddlesworth, nr Folkestone, 48, *134*, 157, *166*; Paddlesworth, nr Snodland, *134*, 158, *213*
Paddock Wood, 18, 53
Palaeolithic, 98, 99; implements, 100; rems., 114
Palmstead, Upper Hardres, 20, 133, 137, 171, 284
Pancras, St, 241, 243, 294
pannage, 26, 30–1, 54, 156, 157; rights, 156, 157, 162, 163, 165
Paradise, Hartlip, 138
parishes, 12, 16, 40, 57, 59, 83, 88, 150–5, 159, 171, 175, 184, 185, 199, 203, 205, 222, 261, 262, 269, 271, 276, 282, 312, 315, 316, 317–18, 325, 326, 332, 345–6; 'bookland', 199, 224, 263, 274, 316; boundaries, *see under* boundaries; Chartland, 52; civil, 278; daughter, 275, 279, 280, 316, 339; dependent, 156–8, 191–2, 194, 195, 316; detached, 171, 279; Downland, 56, 126, 137, 140, 157, 178, 251, 321; formation, 204, 223; forest, 251, 275; manorial, 274, 275, 321; maritime, 233; minster, 155, 192, 219–20, 274–5, 280; names, 182–3; organization, 38–9, 325–6; pastoral, of Downland or *wald*, 323; size, 56, 140, 192, 195, 203, 223, 260, 262; small, 275, 279; 'steads' in, 171–2; strip, 151, 262, 280–1; subsidiary/subord., 220, 251, 256, 275; Wealden, 56, 140, 263, 264, 274; Wilderness, 236–9; wood-pasture, 322
park, 204
Park, *308*
park names, 155
Parkgate, Elham, *283*
parkland, 52
Park Wood, Boxley, *152*; Park Wood, Lyminge, *283*; Park Wood, Hollingbourne, *154*, *308*; Park Wood, Swingfield, *166*
Park Woods, *153*
parochial development, 262; independence, 263; organization, 185, 198; rights, 220;

structure, 182, 205, 261, 271–2, 325; topography, 189, 261–2; unit, 274–8
parrock, 142
Parson's Land Wood, *152*
pastoral, 32, 38, 42, 70; enclosure, 142; dispersal settle. in, 334; lands, 66, 72, 126, 141, 322; people, 253; place-names, 32–3; units, 147; usage, 54, 122, 140, 141, 147–50, 159–72, 177–8, 179–80, 259, 329; zone, 125
pastoralism, 336–7
pasture, 32, 38, 58, 61, 87, 123, 124, 268, 277, 316, 327, 333; ash, 327; attached, 58, 66; cattle, 317; common, 40, 51, 54, 147, 281, 282, 284, 317, 319, 326; detached, 57, 58, 59, 66–7, 123, 155, 159, 171, 263, 317, 326, 330; early colonized woodland, 344, 345, 347; gates, 160; goat, 163; hill, 155; horse, 163; intercommonable, 138–9, 141, 144–6, 155, 177, 205, 276, 330; marshland, 58, 59, 161; ox, 163, 165; rights, 150; royal, 315; sheep, 53, 54, 70, 120, 121–7, 141, 196, 263; swine, 141, 142, 143, 150, 163–5, 263, 268, 317; upland, 145, 148–9, 160–1; wood, 30–1, 66, 78, 88, 90, 123, 126–7, 141–4, 147, 162, 206, 273, 276, 336
Patrixbourne, 79, *80*, 82–3, 197, 262, 267, 276, 295; sec. m. ch., *188*
Paulinus, St, of Rochester, 98, 231, 240
Payden, Wichling, 164, *309*
pays, 6, 13, 43–5, 46, 47, 62, 65, 68, 185, 191, 233, 234; settle. and, 338–40
Pay Street, Folkestone, *166*
pearroc, 130, 142, 163, 283, 329
Peartree Wood, *288*
peasant, 11, 177, 268, 349
Peckham Hurst, *217*
Pelagius, St, 241, 243
Pembury, chp. of St Mary, 256
Penenden, Maidstone, *152*; Penenden Heath, 87, 299
Pennine Counties, 4, 5, 334, 339
Pennycrych, 105, 107
Penshurst, 268, 270; dau. ch. at, 265, St John the Baptist, *215*
Perry Farm, 145
Peter, St, 226, 238, 250, 256, 348
Peter, St, of Canterbury, 240
Peter, St & St Paul, 194, 227, 231, 233, 238, 240, 241, 246, 250, 251, 256, 257, 258, 260, 269
Petersfield, Hants., 30
Petham, 138, *188*, 197, 198, 206, 207, 320
Pett, *154*
Petting Grove, *148*
Pettwood, 319
Pett Wood, *309*
petts, 50, 161, 162
Petts Farm, *152*
Pevington, *85*, 89, 191, 199, *201*, 265
pharos, 193
Phen Farm, 51
Picklands Wood, 319
Pickleden, 164, *166*

pigs, *see* swine
pilgrimages, 16, 249
pilgrims, 253
Pilgrims' Way, 17, 35, *36*, 39, *45*, 49, *76*, 79, *84–5*, 86, 87, 99, 106, 115, 116, 117, 132, *134*, *148–9*, *152–4*, *188*, *200–1*, *209*, *210*, *211*, *212*, 266, *288*, 297, 299, *308*, *309*; route junction on, 242
pilgrim ways, 93, 245, 267
Pipsden Crouch, 183
pirige, 144
Pising, East Langdon, 175
Pistock, Tunstall, *306*, 317, 321
Pitfeld, *134*
Pitstock, Rodmersham, 168, *306*, 317, 319
place-names, 6, 11–12, 32–3, 75, 89, 93–5, 103, 108, 109, 120, 122, 127, 169, 205, 259, 260, 269, 292, 302, 314, 323, 334, 348; British, 29, 266; Celtic, 17, 20, 92, 95, 103, 104–7, 260, 341; in *chart*, 50–1; Christian, 265, 266; crops, 144; Downland, 126–35, 138–9, 141–4, 146–7, 147–9, 151, 155, 156, 157, 159, 160, 161, 162, 163, 179; ecclesiastical, 182–4, 193; elements, 91, 115; English, 104, 117; forest reclamation, 253; French origin, 138; habitation, 184; heathen sites, 265–6; in *ingas*, 14, 161; Latin, 112; local, 329, 330, 346; med., 20, 314; minor, 69, 206, 292, 319, 324, 329, 345; minster, 193; orientation, 265, 267; parish boundaries, 144–6, 278; pastoral, 32, 145, 147, 148–9, 150, 155, 157, 158, 161, 179, 283–4; pre-Christian, 294; pre-Conquest, 11, 20, 314; pre-English, 87, 89, 103, 117; pre-Jut., 103, 108; problem-names, 103, 107–13; of regions, 104; of rivers, 92, 95, 104; settles., 104, 145, 184; in *stān*, 103, 113–16; territorial subdivision, 265, 267; typology, 6, 136; upland *wald* of Midlands, 346–8; Wealden, 34, 145–9; woodland, 25–7, 29, 183, 278, 282, 317, 347; wood-pasture, 141–4; yoke, 324
plants: bluebell, 129; clematis, 26; dog's mercury, 129; dogwood, 26; fern, 162; forest plants, 161; guelder rose, 26; nettles, 172; wood anemone, 129
Plaxtol, Wrotham, 207, 216, 222, 226, 271
plough, land, 61; turn-wrest, 24
Plot, Robert, 324
Pluckley, *85*, 89, 191, 199, 201, 294; ch. of St Nicholas, 250, 251, 253, 265
Plumstead, *148*, 251; Plumstead Common, *148*
Plym, r., Devon, 73
Plympton, 73
Plymstock, 73, 168, 317
Podkin Wood, *152*
Pokeridden, *148*, 164
Polehill Wood, *153*
Polhill Wood, *152*
Pollyfield, 151, *153*
Pond Farm, *308*
ponds, 12; stock, 169

pools, 90, 161; 'miry', 169
population, 24–5, 43, 55, 56; to acreage, 61; British, 342; continuity of, 341; decline, 184; at end Rom. period, 342; expanding, 55, 56, 67, 139, 140, 177, 219, 282; Germanic, 342; pressure, 336, 337, 340; scattered, 263; sparse, 56, 62–3, 126, 275, 335
port (market), 316
ports, 58, 253
Portus Lemanis, 77
post-Conquest, 51–2, 55, 65, 66, 71, 137, 144, 170, 172, 186, 205, 220, 226, 233, 240, 241, 251, 252, 256, 268, 273, 293, 295, 297, 318, 333, 335, 337, 344
Postling, 180, 187, 221, 248; ch. of St Mary & St Radegund, 297
potteries, 96; Romano-Saxon, 113; pottery kilns, 97
Potter's Wood, *153*
Poulton, *167*
Pratts Grove, *148*
preceptories, 206, 227
precincts, 270, 271
pre-Conquest, 2, 19, 31, 34, 73, 75, 83, 117, 120, 122, 137, 164, 171, 172, 174, 175, 176, 179, 189, 205, 272, 278, 297, 316, 336, 343, 347
prehistoric, 17
Presteshelle, in Maidstone, 69, 267
Preston, 266
Preston, Aylesford, 266
Preston by Faversham, *111*, 150, *202*, 266, 297
Preston by Wingham, *80*, 266
Preston nr Minster-in-Thanet, 266
Preston in Shoreham, *209*, 266
Prestwold, Leics., 345
priest, 275, priest's *tūn*, 266, 328
Priestwood, 133, *134*; Priestwood Green, *134*
Prim Farm, Stelling, *283*
priories, 182
properties, landed, 324
Puckle Hill, *287*, 292
Puckleshall (hospital), 307
Punish, *134*
pur, 162
Purty's Shaw, *288*
Pytchley, Northants., 347

Quantnell Wood, *154*
Quarry Hills, *see* Stone Hills
quarries, 100; quarrying, 50; quarrymen, 40
Queen Down, *153*; Queen Down Warren, 305
Queniborough, Leics., 348
Quilters Wood, *283*

Radegund, St, 239, 256
Radfield, *201*, *307*, 315, 319–20, 327; chapelry, 313, 318
railways, 45, 53

Rainham, 28, *76*, 101, 103, 109, 151, *153*, 156, 159, *200*, 312; ch. of St Margaret, 244; Rainham Park, *153*
Rakeshole, Elham, *166*
Rams Bottom Wood, *289*
Ramsden, *148*, 150, 151, 164
Ramsgate, 183, 191
Rams Green, *291*
Ramswood, *148*
Randall Heath, *287*
Ranscombe, 105, *288*
rates, parish, 278
Ratling, Nonington, 189, 273
Ratly Hills, 292; Ratly Hills Wood, *288*
Rats Castle, 51, 139
Raynehurst and Timberwood, *287*
Ravensbourne, r., 98
Rawtenstall, Lancs., 321
rectories, 182
Reculfmynster, 266
Reculver, 10, 16, *45*, 105, 116, 117, 249; chp. of St James nr., 206, 233; cross, 194; dau. chs. of, 251, 264; estate-centre, *76*, 101, 107, 196; manor, 159–60; minster, 124, 187, *188*, 190, 193, 195, 196, 246, 266, 275; m.ch., 191, St Mary, 245, 246; Rom. bricks in minster, 194, 293; Rom. fort, 191, 193; Rom. settle., 101, 107, 195; Saxon burials, 103
Redborough, *310*
rede, 129, 130, 162, 292, 329
Rede Court, *288*, 292
Redham Mead, *290*
Redoak, Elham, *283*
Redsells Wood, 308
Redsole, Paddlesworth, *166*
Red Wood, *134*
Reed Wood, *153*, *309*
Reeds, *283*
Reeds Croft Wood, *152*
Reed's Shaw, *153*; Reed's Wood, *153*
Reformation, 182, 186, 226, 227, 240, 298
regio, regiones, 8, 9–11, 16, 92, 117, 119, 129, 155, 168, 170, 193, 196, 261, 267, 276, 302, 320, 328, 331; of Faversham, 320; of Milton Regis, 311–15, 316, 318, 319, 332; Jut., 271
regions of Kent, words used to describe, 3–6
Regulbium, 107
Reinden, 164, *166*, *283*; Reinden Wood, *166*
relics, 233
religion, heathen, 49, 86, 108, 116, 242, 269, 328
religious centre, 87, 99, 115, 266
rents, an acre, 326; annual, 159; fixed money, 56; food, 72; quit, 159; value of, 223–4
Rhode Wood, *309*
Rhodes Minnis, 138, 145, 146, 147, 330
Richborough, 21, *45*, *81*, 104, 108, 112; ch. of St Augustine, 107, *188*, 195, 230, 244, 245, 255, 294; Jut. settle., 101; Rom. fort, 101; Rom. settle., 103, 107
Ricklands Wood, *307*

Riddles, *306*
'ridge', 124, 161, 162
Ridge, *166*
Ridgemere Lane, Barkby, Leics., 348
ridgeway, 269: Hoo Ridgeway, 287–8; prehistoric, 77, 82, 109, 132, 245
Ridge Wood, 132, *134*
Ridley, *134*, 140, 204; ch. of St Peter, *211*, 256
rights, burial, 318; common, 325, 326–30; 'folk', 172
Rigshill, 135
Ringhead, *81*
Ringleton, 139
Ringwould, 127, 128, 251; ch. of St Nicholas, 253
Ripple, *81*, 127
rites, Christian, 116; pagan, 116, 249
Riverhead, 71
riverine site, 71, 72, 90
River Minnis, 330
rivers, 72, 79, 87, 90, 117; Celtic names of, 73–4, 75, *76*, 77, 92, 95, 104; crossings, 98, 99, 100, 198; early chs. on banks of, 260, 295–6; early English names, 74, 82; early settle., 73; estates, 73, 76–87, 98, 105, 127, 143; minster on banks, 193, 195; navigability of, 71, 72; people, 73, 82; pre-English names, 91, 105; territory, 87, 127; valleys, 96, 344
Road, *309*
roads, 43, 53, 253, 267; Canterbury, 18, 20, 206; ch. built on, 245; Dover, 21–2; London, 18, 269; Otford, 269; post-Rom., 267–70; Roman, 10, 18, 20, 21–2, *45*, 46, *76*, 78, 79, *80*, *81*, 82, 83, *84*, *85*, 86, 87, 115, *152*, *188*, 200–2, 242, 243, 245, 267, 268, 311, 313, 322, 325, abandoned, 319; road-sides, 206; state of, 54; systems, 26, 38, 123; topography, 267; trunk, 340; *see also* Stone Street, Watling Street; droveways, lanes, tracks
Robert of Winchelsea, 240
Rochester, 43, *45*, 46, 47, 100, 106, 107, 109, 116, *152*, 195, 222, 249, 251, 312, 328, 329, 330; cath. of St Andrew, 182, *188*, 190, 193, 195, *288*, 242, 245; dau. chs., 197, 198, *200*; diocese documentation, 139–40, 185, 187, *188*, 189, 190, 194, 196, 203, 242; ecclesiastical centre, 239; estate-centre, *76*, 114; estates of, 173, 176; manorial chs., 204; monastic manor, 117; Rom. settle., 99, 103; saints of, 240; Saxon burials, 103; settle., 233
Rockingham Forest, Northants., 347
rock-shelters, 17
rod, 130, 146, 161, 162, 165, 319, 329
rōd, 162
Rodmersham, 160, *201*, 251, 272, 284, 315, 317, 318–19, 320; depend. of Milton Regis, 251, 270, 313; ch. of St Nicholas, *306*, 318; Rodmersham Green, *306*
Rogley, 122
Roll Lodge Shaw, *152*

418

Roman, 20, 21, 29, 65, 75, 86, 97, 99, 100, 101; altar, 114; basilica, 244; brickwork, 57, 77, 97, 99, 102, 181, 293–4; buildings, 98, 100, *110*, 244, 293, 312; burial ground, 101; coins, 193; cremations, 101, *110*, *111*, 248, 299; farms/estates, 95; ford, 77; forts, 96, 98, 101, 193, 294; invasions, 95; lighthouse/*pharos*, 114; occupation 96, 99, 100, 101, *110*, 113; posting-station, 99, 101, 193; pottery, 101; pottery klns, 319–20; pre-Rom., 17, 76; recession of Rom. settle., 2, 342; rems., 17–18, 57, 77, 78, 79, 82, 87, 99, 100, 108, 109, 114, 116, 193, 244, 248; ritual site, 101, 116; Romanized, 86, 107, 313; sites, 99, 100, 102, 103, *111*; temple, 20, 79, 101, 242; villas, 77, 78, 96, 97, 98, 99, 100, 101, 116, 260, 266, 299
Romano-British, 1, 30, 47, 69, 77, 90, 96, 108, 112, 119, 340, 344; 'boundary', 327; building, 241; burial ground, *110*, 292; communities, 181, 193; enclosure, 312; 'inheritance', 179; mausoleum, 114, 115, 299; military site, 242, 243; origin, 311; people, 117; remains, 78, 82, 102, 114, 193, 260; settle., *see under* settlement; territories, 320; traditions, 330
Rome, 242
Romney, 58, *188*, 194, 196; ch. of St Martin, 244; Romney Marsh, 6, 23, 28, 29, 33, 36, 38, 41, 44, 57, 60, 61, 62, 63, 64, 66, 74, 170, 184, 185, 234, 264, 294; settle., 59
Roots Wood, *152*
Rose's Wood, *153*
rother, 162
Rother, r., *see* Limen, r.; Rother Levels, 57
Ross-shire, 25
Roxborough Wood, Denton, *166*
Roydon Hall, 63
Royton, *201*
Rudstone, E.R. Yorks., 115
Ruffetts, The, *154*, *308*
Rugmer Hill, 149
Rumwold, St, 233, 241, 243, 244
Rumsted, Hucking, *154*, 159, 171, *308*
Rutupiae, 107
Ruxley, 151, 220; ch. of St Botolph, 257–8
Ryarsh, 132, *134*, 277; ch. of St Martin, 212
Ryestreet, *290*; Ryestreet Common, *290*
Ryetop Wood, *153*

St Anthony-in-Roseland, Cornwall, 184
St Giles at Sarre, 182
St James-in-Grain, 182, 184, 198, *200*
St John's-in-Thanet (Margate), 101, 182, 191, 206, 219; altars at, 226
St Lawrence-in-Thanet (Ramsgate), 182, 183, 191; altars at, 226
St Leonard's, West Malling, 212
St Leonard's Wood, *212*; St Leonard's Tower, 183
St Margaret-at-Cliffe, *81*, 183, 203, 248
St Margaret's Crouch (Hawkhurst), 183
St Margaret-at-Helles, 77, *148*, 156, 157, 183, 231

St Martin's Pountney, 183
St Mary Cray, 75, *148*, 150, 151, 183, 198, 280
St Mary's Hoo, 182, 184, 203, 271, *291*
St Mary-in-the-Marsh, 183, 184, 266
St Mary's Marsh, *289*
St Mary-at-the-Ness, 183
St Nicholas-at-Wade, 182, 191, 203, 251
St Paul's Cray, 75, *148*, 150, 151, 183–4, 231, 280
St Peter-in-Thanet (Broadstairs), 182, 183, 191, 206, 226, 256; altars at, 226
St Stephen's Chapel, *152*
saints, 16, 182, 187, 245, 253; assoc. with Canterbury and Rochester, 239, 240; with healing, 253; with travellers, 253; with wild places, 252; child, 243; names, 183, 207, 226, 235, 239–40, 246–7, 250–7; non-local, 240–1; patron, 228, 230, 231, 232, 233, 238, 242, 243, 251, 266, 269; royal, 239–40, 255; royal women, 239, 246–7, 248; Saxon, 254–5, 312, 314; Wilderness, 326; *see also* dedications, church, *and under* individual saints' names
Salisbury Plain, 28, 47
Salmestone, St Augustine's Abbey, 206
Salter's Heath, *209*; Salter's Cross, *288*
Saltonstall, W.R. Yorks., 321
Sandhurst, 29, 52, 251, *308*; ch. of St Nicholas, 253
Sandhurst, Doddington, *310*
Sandling, *152*; Sandling Wood, *152*
Sandwich, 46, *81*, 195, 222; chp. of St Bartholomew's hospital, 206, 232, 298; ch. of St James, 233; St Clement, 233
Sandwich, Sir Henry de, 219
Sandy Hill, *288*
Sarre, 61, 62, *76*, 101, 105, 107; St Giles ch. and fair, 232
Saviour, St, dedications, 21
Saxon shore, 193
Scandinavian, 5
Scarborough, N.R. Yorks., 32
Scarletts, 145
scēad, 162
scēaga, 131
scēap, 160, 170
scearu, 162
scēat, 162
sceld, 162
sceorf, 162
Schamele, Sittingbourne, 266
scīr, 160, 292
Scraye, Lathe of, 327
Scrubbs Wood, *152*
Scrub Wood, *309*
Scuttington, *307*, 319
scylf, 162
sea-farers, 206
Seal, 88, 269, 277; dau. ch. of St Peter & St Paul, *210*, 265; Seal Chart, 50, 51, 88, *210*
sea-wall, 60
Seed, 135, *310*
sele, 277

'stone' names, 113–16, 260, 299; *see also stān*
stone, 162; stone, building, 100
Stone, 77, 98, *148*; subsid. chp., 320
Stone, Bapchild, 114, 116, 306
Stone in Buckland, *110*
Stone in Cranbrook, 114–15
Stone-by-Dartford, 114, 282
Stone-by-Faversham, *110*, 113, 114, 115, *201*, 294, 297; ruined ch., 299; Rom. rems., 114, 115, 299
Stone Acre Wood, *153*
Stone Grave, Snodland, 100, 114
Stonehill Green, *148*
Stone Hills, 35, 37, 47, 50, 53, 79, 88, 197, 199, 294
Stone House Wood, *288*
Stonehouse in Frindsbury, 113, *288*
Stone-in-Oxney, 113, 114
Stone in Saltwood, 114
Stone in Thanet, 114
stone-pits, 50
Stonepitts, Seal, 50, 113
Stone Street, 20, 87, 100, 114, 277, 320
Stony Lane Wood, Swingfield, 133, *166*, 283
Stony Warren, 115
Stour, East, r., 297
Stour, Great, r., 21, 46, 47, 49, 50, 51, 70, 71, 83, 86, 121, 280, 295, 297, 329; estates on, 86; headsprings, 258; Levels, 29, 57, 58, 61, 62, 67, 83; valley, 25, 37, 100, 101, 109, 127, 129, 157, 158, 170, 220, 231, 234, 250, 265, 277, 330
Stour, Lesser or Little, r., 47, 48, 82, 83, 164, 295; valley, 79
Stourmouth, *80*, 294
Stowting, 49, *76*, 88, 102, 108, 297
streams, 12, 90
Street, r., 311
Streetwell, Lenham, 297
Strood, 251, 284, *288*
stubb, 130
Stubs Wood, *154*
Sturigao, 86
Sturry, 76, *80*, 103, 164, 264, 295; estate at, 86; lathe centre, 117; m.ch., *188*, 194, 195, St Nicholas, 251, 257; Rom. rems., 101
Styants Wood, *210*
Suffolk, 31, 32, 66, 185, 334, 344, 347; border parishes, 334
Summerfield, 145
Summerlees, 122
Sunderland, *307*
Sundridge, 37, 38, 52, 106, *148*, 262, 281; dau. ch. at, 209, 265, 269; unknown dedication, 226
Supperton, Wickhambreaux, 144
Surrey, 4, 7, 21, 53, 335; border, 37, 47, 53, 79, 114, 129, 199, 250, 275, 280
Sussex, 2, 4, 5, 7, 25, 28, 29, 30, 32, 37, 47, 53, 54, 66, 78, 87, 88, 104, 168, 273, 334, 335, 336; Weald of, 6, 35, 41, 339
Sutton, 70, 158, 267
Sutton Baron, *305*, 323; the Plots of, 324–5, 349

Sutton-at-Hone, 77, *148*, 150, 151, 156, 158, 267, 297; dau. ch. of, 198; St John's Jerusalem, 183, 206; sec. m.ch., *188*, 197, 231–2, St John the Baptist, 231, 252
Sutton-by-Dover, *81*, 158, 267
Sutton Valence, 51, *84*, 88, 124, 328; dau. ch. at, 199, *200*, 265, 267, 279, St Mary, 250; Norman castle, 294
Swale, r., 29, 33, 57, 97, 101, 104, 106, 311, 312, 319; marshlands, 315
Swalecliffe, 86, 106, 164, 264
swān, 130, 142, 164
swānatūn, 322
Swanley, 33, *148*, 151
Swanscombe, 113
Swanton, Bredgar, 164, *308*, 314, 322, 349
Swanton, Lydden, 33, 80, 164, *166*
Swanton Street, Bredgar, *308*
Swarling, Petham, 207
Swarton, *80*
swelgend, 162
swine, 32, 33, 34, 38, 54, 123; swine herds, 36, 54, 142; names in; 164; pastures, 34–5, 119, 120, 123, 143, 163–5
Swinford, 33
Swinford, Leics., 348
Swingfield, 133, 164, 165, *166*, 179, 283; ch. of St John, *166*, 183; Swingfield Minnis, *166*, 283, 330; ch. of St John, 206
Swingate, *152*
Swyre's Shaw, *288*
Syle Wood, *152*
Syndale, *36*, 37, 112, 327

Taddington Wood, *152*
Tanat, r., Wales, 104
Tanatos, 104
Tanker Dean Wood, *153*
Tappington, Denton, 133, 166
Tanners Cross, *210*
Tatwine, St, 240
Taw, r., Devon, 73
Tawstock, Devon, 73, 166, 317
Tawton, Devon, 73, 77
taxation, 62
teāg, 124, 130, 142, 163; *see also* 'tye'
temples, 96, 166; heathen, 242, 243, 265, 293, 299
Temple, *288*
Temple Ewell, *81*, 138, 147, *167*, 297
Temple Marsh, *288*; Temple Wood, *288*
tenants, 56, 175, 178; forest, 56; Saxon, 177
Tenterden, 38, 147, 161; *dens* of 123; ch. of, St Mildred, 230–1, 236
territory, agrarian, 9; ecclesiastical, 261, 264, 280, 281, 332; dependent, 72, 342; pastoral, 56; pre-Christian, 280; R-B, 280, 320, 321, 331, 342–3; rural, 342–3; springhead, 74, 311; subdivision of, 332; virgin, 340
Test, r., Hants., 260
Teston, 70, 99, 114, 115; date of origin, 260–1; early ch. at, *188*, 195, St Peter & St Paul, *218*, 260; Rom. villa, 100, 260

Textus Roffensis, 185, 189, 205, 269, 270
Teynham, 59, *76*, 87, 89, 123, 144, 171, 193, 281, 298, *307*, 311, 314, 322, 327, 329; *dens* of, 123; dau. chs. of, 157, 171, 201, 251, 320; Jut. estate, 101; minsterland, 192, 332; m.ch. at, *188*, 189, 190, 191, 320; R-B boundary, 319–20, 331; Rom. cremation, *110*
Thames, r., 7, 28, 271, 284; estuary, 29; valley, 18
Thanet, Isle of, 17, 29, 32, 38, 43, *45*, 57, 65, 92, 104, 107, 114, 123, 234, 274; St Mildred's minster in, 231
Thanington, 37–8, 251; ch. of St Nicholas, 231
thegns, 186, 199
St Theodore, 240
St Thomas, 226
St Thomas Becket, 184, 240, 249, 252, 256, 292, 299
Thorne in Thanet, 221
Thorne, Henry, 221
Thorpe Underwood, Northants., 347
Three Crouches, Frindsbury, 183, *288*
Throapham, Yorks., 262
Throwley, nr Faversham, 169, *201*, 265
Throwley Forstal, Throwley, 40, 169
Thurnham, *36*, *84*, 86, 102, 150, *153*, 161, 314; dau. ch. at, *200*; interlocking p.b., 151
thwit, 130, 146
Tickenhurst, 150, 155
Tickham, *307*
'tigh', 124; *see also* 'tye'
Tilden, *36*, 37
Tilmanstone, 81
Tilton, Leics., 347
timber, 347; *see also* 'dray'
Timberden, *148*
Timberwood, *289*
Timbold Hill, *309*, 327
tin, 64
Tithe Index, 278, 279, 318, 319
tithes, 278, 320
Tithe Surveys, 33
'tithings', 52, *198*, 219, 270, 271
toll, 27, 161
Tommydown Wood, 153
Tonbridge, 37, 56, 72, 184, 192, 198; Lowy of, 123; sec. m.ch., *188*, 197, St Peter & St Paul, *215*
Tonge, 59, 160, 332; dau. ch. at, *201*, 313, St Giles, *317*, 318; dependent of, Milton Regis, 315, 138–20; fair of St Giles, 232; hospital of St James, 206; R-B b., 331
topography, 6, 35–6, 43, 65, 93, 126, 127; analysis, 259–301, 329, 330; of boundaries, 278–92, 329, 330; development, 262; ecclesiastical, 192, 193–4, 264, 315, 320; evidence, 69, 75, 135, 259–301, 316, 344; influence of, 10; parochial, 261–2, 274–8, 332, 348; of upland *wald*, 347–8; reconstruction, 259–332
Tottington, 115; chp. of St Stephen, *213*
towns, 68, 123, 271, 279; king's, 112;

market, 40, 72, 74, 316; post-Rom., 78; pre-Conquest, 87; 'primary', 74, 78; Rom., 99, 100, 193; thoroughfare, 316, 349
Toy's Hill, Westerham, 50
tracks, 26, 347; cart, 36–7; prehistoric, 17, 39, 49, 93, 109, *110–11*, 187, 245, 267, 268, 317, timber, *see* 'dray'; ways, 38, 43, 58, 109, 160, maps, 209–18, 253; *see also* droveways, lanes, roads
trade, 40, 316; centre, 83
transhumance, 35–9, 58, 61, 63, 67, 122, 126, 141, 155–6, 159, 160, 161, 178, 263, 273, 333, 336, 337; decline of, 55; economy, 26, 30–1
translation of relics, 233
transport, water, 100; road, 336
Trapham, Wingham, 145
travellers, 206, 226, 232, 233, 253, 269, 270
trees, 26–7, 59, 161, 172, 315; alder, 26; apple, 161, 162, 172; beech, 26, 30, 34, 161, 163, 172; birch, 26; crab apple, 26; chestnut, 26, 30, 314, 316; elder, 26, 161, 162; elm, 26, 161, 172; hazel, 26; holly, 26, 60; hornbeam, 26, 30; lime, 172; maple, field, 26, 161; nut, 172; oak, 26, 30, 34, 161, 162, 163, 172, bog-, 29, mast, 163; pear, 26, 144, 161, 162, 172; plum, 26, 172; spindle, 26; thorn, 161,162; wayfaring, 26; whitebeam, 26; wild cherry, 26; wild service tree, 26; willow, 26; yew, 26; in place-names, 26
trench, 27
Tribal Hidage, 11
Trimworth nr Wye, 158, 189, *202*
Trottiscliffe, *76*, 108, 132, *134*, 195, 275, 297, 332; estate, 88; megaliths nr, 115; m.ch., *188*, 194, 265, St Peter & St Paul, *212*, 245; Rom. rems., 102
Tryndhurst, 122
Tubbenden, *148*, 150, 151, 164
Tumble Tye, Capel-le-Ferne, *166*
tumulus, *110*
tūn, 73, 76, 77, 91, 158, 162, 321, 346; king's, 315
Tunbrick Cross, *287*
Tunbridge Wells, 96, 268
Tunbury Wood, *152*
Tunstall, nr Milton, 168, 284, 314, 317, 320–3; chapelry at, 158, *201*, 315, St John the Baptist, 270, *306*, 320; dependent on Milton Regis, 274, 313; manor at, 321, 322
Twelve Acre Wood, 132, *134*
Twitham, 145, 146, 150, 155
Twitton, 99, 146, *148*
Twydal, 198, *200*
Twysden family, 63, 220
Twyssenden in Goudhurst, 220
'tye' (*teāg*), 33, 130, 142, 147
Tyehurst, 147
Tyland Scrubs, *152*

Ulcombe, 50, *84*, 179, 199, *200*, 281; ch. of All Saints, 250

423

Under River, 277
units, agrarian, 8, 9, 276; ecclesiastical, 276; med. administrative, 343; parochial, 274–8; territorial, 8, 10, 261, 277
Upchurch, 60, 159, 179, 183, 312; dau. ch. at, *200*, St Mary, *305*; Holywell in, 296
upland, wooded, 78, 326, 330
Upland, 34, 44, 46, 57, 58, 61, 63, 67, 68, 123; communities, 141; *dens* on, 123–7, 271; estates, 56; *see also* Foothills
Upminster, minster at, 187, 190, 266
Upper Hardres, *80*, 133, 137, 171, 265, 267, 277, 278, *283*; interlocking p.b., 284; Upper Hardres Wood, *283*
Upper Rodmersham, *306*, 319
Upper Standen, Hawkinge, *166*
Upton, Alkham, *166*
Upton Wood, Sibertswold, *167*

vaccaries, 125, 126, 142, 146, 163, 165, 168–71, 315, 317, 320
Vagniacae (Springhead), 99, 299
valleys, 47, 48, 50, 89, 172; *see also* Darent, Medway, Stour
vehicles, horse-drawn, 37
verno, 107
vicarages, 182
villae regales, 8, 9, 10, 83, 86, 117, 191, 195, 196, 242, 311, 313
villages, 18, 39, 40, 42, 123, 204, 222; Anglo-Saxon, 8; common-field, 348; deserted, 42; green, 52; Midland, 39, 40–1, 72
'villes', 270
Vincent, St, 241, 242

Waddling Wood, Whitfield, *81*, 127
Wadenhall, Waltham, 198, 207, 220
Wadling or *Wolding* Wood, Ripple, 127
wǣl, 162, 169
Wainscot, *alias* Parlabiens Yoke, *288*
wakes, 227
wald, 20, 25, 30, 90, 129, 130, 140, 143, 146, 151, 161, 162, 163, 252, 276, 314, 322, 329, 330, 346; clearance, 15, 139; country, 345; early colonized, 49, 199, 344, 347; evolution of, 335; droves in, 161; outlying, 189, 199, 206, 282, 284; pastoral settle., 324; permanent colonization, 177–9, 181, 197; place-names, 83, 86, 127–8, 139, 150, 253; reclamation, 133, 136, 186, 204, 206, 253; upland, 328, 347–8
Walddraitton, Cambs., 347
Walden, 78, *148*, 150, 151, 164
Walderchain, 48, *80*, 83, 127, 128
Waldershare, *81*, 86, 144, 145, 278
Walderslade, 47, 127, 152, 330
Waldington, 127
Wales, 4–5, 42, 119, 183, 184
Walgrave, Northants., 347
Wallinghurst, 106
Walmer, *81*, 107
Walmestone, 273
Waltham, 20, 48, 127, 128, 137, 144, 157, 158, 171, 220, 320; sec. m.ch. at, *188*, 197,

198, St Bartholomew, 253; subord. chs. of, 198, 207
Waltham, Leics., 345
Walton, Leics., 18
Walton by Eastry, 105, 107
Walton by Folkestone, 105, 106, 107
Walton Holt, Leics., 346
Wantage, 89
Wantsum, r., 30, 104, 105, 107
Warbank, Keston, 98
Warden, ch. of St James, 233
Wardwell Wood, *305*
ware, 162
Warehorne, 206
warren, 27, 131, 155
Warren, The, *308*
Warren Farm, *152*; Warren Street, *309*; Warren Wood, 308
Warwickshire, 6, 24, 25, 336, 339, 340; north, 334
Washenden, 122
waste land, 71
Wastelands Shaw, *154*, *305*
water, drinking, 169; healing, 296; nymphs, 116, 249, 299; spirits, 296; supply, 72
Water Lane, 37
Wateringbury, *218*, 277, 280, 297; ch. of St John the Baptist, *218*, 250; Wateringbury Chart, *217*; Wateringbury Cross, *218*
Watling Street, 22, 23, 30, 35, 37, 47, 87, 98, 99, 101, 109, *110–11*, 116, 117, *148–9*, 245, *287–8*, 292, 297, *305*, *306*, 311, 312, 313, 317, 319, 340
'weald marsh', 30
Weald, the, 6, 19, 23, 24, 25, 28, 33, 41, 42, 44, *45*, 47, 50, 52–7, 61, 64, 68, 70, *76*, 79, *84–5*, 86, 88, 96, 105, 114, 120, 121, 124, 127, 128, 132, 141, 147, 156, 161, 165, *188*, 192, 198, 222, 224, 262, 263–4, 266, 267, 268, 272, 275, 294, 296, 327, 339; of Andred, 41, 53, 104, 325; archaeol. complexes in, 114–15; chs., 186, 205, 222, 232, 256, 274, 295; colonization of, 97; ch. dedications, 234–9; *dens* in, 34–5, 123, 125–6, 163, 263; development of settle., 54–5, 65, 120–1, 136, 147–9, 163, 172, 263, 264, 335; droveways, 36–8; exploitation, 125, 162; forest, 26, 29, 162; High and Low, 27, 52, 53, 65, 339; manorial/ecclesiastical structure, 55–6, 67, 159; orchard country, 18, 53; parishes, 56, 140, 168, 192, 219, 222–3, 251, 262–4, 275, 323; pastoral economy, 56, 161, 163; pasture, 54, 56, 188, 126, 147–9, 174, 263; place-names, 27, 34–5, 106, 123–4, 127, 168; roads, 35–6, state of, 53–4, 207, 219; settle. on p.b., 145; subord. nature of settles., 155, 156; swine pastures, 35, 36, 37, 38, 261, 323; uncolonized, 79; yeoman class, 55, 323, 325
wealth, 105, 107
weard-setl, 162
Wednesbury, Staffs., 294
Week Street, Maidstone, 87, 100

wēl, 91
wella, 91
Welland valley, Leics., 344, 346
wells, 90, 169; St Anne's, Maidstone, 249, 296; St Augustine's, Ebbsfleet, 296; St Eanswythe's Water in the Bail, Folkestone, 296, 298; St Edith's, Kemsing, *210*, 296; St Ethelburga's, Lyminge, 296; St Eustace's, Withersdane in Wye, 296; Godwell, Offham, *212*; Halygarden, *213*; holy wells, 93, 109, 206, 232, 239, 245, 249, 259, 296, 300, 341; Our Lady's, Dover, 296; Pilgrims', Canterbury cath., 296; St Thomas, 116, *209*, 296; St Thomas's Watering, Frindsbury, 296
Welsh Marches, 145, 334, 335, 339
Wentwood, *305*
Werburga, St, 240, 248, 292
Wessex, 4, 5
West Barming, *218*
Westbere, 86
Westborough, *84*
West Cliffe, *81*
West Country, 4, 119, 183, 268, 334
Westcourt Marshes, *287*
Wested, 151
Westenhanger, nr Hythe, 184
Westerham, 51, *76*, 78, 87, 88, 98, 250, 296, 297; depend. chapelry of, 265, 280; estate 79, 82; m.ch. at, *188*, 194; Westerham Hill, 47
Western Heights, Dover, 114
West Farleigh, 280; ch. of All Saints, *218*, 250
Westfield Sole, *152*; Westfield Wood, *152*
West Hougham, Hougham, *167*
West Kingsdown, *see* Kingsdown-by-Wrotham
West Langdon, *81*, 158
West Lees, 283
West Malling, 182, 267, 277; Abbey, *213*; chp. of St Leonard, 207, *212*, 250, 298; ch. of St Mary, *213*
Westmorland, 24, 334, 335
West Peckham, 250; ch. of St Dunstan, *217*; commandery, *217*
Westrill, Leics., 348
West Studdal, *81*, 127
Westwell, *76*, 88, 102, *170*, 282; dau. chs. of, 199; sec. m.ch., *188*, 197, St Mary, 245, 297
West Wickham, 175
West Wood, *153*
Westwood Court, Sheldwich, *170*
Wharram Percy, E.R. Yorks., 13
wheat, cultivation of, 144
Wheelbarrow Town, Elham, *80*, 127, 145, 146, *283*
Whiteacre, Waltham, 144
Whitegate Wood, *153*
White Horse Stone, 100, 115
Whitehorse Wood, 132, *134*
Whites Wood, *152*
Whitfield, *81*, 158

Whitley Row, 52, 145 ; Whitley Scrubs, 51, *214*
Whitstable, 86, 164
Whittaker Wood, *154*
Whittakers Wood, Stockbury, 144
Whittonstall, Northumb., 321
Whorne's Place, Cuxton, 328, 329
wīc+hām, 113
wīchām, 91
Wichling, *36*, 85, 164, 313, 326, 329; detached chapelry at, *201*, 204, 327, St Margaret, *309*; R-B boundary, 327; Wichling Green, *309*
'wick', 162, 168
'wickham', 162
Wickham, Cuxton, 113
Wickham, Otford, 99, 113
Wickhambreaux, *76*, *80*, 82, 113, 117, 144, 164, 295; dau. chs. of, 197; estate, 90; primary m.ch., *188*, 194, 242, 264, St Andrew, 245; sheep-station, 170–1; Rom. pottery, 101
Wickham Bushes, Lydden, *166*
Wickhurst, 159
wīg, 86, 91, 193
Wigston Magna, Leics., 40
Wihtred, King, 187, 190, 266
'wild', 127
Wildage, Elham, *80*, 127, 133, *283*, 284
Wilderness, 238; church in, 250–5, 256, 257; dedications, 236–7, 252, 253, 326
Wildfoots, *307*
Wildmarsh, 30, 110
William I, 173, 191
William, St, of Rochester, 240
Willinghurst Woods, *215*
Willow Wick, *291*; Willow Wood, *309*
wills, 143
Wilmington, 77, *148*, 151, 155, 157, 198
Wiltshire, 17, 73, 262; Wiltshire Downs, 281
Wimbourne, Dorset, 73, 74, 77, 82, 275
wincel, 162
Winchcombe, 105
Winchelesmere (Wichling), 327
Winchester, 232
Wingham, *76*, *80*, 117, 145, 146, 150, 155, 279; College, 273; dependent chs. of, 251, 272–3, 274; estate, 83, 90, 127; minster, *188*, 189, 190, 191, 192, 264, St Mary, 245, 246; Rom. settle., 109, 193; Rom. villa, 101
Wingham, r., 83
Wingham Barton, Ash, 144
Wingmore, Elham, *283*
Winstead, Cobham, *287*
Winterdown, Acrise, *166*, *283*
Winterham Hill, *287*
Wistow, Leics., 182
Withcote, Leics., 347
Withington, Glos., 13
Wittersham, 266
wold names, *80*, *81*, 127, 345, 346
Wold, 127
'wolds', 335, 346

425

Wolds, Leics., 334, 345; Lincs., 19; Yorks., 47
Wolverhampton, Staffs., 294
Wolverton, Alkham, *167*, 189
Womenswold, *80*, 83, 127, 164; dependent chapelry, 265, 273, 274
Wood, *alias* Woodchurch-in-Thanet, 29, 182; dau. ch. at, 251
Woodgate, *305*
Woodgate Way, Barkby, Leics., 347
Wood Hill, *134*
woodland, 1, 19, 25–31, 32, 42, 43, 53, 66, 71, 75, 127, 128, 136, 238, 252, 272, 278, 284, 314, 317, 321, 331, 333, 345–6; ancient, 155, 329, replanting of, 342; animals, 130; clearance, 29, 30, 41, 54, 70, 128, 130, 172, 179, 253, 259, 276, 284, 313, 340; colonization, 146, 268, 334, 335; common, 282, 284; community, 316; country, 145, 150; fuel, 112; 'managed', 31; old, 275, 277, 319, 321, 347; outlying, 321, 330, 339; pasture, 30–1, 49, 126–7, 129, 130, 143, 147, 171, 172; places, 315; poor, 121, 277; recolonization, 344; regeneration, 2, 95, 342; surviving, 128, 132, 133, 146, 302, 319, 335, 345; swine pastures, 143; topography, 119, 128, 129, 135, 159, 348; uncleared, 336; uncolonized, 10, 30, 146, 252, 276; west Midlands, 348
Woodland Park, *289*
Woodlands, 79, 133, *134*, *148*, 157, 185, 269; ch. at, *210*
woods, 2, 11, 12, 13, 20, 25–32, 34, 47, 52, 53, 120, 123, 127–35, 161, 162, 172, 199, 278, 335; ancient, 130; clearance, 292; Downland, 14; isolated, 346; scattered, 347
Woodnesborough, *81*, 107, 127, 139, 150, 155; ch. by barrows, St Mary, 245, 294, 295; Rom. settle., 103
Woodside Green, *309*
Woodstock in Tunstall, 30, 31, 168, *306*, 314, 317, 321
Wood Street, *305*, *307*, 319
wool, 33; production, 34, 170–1
Woolage, *80*
Woolpit Ash, *154*
Woolwich, 22, 37, 38, *148*
Wootton, 48, *80*, 82, 128, 133, 164, *166*, 283, 325
Worcestershire, 24

Worldswonder Farm, Elham, *283*
Wormshill, *36*, 161, 313, 326, 332; dau. ch. at, *201*, St Giles, 270, *308*; *Godeselle*, 328; manor, 327–8
Worsenden, 122
'worth', 143, 157–8, 162
Worth, *81*, 264, chp. of ease, 220; Rom. temple and burials, 101
Wouldham, 150, *152*, 280, 295, 330; Wouldham Marshes, *288*
Wreake valley, Leics., 347
Wrinsted, *201*, 309, 326, 327, 328
Wrotham, 16, 37, 40, 41, 49, 75, *76*, 78, 88, 89, 102, 108, 116, *134*, 183, 184, 185, 194, 274, 302; chp. of St Clere, 205–6, *210*, 220; dau. chs., 157, 171, 207, 220, 264, 265; hundred of, 271, 343; Jut. estate at, 342; minster, *188*, 265, St George, *211*, 226–7, 245, 256; minsterland, 271, 272; Wrotham Heath, *211*
wudu, 130, 146, 160
Wybornes, *291*; Wybornes Wood, *289*
Wye, *45*, 49, 70, 71, 90, 116, 133, 147, 158, 193, 198, 250, 258, 297, 329, 330, 342; heathen worship at, 86, 249, 265; estate at, *76*; Jut. burial ground, 101; lathe centre, 117; minster, *188*, 190, 195, 274, 275, St Martin & St Gregory, 242, 243, 244, 245; *villa regalis*, 8, 9, 86, 191; well of St Eustace at Withersdane, 296, 298
Wymeswold, Leics., 345

Yalding, 70, 149, 195, 197, 198, 280, 295; sec. m.ch., *188*, St Peter & St Paul, *218*
Yaugher Woods, *153*
Yelsted, Stockbury, 151, *153*; Yelsted Lane, *152*
yeomen, 55, 56, 63, 67, 325; landholders, 323
Yewtree Farm, Stelling, *283*; Yewtree Shaw, *152*
Yoakes Court, Old Romney, 324
Yockletts, 137
'yoke' names, 179, 324
yokeland, 178–9, 323–5; yokeland gentry names, 324
'yokes', 179, 322
Yokes Court, Frinsted, *309*, 324, 328
York Farm, Gillingham, 324
Yorkshire, 21, 24, 73, 240, 336, 340
Yotes Court, Mereworth, 324
Youngs Farm, Lower Hardres, 138